IMPLEMENTING SIX SIGMA

IMPLEMENTING SIX SIGMA

Smarter Solutions Using Statistical Methods

FORREST W. BREYFOGLE III
Smarter Solutions, Inc.
Austin, TX

A Wiley-Interscience Publication
JOHN WILEY & SONS, INC.
New York • Chichester • Weinheim • Brisbane • Singapore • Toronto

Copyright © 1999 by John Wiley & Sons. All rights reserved.

Published simultaneously in Canada.

Library of Congress Cataloging-in-Publication Data:

Breyfogle, Forrest W., 1946–
    Implementing Six Sigma: Smarter Solutions Using
Statistical Methods/ by Forrest W. Breyfogle
III.
        p.   cm.
    Includes bibliographical references and index.
    ISBN 0-471-29659-7 (alk. paper)
    1. Quality control—Statistical methods. 2. Production
management—Statistical methods. I. Title.
TS156.B75   1999
658.5'62—dc21   98-31917

Printed in the United States of America.

10 9 8 7 6 5

To my wife, Becki

CONTENTS

20   Comparison Tests: Attribute (Pass/Fail) Response   337

21   Bootstrapping   342

22   Variance Components   351

FOREWORD by Frank Shines, Jr.

Implementing Six Sigma is a book for anyone who wants to make a difference in their organization. From the project manager or employee team member who just wants a step-by-step approach on what needs to be done during a Six Sigma project, to a highly trained quality engineer who needs a statistical reference manual or sample, real-life solutions to the most sophisticated testing, development and manufacturing problems, *Implementing Six Sigma* can meet the need. Let me tell you a true story to illustrate the point.

In September of 1993 I called the master of statistical methods, Dr. W. Edwards Deming to get his advice on a product quality problem I was trying to resolve for a major industrial motors manufacturer. I remember Deming asking me to speak louder as his hearing was beginning to fail him at the time. (As we all know, he passed away in his sleep at age 93 about two months later.) In classic Deming fashion, he chose his words wisely and carefully to give me the insight (not the answer) I needed to resolve this problem and then referred me to his latest book, *The New Economics,* for future reference. "I have distilled all that I have learned in this book," I recall him saying.

Coupling the insights I gained from that conversation with Deming with the practical methods of Forrest Breyfogle's *Statistical Methods for Testing, Development, and Manufacturing,* we (Forrest Breyfogle, Tom Common, Quality Engineer, and Dr. Pete Wung, R&D) were able to resolve—in a few weeks—an ineffective product quality process which had plagued the company for nearly seven years.

And now, Breyfogle has done it again with his latest books, *Implementing Six Sigma.* Here Breyfogle has created a practical and effective methodology, the S^4 (Smarter Six Sigma Solutions) program, which guides the user through the process of:

- Incorporating the organization's strategic vision into the aim of the Six Sigma project charter
- Planning for and kicking off the project by attaining executive sponsorship and selecting the proper project team "champions"
- Conducting executive, management and team education and training
- Developing the proper organizational infrastructure and management and employee buy-in required to reduce resistance to change
- Implementing the project charter using Measurement, Analysis, Improvement, and Control phases

I have seen many Six Sigma approaches, but Breyfogle's Smarter Six Sigma Solutions approach is the most comprehensive of them all. The S^4 approach considers the importance of applying Six Sigma within a business context, by considering:

- Organizational strategy and vision
- A communications and education strategy
- The corporate culture and history
- Business economics and project prioritization
- Organizational and individual skills and competencies
- The pace and degree at which the organization can assimilate the change

In my experience working on projects throughout Europe and the Americas, whether for the military, industry or in the consulting profession, this is the finest collection of practical methods and sophisticated statistical problem-solving tools for today's real-life problems faced by those in both manufacturing and services.

FRANK SHINES, JR.

IBM Global Services
Principal, Measurement Methods Consulting

FOREWORD by Paul Tobias

The key to business success is doing the *right* thing *faster* and *better* and more *efficiently* than your competition. The *Six Sigma* approach aims at achieving this and Forrest Breyfogle has written the most systematic and comprehensive manual available on the subject.

Forrest combines the best parts of the *Six Sigma* philosophy with a large helping of up-to-date, powerful and useful statistical tools. He ties this practical package together with his own trademarked theme of *Smarter Six Sigma Solutions* (S$^{4\,SM}$). Focus is always on the practical: what are the right goals and how do you go about achieving them? High level goals are reduced to concrete industrial questions that managers and engineers can solve using the techniques described in *Implementing Six Sigma*. Every technique is described in detail and illustrated with concrete examples taken from industrial situations.

The *Six Sigma* version of the Quality Improvement initiative spread like wildfire across American industry during the 1980's. Starting at Motorola, *Six Sigma* was adopted by corporate leaders such as General Electric, Sony, Lockheed Martin, Raytheon and AlliedSignal. Documented success stories record many millions of dollars of savings due to following the tenets of *Six Sigma*. But there have also been *Six Sigma* program failures. This will occur when deployment is weak and there is insufficient focus on setting achievable goals and training employees in the use of proper problem-solving techniques. Following *Implementing Six Sigma* will avoid that trap.

Forrest has practiced what he has preached for many years, starting as a statistician in IBM (where we first met) and continuing to the present day, where he consults, trains, and helps large and small corporations implement S^4. This book grew out of his earlier textbook, *Statistical Methods for Testing, Developing and Manufacturing,* and his many years of applying statistics methods to successfully solve industrial problems and achieve business goals.

To me, the most impressive and useful aspect of *Implementing Six Sigma* is its wide scope. No other book available today comes anywhere near as close as this one in assembling all the needed quality and statistics tools in one place. Basic techniques such as FMEA, QFD, and process flowcharting are explained, along with a bevy of powerful statistical techniques and concepts such as:

- Exploratory data analysis (graphical techniques)
- Statistical process control
- Regression model fitting
- Analysis of variance
- Process capability indices
- Designed experiments and response surfaces
- Bootstrapping techniques
- Comparison methods
- Measurement capability analysis (gauge studies).

There is even an extensive discussion of reliability testing and analysis methods, including both repairable systems and non-repairable components. And all this material is presented in a practical straightforward way as the natural tool to use to solve a real problem or reach a desired goal.

This book should be a heavily thumbed reference for managers implementing, and workers participating in, any industrial quality improvement program. In addition, whole sections can be used as resource materials for literally dozens of short courses focusing on useful statistical tools.

PAUL TOBIAS

SEMATECH
Manager, Statistical Methods Group

FOREWORD by Bill Wiggenhorn

I enthusiastically agreed to contribute when Forrest Breyfogle asked me to provide foreword comments for this new book on Six Sigma. The Six Sigma story, which originated at Motorola, is an exciting one. It is a concept that works and, as Forrest relates, results in remarkable and tangible quality improvements when implemented wisely. Today, Six Sigma processes are being executed in a vast array of organizations throughout the world and in every variety of functions. History will document how this elegant process changed our world and gave new meaning to the term "quality."

In preparing these remarks, I reflected on the beginnings of Six Sigma and the pioneers who had the courage, intellect, and vision to make it a reality. The father of Six Sigma was the late Bill Smith, a senior engineer and scientist in our communications products business. It was Bill who crafted the original statistics and formulas that were the beginnings of the Six Sigma culture. He took his idea, and his passion for it, to our CEO at the time, Bob Galvin. Bob could see the strength of the concept, but reacted mostly in response to Bill's strong belief and passion for the idea. He urged Bill to go forth and do whatever was needed to be done to make Six Sigma the number one component in Motorola's culture. Not long afterwards, Senior Vice President Jack Germaine was named as quality director and charged with implementing Six Sigma throughout the corporation. Jack had a big job and was armed with few resources. So he turned to Motorola University to spread the Six Sigma word throughout the company and around the world. Soon, Six Sigma training was required for every employee. The language of quality became the common Motorola language. Whether it was French, Arabic, or Texan everyone understood the six steps, defect measurement and elimination, and parts per million. The training and concepts were not limited to the factory floor. Every single person was expected to understand the process and apply it to everything that they did. Some shied away, saying they were exempt from manufacturing processes. Some challenged the soundness of the statistics. Even so, the company stood behind the commitment and the mandate.

The result was a culture of quality that permeated throughout Motorola and led to a period of unprecedented growth and sales. The crowning achievement was being recognized with the Malcolm Baldrige National Quality Award. At the time, Bill remarked that Motorola was the only company who could receive the award. We were, to his knowledge, the only applicant who had the processes, measurements, and documentation in place to tell our quality story.

The rest, as they say, is history. Today, Six Sigma tools, research, training, and consulting have proliferated throughout business, industry, and education. This new volume is one example.

In his work, Forrest provides a user friendly how-to guide for organizations using Six Sigma to improve their bottom line. The text not only illustrates how manufacturing can utilize and benefit from Six Sigma but also how service, business, development, and other functions can apply and benefit from the techniques.

The text illustrates how most organizations can become more competitive, reduce defect levels, and improve cycle times. It consolidates not only the traditional Six Sigma process measurements and improvement tools, but also many other useful methodologies into one easy to understand text. The sections entitled Smarter Six Sigma Solutions Assessments, at the end of many chapters, offer additional insight into the selection of the best approach for a given situation. The author's real life examples provide a perceptive focus on both the mechanics and the wide range of application possibilities for Six Sigma tools. In addition, this is a Six Sigma guide that can be successfully used by management, technicians, engineers, administrators, and other practitioners.

Finally, this volume captures the spirit of Six Sigma with a common sense approach sure to be appreciated by the pioneers of Six Sigma.

BILL WIGGENHORN

Senior Vice President of Motorola Training and Education
President, Motorola University

PREFACE

In recent years there has been much interest in the application of statistical techniques to process improvement. Within organizations the CEO is hearing about the monetary benefits that others have achieved through "Six Sigma" (originated by Motorola) and are ready to cash-in on the benefits offered by the techniques within their organization. Other organizations are dealing with the statistical requirements that their customers are putting on them, such as statistical process control (SPC), design of experiments (DOE), and ongoing reliability testing (ORT).

This text is a practical guide for both industry and academia. For industry this text is useful to guide an organization to the *wise* implementation of the tools often associated with Six Sigma (and more). It provides many practical examples and has application exercises. In addition, it offers a practical classroom structure where students can learn practical tools and a road map that they can immediately apply within their organization or chosen profession.

When writing *Statistical Methods for Testing, Development and Manufacturing,* which was published in 1992, I was employed by IBM. The company at that time was working at implementing a Six Sigma program. In that same year I left IBM and founded Smarter Solutions. The primary mission of Smarter Solutions is to help organizations *wisely* apply Six Sigma statistical techniques through customized consulting and training. While teaching Six Sigma techniques to a variety of organizations it became obvious that there was a very important need to create a step-by-step guide for implementing a Six Sigma business strategy *wisely* within a variety of organizations. (A Six Sigma initiative program is not nearly as effective.) This text is my answer to this need, which contains concepts from my first text along with many additions and a complete restructuring. This text also contains exercises that can be used within S^4 workshops and classes.

Six Sigma can be very beneficial to improving the bottom line—if implemented *wisely*. However, if the techniques are not used *wisely*, there is a very large danger that the program will be counterproductive and frustrating. Organizations can sometimes get too involved in "how to count defects" and report defect rates that they lose sight of the real value of Six Sigma—orchestrating process improvement and reengineering (and bottom-line benefits) through the *wise* implementation of statistical techniques. A Six Sigma program needs to be orchestrated toward achieving Smarter Solutions[SM] (Smarter Solutions, Smarter Six Sigma Solutions, and S^4 are service marks of Forrest W. Breyfogle III).

If an organization does not apply Six Sigma techniques *wisely*, it will fail. When this occurs there is the tendency to believe that the statistical techniques are not useful, when in fact the real problem is how the program was implemented and/or how the techniques were not effectively applied. There is another danger with Six Sigma techniques. Often organizations assume that everyone calculates Six Sigma metrics such as process capability the same. This is not true; hence, major communication problems can result between organizations, which can cost a lot of money. This text describes the differences and issues that can occur with some metrics and other implementation procedures.

This text will use the terms "Smarter Six Sigma Solutions[SM] (S^4 [SM])" as adjectives with many common Six Sigma terms (e.g., black belt, green belt, champion, executive, workshop) to differentiate the suggested overall Six Sigma training and implementation process of this text from other Six Sigma programs. As a part of this Six Sigma implementation process, this text periodically offers S^4 assessment thoughts to describe various considerations relative to the *wise* implementation of a Six Sigma methodology. Another description for this S^4 activity is "Smarter Six Sigma Solutions" assessments because a major focus is the determination that the right measurements and actions are being taken relative to bottom-line benefits. With S^4 activities an environment is created where there is knowledge-centered activity (KCA) focus. KCA describes efforts for *wisely* obtaining knowledge and/or *wisely* utilizing the knowledge of organizations and processes.

This text can be useful for many situations. It can fulfill the following needs:

- An executive wants to implement a Six Sigma program within their company. Their organization wants a guide that leads to a Smarter Solutions benefit (i.e., an S^4 training and implementation process to implementing a Six Sigma business strategy).
- An organization needs a text to use within Six Sigma workshops.
- A practitioner is confused by many aspects and inconsistencies in implementing a Six Sigma business strategy. He/she wants a better understanding of alternative approaches so they can choose the best approach

for their situation which yields Smarter Solutions results. This understanding will also reduce the likelihood of a Six Sigma requirement/issue misunderstanding with a supplier/customer.

- A university wants to offer a practical statistics course where students can see the benefits and application of *wisely* applied statistical techniques to their chosen profession so their students will achieve Smarter Solutions benefit.

- A high-level manager wants to read parts of a text to see how their organization might benefit from a Six Sigma business strategy and statistical techniques. From this investigation the manager might want to see the results of more statistical design of experiments (DOE) before certain issues are considered resolved (in lieu of previous one-at-a-time experiments). The manager might also have a staff person use this text as a guide for a more in-depth reevaluation of the traditional objectives, definitions, and procedures within his or her organization.

- An engineer or technician who has minimal statistical training wants to easily determine how to address such issues as sample size requirements and perhaps offer a Smarter Solutions approach that better addresses the "real" issue.

- Individuals want a concise explanation of design of experiments (DOE), response surface methods (RSM), reliability testing, statistical process control (SPC), quality function deployment (QFD), and other statistical tools within one text (and how a total problem solution considers a blend of all these techniques that can lead to Smarter Solutions benefit).

This text is subdivided into the following parts:
- Part I: S^4 Deployment Strategy Phase
- Part II: S^4 Measurement Phase
- Part III: S^4 Analysis Phase
- Part IV: S^4 Improvement Phase
- Part V: S^4 Control Phase

The first part describes the benefits and how to deploy an S^4 program with a knowledge-centered activity (KCA) focus. This is where the *wise* application and integration of Six Sigma tools along with S^4 project definition leads to bottom-line improvement. The remaining parts describe the aspects often associated with a four-week S^4 Six Sigma training program and the implementation of a S^4 program.

To meet the needs of a diverse audience, the following was done structurally within this text to improve the ease of use:

- Chapters and sections are typically small, descriptive, and contain many examples. Because of this the table of contents can prove to be very useful to quickly locate techniques and examples that can give guidance to help solve a particular problem.

- The glossary can be a useful reference point whenever a concise definition or an unfamiliar statistical term or symbol is encountered in a chapter.
- Detailed mathematical expressions and other considerations are collected in the appendices to prevent disruption of the flow of dialogue in the chapters and to make it easier for the reader to find and use these tools.
- Sections entitled "Smarter Six Sigma Solutions (S^4) Assessment" are included at the end of many chapters for the purpose of stimulating thought to alternative approaches that can be more beneficial than those initially considered.
- Examples describe the mechanics of implementation and application possibilities along with the integration of techniques that lead to S^4 bottom-line benefits.

CLASSICAL TRAINING AND TEXTBOOKS

Many (if not most) engineers believe that statistics is "only" applicable to baseball and is not helpful to their situation because "too many samples are always required." Bill Sangster, past Dean of the Engineering School at Georgia Tech states that: "Statistics in the hands of an engineer are like a lamppost to a drunk. They're used more for support than illumination" (*The Sporting News* 1989).

It is unfortunate that in the college curriculum of many engineering disciplines there is only a small amount of time allocated to training in statistics. It is also unfortunate that within these classes and other "weeklong short classes" the students often cannot relate to how the techniques can be helpful in solving problems in their discipline.

Statistical texts normally identify techniques to use when solving classical problems of various types. A practitioner could use a text to determine, for example, the sample size that is needed to check a failure rate criterion. However, the practitioner may find that the execution of this "simple test plan" is impossible because the low failure rates of today can require a very large sample size and a very long test duration. Instead of blindly running this type of test, this text suggests that there may be other considerations that can make the test more manageable and meaningful. Effort needs to be expended upon a basic strategy and the definition of problems that focus on meeting the real needs of customers with less time, effort, and costs.

This text breaks from the traditional bounds maintained by many texts. In this guide, emphasis is given to identifying techniques for restructuring, if necessary, the original (or defining the "right") question and then designing a more informative test plan/procedure that requires fewer samples and gives more information with often less test effort.

Both development and manufacturing engineers, in addition to service providers, need concise training on how statistics is applicable to their profession with a "do it (my job) smarter" philosophy. Managers need concise training so that they can give direction to their employees in order to accomplish tasks in the most efficient manner and present information in a concise fashion. If all individuals within an organization would apply S^4 statistical techniques, many meetings that are conducted for the purpose of problem discussion would either be avoided or yield increased benefits with more efficiency. Engineering management and general problem solvers need to have statistical concepts presented to them in an accessible format so they can understand how to use these tools for illumination. This guide addresses these needs.

Theoretical derivations and manual statistical analysis procedures can be very laborious and confusing to many practitioners. In this guide there is minimal discussion on these issues; these topics are presently covered sufficiently in other texts. This information was excluded for the purpose of making the text more readable by a diverse audience that does not have an interest in detailed theoretical or manual considerations. In lieu of theory, illustrations are sometimes included for the purpose of showing why the concepts "work." In lieu of illustrating manual analysis concepts, computer analysis techniques are discussed because most practitioners would implement the concepts using one of the many commercially available computer packages.

This guide also has a "keep-it-simple" (KIS) objective. To achieve maximum effectiveness for developing or manufacturing a product, many "quick tests" (in lieu of one "big" test) could be best for a given situation. Engineers do not have enough time to investigate statistical literature to determine, for example, the "best" theoretically possible DOE strategy to use for a given situation. An engineer needs to spend his or her time choosing a good overall statistical strategy assessment that minimizes the risk of customer dissatisfaction. These strategies often need a blend of statistical approaches with technical considerations.

Classical statistical texts and classes usually emphasize either DOE, statistical process controls, or reliability testing. This guide illustrates that the mixture of all these techniques with brainstorming yields a very powerful combination when developing and producing a high-quality product in a timely fashion. Engineers need to be equipped with all these skills in order to maximize the effectiveness of their job performance.

Classical statistical texts do not typically emphasize "defining the problem(s)." For example, a classical text may give a procedure to choose the sample size to verify a failure criterion. A more important consideration would be to determine how to implement a DOE that considers how several factors could be changed to improve the quality of the product. This guide emphasizes defining the "best" problem to solve for a given situation; individuals should continually assess their work environment by asking: Are we trying to answer the right question, and are we using the best basic test, development, and manufacturing strategies?

Examples in this text presume that samples and trials can be expensive. The focus of this text is to give direction that leads to using a minimum number of samples or trials while striving for the maximum amount of useful information. To achieve this, some examples will illustrate the blending of engineering judgment with statistics as part of a decision process.

Examples also presume that the reader considers that time is money. "Analysis paralysis" (i.e., analyzing the data to "death") is discouraged. Also, emphasis is given not to lose the "big picture" by too close examination of phenomena that may be statistically interesting but of little value to meet the needs of the customer. In many industries, problems are getting more difficult to solve using traditional techniques.

Failure rates are getting lower and the product applications are getting more complex. A classic question in this type of industry is: "What sample size do I need to verily a failure criterion?" The answer to this type of question is that, in general, it will be "too large." In lieu of addressing a sample size issue, individuals should consider what will be done "for the customer" with information obtained from the test. To make this self-evaluation, consider that a test was designed such that the criterion was met if no failures occurred. What would be the reaction from management if several failures occurred during the test? Might the failures be "talked away" (i.e., the numbers game)? If the process is not changed so that the root cause is avoided in the future, there may not be much gained from the test effort. Another example is that it is generally ineffective to arbitrarily conduct a test for the purpose of observing and fixing failures that occur. This approach is in general inefficient for problem determination. When testing to find a problem, it is usually better to structurally change things and observe the response.

NOMENCLATURE AND SERVICE MARKS

I have tried to be consistent with other texts when assigning characters to parameters (e.g., μ represents mean or average). However, there is an overlap in nomenclatures commonly found in texts that address differing areas of statistics. Because this guide spans many areas of statistics, compromises had to be made. Appendix E summarizes the assignments that are used globally in this guide.

In this guide both continuous response and reliability analyses are discussed. The independent variable x is used in models that typically describe continuous responses, while t is used when time is considered the independent variable in reliability models.

Smarter Solutions, Smarter Six Sigma Solutions, and S^4 are service marks of Forrest W. Breyfogle III.

ACKNOWLEDGEMENTS

I am appreciative of the help of many individuals. My wife, Becki, was very supportive of the time and effort required for this undertaking. Stan Wheeler gave very helpful suggestions and guidance. Mark Lehman gave timely help with the initial manuscript and supporting programming. Many improvements resulted from the suggestions of Pat Spagon, Wes Breyfogle, and Fred Bothwell. Also, the contributions in methodology, text, and/or assistance in other capacities from David Laney, Mark Kiemele, Rai Chowdhary, Jim Fish, Mary McDonald, Allen Johnson, Brenda Sabbagh, Ron Hanna, Mary Jo McCarthy, and Kathy Flories were very beneficial. I am also appreciative of the inputs from Dan Breyfogle and the many others who suggested book titles. Finally, I am very appreciative of the written suggestions Lloyd S. Nelson gave me with regard to *Statistical Methods for Testing, Development and Manufacturing,* which I addressed in this text.

CONTACTING THE AUTHOR

Your comments and suggestions for improvement to this book are greatly appreciated. Any suggestions you give will be seriously considered for future editions (I work at practicing what I preach). Also, I conduct both public and in-house Six Sigma workshops from this text utilizing S^4 techniques. Contact me if you would like information about these workshops or need catapults to conduct the described team exercises. My email address is forrest@ smartersolutions.com. You might also find the articles and additional implementation ideas at www.smartersolutions.com. to be beneficial.

FORREST W. BREYFOGLE III

Smarter Solutions, Inc.
Austin, Texas

PART I

S⁴ DEPLOYMENT STRATEGY PHASE

Within this part (Chapters 1–2) there is discussion on the meaning and benefits of a *wisely* implemented Six Sigma program (i.e., S⁴ implementation). Six Sigma issues involving knowledge-centered activity (KCA) opportunities, deployment, training, project selection, and management needs are also included.

1

SIX SIGMA OVERVIEW AND IMPLEMENTATON

As the competition continues to get tougher, there is much pressure on product development, manufacturing, and service organizations to become more productive and efficient. Developers need to create innovative products in less time, even though the product may be very complex. Manufacturing organizations experience growing pressure to improve quality while decreasing costs and increasing production volumes with fewer resources. Service organizations need to reduce cycle times and improve customer satisfaction. A Six Sigma approach can directly affect these needs, if it is conducted *wisely*. Organizations need to give Smarter Six Sigma Solutions (S^4) assessments that are linked to bottom-line benefits (i.e., $marter Six Sigma $olutions).

The term *sigma* is a Greek alphabet letter (σ) used to describe variability, where a classical measurement unit consideration of the program is defects per unit. A sigma quality level offers an indicator of how often defects are likely to occur, where a higher sigma quality level indicates a process that is less likely to create defects. A Six Sigma quality level is said to equate to 3.4 defects per million opportunities (DPMO), as described in section 1.4. [Pat Spagon from Motorola University prefers to use the terminology "sigma quality level" to distinguish this quality measurement from the sigma nomenclature that quantifies the spread of a distribution.]

An S^4 business strategy involves the measurement of how well business processes meet their goal and offers strategies to make needed improvements. The application of the techniques to all functions results in a very high level of quality at reduced costs with a reduction in cycle time, resulting in improved profitability and a competitive advantage. Organizations do not necessarily need to use all the measurement units often presented within a Six Sigma program. It is most important to choose the best set of measurements for their situation and focus their emphasis on the *wise* integration of statistical and other improvement tools offered by a Six Sigma program (i.e., an S^4 program).

An S^4 business strategy can directly attack the cost of poor quality (COPQ). These issues have often been given the broad categories of internal failure costs, external failure costs, appraisal costs, and prevention costs. Another way of looking at COPQ is not doing what is right the first time. COPQ can be thought to include issues such as scrap, reworks, and meetings with no purpose.

Quality cost issues can very dramatically affect a business. However, very important issues are often hidden from view. Organizations can be missing the largest issues when they focus only on the tip of the iceberg, as shown in Figure 1.1. It is important for organizations to direct their efforts so these hidden issues are uncovered (which are often more important than the readily visible issues). Wisely applied Six Sigma techniques can help flatten many of the issues that affect overall cost. However, management needs to ask the right questions so that these issues are effectively addressed. For management to have success with Six Sigma they must have a need, vision, and a plan.

When assessing Six Sigma, an organization should consider the various options: doing nothing, creating a Six Sigma initiative, or creating a Six Sigma business strategy. Let's next consider each of these options. The "doing nothing" option might be the right choice for an organization; however, an organization needs to make this decision after comparing the cost-of-doing-nothing to the cost-of-doing-something. The "creating Six Sigma initiative" option typically is viewed by members of an organization as the "program of the month" and is usually abandoned quickly without much, if any, benefits (there could be detriments with employee attitudes). The "Six Sigma business

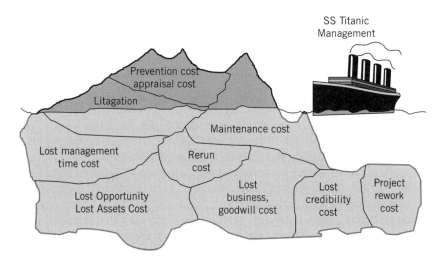

FIGURE 1.1 Cost of poor quality. (Reproduced with permission of RAS Group.)

strategy" has the most benefit, if it is executed *wisely*. This text describes the S^4 business strategy, which involves executive ownership, a support intrastructure, projects with bottom-line results, full-time S^4 black belts, S^4 green belts, reward/motivation considerations, finance engagement (i.e., to determine the cost of doing nothing and return on investment for projects), and training in all rolls (both "hard" and "soft" skills).

1.1   BACKGROUND OF SIX SIGMA

Six Sigma is a business initiative first espoused by Motorola in the early 1990s. Recent Six Sigma success stories, primarily from the likes of General Electric, Sony, AlliedSignal, and Motorola, have captured the attention of Wall Street and have propagated the use of this business strategy. The Six Sigma strategy involves the use of statistical tools within a structured methodology for gaining the knowledge needed to achieve better, faster, and less expensive products and services than the competition. The repeated, disciplined application of the master strategy on project after project, where the projects are selected based on key business issues, is what drives dollars to the bottom line, resulting in increased profit margins and impressive return on investment from the Six Sigma training. The Six Sigma initiative has typically contributed an average of six figures per project to the bottom line. The Six Sigma project executioners are sometimes called "black belts," "top guns,","change agents," or "trailblazers," depending on the company deploying the strategy. These people are trained in the Six Sigma philosophy and methodology and are expected to accomplish at least four projects annually, which should deliver at least $500,000 annually to the bottom line. A Six Sigma initiative in a company is designed to change the culture through breakthrough improvement by focusing on out-of-the-box thinking in order to achieve aggressive, stretch goals. Ultimately, Six Sigma, if deployed properly, will infuse intellectual capital into a company and produce unprecedented knowledge gains that translate directly into bottom line results (Kiemele 1998).

1.2   GENERAL ELECTRIC'S EXPERIENCES WITH SIX SIGMA

General Electric (GE) CEO Jack Welch describes Six Sigma as "the most challenging and potentially rewarding initiative we have ever undertaken at General Electric" (Lowe 1998). The GE 1997 annual reports states that Six Sigma delivered more than $300 million to its operating income. In 1998 they expect to more than double this operating profit impact. GE listed in their annual report the following to exemplify these Six Sigma benefits (GE 1997):

- "Medical Systems described how Six Sigma designs have produced a 10-fold increase in the life of CT scanner x-ray tubes—increasing the "uptime" of these machines and the profitability and level of patient care given by hospitals and other health care providers."
- "Superabrasives—our industrial diamond business—described how Six Sigma quadrupled its return on investment and, by improving yields, is giving it a full decade's worth of capacity despite growing volume— without spending a nickel on plant and equipment capacity."
- "Our railcar leasing business described a 62% reduction in turnaround time at its repair shops: an enormous productivity gain for our railroad and shipper customers and for a business that's now two or three times faster than its nearest rival because of Six Sigma improvements. In the next phase across the entire shop network, black belts and green belts, working with their teams, redesigned the overhaul process, resulting in a 50% further reduction in cycle time."
- "The plastics business, through rigorous Six Sigma process work, added 300 million pounds of new capacity (equivalent to a "free plant"), saved $400 million in investment and will save another $400 million by 2000."

1.3   ADDITIONAL EXPERIENCES WITH SIX SIGMA

A *USA Today* article presented differences of opinions about the value of Six Sigma in "Firms Air for Six Sigma Efficiency" (Jones 1998). One stated opinion was Six Sigma is "malarkey," while Larry Bossidy, CEO of AlliedSignal counters: "The fact is, there is more reality with this (Six Sigma) than anything that has come down in a long time in business. The more you get involved with it, the more you're convinced." Some other quotes from the article are as follows:

- "After four weeks of classes over four months, you'll emerge a Six Sigma "black belt." And if you're an average black belt, proponents say you'll find ways to save $1 million each year."
- "Six Sigma is expensive to implement. That's why it has been a large-company trend. About 30 companies have embraced Six Sigma including Bombardier, ABB (Asea Brown Boveri) and Lockheed Martin."
- " . . . nobody gets promoted to an executive position at GE without Six Sigma training. All white-collar professionals must have started training by January. GE says it will mean $10 billion to $15 billion in increased annual revenue and cost savings by 2000 when Welch retires."
- "Raytheon figures it spends 25% of each sales dollar fixing problems when it operates at four sigma, a lower level of efficiency. But if it raises its quality and efficiency to Six Sigma, it would reduce spending on fixes to 1%."

- "It will keep the company (AlliedSignal) from having to build an \$85 million plant to fill increasing demand for caperolactan used to make nylon, a total savings of \$30-\$50 million a year."

- "Lockheed Martin used to spend an average of 200 work-hours trying to get a part that covers the landing gear to fit. For years employees had brainstorming sessions, which resulted in seemingly logical solutions. None worked. The statistical discipline of Six Sigma discovered a part that deviated by one-thousandth of an inch. Now corrected, the company saves \$14,000 a jet."

- "Lockheed Martin took a stab at Six Sigma in the early 1990s, but the attempt so foundered that it now calls its trainees "program managers," instead of black belts to prevent in-house jokes of skepticism. . . . Six Sigma is a success this time around. The company has saved \$64 million with its first 40 projects."

- "John Akers promised to turn IBM around with Six Sigma, but the attempt was quickly abandoned when Akers was ousted as CEO in 1993."

- "Marketing will always use the number that makes the company look best. . . . Promises are made to potential customers around capability statistics that are not anchored in reality."

- "Because manager's bonuses are tied to Six Sigma savings, it causes them to fabricate results and savings turn out to be phantom."

- "Six Sigma will eventually go the way of other fads, but probably not until Welch and Bossidy retire."

- "History will prove those like Smith wrong, says Bossidy, who has been skeptical of other management fads. Six Sigma is not more fluff. At the end of the day, something has to happen."

The *New York Times* (Deutsch 1998) describes additional Six Sigma success stories.

I believe that Six Sigma implementation can be the best thing that ever happened to a company. Or, a company can find Six Sigma to be a dismal failure. It all depends on implementation. The S^4 roadmap within this text can lead an organization away from a Six Sigma strategy built around "playing games with the numbers" to a strategy that yields long-lasting process improvements with significant bottom-line results.

1.4   THE SIX SIGMA METRIC

The concepts described within this section will be covered in greater depth later within this text. This section will give readers who have some familiarity with the normal distribution a quick understanding of the source for the Six Sigma metric.

First let's consider the level of quality that is needed. The "goodness level" of 99% equates to (Harry 1987)

- 20,000 lost articles of mail per hour
- Unsafe drinking water almost 15 minutes per day
- 5000 incorrect surgical operations per week
- 2 short or long landing at most major airports each day
- 200,000 wrong drug prescriptions each year
- No electricity for almost 7 hours per month

I think that most of us agree that this level of "goodness" is not close to being satisfactory. A S[4] program, among other things, can offer a measurement for "goodness" across various products, processes, and services.

The sigma level (i.e., sigma quality level), sometimes used as a measurement within a Six Sigma program, includes a ±1.5σ value to account for "typical" shifts and drifts of the mean. This sigma quality level relationship is not linear. In other words, a percentage unit improvement in parts-per-million (ppm) defect rate does not equate to the same percentage improvement in the sigma quality level.

Figure 1.2 shows the sigma quality level associated with various services (considering the 1.5σ shift of the mean). From this figure we note that the sigma quality level of most services is about four, while world class is considered six. A goal of S[4] implementation is to continually improve processes and become world class.

Figures 1.3 to 1.5 illustrate various aspects of a normal distribution as it applies to Six Sigma program measures and the implication of the 1.5σ shift.

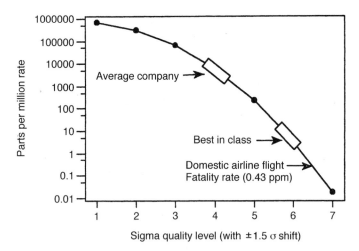

FIGURE 1.2 Implication of sigma quality level. Part per million (ppm) rate for part or process step.

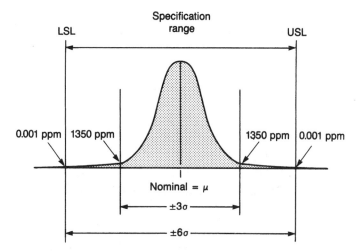

FIGURE 1.3 Normal distribution curve illustrates to Three Sigma and Six Sigma parametric conformance. (Copyright of Motorola, Inc., used with permission.)

Figure 1.3 illustrates the basic measurement concept of Six Sigma where parts are to be manufactured consistently and well within their specification range. Figure 1.4 shows the number of parts per million that would be outside the specification limits if the data were centered within these limits and had various standard deviations. Figure 1.5 extends Figure 1.3 to noncentral data relative to specification limits, where the mean of the data is shifted by 1.5σ. Figure 1.6 shows the relationship of ppm defect rates versus sigma quality

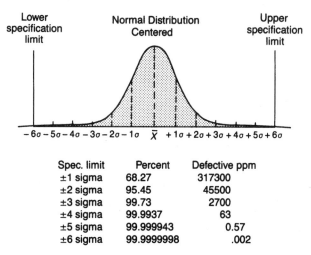

Spec. limit	Percent	Defective ppm
±1 sigma	68.27	317300
±2 sigma	95.45	45500
±3 sigma	99.73	2700
±4 sigma	99.9937	63
±5 sigma	99.999943	0.57
±6 sigma	99.9999998	.002

FIGURE 1.4 With a centered normal distribution between Six Sigma limits, only two devices per billion fail to meet the specification target. (Copyright of Motorola, Inc., used with permission.)

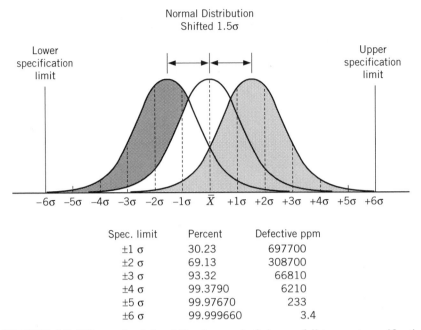

Spec. limit	Percent	Defective ppm
±1 σ	30.23	697700
±2 σ	69.13	308700
±3 σ	93.32	66810
±4 σ	99.3790	6210
±5 σ	99.97670	233
±6 σ	99.999660	3.4

FIGURE 1.5 Effects of a 1.5σ shift where only 3.4 ppm fail to meet specifications. (Copyright of Motorola, Inc., used with permission.)

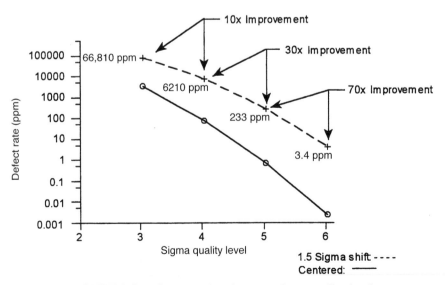

FIGURE 1.6 Defect rates (ppm) versus sigma quality level.

level for a centered and 1.5σ shifted process, along with a quantification for the amount of improvement needed to change a sigma quality level.

A metric that describes how well a process meets requirements is process capability. A Six Sigma quality level is said to translate to process capability index values for C_p and C_{pk} requirement of 2.0 and 1.5, respectively (as described in more detail later within this text). To achieve this basic goal of a Six Sigma program might then be to produce at least 99.99966% "quality" at the "process step" and part level within an assembly (i.e., no more than 3.4 defects per million parts or process steps if the process mean were to shift by as much as 1.5σ). If, for example, there was on the average one defect for an assembly that contained 40 parts and 4 process steps, practitioners might consider that the assembly would be at a four sigma quality level from Figure 1.6, because the number of defects in parts per million is $(\frac{1}{160})(1 \times 10^6) \approx 6210$.

1.5   MOTOROLA'S SIX SIGMA TEN STEPS

Various steps have been proposed by organizations to adopt a Six Sigma type of program for their situation. Figures B.1–B.4 (Motorola BR 392/D) shown in the appendix illustrate a set of 10 steps and methodologies that Motorola used for continuous improvement toward Six Sigma quality level. The basic procedure described in this booklet could be used as a general road map to give direction to the improvement of quality.

The statistical community may note that the statistical procedures suggested in these 10 steps are not new; however, the program name has increased the awareness of upper-level management to the value of using statistical concepts. What appeals to me about this set of steps is that the approach addresses process improvement along with the implementation of statistical techniques. These figures are included within this text to illustrate the basic approach suggested by Motorola, not to dwell on the precise company definitions for all terms and techniques that are described in the document.

The discussion about these Six Sigma implementation steps is from a manufacturing perspective; however, the basic flow is applicable to many other areas of a business. For example, this basic process flow could be used to decrease development cycle time, reduce the chance of design problems escaping to manufacturing, and reduce invoice cycle times.

1.6   TRADITIONAL APPROACH TO THE DEPLOYMENT OF STATISTICAL METHODS

Before the availability and popularity of easy to use statistical software most complex statistical analysis was left to a statistical consultant within an organization. With a statistical consultant, an engineer needed to know what questions to ask. If the engineer does not realize the power of statistics, he or she may not solicit help when statistical techniques are appropriate. If a statistical consultant is approached for assistance by an engineer who has no knowledge of statistics, the statistician should learn all the technical aspects of the dilemma in order to give the best possible assistance. Most statisticians do not have the time, background, or desire to understand all engineering dilemmas within their corporate structure. Engineers need to have at a minimum some basic knowledge of the concepts in this text so that they can first identify an application of the concepts and then solicit help, if needed, in an effective manner.

In any case, detailed knowledge transfer to statisticians can be very time-consuming and in most cases will be incomplete. Engineers that have knowledge of basic statistical concepts can intelligently mix engineering concepts with statistical techniques to maximize test quality and productivity. Earlier problem detection and better quality can then be expected when testing is considered as an integral part of the design and manufacturing process development.

Now easy-to-use statistical software has made the whole process of statistical analyses more readily available to a larger group of people. However, the issue of problem definition and dissemination of the *wise* use of statistical techniques still exists. Even though great accomplishments may be occurring through the use of statistical tools within an organization, there is often a lack of visibility of the benefits to upper management. Because of this lack of visibility, practitioners have to often fight for funds and may be eliminated whenever the times get rough financially.

Typically in this situation executive management does not ask questions that lead to the *wise* application of statistical tools; hence, an internal statistical consultant or practitioner has to spend a lot of their time trying to sell others on how basic problems could be solved more efficiently using statistical methods. In addition, internal statistical consultants or practitioners who help others will only have the time or knowledge to assist with problem resolution as it is currently defined. In a purely consultant role, statistical practitioners will often not be involved in project or problem definition. In addition, the benefits of good statistical work that has been accomplished are not translated into the universal language understood by all executives—namely, money. Hence, the benefits of *wisely* applying statistical techniques is limited to small areas of the business, does not get recognition, and is not accepted as general policy.

1.7   DEPLOYMENT OF SIX SIGMA: PROJECTS WITH BOTTOM-LINE BENEFITS

Often organizations do not look at "their" problems as the result of current process conditions. However, if they did, their situation might be exemplified by Figure 1.7. They might also have a variety of key process output variables (KPOVs), where a KPOV could be a critical dimension, overall cycle time, a DPMO rate (i.e., that could expose a "hidden factory" that has much rework that is not currently being reported), customer satisfaction, and so on.

For this type of situation, organizations often react over time to the up and down movements of the KPOV level in a "fire fighting" mode, "fixing" the problems of the day. Practitioners and management might even think that this

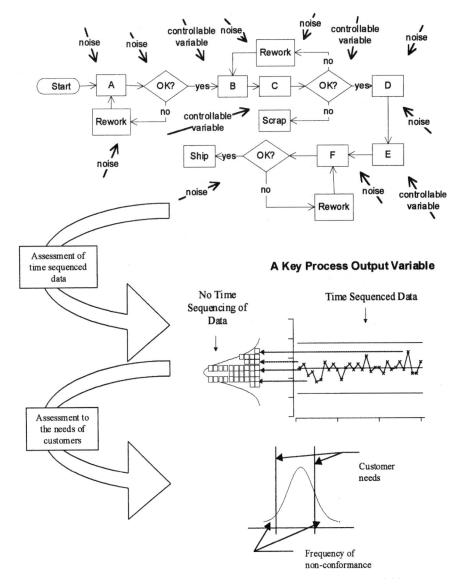

FIGURE 1.7 Exemplary process with a key process output variable.

type of activity is making improvements to the system. However, in reality they are often spending a lot of resources without making any process improvements. Unless process changes are made, the proportion of noncompliance, as shown in the figure, will remain approximately the same.

A practitioner or management might ask about typical sources for process variability. Arbitrary tweaks to controllable process variables that are made frequently and noise (e.g., material differences, operator-to-operator differences, machine-to-machine differences, and measurement imprecision) can impact a KPOV to a level that results in a large nonconforming proportion.

Organizations who frequently encounter this type of situation have much to gain from implementing an S^4 program. They can better appreciate this potential gain when they consider all the direct and indirect costs associated with their current level of nonconformance.

The S^4 methodology described within this text is not only a statistical methodology but also a deployment system of statistical techniques, as described in Figure 1.8. For a program to be successful, it must have upper-level management commitment and the infrastructure that supports this commitment. Deployment of the S^4 techniques is most effective through individuals, sometimes called black belts or agents, who work full time on the implementation of the techniques through S^4 projects selected on business needs (i.e., have a very beneficial ROI). Direct support needs to be given by an executive management committee that has high-level managers who champion S^4 projects.

When an S^4 black belt or green belt utilizes the steps summarized in Figure 1.8, either during a workshop or as a project after a workshop, the type of process improvement exemplified in Figure 1.9 can result, where the process has been simplified, designed to require less testing, and designed to become more robust (i.e., indifferent) to the noise variables of the process. The effort can result in an improvement shift of the mean along with reduced variability that leads to quantifiable bottom-line monetary benefits.

It needs to be emphasized that S^4 black belts need to be selected such that they not only have the capability of learning and applying statistical methodologies. They also need to be proactive people that are good at the so-called soft skills of working with people. S^4 black belts will not only need to analyze information and use statistical techniques to get results, they will also need to be able to work with others through mentoring, teaching, coaching, and selling others on how they can benefit from S^4 techniques.

A rule of thumb for the number of S^4 black belts within an organization is 1% of the total number of employees. S^4 black belts are supported technically through an S^4 master black belt and through the management chain of an organization by way of an S^4 champion. Individuals who are given S^4 training to a lesser extent and support S^4 black belts are called S^4 green belts.

When an organization chooses too implement a Six Sigma program they typically need to use a group outside their company to help them get started. This group can help with setting up a deployment strategy, conducting initial

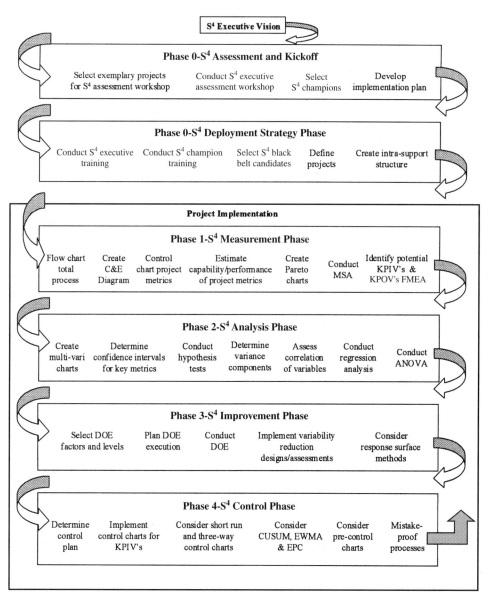

FIGURE 1.8 Pictorial representation of the implementation of an S^4 business strategy.

training, and providing project coaching. The decision on which group is chosen can dramatically affect the success of a program. However, choosing the best group to help an organization implement Six Sigma can be a challenge.

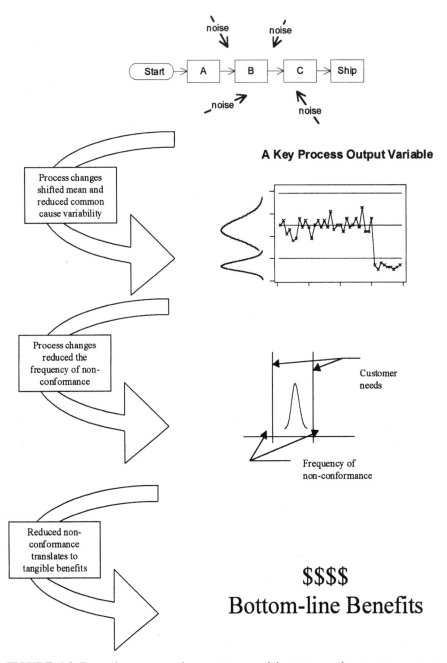

FIGURE 1.9 Exemplary process improvement and impact to a key process output variable.

All Six Sigma implementation programs are not created equal!! I would suggest that you ask the following questions of groups that you are considering using to start a Six Sigma program:

Strategy and Implementation

- What is your basic Six Sigma implementation strategy and flow?
- What do you suggest doing next if we would like to compare the Six Sigma program offered by your organizations with that offered by other organizations? [Note, I suggest that you ask various Six Sigma organizations to conduct a trial executive Six Sigma training session at your facility. Within this session, you should also ask the Six Sigma service provider to describe their basic Six Sigma implementation strategy to exemplary projects that you select (e.g., three). A comparison of the application methodologies can lead to a selection of the best service provider for your particular situation.]
- What book do you use that follows the material taught within the course (so people can get further explanation during workshop or be able to review a concept at a later date)?
- How is your Six Sigma course taught for black belt training (include whether transparencies, PowerPoint (registered trademark of Microsoft), or some other media is used for topic presentations)?
- What is the basic format of your Six Sigma course for executive training and champion training?
- How do you address business and service processes?

Course Material

- What topics do you cover within your black belt workshops?
- What is the format of the handout material?
- Is licensing of instructional material available for use by our internal instructors?
- Is the material in a form that others can easily teach from?
- Have all the courses that your organization sponsored used your material? Note, some Six Sigma providers have subcontracted much of their workshop instruction to other organizations that used their own material.

Computers and Software

- Are attendees required to have computers?
- What software do you see? (Note, I suggest using a general purpose statistical software package such as Minitab.)
- Is the software easy to use and learn?

- Does the software offer other functions besides those taught during the workshop (so people can grow into the application of more sophisticated techniques)?

Exercises

- Describe the frequency of exercises (i.e., manual, computer software, and other hands-on exercises) within the black belt workshop?
- How do you address application of the techniques to real world situations?

Experience of Course Developer(s)/Trainer(s)

- What is the experience of the person(s) responsible for developing the courseware?
- What companies have you helped utilize Six Sigma tools and methodologies?

References

- What have others said about your courses and consulting in the application of Six Sigma tools?

1.8 S⁴ PROJECT INTEGRATION OF THE TOOLS

There are many possible implementation strategies of the tools described within this text for S⁴ projects. The purpose of this section is to give a concise, generic roadmap of how many of the described tools could be utilized within a project. This roadmap can be referenced throughout the reading of this text so insight is not lost of how individual tools can fit into the "big picture."

The glossary and list of symbols in the back of this text can aid with the clarification of terms that are described later within the text. Tools are highlighted to aid the reader in later locating where a tool could be applied.

Step	Action	Participants	Source of Information
1	Identify critical customer requirements from a high level project measurement point of view. Identify **KPOVs** that will be used for project metrics. Implement a balanced scorecard considering **COPQ** and **RTY** metrics.	S⁴ black belt and champion	Current data

2	Identify **team** of key "stakeholders"	S⁴ black belt and champion	Current data
3	Describe business impact. Address financial measurement issues of project.	S⁴ black belt and finance	Current data
4	Plan overall project.	Team	Current data
5	Start compiling project metrics in time series format. Utilize a sampling frequency that reflects "long-term" variability. Create **run charts** and **control charts** of KPOV's.	Team	Current and collected data
6	Determine "long-term" **process capability/ performance** of KPOV's. Quantify nonconformance proportion. Determine baseline performance. **Pareto chart** types of defects.	Team	Current and collected data
7	Create a **flowchart/ process map**.	Team	Organization Wisdom
8	Create a **fishbone diagram** to identify variables that can affect the process output.	Team	Organization Wisdom
9	Create a **cause and effect matrix** assessing strength of relationships that are thought to exist between **KPIV's** and KPOV's.	Team	Organization Wisdom
10	Conduct a **measurement systems analysis.** Consider a **variance components** analysis.	Team	Collected data
11	Rank importance of KPIV's using a **Pareto chart.**	Team	Organization Wisdom
12	Prepare a focused **FMEA.** Assess **current control plans.**	Team	Organization Wisdom

13	Collect data for assessing the KPIV/KPOV relationships that are thought to exist.	Team	Collected data
14	Create **multi-vari charts** and **box plots.**	Team	Passive data
15	Conduct **correlation** studies.	Team	Passive data analysis
16	Access statistical significance of relationships using **hypothesis tests.**	Team	Passive data analysis
17	Conduct **regression** and **analysis of variance** studies.	Team	Passive data analysis
18	Conduct **DOE's** and **Response Surface Methods** analyses.	Team	Active Experimentation
19	Determine optimum operating windows of KPIV's from DOE's and other tools.	Team	Passive data analysis and active experimentation
20	Update **control plan.** Implement **control charts** to timely identify special cause excursions of KPIV's.	Team	Passive data analysis and active experimentation
21	Verify process improvements, stability, and **capability/ performance** using demonstration runs.	Team	Active experimentation

1.9 EXAMPLES IN THIS TEXT THAT DESCRIBE THE BENEFITS AND STRATEGIES OF SIX SIGMA

There are many examples included within this text that give insight to the benefits of implementing S^4 techniques through projects. The following partial list of text examples is included to facilitate the reader for their investigation and/or to give a quick overview of the benefits and implementation methodologies for use within S^4 training sessions.

Generic Process Measurement and Improvement

- Process measurement and improvement within a service organization: Example 5.3.
- A 20:1 return on investment (ROI) study could lead to a methodology that has a much larger benefit through the changing (elimination) of the justification process for many capital equipment expenditures: Example 5.2.
- Tracking a product to a specification and then "fixing" the problem does not reduce the frequency of product nonconformance (but can cost a lot of money). A better summary view of the process (as opposed to only measuring the product) can give direction for design improvements and poka-yoke: Example 43.5.
- Improving internal employee surveys to get more useful results with less effort (also would work with external surveys): Example 43.7.
- A described technique better quantifies the output of a process (including variability) in terms that everyone can understand. The process is a business process that has no specifications: Example 11.5.
- The bottom line can be improved through the customer invoicing process: Example 43.8.
- An improvement in the tracking metric for change order times can give direction to more effective process change needs: Example 43.6.
- Illustrating how the application of S^4 techniques improve the number in attendance at a local ASQ section meeting (the same methodology would apply to many process measurement and improvement strategies): Example 11.5 and Example 19.5.
- Improving product development: Example 43.1.
- A conceptual example can help with a problem that frequently is not addressed—answering the right question: Example 43.9.

Design of Experiments (DOE)

- A DOE strategy during development used one set of hardware components in various combinations to represent the variability expected from future production. A follow-up stress to fail test revealed that design changes reduced the exposure to failure: Example 31.5.
- Several DOE were conducted to better understand and fix a manufacturing problem. A follow-up experiment demonstrated that the implemented design changes not only improved average performance but also reduced the variability in performance between products: Example 19.1, 19.2, 19.3, 19.4.
- The integration of quality functional deployment (QFD) and DOE lead to better meeting customer needs: Example 43.2.

- Implementing a DOE strategy within developme
of no-trouble-founds (NTFs) later reported afte
to customers: Example 30.2.

Testing Products and Product Reliability

- Improving a process that has defects: Example
- A DOE expedites the testing process of a desig
- A strategy to capture combinational problems o
can quickly identify when design problems exis
vides a test coverage statement: Example 42.4.
- An expensive reliability test strategy that requi
chines was replaced with a test that gave much
shorter period of time. The results from this tes
issues that could have been diagnosed as NTF
zations can cost manufacturing a lot of money):
- A customer ongoing-reliability test (ORT) requ
satisfy a customer requirement such that the activity gave more timely
information that could be used for process improvement with less effort
than typical ORT plans: Example 40.7.
- A reduced test of preproduction machines indicates that in order to have
90% confidence that the failure criterion will be met, a total number 5322
test-hours are needed where two failures are permitted: Example 40.3.
- An accelerated reliability test consisting of seven components indicated
a wear-out failure mode where 75% of the units were expected to survive
the median life specifications. Example 41.1.
- Data from the field indicate a nonconstant failure rate for a repairable
system: Example 40.6.

1.10   EFFECTIVE SIX SIGMA TRAINING
AND IMPLEMENTATION

Appendix B.2 exemplifies a basic agenda using the topics within this text to
train S^4 executives (S^4 leadership), S^4 champions, and S^4 black belts. However,
there are many additional issues to be considered within training sessions.

For successful implementation of Six Sigma techniques, the training of
full-time S^4 black belt candidates needs to be conducted such that attendees
can apply the concepts to their project soon after the techniques are covered
within the S^4 workshop. An effective approach to the training of the Six Sigma
concepts described within this book is four weekly modules spread over four
months. Between S^4 workshop sessions, attendees apply the concepts previously learned to their projects. During this time they also get one-on-one
coaching of the application of the S^4 techniques to their project.

Within this training it is also very important that attendees have the resources to quickly learn the concepts and apply the concepts to their S^4 projects. A portable computer should be assigned to all S^4 black belts. The software installed the following:

- An easy-to-use statistical program
- Office suite (programs for word processing, spreadsheets, and presentations)
- Process flowcharting program

In my opinion the most effective basic format to deliver the concepts is as follows:

- Present a topic using a computer projector system in conjunction with a presentation software package.
- Show an example (e.g., using the statistical software).
- Present application exercise where each student is to analyze a given set of data on their computer within the class.
- Periodically present an application exercise where teams within the class work together on a generic application of the concepts recently described (e.g., four or five team members collect and analyze data from a catapult exercise; students use this teaching tool that was developed by Texas Instruments to shoot plastic golf balls and measure the distance they were projected) [*Note:* Team catapult exercises will be described as exercises throughout this text. See the Glossary for a description of the catapult.]
- Periodically discuss how the techniques are applicable to their projects.

I have found that it is very beneficial for each person to create a presentation of how they applied S^4 techniques to their projects. Each person gives a presentation of their project using a computer projector system and presentation software during weeks 2, 3, and 4. The instructor can evaluate the presentation and give the presenter written feedback.

There are differences of opinion on the guidelines to follow for S^4 workshop project selection. Each organization needs to establish their own guidelines. Some things to consider and related issues when determining these guidelines are the following:

Projects

- Create a process for determining S^4 project candidates.
- From a list of candidate S^4 projects determine the potential cost savings (one could use activity-based costing to quantify amount) and the likelihood of success. The product of these two numbers could be compared

to other project numerical values to give direction on which projects should be addressed first.

- An S^4 project should be large enough that a resolution is important to the business but not so large that it can be overwhelming.
- When an S^4 project appears to be too large or small after it is started, rescope the project as soon as possible.
- Projects championed by someone who has responsibility for a process seems to work best.
- Attendees should review the S^4 project periodically with the person who is championing their project and others.
- Upon completion of the S^4 project, work should be documented. Consider having a consistent format that can later be found by others electronically. Among other things include an executive overview, detailed work/analysis, metrics, and benefits.

Metrics and Monetary Issues

- Consider how Defects Per Million Opportunities (DPMO) and process capability will be reported.
- Decisions must be made relative to how monetary S^4 project benefits are determined. Consider whether hard, soft, or both types of savings will be tracked (e.g., hard savings have to show an impact to the accounting balance sheet before reported. Soft savings would include an efficiency improvement that in time would save money because fewer people would later be required to conduct the task). Before making this decision, I suggest first reviewing Examples 5.2 and 5.3. I believe that it is important to have a measurement that encourages the right activity. For the S^4 black belts, one of the primary measurements should be monetary savings. When a strict accounting rule of only "hard money" is counted, the wrong message can be sent. A true "hard money" advocate would probably not allow for cost avoidance (e.g., an S^4 black belt who reduced the development cycle time by 25% would get no credit because the savings were considered "soft money").

Target S^4 Project Completion Dates and Stretch Goals

- Consider having a somewhat flexible amount of time after the last S^4 workshop session to account for project complexity (e.g., one to three months).
- Consider having stretch goals for projects, both individually and collectively. It is very important that management not try to drive improvement only through these numbers. Management must instead orchestrate efforts that lead to the most effective activities that can positively affect these metrics.

Recognition/Certification

- Consider the certification process for someone to become a S[4] black belt. Perhaps they should have demonstrated a savings of at least $100,000 in projects, obtained a certain level of proficiency using S[4] tools, and given good documentation of project results (in a format that could be published).
- Consider how S[4] black belts and others involved within a program will be recognized.

1.11   COMPUTER SOFTWARE

Most tedious statistical calculations can now easily be relegated to a computer. I believe that for a Six Sigma program to be successful, practitioners must have good versatile statistical software used within their training and readily available for use between and after training sessions. The use of statistical software within training sessions expedites the learning of techniques and application possibilities. The availability and use of a common statistical software package within an organization following a training session will improve the frequency of application of the techniques and communications within/between organizations (and their suppliers/customers).

In my opinion an organization should choose a common computer program that offers many statistical tools, ease of use, good pricing, and technical support. *Quality Progress* (a magazine of the American Society for Quality, Milwaukee, WI) periodically publishes an article that describes the features of computer program packages that can aid the practitioner with many of these tasks. The charts, tables, and analyses produced in this text were created with Minitab, SAS, or GRAFSTAT (an APL programming language statistical package developed by IBM).

Reiterating, I believe that S[4] black belt workshops should include only the minimal amount of manual exercises needed to convey basic understanding. Typically, we no longer do manual manipulation of statistical data; hence, a majority of instruction within an S[4] workshop should center around use of this computer program on a portable computer assigned to the individual. After workshop sessions are complete, the student will then have the tools to efficiently apply S[4] techniques immediately.

It needs to be emphasized that even though computer software packages are now very powerful, problem solutions and process improvements are not a result of statistical computer programs. Unfortunately, computer program packages do not currently give the practitioner the knowledge to "ask the right question." This text addresses this most important task along with giving the basic knowledge of how to use computer program packages most effectively.

1.12 S⁴ ASSESSMENT

When organizations are considering making a change, they will consider associated costs. However, they often do not give adequate focus to the cost of not making a change. When organizations are considering the costs of implementing an S^4 program, they should not only look at direct costs of implementation but also the costs associated with not implementing an S^4 a program.

Consider what can be learned from the shortcomings of the implementation of total quality management (TQM) [Schmidt, Kiemele, and Berdine 1997]. TQM activities did not lead to a focus on the overall system and the bottom-line improvement metrics. S^4 projects need to be of a manageable size with consideration to the impact to the overall system and bottom-line improvements. Consider also including cost avoidance and soft savings within the bottom-line improvement of an S^4 project.

Various questions can arise when implementing an S^4 program. Many issues and resolution alternatives are discussed later in this text. For now let's consider one question: For my process, how am I going to define opportunities for defects? When addressing this question it is important to remember that we do not want to "play games" with the numbers. For a given situation, the opportunities for defects can often be counted many different ways. Consider creating a number that is consistent with the needs of the customer and leads to effective process improvement. The metric might not be perfect, but it should also be such that it can be used as a baseline for future process improvement activities.

It is important that management not only drive through the metrics, but also focus on asking the right questions that lead to the right activity. A Six Sigma program can fail because emphasis was only on output measurements, not real process improvement (i.e., "beating up people" when they don't meet an arbitrarily set target). This type of management focus will surely create creativity—how to make my numbers look good so I look good (the heck with real process improvement). Consider making the primary focus of a Six Sigma program a structured strategy for improvement—not a bureaucratic system for data collection and reporting.

Finally, let's consider communications between practitioners and executives. The quality community for years has complained that management has not listened and supported their quality initiatives. The quality professionals blame management. I don't agree. In my opinion we in the quality and process improvement field are to blame because in the past we often showed a lack of ability to communicate well in terms that executives understand. To illustrate my point, consider that we travel to a country and do not speak the language of the country. We should not expect everyone in the country to learn our language so they can communicate with us. We either have to learn their language or figure an alternative way to communicate through a "common language" (e.g., hand gestures). Similarly, a quality professional should not expect executives to take the time to learn everything there is to know about the language of the quality profession. The quality practitioner often needs to do a better job of communicating to executives using a language that they understand (whenever possible)—namely, money.

One might argue that this communication strategy in money terms cannot be done and should not be done for a particular situation. The statement might be made that there are a lot of activities that cannot be translated to money. I won't agree or disagree; however, I do believe that more issues can be translated to monetary terms than are currently receiving this translation (even using an estimate based on opinion to "size" a situation). More importantly than anything, consider a situation where there is no communication problems between practitioners and the right things are getting done. For this situation there is no reason to address changing the communication structure. However, if there are communication problems between executive management and practitioners, perhaps more issues (and Six Sigma project work) should be communicated in monetary terms. Because of this change, a practitioner could receive more recognition for his or her accomplishments and additional support for future efforts.

2

KNOWLEDGE-CENTERED ACTIVITY (KCA) FOCUS AND PROCESS IMPROVEMENT

In addition to being a road map for Six Sigma implementation, a basic theme of this text is to always strive for improvement (i.e., do it smarter) and not "play games" with the numbers. With this approach, management needs to ask the right questions that lead to the *wise* use of statistical techniques for the purpose of obtaining knowledge from facts and data. Management needs to encourage the *wise* application of statistical techniques for a Six Sigma program to be successful. They also need to operate under the philosophy of "show me the data."

This text suggests periodic process reviews and projects based on S^4 assessments that lead to a knowledge-centered activity (KCA) focus in all aspects of the business. This text uses the term KCA to describe efforts for *wisely* obtaining knowledge or *wisely* utilizing the knowledge of organizations and processes. The strategies and techniques described within this text are consistent with the philosophies of such quality authorities as W. Edwards Deming and J. M. Juran. This chapter discusses, as a point of reference, the steps to both Deming's 14 points of management philosophy and Juran's control sequence and breakthrough sequence. Also included in this chapter are the steps for effective decision making and the management attitude needed to support this activity.

2.1 MANAGEMENT STRUCTURE VERSUS TEAM-BASED DECISION MAKING

Management structure can discourage effective decision making (Scholtes 1988). American managers have often conduct much of their business through an approach that is sometimes called *management by results*. This type of management tends to focus only on the end result—that is, process yield, gross margin, sales dollars, return on investment, and so on. Emphasis is placed on a chain of command with a hierarchy of standards, objectives, controls, and accountability. Objectives are translated into work standards or quotas that guide the performance of employees. Use of these numerical goals can cause short-term thinking, misdirected focus fear (e.g., of a poor job performance rating), fudging the numbers, internal conflict, and blindness for customer concerns. This type of management is said to be like trying to keep a dog happy by forcibly wagging its tail.

Quality leadership is an alternative that emphasizes results by working on methods. In this type of management, every work process is studied and constantly improved so that the final product or service not only meets but exceeds customer expectations. The principles of quality leadership are customer focus, obsession with quality, effective work structure, control yet freedom (e.g., management in control of employees yet freedom given to employees), unity of purpose, process defect identification, teamwork, and education and training. These principles are more conducive to long-term thinking, correctly directed efforts, and a keen regard for the customer's interest.

Quality leadership does have a positive effect on the return on investment. In 1950 Deming described this chain reaction of getting a greater return on investment as follows: improve quality $\rightarrow$ decrease costs $\rightarrow$ improve productivity $\rightarrow$ decrease prices $\rightarrow$ increase market share in business $\rightarrow$ provide jobs $\rightarrow$ increase return on investment. Quality is not something that can be delegated to others. Management must lead the transformation process.

To give quality leadership, the historical hierarchical management structure of Figure 2.1 needs to be changed to more a structure that has a more unified purpose as represented in Figure 2.2 using teams. A single person using S^4 concepts can make a big difference in an organization. However, one person rarely has enough knowledge or experience to understand everything within a process. Major gains in both quality and productivity can often result when a team of people pool their skills, talents, and knowledge.

Teams need to have a systematic plan to improve the process that creates mistakes/defects, breakdowns/delays, inefficiencies, and variation. For a given work environment, management needs to create an atmosphere that supports team effort in all aspects of business. In some organizations, management may need to create a process that describes hierarchical relationships between teams, the flow of directives, how directives are transformed into action and improvements, and the degree of autonomy and responsibility of the teams. The change to quality leadership can be very difficult. It requires dedication and patience to transform an entire organization.

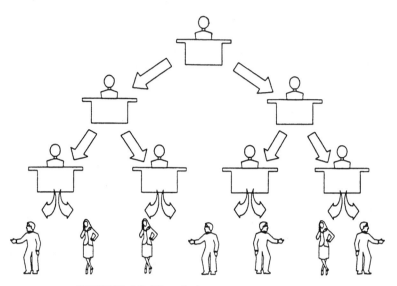

FIGURE 2.1 Historical management structure.

2.2   DEMING'S 14 POINTS FOR MANAGEMENT

Deming had a great influence on the rise of quality and productivity within Japan. The Japanese have embraced his concepts and have named their highest-quality award after him.

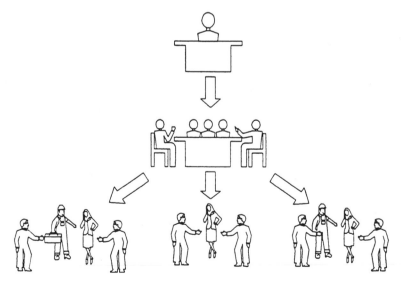

FIGURE 2.2 Management teams.

Based on many years of industrial experience, I agree with Deming's basic philosophy and believe that many companies need to make the changes proposed by Deming in order to become more competitive. This text is a "how-to" guide toward the implementation of many of Deming's concepts.

The following discussion is a summary of Deming's 14 points for management (Deming 1982):

1. *"Create constancy of purpose toward improvement of product and service, with the aim to become competitive and to stay in business and to provide jobs."* For the company that wants to stay in business, the two general types of problems that exist are the problems of today and the problems of tomorrow. It is easy to become wrapped up with the problems of today; however, the problems of the future command first and foremost constancy of purpose and dedication to keep the company alive. Obligations need to be made to cultivate innovation, fund research and education, and improve the product design and service, remembering the customer is the most important part of the production line.

2. *"Adopt the new philosophy. We are in a new economic age. Western management must awaken to the challenge, must learn their responsibilities, and take on leadership for change."* Government regulations and antitrust activities need to be changed to support the well-being of people (not depress it). Commonly accepted levels of mistakes and defects can no longer be tolerated. People must receive effective training so that they understand their job and also understand that they should not be afraid to ask for assistance when it is needed. Supervision must be adequate and effective. Management must be rooted in the company and must not job hop between positions within a company.

3. *"Cease dependence on inspection to achieve quality. Eliminate the need for inspection on a mass basis by building quality into the product in the first place."* Inspection is too late, ineffective, and costly to improve quality. It is too late to react to the quality of a product when the product leaves the door. Quality comes from improving the production process, not inspection. Corrective actions are not inspection, scrap, downgrading, and rework on the process.

4. *"End the practice of awarding business on the basis of price tag. Instead, minimize total cost. Move toward a single supplier for any one item, on a long-term relationship of loyalty and trust."* Price and quality go hand in hand. Trying to drive down the price of anything purchased without regard to quality and service can drive good suppliers and good service out of business. Single-source suppliers are desirable for many reasons. For example, a single-source supplier can become innovative and develop an economy in the production process that can only result from a long-term relationship with their purchaser. Another advantage is that often the lot-to-lot variability within the process of one supplier process is enough to disrupt the purchaser's pro-

cess. Only additional variation can be expected with two suppliers. To qualify a supplier as a source for parts in a manufacturing process, perhaps it is better to first discard manuals that may have been used as guidelines by unqualified examiners when visiting suppliers to rate them. Instead suppliers could be asked to present evidence of active involvement of management that encourages the application of many of the S^4 concepts discussed in this text. Special note should be given to the methodology used for continual process improvement.

5. *"Improve constantly and forever the system of production and service, to improve quality and productivity, and thus constantly decrease costs."* There is a need for constant improvement in test methods and a better understanding of how the customer uses and misuses a product. In the past, American companies have often worried about meeting specifications, while the Japanese have worried about uniformity (i.e., reducing variation about the nominal value). Continual process improvement can take many forms. For example, never-ending improvement in the manufacturing process means that work must be done continually with suppliers to improve their processes. It is important to note that putting out "fires" is not a process improvement.

6. *"Institute training on the job."* Management needs training to learn about the company from incoming materials (with an appreciation of variation) to customer needs. Management must understand the problems the worker has in performing his or her tasks satisfactorily. A large obstacle exists in training and leadership when there are flexible standards to acceptable work. The standard may often be most dependent on whether a foreperson is having difficulty in meeting a daily production quota. It should be noted that money and time spent will be ineffective unless the inhibitors to good work are removed.

7. *"Institute leadership. The aim of supervision should be to help people and machines and gadgets to do a better job. Supervision of management is in need of overhaul, as well as supervision of production workers."* Management is to lead, not supervise. Leaders must know the work that they supervise. They must be empowered and directed to communicate and act on conditions that need correction. They must learn to fix the process, not react to every fault as if it were a special cause, which can lead to a higher defect rate.

8. *"Drive out fear, so that everyone may work effectively for the company."* No one can give their best performance without feeling secure. Employees should not be afraid to express their ideas or ask questions. Fear can take many forms, resulting in impaired performance and padded figures. Industries should embrace new knowledge because it can yield better job performance, not be fearful of this knowledge because it could disclose some of our failings.

9. *"Break down barriers between departments. People in research, design, sales, and production must work as a team to foresee problems of pro-*

duction and in use that may be encountered with the product or service." Teamwork is needed throughout the company. Everyone can be doing superb work (e.g., design, sales, manufacturing), and yet the company can be failing. Why? Functional areas are suboptimizing their own work and not working as a team for the company. Many types of problems can occur when communication is poor. For example, service personnel working with customers know a great deal about their products; however, it is unfortunate that there is often no routine procedure for disseminating this information.

10. *"Eliminate slogans, exhortations, and targets for the work force asking for zero defects and new levels of productivity. Such exhortations only create adversary relationships, as the bulk of the causes of low quality and low productivity belong to the system and thus lie beyond the power of the work force."* Exhortations, posters, targets, and slogans are directed at the wrong people, causing general frustration and resentment. Posters and charts do not consider the fact that most trouble comes from the basic process. Management needs to learn that its main responsibility should be to improve the process and remove any special causes found by statistical methods. Goals need to be set by an individual for the individual, but numerical goals set for other people without a road map to reach the objective have an opposite effect in achieving the goal.

11a. *"Eliminate work standards (quotas) on the factory floor. Substitute leadership."* It is incompatible to achieve never-ending improvement with a quota. Work standards, incentive pay, rates, and piece work are manifestations of management's lack of understanding, which leads to inappropriate supervision. Pride of workmanship needs to be encouraged, while the quota system needs to be eliminated. Whenever work standards are replaced with leadership, quality and productivity increase substantially and people are happier on their jobs.

11b. *"Eliminate management by objective. Eliminate management by numbers, numerical goals. Substitute leadership."* Goals such as "improve productivity by 4 percent next year" without a method are a burlesque. The data behind plots that track these targets are often questionable; however, a natural fluctuation in the right direction is often interpreted as success, while small fluctuation in the opposite direction causes a scurry for explanations. If there is a stable process, a goal is not necessary because the output level will be what the process produces. A goal beyond the capability of the process will not be achieved. A manager must understand the work that is to be done in order to lead and manage the sources for improvement. New managers often short-circuit this and instead focus on outcome (e.g., getting reports on quality, proportion defective, inventory, sales, and people).

12a. *"Remove barriers that rob the hourly worker(s) of their right to pride of workmanship. The responsibility of supervisors must be changed from sheer numbers to quality."* In many organizations the hourly worker becomes a commodity. They may not even know whether they will be working next week. Management can face declining sales and increased costs of almost everything; however, it is helpless to face the problems of people. The establishment of employee involvement and participation plans have all been a smoke screen. Management needs to listen and correct problems with the process that are robbing the worker of pride of workmanship.

12b. *"Remove barriers that rob people in management and in engineering of their right to pride of workmanship. This means, inter alia, abolishment of the annual or merit rating and of managing by objective."* Merit rating rewards people that are doing well in the system; however, it does not reward attempts to improve the system (i.e., don't rock the boat). The performance appraisal erroneously focuses on the end product, not leadership to help people. People that are measured by counting are deprived pride of workmanship. The indexes for these measurements can be ridiculous. For example, an individual is rated on the number of meetings he or she attends; hence in negotiating a contract, the worker extends the number of meetings needed to reach a compromise. One can get a good rating for "fire fighting" because the results are visible and quantifiable, while another person only satisfied requirements because he or she did the job right the first time (i.e., mess up your job and correct it later to become a hero). A common fallacy is the supposition that it is possible to rate people by putting them in rank order from last year's performance. There are too many combinations of forces (i.e., the worker, co-workers, noise, confusion, etc.). Apparent differences in people will arise almost entirely from these actions in the system. A leader needs to be a colleague and counselor that leads and learns with his or her people on a day-to-day basis, not be a judge. In absence of numerical data, a leader must make subjective judgment when discovering who, if any, of his or her people are outside the system (on the good or the bad side) or within the system.

13. *"Institute a vigorous program of education and self-improvement."* An organization needs good people that are improving with education. Management should be encouraging everyone to get additional education and self-improvement.

14. *"Put everybody in the company to work to accomplish the transformation. The transformation is everybody's job."* Management needs to take action to accomplish the transformation. To do this, first consider that every job and activity is part of a process. A flow diagram breaks a process into stages. Questions then need to be asked about what changes could be made to each stage to improve the effectiveness of other upstream or downstream stages. An organization structure is needed to guide continual improvement of quality. Statistical process control (SPC) charts are useful to quantify chronic problems and identify the sporadic problems. Everyone can be a part of the team effort to improve the input and output of the stages. Everyone on a team has a chance to contribute ideas and plans. A team has an aim and goal toward meeting the needs of the customer.

2.3   COMMON CAUSES VERSUS SPECIAL CAUSES AND CHRONIC VERSUS SPORADIC PROBLEMS

J. M. Juran (Juran and Gryna 1980) considers the corrective action strategy for sporadic and chronic problems, while W. Edwards Deming addresses this basic issue using a nomenclature of special causes and common causes (Deming 1986). Process control charts are tools that can be used to distinguish these two types of situations.

Sporadic problems are defined to be an unexpected change in the normal operating level of a process, while chronic problems exist when the process is at a long-term unacceptable operating level. With sporadic problems the collective action is to bring the process back to the normal operating level, while the solution to chronic problems is a change in the normal operating level of the process. Solving these two types of problems involves different basic approaches.

The Juran's control sequence (Juran and Gryna 1980) is basically a feedback loop that involves the following steps:

1. Choose the control subject (i.e., what we intend to regulate).
2. Choose a unit of measure.
3. Set a standard or goal for the control subject.
4. Choose a sensing device that can measure the control subject in terms of unit of measure.
5. Measure actual performance.
6. Interpret the difference between the actual and standard.
7. Take action (if any needed) on the difference.

Process control charting techniques discussed in this text are useful tools to monitor the process stability and identify the existence of both chronic and sporadic problems in the process.

Chronic problems often involve extensive investigation time and resources. Juran describes the following breakthrough sequence for solving this type of problem:

1. Convince others that a breakthrough is needed—that is, convince those responsible that a change in quality level is desirable and feasible.
2. Identify the vital few projects—that is, determine which quality problem areas are most important.
3. Organize for breakthrough in knowledge—that is, define the organization mechanisms for obtaining missing knowledge.
4. Conduct the analysis—that is, collect and analyze the facts that are required and recommend the action needed.

5. Determine the effect of proposed changes on the people involved and find ways to overcome the resistance to change.
6. Take action to institute the changes.
7. Institute controls to hold the new level.

The Pareto chart is a tool that is used to identify the most likely candidates or areas for improvement. Within a given area of improvement, DOE techniques can often be used to efficiently determine which of the considered changes are the most important alterations that should be made to the process.

It is important to note that special causes (sporadic problems) usually receive more attention because of high visibility. However, more gains can often be made by constant effort of continually working on common cause (chronic problems). The terms *common cause* and *special cause* will be used in the remaining portion of this text.

2.4 PROBLEM SOLVING AND DECISION MAKING

The following are steps to effective decision making:

- Become aware of a problem or needed action.
- Define the problem or needed action.
- Consider alternatives and their consequences.
- Select an approach.
- Implement the approach.
- Provide feedback.

This may not be an all inclusive list; however, often deviations from the flow are large. For example, someone may determine a "quick fix" to a "crisis" in the manufacturing line. The person may have created other problems with the quick fix because he or she did not discuss the alternatives with other individuals. In addition, there may be no feedback to determine if the problem fix was effective for future production.

An additional concern arises in that the "wrong" basic problem is often solved (often called a type III error). [Type I and type II errors, discussed in depth later, address (a) the risk of rejecting a null hypothesis when it is true and (b) the risk of failing to reject the null hypothesis when it is not true.] To address this issue, consider a manufacturing facility that produces printed circuit boards. This company may need to reduce their total defect rate at final test. Without proper understanding and investigation, the problem initially may be defined as follows: How should we get the assembly line employees to work more carefully so that they will reduce variability at their stations? However, perhaps a better starting point would be to state the problem as being too high of a defective rate at the end of the manufacturing process. From this more general definition, Pareto charts can be used to direct efforts toward the sources that are causing most of the failures. The S^4 road map can then be used to consider alternatives and possible experiments for data collection as part of the decision-making process that leads to quantifiable improvement.

2.5   GOAL SETTING, SCORECARD, AND MEASUREMENTS

We are trained to think that goals are very important, and they are. Goals are to be SMART (i.e., simple, measurable, agreed to, reasonable, time-based). However, these guidelines are often violated. Arbitrary goals set for individuals or organizations where they have no controls over the outcome can be very counterproductive and very costly. To illustrate my point, consider two situations in your personal life.

Situation 1

You have a lot of work that needs to get done around your house or apartment. A goal can be very useful to get more work done on a Saturday. Consider two scenarios relative to this desire:

- You can set a goal for the number of tasks you would like to accomplish, create a plan on how to accomplish these tasks most efficiently, and track how well you are doing during the day to meet your goal. You would probably get more done with this strategy than just randomly attacking a list of to-do items.
- Your spouse or friend can set an arbitrary goal for the number of tasks you are to accomplish. If they don't create a plan and the goals are set arbitrarily, you probably will not accomplish as much as you would under the previous scenario because there is no plan and you do not necessarily have to buy into the tasks that are to be accomplished.

Situation 2

You would like to make 50% return on your investment next year. Consider two scenarios relative to this desire:

- You choose some mutual funds that have tracked well over the last few years; however, their yield was not as large as you desired. Because this goal is important to you, you decide to track the yield of your portfolio daily and switch money in and out of the funds in order to meet your goal.
- You evaluate some quality mutual funds that have tracked well over the last few years. You decide that your goal was too aggressive because these funds have not had the yield that you would like to obtain. You

alter your plan and choose an investment plan of buying and holding a balanced portfolio of quality mutual funds.

Situations 1 and 2 are very different relative to goal setting. In the first situation, goal setting can be very useful when there is buy into the plan because we do have some control over the outcome.

In the second situation, goal setting could be very counterproductive because we do not directly control the outcome of the process (i.e., how well the stock market will do next year). The first option scenario to situation 2 will probably add additional variability to your investment process and can cause significant losses. The second plan to address this goal is the best because we did research choosing the best process for our situation and took the resulting yield, even though we might not achieve our goal.

Management can easily get into the trap of setting arbitrary goals for people where the outcome is beyond the scope of control of the employee. To illustrate this point, consider a manufacturing process that has 90% of its problems from supplier quality issues. Often the approach to meet aggressive goals for this situation is to "beat up" on suppliers whenever quality problems occur or add inspection steps. This may be the only course of action that manufacturing employees can take, which will not be very productive with regard to meeting any improvement goals.

However, if management extends the scope of what employees can do to fix a problem, then things can change. Perhaps manufacturing employees should be more involved with the initial supplier selection, or perhaps manufacturing employees should work with engineering to conduct a DOE for the purpose of changing settings of the manufacturing process (e.g., process temperature or pressure) so high-quality product can be achieved with raw material of lesser quality.

Note that I do not mean to imply that stretch goals are not useful, because they are. Stretch goals can get people to think "out of the box." However, goals alone without a real willingness to change and a road map to conduct change can be detrimental.

There is another consideration when setting goals—the scorecard. Vince Lombardi said "if you are not keeping score, you are just practicing." A scorecard worksheet can be useful for metric development where organization, product, process, and people are each assessed against performance, schedule, and cost (Schmidt, Kiemele, and Berdine 1997). The implication of this is that organizations should not just measure against sigma quality levels and/or process output defect rates. Balanced scorecard issues when creating performance measurement and management systems should consider the following:

- Hidden factory issues (i.e., reworks within an organization that have no value): Consider metrics that use rolled throughput yields and defects per million opportunity (DPMO) at the operation step to quantify the impact of these issues.

- Activity-based costing (ABC) of process steps.
- Cost of poor quality.
- S^4 project monetary benefits.

How much success a S^4 program receives can depend upon how goals are set and any boundaries that are given relative to meeting these objectives. In addition, if the scorecard is not balanced, people can be driving their activities toward a metric goal in one area which adversely affects another metric or area. The result is that even though the person appears successful since they met their goal, the overall organization can suffer.

2.6   ANSWERING THE RIGHT QUESTION

Sometimes practitioners of Six Sigma techniques need to consider a different approach to a problem or project in order to most effectively resolve the issue. The "S^4 assessment" sections at the end of many chapters can help with the creation of a do-it-smarter approach for a given situation. This section offers some additional thoughts on the topic.

Large objectives can be achieved considering the methodologies described within the S^4 assessment sections; however, there is a price to pay: Objectives may need redefinition. The unwise application of classical statistical problem definitions might assume no engineering knowledge (e.g., will this product meet the failure rate criterion?). Typically, within any product or process development there are individuals who have engineering knowledge of where product risks exist. Combining all sources of knowledge structurally is important to problem redefinition and a S^4 philosophy. If test efforts are directed toward these risk areas, favorable customer satisfaction and higher product quality can result with less test effort.

An S^4 philosophy means directing efforts toward objectives that have the most benefit by compiling and converting data into knowledge. If this is not done, development and manufacturing work can have many misdirections. Efforts must be taken to avoid magnifying the small and missing the big. More emphasis also needs to be placed on having a product that is satisfactory to "all" customers as opposed to "certifying" an "average" criterion. Sometimes only very simple changes are needed to make a process much better.

When choosing an effective test strategy, one needs to gain an appreciation of the fact that a DOE (where several factors are considered in one experiment) is a tool that can often help solve problems quicker than a one-at-a-time approach. When developing a process or product or fixing a problem, the "let's try this next" (i.e., one-at-a-time) strategy often prevails when attempting to get a "quick" solution. This type of test strategy can yield erroneous conclusions and the problems may never really get "fixed." Individuals should, in general, consider the more efficient alternative of evaluating several factors simultaneously using a DOE strategy.

When setting up tests using an S^4 strategy, some problems can be broken up into subgroupings for statistical assessment. However, for this strategy to be successful all areas of management in an organization must have an appreciation for the value of statistical concepts. If an S^4 strategy is incorporated, less emergency testing and fixing (i.e., less "fire fighting") in both product development and the manufacturing process can be expected. One might say: Use statistics for fire prevention. Constant job pressure to fix individual problems "now" can be very stressful. With less fire fighting, there could be less employee stress, which could lead to healthier and happier employees.

In development, S^4 techniques can lead to earlier problem detection and fewer problem escapes, with reduced development time. In manufacturing, these techniques can lead to reduced problem escapes, fixing the problem the first time, and better process understanding. The economics associated with these results can be very significant.

When developing and maintaining processes, emphasis should be given to reducing manufacturing variability—preferably during initial design stages of the development effort. If there is less variability in the process, there will be fewer defects or out-of-compliance product-fewer "fires" will need to be fought. Simple experiments in critical process steps initially can be very beneficial to reducing variability.

Consider the situation where a product failure rate criterion is to be certified before first customer shipment. Samples that are taken should not be assumed to represent a random sample of future machine builds. Random samples can only be presumed to represent the population from which they are taken. With an early production sample, the production volume may not be much larger than the sample used in the test. In addition, the lack of precision of acceleration test factors that may be used in a test adds to the uncertainty about confidence statements relative to certifying that a failure criterion is not exceeded.

Instead of taking a "random sample" of the first production builds, an S^4 strategy may be to make the sample represent future builds with configurations, part tolerances, and/or process tolerances that are typical of what is expected to be within a customer environment. DOE designs are useful when implementing such a test strategy. Within this approach many manufacturing and design factors are structurally changed to assess whether the product will perform satisfactorily within the designed or manufactured "space." The input parameters to a DOE can be set to their specification limits, and the output response is then evaluated to determine if it is "acceptable." This basic test approach can often require more initial planning and effort; however, this strategy typically leads to a much better understanding of the process which can lead to early improvements, resulting in a smaller number of future "fire fights." Overall this strategy can yield higher quality with reduced costs.

In addition to input differences with this philosophy, other output considerations beyond a defect rate can give more "statistical power" and insight to the process and design (e.g., the amount of temperature increase a machine could withstand before failure). In addition, in an established process, surprising conclusions may often result by looking at the data differently. Data analysis paralysis should be avoided. For example, a DOE analysis may indicate that a factor affects the response; however, this may have no practical importance if all DOE trial responses are well within specification. Also consider how information is presented to others. Graphical techniques not only can be very powerful in giving additional knowledge, but can also be a form that is useful in presentations to management.

Another S^4 consideration may be to assess the "design or manufacturing safety factor." With this technique stress factors are changed until failures occur. Probability plotting techniques are then used to project failure rates back to nominal conditions. This technique can be either considered with random samples or considered structurally with fractional factorial experiment designs. True randomization of the current "build vintage" will be sacrificed when using DOE concepts with this approach; however, a more desirable output of earlier problem detection and resolution may be achievable by reconsidering the test objective. This, in combination with good data analyses, can yield a more useful test result.

For a given situation, defining the best problem to solve and convincing others that this is the best problem to solve can be much more difficult than the analytical portion of the problem. It is hoped that the examples discussed in this text can be used as a model for you to help define and convince others of the best problem to solve for your specific situation.

2.7 S⁴ ASSESSMENT

This section describes classical management tools and methodologies that should be considered and integrated when appropriate within an S^4 program.

Management in recent years has encouraged the use of teams. Teams can be very powerful; however, process improvement teams sometime do not operate under a road map that leads them to quick success. A *wisely* applied S^4 implementation process can be a very effective methodology that orchestrates and expedites beneficial change. When creating the organizational infrastructure that supports a Six Sigma program, it is important to utilize Deming's 14 points.

Even organizations that have been trained in statistical process control techniques (SPC) are often guilty of reacting to the problems of the day as though they were special causes. Consider using control charting techniques at various levels within an organization. When this is done the control chart can serve a different purpose.

A high-level view (e.g., daily defect rate) might give us the insight that most of our day-to-day problems are common causes. With this knowledge we can then create an S^4 team that leads the effort toward quantifiable results. At a lower-level view, perhaps temperature was identified through DOE to be a key process input variable (KPIV) to a process. A control chart could then be used to track process temperature. When temperature goes out of control, the process should be shut down for problem resolution immediately before many poor-quality production parts are manufactured.

One should note that this form of thinking is consistent with "systems thinking" as described by Senge (1990). With systems thinking we don't lose sight of the big picture. If we don't do this and instead choose to break a complex system into many elements, the optimization of each element does not typically lead to total system optimization (e.g., optimizing purchasing costs by choosing cheaper parts can impact manufacturing costs through an increase in defect rates).

2.8 EXERCISES

1. *Catapult S^4 workshop exercise* (see Glossary for description of catapult): A company makes widgets, where the throw distance of the catapult is a measure of the quality of the widget. Each catapult represents a manufacturing plant at a different location. Teams of three to six people are assigned a catapult. Each person is assigned a role as plant manager, quality inspector, or operator (remaining people on team). The workshop instructor has three roles: president, quality manager, and chief engineer. Before attendees arrive to the workshop the instructor sets up the catapult to shoot a plastic golf ball that approximately hits a target distance (e.g., 75 inches). As chief engineer the instructor very briefly describes the shot process. He/she then asks if there are any questions. If not, he/she then explains how he/she will be out of the country for the next six months. As quality manager the instructor very briefly explains the inspection of the shot to the inspectors (e.g., if a throw is not within three inches of 75, the part is nonconforming) and gives them a tally sheet. As president the instructor explains to the plant managers that the company is having tough times. He/she explains that an executive committee went to a resort area to come up with the criterion that widgets need to be produced at a rate of at least 50 per day with an initial product yield of 99.99% that is to increase to 99.999% within 10 days. They also discussed how 50% of the production facilities would need to be closed because of economic needs. He/she also explained that a day is two minutes long and that when one day ends, the other begins immediately. Each plant manager is

given a transparency to track both volume of conforming parts and yields of good parts. The instructor immediately starts the exercise and announces whenever a new day is to begin. As president the instructor walks around the room, asking the plant managers for status and then commenting on how poorly they are doing and how they should get their operators to improve volume and quality. I typically set up my tracking charts for "10 days" (i.e., 20 minutes); however, I usually stop production after about "6 days" (i.e., 12 minutes) of chaos. Each team is given a small amount of time to prepare their status transparency that the plant managers present to the class. The president "beats up" on the plant managers for not meeting targets. After all plant site presentations are given, the instructor discusses with the class what was wrong with this picture relative to Deming's 14 points, the measurement system, the S^4 application, and so on.

2. Describe a situation where you think management, organizations, or society is addressing the wrong problem.

3. List some compensation issues that need to be addressed in team work environments and with S^4 implementation leads and teams.

4. Deming's fourth point suggests working with a small number of suppliers. Describe what should be looked for when evaluating a supplier.

5. Describe positive and negative aspects of ranking employees.

6. Describe the type of product variability (i.e., common or special cause) which is consistent but at an undesirable high level of 10%.

7. Describe a situation where a process exhibits a special cause problem.

8. Describe past instances where an existing process exhibited a breakthrough for process improvement.

9. Describe tools that can help initiate breakthrough change.

10. Even when all brainstorming rules are followed, what is a common execution problem when preparing and executing a brainstorming session?

11. Over time a process has experienced consistent variability, but a larger amount than desired. Should management be told that the process is "out-of-control"? Explain.

12. A new operator did not understand his job within manufacturing. The first day of employment he made more mistakes than other operators who performed a similar task. Describe the type of "cause" for recent problems within this process.

13. Describe the type of problem existing when a reporter every day justifies the closing price of the stock market.

14. A company needs to reduce its product development time to be competitive. Describe a basic strategy for making process improvements.

15. Describe how the techniques within this chapter can be useful and can be applied to S^4 projects.

PART II

S⁴ MEASUREMENT PHASE

This part (Chapters 3–14) addresses issues such as process definition, process performance, and the quantification of variability. Potential key process input variables (KPIVs) and key process output variables (KPOVs) are identified through consensus. Tools included within this section are basic analysis tools: Six Sigma measures, Measurement systems analysis, failure mode and effects analysis (FMEA), and quality function deployment (QFD).

3

OVERVIEW OF DESCRIPTIVE STATISTICS AND EXPERIMENTATION TRAPS

This chapter gives an overview of some basic descriptive statistics used when sampling from a population. Some of the methodologies discussed are data gathering, presentation, and simple statistics. There is an introductory discussion of confidence level and hypothesis testing, which will be discussed in more depth later. Also, there is discussion about the types of data (attribute versus continuous data) and the ineffectiveness of visual inspections.

To get a valid answer, care must be exercised when performing experiments and conducting analyses. This chapter also includes examples of experiment traps that need to be consciously avoided when conducting an experiment.

3.1 VARIABILITY AND PROCESS IMPROVEMENTS

Variability is everywhere. Consider a person who parks his/her car inside his/her garage. The final position of the car is not the same exact place day after day. The driver has variability when parking the car. Variability in parking position can be measured over time. When nothing unusual occurs this source of variability in parking position is considered common cause. However, if a cat were to jump in front of the car during parking, this might distract the driver and cause additional variability (i.e., special cause).

If his/her variability (either common or special cause) when parking is too large from the center parking position in the garage, he/she could hit the garage door frame. If parking variability is too large because of special causes (e.g., the cat) attempts need to be given to avoid the source of special cause. If parking variability is too large from common cause the process of parking needs to be changed.

For the purpose of illustration, consider a person who wants to determine his/her average parking position and the consistency he/she has in parking his/her car inside the garage. It is not reasonable to expect that he/she would need to make measurements every time that the car is parked. During some period of time (e.g., one month), he/she could periodically take measurements of the parked position of the car. These measurements would then be used to estimate, for example, an average parking position for that period of time.

Similarly, all automobiles from a manufacturing line will not be manufactured exactly the same. Automobiles will exhibit variability in many different ways. Manufacturers have many criteria (or specifications) that must consistently be achieved. These criteria can range from dimensions on parts in the automobile to various performance specifications. An example criterion is the stopping distance of the automobile at a certain speed. To test this criterion, the automobile manufacturer obviously cannot test every vehicle under actual operating conditions to determine whether it meets this criterion. In lieu of this, the manufacturer could test against this criterion using a sample from the population of automobiles manufactured.

3.2   SAMPLING

A sample is a portion of a larger aggregate (population) from which information is desired. The sample is observed and examined, but information is desired about the population from which the sample is taken. A sample can yield information that can be used to predict characteristics of a population; however, beginning experimenters often have a misconception about the details of performing such a test. They might consider taking a sample (e.g., 10) from today's production, making a measurement, averaging the results, and then reporting this value to management (for the purpose of making a decision).

Arbitrary sampling plans such as this can yield erroneous conclusions because the test sample may not accurately represent the population of interest. A sample that is not randomly selected from a population can give experimental bias, yielding a statement that is not representative of the population that is of interest. A sample of automobiles to address some criterion characteristic, for example, should be taken over some period of time with the consideration of such parameters as production shifts, workers, and differing manufacturing lines (i.e., a random sample without bias). A response (x) from samples taken randomly from a population is then said to be a random variable.

Another consideration when sampling is that if there is much variability within a population, then there may not be much confidence in the value that is reported (e.g., average or mean response). A confidence interval statement quantifies the uncertainty in the estimate because the width of the interval is a function of both sample size and sample variability. When a population characteristic such as the mean is noted to be within a confidence interval, the risk of the true value being outside this range is a quantifiable value.

Still another point not to overlook when evaluating data is that there are other estimates besides the mean that can be a very important part of expressing the characteristic of a population. One of these considerations is the standard deviation of a population, which quantifies the variability of a population. Another consideration is the capability of a process or a population percentage value compliance statement.

3.3   SIMPLE GRAPHIC PRESENTATIONS

It can be meaningful to present data in a form that visually illustrates the frequency of occurrence of values. This display of data could be accomplished using a dot plot or histogram.

A dot plot is a simple procedure to illustrate data positioning and its variability. Along a numbered line a dot plot displays a dot for each observation. Dots are stacked when data are close together. When too many points exist vertically, each dot may represent more than one point.

A histogram is another form of plot to make such illustrations. To create a histogram when the response only "takes on" certain discrete values, a tally is simply made each time a discrete value occurs. After a number of responses are taken, the tally for the grouping of occurrences can then be plotted in histogram form. For example, Figure 3.1 shows a histogram of 200 rolls of two dice, where the sum of the dice was two for eight of these rolls.

However, when making a histogram of response data that are continuous, the data need to be placed into classes (i.e., groups or cells). For example, in a set of data there might be six measurements that fall between the numbers

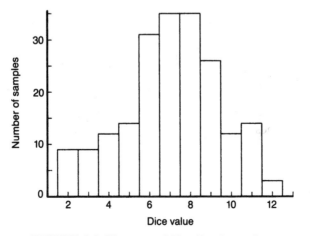

FIGURE 3.1 Histogram: 200 rolls of two dice.

of 0.501 and 1.500; these measurements can be grouped into a class that has a center value of 1. Many computer programs internally handle this grouping. Appendix B discusses a manual approach.

It should be noted that even though histograms are commonly used to illustrate data, the probability plotting techniques described in a later chapter often can give a more informative visual illustration about the population from which the data are sampled.

3.4   EXAMPLE 3.1: HISTOGRAM

A sample yields the following 24 ranked (low to high value) data points:

2.2   2.6   3.0   4.3   4.7   5.2   5.2   5.3   5.4   5.7   5.8   5.8

5.9   6.3   6.7   7.1   7.3   7.6   7.6   7.8   7.9   9.3   10.0   10.1

A computer-generated histogram plot of these data is shown in Figure 3.2.

3.5   SAMPLE STATISTICS (MEAN, RANGE, STANDARD DEVIATION, AND MEDIAN)

A well-known statistic for a sample is the mean ($\bar{x}$). The mean is the arithmetic average of the data values (x_1, x_2, x_3, ..., x_i), which is mathematically expressed in the following equation using a summation sign Σ for sample size (n) as:

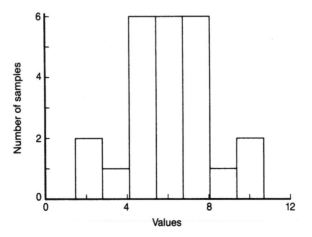

FIGURE 3.2 Histogram of the data.

$$\bar{x} = \frac{\sum\limits_{i=1}^{n} x_i}{n}$$

A sample yields an estimate $\bar{x}$ for the true mean of a population μ from which the sample is randomly drawn. Consider, for example, that the number of earned runs given by a baseball pitcher during six randomly chosen games of his career were 6, 2, 3, 3, 4, and 5. An estimate for his actual "earned run average" (for all the games that were pitched) is

$$\bar{x} = \frac{6 + 2 + 3 + 3 + 4 + 5}{6} = 3.82$$

Range is a statistic that describes data variability. It is simply the difference between the highest and lowest value of a set of data. The range for the previous set of data is 4 (i.e., $6 - 2 = 4$). Range values can give a quick assessment of data variability; however, values are dependent upon the sample size, and outlier data can give distorted results. A better measure of data variability is standard deviation.

Standard deviation is a statistic that quantifies data variability. A baseball manager, for example, might not only be interested in the average runs given by a pitcher but also his consistency between games. One equation form for the standard deviation mean(s) of a sample is

$$s = \left[\frac{\sum\limits_{i=1}^{n} (x_i - \bar{x})^2}{n - 1} \right]^{1/2}$$

A sample yields an estimate s for the true population standard deviation σ. When data have a bell-shaped distribution (i.e., are normally distributed), approximately 68.26% of the data is expected to be within a plus or minus one standard deviation range around the mean. For this example, the standard deviation estimate of the runs given by the baseball pitcher would be

$$s = \left[\frac{(6 - 3.83)^2 + \cdots}{6 - 1} \right]^{1/2} = 1.472$$

It should be noted that the standard deviation of a population, when all the data is available, is calculated using a denominator term n, not $n - 1$. Some calculators offer both standard deviation calculation options. The $n - 1$ term in the denominator of the previous equation is commonly called "degrees of freedom." This term will be used throughout this text and is assigned the

Greek letter ν (pronounced nu, as noted in Appendix E). The number of degrees of freedom is a function of the sample size and is a tabular input value often needed to make various statistical calculations.

Variance is the square of the standard deviation. Variance is equivalent to moment of inertia, a term encountered in engineering. For this illustration, the sample variance s^2 is

$$s^2 = 1.472^2 = 2.167$$

The curves shown in Figure 3.3 have a frequency distribution shape that is often encountered when "smoothing" histogram data. The mathematical model corresponding to the frequency distribution is the probability density function (PDF). Each of these density function curves are bell-shaped and are called a *normal probability density function.*

For a given sample size, a smaller standard deviation yields more confidence in the results of the experiment. This is pictorially illustrated in Figure 3.3, where case 2 has more variability than case 1, which will cause more uncertainty in any estimated population parameter mean (e.g., true population mean). Calculation of the confidence interval that quantifies this uncertainty will be discussed in a later chapter.

The sample median is the number in the middle of all the data. It can be represented as x_{50} or $\tilde{x}$. The 50 denotes that 50% of the measurements are lower than the x value (similarly, e.g., x_{30} indicates the 30th percentile). To determine the median of data, the data first need to be ranked. For the preceding set of data, the median is the mean of the two middle values, because there is an even number of data points, which is

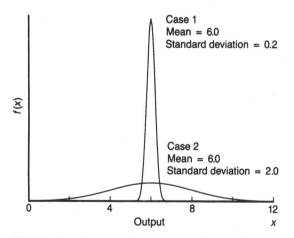

FIGURE 3.3 PDF: Effects of population variability.

$$2\ 3\ 3\ 4\ 5\ 6\text{:median} = \frac{3 + 4}{2} = 3.5$$

However, if the data were 1 2 4 5 6, the sample median would be 4, the middle of an odd number of data points.

3.6 ATTRIBUTE VERSUS CONTINUOUS RESPONSE DATA

The data discussed in the previous section are continuous data (or variable data). Continuous data can assume a range of numerical responses on a continuous scale, as opposed to data that can assume only discrete levels, whereas attribute data have the presence or absence of some characteristic in each device under test (e.g., proportion nonconforming in a pass/fail test).

An example of continuous data are the micrometer readings of a sample of parts. Examples of attribute data are which operator or machine manufactured a part. Another example of attribute data is when an inspector records the number of defects on a part. Still another example of attribute data is the output of an inspection process where parts are either passed or failed (as opposed to measuring and recording the dimension of the part).

One should strive for continuous data information over attribute information whenever possible because continuous data give more information for a given sample size. Sometimes people who build the infrastructure within an organization for how a Six Sigma business strategy will be implemented lose sight of this metrics because ppm and DPMO are attribute measurements.

There is another type of response covered within this text. The author calls this response logic pass/fail. This type of response is most common in the computer industry where a certain machine configurations will not work together. The presumption is that they will always not work together because there perhaps is a logic problem in the software (hence the term *logic*). This is not to be confused with the an attribute response where a conformance is measured in noncompliance rates or proportions. The logic pass/fail response is discussed within the chapter on pass/fail functional testing.

3.7 VISUAL INSPECTIONS

Visual inspections or checking still often remain a very large single form of inspection activity to determine if a product is satisfactory (i.e., pass/fail or attribute data). However, often characteristics do not completely describe what is needed, and inspectors need to make their own judgment. When inspections are required, standards need to be set up so that consistent decisions are made.

Another problem that can occur is that a visual inspection does not address the real desires of the customer. A classified defect found within a manufacturing organization may or may not be a typical customer issue. Also, there can be issues that a customer thinks are important which are not considered by the test.

Visual inspections often have another implication in that they often lead to the thinking that quality can be inspected into a product. This can be a very expensive approach. In addition, people typically believe that a test does better at capturing defects than it really does. An exercise at the end of this chapter and also the measurement systems analysis chapter illustrates the typical ineffectiveness of these tests.

Whether the inspections are visual or not, the frequency of defects and types of defects need to be communicated to the appropriate area for process improvement considerations. The techniques described later within this text can improve the effectiveness of these tests and reduce the frequency of when they are needed.

3.8 HYPOTHESIS TESTING AND THE INTERPRETATION OF ANALYSIS OF VARIANCE COMPUTER OUTPUTS

The purpose of this section is give a quick overview of hypothesis testing and how it relates to the interpretation of analysis of variance outputs. Both hypothesis testing and analysis of variance methods are described in more depth later. The purpose for discussing these concepts now is twofold. First, this explanation can give management a quick overview of the concepts. Second, a basic understanding of the concepts is needed for some topics (e.g., measurement systems analysis) covered before a more formal explanation.

Hypothesis tests are involved when decisions need to be made about a population. Hypothesis tests involve a null hypothesis and an alternate hypothesis. Examples of hypotheses are as follows:

- *Null:* Mean of population equals the criterion. *Alternative:* Mean of population differs from the criterion.
- *Null:* Mean response of machine A equals mean response of machine B. *Alternative:* Mean response of machine A differs from machine B.
- *Null:* Mean response from the proposed process change equals the mean response from the existing process; *Alternative:* Mean response from proposed process change does not equal the mean response from the existing process.
- *Null:* There is no difference in fuel consumption between regular and premium fuel. *Alternative:* Fuel consumption with premium fuel is less.

Two risks can be involved within a hypothesis test. These risks are typically assigned the nomenclature α and β. Within this section we will only consider the α risk.

Assume that we collect data and want to determine if there is a difference between the mean response of two machines or two departments. Our null hypothesis would be that the mean responses of the two machines (or departments) are equal, while the alternate hypothesis would be that the mean response of the two machines (or departments) are not equal.

When analyzing the data we have intent of showing a difference. In all likelihood the means of the sampled data from our two populations will not be exactly the same whether or not there is in fact a true difference between the populations. The question is whether the difference of *sample* means is large enough such that we can consider that there is a difference in the *population* means.

If we conducted a statistical analysis that indicated that there is a difference, then we would say that we reject the null hypothesis (i.e., that the two means of the population are the same) at an α risk of being in error. This α risk addresses the possibility (by the luck of the draw—we are assuming random sampling techniques are followed) that a large enough difference occurred between our samples by chance but in fact there was no difference in the population means. Hence, if we rejected the null hypothesis with an α risk of 0.05, there would be one change in 20 that we were wrong.

Many types of hypothesis tests will be discussed later in this text. The statistical method used when making the hypothesis test will vary depending upon the situation. We will later discuss how one experiment can address many hypotheses at once. To illustrate this (which will help with interpretation of analysis of variance tables), consider that a design of experiments (DOE) evaluation was to assess the impact of five input variables (or factors). These factors are designated as factor A, factor B, factor C, factor D, and factor E. Each of these factors had two levels (e.g., machine 1 vs. machine 2, operator 1 vs. operator 2, day 1 vs. day 2, machine temperature 1 vs. machine temperature 2). An experiment was then conducted and the results were analyzed using a statistical computer software package to give the output shown in Table 3.1.

For now we will only consider the values designed as p within the table for each of the five factors, which corresponds to α in our previous discussion. Basically with this analysis there are five null hypotheses, each taking the form that there is no difference between the two levels of the factor. Consider that we set a criterion of $\alpha = 0.05$. That is, if our analysis indicated a less than 1 chance in 20 of being wrong, we would reject the null hypothesis. From this table we note that the p value for factors B and C are much less than this criterion; hence, for these factors we would reject the null hypothesis. However, for factors A, D, and E the p value is not less than 0.05; hence, we can say that we do not have enough information to reject the null hypothesis at $\alpha = 0.05$.

TABLE 3.1 Analysis of Variance Output Illustration

Source	df	Seq SS	Adj SS	Adj MS	F	P
A	1	0.141	0.141	0.141	0.34	0.575
B	1	31.641	31.641	31.641	75.58	0.000
C	1	18.276	18.276	18.276	43.66	0.000
D	1	0.331	0.331	0.331	0.79	0.395
E	1	0.226	0.226	0.226	0.54	0.480
Error	10	4.186	4.186	0.419		
Total	15	54.799				

As discussed earlier, there is a statistical procedure used by the computer program to calculate these probability values. The statistic used to calculate these values is the F statistic. Sometimes there is more than one statistical approach to analyze data. Table 3.2 shows the output using another statistic, the t statistic. As you can see, many of the table outputs are different; however, the probability (p) values are the same.

Using this type of Six Sigma analysis tool, we can gain a lot of knowledge about our process. We know that if process improvement is needed, we should focus on factors B and C (not A, D, and E).

3.9 EXPERIMENTATION TRAPS

Randomization is used in experiments when attempting to avoid experimental bias. However, there are other traps that can similarly yield erroneous conclusions. For example, erroneous statements can result from not considering measurement error, poor experiment design strategy, erroneous assumptions, and/or data analysis errors.

Invalid conclusions can easily result when good statistical experimentation techniques are not followed. Perhaps more erroneous conclusions occur because of this than from inherent risks associated with the probability of getting a sample that is atypical. The next four sections illustrate examples associated

TABLE 3.2 Estimated Effects and Coefficients Output Illustration

Term	Effect	Coefficient	SD Coefficient	T	P
Constant		4.844	0.1618	29.95	0.000
A	−0.187	−0.094	0.1618	−0.58	0.575
B	−2.812	−1.406	0.1618	−8.69	0.000
C	2.138	1.069	0.1618	6.61	0.000
D	−0.288	−0.144	0.1618	−0.89	0.395
E	−0.238	−0.119	0.1618	−0.73	0.480

with poor experiment methodology. These problems emphasize the risks associated with not considering measurement error, lack of randomization, confused effects, and not tracking the details of the implementation of an experiment design.

3.10   EXAMPLE 3.2: EXPERIMENTATION TRAP—MEASUREMENT ERROR AND OTHER SOURCES OF VARIABILITY

Consider that the data in Table 3.3 are the readings [in 0.001 of a centimeter (cm)] of a functional "gap" measured between two mechanical parts. The design specifications for this gap was 0.008 ± 0.002 cm. The sample was taken from a population where the mean was 0.006 and the standard deviation was 0.002; hence, the part measurements will not be consistently within specification (which is unknown to the experimenter). This type of data could be expected from the measurements in a manufacturing line, where the 16 random samples were taken over a long period of time.

However, there are two areas that are often not considered in enough detail when making such an evaluation. First, how samples are selected when making such an assessment of the capability/performance of the response. Second, the precision and accuracy of the measurement system are often overlooked.

Relative to the sampling methodology, consider the experimenter who is being pressed for the characterization of a process. He/she may take the first product parts from a process and consider this to be a random sample of future process builds. This type of assumption is not valid because it does not consider the many other variabilities associated with processes—for example, raw material lot-to-lot variability that might occur over several days.

Relative to the measurement systems analysis, it is often assumed that gauges are more precise than they really are. It is typically desirable to have a measurement system that is at least 10 times better than the range of the response that is of interest. Measurement error can cause ambiguities during data analysis. The basic sources for error need to be understood so that a conscious effort can be taken to manage and reduce their magnitude so that clear and valid conclusions result. The variability from a measurement tool can be a large term in this equation, which can lead to erroneous conclusions about what should be done to reduce process variability.

The measured variability of parts can have many sources such as repeatability [the variability associated with the ability of appraisers getting a similar reading when given the same part again] (σ_1^2), reproducibility [the variability associated with the ability of differing appraisers obtaining a similar reading for the same part] (σ_2^2), measurement tool-to-tool (σ_3^2), within lots (σ_4^2) and between lots (σ_5^2). The total variability (σ_T^2) for this example would be equal to the sum of the variance components, which are

TABLE 3.3 Ten Random Samplings from a Normal PDF Where $\mu = 6$ and $\sigma = 2$

Within-Group Sample Number	Sampling Group Numbers									
	1	2	3	4	5	6	7	8	9	10
1	2.99	7.88	9.80	6.86	4.55	4.87	5.31	7.17	8.95	3.40
2	6.29	6.72	4.04	4.76	5.19	8.03	7.73	5.04	4.58	8.57
3	2.65	5.88	4.82	6.14	8.75	9.14	8.90	4.64	5.77	2.42
4	10.11	7.65	5.07	3.24	4.52	5.71	6.90	2.42	6.77	5.59
5	5.31	7.76	2.18	8.55	3.18	6.80	4.64	10.36	6.15	9.92
6	5.84	7.61	6.91	3.35	2.45	5.03	6.65	4.17	6.11	4.63
7	2.17	7.07	4.18	4.08	7.95	7.52	2.86	6.87	5.74	7.48
8	4.13	5.67	8.96	7.48	7.28	9.29	8.15	8.28	4.91	8.55
9	7.29	8.93	8.89	5.32	3.42	7.91	8.26	6.60	6.36	6.10
10	5.20	4.94	7.09	3.82	7.43	5.96	6.31	4.46	5.27	6.42
11	5.80	7.17	7.09	5.79	5.80	6.98	8.64	7.08	5.26	4.46
12	5.39	2.33	3.90	4.45	6.45	6.94	1.67	6.97	5.37	7.02
13	10.00	3.62	5.68	5.19	7.72	7.77	7.49	4.06	2.54	5.86
14	9.29	7.16	7.18	5.57	3.53	7.12	6.14	10.01	6.69	4.80
15	4.74	9.39	7.14	4.42	7.69	3.71	2.98	2.20	7.89	9.60
16	5.19	7.98	2.36	7.74	5.98	9.91	7.11	5.18	5.67	5.92
$\bar{x}$	5.77	6.74	5.96	5.42	5.74	7.04	6.23	5.97	5.88	6.30
s	2.41	1.86	2.30	1.59	1.97	1.69	2.19	2.38	1.42	2.14

$$\sigma_T^2 = \sigma_1^2 + \sigma_2^2 + \sigma_3^2 + \sigma_4^2 + \sigma_5^2$$

Measurements will include all these sources of variability. The precision of the measurements of parts is dependent on σ_T^2. In addition, the accuracy depends upon any bias that occurs during the measurements.

Someone in manufacturing could be confronted with the question of whether to reject initial product parts, given the information from any column of Table 3.3. With no knowledge about the measurement system, a large reproducibility term, for example, can cause good parts to be rejected and bad parts to be accepted. (Variance components and measurement systems analysis, which are discussed later, can provide an estimate of the parameters in this equation.)

3.11   EXAMPLE 3.3: EXPERIMENTATION TRAP—LACK OF RANDOMIZATION

The following measurements were made to assess the effect of pressure duration on product strength:

Test Number	Duration of Pressure (sec)	Strength (lb)
1	10	100
2	20	148
3	30	192
4	40	204
5	50	212
6	60	208

From the data plot of Figure 3.4, the strength appears to have increased with duration; however, from the preceding table it is noted that the magnitude of pressure duration was not randomized relative to the test number. The collection of data was repeated in a random fashion to yield the following:

Test Number	Duration of Pressure Mean (sec)	Strength (lb)
1	30	96
2	50	151
3	10	190
4	60	200
5	40	210
6	20	212

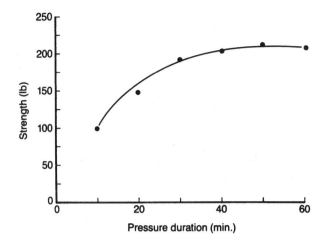

FIGURE 3.4 Plot of the first set of experimental data.

From the data plot in Figure 3.5, strength does not now appear to increase with duration. For an unknown reason the initial data indicates that strength increases with the test number. Often such unknown phenomena can cloud test results. Perhaps the first two samples of the initial experiment were taken when the machine was cold, and this was the real reason that the strength was lower. Randomization reduces the risk of an unknown phenomenon affecting a response, which can lead to an erroneous conclusion.

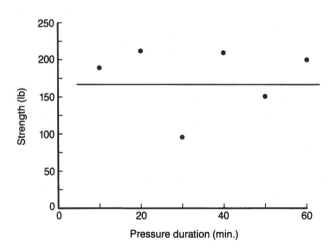

FIGURE 3.5 Plot of the second set of experimental data.

3.12   EXAMPLE 3.4: EXPERIMENTATION TRAP—CONFUSED EFFECTS

The following strategy was used to determine if resistance readings on wafers are different when taken with two types of probes and/or between automatic and manual readings. Wafers were selected from 12 separate part numbers G_1 through G_{12}, as shown in Table 3.4.

However, with this experiment design, the differences between probes are confused with the differences between part numbers. For example, wafer G_1 is never tested with probe type 2: hence, this part number could affect our decision whether probe type significantly affects the resistance readings. Table 3.5 indicates a full factorial design that removes this confusing effect. Note that future chapters will illustrate other test alternatives to full factorial experiment designs that can reduce experiment time dramatically.

3.13   EXAMPLE 3.5: EXPERIMENTATION TRAP—INDEPENDENTLY DESIGNING AND CONDUCTING AN EXPERIMENT

A system under development had three different functional areas. In each of these areas there were two different designs that could be used in production.

To evaluate the designs, an engineer built eight special systems, which contained all combinations of the design considerations (i.e., a full factorial DOE). The systems were built according to the following matrix, where the functional areas are designated as A, B, and C and the design considerations within these areas are designated either as plus mean $(+)$ or minus mean $(-)$.

System Number	Functional Area A B C
1	+ + +
2	+ + −
3	+ − +
4	+ − −
5	− + +
6	− + −
7	− − +
8	− − −

The engineer than gave the eight systems to a technician to perform an accelerated reliability test. The engineer told the technician to note the time when each system failed and call his/her after all the systems had failed. The engineer did not tell him that there were major differences between each of

TABLE 3.4 Initial Experiment Strategy

	Automatic	Manual
Probe type 1	G_1, G_2, G_3, G_4	G_1, G_2, G_3, G_4
Probe type 2	$G_5, G_6, G_7, G_8, G_9, G_{10}, G_{11}, G_{12}$	$G_5, G_6, G_7, G_8, G_9, G_{10}, G_{11}, G_{12}$

the test systems. The technician did not note any difference because the external appearance of the systems were similar.

After running the systems for one day, the technician accidentally knocked one of the systems off the table. There was no visible damage; however, the system now made a different sound when operating. The technician chose not to mention this incident because of the fear that the incident might affect his work performance rating. At the end of the test, the technician called the engineer to give the failure times for the eight systems.

During the analysis, the engineer did not note that one of the systems had an early failure time with an unexpected mode of failure. Because of schedule pressures from management, the engineer's decision was based only on "quick and dirty" statistical analysis of the mean effects of the factors without residual analysis (discussed later in this text). Unknown to the engineer, the analytical results from this experiment led to an erroneous decision that was very costly.

This type of experiment trap can occur in industry in many forms. It is important for the person who designs a test to have some involvement in the details of the test activity. When breaking down the communication barrier that exists in this example, the test designer may also find some other unknown characteristic of the design/process that is important. This knowledge along with some interdepartmental brainstorming can yield a better overall basic test strategy.

TABLE 3.5 Revised Experiment Strategy

	Auto		Manual	
	Probe 1	Probe 2	Probe 1	Probe 2
G_1	—[a]	—	—	—
G_2	—	—	—	—
.	.	.	.	.
.	.	.	.	.
.	.	.	.	.
G_{11}	—	—	—	—
G_{12}	—	—	—	—

[a] A dash indicates the tabular position of a datum point.

Wisely applied DOE techniques can be very beneficial to improve the bottom line. A DOE does not have to investigate all possible combinations of the factor levels. The text will later describe how seven two-level factors can be assessed in only eight trials.

3.14 SOME SAMPLING CONSIDERATIONS

Readers might state that it is hard to believe that they could ever fall into one or more of the preceding example traps. However, within an individual experiment these traps can be masked; they may not be readily identifiable to individuals who are not aware of the potential pitfalls.

The reader may conclude from the previous examples that this text will suggest that all combinations of the parameters (factors) need direct experimental assessment during test. This is not usually true; experimental design techniques are suggested that are manageable within the constraints of industry. This objective is achieved by using design matrices that yield much information for each test trial.

Random sampling plans are based on the assumption that errors are independent and normally distributed. In real data this independence assumption is often invalid, which can yield serious inaccuracies. If appropriate, randomization is introduced when conducting an experiment, as an approximation alternative. The adoption of the randomization approach has the advantage that it does not require information about the nature of dependence. However, there are situations where randomization is not appropriate. To illustrate this, consider stock market prices. The magnitude of the closing price on a given day is dependent on its closing price the previous day.

One approach to this data-dependence issue is to use a specific model for dependence. If such a model is valid, it is possible to develop procedures that are more sensitive than those that depend only on randomization. Box et al. (1978) illustrates with elementary examples that the ability to model dependence using time series can lead to problem solutions in the areas of forecasting, feedback control, and intervention analysis.

The sampling plans discussed later in this text assume that the process is stable. If the measurements are not from a stable process, the test methodology and confidence statements can be questionable. Even if an experiment strategy is good, the lack of stability can result in conclusions that can be erroneous.

3.15 S⁴ ASSESSMENT

It is important that management ask questions that encourage the collection and analyses of data so that much can be gained from the efforts of employees. If care is not exercised, an experimenter may simply collect data, compile the data using traditional statistical techniques, and then report the results in a form that leads to fire fighting or one-at-a-time fix attempts. For example, the direction of management might lead an experimenter to collect data and report the following with no suggestions on what steps should be taken to improve unfavorable results:

- Confidence interval on the population mean and standard deviation
- Hypothesis statement relative to an average criterion
- Process capability statement relative to a specification

When unfavorable results exist, there are many other issues that should be considered. These issues can be more important to consider than the simple reporting of the results from randomly collected data. Unfortunately, these issues can involve how the data are initially collected. A lot of resource can be wasted if thought is not given up front for the best approach to take when working to resolve an unsatisfactory situation.

For example, understanding the source of the variability in measurements may be more beneficial. A random effects model (variance components analysis) could be used in an experiment design having such considerations. Or, perhaps there should be an emphasis to understand what factors affect the average response output of an experiment.

Another possibility for inefficient data collection is the proportion of product that either passes or fails a specification. An experimenter may want to make a confidence statement about the population of this attribute information. Another application of an attribute statistic is the comparison of two populations (e.g., two machine failure rates). In these cases it is often easy for a practitioner to overlook how he/she could have benefited more if they would have considered changing traditionally reported attribute statistics to a variable assessment, so more information can be obtained about a process with less effort.

3.16   EXERCISES

1. Describe a situation where you or your organization exhibits variability.

2. Roll two dice 10 times and create a histogram. Roll two dice 50 times and create a histogram. Comment on the shape of the distributions.

3. Manually calculate the mean, standard deviation, variance, and median of the following four data sets. Comment on the results.
a.	100	100	100	100	100
b.	50	75	100	125	150
c.	50	100	100	100	150
d.	75	75	75	100	175

4. Count the number of times the sixth letter of the alphabet occurs in the paragraph and compare to others within the S^4 workshop. Save the results from your count and also save the results from other members of the workshop.

> The farmer found that his field of alfalfa had a certain type of fungus on it. The fungus was part of a family of parasitic microbes. The only answer that the farmer had found to fight the feisty fungus was to spray his fields with a toxic chemical that was not certified. It was the only method that offered him any hope of success. Unfortunately, when the farmer began to spray his fields, the federal agent from the FDA was in the area. The federal agent's opinion of the fungus was that it was not at a stage of significant concern. He offered the farmer a choice: Stop the contamination of the flora of the region or face a fine of substantial amount. The farmer halted the spraying of his alfalfa fields.

5. Manually calculate the mean, median, standard deviation, and variance of the class results for exercise 4. Show the position of these parameters on a histogram.

6. Describe a television or radio commercial that could be questioned because of the wording in their claim.

7. Describe what affects the magnitude of the level of confidence in the results, given a sample that has continuous response outputs.

8. Describe the source of measurement variability of a plastic part. Describe other sources of variability if the part were made from a cavity of a multicavity tool where there are many multicavity tools and many injecting molding machines.

9. A potential problem exists with machines that are stored within a large warehouse, where the shipping boxes are stacked high and packed close together. Management wants a test conducted on a sample of the product to assess the magnitude of the problem. Describe a major physical problem with implementing the task.

10. Describe a nonmanufacturing application of DOE.

11. Describe how you could personally apply control charting and DOE techniques at work or at home.

12. Describe how the techniques within this chapter are useful and can be applied to S^4 projects.

4

PROCESS FLOWCHARTING/ PROCESS MAPPING

For quality systems it is advantageous to represent system structure and relationships using flowcharts. A flowchart provides a picture of the steps that
are needed to create a deliverable. The process flowchart document can maintain consistency of application, identify opportunities for improvement, and
identify key process input variables. It can also be very useful to train new
personnel and expediently describe activities during audits.

A flowchart provides a complete pictorial sequence of what happens from
start to finish of a procedure. Applications include procedures documentation,
manufacturing processes, work instructions, and product development steps.
Flowcharting can minimize the volume of documentation, including ISO 9000
documentation.

However, organization can sometime spend a very large amount of resources, as part of a "program," creating flowcharts that are never referenced
or used for insight to process improvement. In lieu of a major process documentation effort within an organization, it can be better to create flowcharts
after unsatisfactory baseline measurements of the overall process are identified. The overall measurement outputs from a process can give insight to the
level of detail and how the flowcharting process should be conducted. In
addition, this baseline measurement should be used to quantify the monetary
benefits of the S^4 projects.

Flowcharting of key processes for S^4 projects should lead to the establishment and documentation of a standard operating procedure (if one does not
currently exist) that is used by all. The following of a standard operating
procedure that is documented can dramatically reduce variability and cycle
time, along with improving the product quality. In addition, a flowchart can
give insight to process improvement focus areas and other measurement
needs.

An alternative (or supplement) to a detailed process flowchart is a high level process map that shows only a few major process steps as activity symbols. For each of these symbols key process input variables (KPIVs) to the activity are listed on one side of the symbol, while key process output variables (KPOVs) to the activity are listed on the other side of the symbol. These KPIVs and KPOVs can then be used as inputs to a cause-and-effect matrix, which is described in a later chapter.

4.1 DESCRIPTION

Figure 4.1 exemplifies the form of a process flowchart. Frequently used symbols to describe the activities associated with a process map are as follows:

- **Terminal:** Symbol that defines start and end of a flowchart.
- **Activity symbol:** Symbol that contains a description of a step of the process.
- **Decision symbol:** Symbol that contains a question following an activity symbol (e.g., passes test?). The process branches into to or more paths. Each path is labeled to correspond to the answer of the question.
- **On-page connector:** Symbol identifies the connection points in a loop or the continuation in a flow. Tie-in symbols contain the same letter.
- **Off-page connector:** Initiating symbol contains a letter or number in the form "to page x," while the receiving symbol contains a letter or number in the form "from page y."

An arrowhead on the line segments that connect symbols show direction of flow. The conventional overall flow direction of a flowchart is top to bottom or left to right. Usually the return loop flow is left and up. When a loop feeds into a box, the arrowhead may terminate at the top of the box, at the side of the symbol, or at the line connecting the previous box. The use of on-page connectors on a page can simplify a flowchart by reducing the number of interconnection lines.

An illustration of a process can proceed down the left side of a page and then proceed down the right side of a page. A line or on-page connector can connect the last box of the left column with the first box of the right column.

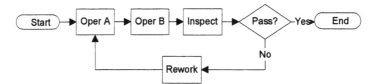

FIGURE 4.1 Process flowchart.

Boxes should be large enough to contain all necessarily information to describe who does what. Notes can contain nondirective information.

4.2   DEFINING A PROCESS AND DETERMINING KEY PROCESS INPUT/OUTPUT VARIABLES

First consider and describe the purpose and the process that is to be evaluated. Much time can be wasted trying to formally document every process within an organization. Example reasons to formally document and evaluate a process include the reduction of cycle time, reduction of defects, improved consistency of operators, reduction of new operator training time, reduction of product variability, and reduction of hidden factory reworks. When defining the purpose, consider the bottom-line benefits of the activity. Consider also the potential impact of the process that is to be evaluated to the high-level metrics that are important to management. Start with processes that have the most impact on deliverables, and then work downward from there.

Define all steps to create a product or service deliverable. This can be done several different ways. One common approach is to conduct a meeting of those familiar with a process. The team then describes the sequence of steps on a wall or poster chart using self-stick removable notes. Each process step is described on one self-stick removable note. With this approach the team can easily add and rearrange process steps. After the meeting, one person typically documents and distributes the results.

I prefer to use another approach when documenting and defining new processes. When conducting a team meeting to either define or review a process, I prefer to use a computer process flow-charting program in conjunction with a projector that projects the computer image to a screen. This approach can save a lot of time, greatly improve the accuracy, and dramatically reduce the number of types the process description needs to be reworked. Computer process charting programs offer the additional benefit of easy creation and access to subprocesses. These subprocesses can be shown as a process step that is highlighted and accessed by double clicking with a mouse.

After the process is described, brainstorming sessions can be conducted to list ideas for improvement. For the process, value-add and no-value-add steps can be identified along with key process input variables and key process output variables. These ideas can then be prioritized and action plans created.

4.3   EXAMPLE 4.1: DEFINING A DEVELOPMENT PROCESS

A computer manufacturer wants to define and improve its functional tests of a new computer design during development.

Often this type of activity is not viewed as a process because the process output crosses product boundaries. When evaluating a new product, the tendency is to determine what should be done to test a new specific computer design. People will often have the tendency to say that a new product design is a lot different than the previous product design and needs special considerations.

The structure of management and its roles and responsibilities often discourage viewing situations as processes. A new product typically will have a product manager. His/her responsibility will be to get the product through the various phases of development as quickly as possible. Their personal rewards reflect how well they conducted this activity. Their personal measurements often do not involve processes at all. When we look at the situation from this point of view, it is not hard to understand why they might not view the situation as a process. Even if they did view the situation as a process, the "what's in it for me" impetus for change would not be very strong.

The point that someone makes about a new product being different than the previous can be very true; however, often the previous product was a lot different than its predecessor. Viewing the process at a higher level can change our point of view. At a very high level we might consider the process cycle simply as four steps (design, test, manufacture, customer use). If we do this, product-to-product differences could simple be considered as noise to the process. We could then consider differences between product-to-product technology, individuals on development team, and so on, as common cause "noise to the process" unless something special occurs (e.g., a dramatically different design or an unusually major change was made to the development cycle). This perspective on the basic situation can completely change how we view the metrics of a product and what should be done different to improve.

The original problem of concern was functional testing of a computer design. The following implementation steps for defining a process (basically a process in itself) presumes that a nondocumented process previously has been conducted for earlier vintage products and that the process inputs/outputs to the process are known.

Using a computer process flow program, create a process flow that gives a high-level view of the functional test process. This process flowchart might only list the various test phases as Phase 1, Phase 2, ..., Phase 6.

Representatives who are familiar with the process are invited to a meeting (e.g., two hours) where the creation of the process is facilitated using a computer process flow program and projection system. When defining the process steps, keep the view at a fairly high level. Define subprocess steps that need further expansion off-line with other teams. Document the process as it currently exists. Describe entry requirements and deliverables to the various test phases processes. Create a list of any suggested changes to the process for future reference. The overall process meeting may take more than one session.

Between meetings the facilitator cleans up the process flowcharts and distributes them to attendees for their review and comments. Subprocess meetings are similarly conducted as needed. Upon completion of all process and subprocess meetings (and reviews), the facilitator compiles the work and puts it into a document.

Process improvement brainstorming session(s) can then be conducted. For the process, value-add and no-value-add steps can be identified along with key process input variables and key process output variables. During these session(s), each step of the process can be reviewed to stimulate both minor process improvement or more major process reengineering possibilities. A meeting can then be conducted to discuss the process change brainstorming issues and prioritize the improvement ideas. Action items and responsibilities can then be assigned. Customers and suppliers can then be asked for inputs to what they think should be done to improve the process. Monetary implication of changes should be made whenever possible.

4.4   FOCUSING EFFORTS AFTER PROCESS DOCUMENTATION

Many organizations are now documenting processes. However, often an organization does have a structured approach that leads to the next step after the documentation of a process is complete. Organizations need to have a methodology that leads them to focus areas for process improvement (or reengineering) and also the quantification of bottom-line benefits when they are made.

An approach that some Six Sigma teams use to give them insight to where focus efforts should be given is to assess all process steps to determine whether the step is "value add" or "no value add" to the end result of the process. Within this assignment, steps such as "inspection" would be given an assignment of "no value add." These assignments can then given insight to where improvement efforts should be directed.

Another consideration is to immediately conduct a cause-and-effect diagram upon the completion of a process flow diagram. Consideration is then given to how the items within a cause-and-effect diagram of a response variable, problem, goal, or objective should be addressed. When doing this, each item is assigned a classification of control, noise, or experimental. After this is completed, investigation is then given to ensure that all standard operating procedures for the process are in place and are followed to minimize the impact of the identified causes (Schmidt et al. 1997).

Another approach is to use activity based costing (ABC) for process steps. This approach offers the added flexibility of combining costs with process steps within a computer model to give insight to the prioritization of focus areas for improvement opportunities and the quantification of return on investment (ROI) for process changes (Spagon 1998).

4.5   S⁴ ASSESSMENT

It might sound like a worthy goal to document all processes within an organization. However, before initiating such a task, assess the amount of effort involved to initially create and then maintain the documentation. Consider the level of detail to include within the documentation, and also consider the order in which the various processes will be described. Then honestly assess the value of the overall effort upon completion relative to employees actually referencing and following the documented processes.

An initial assessment to document all processes may not indicate as much value as initially expected. This does not mean that time spent documenting current processes and defining improvement opportunities is not beneficial. Large rewards can be expected when the effort is spent wisely. Much value can be gained if process definition activities are linked with process metrics. This focus can also lead to the prioritization of process documentation activities. This approach often starts with a high-level view of the processes. Drill downs from this vantage point can be prioritized so that problematic areas are addressed first. After processes are developed, put them in a place where they can easily be referenced. Electronic filing of the information on a readily available media such as a website can be very beneficial.

Whether the consideration of a process improvement activity originated from an ISO 9000 requirement or from an S⁴ project, it is important to get buy-in at all levels. Practitioners need to determine the best way to get the right people involved within a team environment during the process creation. In addition to the definition of process steps, input is needed to key process input variables and key process output variables. If people who are involved within the process are a part of the process documentation and refinement process, they will more likely follow the documented process and the process definition will be more precise. This is different from a common practice of creating a process in a nonteam environment that is later reviewed for input. This practice is an analogy to the ineffective manufacturing method of "testing quality into a product," where the product is the document that was created.

When team meetings are conducted to create processes, it is essential to be considerate of the time of attendees. The practitioner who is responsible for defining processes is probably infringing on their normal day-to-day activities and deliverables to their management. As with all meetings, the facilitator should be well prepared. This is especially important for the practitioner because he/she wants to build the reputation of having efficient and effective meetings where they can see the benefits of their attendance and participation. If a good reputation is established, more attendees will attend and help during future meetings.

A projector that displays the images from a computer process flowcharting program can be very valuable to improve meeting efficiency. Consider having meetings of one or two hours' duration, depending upon the complexity of the process. Start and compete the meetings on time. Keep the meeting flowing with a focus on the objectives of the meeting. It seems that many organizations have too many meetings that are inefficiently conducted. The practitioner who is facilitating the meeting should not fall into this trap.

Perhaps the process of preparing and conducting meetings is where many organization should focus some of their initial process documentation and improvement activities. If you agree with this thought, consider how you could sell the idea to others. Consider what metrics are appropriate and do some informal data collection (e.g., track the number of hours per week that you are attending meetings or estimate how much time is wasted in meetings because people arrived late or the presenter was not prepared). Even with limited data, perhaps you can present this information to your manager in a charting format using monetary terms to get him/her thinking of the implications and possibilities. You might then get the task of working with your colleagues to create a process that will be followed preparing and conducting each meeting. This work initiative by you could be the best thing the company does for the year. Think of the benefits to you. You might get some form of monetary reward or at least the good feeling that you are not wasting as much time within meetings!

4.6 EXERCISES

1. *Catapult Exercise*
   a. *Executing a process:* Teams are handed a tape measure, a golf ball, and a catapult that has previously been set up. They can use no other equipment. They are told that each person is to shoot five shots, where the time between shots is not to exceed 10 seconds. The distant from the catapult base to impact is recorded. Operators and inspector of shot distances are rotated until a total of 100 shots are completed. The range of shot distances is noted and compared to a range specification (e.g., 6 inches) determined by the instructor. (The data are saved in a time series format for future exercises. Note in the data who was the operator and inspector for each shot.) Compare the range of shot distances for each catapult to the objective.
   b. *Process documentation:* Teams are to create a flowchart of the catapult process, list potential improvement ideas, and then repeat the previous exercise. They are given the option of using additional material. For example, a carbon paper and blank paper combination (or aluminum foil) could aid the identification of the projection impact point. Or, talcum powder could be put onto the ball before the ball is shot to aid with marking ball impact position. In addition, tape is provided to hold the catapult and tape measurer to the floor. Measurements are to be made as precisely as possible (e.g., nearest 0.1 inch). Compare the range of shot distances to the previous results. Save the data in a time series format for future exercises. Record who was the operator and inspector for each shot. Compare the range of these shot distances for each catapult to an objective provided by the instructor (e.g., 6 inches). Also compare range of distances to the previous exercise.

2. *Catapult Exercise COPQ:* Create histograms for the two sets of data created from shooting the catapult. Determine the center of the process and then establish upper and lower specification limits from the center using a distance specified by the instructor (e.g., ±3 inches from mean projection distance). A part can be reworked if it is outside the specification but close to the limit (e.g., 1 inch, as specified by instructor). Compute the cost of poor quality for each set of data given the following unit costs: inspection costs of $10.00, defect costs of $20.00, rework costs of $100.00, and scrap costs of $200. Estimate annual savings from process change; considering 10,000 "catapult projections" are made annually.

3. *Catapult Exercise Data Analysis:* Consider how an activity-based costing procedure could be used to compare the two processes for shooting and measuring the projection distance. Compare this methodology to the previously described cost of poor-quality procedure.

4. Create a process flowchart that describes your early morning activities. Consider the day of the week within the process flowchart. List key process input variables and key process output variables. Identify steps that add value and steps that do not add value. Consider what could be done to improve the process.

5. Create a process flowchart that describes the preparation and conducting of a regular meeting that you attend. List key process input variables and key process output variables. Identify steps that add value and steps that do not add value. Consider what could be done to improve the process.

6. List a process that impacts you personally at school or work. Consider what metrics could be created to get focus on how much the process needs improvement.

7. Describe how you are going to document a process for your S⁴ project.

5

BASIC TOOLS

Among other topics, Chapters 2 and 3 discussed histograms, sample mean, sample standard deviation, attribute/continuous data, and special/common cause. This chapter continues the discussion of basic techniques and offers a collection of data analysis, data presentation, and improvement alternatives.

Within this chapter a wide variety of tools are briefly described for the purpose of aiding with the efficient building of strategies for collecting and compiling information that leads to knowledge. With this knowledge we can make better decisions. The mechanics of implementing many of the topics described within this section will be covered in more depth later within this text.

5.1 DESCRIPTIVE STATISTICS

A tabular output of descriptive statistics calculated from data summarize information about the data set. The following computer output exemplifies such a summary where 14 samples (having data values designated as x_1, x_2, x_3, . . . , x_{14}) were taken from both a current product design and new product design (lower numbers are better).

DESCRIPTIVE STATISTICS

Variable:	n	Mean	Median	TrMean	SD	SE Mean
Current:	14	0.9551	0.8970	0.9424	0.1952	0.0522
New:	14	0.6313	0.6160	0.6199	0.1024	0.0274

Variable:	Minimum	Maximum	Q1	Q3
Current:	0.7370	1.3250	0.7700	1.1453
New:	0.5250	0.8740	0.5403	0.6868

This output has tabular values for the following:

- *Mean:* Arithmetic average of the data values $(x_1, x_2, x_3, \ldots, x_i)$, which is mathematically expressed in the following equation using a summation sign Σ for sample size (n): $\bar{x} = \Sigma_{i=1}^{n} x_i/n$.
- *Median:* The data of n observations are ordered from smallest to largest. For an odd sample size, median is the ordered value at $(n + 1)/2$. For an even sample size, median is the mean of the two middle ordered values.
- *TrMean (trimmed mean):* Average of the values remaining after both 5% of the largest and smallest values (rounded to the nearest integer) are removed.
- *SD:* Sample standard deviation of data, which can be mathematical expressed as $\sqrt{\Sigma(x - \bar{x})^2/(n - 1)}$.
- *SE mean (standard error of mean):* $SD/\sqrt{n}$.
- *Minimum:* Lowest number in data set.
- *Maximum:* Largest number in data set.
- *Q1 and Q3:* The data of n observations are ordered from smallest to largest. The observation at position $(n + 1)/4$ is the first quartile $(Q1)$. The observation at position $3(n + 1)/4$ is the third quartile $(Q3)$

5.2   RUN CHART (TIME SERIES PLOT)

A run chart or time series plot permits the study of observed data for trends or patterns over time, where the x-axis is time and the y-axis is the measured variable. A team can use a run chart to compare a performance measurement before and after a solution implementation to measure its impact. Generally, 20–25 points are needed to establish patterns and baselines.

Often a problem exists with the interpretation of run charts. There is a tendency to see all variation as important (i.e., reacting to each point as a special cause). Control charts offer simple tests that are to identify special cause occurrences from common cause variability through the comparison of individual datum points and trends to an upper control limit (UCL) and a lower control limit (LCL).

5.3   CONTROL CHART

Control charts offer the study of variation and its source. Control charts can give process monitoring and control and can also give direction for improvements. Control charts can separate special from common cause issues of a process. This is very important because the resolution approach is very different for these two types of situations. Reacting to fix "the problem of the day" when it is a common cause issue as though it were a special cause adds little (if any) value to the long-term performance of the process.

A typical explanation of the value for control charts is that control charts can give early identification of special causes so that there can be timely resolution (before many poor-quality parts are produced). This can be a benefit; however, often organizations focus only on the output of a process when applying control charts. This type of measurement is not really "controlling" the process and may not offer timely problem identification. To control a process using control charts, the monitoring should be of key process input variables where the process flow is stopped for resolution when this variable goes out of control.

I like to also use control charts when examining a process from a higher view point. In my opinion, this application may offer more value to an organization than using process control charts to truly control processes through the observation and reaction to key process input variable data. Deming (1986) states that 94% of the troubles belong to the system (common) cause and that only 6% are special cause. A control chart might illustrate to management (and others) that "fire-fighting" activities of the past have been the result of common cause issues. Because most of these issues were not special cause issues, this expensive approach to issue resolution had no lasting value. An argument can then be made to track the day-to-day issues using control chart. If the process is shown to be in control, issues should be looked at collectively over some period of time, where the most frequent occurring issues are resolved first using overall process improvement techniques.

The construction and interpretation of the many types of control charts (for both attribute and continuous data) are described in Chapter 10. This chapter illustrates how upper and lower control limits (UCL and LCL) are calculated for various types of data. These control limits are a function of data variability, not specification limits.

5.4 PROBABILITY PLOT

Probability plots are most often associated with tests to assess the validity of normality assumptions. When data are a straight line on a normal probability plot, the data are presumed to be from a normal distribution (bell-shaped curve). Probability plots similarly apply to other distributions such as the Weibull distribution.

Probability plots can also be used to make percentage of population statements. This can be very useful in describing the performance of business and other processes. Probability plotting techniques are described later within this text.

5.5   CHECK SHEETS

Check sheets have the systematic recording and compiling of data from historical or current observations. This information can indicate patterns and trends. After agreement is reached on the definition of events or conditions, data are collected over a period of time and presented in tabular form similar to the following:

	Week			
Problem	1	2	3	Total
A	III	IIIII	II	10
B	I	II	II	5
C	IIII	I	I	6

5.6   PARETO CHART

Pareto charts are a tool that can be helpful, for example, to identify the source of chronic problems/common causes in a manufacturing process. The Pareto principle basically states that a "vital few" of the manufacturing process characteristics cause most of the quality problems on the line, while a "trivial many" of the manufacturing process characteristics cause only a small portion of the quality problems.

A procedure to construct a Pareto chart is as follows:

1. Define the problem and process characteristics to use in the diagram.
2. Define the period of time for the diagram—for example, weekly, daily, or shift. Quality improvements over time can later be made from the information determined within this step.
3. Total the number of times each characteristic occurred.
4. Rank the characteristics according to the totals from step 3.
5. Plot the number of occurrences of each characteristic in descending order in a bar graph form along with a cumulative plot of the magnitudes from the bars. (Sometimes Pareto charts do not have a cumulative percentage overlay).
6. Trivial columns can be lumped under one column designation; however, care must be exercised not to forget a small but important item.

Note that a Pareto chart may need to consider data from different perspectives. For example, a Pareto chart of defects by machine may not be informative, while a Pareto chart of defects by manufacturing shifts could illustrate a problem source. Example 5.1 exemplifies a Pareto chart.

5.7   BRAINSTORMING

A brainstorming session can be a very valuable means to generate new ideas and get group involvement. There are many ways to conduct a brainstorming session. There are also many ways to compile the information from a brainstorming session. The generation of ideas can be generated formally or informally within a session. Flexibility should exist when choosing an approach because each team and group seems to take a personality of its own. Described next is a formal process, which can be modified to suit specific needs.

To begin this process of gathering information by brainstorming, a group of people is assembled in a room where it is preferable that tables are positioned in a manner to encourage discussion (e.g., the tables are positioned in the shape of a U). The people who are assembled should have different perspectives on the topic that is to be addressed. The problem or question is written down so that everyone can see it, and the following basic rules of the exercise are followed by the meeting leader (and explained to the members). It is preferable that the meeting leader (i.e., facilitator) have experience in conducting a brainstorming session. At a minimum a facilitator should have been a member of a previous brainstorming session.

1. Ask each member in rotation for one idea. This continues until all ideas are exhausted. It is acceptable for a member to pass a round.
2. Rule out all judgments. No idea is evaluated or criticized before considering all thoughts relevant to the problem.
3. Encourage wild ideas. It may be difficult to generate them; hence, wild ideas should not be discouraged because they encourage other wild ideas. They can always later be tamed down.
4. Encourage good natured laughter and informality.
5. Target for quantity, not quality. When there are many ideas, there is more chance of a good one being within the group.
6. Look for improvements and combinations of ideas. Participants should feel free to modify or add to the suggestions of others.

For the most effective meeting the leader should consider the following guidelines:

1. The problem needs to be simply stated.
2. Two or more people should document the ideas in plain sight so that the participants can see the proposed ideas and build on the concepts.
3. The person's name should be placed next to the idea so that the flow of ideas is not disrupted.
4. Ideas typically start slowly and build speed. Change in speed often occurs after someone proposes an offbeat idea. This change typically encourages others to try to surpass it.

5. A single session can produce over 100 ideas, but many will not be practical.
6. Many innovative ideas can occur after "sleeping on it."

A follow-up session can be used to sort the ideas into categories and rank the ideas. When ranking ideas, members vote on each idea that they think has value. For some idea considerations it is beneficial to have a discussion of the pros and cons about the idea before the vote. A circle is drawn around the ideas that receive the most votes. Through sorting and ranking, many ideas can be combined while others are eliminated.

Brainstorming can be a useful tool for a range of questions, from defining the right question to ask to determining the factors to consider within a DOE. Brainstorming sessions can be used to determine, for example, a more effective general test strategy that considers a blend of reliability testing, SPC, and DOE. The cause-and-effect diagramming tool, as discussed later in this chapter, can be used to assemble thoughts from the sessions. Personally I like to facilitate brainstorming sessions using a computer projector system. This approach can expedite the recording of ideas and dissemination of information after the session.

Computers are sometimes now used with specialized software in a network to aid with administering brainstorming sessions. This tool can be a very effective means to gather honest opinions because inputs are often anonymous.

5.8 NOMINAL GROUP TECHNIQUE (NGT)

Nominal group technique expedites team consensus on relative importance of problems, issues, or solutions. A basic procedure for conducting an NGT session is described below; however, voting procedures can differ depending upon team preferences and the situation.

An NGT is conducted by displaying a generated list of items, perhaps from a brainstorming session, on a flipchart or board. A final list is made by eliminating duplications and making clarifications. The new final list of statements is then prominently displayed, where each item is assigned a letter (i.e., A, B, . . . Z). On a sheet of paper, each person ranks the statements, assigning the most important a number equal to the number of statements and the least important the value of one. Results from the individual sheets are combined to create a total overall prioritization number for each statement.

5.9 FORCE FIELD ANALYSIS

Force field analysis can be used to analyze what forces in an organization are supporting and driving toward a solution and which are restraining progress.

The technique forces people to think together about the positives and negatives of a situation and the various aspects of making a change permanent.

After an issue or problem is identified, a brainstorming session is conducted to create a list driving forces and then a list restraining forces. A prioritization is then conducted of the driving forces that could be strengthened. There is then a prioritization of the restraining forces that could be reduced to better achieve the desired result. An example presentation format for this information is shown in Figure 5.1, where the weight of the line is an indication of the importance of a force.

5.10   CAUSE-AND-EFFECT DIAGRAM

An effective tool as part of a problem-solving process is the cause-and-effect diagram, also known as an Ishikawa diagram (after its originator Karoru Ishikawa) or fishbone diagram. This technique is useful to trigger ideas and promote a balanced approach in group brainstorming sessions where individuals list the perceived sources (causes) of a problem (effect). The technique can be useful, for example, to determine the factors to consider within a regression analysis or DOE.

When constructing a cause-and-effect diagram, it is often appropriate to consider six areas (causes) that can contribute to a characteristic response (effect): materials, machine, method, personnel, measurement, and environment. Each one of these characteristics is then investigated for subcauses. Subcauses are specific items or difficulties that are identified as a factual or potential cause to the problem (effect). Figure 5.2 exemplifies a cause-and-effect diagram. In this figure the most likely causes, which are circled, could be used, for example, as initial factor considerations within a DOE. Besides the identification of experimental factors within the cause-and-effect diagram, it can also be beneficial to identify noise factors (e.g., ambient room temper-

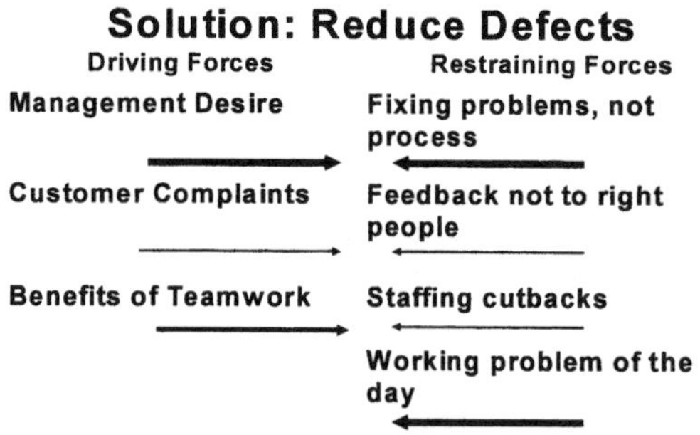

Solution: Reduce Defects

Driving Forces	Restraining Forces
Management Desire	Fixing problems, not process
Customer Complaints	Feedback not to right people
Benefits of Teamwork	Staffing cutbacks
	Working problem of the day

FIGURE 5.1 Force field analysis.

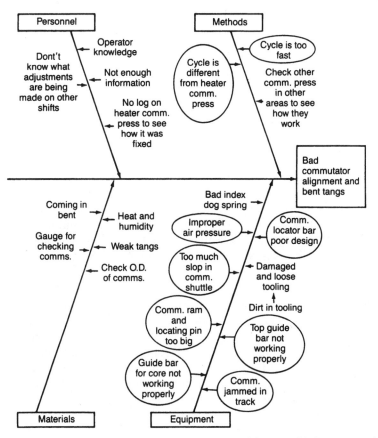

FIGURE 5.2 Completed cause-and-effect diagram with most likely causes circled. "Comm." = commutator. [From Ball and Barney (1982) p. 23, with permission.]

ature and a raw material characteristic that cannot be controlled) and factors that can be controlled (e.g., process temperature or speed).

5.11   AFFINITY DIAGRAM

Using an affinity diagram a team can organize and summarize the natural grouping from a large number of ideas and issues. From this summary teams can better understand the essence of problems and breakthrough solution alternatives.

To create an affinity diagram, boldly record each brainstorming idea individually on a "self-stick removable note," using at a minimum a noun and verb to describe each item. An affinity diagram often addresses 40–60 items but can assess 100–200 ideas. Next place the "self-stick removable note" on a wall and ask everyone to move the notes (without talking) to where they think the issue best fits them. Upon completion of this sorting, create a summary or header sentence for each grouping. Create subgroups for large groupings as needed with a subhead description. Connect all finalized headers with their groupings by drawing lines around the groupings.

5.12   INTERRELATIONSHIP DIGRAPH (ID)

An interrelationship digraph permits systematic identification, analysis, and classification of cause-and-effect relationships. From these relationships teams can focus on key drivers or outcomes to determine effective solutions.

To create an ID assemble a team (of size 4–6) that has intimate knowledge of the subject. Arrange the 5–25 items or statements from another tool (e.g., affinity diagram) in a circular pattern on a flipchart. Draw a relationship between the items by choosing any one of the items as a starting point, where a stronger cause or influence is indicated by the origination of an arrow. Upon the completion of a chart, get additional input from others and then tally the number of outgoing and input arrows for each item. A high number of outgoing arrows indicates that the item is a root cause or driver that should be addressed initially. A high number of incoming arrows indicates a key outcome item. A summary ID shows the total number of incoming and outgoing arrows next to each item. Driver and outcome items can be highlighted using a double box or bold box as a border to the item.

5.13   SCATTER DIAGRAM (PLOT OF TWO VARIABLES)

A scatter diagram is a plot to assess the relationship between two variables. This plot offers a follow-up procedure to assess the validity of a consensus relationship from a cause-and-effect diagram. When creating a scatter diagram, 50–100 pairs of samples should be plotted such that the independent variable is on the x-axis, while the dependent variable is on the y-axis.

A scatter diagram relationship does not predict a true cause-and-effect relationship. The plot only shows the strength of the relationship between two variables, which may be linear, quadratic, or some other mathematical relationship. The correlation techniques described in a later chapter can be used to test the significance of relationships.

5.14   EXAMPLE 5.1: IMPROVING A PROCESSS THAT HAS DEFECTS

As noted earlier, process control charts are useful to monitor the process stability and identify when special cause situations occur. A process is gen-

erally considered to be "'in control" whenever the process is sampled periodically in time and the measurements from the samples are within the upper
control limit (UCL) and lower control limit (LCL), which are positioned
around a center line (CL). Note that these control limits are independent of
any specification limits.

Consider the final test of a printed circuit-board assembly in a manufacturing facility that had a hypothetical process control p chart (i.e., fraction
nonconforming control chart) shown in Figure 5.3 (a run chart without control
limits could cause the organization to react to the individual ups and downs
of the chart as special cause). In this chart it is noted that sample number 1
had a defect rate approximately equal to 0.18, while the overall average defect
rate was 0.244.

This process is in control (i.e., no special causes are noted); however, the
defect rate needs to be reduced so that there will be less rework and scrap
(i.e., reduce the magnitude of common causes). A team was then formed. The
team noted the following types of production defects for the 3200 manufactured printed circuit boards (Messina 1987):

440	Insufficient solder
120	Blow holes
80	Unwetted
64	Unsoldered
56	Pinholes
40	Shorts
800	

From the Pareto Chart of the solder defects shown in Figure 5.4, it becomes
obvious that the insufficient solder characteristic should be "attacked first."

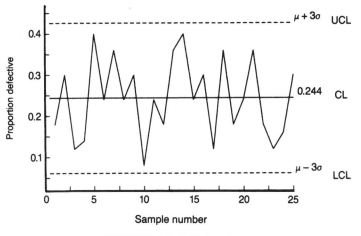

FIGURE 5.3 Initial p chart.

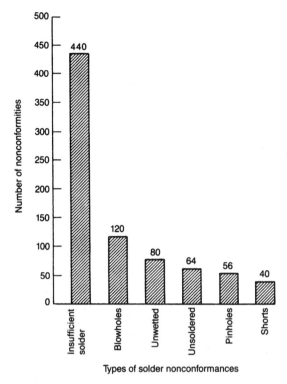

FIGURE 5.4 Pareto chart of solder defects. [From Messina (1987), with permission.]

A brainstorming session with experts (i.e., engineers, technicians, manufacturing workers, chemists, management, etc.) in the field could then be conducted to create a cause-and-effect diagram for the purpose of identifying the most likely sources of the defects. Regression analysis followed by a DOE might then be most appropriate to determine which of the factors has the most impact on the defect rate. This group of technical individuals can perhaps also determine a continuous response to use in addition to or in lieu of the preceding attribute response consideration. One can expect that a continuous response output would require a much smaller sample size.

After changes are made to the process and improvements are demonstrated on the control charts, a new Pareto chart can then be created. Perhaps the improvements will be large enough to the insufficient solder characteristic that blow holes may now be the largest of the "vital few" to be attacked next. Process control charts could also be used to track insufficient solder individually so that process degradation from the "fix level" can be identified quickly.

Changes should then be made to the manufacturing process after a confirmation experiment verifies the changes suggested by the experiments. The data pattern of the p chart should now shift downward in time because of these changes, to another region of stability. As part of a continuing process improvement program, the preceding steps can be repeated to identify other areas to improve.

5.15 EXAMPLE 5.2: REDUCING THE TOTAL CYCLE TIME OF A PROCESS

Sometimes individuals are great at fixing the small problems; however, they sometimes miss the "big picture." This example addresses a big-picture issue.

Consider the development cycle time of a complex product that needs shortening so that the needs of the customer can more expediently be met. The total development process is described in Figure 5.5.

The total development cycle time of a product is typically between 2 and 3 years. Because absolute numbers were not available from previous development cycles, brainstorming sessions were conducted to identify possible sources of improvement. Several sessions were conducted to identify areas that could be targeted for improvement (i.e., processes). Consider that after all the group sessions were completed, the total list was presented back to each group for quantification in the form of a survey. Such a survey might

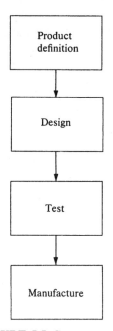

FIGURE 5.5 Current process.

ask for the amount of perceived improvement for each of the items, resulting in a Pareto chart.

Management might be surprised to learn that an item such as the procurement of standard equipment and components was the biggest deterrent to a shortened development cycle time. Management might have expected to hear something more complex such as availability of new technology.

A team was then formed for the purpose of improving the procurement cycle. The current procurement process was defined by the team, as in Figure 5.6.

To better understand the existing process, the team considered a sample situation where a new piece of computer equipment is needed by an employee in her office. The equipment costs $1000. There should be much improvement in work efficiency after the equipment item is installed. An overhead rate of $100/hr exists (i.e., it costs the company $100 for the employee's salary, benefits, space allotment, etc.) and an improvement in efficiency of $1/8$ is expected when the equipment is available for use (i.e., 5 hr for every 40-hr week). The estimated cost to procure the item is noted in the following breakdown. Because the cost is over $500, the approval process is lengthy. The itemized costs include lost efficiency because of the time it takes to receive the item (e.g., consider that the company might not have to spend so much money subcontracting out work if the employee could get more done in less time).

Because of this, time expenditures and lost revenue increased the purchase price by a factor larger than 20 (i.e., $22,100 compared to $1000; see Table 5.1). This process flow encourages the purchase of antiquated equipment. To illustrate this point, consider that during the 36 weeks of justification and budgeting a new more expensive piece of equipment is marketed. This equipment offers the opportunity of having much more productivity, which would be cost effective. But, if the purchase of this equipment would require additional delays, the employee would probably opt to purchase the "obsolete" piece of equipment in lieu of going through another justification and budget cycle. This action could cause a decrease in product quality and/or an increase in product development time.

In addition, the team also noted that with this process, it becomes only natural to play games. A department may often "justify" equipment with the anticipation that in 36 weeks it can replace this "justified" equipment with some other piece of equipment that it really needs. However, what is done if there is allotted money and they find that they really don't need the justified equipment or any substitute equipment? The team discovered that departments typically buy some equipment anyway because they may lose their typical allotted monies in the next budget cycle

The team next had a brainstorming session with people who often procure this type of equipment along with key people from the purchasing department (including managers). One outcome from this session might be that some capital equipment monies would be budgeted in the future more like existing

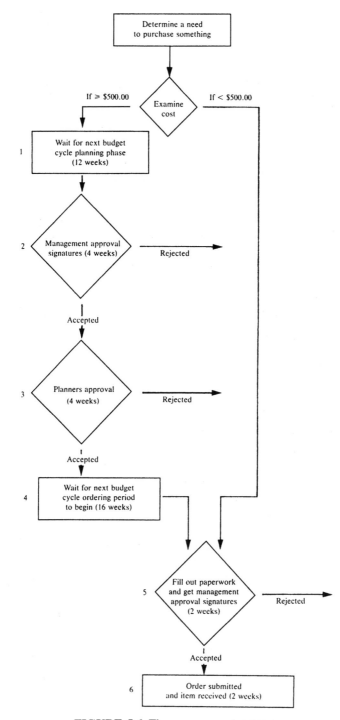

FIGURE 5.6 The procurement process.

TABLE 5.1 Lost Time and Revenue in Equipment Procurement

Step Number	Item	Cost
1	List efficiency while waiting for next budget cycle time to begin: (12 weeks) (5 hr/week) ($1000/hr) =	$6,000
2	Time writing justification and time for approval signatures: (4 hr × $100/hr) =	$400
2	Lost efficiency while waiting for equipment approval: (4 weeks) (5 hr/week) ($100/hr) =	$2,000
3	Planners' time for approving item: (2 hr × $100/hr) =	$200
3	Lost efficiency during planners' approval step: (4 weeks) (5 hr/week) ($100/hr) =	$2,000
4	Lost efficiency while waiting for next budget ordering cycle time to begin: (16 weeks) (5 hr/week) ($100/hr) =	$8,000
5	Time writing purchase order and time for approval signatures: (4 hr × $100/hr) =	$400
5	Lost efficiency while waiting for purchase order approval: (2 weeks) (5 hr/week) ($100/hr) =	$1,000
6	Time people spend in delivery of the item to correct internal location: (1 hr × $100/hr) =	$100
6	Lost efficiency while waiting for delivery of item: (2 weeks) (5 hr/week) ($100/hr) =	$1,000
	Total "process expense"	$21,100
	Item expense	1,000
		$22,100

expense monies. Each department would then be allotted a certain amount of money for engineers, administrators, technicians, and so forth, for improvements to their office equipment and other expenditures. Department managers would have the sole responsibility to authorize expenditures from these resources wisely. The team also noted that the future budget allotment for a department should not be reduced if they did not spend all their budget monies. Also, very large expenditures would be addressed in a different process flow.

5.16   EXAMPLE 5.3. IMPROVING A SERVICE PROCESS

Consider an S^4 project with a claims processing center, accounts payable organization, or typing center. Measurement data may not be recorded at all

EXAMPLE 5.3. IMPROVING A SERVICE PROCESS   **89**

within the organization. If there is documentation, periodic reporting may only be a set of numbers from one or two periods of time.

A first step for an S^4 black belt would be to work with management and a team from the area to determine a set of measurements that reflect the needs of customers and the business. The team might agree to a daily or weekly reporting time period. Example metrics determined by the team for these time periods might include the number of forms processed, the average number of forms processed per individual, the rejection rate of forms from the final customer, the rejection rate of forms that are found unsatisfactory before delivery of the document, and the time to complete a form (from initial request to final delivery). Some of these rejection rates could be converted to a DPMO rate (e.g., by considering an estimation of the number of opportunities, perhaps keystroke entries into a form). Monetary implications should be estimated for these measurements whenever possible. These measurements could be tracked over time in a control chart format.

The S^4 black belt could then work with the team to describe the process as exemplified in Figure 5.7. The team could then create a cause-and-effect diagram to aid in the identification of process improvement opportunities. During this session, team members most familiar with the process were asked to quantify the benefit of how they thought the proposed process change would benefit efficiency. Figure 5.8 is a Pareto chart that illustrates the relative magnitude of these items. Note that tasks 1, 2, and 3 in the Pareto chart affected other areas of the business; hence, they were not included in the previous process flowchart.

The implication of the issue "purchase two additional printers" needs next to be addressed because this is perceived as the most important change to make. To address this issue it was noted that if two printers were purchased, each operator could have a dedicated printer, which was thought to be much more efficient than the current queuing of jobs on the shared printers. The operators spent a lot of time walking to the printers and sorting through printer outputs to find their jobs. The cost for two printers would be

Cost for two printers = (2 printers)($2000/printer) = $4000

Given a 40% efficiency and the additional factors of a 160-hr work month for five employees at a company burden rate of $100/hr, the estimated annual cost savings after purchasing the equipment would be

0.40(160 hr/month)(12 month/yr)($l00/hr)(5 people) = $384,000

The percentile estimates made by the operators could have considerable error, and yet the purchase of these printers would still be cost effective. It is also expected that there will be fewer operator errors after the purchase of the printers because the removal of job queuing and sorting of printer outputs

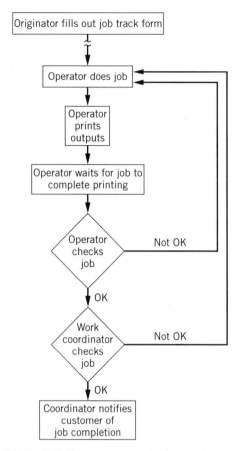

FIGURE 5.7 Current process in the service center.

will eliminate one major source of frustration in the center. A similar analysis might also be done of the lesser "leverage" items that were mentioned in the brainstorming session.

After the purchase of the equipment we would expect that a control chart of our metrics would go out of control to the better (i.e., we made a significant improvement in performance of the process). After this change is implemented we could better quantify from these metrics the true cost savings to the process from the changes.

5.17 EXERCISES

1. *Catapult Exercise:* Using the catapult exercise data sets from Chapter 4, create or determine the following for each set of data: run chart, histogram, mean, standard deviations, median, quartile 1, and quartile 3.

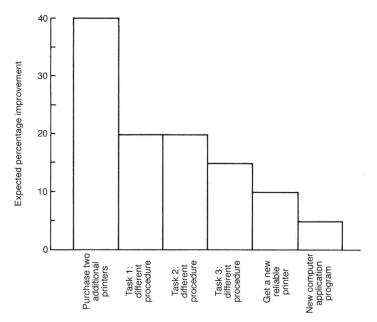

FIGURE 5.8 Pareto chart of opportunities for improvement.

2. *Catapult Exercise:* Create a cause-and-effect diagram of factors that affect throw distance. Label the factors as noise, controllable, or experimental. Select an experimental factor from the control chart (e.g., arm length). Make adjustments to this factor and monitor the projection distance. Collect 20 data points. Consider how the experiment will be executed (e.g., randomized or not). Create a scatter diagram. Save the data for a future exercise.

3. *M&M's Candy Exercise:* Open a bag of M&M's, count the number of each color, and present information in a Pareto chart. Save the data for a future analysis.

4. Determine the mean, standard deviation, variance, median, and number of degrees of freedom for the following sampled sequential data:

    9.46, 10.61, 8.07, 12.21, 9.02, 8.99, 10.03, 11.73, 10.99, 10.56

5. Create a run chart of data in the previous exercise.

6. Create a scatter plot of the following data. Describe the results.

Temp.	Strength	Temp.	Strength	Temp.	Strength
140.6	7.38	140.5	6.95	142.1	3.67
140.9	6.65	139.7	8.58	141.1	6.58
141.0	6.43	140.6	7.17	140.6	7.42
140.8	6.85	140.1	8.55	140.5	7.53
141.6	5.08	141.1	6.23	141.2	6.28
142.0	3.80	140.9	6.27	142.2	3.46
141.6	4.93	140.6	7.54	140.0	8.67
140.6	7.12	140.2	8.27	141.7	4.42
141.6	4.74	139.9	8.85	141.5	4.25
140.2	8.70	140.2	7.43	140.7	7.06

7. Describe how the techniques within this chapter are useful and can be applied to S^4 projects.

6

PROBABILITY

Processes are to deliver product, either meeting or exceeding the expectations of their customers. However, the output of many processes are subject to the effects of chance. Because of this, companies need to consider chance (or probability) when they make assessments of how well they fulfill customer expectations. This chapter gives a very brief description of some basic probability concepts and the applicability to techniques described within this text.

6.1 DESCRIPTION

Data can originate as samples of measurements from production samples (e.g., closing force for car doors) or a business process (e.g., invoice payment times). Measurements can also result from experimental evaluation (e.g., does an increase in the temperature of the process improve the yield of the process?). In all these cases if the experiment were repeated, we should get a comparable value to an initial response; however, we probably would not get exactly the same response. Because of this, we need to assess occurrence probabilities when making decisions from data (e.g., should we increase the temperature of the process to improve yield?).

When conducting an experiment (or making an evaluation) in which results will not be essentially the same even though conditions may be nearly identical, the experiment is called a random experiment. Random events can be associated with flip of a coin and the roll of die. In these cases the probability of an event is known (assuming the coin and die are fair). In the case of a flip of the coin there is one chance in two that the flip will result in "heads" (probability $= 1/2 = 0.5$). Similarly, with a six-sided die there is one chance in six that a two will occur on a single roll of the die (probability $= 1/6 = 0.167$).

In manufacturing we might similarly have a nonconformance rate of one in a hundred. Hence, any given customer would have a $1/100$ (or 0.01) probability of obtaining a product that is nonconforming. The difference between the roll of a die and this scenario is that for the manufacturing situation we typically do not know the probability of the underlying population from which we are sampling. This uncertainty relative to sampling needs consideration when we make decisions about process characterization and improvements.

These situations could also be described using a percent of population statement rather than the probability of occurrence of a single event. In the case of the flip of the coin we could state that 50% of the time a flip of the coin would be heads. Similarly we could state that 16.67% of the time a two will occur with the roll of the die. In the case of the roll of the die, we could expand our population percentage statement to a region of values. For example, 33.3% of the time a two or less will occur with the roll of the die (i.e., 16.67% for a roll of 1 plus 16.67% for a roll of 2).

If $P(A)$ represents the probability of A occurring, $P(A') = 1 - P(A)$ represents the probability of A not occurring. In the above example the probability was 0.33 of rolling a two or less; hence, the probability of not rolling a two or less is 0.67 (which is the same as the probability of rolling either a 3, 4, 5, or 6).

Sample space is a set that consists of all possible outcomes of a random experiment. A sample space that is countable is said to be discrete sample space (e.g., roll of die), while one which is not countable is to be a continuous sample space (e.g., viscosity of incoming raw material to a production process).

6.2 MULTIPLE EVENTS

If A and B are events, the following describes possible outcomes:

- Union $(A \cup B)$ is the event "either A or B or both."
- Intersection $(A \cap B)$ is the event "both A and B."
- Negation or opposite of A (A') is the event "not A."
- Difference $A - B$ is the event "A but not B."

Consider the situation where for two flips of a coin A is the event "at least one head (H) occurs" and B the event "the second toss results in a tail (T)." These events can be described as the sets

$$A = \{HT, TH, HH\}$$

$$B = \{HT, TT\}$$

For this situation we note the space describing possible outcomes as

$$(A \cup B) = \{HT, TH, HH, TT\}$$

Other events within this space are described as

$$(A \cap B) = \{HT\}$$

$$A' = \{TT\}$$

$$A - B = \{TH, HH\}$$

6.3   MULTIPLE EVENT RELATIONSHIPS

If A and B are two events that cannot occur simultaneously, then the probability that event A or event B will occur is

$$P(A \cup B) = P(A) + P(B)$$

If A and B are two events that can occur simultaneously, then the probability that event A or event B will occur is

$$P(A \cup B) = P(A) + P(B) - P(A \cap B)$$

To illustrate the application of this equation, consider that a process has two steps, where the probability of failure for the first step is 0.1 and the probability of failure at the second step is 0.05. The probability of failure from either step within the process is

$$P(A \cup B) = P(A) + P(B) - P(A \cap B) = 0.1 + 0.05 - (0.1)(0.05) = 0.145$$

If the occurrence of A influences the probability that event B will occur, then the probability that event A and event B will occur simultaneously is the following [$P(B|A)$ is the probability of B given that A has occurred]:

$$P(A \cap B) = P(A) \times P(B|A)$$

To illustrate the application of this equation, consider that the probability of drawing two aces from a deck of cards is

$$P(A \cap B) = P(A) \times P(B|A) = (4/52)(3/51) = 0.0045$$

If A and B are two independent events, then the probability that events A and B will occur simultaneously is

$$P(A \cap B) = P(A) \times P(B)$$

To illustrate the application of this equation, consider again the above process that had steps, where the probability of failure for the first step is 0.1 (i.e., yield is 0.9) and the probability of failure at the second step is 0.05 (i.e., yield is 0.95). The overall yield of the process is

$$P(A \cap B) = P(A) \times P(B) = (1 - 0.1)(1 - 0.05) = 0.855$$

Note that this answer is consistent with the earlier calculation (i.e., $0.855 = 1 - 0.145$).

6.4 BAYES' THEOREM

When there are two possible events A and B, the probability of Z occurring can be described by the theorem of total probability, which takes the form

$$P(Z) = [P(A) \times P(Z|A)] + [P(B) \times P(Z|B)]$$

A relationship that is often very useful is Bayes' theorem, which takes the form

$$P(A|Z) = \frac{P(A \cap Z)}{P(Z)}$$

To address the application of this theorem, consider the following. A production process has a product nonconformance rate of 0.5%. There is a functional test for nonconformance. A "failed test" response is supposed to indicate that a defect exists; however, the test is not perfect. For a product that has a defect, the test misses the defect 2% of the time (i.e., it reports a false "product conformance"). For machines without the defect, the test incorrectly indicates 3% of the time that they have the defect (i.e., it reports a false "product nonconformance").

The probability that a sampled machine picked at random will test satisfactory equates to the summation of the appropriate legs of the tree diagram shown in Figure 6.1, which is

$$P(\text{failed}) = [P(A) \times P(\text{failed}|A)] + [P(B) \times P(\text{failed}|B)]$$
$$= [(0.005)(0.98) + (0.995)(0.03)] = 0.03475$$

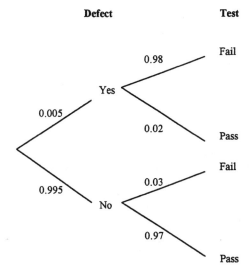

Defect   **Test**

FIGURE 6.1 Tree diagram.

where event A is the occurrence of nonconforming products and event B is the occurrence of conforming products.

From Bayes' theorem we have

$$P(\text{has a defect|failed}) = \frac{\text{Probability of being correct when defect occurs}}{P(\text{failed})}$$

$$= \frac{0.005(9.8)}{0.03475} = 0.141$$

Even though the test success rates of 98% and 97% seem high, for a test failure there is only a probability of 0.141 that the product is a true failure. The above example could similarly address the probability of a defect when the test indicated no failure. For this situation we would really like to know the first stage of the result: Does the product have a defect? The truth of this assessment is hidden because our measurement system is not perfect. The second stage of the assessment is not hidden. Hence, the best we can do is to make a prediction about the first stage by examination of the second stage.

6.5 S⁴ ASSESSMENT

Organizations often do not consider the impact of the measurement system on the validity of their actions. The probability might be relatively high that the product they reject is satisfactory, while the product they pass is unsatisfactory. Gauge R&R studies and Bayes' theorem can quantify these risks.

This information could lead to a concentrated effort on improving the measurement system, resulting in improvement to the bottom line (i.e., less satisfactory product being rejected and less product returns from customers because of nonconforming product).

6.6 EXERCISES

1. Your friend wants to have a friendly wager with you. He/she wants to bet $10.00 that two people within your organization of 30 have the same birthday. Determine whether it would be wise to take this wager by calculating the probability of occurrence.

2. A process had three steps. The probability of failure for each step equated to the roll of two dice. The probability of failure for the first step was equivalent to rolling two one's (i.e., "snake eyes"). The probability of failure for the second step was the equivalent of the roll of a seven. The probability of failure for the third step was the equivalent of rolling 11 or higher. Determine the probability of a part being manufactured with no failure.

3. For the described Bayes' example determine the probability that there is actually a defect when it passes the test.

4. A production process has a product nonconformance rate of 1%. There is a functional test for nonconformance. A "failed test" response is supposed to indicate that a defect exists; however, the test is not perfect. For product that has a defect, the test misses the defect 3% of the time (i.e., it reports a false "product conformance"). For machines without the defect, the test incorrectly indicates 4% of the time that they have the defect (i.e., it reports a false "product nonconformance"). Determine the probability of a defect when no defect was indicated by the test.

5. Describe how the techniques within this chapter are useful and can be applied to S^4 projects.

7

OVERVIEW OF DISTRIBUTIONS AND STATISTICAL PROCESSES

A practitioner does not need an in-depth understanding of all the detailed information that is presented in this chapter to solve most types of problems. A reader may choose to initially scan this chapter and then refer to this information again as needed in conjunction with the reading of other chapters in this text.

This chapter gives an overview of some statistical distributions (e.g., normal PDF) that are applicable to various engineering situations. In some situations a general knowledge of distributions can be helpful when choosing a good test/analysis strategy to answer a specific question. Detailed analysis techniques using these distributions are discussed in later chapters. Additional mathematics associated with these distributions is in the Appendix.

Hazard rate, the homogeneous Poisson process (HPP), and the nonhomogeneous Poisson process (NHPP) with Weibull intensity are also discussed in this chapter. The hazard rate is the instantaneous failure rate of a device as a function of time. The HPP and NHPP are used later in this text to model the failure rate for repairable systems. The HPP can be used to model situations where a failure rate is constant with respect to time. The NHPP can be used to model situations in which the failure rate increases or decreases with time.

7.1 AN OVERVIEW OF THE APPLICATION OF DISTRIBUTIONS

The population of a continuous variable has an underlying distribution. This distribution might be represented as a normal, Weibull, or lognormal distribution. This distribution is sometimes called the parent distribution. From a population samples can be taken with the objective of characterizing a population. A distribution that describes the characteristic of this sampling is called the sampling distribution or child distribution.

The shape of the distribution of a population does not usually need to be considered when making statements about the mean because the sampling distribution of the mean tends to be normally distributed (i.e., the Central Limit Theorem, which is discussed later in this text); however, often more useful knowledge relative to the needs of the customer is obtained by better understanding percentiles of the population. To be able to get this information, knowledge is needed about the shape of the population distribution. Instead of representing continuous response data using a normal distribution, the three-parameter Weibull distribution or lognormal distribution may, for example, better explain the general probability characteristics of the population.

The normal distribution is often encountered within statistics. This distribution is characterized by the bell-shaped Gaussian curve. The normal PDF is applicable to many sampling statistical methodologies when the response is continuous.

The binomial distribution is another common distribution. In this distribution an attribute pass/fail condition is the response that is analogous to a flip of the coin (one chance in two of passing) or a roll of a die (one chance in six of getting a particular number, which could equate to either a passing or failing probability). An application for the hypergeometric distribution is similar to the binomial distribution, except this distribution addresses the situation where the sample size is large relative to the population. These distributions are compared further in the binomial/hypergeometric distribution section of this chapter.

In addition to a continuous output or a pass/fail response, another attribute output possibility is that multiple defects or failures can occur on a sample (e.g., the sample has several defects and failures). The Poisson distribution is useful to design tests when the output takes this form.

Reliability tests are somewhat different from the previously noted sampling plans. For a reliability test, the question of concern is how long the sample will perform before failure. Initial start-up tests can be binomial (i.e., samples either pass or fail start-up). If the sample is not DOA (dead on arrival), then a reliability test model can be used to analyze the failure times from the samples.

If reliability test samples are not repairable (e.g., spark plugs in an automobile), the response of interest is percentage failure as a function of usage. The Weibull and lognormal distributions (which are discussed later in this chapter) typically can model this scenario.

If the reliability test samples are repairable (e.g., an automobile), the natural response of interest is a failure rate model (i.e., intensity function). In this type of test, systems are repaired and placed back on test after failures have occurred. The HPP is used to describe system failure rate when it has a constant (i.e., a constant intensity function) value that is independent of usage that the system has previous experienced. The NHPP can be used to model system failure rate when the instantaneous failure rate (i.e., intensity function) either increases or decreases as a function of system usage. Both of these models use the Poisson distribution to calculate the probability of seeking a certain number of failures during a fixed interval of time.

The following discussion in this chapter expands on the preceding overview. The mathematics associated with these distributions is found in Appendix A. In this chapter there is also discussion on the application of other frequently encountered distributions that have tabular probability values, which are found at the end of this text. These distributions are referenced as sampling distributions. Sampling distributions are derived from the parent distribution by random sampling. Later chapters in this text expand upon the practical implementation of these distributions/processes.

7.2 NORMAL DISTRIBUTION

The following two scenarios exemplify data that follow a normal distribution.

A dimension on a part is critical. This critical dimension is measured daily on a random sample of parts from a large production process. The measurements on any given day are noted to follow a normal distribution.

A customer orders a product. The time it takes to fill the order was noted to follow a normal distribution.

Figure 7.1 illustrates the characteristic bell shape of the normal PDF, while Figure 7.2 shows the corresponding S shape of the normal CDF. These curves were generated for $\mu = 0$ and $\sigma = 1$. The area shown under the PDF cor-

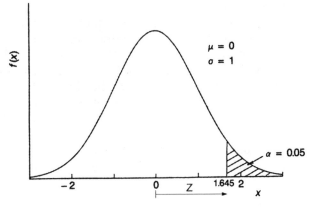

FIGURE 7.1 Normal PDF.

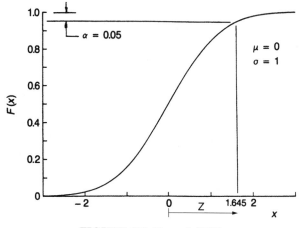

FIGURE 7.2 Normal CDF.

responds to the ordinate value of the CDF. Any normal X variable governed by $X \sim N(\mu;\sigma^2)$ [this is a shorthand notation for a normally distributed random variable X with mean μ and variance σ^2] can be converted into variable $Z \sim N(0;1)$ using the relationship

$$Z = \frac{X - \mu}{\sigma}$$

A commonly applied characteristic of the normal distribution is the relationship of percent of population to the standard deviation. To pictorially illustrate this relationship, it can be noted from the normal PDF equation in Appendix A that the CDF is dependent only on the mean μ and standard deviation σ. Figure 7.3 pictorially quantifies the percent of population as a function of standard deviation.

In Appendix D, area under the standardized normal curve values is shown in Tables A, B, and C. To conceptually illustrate the origin of these tables, the reader can note from Table B that $U_\alpha = U_{0.05} = 1.645$, which is the area shaded in Figure 7.1. Also the quantity for U_α is noted to equal the double-sided value in Table C when $\alpha = 0.10$ (i.e., the single-sided probability is multiplied by 2). In addition, the single-sided value equates to the value that can be determined from Table A for $Z_\alpha = Z_{0.05}$ (i.e., a more typical table format).

As an additional point to illustrate the preceding concept, the reader can also note that the 2σ value of 95.46% from Figure 7.3 equates to a double-tail (α) area of approximately 0.05 [i.e., $(100 - 95.46)/100 \approx 0.05$]. For an $\alpha = 0.05$, Table C yields a value of 1.960, which approximately equates to the σ value of 2.0 shown in Figure 7.3 (i.e., $\pm 2\sigma$ contains approximately 95% of the population).

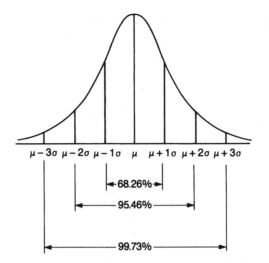

FIGURE 7.3 Properties of a normal distribution.

As a side note, most texts consider only one type of table for each distribution. The other table forms were included in this text so that the practitioner can more readily understand single- and double-tail probability relationships and determine the correct tabular value to use when solving the types of problems addressed in this text.

The reader should be aware how a text or computer program computes a Z statistic. The area for a Z value is sometimes computed from the center of the distribution.

7.3   EXAMPLE 7.1: NORMAL DISTRIBUTION

The diameter of bushings is $\mu = 50$ mm with a standard deviation of $\sigma = 10$ mm. Let's estimate the proportion of the population of bushings that have a diameter equal to or greater than 57 mm.

For $P(X \geq 57$ mm$)$, the value of Z is

$$Z = \frac{X - \mu}{\sigma} = \frac{57 \text{ mm} - 50 \text{ mm}}{10 \text{ mm}} = 0.7$$

Table A yields $P(X \geq 57$ mm$) = P(Z \geq 0.7) = 0.2420$ (i.e., 24.20%).

7.4   BINOMIAL DISTRIBUTION

A binomial distribution is useful when there are only two results in a random experiment (e.g., pass or failure, compliance or noncompliance, yes or no, present or absent). The tool is frequently applicable to attribute data. Altering the first scenario discussed under the normal distribution section to a binomial distribution scenario yields the following:

> A dimension on a part is critical. This critical dimension is measured daily on a random sample of parts from a large production process. To expedite the inspection process, a tool is designed to either pass or fail a part that is tested. The output now is no longer continuous. The output is now binary (pass or fail for each part); hence, the binomial distribution can be used to develop an attribute sampling plan.

Other application examples are as follows:

- Product either passes or fails test; determine the number of defective units.
- Light bulbs work or do not work; determine the number of defective light bulbs.
- People respond yes or no to a survey question; determine the proportion of people who answer yes to the question.
- Purchase order forms are either filled out incorrectly or correctly; determine the number of transactional errors.
- The appearance of a car door is acceptable or unacceptable; determine the number of parts of unacceptable appearance.

The following binomial equation could be expressed using either of the following two expressions:

- The probability of exactly x defects in n binomial trials with probability of defect equal to p is [see $P(X = x)$ relationship]
- For a random experiment of sample size n where there are two categories of events, the probability of success of the condition x in one category (where there is $n - x$ in the other category) is

$$P(X = x) = \binom{n}{x} p^x(q)^{n-x}, \qquad x = 0, 1, 2, ..., n$$

where $(q = 1 - p)$ is the probability that the event will not occur. Also, the binomial coefficient gives the number of possible combinations respect to the number of occurrences, which equates to

$$\binom{n}{x} = {}_nC_x = \frac{n!}{x!(n - x)!}$$

From the binomial equation it is noted that the shape of a binomial distribution is dependent on the sample size (n) and the proportion of the population having a characteristic (p) (e.g., proportion of the population that is not in compliance). For an n of 8 and various p values (i.e., 0.1, 0.5, 0.7, and 0.9), Figure 7.4 illustrates these four binomial distributions (for the probability of an occurrence P), while Figure 7.5 shows the corresponding cumulative distributions.

When the number of occurrences of the event is zero ($x = 0$), the binomial equation becomes

$$P(X = 0) = \frac{n!}{x!(n - x)!} \, p^x q^{n-x} = q^n = (1 - p)^n$$

$P(X = 0)$ has application as a Six Sigma metric and is sometimes called first time yield (Y_{FT}) and equates to $Y_{FT} = q^n = (1 - p)^n$.

7.5 EXAMPLE 7.2: BINOMIAL DISTRIBUTION—NUMBER OF COMBINATIONS AND ROLLS OF DIE

The number of possible combinations of three letters from the letters of the word "quality" (i.e., $n = 7$ and $x = 3$) is

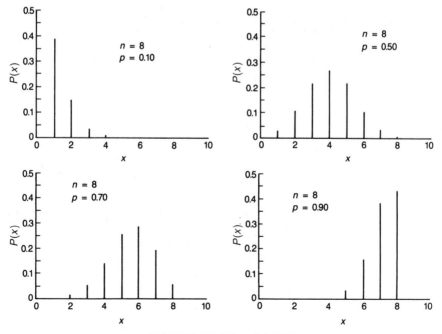

FIGURE 7.4 Binomial PDF.

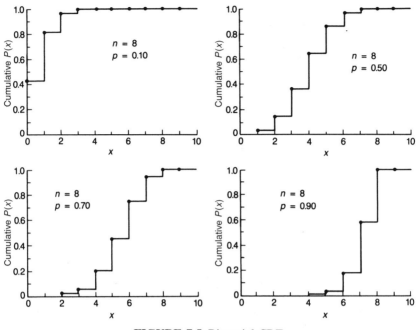

FIGURE 7.5 Binomial CDF.

$$_nC_r = \frac{n!}{x!(n-x)!} = \frac{7!}{3! \times 4!} = \frac{7 \times 6 \times 5 \times 4 \times 3 \times 2}{3 \times 2 \times 4 \times 3 \times 2} = 35$$

Consider now that the probability of having the number "2" appear exactly three times in seven rolls of a six-sided die is

$$P(X = 3) = \binom{n}{x} p^x(1-p)^{n-x} = (35)(0.167)^3(1 - 0.167)^{7-3} = 0.0784$$

where the number 35 was determined previous under a similar set of numeric values and 0.167 is the probability of a roll of "2" occurring (i.e., $\frac{1}{6}$ = 0.167). Hence, the probability of getting the number "2" to occur exactly three times in seven rolls of a die is 0.0784.

Similarly, we could calculate the probability of "2" occurring for other frequencies besides three out of seven. A summary of these probabilities (e.g., the probability of rolling a "2" one time is 0.390557) is as follows:

$$P(X = 0) = 0.278301$$

$$P(X = 1) = 0.390557$$

$$P(X = 2) = 0.234897$$

$$P(X = 3) = 0.078487$$

$$P(X = 4) = 0.015735$$

$$P(X = 5) = 0.001893$$

$$P(X = 6) = 0.000126$$

$$P(X = 7) = 3.62E\text{-}06$$

The probabilities from this table sum to one. From this summary we note that the probability, for example, of rolling a "2" three, four, five, six, or seven times is 0.096245 (i.e., 0.078487 + 0.015735 + 0.001893 + 0.000126 + 3.62256×10^{-6}).

7.6   EXAMPLE 7.3: BINOMIAL—PROBABILITY OF FAILURE

A part is said to be defective if a hole that is drilled into it is less or greater than specifications. A supplier claims a failure rate of 1 in 100. If this failure rate were true, the probability of observing one defective part in 10 samples is

$$P(X = 1) = \frac{n!}{x!(n - x)!} p^x q^{n-x} = \frac{10!}{1!(10 - 1)!} (0.01)^1 (0.99)^{10-1} = 0.091$$

The probability of the test having a defect is only 0.091.

This exercise has other implications. An organization might choose a sample of 10 to assess a criterion failure rate of 1 in 100. The effectiveness of this test is questionable because the failure rate of the population would need to be a lot larger than 1/100 for their to be a good chance of having a defective test sample. That is, the test sample size is not large enough to do an effective job.

7.7   HYPERGEOMETRIC DISTRIBUTION

Use of the hypergeometric distribution in sampling is similar to that of the binomial distribution except that the sample size is "large" relative to the population size. To illustrate this difference, consider that the first 100 parts of a new manufacturing process were given a pass/fail test where one part failed. A later chapter shows how a confidence interval for the proportion of defects within a process can be determined given the one failure in a sample of 100. However, in reality the complete population was tested; hence, there is no confidence interval. The experimenter is 100% confident that the failure rate for the population that was sampled (i.e., the 100 parts) is 0.01 (i.e., 1/100). This illustration considers the extreme situation where the sample size equals the population size. The hypergeometric distribution should be considered whenever the sample size is larger than approximately 10% of the population. Appendix A shows the mathematics of this distribution.

7.8 POISSON DISTRIBUTION

A random experiment of a discrete variable can have several events and the probability of each event is low. This random experiment can follow the Poisson distribution. The following two scenarios exemplify data that can follow a Poisson distribution.

> There are a large number of dimensions on a part that are critical. Dimensions are measured on a random sample of parts from a large production process. The number of "out-of-specification conditions" are noted on each sample. This collective "number-of-failures" information from the samples can often be modeled using a Poisson distribution.

> A repairable system is known to have a constant failure rate as a function of usage (i.e., follows an HPP). In a test a number of systems are exercised and the number of failures are noted for the systems. The Poisson distribution can be used to design/analyze this test.

Other application examples are estimating the number of cosmetic non-conformances when painting an automobile, projecting the number of industrial accidents for next year, and estimating the number of unpopped kernels in a batch of popcorn.

The probability of observing exactly x events in the Poisson situation is given by the Poisson PDF:

$$P(X = x) = \frac{e^{-\lambda}\lambda^x}{x!} = \frac{e^{-np}(np)^x}{x!}, \qquad x = 0, 1, 2, 3, \ldots$$

where e is a constant of 2.71828, x is the number of occurrences, and λ can equate to a sample size multiplied by the probability of occurrence (i.e., np). $P(X = 0)$ has application as a Six Sigma metric for yield, which equates to $Y = P(X = 0) = e^{-\lambda} = e^{-D/U} = e^{-DPU}$, where D is defects, U is unit, and DPU is defects per unit.

The probability of observing a or fewer events is

$$P(X \le a) = \sum_{x=0}^{a} P(X = x)$$

The Poisson distribution is dependent only on one parameter, the mean (μ) of the distribution. Figure 7.6 shows Poisson distributions (for the probability of an occurrence P) for the mean values of 1, 5, 8, and 10, while Figure 7.7 shows the corresponding cumulative distributions.

7.9   EXAMPLE 7.4: POISSON DISTRIBUTION

A company observed that over several years they had a mean manufacturing line shutdown rate of 0.10 per day. Assuming a Poisson distribution, determine the probability of two shutdowns occurring on the same day.

For the Poisson distribution, $\lambda = 0.10$ occurrences/day and $x = 2$ results in the probability

$$P(X = 2) = \frac{e^{-\lambda}\lambda^x}{x!} = \frac{e^{-0.1}0.1^2}{2!} = 0.004524$$

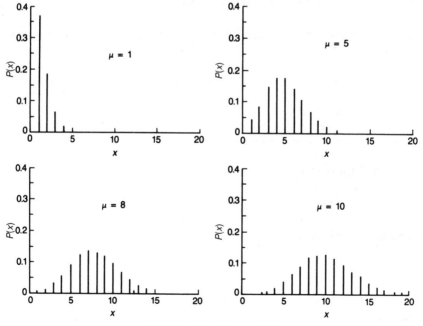

FIGURE 7.6 Poisson PDF.

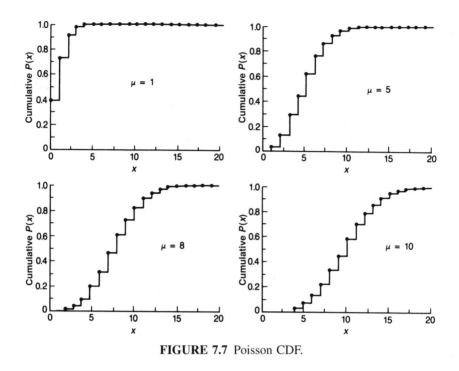

FIGURE 7.7 Poisson CDF.

7.10   EXPONENTIAL DISTRIBUTION

The following scenario exemplifies a situation that follows an exponential distribution:

> A repairable system is known to have a constant failure rate as a function of usage. The time between failures will be distributed exponentially. The failures will have a rate of occurrence that is described by an HPP. The Poisson distribution can be used to design a test where sampled systems are tested for the purpose of determining a confidence interval for the failure rate of the system.

The PDF for the exponential distribution is simply

$$f(x) = (1/\theta)e^{-x/\theta}$$

Integration of this equation yields the CDF for the exponential distribution

$$F(x) = 1 - e^{-x/\theta}$$

The exponential distribution is only dependent on one parameter (θ), which is the mean of the distribution (i.e., mean time between failures). The instantaneous failure rate (i.e., hazard rate) of an exponential distribution is constant and equals $1/\theta$. Figure 7.8 illustrates the characteristic shape of the PDF, while Figure 7.9 shows the corresponding shape for the CDF. The curves were generated for a θ value of 1000.

7.11   EXAMPLE 7.5: EXPONENTIAL DISTRIBUTION

The reported mean time between failure rate of a system is 10,000 hours. If the failure rate follows an exponential distribution, the time when $F(x)$ is 0.10 can be determined from substitution into the relationship.

$$F(x) = 1 - e^{-x/\theta} = 0.10 = 1 - e^{-x/10,000}$$

which is 1054 hours.

7.12   WEIBULL DISTRIBUTION

The following scenario exemplifies a situation that can follow a two-parameter Weibull distribution:

> A nonrepairable device experiences failures through either early-life, intrinsic, or wear-out phenomena. Failure data of this type often follow the Weibull distribution.

The following scenario exemplifies a situation where a three-parameter Weibull distribution is applicable:

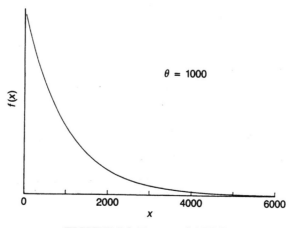

FIGURE 7.8 Exponential PDF.

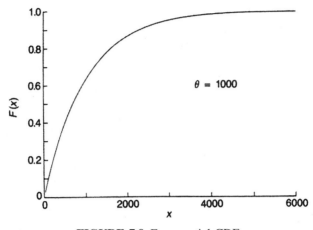

FIGURE 7.9 Exponential CDF.

A dimension on a part is critical. This critical dimension is measured daily on a random sample of parts from a large production process. Information is desired about the "tails" of the distribution. A plot of the measurements indicate that they follow a three-parameter Weibull distribution better than they follow a normal distribution.

As illustrated in Figures 7.10 and 7.11, the Weibull distribution has shape flexibility; hence, this distribution can be used to describe many types of data.

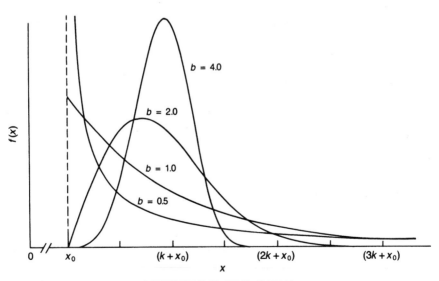

FIGURE 7.10 Weibull PDF.

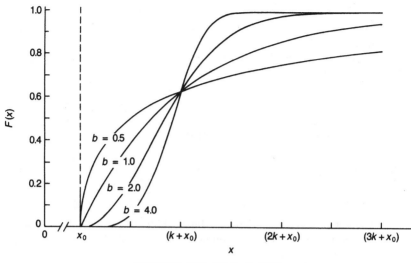

FIGURE 7.11 Weibull CDF.

The shape parameter (b) in the Weibull equation defines the PDF shape. Another parameter is k (scale parameter or characteristic life), which describes conceptually the magnitude of the x-axis scale. The other parameter contained within the three-parameter model is the location parameter (x_0), which is the x-axis intercept equating to the value where there is zero probability of lesser values.

For reliability models, x_0 usually equals zero. The proportion of failures $F(x)$ at a certain time reduces to simply

$$F(x) = 1 - \exp\left[-\left(\frac{x}{k}\right)^{b}\right]$$

Appendix A has more detailed information on the mathematical properties of the Weibull distribution.

7.13   EXAMPLE 7.6: WEIBULL DISTRIBUTION

A component has a characteristic life of 10,000 hours and a shape parameter of 1. It is expected that 90% of the systems are expected to survive x determined from substituting into the relationship

$$F(x) = 1 - \exp\left[-\left(\frac{x}{k}\right)^{b}\right] = 0.10 = 1 - \exp\left[-\left(\frac{x}{10{,}000}\right)^{1}\right]$$

which is 1054 hours. Note that this is the same result as the exponential distribution example. The parameters within this example are a special case of the Weibull distribution, which equates to the exponential distribution. Here the scale parameter of the Weibull distribution equates to the mean of the exponential distribution.

7.14 LOG-NORMAL DISTRIBUTION

The following scenario exemplifies a situation that can follow a log-normal distribution:

> A nonrepairable device experiences failures through metal fatigue. Time of failure data from this source often follows the lognormal distribution.

Like the Weibull distribution, the lognormal distribution exhibits many PDF shapes, as illustrated in Figures 7.12 and 7.13. This distribution is often useful in the analysis of economic, biological, life data (e.g., metal fatigue and electrical insulation life), and the repair times of equipment. The distribution can often be used to fit data that has a large range of values.

The logarithm of data from this distribution is normally distributed; hence, with this transformation, data can be analyzed as if they came from a normal distribution. Note in Figures 7.12 and 7.13 that μ and σ are determined from the transformed data.

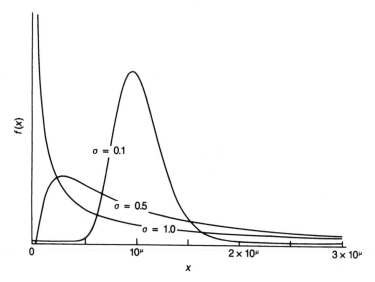

FIGURE 7.12 Lognormal PDF.

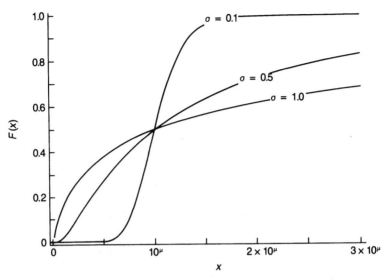

FIGURE 7.13 Lognormal CDF.

7.15 TABULATED PROBABILITY DISTRIBUTION: CHI-SQUARE DISTRIBUTION

The chi-square distribution is an important sampling distribution. One application of this distribution is where the chi-square distribution (Table G) is used to determine the confidence interval for the standard deviation of a population.

If x_i, where $i = 1, 2, \ldots, \nu$, are normally and independently distributed with means μ_i and variances σ_i^2 the chi-square variable can be defined as

$$\chi^2(\nu) = \sum_{i=1}^{\nu} \left[\frac{x_i - \mu_i}{\sigma_i} \right]^2$$

In Figure 7.14 the chi-square distribution is shown to be a family of distributions that is indexed by the number of degrees of freedom (ν). The chi-square distribution has the characteristics $\mu = \nu$ and $\sigma^2 = 2\nu$.

Table G gives percentage points of the chi-square distribution. From this table, for example, $\chi^2_{\alpha;\nu} = \chi^2_{0.10;50} = 63.17$, which is illustrated pictorially in Figure 7.14.

7.16 TABULATED PROBABILITY DISTRIBUTION: t DISTRIBUTION

Another useful sampling distribution is the t distribution. Applications of the t distribution include the confidence interval of the population mean and con-

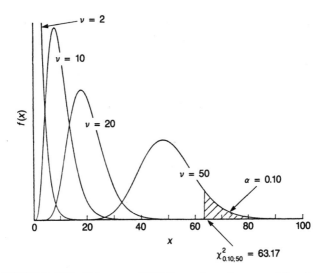

FIGURE 7.14 Chi-square PDF for various degrees of freedom.

fidence statistics when comparing sampled population means. In these equations, probability values from the t distribution (see Tables D and E) are used to determine confidence intervals and comparison statements about the population mean(s).

In Figure 7.15 the t distribution is shown to be a family of distributions that is indexed by the number of degrees of freedom (v). The distribution is

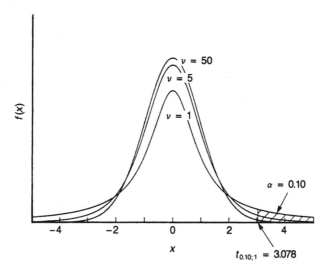

FIGURE 7.15 t PDF for various degrees of freedom.

symmetrical; hence, $t_{1-\alpha;v} = -t_{\alpha;v}$. Tables D and E give probability points of the t distribution. Table D considers the single-sided probability of the distribution tail, while Table E contains the probability of both tails (i.e., double-sided). From Table D, for example, $t_{\alpha;v} = t_{0.10;1} = 3.078$, which is illustrated pictorially in Figure 7.15. A double-sided value equates to the single-sided value when the single-sided probability is multiplied by 2. For example, the double-sided 0.20 level equates to the 0.10 single-sided value (i.e., from Table E, $t_{\alpha;v}$ (double-sided) $= t_{0.20;1} = 3.078$ equates to the preceding value).

As the number of degrees of freedom approaches infinity, the distribution approaches a normal distribution. To illustrate this note that from Table D, $t_{0.10;\infty} = 1.282$, which equates to the value $U_{0.10}$ in Table B and $Z_{0.10}$ in Table A.

7.17   TABULATED PROBABILITY DISTRIBUTION: *F* DISTRIBUTION

The F distribution is another useful sampling distribution, which is the t distribution squared. An application of the F distribution (see Table F) is the test to determine if two population variances are statistically different in magnitude.

The F distribution is a family of distributions defined by two parameters, v_1 and v_2. Figure 7.16 shows example shapes for this distribution. Table F gives percentage points of the F distribution. From this table, for example, $F_{\alpha;v_1;v_2} = F_{0.10;40;40} = 1.51$, which is illustrated pictorially in Figure 7.16.

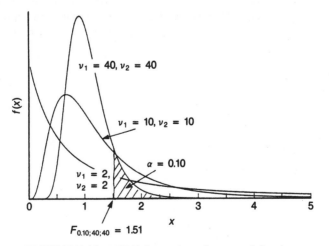

FIGURE 7.16 *F* PDF for various degrees of freedom.

7.18   HAZARD RATE

Hazard rate is the probability that a device on test will fail between (t) and an additional infinitesimally small increment unit of time (i.e., $t + dt$), if the device has already survived up to time (t). The general expression for the hazard rate (λ) is

$$\lambda = \frac{f(t)}{1 - F(t)}$$

where $f(t)$ is the PDF of failures and $F(t)$ is the CDF of failures at time t. The $[1 - F(t)]$ quantity is often described as the reliability of a device at time t (i.e., survival proportion).

The hazard rate (failure rate) can often be described by the classical reliability bathtub curve shown in Figure 7.17. For a nonrepairable system, the Weibull distribution can be used to model portions of this curve. In the Weibull equation a value of $b < 1$ is characteristic of early-life manufacturing failures, a value of $b > 1$ is characteristic of a wear-out mechanism, and a value of $b = 1$ is characteristic of a constant failure rate mode (also known as intrinsic failure period).

The hazard rate equations for the exponential and Weibull distributions are shown in Appendix A.

7.19   NONHOMOGENEOUS POISSON PROCESS (NHPP)

The Weibull distribution can be used to estimate the percent of the population that is expected to fail by a given time. However, if the unit under test is repaired, then this percentage value does not have much meaning. A more desirable unit of measure would be to monitor the system failure rate as a

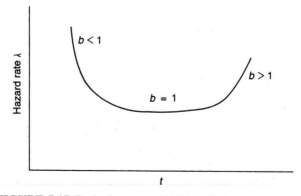

FIGURE 7.17 Bathtub curve with Weibull shape parameters.

function of usage. For a repairable system, this failure rate model is called the intensity function. The NHPP with Weibull intensity is a model that can consider system repairable failure rates that change with time. The following scenario exemplifies the application of this NHPP.

> A repairable system failure rate is not constant as a function of usage. The NHPP with Weibull intensity process can often be used to model this situation when considering the general possibilities of early-life, intrinsic, or wear-out characteristics.

The NHPP with Weibull intensity function can be expressed mathematically as

$$r(t) = \lambda b t^{b-1}$$

where $r(t)$ is instantaneous failure rate at time t and λ is the intensity of the Poisson process.

7.20 HOMOGENEOUS POISSON PROCESS (HPP)

This model considers that the failure rate does not change with time (i.e., a constant intensity function). The following scenario exemplifies the application of the HPP.

> A repairable system failure rate is constant with time. The failure rate is said to follow an HPP process. The Poisson distribution is often useful when designing a test of a criterion that has an HPP.

The HPP is a model that is a special case of the NHPP with Weibull intensity, where b equals 1. With this substitution the HPP model is noted to have a constant failure rate. It can be noted that the intensity of the HPP equates to the hazard rate of the exponential distribution (i.e., they both have a constant failure rate).

$$r(t) = \lambda$$

7.21 APPLICATIONS FOR VARIOUS TYPES OF DISTRIBUTIONS AND PROCESSES

Table 7.1 summarizes the application of distributions and processes to solve a variety of problems found in this text.

For engineering applications the previous sections of this chapter have shown common density functions for continuous responses and the discrete

TABLE 7.1 Distribution/Process Application Overview

Distribution or Process	Applications	Examples
Normal distribution	Can be used to describe various physical, mechanical, electrical, and chemical properties.	Part dimensions Voltage outputs Chemical composition level
Binomial distribution	Can be used to describe the situation where an observation can either pass or fail.	Part sampling plan where the part meets or fails to meet a specification criterion
Hypergeometric distribution	Similar to the binomial distribution; however, the sample size is large relative to the population size.	Binomial sampling where a sample of 50 is randomly chosen from a population of size 100
Lognormal distribution	Shape flexibility of density function yields an adequate fit to many types of data. Normal distribution equations can be used in the analysis.	Life of mechanical components that fail by metal fatigue Describes repair times of equipment
Weibull distribution (2-parameter)	Shape flexibility of density function conveniently describes increasing, constant and decreasing failure rates as a function of usage (age).	Life of mechanical and electrical components
Weibull distribution (3-parameter)	Shape flexibility of two-parameter distribution with the added flexibility that the zero probability point can take on values that are greater than zero.	Mechanical part tensile strength Electrical resistance
Exponential distribution	Shape can be used to describe device system failure rates that are constant as a function of usage.	MTBF or constant failure rate of a system
Poisson distribution	Convenient distribution to use when designing tests that assumes that the underlying distribution is exponential.	Test distribution to determine whether a MTBF failure criterion is met
HPP	Model that describes occurrences that happen randomly in time.	Modeling of constant system failure rate
NHPP	Model that describes occurrences that either decrease or increase in frequency with time.	System failure rate modeling when the rate increases or decreases with time

distribution function for a binary response. In addition, this discussion has shown some models to describe the instantaneous failure rate of a process.

The equation forms for the discrete distributions noted in Appendix A are rather simple to solve even though they initially look complex. By knowing the sample size and the percentage of good parts, the mechanics of determining the probability (chance) of getting a "bad" or "good" individual sample involves only simple algebraic substitution. Unfortunately in reality the percent of good parts is the unknown quantity, which cannot be determined from these equations without using an iterative solution approach.

An alternative approach to this binomial criterion validation dilemma is to use another distribution that closely approximates the shape of the binomial distribution. As mentioned earlier, the Poisson distribution is applicable to address exponential distribution problems. The Poisson distribution can also be used for some binomial problems. This can be better understood by noting how the binomial distribution shape in Figure 7.4 skews toward the shape of the exponential distribution in Figure 7.8 when the proportion defective (p) is a low number. However, when the proportions of good parts approach 0.5, the normal distribution can be utilized. This can again be conceptually understood by comparing the distribution shapes between Figure 7.4 (when p is near 0.5) and Figure 7.1.

Table 7.2 gives some rules of thumb to determine when the preceding approximations can be used, along with determining whether the binomial distribution is applicable in lieu of the hypergeometric distribution.

The distributions previously discussed are a few of the many possible alternatives. However, these distributions are, in general, sufficient to solve most industrial engineering problems.

An exception to this statement is the multinomial distribution, where the population can best be described with more than one distribution (e.g., bimodal distribution). This type of distribution can occur, for example, when a supplier sorts and distributes parts that have a small plus or minus tolerance at an elevated piece price. The population of parts that are distributed to the larger plus or minus tolerance will probably have a bimodal distribution.

TABLE 7.2 Distribution Approximations

Distribution	Approximate Distribution	Situation
Hypergeometric	Binomial	$10n \leq$ population size (Miller and Freund 1965)
Binomial	Poisson	$n \geq 20$ and $p \leq 0.05$. If $n \geq 100$, the approximation is excellent as long as $np \leq 10$ (Miller and Freund 1965)
Binomial	Normal	np and $n(1 - p)$ are at least 5 (Dixon and Massey 1969)
		$n =$ sample size; p proportion (e.g., rate of defective parts)

A specific example of this situation is the distribution of resistance values for resistors that have a $\pm 10\%$ tolerance. A manufacturer may sort and remove the $\pm 1\%$ parts that are manufactured thereby creating a bimodal situation for the parts that have the larger tolerance.

7.22   S⁴ ASSESSMENT

When there is an alternative, attribute sampling inspection plans are not, in general, as desirable as a continuous sampling plan, which monitors the measurement values. For the parts in the above sampling plan, no knowledge is gained as to the level of goodness or badness of the dimension relative to the criterion. Attribute test plans can often require a much larger sample size than sampling plans that evaluate measurement values.

7.23   EXERCISES

1. *Catapult Data Analysis:* Using the catapult exercise data sets from Chapter 4, determine Z for an X value that is specified by the instructor (e.g., 78 inches). Determine the probability of a larger value. Show this probability relationship in a histogram plot of the data.

2. *M&M's Candy Data Analysis:* In an exercise within Chapter 5 a bag of M&M's candy was opened. Compile the total number of brown colors from all attendees. Plot the data. Estimate the number of browns expected 80% of the time.

3. The diameter of a shaft has $\mu = 75$ mm with a standard deviation of $\sigma = 8$ mm. Determine the proportion of the population of bushings that have a diameter less than 65 mm.

4. Determine the proportion of the population described in the previous exercise that has a diameter between 55 mm and 95 mm.

5. An electronic manufacturer observed a mean of 0.20 defects per board. Assuming a Poisson distribution, determine the probability of three defects occurring on the same board.

6. Give an example application of how each of the following distributions could be applicable to your personal life: normal, binomial, hypergeometric, Poisson, exponential, Weibull, log normal, NHPP, HPP.

7. List the important parameters for each of the following: Normal distribution (e.g., mean and standard deviation), binomial distribution, Poisson distribution, exponential distribution, two-parameter Weibull distribution, lognormal distribution, NHPP, HPP.

8. Determine the following values from the appropriate table:

U (one-sided): probability $= 0.10$

U (two-sided): probability $= 0.20$

Z: probability $= 0.10$

Chi-square: probability $= 0.10$, degrees of freedom $= 20$

t distribution, one-sided: probability $= 0.05$, degrees of freedom $= 5$

t distribution, two-sided: probability $= 0.10$, degrees of freedom $= 5$

F distribution: probability $= 0.05$, degrees of freedom in numerator $= 10$, degrees of freedom in denominator $= 5$

9. One hundred computers were randomly selected from 10,000 manufactured during last year's production. The times of failure were noted for each system. Some systems had multiple failures, while others did not work initially when the customer tried to initially use the system. Determine what modeling distribution(s) could be appropriate to describe the failures.

10. Note the distribution(s) that could be expected to describe the following:

(a) Diameters produced for an automobile's piston

(b) Time to failure for the brake lining of an automobile

(c) A random sample of 10 electronic computer cards from a population of 1000 that either pass or fail test

(d) A random sample of 10 cards from a population of 50 that either pass or fail test

(e) Test evaluating a computer system MTBF rate

(f) Distribution of automobile failures that has a constant failure rate

(g) The time to failure of an inexpensive watch

11. An electronic subassembly is known to have a failure rate that follows a Weibull distribution where the shape parameter is 2.2 and its character life is 67 months. Determine the expected failure percentage at an annual usage of 12 months.

12. At 10,000 hr, 20% of an electrical component type fail. Determine its reliability at 10,000 hr.

13. A component has a Weibull probability plot with a slope of 0.3 and then later changes to 2.0. Describe what physically happened.

14. A repairable system has an intensity of 0.000005 and a b constant of 1.3. Determine its failure rate at 1500 hours.

15. Describe how the techniques within this chapter are useful and can be applied to S^4 projects.

8

PROBABILITY AND HAZARD PLOTTING

Chapter 7 discussed various types of probability density functions (PDFs) and their associated cumulative distribution functions (CDFs). This chapter illustrates the concepts of PDF, CDF, probability plotting, and hazard plotting.

Probability plotting, in particular, is a very powerful tool that is used in many different situations throughout this text. When sampling from a population, a probability plot of the data can often yield a better understanding of the population than traditional statements made only about the mean and standard deviation.

8.1 DESCRIPTION

Percent characteristics of a population can be determined from the cumulative distribution function (CDF), which is the integration of the probability density function (PDF). Probability and hazard plots are useful to visually assess how well data follow distributions and estimate from data the unknown parameters of a PDF/CDF. These plots can also be used to estimate the percent less than (or greater than) characteristics of a population.

A basic concept behind probability plotting is that if data plotted on a probability distribution scale (e.g., normal probability paper, see Table Q1) follow a straight line, then the population from which the samples are drawn can be represented by that distribution. When the distribution of data is noted, statements can be made about percentage values of the population, which can often be more enlightening than the mean and standard deviation statistics.

There are many different types of probability papers (i.e., coordinate systems) to address data from differing distributions (e.g., normal PDF or Weibull

124

PDF). Some computer programs can generate probability plots conveniently and yield precise parameter estimations. However, manual plots can also be generated using probability paper, which can be obtained from sources such as TEAM (see reference section). Some blank probability papers are included near the end of this text so that the reader will have the opportunity to immediately apply this powerful tool to a variety of problems.

Probability and hazard plots of the same data are interchangeable for practical purposes (Nelson 1982). For ease of manual calculations, this text will use probability plotting when the data are not censored (e.g., all component failure times are available from a reliability test), while hazard plotting will be used when there are censored data (e.g., all the components did not fail during a reliability test).

8.2 PROBABILITY PLOTTING

When creating a histogram, data are grouped into intervals. A PDF can describe the shape of a histogram, where the area under the PDF is equal to 100% of the population. The median of the variable described by a PDF, for example, is the value where the area under the curve is split 50/50 [i.e., 50% of the population is less than (or greater than) the median value]. Other percentiles of population values can similarly be determined; however, because this percentage value is the area under a curve, it is difficult to get an accurate value for any given value of the variable on the abscissa of a PDF.

As noted earlier, the PDF is integrated to yield the CDF, which graphically yields population percentile (less than or greater than) values on one axis of the plot. However, drawing a line through test data to determine population characteristics is not accurate because the data do not typically follow a straight line on commonly used graph papers.

To address this nonlinear plotting situation, probability paper can be used because the axes are transformed such that a particular CDF shape will appear as a straight line if the data are from that distribution. The mathematics behind this transformation is illustrated for the Weibull PDF (see Appendix B.5). The following example illustrates this transformation from a conceptual point of view.

8.3 EXAMPLE 8.1: PDF, CDF, AND THEN A PROBABILITY PLOT

Consider the following 25 ranked (low to high) measurements:

3.8   4.6   4.6   4.9   5.2   5.3   5.3   5.4   5.6   5.6   5.7   5.8   5.9

6.0   6.1   6.1   6.3   6.3   6.4   6.5   6.6   6.8   7.0   7.4   7.6

In these data there is, for example, one output response between 3.6 and 4.5, while there are seven between 4.6 and 5.5. These ranked values can be grouped into cells (see Table 8.1) and then be plotted to create the histogram shown in Figure 8.1. These measurements form a bell-shaped PDF that is characteristic of a normal distribution. Figure 8.2 illustrates an integration plot of the data from Figure 8.1, yielding the characteristic S-shaped curve of the normal CDF.

Figure 8.3 next illustrates a transformation of the raw data via a normal probability plot. To make this plot, the following probability plot coordinate positions were used in conjunction with the original data set. The origin of these positions will be discussed in the next section of this chapter:

Data point:	3.8	4.6	4.6	4.9	5.2	5.3	5.3	5.4	5.6
Plot position:	2.0	6.0	10.0	14.0	18.0	22.0	26.0	30.0	34.0
Data point:	5.6	5.7	5.8	5.9	6.0	6.1	6.1	6.3	
Plot position:	38.0	42.0	46.0	50.0	54.0	58.0	62.0	66.0	
Data point:	6.3	6.4	6.5	6.6	6.8	7.0	7.4	7.6	
Plot position:	70.0	74.0	78.0	82.0	86.0	90.0	94.0	98.0	

8.4   PROBABILITY PLOT POSITIONS AND INTERPRETATION OF PLOTS

Probability paper has one axis that describes percentage of the population, while the other axis describes the variable of concern. For example, a straight line on probability paper intersecting a point having the coordinates 30% (less than) and 2.2 can be read as "30% of the population is estimated to have values equal to or less than 2.2." Note that this could mean that 30% of the devices exhibit failure before a usage of 2.2 or that a measurement is expected

TABLE 8.1 Data Groupings

Response	Test Data[a] (number of items)	Test Data[b] Integration (number of items less than or equal to a value)
3.6–4.5	1	1
4.6–5.5	7	8
5.6–6.5	12	20
6.6–7.5	4	24
7.6–8.5	1	25

[a]For Figure 8.1.
[b]For Figure 8.2.

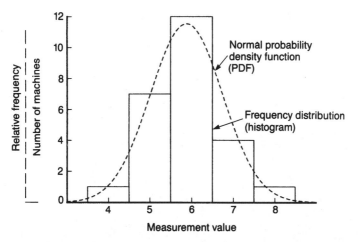

FIGURE 8.1 Frequency distribution and normal PDF.

to be less than 2.2 for 30% of the time. The precise statement wording depends on the type of data under consideration.

Consider an evaluation in which components were to be tested to failure; however, some of the samples had not yet experienced a failure at the test termination time. Only measured data (e.g., failure times) can be plotted on probability paper; individual censored datum points (e.g., times when components were removed from test without failure) cannot be plotted. When there are censored data, these data affect the percentage value plot considerations of the uncensored data. Because the adjustment of these plot positions

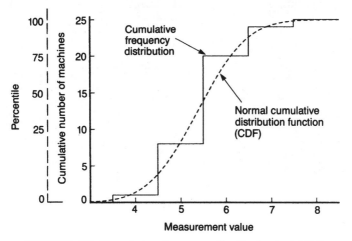

FIGURE 8.2 Cumulative frequency distribution and CDF.

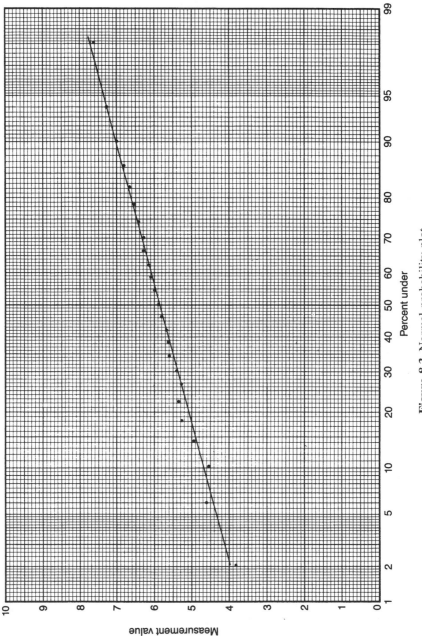

Figure 8.3 Normal probability plot.

utilizes a cumbersome and difficult algorithm, this text will use hazard plots, as discussed later in this chapter, to address the manual analysis of data that contains some censored data points.

With uncensored data, the coordinate position of each plot point relates to the measured value and a percentage value. For a sample of uncensored data, a simple generic form commonly used to determine the percentage value for ranked data (F_i) (Nelson 1982) is

$$F_i = \frac{100(i - 0.5)}{n}, \qquad i = 1, 2, \ldots, n$$

where n is the sample size and i is the ranking number of the data points. For convenience, values from this equation are tabulated within Table P for sample sizes up to 26. Appendix B discusses some other probability plot position equations that may, in general, yield a more precise plot position for a given set of data.

There are many types of probability paper. Within this text, normal, log-normal, and Weibull are discussed. Data from a distribution follow a straight line when plotted on a probability paper created from that distribution. Hence, if a distribution is not known, data can be plotted on different papers in an attempt to find the probability paper distribution that best fits the data. In lieu of a manual plot, a computer program could be used to generate a probability plot and make a lack of fit assessment of how the data fit the model.

Probability plots have many applications. These plots are an excellent tool to gain better insight into what may be happening physically in an experiment. A probability plot tells a story. For example, a straight line indicates that a particular distribution may adequately represent a population, while a "knee" can indicate that the data are from two (or more) distributions. One data point that deviates significantly from an otherwise straight line on a probability plot could be an outlier that is caused, for example, by an erroneous reading. Later chapters of this text discuss the application of probability plotting relative to measured data, utilizes the technique to determine the reliability of a device, and discusses applications relative to DOE analyses.

Other texts discuss the mathematics that is used to perform the various formal lack-of-fit tests. A manual lack-of-fit check procedure is discussed in Appendix B. However, in many situations a simple visual examination can be adequate if care is taken not to overreact and conclude that a distribution assumption is not valid because the data do not visually fit a straight line "well enough." Visually assessing data fit is further illustrated by Daniel and Wood (1980), where 40 normal probability plots of 16 independent standard normal deviates ($\mu = 0$ and $\sigma = 1$) contain more dispersion than may intuitively be expected.

8.5   HAZARD PLOTS

Most nonlife data are complete (i.e., not censored). Reliability test of life data may also be complete when the time to failure of each sample is noted. However, reliability tests of this type commonly contain failure times for some samples and cumulative usage's for other test samples that have not experienced failure. There are several types of censoring possible (Nelson 1982); however, this text considers only multiple time censoring where failure times are noted and test samples may be removed from test at any time (in general, some can be removed earlier than others). Graphically, this is shown in Figure 8.4.

As noted earlier, this problem is addressed manually in this text using hazard plots. The following procedure can be used to plot data on hazard paper (see Tables R1 to R3 for blank normal, lognormal, and Weibull hazard papers).

1. Ranked data are assigned a reverse rank number (j), which is independent of whether the data points were from censoring or failure. A "+" sign indicates that the device has not yet failed at the noted time.
2. A hazard value ($100/j$) for each *failure* point is determined, where j is the reverse ranking.
3. Cumulative hazard values are determined for these failure points. This value is the sum of the current hazard value and the previous failed cumulative hazard value. These hazard values may exceed 100%.
4. The cumulative hazards are plotted with the failure times on hazard plotting paper.

If the data follow a straight line on the hazard plot, the data are from the distribution described by that paper. The example in the next section illustrates the creation of a hazard plot.

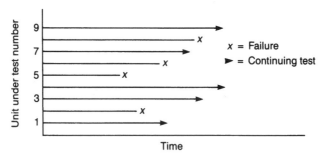

FIGURE 8.4 Multiple censored test.

8.6   EXAMPLE 8.2: HAZARD PLOTTING

Consider that the ranked data from the previous example were from an accelerated reliability test that had some censoring. In Table 8.2 the data (censored data are noted by a + sign) are shown along with the results from applying the steps noted in the previous section.

Time of failure data from a nonrepairable device often follow a Weibull distribution. From the hazard plot of this data in Figure 8.5, it is noted that the data can be fitted by a Weibull distribution because the data follow a straight line on Weibull hazard paper. Percentage values for a failure time are then estimated by using the upper probability scale. For example, 90% of the population is expected to have a value less than 7.0. An example of a reliability statement given these numbers from a test would be as follows: A "best

TABLE 8.2 Hazard Plot Data/Calculations

Time of Failure or Censoring Time (yr)	Reverse Rank (j)	Hazard ($100/j$)	Cumulative Hazard
3.8	25	4.0	4.0
4.5	24	4.2	8.2
4.6	23	4.3	12.5[b]
4.9	22	4.5	17.0
5.2+[a]	21		
5.3	20	5.0	22.0
5.3	19	5.3	27.3
5.4+	18		
5.6	17	5.9	33.2
5.6	16	6.3	39.5
5.7	15	6.7	46.2
5.8+	14		
5.9	13	7.7	53.9
6.0	12	8.3	62.2
6.1	11	9.1	71.3
6.1	10	10.0	81.3
6.3+	09		
6.3	08	12.5	93.8
6.4	07	14.3	108.1
6.5	06	16.7	124.8
6.6	05	20.0	144.8
6.8+	04		
7.0	03	33.3	178.1
7.4	02	50.0	228.1
7.6+	01		

[a] Censoring times are identified by a + sign.
[b] For example, 12.5 = 8.2 + 4.3.

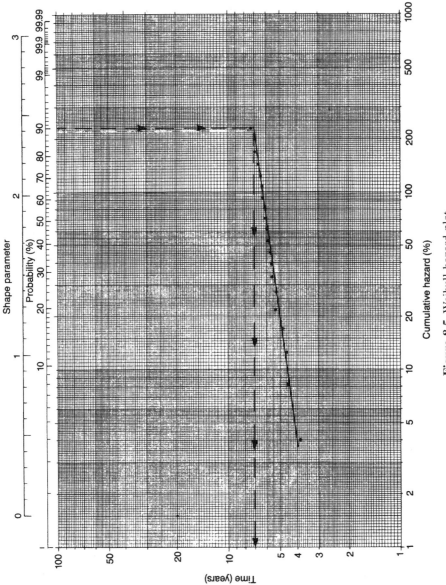

Figure 8.5 Weibull hazard plot.

estimate" is that 90% of the devices will fail in the customer's office before a usage of 7.0 years. A later chapter has more discussion about the application of hazard plots to reliability data.

8.7 SUMMARIZING THE CREATION OF PROBABILITY AND HAZARD PLOTS

A histogram is a graphical representation of a frequency distribution determined from sample data. The empirical cumulative frequency distribution is then the accumulation of the number of observations less than or equal to a given value.

Both the frequency distribution and cumulative frequency distribution are determined from sample data and are estimates of the actual population distribution. Mathematically, the PDF and CDF are used to model the probability distribution of the observations. The PDF is a mathematical function that models the probability density reflected in the histogram. The CDF evaluated at a value x is the probability that an observation takes a value less than or equal to x. The CDF is calculated as the integral of the PDF from minus infinity to x. The procedure often used to determine a PDF for a given set of data is to first assume that the data follow a particular type of distribution and then observe whether the data can be adequately modeled by the selected distribution shape. This observation of data fit to a distribution can be evaluated using a probability plot or hazard plot.

Chapter 7 gave an overview of the common PDFs that describe some typical frequency distribution shapes, and it summarized the application of distributions and processes to solve a variety of problems found in this text.

8.8 PERCENTAGE OF POPULATION STATEMENT CONSIDERATIONS

Appendix B discusses other things to consider to make when generating either manual or computer probability plots. This appendix discusses techniques for determining the best-fit line on a probability plot and whether this line (i.e., the PDF) adequately describes the data.

Confidence interval statements relative to a percent of population plot can take one of two general forms. For example, in Figure 8.3 the following two questions could be asked:

1. The population percentile estimate below 7.0 is 90%. What are the 95% confidence bounds for this percentile estimate?
2. The 90% population percentile is estimated to have a value of 7.0. What are the 95% confidence bounds around this estimate?

This text does not address the confidence interval calculations for percentiles. Nelson (1982) includes an approximation for these limits, while King (1980b) addresses this issue by using graphical techniques with tabular plot positions. Statistical computer programs can offer confidence intervals for probability plots.

This text focuses on the normal, Weibull, and log-normal distributions to solve common, industrial problems. Nelson (1982) and King (1980b, 1981) discuss other distributions that may be more appropriate for a given set of data.

8.9   S⁴ ASSESSMENT

The most frequent application of probably plots is the test for data normality. This can be beneficial; however, a probability plot can also describe percentage statements. This approach can be especially useful to describe the transactional processes (e.g., 80% of the time, orders take 2–73 days to fulfill), where specifications often don't exist. This can be more meaningful than fabricating criteria so that a process capability index can be created for this business process. A two-parameter Weibull plot is often very useful for this situation because this distribution is truncated at zero, which is often the case when time (e.g., delivery time) is the reported metric.

8.10   EXERCISES

1. *Catapult Exercise Data Analysis:* Using the catapult exercise data sets from Chapter 4, create two normal probability plots. Assess how well data fits a normal distribution and whether there are any outliers. Determine from the chart the probability of a larger value than the value use in the previous exercise (e.g., 75 inches). Estimate from the probability plot the range of values expected 80% of the time. Determine these values mathematically using the Z table (i.e., Table A).

2. Consider a situation where a response equal to or greater than 12.5 was undesirable. The collection of data was very expensive and time-consuming; however, a team was able to collect the following set of random measurements: 9.46, 10.61, 8.07, 12.21, 9.02, 8.99 10.03, 11.73, 10.99, 10.56.

   (a) Conduct an attribute assessment.

   (b) Make a visual assessment of data normality using a histogram. From the plot estimate the mean and percentage of time 12.5 or larger.

   (c) Make a visual assessment of data normality using a normal probability plot. From this plot estimate the median and percentage of time 12.5 or larger. Estimate the response level where 10% is below. Estimate the response level that 10 % of the population does not exceed. Estimate the range of response exhibited by 80% (i.e. $\pm 40\%$ from the median) of the population.

(d) Use the Z table (i.e., Table A) to refine these estimates.

3. Describe a business process application and/or S^4 project application of the normal probability plot that can improve the explanation and understanding of a process output (e.g., 80% of the payment for invoices are between -5 and 120 days delinquent).

4. Give an example of censored data from a reliability test and a nonreliability test.

5. Describe how the techniques within this chapter are useful and can be applied to S^4 projects.

9

SIX SIGMA MEASUREMENTS

This chapter summarizes metrics that are often associated with Six Sigma (Harry 1994a, 1994b). It is not suggested that an organization utilize all the described metrics. Some of these metrics are very controversial. The real value of an S^4 program is the process of continuous improvement that produces good results despite the possible shortcoming of some of its metrics.

The intent of this chapter is to provide a concise overview of Six Sigma metric alternatives so that an organization can better select metrics and calculation techniques that are most appropriate for their situation. Even if an organization does not utilize the described methodologies, a basic knowledge is still needed so that there is good communication with other organizations, suppliers, and customers that might be using or developing their application of Six Sigma techniques. Improved communication of the described metrics could make a very significant impact to the bottom line of an organization by reducing the chance for misunderstandings that lead to defects.

9.1 CONVERTING DEFECT RATES (DPMO OR PPM) TO SIGMA QUALITY LEVEL UNITS

Chapter 1 showed the sigma quality level relationship from a normal distribution to a parts-per-million (ppm) defect rate. This discussion also described the impact of a shift of the mean by 1.5σ, which is often assumed within a Six Sigma program to account for "typical" process drifting.

Sometimes organizations calculate a ppm defect rate or defects per million opportunities (DPMO) rate and then convert this rate to a Six Sigma measurement unit that considers this 1.5σ shift. Table S describes the relationship of ppm defect rates to sigma quality level units with and without the shift the by 1.5σ. This sigma quality level relationship with the 1.5σ shift can be approximated (Schmidt and Launsby 1997) by the equation

$$\text{Sigma quality level} = 0.8406 + \sqrt{29.37 - 2.221 \times \ln(\text{ppm})}$$

9.2   SIX SIGMA RELATIONSHIPS

The following summarizes Six Sigma nomenclature, basic relationships, yield relationships, and standardized normal distribution relationships for Z that will be described throughout this chapter:

Nomenclature

- Number of operation steps $= m$
- Defects $= D$
- Unit $= U$
- Opportunities for a defect $= O$
- Yield $= Y$

Basic Relationships

- Total opportunities: $TOP = U \times O$
- Defects per unit: $DPU = \dfrac{D}{U}$
- Defects per unit opportunity: $DPO = \dfrac{DPU}{O} = \dfrac{D}{U \times O}$
- Defects per million opportunity: $DPMO = DPO \times 10^6$

Yield Relationships

- Throughput yield: $Y_{TP} = e^{-DPU}$
- Defects per unit: $DPU = -\ln(Y)$
- Rolled throughput yield: $Y_{RT} = \Pi_{i=1}^{m} Y_{TPi}$
- Total defects per unit: $TDPU = -\ln(Y_{RT})$
- Normalized yield: $Y_{\text{norm}} = \sqrt[m]{Y_{RT}}$
- Defects per normalized unit: $DPU_{\text{norm}} = -\ln(Y_{\text{norm}})$

Standardized Normal Distribution Relationships for Z

- $Z_{\text{equiv}} \cong Z \sim N(0;1)$
- Z "long-term": $Z_{LT} = Z_{\text{equiv}}$

- Z "short-term" relationship to Z "long-term" with 1.5 standard deviation shift: $Z_{ST} = Z_{LT} + 1.5_{\text{shift}}$
- Z Benchmark: $Z_{\text{Benchmark}} = Z_{Y_{\text{norm}}} + 1.5$

9.3 PROCESS CYCLE TIME

The time it takes for a product to go through an entire process is defined as process cycle time. Process cycle time is an important parameter relative to meeting the needs of customers. The inspection, analysis, and repair of defects extends the process cycle time.

Within a manufacturing just-in-time environment, process cycle time could be calculated as the time it takes for material arriving at the receiving dock to become a final product received by the customer. An objective of a Six Sigma program might be to significantly reduce this cycle time.

Real process cycle time includes the waiting and storage time between and during operations. Theoretical process cycle time does not include waiting, shutdown, and preparation time. Real daily operating time equates to the time when processes are functioning. This time considers maintenance periods and rest periods. The relationship between real daily operating time and theoretical process cycle time is

$$\text{Theoretical process cycle time} = \frac{\text{Real daily operating time}}{\text{Number of units required daily}}$$

Process-cycle-time analysis consists of comparing real and theoretical process cycle times. Factors that constitute additional steps to the theoretical process cycle time include inspection, shipping, testing, analysis, repair, waiting time, storage, operation delays, and setup times. The identification and resolution of causal differences can reduce the real process cycle time. Possible solutions include improved work methods, changed production sequence, transfer of part inspection ownership to production employees, and reduction in batch size.

Reducing real process cycle time can reduce the number of defective units and improve process performance. Other advantages include the reduction in inventory costs, reduction in production costs, increased internal/external customer satisfaction, improved production yields, and reduction in floor space requirements. Process-cycle-time reductions have advantages but must not be achieved by jeopardizing product quality. Hence, quality assessments should be made before implementing process-cycle-time reduction changes.

9.4 YIELD

Yield is the area under the probability density curve between tolerances. From the Poisson distribution, this equates to the probability with zero failures. Mathematically, this relationship is

$$Y = P(x = 0) = \frac{e^{-\lambda}\lambda^x}{x!} = e^{-\lambda} = e^{-D/U} = e^{-DPU}$$

where λ is the mean of the distribution and x is the number of failures. This relationship is shown pictorially in Figure 9.1.

9.5 EXAMPLE 9.1: YIELD

Five defects are observed in 467 units produced. The number of defects per unit (DPU) is 0.01071 (i.e., 5/467). The probability of obtaining units with zero defects (yield) is

$$Y = P(x = 0) = e^{-DPU} = e^{-0.01071} = 0.98935$$

9.6 *Z* VARIABLE EQUIVALENT

The Poisson distribution can be used to estimate the Z variable. This is accomplished by determining the Z value for the defects per unit (DPU) from the normal distribution table. This Z value is defined as the Z variable equivalent (Z_{equiv}) and is sometimes expressed using the following relationships with Z "long-term" (Z_{LT}) and Z "short-term" (Z_{ST}):

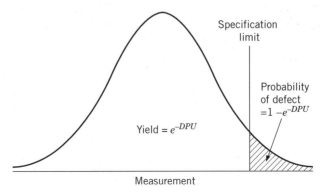

FIGURE 9.1 Yield plot.

$$Z_{LT} = Z_{\text{equiv}}$$

$$Z_{ST} = Z_{LT} + 1.5_{\text{shift}}$$

The value for Z_{ST} can be converted to a parts per million (ppm) defect rate by use of the "conversion of Z variable to ppm" table (Table S).

9.7   EXAMPLE 9.2: Z VARIABLE EQUIVALENT

For the previous example the *DPU* was calculated as 0.01071. Determine Z_{equiv} and Z_{ST}. Estimate the ppm defect rate.

From a normal distribution table (Table A) a DPU value of 0.01071 results in a Z_{equiv} value of 2.30. The resulting value for Z_{ST} is

$$Z_{ST} = Z_{LT} + 1.5_{\text{shift}} = 2.30 + 1.5 = 3.8$$

The process is then said to be at a 3.8 sigma quality level. Converting the Z Variable to ppm using the shifted value within Table S yields a ppm rate of 10,724.

9.8   DEFECTS PER MILLION OPPORTUNITIES (DPMO)

Some organizations give focus only to the rate of defects at the end of a process. For example, if there were 200 units produced and 10 units failed test, the reported defect rate is 5% (i.e., [10/200]100 = 5).

A defect per unit calculation can give additional insight into a process by including the number of opportunities for failure. A defect per unit metric considers the number of opportunities for failure within the calculations. To illustrate the methodology, consider a process where defects were classified by characteristic type and the number of opportunities for failure (*OP*) were noted for each characteristic type. The number of defects (*D*) and units (*U*) are then monitored for the process over some period of time. Calculations for the metrics in spreadsheet format are as follows:

Characteristic Type	Defects	Units	Opportunities	Total Opportunities	Defects Per Unit	Defects Per Total Opportunities	Defects Per Million Opportunities
Description	D	U	OP	TOP	DPU	DPO	$DPMO$
				$= U \times OP$	$= D/U$	$= D/TOP$	$= DPO \times 1{,}000{,}000$

An application example might have 15 or 20 different description types. Totals could then be determined for the Defects (*D*) and Total Opportunities (*O*) columns for each description type. The overall Defects Per Total Opportunities (*DPO*) and Defects per Million Opportunities (*DPMO*) could then be calculated from these totals. A Pareto chart of the defect characteristic type by *DPMO* can give insight to where process improvement efforts should focus.

An electronic industry application example of *DPMO* is the soldering of components onto printed circuit boards. For this case, the total number of opportunities for failure could be the number of components plus the number of solder joints (sometimes insertion is also included as a opportunity for failure). A benefit of using *DPMO* for this situation is that many different part numbers pass through a printed circuit-board assembly process. Each of these part numbers typically contain a different number of solder joints and components. With a *DPMO* metric we can now have a uniform measurement for the process, not just the product. Measurements that focus on the process, as opposed to the product, lead more directly to effective process improvement activities.

9.9 EXAMPLE 9.3: DEFECTS PER MILLION OPPORTUNITIES (DPMO)

A process had defects described as type A, B, C, D, E, and F. Example originations for these data include the manufacturing of printed circuit boards and the generation of purchase orders. Data were collected over some period of time for defects (*D*), units (*U*), and opportunities per unit (*OP*). These input data and calculations are as follows:

Characteristic	D	U	OP	TOP	DPU	DPO	DPMO
Type A	21	327	92	30,084	0.064	0.0007	698
Type B	10	350	85	29,750	0.029	0.0003	336
Type C	8	37	43	1,591	0.216	0.0050	5,028
Type D	68	743	50	37,150	0.092	0.0018	1,830
Type E	74	80	60	4,800	0.925	0.0154	15,417
Type F	20	928	28	25,984	0.022	0.0008	770
Totals:	201			129,359		0.0016	1,554

Calculations for totals are

$DPO = 201/129,359 = 0.0016$

$DPMO = DPO \times 1,000,000 \cong 1554$ (difference is due to round-off error)

Figure 9.2 shows a Pareto chart of *DPMO* by characteristic type.

9.10 ROLLED THROUGHPUT YIELD

When organizations only focus on a defect rate at the end of a process, they can lose sight of reworks that occur within processes. Reworks within an

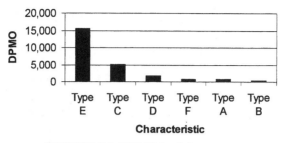

FIGURE 9.2 DPMO by failure type.

operation have no value and comprise what is termed the "hidden factory." Rolled throughput yield measurements can give visibility to process steps that have high defect rates and/or rework needs.

One method to determine the rolled throughput yield is to determine the yield for each process operation. Multiply these process operation step yields to get the rolled throughput yield for a process. A cumulative throughput yield up through a process step can be determined by multiplying the yield of the current step by the yields of previous steps.

Process yield can pictorially be described using two plots on one chart. In both cases the x axis lists the step numbers sequentially. One of the plots shows yield for each process step, while the other plot shows degradation in yield with the progression of process steps.

Rolled throughput yield could be calculated from the number of defects per unit (DPU) through the relationship

$$Y_{RT} = e^{-DPU}$$

where the number of defects per unit within a process is the total of the defects for each operation divided by the number of units produced.

The total number of units needed to produce one unit that has no defects is

$$\text{Units produced} = 1 + (1 - e^{-DPU})$$

The real time to create conforming units then becomes

$$T_{\text{real}} = T_{\text{base}}[1 + (1 - e^{-DPU})]$$

where the base time is the average time for activities described within the process. The real time described in this equation does not include the analysis, repair, and testing time for nonconforming units. Adjustments should be made to this calculated value for these issues.

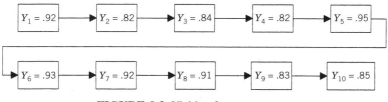

FIGURE 9.3 Yields of process steps.

9.11   EXAMPLE 9.4: ROLLED THROUGHPUT YIELD

A process has 10 operation steps Y_1–Y_{10} shown pictorially in Figure 9.3. Example sources for these data are a manufacturing assembly operation and the administrative steps for the execution of a purchase order. A summary of these yields and calculated cumulative rolled throughput yields is as follows:

	Y_1	Y_2	Y_3	Y_4	Y_5	Y_6	Y_7	Y_8	Y_9	Y_{10}
Oper. Yield	0.92	0.82	0.95	0.82	0.84	0.93	0.92	0.91	0.83	0.85
Cum. Yield	0.92	0.75	0.72	0.59	0.49	0.46	0.42	0.38	0.32	0.27

The rolled throughput yield of the process is 0.27. Figure 9.4 is a plot of this information showing both operation step and cumulative rolled throughput yields.

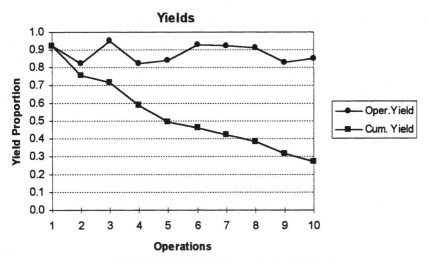

FIGURE 9.4 Rolled throughput yield.

9.12   EXAMPLE 9.5: ROLLED THROUGHPUT YIELD

A process produces a total of 400 units and has a total of 75 defects. Determine the number units it would take to produce 100 conforming units. Calculations are

$$DPU = 75/400 = 0.1875$$

$$Y_{RT} = e^{-DPU} = e^{-0.1875} = 0.829029$$

Units produced $= 1 + (1 - e^{-DPU}) = 1 + (1 - e^{-0.829029}) = 1.170971$

To achieve 100 conforming units, 117 (i.e., 1.17×100) would need to be produced.

9.13   YIELD CALCULATION

A process had D defects and U units within a period of time for operation steps (m). The following exemplifies table entries to determine rolled throughput yield and defects per unit:

Operation	Defects	Units	DPU	Operation Throughput Yield
Step Number	D	U	$DPU = D/U$	$Y_{TPi} = e^{-DPU} = e^{-D/U}$
Summations:	Sum of defects	Sum of units	Sum of DPUs	$Y_{RT} = \prod_{i=1}^{m} Y_{TPi}$
Averages:	Average of the number of defects per operation	Average of the sum of units per operations	Average of DPUs per operation	$TDPU = -\ln(Y_{RT})$

9.14   EXAMPLE 9.6: YIELD CALCULATION

A process has 10 operation steps. Shown is a summary of the number of defects and units produced over time. Calculated for each step is DPU and operation yield along with rolled throughput yield (Y_{TPi}) and defects per unit (DPU). Summary calculations are total defects per unit $(TDPU)$ and rolled throughput yield (YRT).

Operation	Defects	Units	*DPU*	Throughput Yield
1	5	523	0.00956	0.99049
2	75	851	0.08813	0.91564
3	18	334	0.05389	0.94753
4	72	1202	0.05990	0.94186
5	6	252	0.02381	0.97647
6	28	243	0.11523	0.89116
7	82	943	0.08696	0.91672
8	70	894	0.07830	0.92469
9	35	234	0.14957	0.86108
10	88	1200	0.07333	0.92929
Sum of operation = steps	479	6676	0.73868	$0.47774 = Y_{RT}$ (rolled throughput yield)
Avg. of operation = steps	47.9	667.6	0.07387	$0.73868 = TDPU$ (total defects per unit)

Example calculations are as follows:

For Step 1

$$DPU = 5/523 = 0.00956$$

$$\text{Operation yield} = e^{-0.00956} = 0.99049$$

For Operation Yield Totals

$$Y_{RT} = \text{rolled throughput yield}$$

$$= 0.99049 \times 0.91564 \times \cdots \times 0.92929$$

$$= 0.47774$$

$$TDPU = \text{total defects per unit} = -\ln(0.47774) = 0.73868$$

9.15   EXAMPLE 9.7: NORMAL TRANSFORMATION (Z VALUE)

Some Six Sigma calculations involve the transformation of yields into Z values. Standardized normal distribution relationships for Z can be determined using a standardized normal curve table, spread sheet equations, or statistical programs.

The yields for the operation steps described in an earlier example were as follows:

	M_1	M_2	M_3	M_4	M_5	M_6	M_7	M_8	M_9	M_{10}
Oper. Yield:	0.92	0.82	0.95	0.82	0.84	0.93	0.92	0.91	0.83	0.85
Oper. Z Value:	1.4051	0.9154	1.6449	0.9154	0.9945	1.4758	1.4051	1.3408	0.9542	1.0364

To exemplify the conversion of yield to Z, consider process step 1. For the Standardized Normal Curve table in the Appendix the table entry value is 0.08 (i.e., $1.00 - 0.92 = 0.08$). This value yields an interpolated Z value between 1.4 and 1.41. The above tabled value of 1.4051 was determined mathematically using a statistical program. This value is consistent with the Standardized Normal Curve computation approach.

9.16   NORMALIZED YIELD AND Z VALUE FOR BENCHMARKING

Typically, yields for each of the m steps within a process differ. Rolled throughput yield (Y_{RT}) gives an overall yield for the process. A normalized yield value (Y_{norm}) for the process steps is expressed as

$$Y_{norm} = \sqrt[m]{Y_{RT}}$$

The defects per normalized unit (DPU_{norm}) is

$$DPU_{norm} = -\ln(Y_{norm})$$

The following Six Sigma relationships are used to determine a benchmark value for Z ($Z_{Benchmark}$). The normality approximation for Z equivalent (Z_{equiv}) and the relationship of Z equivalent to Z long term (Z_{LT}) are expressed as

$$Z_{equiv} \cong Z \sim N(0 ;1)$$
$$Z_{equiv} = Z_{LT}$$

The Z "long-term" to Z "short-term" (Z_{ST}) relationship with a 1.5 standard deviation shift is

$$Z_{ST} = Z_{LT} + 1.5_{shift}$$

The Z value for benchmarking ($Z_{Benchmark}$) is then

$$Z_{Benchmark} = Z_{Y_{norm}} + 1.5$$

9.17   EXAMPLE 9.8: NORMALIZED YIELD AND Z VALUE FOR BENCHMARKING

A previous example had a rolled throughput yield of 0.47774 for 10 operations. The following shows calculations to determine normalized yield (Y_{norm}) defects per normalized unit (DPU_{norm}), and $Z_{benchmark}$.

$$Y_{\text{norm}} = \sqrt[m]{Y_{RT}} = \sqrt[10]{0.47774} = 0.92879$$

$$DPU_{\text{norm}} = -\ln(Y_{\text{norm}}) = -\ln(0.92879) = 0.07387$$

$$Z_{\text{Benchmark}} = Z_{Y_{\text{norm}}} + 1.5 = 1.47 + 1.5 = 2.97$$

9.18 BENCHMARKING

Benchmarking involves the search of an organization for the best practices, adaptation to the practices to their processes, and improving with the focus of becoming the best in class. Benchmarking can involve comparisons of products, processes, methods, and strategies. Internal benchmarking makes comparisons between similar operations within an organization. Competitive benchmarking makes comparisons with the best direct competitor. Functional benchmarking makes comparisons of similar process methodologies. Generic benchmarking makes comparisons of processes with exemplary and innovative processes of other companies. Sources of information for benchmarking include the internet, in-house published material, professional associations, universities, advertising, and customer feedback.

World class organizations are those considered to be at 6σ performance in the "short term" or 4.5σ in the "long term." Average companies are said to show a 4σ performance. The difference between 4σ and 6σ performance means producing 1826 times fewer defects and increasing profits by at least 10%.

9.19 SIX SIGMA ASSUMPTIONS

The validity of several assumptions can affect the accuracy of many of the Six Sigma metrics described in this chapter and process capability discussed later in this text. A very significant consideration is the characterization of each process parameter by a normal distribution. A question is then, How common is the normal distribution in the real world? Gunther (1989) states that there are certainly many situations where a non-normal distribution is expected and describes these two situations:

- Skewed distribution with a one-sided boundary is common for processes in which process measurements are clustered around low values with a heavy tail to the right.
- Heavy-tailed distributions where the tails have a larger proportion of the values than for a normal distribution which can be caused by natural variation from a variety of sources.

Another Six Sigma calculation assumption is that the process mean shifts 1.5σ. In addition, it is assumed that the process mean and standard deviation are known and that the process capability parameters C_p and C_{pk} are point values (that everybody calculates using the same methodology). Also, it is assumed that defects are randomly distributed throughout units and that there is independence between part/process steps.

9.20 S⁴ ASSESSMENT

A variety of responses could be expected when many are asked their perception of Six Sigma. Among other things, responses would depend upon a person's background and their position within an organization. One possible response could involve the unique metrics of Six Sigma. Another possible response is that Six Sigma can offer a methodology to integrate meaningful metrics with effective process improvements.

I have seen organizations get very frustrated and then drop a Six Sigma initiative because management tried to drive improvement through the metrics. Another common problem with the implementation of Six Sigma is creating Six Sigma metrics using very limited data that do not represent the population of interest. In addition, the comparison of suppliers by examining only reported Six Sigma metrics without an understanding of how the metrics were originated can lead to distorted results because the data might not have been similarly obtained.

It is difficult, expensive, and takes a lot of time to collect good data and create a metric that is meaningful. This task can be even more difficult if metrics are forced into a "one size fits all" Six Sigma format. Metrics are important; however, some formats are more beneficial for a given situation.

Metrics that convey monetary issues get the most visibility and should be considered a part of an overall measurement strategy. However, metrics by itself does not fix anything. If a metric chart is used only for information and has no backup chart that gives insight to what should be done differently, perhaps this chart should be eliminated from regular meetings.

Organizations should not lose sight that charts and measurements cost money. If organizations spend a lot of time and money collecting data and creating some Six Sigma charts that don't have value add, there will probably come a time when they question the effectiveness of their Six Sigma program and perhaps drop the effort.

The major value add of a Six Sigma program should be to determine using statistical techniques, what should be done differently, to improve. If this is the focus of a Six Sigma initiative, customer satisfaction, cycle times, defect rates, and so on, will improve (i.e., Six Sigma metrics will improve).

9.21   EXERCISES

1. *Catapult Exercise Data Analysis:* Using the catapult exercise data sets from Chapter 4, determine the process yields and ppm defect rates for specifications supplied by the instructor (e.g., 75 ± 3 inches).

2. *Cards Exercise:* The purpose of this exercise is to demonstrate the impact of process variation on rolled throughput yield, product cost, and cycle time. Each team of 4–12 people needs three poster chart sheets as targets, one deck of 52 cards, a stop watch, three pads of paper, and a tally sheet. There are three process steps, where good products advance to the next process step while defects are recycled. At each process step an operator drops a card, where the card is held vertically (or as specified by instructor) at arm's length parallel to the floor (shoulder's height). If the card lands complete within the poster chart a material handler moves the card to the next process step. If the card does not land correctly, it is considered a defect and returned to the operator. A recorder documents performance data for the step. Each team will need a timekeeper who measures time to completion, a customer who receives/counts the number of cards completed satisfactory, and a data entry clerk to tally the results.

Each team starts with a full deck of 52 cards and stops when 25 good units are received. The following is used within the computations and presented to the group: total good units moved to subsequent step or customer, total drops at each step, total number of cards never used by first operator (will need to segregate recycled units from never used units), and total time from first drop to customer order completion. Teams are given a trial run of five units, where cards are returned to first operator. Each team is to maximize yield, while minimizing scrap and rework, total cost, and total cycle time. Teams determine these metrics from the following relationships: Yield = materials yield − shipment quantity/ total input into step 1; RTY = multiplication of yield (units in spec/total drops) for all three process steps (materials cost is $5 per unit introduced into step 1, process cost is $2 per drop, scrap is $1 per unit in process at end of game); and cycle time = total time/number of units shipped to customer. Upon completion, give an assessment of the process relative to variability and control. Consider how this affects the metrics (Zinkgraf 1998).

3. Six defects are observed in 283 units produced. Determine the probability of obtaining units with zero defects (yield).

4. For a *DPU* value of 0.02120, determine Z_{equiv} and Z_{ST}. Estimate the ppm defect rate.

5. The following data were collected over time. Create a table showing *TOP*, *DPU*, *DPO*, and *DPMO* for each characteristic along with the grand

DPMO. Create a Pareto chart for characteristic type ranked by *DPMO* values. Describe manufacturing, business process, and/or Six Sigma project situations for the origination of these data. Include characteristics to monitor.

Characteristic	D	U	OP
Type A	56	300	88
Type B	44	350	75
Type C	30	55	32
Type D	83	50	60
Type E	95	630	70
Type F	53	800	40

6. A process has 10 steps with yields

Y_1	Y_2	Y_3	Y_4	Y_5	Y_6	Y_7	Y_8	Y_9	Y_{10}
0.82	0.81	0.85	0.78	0.87	0.80	0.88	0.83	0.89	0.90

Create a table that shows operation step yields and cumulative rolled throughput yields. Determine the overall process rolled throughput yield. Plot the results. Describe manufacturing, business process, and/or Six Sigma project situations for the origination of this data. Include example operation steps to monitor.

7. A process has 10 steps with the following data:

Operation	Defects	Units
1	12	380
2	72	943
3	22	220
4	85	1505
5	23	155
6	23	255
7	102	1023
8	93	843
9	55	285
10	68	1132

Calculate *DPU* and operation yield for each step. Determine the rolled throughput yield and total defects per unit. Describe manufacturing, business process, and/or Six Sigma project situations for the origination of these data. Include example operation steps to monitor.

8. A process produces a total of 300 units and has a total of 80 defects. Determine the number units it would take to produce 100 conforming units.

9. Determine the Z value for each of the following 10 process steps that had the following yields:

Y_1	Y_2	Y_3	Y_4	Y_5	Y_6	Y_7	Y_8	Y_9	Y_{10}
0.82	0.81	0.85	0.78	0.87	0.80	0.88	0.83	0.89	0.90

10. A process had a rolled throughput yield of 0.38057 for 10 operations. Determine normalized yield (Y_{norm}), defects per normalized unit (DPU_{norm}), and $Z_{benchmark}$.

11. You are given the following information for analysis with the purpose of selecting the best supplier that is to manufacture to a specification of 85–115. Suppliers claimed the following: supplier 1—$\bar{x} = 100$, $s = 5$; supplier 2—$\bar{x} = 95$, $s = 5$; supplier 3—$\bar{x} = 100$, $s = 10$; supplier 4—$\bar{x} = 95$, $s = 10$. Determine ppm noncompliance rates and yields. Discuss any concerns you have about making a decision with just the information.

12. Describe how the techniques within this chapter are useful and can be applied to S^4 projects.

10

BASIC CONTROL CHARTS

In the second half of the 1920s, Dr. Walter A. Shewhart of Bell Telephone Laboratories developed a theory of statistical quality control. He concluded that there were two components to variations that were displayed in all manufacturing processes. The first component was a steady component (i.e., random variation) that appeared to be inherent in the process. The second component was an intermittent variation to assignable causes. He concluded that assignable causes could be economically discovered and removed with an effective diagnostic program but that random causes could not be removed without making basic process changes. Dr. Shewhart is credited with developing the standard control chart test based on 3σ limits to separate the steady component of variation from assignable causes. Shewhart control charts came into wide use in the 1940s because of war production efforts. Western Electric is credited with the addition of other tests based on sequences or runs (Western Electric 1956).

Deming (1986) notes: "A fault in the interpretation of observations, seen everywhere, is to suppose that every event (defect, mistake, accident) is attributable to someone (usually the one nearest at hand), or is related to some special event. The fact is that most troubles with service and production lie in the system." Deming adds: "Confusion between common causes and special causes leads to frustration of everyone, and leads to greater variability and to higher costs, exactly contrary to what is needed. I should estimate that in my experience most troubles and most possibilities for improvement add up to proportions something like this: 94% belong to the system (responsibility of management), 6% special."

In an earlier chapter it was noted that Juran classifies manufacturing process problems into two categories, sporadic and chronic. Similarly, there was discussion about Deming's categorization of process situations that result from common causes and special causes. It was emphasized that corrective action can be very different depending on which of the two categories exists in a given situation. The process control charts discussed in this chapter are tools that can identify when common or special causes (sporadic or chronic problem) exists so that the appropriate action can be taken.

The techniques covered in this chapter are normally associated with manufacturing processes. However, these analysis techniques can be used to assess parameters in other areas of the business (e.g., the time required to process an invoice). Also, these techniques can be very beneficial to get both a high-level and low-level view of the process.

There are some additional control charting techniques described within a later chapter of this text. I subdivided the control charting techniques into two chapters with the thought that the topics within this first chapter would be most appropriately covered during the first week of an S^4 training course, while the topics within the later chapter could be covered during the fourth week of an S^4 training course.

10.1 AQL (ACCEPTABLE QUALITY LEVEL) SAMPLING CAN BE DECEPTIVE

The intent of this section is not to give instruction on how to create an acceptable quality level (AQL) sampling plan. There are many other sources for this type of information. The intent of this section is to show how an AQL pass/fail sample lot test strategy for product is not effective. A more effective approach is to monitor the process using techniques such as control charts.

With AQL sampling plans, a lot is inspected to determine if it should be accepted or rejected. Sampling plans are typically determined from tables as a function of an AQL criterion and other characteristics of the lot. Pass/fail decisions for an AQL evaluated lot are based only on the lot's performance, not on previous product performance from the process. AQL sampling plans do not give you a picture of how a process is performing.

AQL sampling plans are inefficient and can be very costly, especially when high levels of quality are needed. Often, organizations think that they will achieve better quality with AQL sampling plans than they really can. The trend is that organizations are moving away from AQL sampling plans; however, many organizations are slow to make the transition. The following describes the concepts and shortcomings of AQL sampling plans.

When setting up an AQL sampling plan, much care needs to be exercised when choosing samples. Samples must be a random sample from the lot. This can be difficult to accomplish. Neither sampling nor 100% inspection guarantees that every defect will be found. Studies have shown that 100% inspection is at most 80% effective.

There are two kinds of sampling risks:

- Good lots can be rejected.
- Bad lots can be accepted.

The operating characteristic (OC) curve for sampling plans quantifies these risks. Figure 10.1 shows an ideal operating curve. Because we cannot achieve an "ideal" OC curve, we describe OC curves using the following terms:

Acceptable Quality Level (AQL)

- AQL is typically considered to be the worst quality level that is still considered satisfactory.
- According to Mil-STD-105E, AQL is the maximum percent defective that for purposes of sampling inspection can be considered satisfactory as a process average.
- The probability of accepting an AQL lot should be high. A probability of 0.95 translates to an α risk of 0.05.

Rejectable Quality Level (RQL)

- This is considered to be unsatisfactory quality level.
- This is sometimes called *lot tolerance percent defective* (LTPD).
- This consumer's risk has been standardized in some tables as 0.1.
- The probability of accepting an RQL lot should be low.

Indifference Quality Level (IQL)

- Quality level is somewhere between AQL and RQL.
- This is frequently defined as quality level having probability of acceptance of 0.5 for a sampling plan.

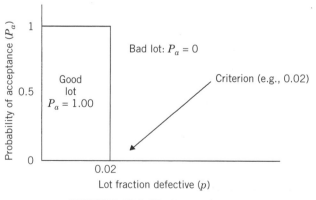

FIGURE 10.1 Ideal operating curve.

An OC curve describes the probability of acceptance for various values of incoming quality. *Pa* is the probability that the number of defectives in the sample is equal to or less than the acceptance number for the sampling plan. The hypergeometric, binomial, and Poisson distributions describe the probability of acceptance for various situations.

The Poisson distribution is the easiest to use when calculating probabilities. The Poisson distribution can often be used as an approximation for the other distributions. The probability of exactly *x* defects [*P*(*x*)] in *n* samples is

$$P(x) = \frac{e^{-np}(np)^x}{x!}$$

For "*a*" allowed failures, $P(x \leq a)$ is the sum of $P(x)$ for $x = 0$ to $x = a$.

Figure 10.2 shows an AQL operating characteristic curve for an AQL level of 0.9%. Someone who is not familiar with the operating characteristic curves of AQL would probably think that passage of this AQL 0.9% test would indicate goodness. Well this is not exactly true because from this operating curve (OC) it can be seen that the failure rate would have to be actually about 2.5% to have a 50%/50% chance of rejection.

AQL sampling often leads to activities that are associated with attempts to "test quality into a product." AQL sampling can reject lots that are a result of common-cause process variability. When a process output is examined as AQL lots and a lot is rejected because of common cause variability, customer quality does not improve.

In lieu of using AQL sampling plans to periodically inspect the output of a process, more useful information can be obtained by using control charts to first identify special cause issues. Process capability studies can then be used to quantify the common cause of the process. If a process is not capable, something needs to be done different to the process to make it more capable.

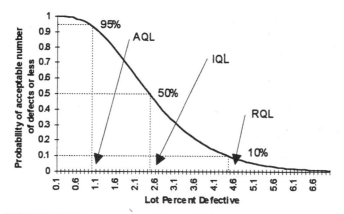

FIGURE 10.2 An operating characteristic curve. $n = 150$, $c = 3$.

10.2 EXAMPLE 10.1: ACCEPTABLE QUALITY LEVEL

For N (lot size) = 75 and AQL = 4.0%, MIL-STD-105E yields for a general inspection level II a test plan where

- Sample Size = 13
- Acceptance Number = 1
- Rejection number = 2

From this plan we can see how AQL sampling protects the producer. The "failure rate at the acceptance number" is 7.6% [i.e., $(1/13)(100) = 7.6\%$], while the "failure rate at the rejection number" is 15.4% [i.e., $(2/13)(100) = 15.4\%$].

10.3 MONITORING PROCESSES

A process is said to be in statistical control when special causes don't exist. Figure 10.3 illustrates both an "out-of-control" and an "in-control" process condition. When a process is in statistical control, this does not imply that the process is producing the desired quality of products relative to specification limits. The overall output of a process can be in statistical control and still be producing defects at a rate of 20%; this is considered a process capability/performance issue, not a process control issue. However, a process can be in statistical control and not be capable of consistently producing

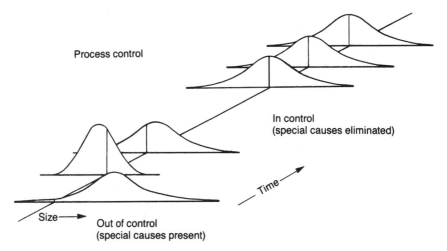

FIGURE 10.3 Process control. [From *Continuing Process Control and Process Capability Improvement*, Ford Corporate Quality Education and Training Center (1987), with permission.]

product that is within specification limits, as shown in Figure 10.4. This can occur because the process mean is shifted excessively from the nominal target value, or because the variability is excessive. Process capability/performance studies can be used to assess this situation. This type of problem is a fault of the system (a Deming description) and needs to be addressed as a common-cause problem.

We would like to be able to create a control charting strategy for a process where we can separate special-cause events from common-cause events (fault of the system). The question of concern is whether for a given process one person might set up a control charting strategy that indicates that the system is out of control while another sets up a control charting strategy that indicates that the system is in control. The answer is yes, this is quite possible. Think about the significance of this. For a given process, one control charting plan can indicate the occurrence of many special cause problems (perhaps leading to many fire-fighting activities), while the other person would be working on common cause issues (process improvement) if the process capability/performance were not adequate.

To illustrate how this could happen, consider a manufacturing process that produces a widget (the same methodology would apply to business processes). There is one dimension on this widget that is considered very important and needs to be monitored by way of a control chart. Consider that new raw material is supplied daily and that the measurement of this part is quite expensive.

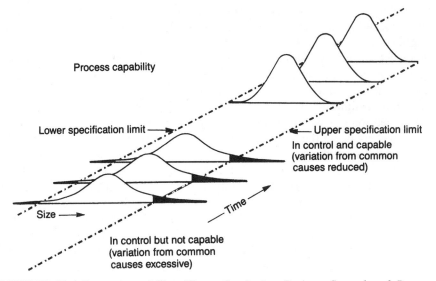

FIGURE 10.4 Process capability. [From *Continuing Process Control and Process Capability Improvement,* Ford Corporate Quality Education and Training Center (1987), with permission.]

Using a traditional sampling approach, one person might choose to sample five parts daily that are created consecutively (a more frequent sampling plan was thought to be too expensive), while another person might choose to sample one part every five days (again, he/she thought a more frequent sampling plan was thought to be too expensive).

Consider now that both of these people plotted information on $\bar{x}$ and R charts (described later) using a subgroup size of five, and the process was not capable of consistently producing an adequate dimension because of variability in raw material (however, they did not know this). The question is whether the two control charting strategies would lead to the same basic actions. The answer is no. The upper and lower control chart limits that are to identify special cause and common cause are not determined from tolerances. They are determined from the variability of the process. The sampling of five consecutive parts would typically have a lower standard deviation than the sampling of five parts throughout the week; hence, the control charts that used five consecutive parts could be out of control frequently because of the variability from daily changes in raw material. For this situation there could be frequent panic because the production line is supposed to stop when this occurs until the problem is resolved. In addition, the next obvious question is, What should be done with the parts produced since the previous inspection, a day earlier (perhaps we need to institute a sorting plan for today's production)? On the next day (since the material changed) the process might be "in control" so everybody takes a sigh of relief that the problem is "fixed" now—until another batch of material arrives that adversely affects the widget.

The sampling plan of five parts weekly would not indicate an out of control condition; however, a process capability/performance study would not be satisfactory, indicating that a common cause problem exists. This process study might indicate that there is an overall 10% problem (i.e., 10% of the widgets produced are not conforming to specification). This problem then could be translated into a monetary and customer satisfaction terms that everyone can understand. A team could then tackle this problem by collecting data that give more insight into what could cause the problem. A lot of ideas could be mentioned, one of which is a raw material. The collection of these data and then analysis using the techniques described later in this text would indicate there is a "system problem" with raw material. A quick fix might be to inspect raw material or work with the supplier to tighten up tolerances.

A potentially more desirable solution might be to conduct a DOE to determine if there are process settings that would make the process more robust to differences in raw material. Perhaps through this experiment we would find that if process temperature were increased, raw material variability would no longer affect widget quality. We have now gained knowledge about our process, where a control chart should be considered for temperature, because it is a key process input variable. A frequent sampling plan should be considered for this measure because the quality of the process output depends on the performance of this key process input variable. When this "upstream" process measurement goes out of control, the process should be shut down immediately to resolve this key process input problem.

Consider how control charts were used initially in the above illustration. For the sampling plan of five parts weekly (we could analyze also as an individual chart) the overall measurement was at a high level (30,000-ft level). It considered material variability as common cause to the system. The more frequent plan treated the material variability as special cause. Not everyone in the statistical community agrees as to whether material variability should be considered special or common cause. When making this decision for yourself, consider that Deming described "system problems" to be common cause that needed to be addressed by management. The question is whether you consider the typical variability raw material as a "system problem," as opposed to a problem that was caused by something outside the system. The later description of temperature monitoring using control charts had a lower level view of the process (e.g., 100-ft level), where this key process input variable was chosen through DOE techniques to be important to the quality of the process.

10.4 RATIONAL SAMPLING AND RATIONAL SUBGROUPING

The effective use of control charts is dependent upon both rational sampling and subgrouping. Efforts should focus on using the simplest technique that provides the best analysis.

Rational sampling involves the best selection of the best what, where, how, and when for measurements. Sampling frequency is rational if it is frequent enough to monitor process changes. Other issues include the creation of both product and process measurements that either directly or indirectly affect internal/external customer satisfaction. Sampling plans should lead to analyses that give insight not just present numbers.

Traditionally, rational subgrouping issues involve the selection of samples that yield relatively homogeneous conditions within the subgroup for a small region of time or space (perhaps five in a row). Hence, the within-subgroup variation defines the limits of the control chart on how much variation should exist between the subgroups. For a given situation, differing subgrouping methodologies can dramatically affect the measured variation within subgroups, which in turn affects the width of the control limits.

Subgrouping can affect the output and resulting decisions from $\bar{x}$ and R charts. Average charts identify differences between subgroups, while the range charts identify inconsistency within the subgroups. The variation within subgroups determines the sensitivity of the control charts. Because of this it is important to consider the sources of variation for the measurement and then organize the subgroups accordingly.

Consider the hourly sampling of five parts created one after another from a single cavity mold. This subgroup size is five and the frequency of sampling is hourly. Sources of variability are cycle-to-cycle and hour-to-hour. A process could have low variability between cycles in conjunction with raw material variability that affects the hour-to-hour measurements. The measurement of five consecutive pieces for this process yields control limits that are small. Concerns for immediate investigation can then result from many apparent out of control conditions. However, if this process consistently meets the needs of the customer, even with many out of control points, perhaps it would not be wiser to spend resources on other areas of the business. Perhaps the business would benefit more from an effort to change the current sampling plan because the hour-to-hour variability in raw material did not jeopardize overall customer satisfaction.

Sometimes the decisions for sampling and subgrouping are more involved. Consider, for example, a four-cavity molding process which has an hourly sampling frequency of five parts. A control chart sampling plan for this situation should consider cavity-to-cavity, cycle-to-cycle, and hour-to-hour varitions. Inappropriate activities can result when these sources are not considered collectively within sampling plans. Section 35.1 offers a sampling alternative for this situation.

10.5 STATISTICAL PROCESS CONTROL CHARTS

Shewhart control charts (Shewhart 1931) track processes by plotting data over time in the form shown in Figure 10.5. This chart can track either variables or attribute process parameters. The types of variable charts discussed within this text are process mean ($\bar{x}$), range (R), standard deviation (s), and individual values (X). The attribute types discussed are proporiton nonconforming (p), number of nonconforming items (np), number of nonconformities (c), and nonconformities per unit (u).

The typical control limits are plus and minus three standard deviation limits using at least 20 data points (some illustrative examples in this text have less data). When a point falls outside these limits, the process is said to be out of

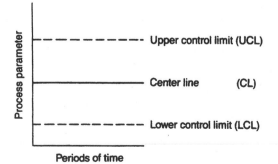

FIGURE 10.5 Shewhart control chart format.

control. Interpretations of other control chart patterns are discussed in Section 10.6. It should be emphasized that the process (not the specification) determines the process control limits noted in the following sections.

The terms *variable data* and *continuous data* describe the same situation. These situations involve measurements such as cycle time, weight, temperature, and size. A rough rule of thumb is to consider data as continuous if at least 10 different values occur and no more than 20% of the data set are repeat values.

10.6 INTERPRETATION OF CONTROL CHART PATTERNS

When a process is in control, the control chart pattern should exhibit "natural characteristics" as if it were from random data. Unnatural patterns involve the absence of one or more of the characteristics of a natural pattern. Some example unnatural patterns are mixture, stratification, and/or instability.

Unnatural patterns classified as mixture have an absence of points near the center line. These patterns can be the combination of two different patterns on one chart: one at a high level and one at a low level. Unnatural patterns classified as stratification have up-and-down variations that are very small in comparison to the control limits. This pattern can occur when samples are taken consistently from widely different distributions. Unnatural patterns classified as instability have points outside the control limits. This pattern indicates that something has changed within the process (either "goodness" or "badness").

Consider further the analysis approach to determine whether there is instability in the process. It should be remembered that whenever the process is stated to be out of control there is a chance that the statement was made in error because there is a chance that either abnormally "good" or "bad" samples were drawn. This chance of error increases with the introduction of more criteria when analyzing the charts. When using the following pattern criteria, this chance of error should be considered before making a process out-of-control statement.

Because the upper and lower control limits each are 3σ, consider a control chart that is subdivided into three 3σ regions, as noted in Figure 10.6. Tests for out-of-control conditions relative to these zones are (statistical computer analysis programs may offer other tests) as follows:

1. One point beyond zone A.
2. Two out of three points in zone A or beyond.
3. Four out of five points in zone B or beyond.
4. Eight points in zone C or beyond.

In Figure 10.7 the out-of-control data points are identified with the applicable condition number.

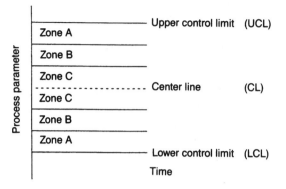

FIGURE 10.6 Shewhart control chart zones.

Another test is the runs test, which indicates that the process has shifted. Sequential data are evaluated relative to the center line. A shift has occurred if:

1. At least 10 out of 11 sequential data points are on the same side of the center line.
2. At least 12 out of 14 sequential data points are on the same side of the center line.
3. At least 14 out of 17 sequential data points are on the same side of the center line.
4. At least 16 out of 20 sequential data points are on the same side of the center line.

Other patterns within a control chart can tell a story. For example, a cyclic pattern that has a large amplitude relative to the control limits may indicate

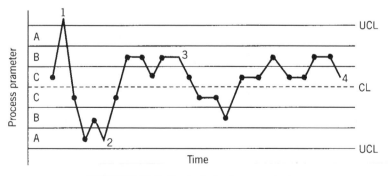

FIGURE 10.7 Control charts: zone tests.

that samples are being taken from two different distributions. This could occur because of operator or equipment differences.

The above battery of runs test is commonly suggested in texts; however, there is a cost in terms of decreasing the ARL of the chart. Lloyd Nelson has noted that he prefers to use nine consecutive points all on the same side of the center line as the only test of this type (Nelson 1993).

10.7 $\bar{x}$ AND R AND $\bar{x}$ AND s CHARTS: MEAN AND VARIABILITY MEASUREMENTS

Consider that a rational subgrouping of m samples of size n are taken over some period of time. The number of m samples should be at least 20 to 25, where n will often be smaller and either 4, 5, or 6. For each sample of size n a mean and range can be determined, where range is the difference between high and low readings.

For a process variable to be in statistical control, both the mean and range (or standard deviation) of the process must be within control. For a new process typically the process mean $(\bar{\bar{x}})$ is not known; hence, it has to be calculated using the equation

$$\bar{\bar{x}} = \frac{\bar{x}_1 + \bar{x}_2 + \cdots + \bar{x}_m}{m}$$

Similarly the mean range value $(\bar{R})$ of the m subgroups is

$$\bar{R} = \frac{R_1 + R_2 + \cdots + R_m}{m}$$

For small sample sizes a relatively good estimate for the population standard deviation $(\hat{\sigma})$ is (see Table J for factor d_2)

$$\hat{\sigma} = \frac{\bar{R}}{d_2}$$

In general, it is better to use the standard deviation from each subgroup instead of the range when tracking variability. This was more difficult in the past before the advent of on-line computers and calculators. However, when sample sizes for n are of a magnitude of 4 to 6, the range approximation is satisfactory and typically utilized.

When the sample size n for the subgroup is moderately large, say ($n > 10$ to 12), the range method for estimating σ loses efficiency. In these situations it is best to consider using $\bar{x}$ and s charts, where s (the sample standard deviation) can be determined using the relationship

$$s = \left[\frac{\sum_{i=1}^{n}(x_i - \bar{x})^2}{n - 1} \right]^{1/2}$$

For m subgroups, $\bar{s}$ can then be determined using the equation

$$\bar{s} = \frac{s_1 + s_2 + \cdots + s_m}{m}$$

The upper control limit (UCL) and lower control limit (LCL) around a center line (CL) for $\bar{x}$ and (R or s) can be determined from the following equations, where the constants (e.g., A_2 and D_3) are taken from Table J:

		UCL = $\bar{\bar{x}} + A_2\bar{R}$	LCL = $\bar{\bar{x}} - A_2\bar{R}$
$\bar{x}$:	CL = $\bar{\bar{x}}$	or	
		UCL = $\bar{\bar{x}} + A_3\bar{s}$	LCL = $\bar{\bar{x}} - A_3\bar{s}$
R:	CL = $\bar{R}$	UCL = $D_4\bar{R}$	LCL = $D_3\bar{R}$
s:	CL = $\bar{s}$	UCL = $B_4\bar{s}$	LCL = $B_3\bar{s}$

If successive group values plotted on the s or R charts are in control, control statements can then be made relative to an $\bar{x}$ chart.

When it is possible to specify the standard values for the process mean (μ) and standard deviation (σ), these standards could be used to establish the control charts without the analysis of past data. For this situation the following equations are used, where the constants are again taken from Table J:

$\bar{x}$:	CL = μ	UCL = $\mu + A\sigma$	LCL = $\mu - A\sigma$
R:	CL = $d_2\sigma$	UCL = $D_2\sigma$	LCL = $D_1\sigma$
s:	CL = $c_4\sigma$	UCL = $B_6\sigma$	LCL = $B_5\sigma$

Care must be exercised when using this approach because the standards may not be applicable to the process, which can result in many out-of-control signals.

10.8   EXAMPLE 10.2: $\bar{x}$ AND R CHART

A grinding machine is to produce treads for a hydraulic system of an aircraft to a diameter of 0.4037 ± 10.0013 in. Go/no-go thread ring gauges are currently used in a 100% test plan to reject parts that are not within tolerance. In an attempt to better understand the process variability so that the process can be improved, variable data were taken for the process. Measurements were taken every hour on five samples using a visual comparator that had an accuracy of 0.0001. The averages and ranges from this test are noted in Table 10.1 (Grant and Leavenworth 1980).

The $\bar{x}$ and R chart parameters are (values are expressed in units of 0.0001 in. in excess of 0.4000 in.) as follows:

For $\bar{x}$ chart:

$$\text{CL} = \bar{\bar{x}} = 33.6 \qquad \text{UCL} = \bar{\bar{x}} + A_2\bar{R} = 33.6 + 0.577(6.2) = 37.18$$

$$\text{LCL} = \bar{\bar{x}} - A_2\bar{R} = 33.6 - 0.577(6.2) = 30.02$$

For R chart:

$$\text{CL} = \bar{R} = 6.2$$

$$\text{UCL} = D_4\bar{R} = 2.114(6.2) = 13.1 \qquad \text{LCL} = D_3\bar{R} = 0(6.2) = 0$$

TABLE 10.1 $\bar{x}$- and R-Chart Data

Sample Number	Subgroup Measurements					Mean $\bar{x}$	Range (R)
1	36	35	34	33	32	34.0	4
2	31	31	34	32	30	31.6	4
3	30	30	32	30	32	30.8	2
4	32	33	33	32	35	33.0	3
5	32	34	37	37	35	35.0	5
6	32	32	31	33	33	32.2	2
7	33	33	36	32	31	33.0	5
8	23	33	36	35	36	32.6	13
9	43	36	35	24	31	33.8	19
10	36	35	36	41	41	37.8	6
11	34	38	35	34	38	35.8	4
12	36	38	39	39	40	38.4	4
13	36	40	35	26	33	34.0	14
14	36	35	37	34	33	35.0	4
15	30	37	33	34	35	33.8	7
16	28	31	33	33	33	31.6	5
17	33	30	34	33	35	33.0	5
18	27	28	29	27	30	28.2	3
19	35	36	29	27	32	31.8	9
20	33	35	35	39	36	35.6	6
						$\bar{\bar{x}} = 33.55$	$\bar{R} = 6.2$

Computer-generated $\bar{x}$ and R control charts are shown in Figure 10.8. Both the $\bar{x}$ (points 10, 12, and 18) and R (points 9 and 13) charts show lack of control. These points should have an assignable cause for being outside the control limits; however, in general, determining the real cause after some period of time may be impossible. In addition, often not much can be done about these past causes beside creating some awareness of trying to prevent a certain type of problem in the future; however, this chart gives evidence that there is opportunity to reduce the variability of the current process. For this example the previously noted abnormal variation in the mean was determined to be from the machine setting, while abnormal variation in the range was determined to be from operator carelessness. After isolating special causes, these points should then, in general, be removed from the data to create new control charts with new limits.

Assuming an average range value of 0.0006, it indicates that the tolerance of ±0.0013 could be consistently obtainable with a stable process that is centered within the specification, if there are no operator and machine problems. However, the $\bar{x}$ chart indicates that the process mean is shifted from the nominal specification. An example in the process capability chapter will later quantify the measurement of process capability/performance.

Whenever natural tolerances are found to be consistently within specification limits, consideration should be given to replacing a 100% inspection plan with periodic variable measurements of samples. For this example this can mean the replacement of the 100% go/no-go test with periodic measurements and control charting of the actual dimensions of five samples, as long as the control chart is in control and has an acceptable level of process ca-

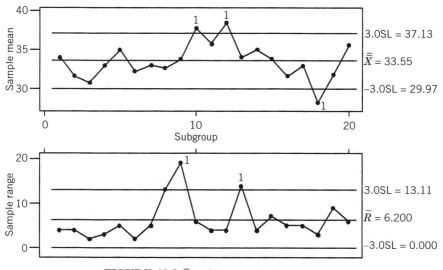

FIGURE 10.8 $\bar{x}$ and R control chart example.

pability. Often this change can yield both a significant savings and improvement in quality, because the process is better understood.

A practitioner might have chosen a different approach to set up this control chart plan. For example, someone might have chosen to use a single value rather than a subgroup size of five. The resulting control chart would then be an *XmR* chart (described in the next session). The creation of *XmR* charts from this data is an exercise at the end of this chapter.

10.9   *XmR* CHARTS: INDIVIDUAL MEASUREMENTS

A chart of individual values is typically referred to as an *I* chart or an *X* chart. A moving-range chart often accompanies these charts; hence, the designation *I–MR* or *XmR* chart. I will use the *XmR* nomenclature.

The criteria of $\bar{x}$ and R charts consider sample sizes greater than one within the sampling groups. For some situations, such as chemical batch processes, only a sample size of one is achievable. Individual measurements of this type can be monitored using X charts. For other situations, someone can choose which type of chart to use.

For an individual-measurement control chart the process average is simply the mean of the n data points, which is

$$\bar{x} = \frac{\sum_{i=1}^{n} x_i}{n}$$

Most frequently, adjacent values are used to determine the moving range; however, someone could use a larger duration when making this calculation. The constants shown would need to be adjusted accordingly. When using adjacent values, moving ranges (MRs) are determined from the data using the equations

$$MR_1 = |x_2 - x_1| \qquad MR_2 = |x_3 - x_2|, \cdots$$

The average moving range $(\overline{MR})$ is the average MR value for the n values described by

$$\overline{MR} = \frac{\sum_{i=1}^{m} MR_i}{m} = \frac{(MR_1) + (MR_2) + (MR_3), \cdots, (MR_m)}{m}$$

Charting parameters for the individual values chart are

$$\text{CL} = \bar{x} \qquad \text{UCL} = \bar{x} + \frac{3(\overline{MR})}{d_2} = \bar{x} + 2.66(\overline{MR})$$

$$\text{LCL} = \bar{x} - \frac{3(\overline{MR})}{d_2} = \bar{x} - 2.66(\overline{MR})$$

The 2.66 factor is $3/d_2$, where 3 is for three standard deviations and d_2 is from Table J for a sample size of 2 (i.e., $3/1.128 = 2.66$). This relationship can be used when the moving range is selected to expand beyond the adjacent samples. For this situation the value for d_2 would be adjusted accordingly.

When using two adjacent values to determine moving range, the charting parameters for the moving range chart are

$$\text{CL} = \overline{MR} \qquad \text{UCL} = D_4\overline{MR} = 3.267(\overline{MR})$$

The 3.267 factor D_4 is from Table J for a sample size of 2.

Some practitioners prefer not to construct moving range charts because any information that can be obtained from the moving range is contained in the X chart and the moving ranges are correlated, which can induce patterns of runs or cycles (ASTM STP15D). Because of this artificial autocorrelation, the assessment of moving range charts (when they are used) should not involve the use of run tests for out-of-control conditions.

10.10   EXAMPLE 10.3: *XmR* CHARTS

The viscosity of a chemical mixing process has the centipoise (cP) measurements noted in Table 10.2 for 20 batches (Messina 1987). Within a service organization, these data could be thought of as the time it takes to complete a process such as a purchase order request.

The MRs are determined from the relationship

$$MR_1 = |x_2 - x_1| = |70.10 - 75.20| = 5.10$$

$$MR_2 = |x_3 - x_2| = |74.40 - 75.20| = 0.80, \ldots$$

The process mean and moving range mean are calculated and used to determine the individual-measurement control chart parameters of

$$\text{CL} = \bar{x} \qquad \text{UCL} = \bar{x} + 2.66(\overline{MR}) \qquad \text{LCL} = \bar{x} - 2.66(\overline{MR})$$

$$\text{CL} = 74.200 \quad \text{UCL} = 74.200 + 2.66(2.267) \quad \text{LCL} = 74.200 - 2.66(2.267)$$

$$\text{UCL} = 80.230 \qquad\qquad\qquad \text{LCL} = 68.170$$

The moving range chart parameters are

TABLE 10.2 X-Chart Data

Batch Number	Viscosity (cP)	Moving Range (MR)
1	70.10	—
2	75.20	5.10
3	74.40	0.80
4	72.07	2.33
5	74.70	2.63
6	73.80	0.90
7	72.77	1.03
8	78.17	5.40
9	70.77	7.40
10	74.30	3.53
11	72.90	1.40
12	72.50	0.40
13	74.60	2.10
14	75.43	0.83
15	75.30	0.13
16	78.17	2.87
17	76.00	2.17
18	73.50	2.50
19	74.27	0.77
20	75.05	0.78
	$\bar{\bar{x}} = 74.200$	$\overline{MR} = 2.267$

$$CL = \overline{MR} = 2.267 \quad UCL = 3.267(\overline{MR}) = 3.267(2.267) = 7.406$$

The XmR computer plots shown in Figure 10.9 indicate no out of control condition for this data. If we consider that the 20 batch readings are a random sample of the process, we could make a probability plot of the raw data to determine the expected range of viscosities that will be experienced by the customer. We also could make process capability assessments relative to specification requirements.

10.11 $\bar{x}$ AND R VERSUS XmR CHARTS

Wheeler (1995a) favors the XmR chart for most real-time applications involving periodic data collection. He suggests the following:

- Charting individual values to achieve a timely response to any shift in process location.
- Charting moving average values when it is more important to know about recent trends than it is to respond to sudden changes.

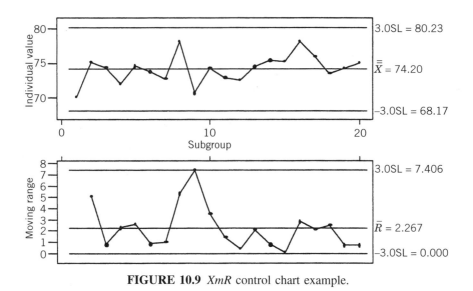

FIGURE 10.9 *XmR* control chart example.

If someone were using "short-term" variability within their Six Sigma process capability assessment (described in a later chapter), there could be a large difference caused by chart methodology selection. For an $\bar{x}$ and R chart, "short-term" variability is estimated from the variability within a subgroup, while in an *XmR* chart variability is estimated from the moving range. If between-subgroup variability was a lot larger than within-subgroup variability (perhaps caused by raw material lot changes between subgroups), the "short-term" standard deviation determined from an $\bar{x}$ and R chart would be lower than it would be if one value were selected from each subgroup and plotted using an *XmR* chart. For this second scenario, standard deviation would be determined from the moving range of the *XmR* chart. Many of the comments within the rational subgroup section of this chapter are also applicable to the selection of chart type.

10.12   ATTRIBUTE CONTROL CHARTS

The standard deviation used to calculate control chart limits for variable data is computed from the data. However, if one examines the binomial and Poisson distribution equations noted in Appendix A, he/she will find that standard deviation is dependent on the mean of the data (not data dispersion as with variables data). Because of this the standard deviation for an attribute control that uses the binomial or Poisson distribution will be derived from a formula based on the mean.

For the binomial-distribution-based and Poisson-distribution-based control charts we assume that when a process is in control the underlying probabilities remain fixed over time. This does not happen very often, which can have a dramatic impact on the binomial-distribution-based and Poisson-distribution-based control chart limits when the sample size gets large. For large sample sizes batch-to-batch variation can be greater than the prediction of traditional theory because of the violation of an underlying assumption. This assumption is that the sum of one or more binomial distributed random variables will follow a binomial distribution. This is not true if these random variables have differing values (Wheeler 1995a). The implication of this is that with very large sample sizes, classical control chart formulas squeeze limits toward the center line of the charts, which can result in many points falling outside the control limits. The implication is that the process is out of control most of the time when in reality the control limits do not reflect the true common-cause variability of the process.

The usual remedy for this problem is to plot the attribute failure rates as individual measurements. One problem with this approach is that the failure rate for the time of interest can be very low. For this situation the control chart limit might be less than zero, which is not physically possible. One approach to get around this problem is to use *XmR* charts to track time between failures.

Another problem with plotting failure rates directly as individual measurements is that there can be a difference in batch sample size. A way to address this problem is to use a *Z* chart. However, this has the same problem as previously described relative to variability being just a function of the mean. Laney (1997) suggests combining the approaches of using an *XmR* chart with a *Z* chart to create *Z&MR* charts for this situation (see Section 10.18).

The following two sections describe and illustrate the application of classical *p* charts, where Section 10.18 describes, through example, the mechanics of executing the *XmR* and *Z&MR* analysis alternatives for an attribute analysis.

10.13 *p* CHART: FRACTION NONCONFORMING MEASUREMENTS

Consider *m* rational subgroups where each subgroup has *n* samples with *x* nonconformities or defective units. The fraction nonconforming (*p*) for a subgroup is

$$p = \frac{x}{n}$$

The process average nonconforming $\bar{p}$ for the *m* subgroups is

$$\bar{p} = \frac{\sum\limits_{i=1}^{m} p_i}{m}$$

where in general m should be at least 20 to 25. The chart parameters for this binomial scenario are

$$CL = \bar{p} \qquad UCL = \bar{p} + 3\sqrt{\frac{\bar{p}(1-\bar{p})}{n}}$$

$$LCL = \bar{p} - 3\sqrt{\frac{\bar{p}(1-\bar{p})}{n}}$$

An LCL cannot be less than zero; hence, this limit is set to zero whenever a limit is calculated below zero.

One of the problems that often occurs with this type of chart is that sample sizes are often not equal. One approach to solve this problem is to use the average sample size with a p value that is most typically determined as the total number of defects from all the samples divided by the total number of samples that are taken. The interpretation of these charts are easy to interpret since the control limits are at the same level for all samples. However, this approach is not very satisfactory when there are large differences in sample sizes. A better way to create this chart (but a more difficult chart to interpret) is to adjust the control chart limits for each sample. For this chart we have

$$\bar{p} = \frac{\sum\limits_{i=1}^{m} D_i}{\sum\limits_{i=1}^{m} n_i}$$

where D_i is the number of nonconformances within the ith sample of m total samples. Control limits for the ith sample is then

$$CL = \bar{p} \qquad UCL = \bar{p} + 3\sqrt{\frac{\bar{p}(1-\bar{p})}{n_i}}$$

$$LCL = \bar{p} - 3\sqrt{\frac{\bar{p}(1-\bar{p})}{n_i}}$$

There is another approach to address unequal subgroup sample sizes but still get constant control limits. The approach is to perform a Z transformation on the data. Section 10.18 describes this technique.

10.14   EXAMPLE 10.4: *p* CHART

A machine manufactures the cardboard can used to package frozen orange juice. Cans are then inspected to determine whether they will leak when filled with orange juice. A *p* chart is initially established by taking 30 samples of 50 cans at half-hour intervals within the manufacturing process, as summarized in Table 10.3 (Montgomery 1985). Within a service organization this data could be thought as defect rates for the completion of a form such as whether a purchase order request was filled out correctly. Note, in this example there was no assessment of the number of error that might be on an individual form (this would involve a *c* or *u* chart). An alternative analysis approach for this data is described in Example 10.5.

The process average is

$$\bar{p} = \sum_{i=1}^{m} \frac{p_i}{m} = \frac{0.24 + 0.30 + 0.16, \ldots}{30} = 0.2313$$

The chart parameters are then

$$CL = 0.2313 \qquad UCL = 0.2313 + 3\sqrt{\frac{0.2313(1 - 0.2313)}{50}} = 0.4102$$

$$LCL = 0.2313 - 3\sqrt{\frac{0.2313(1 - 0.2313)}{50}} = 0.0524$$

The *p* chart of the data is shown in Figure 10.10. Samples 15 and 23 are beyond the limits in the control chart; hence, the process is considered "not in control." If investigation indicates that these two points were caused by an adverse condition (e.g., a new batch of raw material or an inexperienced operator), the process control limits can be recalculated without the data points. Whenever out-of-control conditions exist that cannot be explained, these data points should typically not be removed from the control limit computations. If this initial process control chart also does not have any abnormal patterns, the control limits are used to monitor the current production on a continuing basis.

For an in-control process the magnitude of the average failure rate should be examined for acceptability. A reduction in the overall average typically requires a more involved overall process or design change (i.e., a common

TABLE 10.3 Data for p-Chart Example

Sample Number	Number of Nonconformances	Sample Nonconforming Fraction
1	12	0.24
2	15	0.30
3	8	0.16
4	10	0.20
5	4	0.08
6	7	0.14
7	16	0.32
8	9	0.18
9	14	0.28
10	10	0.20
11	5	0.10
12	6	0.12
13	17	0.34
14	12	0.24
15	22	0.44
16	8	0.16
17	10	0.20
18	5	0.10
19	13	0.26
20	11	0.22
21	20	0.40
22	18	0.36
23	24	0.48
24	15	0.30
25	9	0.18
26	12	0.24
27	7	0.14
28	13	0.26
29	9	0.18
30	6	0.12

cause issue). Pareto charts and DOE techniques can be powerful approaches to aid in determining which changes are beneficial to improving the process.

This section described the traditional control chart analysis approach for this type problem. See Example 10.5 for alternative approaches to the analysis of this data.

10.15 np CHART: NUMBER OF NONCONFORMING ITEMS

An alternative to the p chart when the sample size (n) is constant is a np chart. In this chart the number of nonconforming items is plotted instead of the fraction nonconforming (p). The chart parameters are

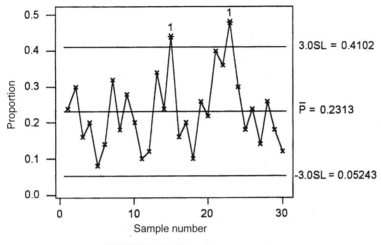

FIGURE 10.10 *p*-Chart example.

$$CL = n\overline{p} \qquad UCL = n\overline{p} + 3\sqrt{n\overline{p}(1 - \overline{p})} \qquad LCL = n\overline{p} - 3\sqrt{n\overline{p}(1 - \overline{p})}$$

where $\overline{p}$ is determined similar to a *p* chart. See Example 10.5 for alternative analysis considerations for this type of data.

10.16   *c* CHART: NUMBER OF NONCONFORMITIES

In some cases the number of nonconformities per unit (i.e., defects) is a more appropriate unit of measure than the fraction nonconforming. An example of this situation is where a printed circuit board is tested. If the inspection process considered the board as a pass/fail entity, then a *p* chart or *np* chart would be appropriate. However, a given printed circuit board can have multiple failures; hence, it may be better to track the total number of defects per unit of measure. For a printed circuit board the unit of measure could be the number of solder joints in 100 cards, while the unit of measure when manufacturing cloth could be the number of blemishes per 100 square yards.

The *c* chart can be used to monitor these processes, if the Poisson distribution is an appropriate model. As noted earlier, the Poisson distribution can be used for various analysis considerations if the number of opportunities for nonconformities are sufficiently large and the probability of occurrence of a nonconformity at a location is small and constant. The chart parameters for the *c* chart are

$$CL = \overline{c} \qquad UCL = \overline{c} + 3\sqrt{\overline{c}} \qquad LCL = \overline{c} - 3\sqrt{\overline{c}}$$

where $\overline{c}$ is the mean of the occurrences and the LCL is set to zero if the calculations yield a negative number. See Example 10.5 for alternative analysis considerations for this type of data.

10.17 u CHART: NONCONFORMITIES PER UNIT

A u chart plots defects that can be used in lieu of a c chart when the rationale subgroup size is not constant. This occurs, for example, when defects are tracked daily and production volume has daily variation. For a sample size n that has a total number of nonconformities c, u equates to

$$u = c/n$$

The control chart parameters for the u chart are then

$$\text{CL} = \bar{u} \qquad \text{UCL} = \bar{u} + 3\sqrt{\bar{u}/n} \qquad \text{LCL} = \bar{u} - 3\sqrt{\bar{u}/n}$$

where $\bar{u}$ is the mean of the occurrences. See Example 10.5 for alternative analysis considerations for this type of data.

10.18   EXAMPLE 10.5: ALTERNATIVES TO p-CHART, np-CHART, c-CHART, AND u-CHART ANALYSES

Earlier some potential problems with a classical p chart analysis were described. This section will illustrate the mechanics of various analysis alternatives using the data in Table 10.3. The implication of these alternate analysis approaches become more dramatic when the sample size is much larger and there are differing sample sizes between samples. The basic alternatives described within this section could be considered for a variety of situations, including DPMO tracking.

   When creating a p chart both the number of opportunities and defects are considered within the calculations are made for each sample. An XmR analysis of attribute data needs only response for each sample. This response could take differing forms to describe each trial, such as failure rate for each trial, inverse of failure rate, and the total number of failures for each trial (i.e., an np value). For this illustration I have chosen to use the proportion that failed for each trial (i.e., the failure rate for each trial). The results of this XmR analysis is shown in Figure 10.11.

   We note that the results of this XmR analysis of the Table 10.3 data is very different from the previous p-chart analysis. This analysis shows no out-of-control points. With this analysis we now would consider the out-of-control points determined in the p-chart analysis to be common cause, not special cause. The reason for differing results between these two analysis approaches is that the XmR control chart analysis considers variability between samples

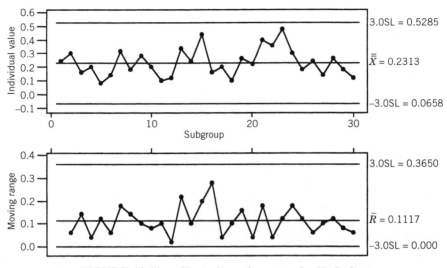

FIGURE 10.11 p-Chart alternative example: XmR chart.

when determining control limits. A p-chart analysis (also for np-chart, c-chart, and u-chart analysis) assumes that dispersion is a function of location and uses theoretical limits. The XmR chart makes no such assumption and uses empirical limits. Wheeler (1995a) states that theoretical limits only offer a larger number of degrees of freedom. However, if the theory is correct, XmR chart will be about the same. However, if the theory is wrong, the theoretical limits will be wrong, yet the empirical limits will be still correct.

However, some issues often need to be addressed when conducting an XmR analysis for this type of situation. First, an XmR analysis is not bounded by physical restraints that might be present. For example, the XmR computer program analysis has a lower control limit below zero that is below zero, which is not physically possible. Hence, this limit needs to be adjusted to zero. Sometimes this problem can be overcome by reassessing our rational subgrouping or viewing the data differently. We might also consider plotting the total number of failures (i.e., an np-chart alternative) or the reciprocal of the failure rate (instead of failure rate).

Another potential issue with the XmR analysis approach for this situation is that this analysis does not consider that there could be differing subgroup sample sizes. If these differences are not large, this issue might not be important; however, if the differences are large, this can adversely affect the analysis.

To address the differing sample size issue for an XmR analysis of this situation, Laney (1997) suggests analyzing the data using a $Z\&MR$ chart, where a Z transformation is made of the nonconformance rates. This transformation is then analyzed as an individual measurement. For this procedure

$$Z_i = \frac{p_i - \bar{p}}{\hat{\sigma}_{pi}} \quad \text{for example:} \quad Z_1 = \frac{p_1 - \bar{p}}{\hat{\sigma}_{p1}} = \frac{0.24 - 0.2313}{0.05963} = 0.145$$

where p_i is the nonconformance proportion at the ith sample and the value for $\hat{\sigma}_{pi}$ is determined from the relationship

$$\hat{\sigma}_{pi} = \sqrt{\frac{\bar{p}(1 - \bar{p})}{n_i}} \quad \text{for example:} \quad \hat{\sigma}_{p1} = \sqrt{\frac{0.2313(1 - 0.2313)}{50}} = 0.05963$$

A Z chart could be created from these calculations where the center line would be zero and the upper/lower control limits would be ± 3 standard deviations. However, this does not resolve the previously discussed problem of limits being calculated from dispersion of the mean. The solution to this dilemma is to analyze the Z-score transformed data as though it were individual measurements. This $Z\&MR$ chart has limits that are calculated the same as XmR charts, except Z values replace the original data values. Figure 10.12 show the results of this analysis. We note that this control chart is very similar in appearance to Figure 10.11; however, we do not have the zero bound problem with this chart. We should note that in general there could be large differences between these two plots when there are differing sample sizes between subgroups.

10.19   CHARTS FOR RARE EVENTS

Imagination is the only limitation to Shewhart's charts. Shewhart charts are applicable to a wide variety of situations; however, the key is to *wisely* im-

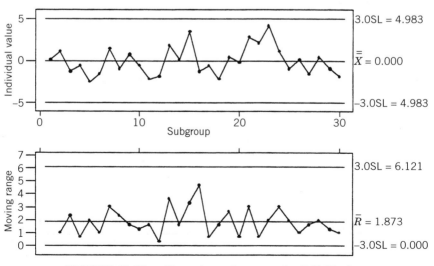

FIGURE 10.12 *p*-Chart alternative example: Z&MR chart.

plement the charts. Consider the need to create a control charting plan for the following situations:

- An organization has an occasional safety problem such as a spill or an injury. Much effort was spent to eliminate the problems, but problems still occur on the average every 7 months.
- A company requires that a supplier conducts an ongoing reliability test (ORT) of an electronic product that the supplier manufactures. The company later integrates this product into a larger system within their manufacturing facility. Through this ORT the supplier is to determine when changes are occurring such that they expect the frequency of failure to degrade within a final customer environment. The supplier is most interested in weekly performance; however, because of sampling costs and constraints they expect failure to occur only once every 7 weeks. They estimated this frequency of occurrence by dividing the total usage (adjusting for any acceleration factors) per week into the expected mean time between failure (MTBF) rate for their product. (The supplier could have determined this expected frequency of failure from a bottoms-up analysis of historical failure rates of the components comprising the product that he/she manufactures.)

Even though these two scenarios are quite different, the analysis challenges and approaches are very similar. In scenario 1 the unit of time was months, while in scenario 2 the unit of time was weeks. Both scenarios involve count data, which can often be represented by a Poisson distribution. For both scenarios a plot count contained the number of failures within their respective time periods. The following description exemplifies the first scenario; however, the same methodology would apply also to the second scenario.

Typically, plots for these scenarios are in the form of c charts. If the duration of time examined is small relative to the frequency of failure, the plot positions for most data points are zero. Whenever even one rare problem or failure occurs during a month, the plot point shifts to one. This occasional shift from zero to one for low failure rates (e.g., 1/7 failures per month) gives little information. A better alternative to the c chart is the XmR chart that examines the change in failure rate between failure occurrences.

10.20   EXAMPLE 10.6: CHARTS FOR RARE EVENTS

A department occasionally experiences a spill, which is undesirable (Wheeler 1996). Everything possible is done to prevent spills; however, over the last few years a spill occurs on the average about once every 7 months. The following describes two methods to analyze data spills.

The first spill occurred on February 23 of year 1. The second occurred on January 11 of year 2. The third occured on September 15 of year 2. The number of days between the first and second spill is 322 days, or an equivalent rate of 1.13 spills per year. The number of days between the second spill and third spill is 247 days, or an equivalent rate of 1.48 spills per year. Dates of occurrence, time between spills, and annual spill rates for these and other occurrences are summarized as follows:

Date of Occurrence	Time Between Spills	Annual Spill Rate
2/23/90		
1/11/91	322.00	1.13
9/15/91	247.00	1.48
7/5/92	294.00	1.24
2/17/93	227.00	1.61
9/28/93	223.00	1.64
3/19/94	172.00	2.12
7/12/94	115.00	3.17

A c-chart analysis for these data (where the time of failure occurrences is converted to the number defects that occurred each month) is shown in Figure 10.13. This chart shows no out of control condition, while the XmR chart analysis shown in Figure 10.14 suggests an increase in spill rate that should be investigated. Counts of rare events is no exception to the rule that count information is generally weaker than measurement data. This example illustrates that the times between undesirable rare events are best charted as rates.

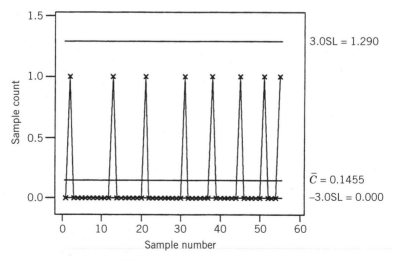

FIGURE 10.13 c-Chart example.

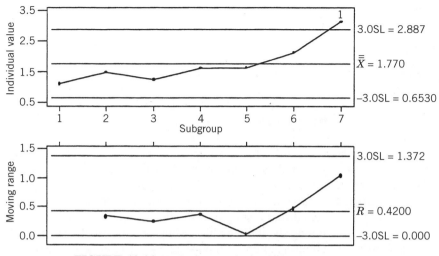

FIGURE 10.14 *XmR*-chart analysis alternative to *c* chart.

10.21 S^4 ASSESSMENT

With the typical low failure rates of today, AQL sampling is not an effective approach to identify lot defect problems. However, often it can be difficult to convince others that AQL does not have much value add (and should be replaced by a better process monitoring system). If AQL testing is common-place within an organization, consider viewing the AQL's department activity as a process where input to the process is various types of batches that enter this process. The output to this process is whether the lot failed or not. Next calculate *p* for some period of time (e.g., weekly) by dividing the number of lots that failed by the number of lots that were tested. Next plot these *p* values on an *XmR* chart and assess the frequency of lots. A Pareto chart could then be created to summarize overall the types of failure captured within the AQL department. To better grasp how many "unacceptable" lots that are perhaps missed by the AQL department because of a low sample size, resampling of some lots that failed can give valuable insight. I would suspect that many of the failed lots would pass the second time (if this is the case, one would suspect that many of the lots that passed might fail if retested). This infor-mation collectively could be very valuable when we want to get a better overall picture of the value of the department and to determine where im-provements could be made.

The presentation of time series data can give insight to when and how process improvements should be conducted. However, it is important to select the best chart and sampling frequency for the given situation.

Control charts are most often associated with the identification of special causes within the control of a process. However, these charts are also very useful at a higher level where focus is given to direct activities ranging from the fire fighting of daily problems (i.e., common-cause issues being attacked as though they were special cause) to fire prevention activities (i.e., common-cause issues being resolved through process improvement activities). When selecting a rational subgrouping for a high level, consider a sampling plan that will give a long-term view of variability (e.g., one sample daily). A probability plot of the data can be a good supplementary tool to better understand and describe pictorially expected variability (e.g., 80% of the time it takes between 2 days and 6 weeks to fulfill our orders).

When this measurement and process improvement strategy is implemented, true change can be detected as a shift of the Shewhart chart. It is hoped that this shift in the control chart is toward the better (perhaps caused through the change resulting from a DOE or improved operator awareness).

Classically, it is stated that a subgroup should be chosen so that opportunities for variation among the units within a subgroup are small. The thought is that if variation within a subgroup represents the piece-to-piece variability over a very short period of time, then any unusual variation between subgroups would reflect changes in the process that should be investigated for appropriate action. The case for this sampling plan is that this sampling approach can quantify the variability from common cause.

Let us elaborate on this thought. Consider a process that has one operator per shift and batch-to-batch raw material changes that occur daily. Consider also that there are some slight operator-to-operator differences and raw material differences from batch to batch (but raw material is always within specification limits). If a control chart is established where five pieces are taken in a row for each shift, the variability used to calculate control chart limits does not consider operator-to-operator and batch-to-batch raw material variability. If the variability between operators and from batch to batch is large relative to five pieces in a row, the process could appear to be going out of control a lot. When a process goes out of control we are told to "stop the presses" and fix the "special-cause" problem. Much frustration can occur in manufacturing because they will probably be trying to fix a "special-cause" problem that they have no control over.

One question that someone might ask is whether the manufacturing line should be shut down because of such a "special cause." Someone could even challenge whether out of control conditions caused by raw material should be classified as special cause. Note that this point does not say that raw material is not a problem to the process even though it is within tolerance. The point is whether the variability between raw material should be treated as a special cause. It seems that there is a very good argument to treat this type of variability as common cause. If this were the case, control limits should then be created to include this variability. Perhaps measurements from one unit could be tracked on a control chart. To address whether the batch-to-batch variability and other variability sources are causing a problem, the "long-term" variability of the process could then be compared to specification needs. If the process is not capable of meeting specification needs, then further analysis of the process using the other tools described in this book would show that the process is not robust to raw material batch-to-batch variations. This knowledge could then perhaps lead to a DOE that fixes this "common-cause" problem.

It should be noted that the above dialogue does not suggest that an infrequent sampling plan using individual charting is the best approach for all processes. What it does suggest is that perhaps we often need to step back and look at the purpose and value of the control charting plan. Surely control charts are beneficial to give direction when a process needs to be adjusted before a lot of scrap is produced. However, control charts can also be very beneficial at a higher plane of vision that reduces day-to-day fire fighting of common-cause problems as though they were special cause.

A process that is in-control is not necessarily without problems. When analyzing the average failure rate of a stable process, consider the acceptability of the expected failure rate. A reduction in the overall average typically requires a more involved overall process or design change because the non-conformances are considered chronic-problem or common-cause issues. A Pareto chart in conjunction with a DOE can often be a very powerful approach to aid in determining which changes are beneficial to improving the process. A control chart tracking of the largest Pareto chart items can give us insight to when our process improvements focused on these items is effective (i.e., should go out of control to the better). We should also consider translating any of these quantifiable defect rate improvements to monetary benefits for presentation to management.

10.22   EXERCISES

1. *Catapult Exercise Data Analysis:* Combine the catapult exercise data sets from Chapter 4 to create an $\bar{x}$ and R chart that shows the impact of the process change. Describe the results.

2. *M&M's Candy Data Analysis:* In Chapter 5 an exercise was described where bags of M&M's were opened by S^4 workshop attendees. The number of each color was counted and documented. Create a p chart and c chart for the number for each color of M&M's. Comment on the results and which chart seems to be most appropriate for the given situation.

3. Create a control chart of the following data (AIAG 1995). Comment.

4. Make an assessment of the statistical control of a process using *XmR* charts: 3.40, 8.57, 2.42, 5.59, 9.92, 4.63, 7.48, 8.55, 6.10, 6.42, 4.46, 7.02, 5.86, 4.80, 9.60, 5.92.

Subgroup	Measurement				
	1	2	3	4	5
1	0.65	0.70	0.65	0.65	0.85
2	0.75	0.85	0.75	0.85	0.65
3	0.75	0.80	0.80	0.70	0.75
4	0.60	0.70	0.70	0.75	0.65
5	0.70	0.75	0.65	0.85	0.80
6	0.60	0.75	0.75	0.85	0.70
7	0.75	0.80	0.65	0.75	0.70
8	0.60	0.70	0.80	0.75	0.75
9	0.65	0.80	0.85	0.85	0.75
10	0.60	0.70	0.60	0.80	0.65
11	0.80	0.75	0.90	0.50	0.80
12	0.85	0.75	0.85	0.65	0.70
13	0.70	0.70	0.75	0.75	0.70
14	0.65	0.70	0.85	0.75	0.60
15	0.90	0.80	0.80	0.75	0.85
16	0.75	0.80	0.75	0.80	0.65

5. Consider that someone decided to use an *XmR* strategy in lieu of the $\bar{x}$ and *R* strategy described in Example 10.1. Consider five scenarios for the resulting data as the five columns of Table 10.1. That is, one set of *XmR* data would be 36, 31, 30, . . . , 35, 33, while another data set would be 35, 31, 30, . . . , 36, 35. Compare and describe result differences from Example 10.1.

6. Discuss the concepts of special and common cause relative to Shewhart charts. Describe the statistical meaning of the term "in-control." Describe a nonmanufacturing application of control charts.

7. A process produces an output that is measured as a continuous response. The process is consistent from day to day.
   (a) Given only this information, comment on what can be said, if any-thing, about the capability of the process.
   (b) Give an example of a service, manufacturing, and personal process where this might apply.

8. Management initially wanted the evaluation of a random sample to assess a process that is considered a problem whenever the response is larger than 100. They believe an unsatisfactory rate of 2% is tolerable but would like a rate not to exceed 3%. Describe control charting alternatives that could have been used earlier within the process to give the requested response. Describe the advantages of the alternative strategies over the currently proposed a single-sample approach.

9. A manufacturing company was conducting a go/no-go test on a critical dimension that had a dimension of 0.100 ± 0.002 in. The company

thought they were getting a reject rate of 10%. Describe what, if anything, could be done differently within their sampling plan to better understand the process.

10. Manufactured parts experience a high-temperature burn-in test of 6–12 hours before shipment. The parts either pass or fail the test. Create a plan that identifies special from common causes and also gives manufacturing feedback to common-cause issues. Describe a strategy that could be used to reduce the frequency of manufacturing common-cause failures. Describe what could be done to assess the effectiveness of the test relative to capturing the types of problems encountered within a customer environment.

11. Describe how the techniques within this chapter are useful and can be applied to S^4 projects.

11

PROCESS CAPABILITY AND PROCESS PERFORMANCE

Process capability/performance studies are to assess a process relative to specification criteria. Statisticians often challenge how well commonly used capability indices do this; however, the fact remains that customers often request these indices when communicating with their suppliers. A customer might set process capability/performance targets and then ask their suppliers for their level of conformance to these targets.

The equations for process capability/performance indices described within this chapter are basically very simple; however, they are very sensitive to the input value for standard deviation (σ). Unfortunately, there can be differences of opinion on how to determine standard deviation in a given situation. This chapter will discuss some of these alternatives and their differences.

The equations described within this chapter are for normally distributed data. Computer programs can often address situations where data are not from a normal distribution.

11.1 DEFINITIONS

It is important to note that the following definitions are not used by all organizations. Some differences of opinion are described at the end of this section. AIAG (1995b) defines the following:

Inherent Process Variation. That portion of process variation due to common causes only. This variation can be estimated from control charts by $\bar{R}/d_2$, among other things (e.g., $\bar{s}/c_4$).

Total Process Variation. This is the variation due to both common and special causes. This variation may be estimated by s, the sample standard deviation, using all of the individual readings obtained from either a detailed control chart or a process study; that is, $s = \sqrt{\sum_{i=1}^{n}(x_i - \bar{x})^2/(n-1)} = \hat{\sigma}_s$, where x_i is an individual reading, $\bar{x}$ is the average of individual readings, and n is the total number of all of the individual readings.

Process Capability. The 6σ range of a process's inherent variation, for statistically stable processes only where σ is usually estimated by $\bar{R}/d_2$.

Process Performance. The 6σ range of a process's total variation, where σ is usually estimated by s, the sample standard deviation.

AIAG (1995b) describes the indices:

C_p. This is the capability index which is defined as the tolerance width divided by the process capability, irrespective of process centering.

C_{pk}. This is the capability index which accounts for process centering. It relates the scaled distance between the process mean and the closest specification limit to half the total process spread.

P_p. This is the performance index which is defined as the tolerance width divided by the process performance, irrespective of process centering. Typically, this is expressed as the tolerance width divided by six times the sample standard deviation. (It should be used only to compare to or with C_p and C_{pk} and to measure and prioritize improvement over time.)

P_{pk}. This is the performance index which accounts for process centering. (It should be used only to compare to or with C_p and C_{pk} and to measure and prioritize improvement over time.)

As noted earlier, it is important to understand that these definitions are not followed by all organizations.

- Some organizations interpret process capability as how well a product performs relative to customer needs (i.e., specification). This interpretation is closer to the above definition for process performance.
- Some organizations require/assume that processes are in control before conducting process capability/performance assessments. Other organizations lump all data together which result in special-cause data increasing the value for "long-term" variability.
- The term *process performance* is not always used to describe P_p and P_{pk}.

11.2 MISUNDERSTANDINGS

Practitioners need to be very careful of the methodology they use to calculate and report process capability/performance metrics. The author has seen a situation where a customer was asking for C_p and C_{pk} metrics; however if you read their documentation carefully, they really were stipulating the use of a "long-term" estimate for standard deviation. This supplier was initially operating under the school of thought that C_p and C_{pk} are to be a measure of "short-term" variability. A misunderstanding between the customer and supplier about how this metric is determined could be very costly.

Another source of confusion could be the use of a statistical computer program package to calculate these indices. The author has seen a supplier enter randomly collected data into a computer program, thinking that the usual sampling standard deviation formula would be the source for the standard deviation value used within the capability computations. The computer program by default was presuming that the data were collected sequentially. The computer program was estimating a "short-term" standard deviation by calculating the average moving range of the sequential entries and then converting this moving range value to a standard deviation. The program listed the response as C_p and C_{pk}. The practitioner thought they were using the program correctly because the computer program stated that the output of the computer program (C_p and C_{pk}) was consistent with the request of their customer. However data were not generated in sequence. If the practitioner had reentered the same data in a different sequence (which would be a reasonable thing to do because since the data are not sequentially generated), a different C_p and C_{pk} metric would probably appear. For this situation of nonsequentially generated data the practitioner should limit his/her calculations to options of this program that lead to a P_p- and P_{pk}-type computation. The underlying assumption with this approach is that the results from this computation presume that the data are collected randomly over a long period of time and accurately describe the population of interest.

The bottom line is that process capability metrics require very good communications and agreements to the techniques used to determine the metrics. These agreements should also include sample size and measurement considerations.

11.3   CONFUSION: SHORT-TERM VERSUS LONG-TERM VARIABILITY

Differences of opinion and confusion exist relative to the terms "short-term" and "long-term" variability. Even though differences in application approach can be many, the following summarizes the basic differences into two major categories.

Opinion 1

Process capability describes the "capability" or the best a process could currently be expected to produce. The intent of process capability is not to address directly how well a process is executing relative to the needs of the customer. Process capability considers "short-term" variability. A "long-term" variability assessment attempts to address directly how well the process is performing relative to the needs of the customer. Typically, analysis focus is on determining "short-term" variability with an assumed adjustment of 1.5σ to compensate for drifts to get "long-term" variability. Special causes from a control chart might be included within the analyses, which has the most impact to "long-term" variability estimates. (This can be a major issue of contention with some practitioners because their point is that predictions cannot be made without process stability. Another point to this consideration, as noted earlier. is that processes can appear to be out of control from day-to-day variability effects, such as raw material, which some would argue is common-cause variability.)

Standard deviation input to process capability and process performance equations can originate from "short-term" or "long-term" considerations. When determining process capability indices from $\bar{x}$ and R control chart data, the standard deviation within subgroups is said to give an estimate for the "short-term" variability of the process, while the standard deviation of the combination of all the data is said to be an estimate for the "long-term" variability of the process.

Within a manufacturing process, "short-term" variability typically would not include, for example, raw material lot-to-lot variability and operator-to-operator variability. Within a business process, "short-term" variability might not include, for example, day-to-day variability or department-to-department variability. Depending upon the situation, these "long-term" variability sources could be considered special cause (not common cause).

Process capability indices C_p and C_{pk} typically assess the potential "short-term" capability by using a "short-term" standard deviation estimate, while P_p and P_{pk} typically assess overall "long-term" capability by using a "long-term" standard deviation estimate. Sometimes the relationship P_p and P_{pk} is referred to as process performance.

Some organizations require/assume that processes are in control before conducting process capability/performance assessments. Other organizations lump all data together, which result in special-cause data increasing the value for "long-term" variability (these organizations might give effort to restrict the application of control charts to the control of inputs to a process).

Opinion 2

Process capability describes how well a process is executing relative to the needs of the customer. The terms "short-term" and "long-term" are not typically considered separately as part of a process capability assessment.

The quantification for the standard deviation term within process capability calculations describes the overall variability of a process. When determining process capability indices from $\bar{x}$ and R control chart data, an overall standard deviation estimate would be used within the process capability equations. Calculation procedures for standard deviations can differ between practitioners, ranging from lumping all data together to determining total standard deviation from a variance components model.

This opinion has more of a "long-term" view for variability; hence, there can be differences of opinion on how factors are viewed for an in-control process. Within manufacturing, raw material lot-to-lot variability and operator-to-operator variability would be more likely considered common-cause issues. Within a business process, day-to-day variability or department-to-department variability would more likely be considered common-cause issues.

Process capability indices C_p and C_{pk} typically address the needs of customers and have a total standard deviation estimate within the calculations. P_p and P_{pk} are not typically used as a metric.

11.4   CALCULATING STANDARD DEVIATION

This section addresses some confusion that is often encountered relative to the calculation of the seemingly simple statistic, standard deviation. Standard deviation is a very integral part of the calculations for process capability; however, often the methodology to make the calculation is not adequately scrutinized. In some cases it is impossible to get a specific desired result if data are not collected in a fashion that is consistent with the described result. For the purpose of this discussion let us consider the following three situations as sources for continuous data (Method 6 describes other alternatives for data collection and analyses):

- *Situation 1.* An $\bar{x}$ and R control chart that has subgroups of sample size of 5.
- *Situation 2.* An X chart that has individual measurements.
- *Situation 3.* A random sample of measurements from a population.

All three of these situations are very real possibilities for the source of information. However there is no one correct method to obtain an estimate for standard deviation a that covers all three scenarios. The following five methods (Pyzedek 1998) of making this calculation describe the applicability of each method to the various situations.

Method 1

"Long-Term" Estimate of σ. One approach for calculating the standard deviation of a sample (s) is to use the formula

$$\hat{\sigma} = \sqrt{\sum_{i=1}^{n} \frac{(x_i - \bar{x})^2}{n - 1}}$$

where $\bar{x}$ is the average of all data, x_i is the data values, and n is the overall sample size.

Sometimes computer programs apply an unbiasing term to this estimate by dividing the above by $c_4(n-1)$ (Minitab 1998). Tabulated values for c_4 at $n-1$ can be determined from Table J or by using the mathematical relationship described in Appendix B9.

- *Situation 1.* When data are from an $\bar{x}$ and R chart, this traditional estimate of standard deviation is only really valid when a process is stable (however, some may use the approach when processes are not stable). Shewhart showed that the estimate will overestimate the process scatter if a process is influenced by a special cause. It should be emphasized that this estimate should never be used to calculate control limits. Control limits are calculated using sampling distributions.
- *Situation 2.* When data are from an individual control, this approach can give an estimate of process variability from the point of view of a customer.
- *Situation 3.* For a random sample of data from a population, this is the only one of the described methodologies that makes sense, because the sequence of when parts were created is needed for the methodologies that are numbered below.

Method 2

"Short-Term" Estimate of σ. A standard methodology for estimating standard deviation from $\bar{x}$ and R control chart data is

$$\hat{\sigma} = \frac{\bar{R}}{d_2}$$

where $\bar{R}$ is the average of the subgroup range values from a control chart and d_2 is a value from Table J, which depends upon subgroup sample size.

- *Situation 1.* When data are from an $\bar{x}$ and R chart, this estimator alleviates the problem of the standard deviation being inflated by special causes because it does not include variation between time periods. Shewhart proposed using a rational subgroup to achieve this. where the subgroup sample is chosen such that the opportunity for special cause is minimized. Often this is accomplished by selecting consecutively produced units from a process. The analysis methodology is inefficient when range is used to estimate standard deviation because only two data values are used from each subgroup. This inefficiency increases as the subgroup size increases. Efficiency increases when subgroup standard deviation is used.

- *Situation 2.* When data are from an individual control chart, this calculation is not directly possible because the calculation of $\bar{R}$ for a subgroup size of one is not possible.
- *Situation 3.* For a random sample of data from a population, this calculation is not possible because the sequencing of unit creation by the process is not known and considered.

Method 3

"Short-Term" Estimate of σ. The following relationship is taken from the equation used to determine the center line of a control chart when the process standard deviation is known:

$$\hat{\sigma} = \frac{\bar{s}}{c_4}$$

where $\bar{s}$ is the average of the subgroup standard deviation values from a control chart and c_4 is a value from Table J, which depends upon subgroup sample size. Subgroup standard deviation values are determined by the formula shown in Method 1.

- *Situation 1.* When data are from an $\bar{x}$ and R or s chart, the comments relative to this situation are similar to the comments in Method 2. When compared to Method 2, this approach is more involved but is more efficient.
- *Situation 2.* When data are from an individual control, this calculation is not directly possible because the calculation of $\bar{s}$ for a subgroup size of one is not possible.
- *Situation 3.* For a random sample of data from a population, this calculation is not possible because the sequencing of unit creation by the process is not known and considered.

Method 4

"Short-Term" Estimate of σ. The following relationship is taken from one of the equation options used to determine the center line of an individual control chart

$$\hat{\sigma} = 1.047 \, (\text{Moving } \tilde{R})$$

where a correction factor of 1.047 is multiplied by the median of the moving range (Moving $\tilde{R}$).

- *Situation 1.* When data are from an $\bar{x}$ and R chart, this approach is not directly applicable.

- *Situation 2.* When data are from an individual control, this calculation is an alternative. If the individual chart values are samples from a process, we would expect a higher value if there is less variability from adjacently created units when compared to the overall variability experienced by the process between sampling periods of the individuals control chart. Research recently has indicated that this approach gives good results for a wide variety of out-of-control patterns.
- *Situation 3.* For a random sample of data from a population, this calculation is not possible because the sequencing of unit creation by the process is not known and considered.

Method 5

"Short-Term" Estimate of σ. The following relationship is taken from one of the equation options used to determine the center line of an individual control chart:

$$\hat{\sigma} = \frac{\overline{MR}}{d_2} = \frac{\overline{MR}}{1.128}$$

where $\overline{MR}$ is the moving range between two consecutively produced units and d_2 is a value from the table on factors for constructing control charts using a sample size of two.

- *Situation 1.* When data are from an $\bar{x}$ and R chart, this approach is not directly applicable.
- *Situation 2.* When data are from an individual control, this calculation is an alternative. Most of the Method 4 comments for this situation are similarly applicable. This is methodology suggested within AIAG (1995b). Some practitioners prefer Method 4 over this Method 5 (Pyzedek 1998).
- *Situation 3.* For a random sample of data from a population this calculation is not possible because the sequencing of unit creation by the process is not known and considered.

Method 6

"Short-Term" Estimate of σ. The following relationship is sometimes used by computer programs to pool standard deviations, where there are *m* subgroups of sample size *n*:

$$\hat{\sigma} = \frac{s_p}{c_4(d)}$$

where

$$s_p = \sqrt{\frac{\displaystyle\sum_{i=1}^{m}\sum_{j=1}^{n}(x_{ij} - \bar{x}_i)^2}{\displaystyle\sum_{i=1}^{m}(n_i - 1)}}$$

and

$$d = \left(\sum_{i=1}^{m} n_i\right) - m + 1$$

The purpose of $c_4(d)$ when calculating $\hat{\sigma}$ is the reduction of bias to this estimate. Tabular values for c_4 are within Table J. If the table does not contain the needed value for d, the equation described within Appendix B9 can be used to calculate a value.

- *Situation 1.* When data are from an $\bar{x}$ and R or s chart, the comments relative to this situation are similar to the comments in Methods 2 and 3. If you want all groups weighed the same regardless of the number of observations, the $\bar{s}$ (or $\bar{R}$) approach is preferred. If you want the variation weighted dependent upon the subgroup size, the pooled approach is appropriate.
- *Situation 2.* When data are from an individual control, this calculation is not directly possible because the calculation of $\bar{R}$ for subgroup size of one is not possible.
- *Situation 3.* For a random sample of data from a population, this calculation is not possible because the sequencing of unit creation by the process is not known and considered.

Other Methods

The following methodologies are described in more detail later in this text. For these approaches, data need to be collected in a manner different from that of the three previously described situations:

- *"Long-Term" Estimate of* σ *(Could Also Obtain a "Short-Term" Estimate).* Variance components analysis using total variability from all considered components.
- *"Short-Term" or "Long-Term" Estimate of* σ. Single-factor analysis of variance.
- *"Short-Term" or "Long-Term" Estimate of* σ. Two-factor analysis of variance.

11.5   PROCESS CAPABILITY INDICES: C_p AND C_{pk}

The process capability index C_p describes the allowable tolerance spread to the actual spread of the data when the data follow a normal distribution. This relationship is

$$C_p = \frac{\text{USL} - \text{LSL}}{6\sigma}$$

where USL and LSL are the upper specification limit and lower specification limit, respectively, and 6σ describes the range or spread of the process. No quantification for data centering is described within this C_p relationship. Options for standard deviation (σ) are described later in this section.

Figure 11.1 illustrates graphically various C_p values relative to specification limits; C_p addresses only the spread of the process; C_{pk} is used concurrently to consider the spread and mean shift of the process as graphically illustrated in Figure 11.2. Mathematically C_{pk} can be represented as the minimum value of the two quantities

$$C_{pk} = \min \left[\frac{\text{USL} - \mu}{3\sigma}, \frac{\mu - \text{LSL}}{3\sigma} \right]$$

The relationship between C_{pk} to C_p is

$$C_{pk} = C_p(1 - k)$$

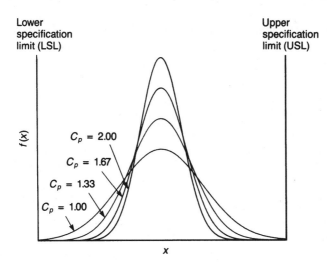

FIGURE 11.1 C_p examples.

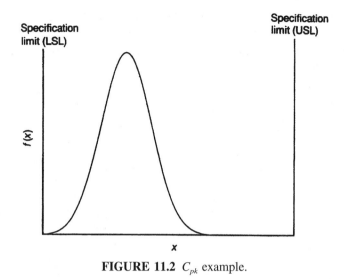

FIGURE 11.2 C_{pk} example.

The k factor quantifies the amount by which the process is off center and equates to

$$k = \frac{|m - \mu|}{(\text{USL} - \text{LSL})/2}$$

where $m = [(\text{USL} + \text{LSL})/2]$ is the midpoint of the specification range and $0 < k < 1$.

Computer programs can offer appropriate options from the above-described methodologies. Referenced strategies to estimate standard deviation (σ) for these equations include the following:

- *"Short-Term" View for* σ. From an $\bar{x}$ and R chart the following estimates are made: $\hat{\sigma} = s = \bar{R}/d_2$, $\hat{\mu} = \bar{\bar{x}}$ (AIAG 1995b).
- *"Long-Term" View for* σ. Total standard deviation from a variance components analysis is now used within the Motorola University Continuous Improvement Curriculum (CIC) training program (Spagon 1998).

Section 11.4 describes other considerations relative to the origination of data.

A minimum acceptable process capability index often recommended (Juran et al. 1976) is 1.33 (4σ); however, Motorola, in its Six Sigma program, proposes directing efforts toward obtaining a minimum individual process step C_p value of 2.0 and a C_{pk} value of 1.5.

11.6   PROCESS CAPABILITY/PERFORMANCE INDICES: P_p AND P_{pk}

These indices are sometimes referred to as "long-term" capability/perform-ance. Not all organizations report information as P_p and P_{pk}. Some organi-zations calculate C_p and C_{pk} such that they report information that is similar to P_p and P_{pk}.

The equations and relationships of P_p and P_{pk} are similar to C_p and C_{pk}. The process capability index P_p describes the allowable tolerance spread to the actual spread of the data when the data follow a normal distribution. This relationship is

$$P_p = \frac{\text{USL} - \text{LSL}}{6\sigma}$$

where USL and LSL are the upper specification limit and lower specification limit. No quantification for data centering is described within this P_p rela-tionship. Calculation alternatives for a are described later in this section. Pic-torially the relationship of P_p and P_{pk} are similar to C_p and C_{pk} relative to specification limits. Differences can be the spread of the distribution for a given processes.

Mathematically, P_{pk} can be represented as the minimum value of the two quantities

$$P_{pk} = \min\left[\frac{\text{USL} - \mu}{3\sigma}, \frac{\mu - \text{LSL}}{3\sigma}\right]$$

Computer programs can offer appropriate options from the above-described methodologies. Referenced strategies to estimate standard deviation (σ) for these equations include the following:

- From an $\bar{x}$ and R chart the following estimates are made (AIAG 1995b): $\hat{\mu} = \bar{\bar{x}}$ and

$$\hat{\sigma} = \sqrt{\sum_{i=1}^{n} \frac{(x_i - \bar{\bar{x}})^2}{n - 1}}$$

where x_i are individual readings from a process that has n total samples (including subgroup samples), and $\bar{\bar{x}}$ is the process mean from the control chart.
- P_p and P_{pk} indices are not now considered within the Motorola University training program. C_p and C_{pk} address total variability (Spagon 1998).

Section 11.4 describes other considerations relative to the origination of data.

11.7 PROCESS CAPABILITY AND THE Z DISTRIBUTION

Capability can be described using the distance of the process average from specification limits in standard deviation units (Z from the standardized normal curve). Consider the noncentering of a process relative to specification limits as process capability, expressions for these process capability relationships are as follows:

- *Unilateral Tolerance:* $Z = \dfrac{\text{USL} - \mu}{\sigma}$ or $Z = \dfrac{\mu - \text{LSL}}{\sigma}$,

  whichever is appropriate.

- *Bilateral Tolerances:* $Z_{\text{USL}} = \dfrac{\text{USL} - \mu}{\sigma}$ $\qquad Z_{\text{LSL}} = \dfrac{\mu - \text{LSL}}{\sigma}$

  $Z_{\text{min}} = $ Minimum of Z_{USL} or Z_{LSL}.

When a process is in statistical control and is normally distributed, calculated Z values can be used to estimate the proportion of output beyond any specification. This computation is made from either a statistical computer program or a standardized normal curve table (Table A). For unilateral tolerancing, this estimated proportion is simply the proportion value corresponding to the Z value. For the bilateral tolerancing, determine the proportions above and below the tolerance limits and add these proportions together. This proportion can be changed to a parts per million (ppm) defect rate by multiplying the value by one million.

An expression for C_{pk} in terms of Z is

$$C_{pk} = \frac{Z_{\text{min}}}{3}$$

From this equation we note the following: A Z_{min} value of 3 for a process equates to a C_{pk} value of 1.00, a Z_{min} value of 4 for a process equates to a C_{pk} value of 1.33, a Z_{min} value of 5 for a process equates to a C_{pk} value of 1.67, and a Z_{min} value of 6 for a process equates to a C_{pk} value of 2.00.

For the original Motorola's Six Sigma program a process was said to be at a six sigma quality level when $C_p = 2.00$ and $C_{pk} = 1.5$. This program considered that on the average, processes had a mean shift of 1.5σ. This 1.5σ adjustment is considered an average adjustment from "short-term" to "long-term" variability. Using the above relationship between C_{pk} and Z_{min}, a Z shift of 1.5 would equate to a change in C_{pk} of 0.5. This shift of 0.5 is the difference between Motorola's Six Sigma program C_p value of 2.00 and the C_{pk} value of 1.5.

The S^4 assessment section in the single-factor analysis of variance chapter has more discussion on "short-term" and "long-term" variability calculations.

11.8   CAPABILITY RATIOS

Sometimes organizations use the following "capability ratios" to describe their processes (AIAG 1995b). These ratios are defined as

$$CR = \frac{1}{C_p}$$

$$PR = \frac{1}{P_p}$$

11.9 C_{pm} INDEX

It is stated by some (Boyles 1991) that C_p and C_{pk} do not adequately address the issue of process centering. Taguchi advocated an alternative and later authors introduced the name C_{pm} for the Taguchi index (Chan et al. 1988). The index of C_{pm} is

$$C_{pm} = \frac{\text{USL} - \text{LSL}}{6\sqrt{(\mu - T)^2 + \sigma^2}}$$

where target (T) is the added consideration.

The relationship of C_{pm} centers around Taguchi's championed approach of reducing variation from the target value as the guiding principle to quality improvement. This equation is consistent with the philosophy of Taguchi relative to his loss function and his philosophy about monetary loss to the customer as well as to society in general when product does not meet the target exactly. These concepts are described in more detail later in this text.

From this equation we note the following:

- More importance is given to target (T).
- Less importance is given to specification limits.
- Variation is expressed from target as two components, namely, process variability (σ) and process centering ($\mu - T$).

11.10   EXAMPLE 11.1: PROCESS CAPABILITY INDICES

From an earlier $\bar{x}$ and R control chart example we concluded that data from a process were out of control. The data from that process are shown in Table

TABLE 11.1. Data and Calculations for Assessment of Process Capability Indices

Sample Number	Subgroup Measurements					Mean	Range	SD	Sum of Squares
1	36	35	34	33	32	34.0	4	1.5811	10.0
2	31	31	34	32	30	31.6	4	1.5166	9.2
3	30	30	32	30	32	30.8	2	1.0954	4.8
4	32	33	33	32	35	33.0	3	1.2247	6.0
5	32	34	37	37	35	35.0	5	2.1213	18.0
6	32	32	31	33	33	32.2	2	0.8367	2.8
7	33	33	36	32	31	33.0	5	1.8708	14.0
8	23	33	36	35	36	32.6	13	5.5045	121.2
9	43	36	35	24	31	33.8	19	6.9785	194.8
10	36	35	36	41	41	37.8	6	2.9496	34.8
11	34	38	35	34	38	35.8	4	2.0494	16.8
12	36	38	39	39	40	38.4	4	1.5166	9.2
13	36	40	35	26	33	34.0	14	5.1478	106.0
14	36	35	37	34	33	35.0	4	1.5811	10.0
15	30	37	33	34	35	33.8	7	2.5884	26.8
16	28	31	33	33	33	31.6	5	2.1909	19.2
17	33	30	34	33	35	33.0	5	1.8708	14.0
18	27	28	29	27	30	28.2	3	1.3038	6.8
19	35	36	29	27	32	31.8	9	3.8341	58.8
20	33	35	35	39	36	35.6	6	2.1909	19.2
				Totals:		671.0	124.0	49.9532	702.4
				Averages:		33.55	6.2	2.4977	

11.1 with some additional computations. Some would argue that the process needs to be brought into statistical control before determining process capability. The purpose of this example is to illustrate the various computation methodologies, not address at this time this issue of debate. An exercise at the end of this chapter addresses the analysis of these data when the out-of-control points are removed because of special-cause resolution.

For this process, specifications are 0.4037 ± 0.0013 (i.e., 0.4024 to 0.4050). Tabular and calculated values will be in units of 0.0001 (i.e., the specification limits will be considered 24 to 50).

Method 1 ("Long-Term" View): Using Individual Data Points

The standard deviation estimate is

$$\hat{\sigma} = \sqrt{\sum_{i=1}^{n} \frac{(x_i - \bar{x})^2}{n - 1}} = \sqrt{\sum_{i=1}^{70} \frac{(x_i - 33.55)^2}{70 - 1}} = 3.52874$$

If we chose to give this standard deviation an adjustment for bias, our results would be

$$\hat{\sigma}_{\text{adjusted}} = \frac{3.529}{c_4(70)} = \frac{3.529}{0.9975} = 3.53776$$

which results in

$$P_p = \frac{\text{USL} - \text{LSL}}{6\hat{\sigma}} = \frac{50 - 24}{6(3.53776)} = 1.22$$

$$P_{pk} = \min\left[\frac{\text{USL} - \hat{\mu}}{3\hat{\sigma}}, \frac{\hat{\mu} - \text{LSL}}{3\hat{\sigma}}\right]$$

$$= \min\left[\frac{50.00 - 33.55}{3(3.53776)}, \frac{33.55 - 24.00}{3(3.53776)}\right]$$

$$= \min[1.55, 0.90] = 0.90$$

Calculating ppm from Z values yields

$$Z_{\text{USL}} = \frac{\text{USL} - \hat{\mu}}{\hat{\sigma}} = \frac{50.00 - 33.55}{3.53776} = 4.65$$

$$Z_{\text{LSL}} = \frac{\hat{\mu} - \text{LSL}}{\hat{\sigma}} = \frac{33.55 - 24.00}{3.53776} = -2.70$$

$$\text{ppm}_{\text{USL}} = \Phi(Z_{\text{USL}}) \times 10^6 = \Phi(4.65) \times 10^6 = 1.7$$

$$\text{ppm}_{\text{LSL}} = \Phi(Z_{\text{LSL}}) \times 10^6 = \Phi(-2.70) \times 10^6 = 3472.7$$

$$\text{ppm}_{\text{total}} = \text{ppm}_{\text{USL}} + \text{ppm}_{\text{LSL}} = 1.7 + 3472.7 = 3474.4$$

Method 2 ("Short-Term" View): Using $\overline{R}$

Converting $\overline{R}$ into σ yields

$$\hat{\sigma} = \overline{R}/d_2 = 6.2/2.326 = 2.66552$$

which results in

$$C_p = \frac{\text{USL} - \text{LSL}}{6\hat{\sigma}} = \frac{50 - 24}{6(2.66552)} = 1.63$$

$$C_{pk} = \min \left[\frac{\text{USL} - \hat{\mu}}{3\hat{\sigma}}, \frac{\hat{\mu} - \text{LSL}}{3\hat{\sigma}} \right]$$

$$= \min \left[\frac{50.00 - 33.55}{3(2.66552)}, \frac{33.55 - 24.00}{3(2.66552)} \right]$$

$$= \min [2.06, 1.19] = 1.19$$

Calculating ppm from Z values yields

$$Z_{\text{USL}} = \frac{\text{USL} - \hat{\mu}}{\hat{\sigma}} = \frac{50.00 - 33.55}{2.66552} = 6.17$$

$$Z_{\text{LSL}} = \frac{\hat{\mu} - \text{LSL}}{\hat{\sigma}} = \frac{33.55 - 24.00}{2.66552} = -3.58$$

$$\text{ppm}_{\text{USL}} = \Phi(Z_{\text{USL}}) \times 10^6 = \Phi(6.17) \times 10^6 = 0$$
$$\text{ppm}_{\text{LSL}} = \Phi(Z_{\text{LSL}}) \times 10^6 = \Phi(-3.58) \times 10^6 = 170$$

$$\text{ppm}_{\text{total}} = \text{ppm}_{\text{USL}} + \text{ppm}_{\text{LSL}} = 0 + 170 = 170$$

Method 3 ("Short-Term" View): Using $\bar{s}$

Converting $\bar{s}$ into sigma yields

$$\hat{\sigma} = \frac{\bar{s}}{c_4} = \frac{1.8966}{0.9400} = 2.6571$$

which results in

$$C_p = \frac{\text{USL} - \text{LSL}}{6\hat{\sigma}} = \frac{50 - 24}{6(2.6571)} = 1.63$$

$$C_{pk} = \min \left[\frac{\text{USL} - \hat{\mu}}{3\hat{\sigma}}, \frac{\hat{\mu} - \text{LSL}}{3\hat{\sigma}} \right]$$

$$= \min \left[\frac{50.00 - 33.55}{3(2.6571)}, \frac{33.55 - 24.00}{3(2.6571)} \right]$$

$$= \min[2.06, 1.20] = 1.20$$

Calculating ppm from Z values yields

$$Z_{USL} = \frac{USL - \hat{\mu}}{\hat{\sigma}} = \frac{50.00 - 33.55}{2.6571} = 6.19$$

$$Z_{LSL} = \frac{\hat{\mu} - LSL}{\hat{\sigma}} = \frac{33.55 - 24.00}{2.6571} = -3.59$$

$$ppm_{USL} = \Phi(Z_{USL}) \times 10^6 = \Phi(6.19) \times 10^6 = 0$$

$$ppm_{LSL} = \Phi(Z_{LSL}) \times 10^6 = \Phi(-3.59) \times 10^6 = 170$$

$$ppm_{total} = ppm_{USL} + ppm_{LSL} = 0 + 170 = 170$$

Methods 4 and 5

These do not apply because data are not from an *XmR* chart.

Method 6 ("Short-Term" View): Pooled Standard Deviation

$$s_p = \sqrt{\frac{\sum_{i=1}^{m}\sum_{j=1}^{n}(x_{ij} - \bar{x}_i)^2}{\sum_{i=1}^{m}(n_i - 1)}} = \sqrt{\frac{702.4}{20 \times 4}} = 2.963106$$

$$d = \left(\sum_{i=1}^{m} n_i\right) - m + 1 = (20 \times 5) - 20 + 1 = 81$$

$$\hat{\sigma} = \frac{s_p}{c_4(d)} = \frac{s_p}{c_4(81)} = \frac{2.963106}{0.9969} = 2.97238$$

which results in

$$C_p = \frac{USL - LSL}{6\hat{\sigma}} = \frac{50 - 24}{6(2.97238)} = 1.46$$

$$C_{pk} = \min\left[\frac{USL - \hat{\mu}}{3\hat{\sigma}}, \frac{\hat{\mu} - LSL}{3\hat{\sigma}}\right]$$

$$= \min\left[\frac{50.00 - 33.55}{3(2.97238)}, \frac{33.55 - 24.00}{3(2.97238)}\right]$$

$$= \min[1.84, 1.07] = 1.07$$

Calculating ppm from Z values yields

$$Z_{\text{USL}} = \frac{\text{USL} - \hat{\mu}}{\hat{\sigma}} = \frac{50.00 - 33.55}{2.97238} = 5.53$$

$$Z_{\text{LSL}} = \frac{\hat{\mu} - \text{LSL}}{\hat{\sigma}} = \frac{33.55 - 24.00}{2.97238} = -3.21$$

$$\text{ppm}_{\text{USL}} = \Phi(Z_{\text{USL}}) \times 10^6 = \Phi(5.53) \times 10^6 = 0$$

$$\text{ppm}_{\text{LSL}} = \Phi(Z_{\text{LSL}}) \times 10^6 = \Phi(-3.21) \times 10^6 = 657$$

$$\text{ppm}_{\text{total}} = \text{ppm}_{\text{USL}} + \text{ppm}_{\text{LSL}} = 0 + 657 = 657$$

Some organizations also convert the $\text{ppm}_{\text{total}}$ rates calculated from "short-term" variability into a "sigma quality level," taking into account a 1.5σ shift. This could be done by using Table S.

This example gives an illustration of the differences that can occur between organizations given the same set of data. These differences could be much larger for some data sets. Hence, it is important to have agreement on the procedures that will be followed. Another point that should be mentioned is that it is preferable to have more data points than 100 to make such an evaluation because of confidence level considerations.

If "special causes," as identified by an $\bar{x}$ and R chart, were removed the current process variability would appear to be low enough such that the process would appear to be currently capable of producing parts consistently within specification limits. If there is no feedback in the manufacturing process, a drift in the mean could occur because of wear in the grinding wheel. For this situation a process control chart could then be used to monitor this shift to help optimize the frequency of machine adjustments and adjustment setting. An EWMA Chart (discussed in Chapter 36) may be more appropriate since grinding wheel wear can cause trials to be nonindependent. An Engineering Process Control (EPC) plan could also be beneficial to the optimization of process adjustment procedures (see Chapter 36).

At the same time, thought should be given to any process changes that could be made to reduce the process variability, which would reduce the sensitivity of the process to this adjustment precision and frequency of calibration. The DOE discussed later in this text can be used to evaluate the effectiveness of these possible changes. These DOE techniques can help avoid the implementation of process changes that perhaps in theory sound good from a "one-at-a-time" experiment but, in general, may not be helpful or could in fact be detrimental to the quality of the process.

11.11   EXAMPLE 11.2: PROCESS CAPABILITY/PERFORMANCE STUDY

The data in Table 11.2 (AIAG 1995b) were presented as a control chart exercise in Chapter 10. The $\bar{x}$ and R chart of the data shown in Figure 11.3 indicates that the process is in control.

TABLE 11.2. Data for Assessment of Process Capability/Performance Indices

								Subgroups								
	1	2	3	4	5	6	7	8	9	10	11	12	13	14	15	16
1	0.65	0.75	0.75	0.60	0.70	0.60	0.75	0.60	0.65	0.60	0.80	0.85	0.70	0.65	0.90	0.75
2	0.70	0.85	0.80	0.70	0.75	0.75	0.80	0.70	0.80	0.70	0.75	0.75	0.70	0.70	0.80	0.80
Samples: 3	0.65	0.75	0.80	0.70	0.65	0.75	0.65	0.80	0.85	0.60	0.90	0.85	0.75	0.85	0.80	0.75
4	0.65	0.85	0.70	0.75	0.85	0.85	0.75	0.75	0.85	0.80	0.50	0.65	0.75	0.75	0.75	0.80
5	0.85	0.65	0.75	0.65	0.80	0.70	0.70	0.75	0.75	0.65	0.80	0.70	0.70	0.60	0.85	0.65
Mean:	0.700	0.770	0.760	0.680	0.750	0.730	0.730	0.720	0.780	0.670	0.750	0.760	0.720	0.710	0.820	0.750
Range:	0.70	0.77	0.76	0.68	0.75	0.73	0.73	0.72	0.78	0.67	0.75	0.76	0.72	0.71	0.82	0.75

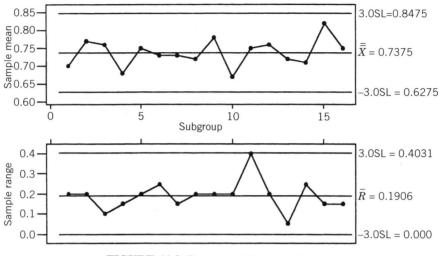

FIGURE 11.3 Example 11.2. $\bar{x}$ and R chart.

The procedure that AIAG (1995a) used to calculate process capability/ performance is described below. Additional calculation procedures for this set of data are discussed as examples within the variance components and single-factor analysis of variance chapters.

We will use the specification limits of

- Lower: 0.500
- Upper: 0.900

The process control chart yielded

$$\text{Subgroup sample size} = 5$$
$$\bar{\bar{x}} = 0.7375$$
$$\bar{R} = 0.1906$$

A "short-term" standard deviation using Method 2 described previously yields

$$\sigma_{\bar{R}/d_2} = s = \frac{\bar{R}}{d_2} = \frac{0.1906}{2.326} = 0.0819$$

For the bilateral tolerances, Z values and C_{pk} are as follows:

$$Z_{USL} = \frac{USL - \hat{\mu}}{\sigma_{\bar{R}/d_2}} = \frac{0.900 - 0.7375}{0.0819} = 1.9831$$

$$Z_{LSL} = \frac{\hat{\mu} - LSL}{\sigma_{\bar{R}/d_2}} = \frac{0.7375 - 0.500}{0.0819} = 2.8983$$

$$C_{pk} = \frac{Z_{min}}{3} = \frac{1.98307975}{3} = 0.6610$$

Proportion out-of-specification calculations are

$$\Phi(Z_{USL}) = 0.0237$$

$$\Phi(Z_{LSL}) = 0.0019$$

$$\Phi(total) = 0.0256 \quad (\textit{Note:} \text{ This equates to a 25554 ppm defect rate,}$$
from a "short-term" variability perspective.)

It also can be determined that

$$C_p = \frac{USL - LSL}{6\sigma_{\bar{R}/d_2}} = \frac{0.9 - 0.5}{0.0819} = 0.8136$$

The "long-term" standard deviation using Method 1 with the mean equal to the control chart average yields

$$\sigma_{sample} = s = \sqrt{\sum_{i=1}^{n} \frac{(x_i - \bar{\bar{x}})^2}{n - 1}} = \sqrt{\sum_{i=1}^{80} \frac{(x_i - 0.7375)^2}{80 - 1}} = 0.0817$$

Using this standard deviation estimate we can determine

$$P_p = \frac{USL - LSL}{6\sigma_{sample}} = \frac{0.9 - 0.5}{6(0.081716)} = 0.8159$$

$$P_{pk} = \min \left[\frac{USL - \bar{\bar{x}}}{3\sigma_{sample}}, \frac{\bar{\bar{x}} - LSL}{3\sigma_{sample}} \right]$$

$$= \min \left[\frac{0.900 - 0.7375}{3(0.0817)}, \frac{0.7375 - 0.500}{3(0.0817)} \right]$$

$$= \min [0.6629, 0.9688] = 0.6629$$

The following should be noted:

- Process capability and process performance metrics are almost identical.
- Calculations for "short-term" variability were slightly larger than "long-term" variability, which is not reasonable because "short-term" variability is a component of "long-term" variability. Using range as described in Method 2 is not as statistically powerful as Method 3 (because only the highest and lowest data points are considered), which yields the better estimate for "short-term" variability (slightly smaller estimate than "long-term" standard deviation in this case) of

$$ s = \frac{\bar{s}}{c_4} = \frac{0.07627613}{0.94} = 0.0811 $$

- The above discussion follows the basic approach described in AIAG (1995b). This booklet focuses on the use of "short-term" variability metrics. Some organizations prefer to focus on using "long-term" standard deviation and ppm metrics. These data will be analyzed again as an example in the variance components and single-factor analysis of variance chapters to illustrate other alternatives for determining process capability/performance metrics.

11.12   EXAMPLE 11.3: PROCESS CAPABILITY NEEDS

Management has given the mandate (all too frequently we have to deal with managers who are not schooled in the principles of Deming) that process steps are to have process indices of $C_p \geq 2.0$ and $C_{pk} \geq 1.5$. Consider the five parts in Figure 11.4 that are to be manufactured and then assembled. The tolerances of the dimensions on the parts were believed achievable using conventional manufacturing practices. We will also consider that C_p and C_{pk} are expressions of "long-term" capability (or equate to P_p and P_{pk}).

For purposes of achieving final measurements that meet customer needs, one could ask whether each dimension should be given equivalent effort of monitoring relative to the process indices. Consider also what procedure would be followed to correct manufacturing processes if the parts are shown not to meet the process capability objective. Because quality cannot be measured into a product, perhaps it would be better to rephrase the initial question to address how S^4 techniques can be applied to better meet the needs of the customer. Let's consider the following discussion when addressing what is to be done.

Measurements that are considered should include other parameters besides just the final characteristics of the part (e.g., final part dimension considerations). Effort should be made to create a process that consistently produces products as close to the nominal specification as possible (not ones that just meet specification).

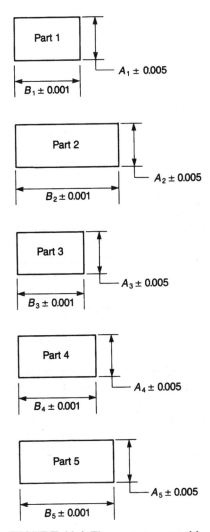

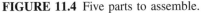

FIGURE 11.4 Five parts to assemble.

The cost to determine many capability indices in a process over time can become very expensive. Often it may be more important to monitor a key process parameter (e.g., a pressure that was prevalent in a manufacturing tool) than to monitor the final specification considerations of the manufactured part. This basic manufacturing philosophy can result in the detection of process degradation shifts before a large volume of "bad" parts is produced.

If the philosophy of striving for nominal considerations during development is stressed, the chance of meeting the desired process capability indices initially will be higher. For this example, effort should be given to make tools and identify economical processes that manufacture the parts with precision and consistency along with the emphasis of continual process improvement in the areas that are important form the perspective of the customer.

Let's now get back to the initial question of concern. It may not be necessary, from a customer's point of view, to collect enough dimensions to calculate the process indices for all dimensions. Assume that the 0.005 tolerance (in inches) is easy to achieve consistently with the current process, if the manufacturing processes is initially shown via a tool sample to produce this dimension well within specification. For this dimension, only periodic measurements may be needed over time.

However, the tolerance of the B dimensions may require a special operation that is more difficult to achieve on a continuing basis. For the process that was chosen initially, assume that the B dimensions are shown to be in control over time for all the B-value considerations. For the purpose of illustration, consider also that the processes had a mean value equal to the nominal specification (i.e., $C_{pk} = C_p$); however, the C_p values for these dimensions ranged from 1.0 to 1.33 for the five parts. A brainstorming session was then conducted because the C_p values were less than the objective of 2.0. The consensus of opinion from this session was that a new, expensive process would be required to replace the existing process in order to achieve a higher C_p value.

The question of concern is now whether this new process should be developed in order to reduce the B-dimensional variability. Before making this decision, the group considered first how these parts are used when they are assembled. The important dimension from a customer's perspective is the overall dimensional consideration of B, which after the assembly process is pictorially shown in Figure 11.5.

Consider that the manufactured B dimensions conformed to a straight line when plotted on normal probability paper (i.e., the parts are distributed normally). In addition, the mean value for each part equaled the nominal specification value, and a 3σ limit equaled the tolerance of 0.001 (i.e., $C_p = C_{pk} = 1.0$).

When these parts are assembled in series, a low dimension for B_1 can be combined with a high dimension for B_2, and so on; hence, it would not be

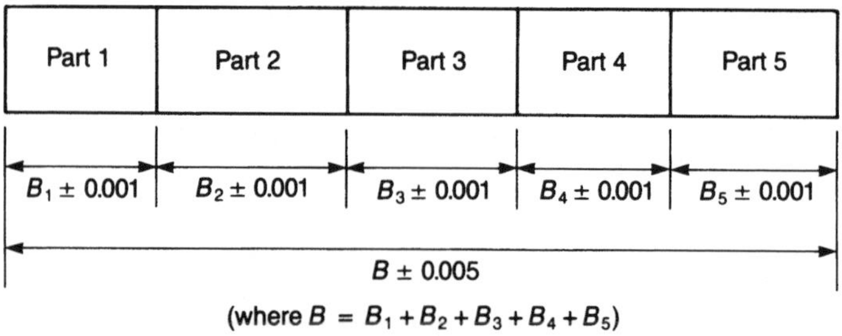

Part 1	Part 2	Part 3	Part 4	Part 5

$B_1 \pm 0.001$ $B_2 \pm 0.001$ $B_3 \pm 0.001$ $B_4 \pm 0.001$ $B_5 \pm 0.001$

$B \pm 0.005$

(where $B = B_1 + B_2 + B_3 + B_4 + B_5$)

FIGURE 11.5 Five assembled parts.

reasonable to just add the tolerance considerations of the individual parts to get the overall tolerance consideration. Because the individual part dimensions are normally distributed, an overall tolerance can be determined as the squares of the individual; hence, the overall assembled expected tolerance for B would be

$$B \text{ tolerance} = \pm (0.001^2 + 0.001^2 + 0.001^2 + 0.001^2)^{1/2}$$
$$= \pm (0.00224)$$

Because 0.00224 describes 3σ, we can see that

$$C_p = \frac{\text{USL} - \text{LSL}}{6\sigma} = \frac{0.010}{2(0.00224)} = 2.23$$

Because $C_p \geq 2.0$, this process index target is met on the overall dimension even though the individual measurements do not meet the target of 2.0.

The purpose of this example is to illustrate that care must be taken not to spend resources unwisely by striving for the tightening of tolerances that may not have much benefit to the customer. There are many ways to determine which parameters should be tracked (e.g., experience, history data, or significant factors from a DOE). Efforts must also be directed toward continually improving processes in those areas that benefit the customer the most. Playing games with the numbers should be avoided.

11.13   PROCESS CAPABILITY CONFIDENCE INTERVAL

Confidence intervals are discussed in more depth later in this text. However, it seems best now to briefly discuss the large uncertainties that can occur when calculating this statistic.

A process capability index calculated from sample data is an estimate of the population process capability index. It is highly unlikely that the true population index is the exact value that we calculated. A confidence interval adds a probabilistic range for the true population value given the results of the sample, including sample size. The confidence interval for C_{pk} and P_{pk} is difficult to calculate directly (later bootstrapping will be used to give an estimate); however, the confidence interval for C_p and P_p is not difficult. The $100(1 - \alpha)$ percent confidence interval expressed in C_p terms is

$$\hat{C}_p \sqrt{\frac{\chi^2_{1-\alpha/2;n-1}}{n-1}} \leq C_p \leq \hat{C}_p \sqrt{\frac{\chi^2_{\alpha/2;n-1}}{n-1}}$$

11.14   EXAMPLE 11.4: CONFIDENCE INTERVAL ON PROCESS CAPABILITY

An organization wants to create a table that can be used to give a quick 95% confidence interval for a population C_p given the sample size and calculated C_p. To create this table, consider assigning a C_p value of 1.0 to calculate the following relationship where a sample size of 10 is used for illustration:

$$\hat{C}_p \sqrt{\frac{\chi^2_{1-\alpha/2;n-1}}{n-1}} \leq C_p \leq \hat{C}_p \sqrt{\frac{\chi^2_{\alpha/2;n-1}}{n-1}}$$

$$(1.0) \sqrt{\frac{\chi^2_{1-0.05/2;10-1}}{10-1}} \leq C_p \leq (1.0) \sqrt{\frac{\chi^2_{0.05/2;10-1}}{10-1}}$$

$$\sqrt{\frac{2.70}{9}} \leq C_p \leq \sqrt{\frac{19.02}{9}}$$

$$0.55 \leq C_p \leq 1.45$$

A 95% confidence interval table including other sample sizes would be

n	C_p Lower Confidence Multiple	C_p Upper Confidence Multiple
10	0.55	1.45
20	0.68	1.31
30	0.74	1.26
40	0.78	1.22
50	0.80	1.20
60	0.82	1.18
70	0.83	1.17
80	0.84	1.16
90	0.85	1.15
100	0.86	1.14

From this table we can then determine the C_p confidence interval for a sample of 10 that had a calculated C_p of 1.5:

$$(1.5)(0.55) \leq C_p \leq (1.5)(1.45)$$

$$0.82 \leq C_p \leq 2.18$$

11.15 PROCESS CAPABILITY FOR NON-NORMAL DISTRIBUTION

The capability measures previously described are not valid for non-normal distributions. Non-normality is common for situations such as flatness, roundness, and particle contamination. One approach to address the non-normal distribution is to make transformations to "normalize" the data. Some statistical software offers Box-Cox Transformation alternatives (Box et al. 1977).

An alternative approach when data can be represented by a probability plot (e.g., Weibull distribution) is to use the 0.135 and 99.865 percentiles from this plot to describe the spread of the data. This methodology is applicable when all individual measurements are combined from an in-control process to determine a "long-term" capability. The capability indices from this procedure are sometimes described as equivalent indices because they use the equivalent percentile points from the normal distribution. Both observed and expected "long-term" ppm nonconformance rates can be determined using this methodology.

Statistical software can expedite calculations and give better estimates because calculations can be based upon maximum likelihood estimates of the distribution parameters. For example, for the Weibull distribution these estimates would be based on the shape and scale parameters, rather than mean and variance estimates as in the normal case.

11.16 PROCESS CAPABILITY FOR ATTRIBUTE DATA

The p chart and other attribute control charts are different from variables data in that each point can directly be related to a proportion or percent of nonconformance relative to customer requirements, while points on a variables chart indicate a response irrespective of specification needs.

AIAG (1995b) defines the following: "For attribute charts, capability is defined simply as the average proportion or rate of nonconforming product, whereas capability for variables charts refers to the total (inherent) variation ($6\hat{\sigma}_{R/d_2}$) yielded by the (stable) process, with and/or without adjustments for process centering to specification targets." AIAG (1995b) also states: "If desired, this can be expressed as the proportion conforming to specification (i.e., $1 - \bar{p}$). For a preliminary estimate of process capability, use historical data, but exclude data points associated with special causes. For a formal process capability study, new data should be run, preferably for 25 or more periods, with the points all reflecting statistical control. The $\bar{p}$ for these consecutive in-control periods is a better estimate of the process's current capability."

Attribute assessments are not only applicable to pass/fail tests at the end of a manufacturing line. They can also be used to measure the "hidden factor" using a DPMO scale. Process improvement efforts for stable processes having attribute measurements can originate with a Pareto chart of the types of non-conformance. Efforts to reduce the most frequent types of defects could perhaps then utilize DOE techniques.

11.17   A PROCESS CAPABILITY/PERFORMANCE METRIC WHEN NO SPECIFICATION EXISTS

Specification requirements are needed to determine C_p, C_{pk}, P_p, and P_{pk}. However, sometimes the output of a process does not have a specification. This happens frequently with business or service processes. Measurements for these situations can be cycle time and costs. Sometimes organizations will use targets as a specification; however, the results can sometimes be deceptive.

A measurement approach I have found very useful for this type of situation is to describe the overall response as expected percentage of occurrences. This approach will be described using three figures. Figure 11.6 shows an X chart and how time-sequenced data can be conceptually accumulated to create a distribution of nonsequenced data. Figure 11.7 then illustrates how 80% of the occurrences are expected to be between response levels A and B. However, it is difficult to determine percentage of populations from a histogram. Figure 11.8 shows how this percentage can be easier shown using a probability plot and how it relates to a probability density function and histogram plot.

For a given set of data a percentage value can be determined mathematically using a Z table (i.e., Table A) or a statistical computer program. The presentation of this type of information with a normal probability can give a good baseline view of the process. Quick estimations are offered through the plot response estimates at differing percentage levels and percentage estimates at differing response levels. This same approach has application flexibility to other probability plots where the distribution is non-normal. I have found the two-parameter Weibull distribution to be very useful to describe many situ-

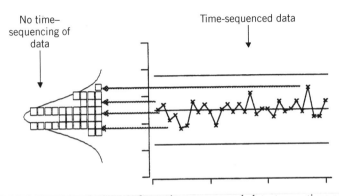

FIGURE 11.6 Conceptual change from time-sequenced data to no time-sequencing of data.

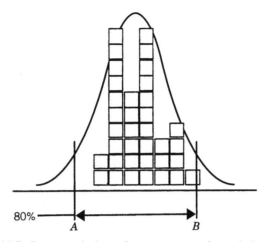

80%

A   B

FIGURE 11.7 Conceptual view of a percentage of population statement.

ations where, for example, time (e.g., cycle time) is the metric and values below zero are not possible.

11.18   EXAMPLE 11.5: A PROCESS CAPABILITY/ PERFORMANCE METRIC WHEN NO SPECIFICATION EXISTS

The busy schedule of people and other factors can make it very difficult to get good attendance at professional society meetings. An average monthly attendance of 10% of the membership is considered very good. As the new local ASQ section chair in Austin, Texas, I thought attendance was important and chose this metric as a measure of success for my term. My stretch goal was to double average monthly attendance from the level experienced during the previous six years.

The process of setting up and conducting a professional society session meeting with program is more involved than one might initially think. Steps to this process include guest speaker/topic selection, meeting room arrangements, and meeting announcements, along with many other issues. I wanted to create a baseline that would indicate expected results if nothing were done differently from our previous meeting creation process. Later I also wanted to test the two process means to see if there was a significance difference of the processes at an α level of 0.05.

This basic form of this situation is not much different from a metric that might be expected from a business or service processes. A process exists and a goal has been set; however, there are no real specification limits. Setting a goal or soft target as a specification limit for the purpose of determining process capability indices could yield very questionable results. The records

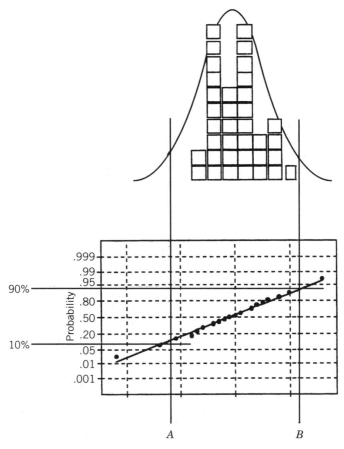

FIGURE 11.8 Conceptual view of a percent of population statement using a normal probability plot.

indicated that our previous section meeting attendance was as follows: (we do not meet during the summer months, and a term is from July 1 to June 30):

9/9/93	10/14/93	11/11/93	12/9/93	1/13/94	2/17/94	3/10/94	4/14/94	5/12/94
66	45	61	36	42	41	46	44	47

9/8/94	10/13/94	11/10/94	12/8/94	1/12/95	2/16/95	3/9/95	4/3/95	5/16/95
46	51	42	42	61	57	47	46	28

9/14/95	10/12/95	11/9/95	12/14/95	1/11/96	2/8/96	3/14/96	4/11/96	5/9/96
45	37	45	42	58	49	39	53	58

9/12/96	10/10/96	11/14/96	12/12/96	1/9/97	2/13/97	3/13/97	4/10/97	5/8/97
44	37	52	33	43	45	35	29	33

An *XmR* chart of the data shown in Figure 11.9 indicates that the process is stable. A "process capability/performance" metric shown in Figure 11.10 could be used to describe the expected response variability from the process. Management and others can then assess if this response range is OK. For this example the figure indicates an estimation that 80% of the time attendance would be between 34 and 57. Other percentage of populations estimates can similarly be taken from this chart. If an improved response is desired from a stable process, process improvements are needed. A later example in the comparison test chapter show some implemented changes that were conducted to encourage better attendance. This example also shows the results of a comparison test that compared the previous meeting mean attendance to the meeting mean attendance response from the new process.

11.19   IMPLEMENTATION COMMENTS

AIAG (1995b) states that "the key to effective use of any process measure continues to be the level of understanding of what the measure truly represents. Those in the statistical community who generally oppose how C_{pk} numbers, for instance, are being used are quick to point out that few "real world" processes completely satisfy all of the conditions, assumptions, and parameters within which C_{pk} has been developed. Further, it is the position of this manual that, even when all conditions are met, it is difficult to assess or truly understand a process on the basis of a single index or ratio number."

AIAG (1995b) further comments that it is strongly recommended that graphical analyses be used in conjunction with process measures. A final

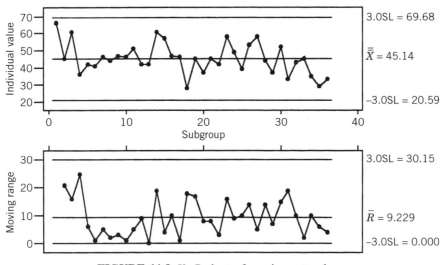

FIGURE 11.9 *XmR* chart of previous attendance.

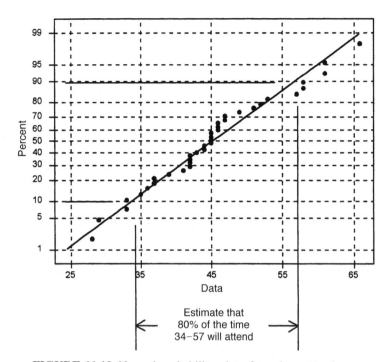

FIGURE 11.10 Normal probability plot of previous attendance.

precaution is given that all capability assessments should be confined to a single process characteristics. It is never appropriate to combine or average the capability results for several processes into one index.

Organizations might be tempted to ask suppliers to report their current process capability indices. The results from this effort can be very deceiving because these indices are statistics that will vary over time, even if the process were exactly the same. Wheeler (1995a) suggests the use of an *XmR* chart to report process indices, where the supplier is meeting the target when the central line meets or exceeds the target and capability indices are "in control."

11.20 S⁴ ASSESSMENT

This chapter, among other things, describes the often overlooked aspect of process capability equations—the methodology used to determine standard deviation. For some situations there can be large differences in this metric depending upon how someone collects and then analyzes the data. Organizations need to determine what is the best metric for their particular situation. Also, there needs to be good communication between organizations and their supplier/customers up front to avoid any costly misunderstandings.

Some considerations when conducting a process capability assessment are as follows:

- It is important to keep priorities balanced. The collection and reporting of data can be expensive. Process capability metrics alone do not directly add value. These metrics only are an estimate of what is expected from the process. Hence, it is important not to spend a large amount of resource *just* to determine a precise process capability value at the expense of process improvement efforts.
- When reporting process measurements, don't forget to consider the language spoken by all—money. Converting the cost of cycle time and average defect costs (direct and indirect impact) to money can be very eye-opening.
- Consider the impact of sample size on process capability calculations.
- A variance-component analysis approach can not only quantify a standard deviation to use within process capability calculations, it can also give insight to where process improvement efforts should be focused. It also can be used whenever there is not a lot of time series data available.
- If variability is larger than desired, consider the impact of the measurement system. One customer of mine had a situation where the contribution from measurement uncertainty was one-half of the total variability of the product output that he was using to determine whether he should ship a product or not.
- Make sure that you and your customer/supplier are in agreement whether reported metrics are to reflect "short-term" or "long-term" variability. Rational subgrouping considerations can make a very big difference in process capability calculations.
- Consider the impact of forcing a specification where one does not exist. I have seen some organizations spend a lot of time creating a very questionable metric by arbitrarily adding a specification value where one was not really appropriate—so they could make a C_{pk} metric. This situation can often occur within business and service processes. Consider using the described probability plotting reporting procedure for this situation.

11.21 EXERCISES

1. *Catapult Exercise Data Analysis:* Using the catapult exercise data sets from Chapter 4, determine the process capability/performance of each data set using specifications supplied by instructor (e.g., 75 ± 3 in.). Compare the results using different calculating procedures.

2. The example $\bar{x}$ and R chart in the control chart chapter indicated that samples numbered 8, 9, 10, 12, 13, and 18 were out of control. The process specifications are 0.4037 ± 0.0013 (i.e., 0.4024 to 0.4050). Tab-

ular and calculated values will be in units of 0.0001 (i.e., the specification limits will be considered 24 to 50). Assume that for each of these data points, circumstances for an out-of-control response were identified and will be avoided in future production. Determine the process capability indices of the remaining 14 subgroups, which are as follows:

1	36	35	34	33	32
2	31	31	34	32	30
3	30	30	32	30	32
4	32	33	33	32	35
5	32	34	37	37	35
6	32	32	31	33	33
7	33	33	36	32	31
8	34	38	35	34	38
9	36	35	37	34	33
10	30	37	33	34	35
11	28	31	33	33	33
12	33	30	34	33	35
13	35	36	29	27	32
14	33	35	35	39	36

3. Determine the capability/performance measures of a process that had a lower specification of 2 and an upper specification of 16 with responses 3.40, 8.57, 2.42, 5.59, 9.92, 4.63, 7.48, 8.55, 6.10, 6.42, 4.46, 7.02, 5.86, 4.80, 9.60, 5.92 (data were collected sequentially). Determine the 95% confidence interval for C_p.

4. A company is incorporating a Six Sigma program. A process is said to be capable of producing a response of 36 ± 12. Someone compiled the following responses from the process, which were not collected in time sequence: 41.3, 30.8, 38.9, 33.7, 34.7, 20.4, 28.3, 35.1, 37.9, 32.6. Determine the best estimate and 95% confidence intervals for capability/performance indices that can be calculated. List any concerns or questions.

5. A machine measures the peel-back force necessary to remove the packaging for electrical components. A tester records an output force that changes as the packaging is separated. Currently, one random sample is taken from three shifts and compared to a $\pm$ specification limit that reflects the customer needs for a maximum and minimum peel-back force range. Whenever a measurement exceeds the specification limits the cause is investigated.

(a) Evaluate the current plan and create a sampling plan utilizing control charts.

(b) Assume that the peel-back force measurements are in control. Create a plan to determine if the process is capable of meeting the $\pm$ specifications.

(c) Discuss alternative sampling considerations.

6. A supplier quotes a C_p value of 1.7. After a discussion with them, you determine that they are calculating standard deviation consistent with your wishes; however, you are concerned that they only had a sample size of 20. Determine a 95% confidence interval for the population C_p.

7. An organization requires a C_p value of 2.00. Given a sample size of 30, determine the minimum level for a sampled C_p value in order to be 97.5% confident that the C_p population value is 2.00 (i.e., a one-sided confidence interval).

8. In an exercise in Chapter 11 you were presented the following information for analysis with the purpose of selecting the best supplier that is to manufacture to a specification of 85–115. Suppliers claimed the following: supplier 1, $\bar{x} = 100$ and $s = 5$; supplier 2, $\bar{x} = 95$ and $s = 5$; supplier 3, $\bar{x} = 100$ and $s = 10$; supplier 4, $\bar{x} = 95$ and $s = 10$. You were to determine ppm noncompliance rates and yields. Because of concerns about the lack of information supplied about the raw data used to make these computations, you asked each supplier for additional information. They could not supply you with the raw data, but all suppliers said their raw data was normally distributed and from a process that was in control. In addition, you did get the following information from them: For supplier 1, results were determined from five samples produced consecutively; for supplier 2, results were determined from 10 samples, where one sample was produced every day for ten days; for supplier 3, results were from 60 samples taken over 30 days; and for supplier 4, results were from 10 samples taken over two days. Determine confidence intervals for C_p and P_p. Comment on the selection of a supplier and what else you might ask to determine which supplier is the best selection. Comment on what you would ask the purchasing department to do different in the future relative to supplier selection.

9. List issues organizations often ignore when addressing capability/performance issues.

10. Describe how the techniques within this chapter are useful and can be applied to S^4 projects.

12

MEASUREMENT SYSTEMS ANALYSIS (GAUGE REPEATABILITY AND REPRODUCIBILITY—GAUGE R&R)

Organizations frequently overlook the impact of not having quality measurement systems. Organizations sometimes do not even consider that their measurements might not be exact. Such presumptions and inadequate considerations can lead to questionable analyses and conclusions.

When appraisers do not measure a part consistently, the expense to a company can be very large when satisfactory parts are rejected and unsatisfactory are accepted. In addition, a poor measurement system can make the process capability assessment of a satisfactory process appear unsatisfactory. This can lead to lost sales and unnecessary expense while trying to fix a manufacturing or business process where the primary source of variability is from the measurement system.

This chapter presents procedural guidelines for the assessment of the quality of a measurement system. Mathematically, measurement systems analysis involves the understanding and quantification of measurement variance, as described in the following equation, to process variability and tolerance spread:

$$\sigma_T^2 = \sigma_p^2 + \sigma_m^2$$

where

$$\sigma_T^2 = \text{Total variance}$$

$$\sigma_p^2 = \text{process variance}$$

$$\sigma_m^2 = \text{measurement variance}$$

Measurement systems analysis assesses the statistical properties of repeatability. reproducibility, bias, stability. and linearity. Collectively, these techniques are sometimes referred to as "gauge R&R" (repeatability and reproducibility).

Focus is given in this chapter to measurement systems where readings can be repeated on each part; however, destructive test situations are also included. The described gauge R&R methodologies are applicable to both initial gauge assessments and studies that help determine whether a measurement system is contributing a large amount to an unsatisfactory reported process capability index.

12.1   TERMINOLOGY

- Bias is the difference between the observed average of measurements and the reference value. Bias is often referred to as accuracy.
- Repeatability is the variation in measurements obtained with one measurement instrument when used several times by one appraiser while measuring the identical characteristic on the same part.
- Reproducibility is the variation in the average of the measurements made by different appraisers using the same measuring instrument when measuring identical characteristics on the same part.
- Percent R&R is the percentage of process variation related to the measurement system for repeatability and reproducibility.
- Stability (or drift) is the total variation in the measurements obtained with a measurement system on the same master or parts when measuring a single characteristic over an extended time period.
- Linearity is the difference in the bias values through the expected operating range of the gauge.
- Percent of tolerance is the percentage of the part tolerance related to the measurement system for repeatability and reproducibility.

12.2   GAUGE R&R CONSIDERATIONS

In a gauge R&R study the following characteristics are essential

- The measurement must be in statistical control, which is referred to as statistical stability. This means that variation from the measurement system is from common causes only and not special cause.
- Variability of the measurement system must be small compared with both the manufacturing process and specification limits.

- Increments of measurement must be small relative to both process variability and specification limits. A common rule of thumb is that the increments should be no greater than one-tenth of the smaller of either the process variability or specification limits.

The purpose of a measurement system is to better understand the sources of variation that can influence the results produced by the system. A measurement is characterized by location and spread, which are impacted by the following metrics:

- *Location:* bias, stability, and linearity metrics
- *Spread:* repeatability and reproducibility

Bias assessments need an accepted reference value of a part. This can usually be done with tool room or layout inspection equipment. A reference value is derived from readings and compared with appraisers' observed averages. The following describes such an implementation method:

- Measure one part in a tool room.
- Instruct one appraiser to measure the same part 10 times, using the gauge being evaluated.
- Determine measurement system bias using the difference between the reference value and observed average.
- Express percent of process variation for bias as a ratio of bias to process variation multiplied by 100.
- Express percent of tolerance for bias as a ratio of bias to tolerance multiplied by 100.

Measurement system stability is the amount of total variation in system's bias over time on a given part or master part. One method of study is to plot the average and range of repeated master or master part readings on a regular basis. Care must be given to ensure that the master samples taken are representative (e.g., not just after morning calibration).

Linearity graphs are a plot of bias values throughout the expected operating range of the gauge. Later sections of this chapter describe how to implement this gauge assessment methodology. Various measures of evaluating the acceptability of the measurement system spread are as follows:

- Percent of tolerance
- Percent of process variation
- Number of distinct data categories

Percent of population metrics equate to standard deviation units from an R&R study multiplied by a constant. This text uses a multiple of 5.15, where the 5.15 multiple converts to 99% of the measurements for a normal distribution. Chrysler Corporation, Ford Motor Company, and General Motors Corporation use this percentage value in AIAG (1995a).

The discrimination of a measurement system is the concern when selecting or analyzing a measurement system. Discrimination or resolution of a measurement system is its capability to detect and faithfully indicate even small changes in the measured characteristic. Measurement systems cannot, because of economic and physical limitations, perceive infinitesimal separate or different measured characteristics of parts or a process distribution. Measured values of a measured characteristic are instead grouped into data categories. For example, the incremental data categories using a rule might be 0.1 cm, while a micrometer might be 0.001 cm. Parts in the same data category have the same value for the measured characteristic.

When the discrimination of a measurement system is not adequate, the identification of process variation or individual part characteristic values is questionable. This situation warrants the investigation of improved measurement techniques. The recommended discrimination is at most one-tenth of six times the total process standard deviation.

Discrimination needs to be at an acceptable level for analysis and control. Discrimination needs to be able to both detect the process variation for analysis and control for the occurrence of special causes. The number of distinct data categories determined from a Gauge R&R study is useful for this assessment. Figure 12.1 illustrates how the number of categories impacts conclusions about control and analysis.

Unacceptable discrimination symptoms can also appear in a range chart, which describes the repeatability of operators within a gauge R&R study. When, for example, the range chart shows only one. two, or three possible values for the range within the control limits, the discrimination for the measurements is inadequate. Another source of inadequate discrimination is when the range chart shows four possible values for the range within control limits, and more than one-fourth of the ranges are zero.

12.3 GAUGE R&R RELATIONSHIPS

A measurement process is said to be consistent when the results for operators are repeatable and the results between operators are reproducible. A gauge is able to detect part-to-part variation whenever the variability of operator measurements is small relative to process variability. The percent of process variation consumed by the measurement (% R&R) is then determined once the measurement process is consistent and can detect part-to-part variation.

When describing % R&R mathematically, first consider

$$\sigma_m = \sqrt{\sigma_e^2 + \sigma_0^2}$$

where

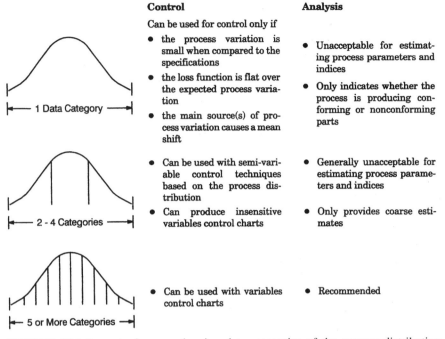

	Control	**Analysis**
	Can be used for control only if	

Control

Can be used for control only if

- the process variation is small when compared to the specifications
- the loss function is flat over the expected process variation
- the main source(s) of process variation causes a mean shift

Analysis

- Unacceptable for estimating process parameters and indices
- Only indicates whether the process is producing conforming or nonconforming parts

(1 Data Category)

- Can be used with semi-variable control techniques based on the process distribution
- Can produce insensitive variables control charts

- Generally unacceptable for estimating process parameters and indices
- Only provides coarse estimates

(2 - 4 Categories)

- Can be used with variables control charts

- Recommended

(5 or More Categories)

FIGURE 12.1 Impact of nonoverlapping data categories of the process distribution on control and analysis activities. [From *Measurement Systems Analysis Reference Manual,* Chrysler Corp., Ford Motor Company, and General Motors Corp. (1995), with permission.]

σ_m = measurement system standard deviation

σ_e = gauge standard deviation

σ_0 = appraiser standard deviation

The measurement system study or an independent process capability study determines the part standard deviation σ_p component of the total gauge R&R study variation in the equation

$$\sigma_T^2 = \sigma_p^2 + \sigma_m^2$$

The percentage of process variation contributed by the measurement system for repeatability and reproducibility (%R&R) is then estimated as

$$\%\text{R\&R} = \frac{\sigma_m}{\sigma_t} \times 100$$

The percent of tolerance related to the measurement system for repeatability and reproducibility is estimated by

$$\%\text{Tolerance} = \frac{5.15\sigma_m}{\text{tolerance}} \times 100$$

where tolerance is upper specification limit minus lower specification limit.

The number of distinct categories that can be reliably obtained from the data is

$$\text{Number of distinct categories} = \left[\frac{\sigma_p}{\sigma_m} \right] \times 1.41$$

If the number of distinct categories is less than two, the measurement system is of no value in controlling the process. If the number of categories is two, it would mean that the data can be divided into high and low groups; however, this is equivalent to attribute data. The number of categories must be five, and preferably more, for the measurement system to be acceptable for the analysis of the process.

One general recognized industry practice suggests a "short method" of evaluation using five samples, two appraisers, and no replication. A gauge is considered acceptable if the gauge error is less than or equal to 20% of the specification tolerance.

Gauge R&R analyses typically offer several different outputs and options that help with the understanding of the sources for R&R issues. Output graphs can describe differences by part, operator, operator*part interaction, and the components of variation. Traditionally, practitioners used manual techniques for gauge R&R studies. Computer Gauge R&R programs now offer additional options such as analysis of variance for significance tests. Because of procedural differences, analysis of variance result outputs can have some differences from manual computations.

The output from a gauge R&R analysis typically includes $\bar{x}$ and R charts. Confusion sometimes occurs during the interpretation of these charts. Unlike control charts, the horizontal axis for these charts is not time. On these charts the x axis is segmented into regions for the various operators and their measurements of the samples. This leads to a very different interpretation methodology from traditional control charts.

The following equations that determine the control limits of a gauge R&R $\bar{x}$ chart are similar to normal control charts:

$$\text{UCL}_{\bar{x}} = \bar{\bar{x}} + A_2 \bar{R}$$

$$\text{LCL}_{\bar{x}} = \bar{\bar{x}} - A_2 \bar{R}$$

In this equation, $\overline{\overline{x}}$ is the overall average (between and within operator), $\overline{R}$ is an estimate of within operator variability, and A_2 is determined from Table J. Out-of-control conditions in an $\overline{x}$ chart indicate that part variability is high compared to repeatability and reproducibility, which is desirable.

The methods to construct an R chart are similar. The inconsistencies of appraisers appear as out of control conditions in the R chart.

12.4   PREPARATION FOR A MEASUREMENT SYSTEM STUDY

Sufficient planning and preparation should be done prior to conducting a measurement system study. Typical preparation prior to study is as follows:

1. Plan the approach. For instance, determine by engineering judgment, visual observations, or gauge study if there is an appraiser influence in calibrating or using the instrument. Reproducibility can sometimes be considered negligible—for example, when pushing a button.
2. Select number of appraisers, number of sample of parts, and number of repeat reading. Consider requiring more parts and/or trials for circle dimensions. Bulky or heavy parts may dictate fewer samples. Consider using at least two operators and ten samples where each operator measures each sample at least twice (all using the same device). Select appraisers who normally operate the instruments.
3. Select sample parts from the process that represent its entire operating range. To achieve this, perhaps select one part daily. Number each part.
4. Ensure that the instrument has a discrimination that is at least one-tenth of the expected process variation of the characteristic to be read. For example, if the characteristic's variation is 0.001, the equipment should be able to read a change of 0.0001.

Ensure that the measuring method of the appraiser and instrument is following the defined procedure. It is important to conduct the study properly. All analyses assume statistical independence of all readings. To reduce the possibility of misleading results, do the following:

1. Execute measurements in random order to ensure that drift or changes that occur will be spread randomly throughout the study.
2. Record readings to the nearest number obtained. When possible, make readings to nearest one-half of the smallest graduation (e.g., 0.00005 for 0.0001 graduations).
3. Use an observer who recognizes the importance of using caution when conducting the study.
4. Ensure that each appraiser uses the same procedure when taking measurements.

12.5 EXAMPLE 12.1: GAUGE R&R

Five samples selected from a manufacturing process are to represent the normal spread of the process. Two appraisers who normally do the measurements are chosen to participate in the study. Each part is measured three times by each appraiser. Results of the test are shown in Table 12.1 (AIAG 1995a).

The computer output for a gauge R&R study is shown next where Figure 12.2 shows the computer graphical output. An analysis discussion then follows.

Gauge R&R Computer Output

Gauge R&R Study—Analysis of Variance Method
*Analysis of Variance Table with Operator*Part Interaction*

Source	DF	SS	MS	F	P
Parts	4	129.467	32.3667	13.6761	0.01330
Operators	1	2.700	2.7000	1.1408	0.34565
Oper*Part	4	9.467	2.3667	0.9221	0.47064
Repeatability	20	51.333	2.5667		
Total	29	192.967			

*Analysis of Variance Table Without Operator*Part Interaction*

Source	DF	SS	MS	F	P
Parts	4	129.467	32.3667	12.7763	0.0000
Operators	1	2.700	2.7000	1.0658	0.3122
Repeatability	24	60.800	2.5333		
Total	29	192.967			

Gauge R&R

Source	VarComp	StdDev	5.15*Sigma
Total Gauge R&R	2.5444	1.59513	8.2149
Repeatability	2.5333	1.59164	8.1970
Reproducibility	0.0111	0.10541	0.5429
Operator	0.0111	0.10541	0.5429
Part-to-Part	4.9722	2.22985	11.4837
Total Variation	7.5167	2.74165	14.1195

Source	%Contribution	%Study Var
Total Gauge R&R	33.85	58.18
Repeatability	33.70	58.05

```
Reproducibility                    0.15              3.84
   Operator                        0.15              3.84
Part-to-Part                      66.15             81.33
Total Variation                  100.00            100.00


Number of Distinct Categories = 2
```

Gauge R&R Output Interpretation

The first analysis of variance analysis considered both operators and operator*part interaction. The second analysis of variance analysis did not consider the operator*part interaction. From these analyses, operator and operator*part interaction were not found to be significant because the probability of significance values (P) for operator or operator*part interaction were not small (e.g., not less than 0.05).

A recreation of the computer output calculations for the ratio variance component to total variance estimates is

$$\text{Variance component \%} = \frac{\text{Variance component}}{\text{Total variance}} \times 100$$

$$\text{Gauge variance component \%} = \frac{2.5444}{7.5167} \times 100 = 33.85\%$$

$$\text{Part-to-part variance component \%} = \frac{4.9722}{7.5167} \times 100 = 66.15\%$$

These results indicate a need to improve the measurement system, because approximately 34% of the total measured variance is from repeatability and reproducibility of the gauge.

The following shows a similar recreation of the previous computer output calculations, except the ratio of variance component to total variance is now expressed in 99 percentile units:

$$\text{\% Study ratio} = \frac{5.15 \times \text{standard deviation of component}}{\text{Total of } 5.15 \times \text{standard deviation of all components}} \times 100$$

$$\text{R\&R \% study Var} = \frac{8.2149}{14.1195} \times 100 = 58.18$$

$$\text{Part-to-part \% Var study} = \frac{11.4837}{14.1195} \times 100 = 81.33$$

TABLE 12.1 Measurements for Gauge R&R Example

	Appraiser 1				
Trials	Part 1	Part 2	Part 3	Part 4	Part 5
1	217	220	217	214	216
2	216	216	216	212	219
3	216	218	216	212	220
Avg.	216.3	218.0	216.3	212.7	218.3
Range	1.0	4.0	1.0	2.0	4.0

Average of averages = 216.3

	Appraiser 2				
Trials	Part 1	Part 2	Part 3	Part 4	Part 5
1	216	216	216	216	220
2	219	216	215	212	220
3	220	220	216	212	220
Avg.	218.3	217.3	215.7	213.3	220.0
Range	4.0	4.0	1.0	4.0	0.0

Average of averages = 216.9

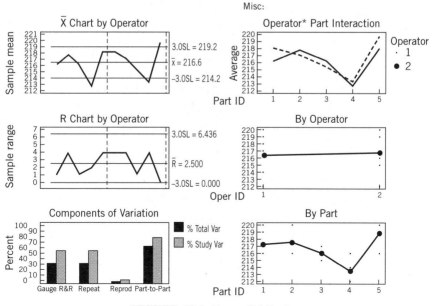

FIGURE 12.2 Gauge R&R plots.

Concern is again appropriate because it is estimated that about 58% of the 99% spread of variability is from the measurement system.

The gauge R&R computer output shows only two distinct categories, another indicator that the effectiveness of this gauge is not good. With only two distinct categories, the data can be divided into high and low groups, which is equivalent to attribute data.

Graphical outputs associated with a gauge R&R study can give additional insight to a gauge and opportunities for improvement. In a gauge R&R study the $\bar{x}$ control chart address measurement variability relative to part-to-part variation. The limits for a control chart in a gauge R&R study describes part-to-part variation. The control limits for these charts are based on repeatability inconsistencies, not part-to-part variation. For this study, the $\bar{x}$ chart by operator plot had only 30%, or less than half, of the averages outside the limits. The measurement system in this example is concluded to be inadequate to detect part-to-part variations, assuming that the parts used in the study truly represent the total process variation. An adequate measurement system is present when a majority of part averages fall outside the limits and appraisers agree on which parts fall outside the limits.

When the R chart of a gauge R&R study is in control, the inspection process by appraisers is similar. If one appraiser is out of control, his/her method differs from the others. If all appraisers have some out-of-control ranges, the measurement system is apparently sensitive to appraiser technique and needs improvement to obtain useful data. For this example there does not appear to be any inconsistency within and between operators.

Other output graphs from a gauge R&R study can give additional insight to sources of variability (e.g., part-to-part, operator, operator*part interaction, and components of variance). These charts, for this example, do not appear to contain any additional information that was already determined through other means.

This example did not include a percent part tolerance; however, similar calculations to the percent study ratio could be made for this calculation. For the percent part tolerance calculations, part tolerance spread replaces the product of 5.15 times part-to-part standard deviation.

12.6   LINEARITY

Linearity is the difference in the bias values through the expected operating range of the gauge. For a linearity evaluation, one or more operators measure parts selected throughout the operating range of the measurement instrument. For each of the chosen parts, the average difference between the reference value and the observed average measurement is the estimated bias. Sources for reference values of the parts include tool room or layout inspection equipment.

If a graph between bias and reference values follows a straight line throughout the operating rate, a regression line slope describes the best fit of bias versus reference values. This slope value is then multiplied by the process variation (or tolerance) of the parts to determine an index that represents the linearity of the gauge. Gauge linearity is converted to a percentage of process variation (or tolerance) when multiplied by 100 and divided by process variation (or tolerance). A scatter diagram of the best-fit line using graphical techniques can give additional insight to linearity issues.

12.7   EXAMPLE 12.2: LINEARITY

The five parts selected for the evaluation represent the operating range of the measurement system based upon the process variation. Layout inspection determined the part reference values. Appraisers measured each part 12 times in a random sequence. Results are shown in Table 12.2 (AIAG 1995a).

Figure 12.3 shows the results of a computer analysis of the data. The difference between the part reference value and the part average yielded bias. Inferences of linear association between the biases (accuracy measurements) and reference value (master part measurement) use the goodness-of-fit (R^2) value. Conclusions are then made from this to determine if there is a linear relationship. Linearity is determined by the slope of the best-fit line, not the goodness-of-fit (R^2). If there is a linear relationship, a decision needs to be

TABLE 12.2 Measurements for Linearity Example

Part: Reference Value:	1 2.00	2 4.00	3 6.00	4 8.00	5 10.00
1	2.70	5.10	5.80	7.60	9.10
2	2.50	3.90	5.70	7.70	9.30
3	2.40	4.20	5.90	7.80	9.50
4	2.50	5.00	5.90	7.70	9.30
5	2.70	3.80	6.00	7.80	9.40
6	2.30	3.90	6.10	7.80	9.50
7	2.50	3.90	6.00	7.80	9.50
8	2.50	3.90	6.10	7.70	9.50
9	2.40	3.90	6.40	7.80	9.60
10	2.40	4.00	6.30	7.50	9.20
11	2.60	4.10	6.00	7.60	9.30
12	2.40	3.80	6.10	7.70	9.40
Part average:	2.49	4.13	6.03	7.71	9.38
Bias:	−0.49	−0.13	−0.03	+0.29	+0.62
Range:	0.4	1.3	0.7	0.3	0.5

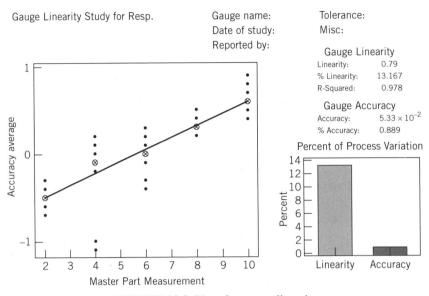

FIGURE 12.3 Plots for gauge linearity.

made to determine if the amount is acceptable. Generally a lower slope is better gauge linearity.

12.8 ATTRIBUTE GAUGE STUDY

Described is a short method for conducting an attribute gauge study. An attribute gauge either accepts or rejects a part after comparison to a set of limits. Unlike a variable gauge, an attribute gauge cannot quantify the degree to which a part is good or bad.

A short attribute gauge can be conducted by first selecting 20 parts. Choose parts, if possible, such that some parts are slightly below and above specification limits. Use two appraisers and conduct the study in a manner to prevent appraiser bias. Appraisers inspect each part twice, deciding whether the part is acceptable or not. If all measurements agree (four per part), gauge is accepted. Gauge needs improvement or reevaluation if measurement decisions do not agree. Choose an alternate measurement system if gauge cannot be improved (because the measurement system is unacceptable) (AIAG 1995a).

12.9 GAUGE STUDY OF DESTRUCTIVE TESTING

Unlike nondestructive tests, destructive tests cannot test the same unit repeatedly to obtain an estimate for pure measurement error. However, an upper bound on measurement error for destructive tests is determinable using the described control chart technique (Wheeler 1990).

When testing is destructive, it is impossible to separate the variation of the measurements themselves from the variation of the product being measured. However, it is often possible to minimize the product variation between pairs of measurement through the careful choice of the material that is to be measured. Through the repeated duplicate measurements on material that are thought to minimize product variation between the two measurements, an upper bound is obtainable for the variation due to the measurement process. The simple control chart methodology illustrated in the following example shows the application of this procedure.

12.10   EXAMPLE 12.3: GAUGE STUDY OF DESTRUCTIVE TESTING

The data in Table 12.3 are viscosity measurements by lot (Wheeler 1990). For this measurement systems analysis study, consider that the readings for the samples represent duplicate measurements because they were obtained using the same methods, personnel and instruments. Because each lot is separate, it is reasonable to interpret the difference between the two viscosity measurements as the primary component of measurement error. To illustrate the broader application of the described approach, consider that these data could also represent a continuous process where the measurements are destructive. If this were the case, measurements need to be taken so that the samples are as similar as possible. This selection often involves obtaining samples as close together as possible from the continuous process.

Figure 12.4 shows a range chart for these data. These duplicate readings show consistency because no range exceeds the control limit of 0.2007. An estimate for the standard deviation of the measurement process is

$$\sigma_m = \frac{\overline{R}}{d_2} = \frac{0.0614}{1.128} = 0.054$$

where $\overline{R}$ is average range and d_2 is from Table J, where $n = 2$.

These calculated ranges do not reflect batch-to-batch variation and should not be used in the construction of the control limits for average viscosity.

TABLE 12.3 Destructive Testing Example: Calculations for Range Chart

Lot:	1	2	3	4	5	6	7
Sample 1:	20.48	19.37	20.35	19.87	20.36	19.32	20.58
Sample 2:	20.43	19.23	20.39	19.93	20.34	19.30	20.68
Range:	0.05	0.14	0.04	0.06	0.02	0.02	0.10

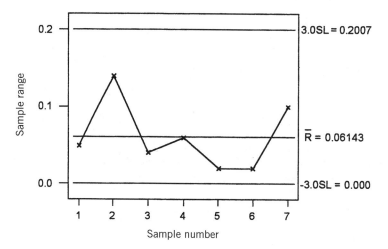

FIGURE 12.4 Range chart of difference between two samples for destructive test.

When tracking the consistency of the process, it is best to use the average of the duplicate readings with an individual chart and a moving range chart (i.e., *XmR* chart), as determined in Table 12.4. The grand average is 20.045 and the average moving range is 0.9175. The *XmR* chart in Figure 12.5 indicates no inconsistency in the process.

There is a need for both types of control charts. The range chart checks for consistency within the measurement process, while the *XmR* chart checks for consistency of the production process. From the individual chart, an estimate for the standard deviation of the product measurements is

$$\sigma_p = \frac{\overline{R}}{d_2} = \frac{0.9175}{1.128} = 0.813$$

where $\overline{R}$ is average range and d_2 is from Table J, where $n = 2$.

The estimated number of distinct categories is then

$$\text{Number of distinct categories} = \left[\frac{\sigma_p}{\sigma_m}\right] \times 1.41 = \frac{0.813}{0.054} \times 1.41 = 2.12$$

TABLE 12.4 Destructive Testing Example: Calculations for *XmR* Chart

Lot:	1	2	3	4	5	6	7
Sample 1:	20.48	19.37	20.35	19.87	20.36	19.32	20.58
Sample 2:	20.43	19.23	20.39	19.93	20.34	19.30	20.68
$\bar{x}$:	20.455	19.300	20.370	19.900	20.350	19.310	20.630
MR		1.155	1.07	0.47	0.45	1.04	1.32

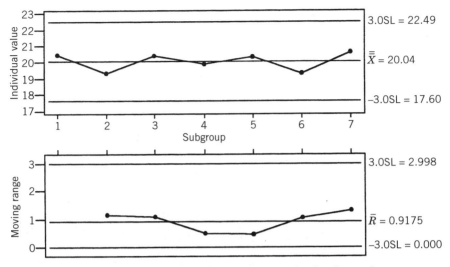

FIGURE 12.5 *XmR* chart of mean of two samples for destructive test.

The magnitude for number of distinct categories suggests that the measurement process adequately detects product variation.

In summary, the pairing of units such that sample-to-sample variation is minimized can give a reasonable estimate of the measurement process using a simple control chart approach. Estimates from these calculations are useful to then determine an estimate for the number of distinct categories for the measurement process.

12.11   S⁴ ASSESSMENT

Often organizations overlook the importance of conducting a measurement systems analysis. For example, much money can be wasted trying to fix a process when the major source of variability is the measurement system. Practitioners often need to give more consideration to the measurement system before beginning experimentation work. To illustrate the importance of pretest measurement systems analysis, consider a DOE. When the measurement system is poor, significance tests can only detect factors with very large effects. There might be no detection of important smaller factor effects. The importance of a measurement system is also not often considered when making sample size and confidence interval calculations. An unsatisfactory measurement system can affect these calculations dramatically.

This chapter describes procedures to determine whether a measurement system is satisfactory. The measurement system is only one source of variability when measuring a product or process. Other possible sources of variability are differences between raw material, manufacturing lines, and test equipment. In some instances it is advantageous to consider these other sources of variability in addition to operator variability within one experiment. The variance components techniques described later in this text use a nested design structure that can quantify the variance components of not only a process but also measurement system parameters. Knowing and then improving the sources of variability for a measurement system can lead to an expedient means of improving the bottom line.

12.12   EXERCISES

1. *Machine Screws Exercise:* Teams are to conduct a gauge R&R study of the length measurement of machine screws. Five machine screws (approximately two inch long) will be supplied to each team for analysis. These machine screws were previously filed or ground such that the length of screws within a set have measurements that span some range (e.g., 0.200 in.). Teams are instructed to conduct a gauge R&R using two appraisers where each part is measured twice by the appraisers. Measurements are to be recorded to the nearest one-tenth of the smallest increment on the rule.

2. *M&M's Candy Exercise:* A team sets up the procedure to conduct an experiment where 20 M&M's candies are taken from a bag. For each team there will be two or three operators. There will be also one to three people who collect and compile the results from the following table format entries:

	Appraiser 1		Appraiser 2		Appraiser 3		Overall
Sample	Test 1: OK?	Test 2: OK?	Test 1: OK?	Test 2: OK?	Test 1: OK?	Test 2: OK?	All Agree?
1							
2							
.							
.							
.							
19							
20							
% Time oper consistent[a]	Answer:		Answer:		Answer:		
% overall Consistent[b]							Answer:

[a] 100 times number of times in agreement for each pair of columns divided by 20.

[b] 100 times number of times "yes" in "all agree" column divided by 20.

3. In an exercise within Chapter 3 a paragraph of text was examined. The number of times the sixth character occurs was counted. Discuss what

could be said about this visual inspection process. Describe what you think should be done to increase awareness of any deficiencies and approaches to make process improvements.

4. Conduct a gauge R&R study of the following data, where five parts are evaluated twice by three appraisers.

	Appraiser A						Appraiser B						Appraiser C				
Part	1	2	3	4	5		1	2	3	4	5		1	2	3	4	5
1	113	113	71	101	113		112	117	82	98	110		107	115	103	110	131
2	114	106	73	97	130		112	107	83	99	108		109	122	86	108	90

5. For the following data conduct a Gauge R&R study to assess whether the gauge is acceptable, may be acceptable, or unacceptable. A specification tolerance is 0.004 (i.e., for a specification of 0.375 ± 0.002, where measurement unit is 0.0001). A table value of 56, for example, equates to a measurement of $0.3700 + (56 \times 0.0001) = 0.3756$ (IBM 1984).

Appraiser	1			2			3		
Sample No.	1st Trial	2nd Trial	3rd Trial	1st Trial	2nd Trial	3rd Trial	1st Trial	2nd Trial	3rd Trial
1	56	55	57	57	58	56	56	57	56
2	63	62	62	64	64	64	62	64	64
3	56	54	55	57	55	56	55	55	55
4	57	55	56	56	57	55	56	57	55
5	58	58	57	59	60	60	57	60	60
6	56	55	54	60	59	57	55	57	56
7	56	55	56	58	56	56	55	55	57
8	57	57	56	57	58	57	57	58	57
9	65	65	64	64	64	65	65	64	65
10	58	57	57	61	60	60	58	59	60

6. Describe how the techniques within this chapter are useful and can be applied to S^4 projects.

13

CAUSE-AND-EFFECT MATRIX AND QUALITY FUNCTION DEPLOYMENT

Processes have inputs and outputs. Some outputs are more important to customers than other outputs. The output of a process might be a product or service. Output variables can include delivery time or a dimension on a part. Input variables to a process can affect output variables. Important key process output issues are sometimes classified with regard to their area of impact—that is, critical to quality (CTQ) [e.g., flatness, diameter, or electrical characteristic], critical to delivery (CTD), and critical to cost (CTC). Important key process input issues are sometimes classified as critical to process (CTP).

Example input variables are operators, machines, process temperatures, time of day, and raw material characteristics. Some output variables to a process are more important to customers (internal and external) of the process than other variables. The performance of these key output variables can be affected by process input variables. However, all process input variables do not equally affect key output variables. To improve a process we would like to determine what are the key process input variables, how they affect key process output variables, and what (if anything) should be done differently with these variables (e.g., control them).

Described within this chapter are tools that can help assess the relationships between key process input and key process output variables. Quality function deployment (QFD) is described first. QFD is a powerful tool; however, it can require a lot of time and resources to conduct. Other simpler-to-use tools such as cause-and-effect matrix are later described within the chapter. Week one of an S^4 blackbelt 4-week workshop may cover only the cause-and-effect matrix from this chapter. Week four could later discuss QFD, if time permits. If a practitioner has identified potential key process input and output variables when defining their process (as described in Chapter 4), they may wish to skip the QFD and customer survey sections and proceed directly to the sections on cause-and-effect matrix and data relationship matrix.

13.1   MEETING THE NEEDS OF THE CUSTOMER

Consider products that a customer has purchased that do not meet his or her expectations. Perhaps a product has a lot of "bells and whistles"; however, it does not meet his or her basic needs. Or, perhaps the product is not user-friendly. Will a customer take the time to complain about the product or service? Will the customer avoid purchasing products from that company in the future?

When addressing the needs of customers, it should be emphasized that the end user of a product is not the only customer. For example. a supplier that manufactures a component part of a larger assembly has a customer relationship with the company responsible for the larger assembly. Procedures to determine the needs of customers can also be useful to define such business procedural tasks as office physical layout, accounting procedures, internal organization structure, and product test procedures. Focusing on the needs of customers goes hand in hand with "answering the right question" and S^4 assessments discussed throughout this text.

QFD can be used in many different areas of the business (e.g., planning, testing, engineering, manufacturing, distribution, marketing, and service). However, it must be understood that a large amount of effort can be required to perform a formal QFD evaluation. If the amount of work is thought to be excessive, the other methodologies discussed within this chapter may be more applicable.

13.2   QUALITY FUNCTION DEPLOYMENT (QFD)

Quality function deployment or the "house of quality" (a term coined in QFD because of the shape of its matrix) is a tool that can be used to give direction on what should be done to meet the needs of the customer. It is a tool that can aid with this process and translate customer requirements into basic requirements that have direction. It is a communication tool that uses a team concept where many organizations (e.g., sales, manufacturing, development) can break down barriers so that product definition and efforts have direct focus toward the needs of the customer. A QFD chart can be used to organize, preserve, and provide for the transfer of knowledge. It can also be used in conjunction with DOE (see Example 43.2).

It should be noted that many problems can be encountered when conducting a QFD. If extreme care is not exercised, wrong conclusions can result from the effort. For example, bias can easily be injected into a survey through the way the questions were asked, the procedure that was used to conduct the survey, or the type of people who were asked questions. Practitioners might ask themselves if they would expect to get the same results if the survey were conducted again (i.e., perhaps the experimental error in the results is too high, and a forced comparison survey procedure should have been utilized). Another way in which an erroneous conclusion can be made is through the data analysis—for example, the technical importance calculations that are made in step 7 of the generic procedures described in the next section. In a given situation it may be more important to weight responses by the importance of overall secondary or primary customer requirements. Perhaps the most important benefit that can result from creating a QFD is via personal interviews with customers. The comments resulting from these discussions can perhaps give the best (although not numerically tangible) direction (Brown 1991).

An overall product QFD implementation strategy involves first listing the customer expectations (voice of the customer). These "whats" are then tabulated along with the listing of design requirements related to meeting these customers' expectations ("hows"). The important "hows" can then be transferred to "whats" of another QFD matrix within a complete QFD matrix-to-matrix process flow. For example, consider the customer requirement of increasing the years of durability for a car. This matrix-to-matrix flow is exemplified in Table 13.1.

The needs of the customer are dynamic. Product features that were considered "wow" features in the past are now taken for granted. For example, a person seeing for the first time a car that does not need a "crank start" would consider this a "wow" change; however, electronic starters are now taken for granted. Noritaki Kano's description of this is illustrated conceptually in Figure 13.1 (King 1987).

The arrow in the middle, "one-dimensional quality," shows the situation where the customers tell the producer what they want, and the producer supplies this need. The lower arrow represents the items that are expected. Customers are less likely to mention them; however, they are dissatisfied if they

TABLE 13.1. QFD Matrices: An Example about Car Durability

QFD Matrix	Example Matrix Outputs
Customer requirement	Years of durability
Design requirement	No visible exterior rust in 3 yr
Part characteristics	Paint weight: 2–2.5 g/m^2
	Crystal size: 3 maximum
Manufacturing operations	Dip tank
	3 coats
Production requirements	Time: 2.0-min minimum
	Acidity: 15–20
	Temperature: 48–55°C

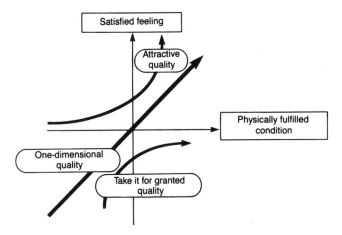

FIGURE 13.1 Satisfied feeling versus condition.

do not receive them. Safety is an example in this category. The top arrow represents wow quality. These are the items that a normal customer will not mention. Innovative individuals within the producers' organization or "leading edge" users need to anticipate these items, which must be satisfiers (not dissatisfiers).

To determine accurate "whats" for the requirement matrix (i.e., accurate one-dimensional quality projections and anticipated attractive quality additions), personal interviews with customers may first be appropriate. Surveys should use the words of the customer when determining these "what" items. These "whats" can then be compiled into primary, secondary, and even tertiary requirements. Follow-up surveys can then be done using test summaries to get importance ratings (e.g., 1–5) for each "what" item. Opinions about competitive products can also be compiled during these surveys.

The "whats" for the other matrices may be determined from internal inputs in addition to pass-down information from higher-state matrices. These "whats" are often more efficiently determined when the QFD team begins with tertiary "whats" and then summarizes these into a shorter list of secondary "whats" followed by another summary into the primary "whats."

The following is a step-by-step QFD matrix creation process, as it relates to Figure 13.2. The steps are applied in Example 13.1. The steps are written around the development of a design requirement matrix; however, the basic procedural flow is similar for other matrices. With this procedure, equations, weights, specific parameters, and step sequence may be altered to better identify important items that need emphasis for a particular situation.

1. A list of customer requirements ("whats") is made in primary, secondary, and tertiary sequence. Applicable government regulation items should also be contained within this list.

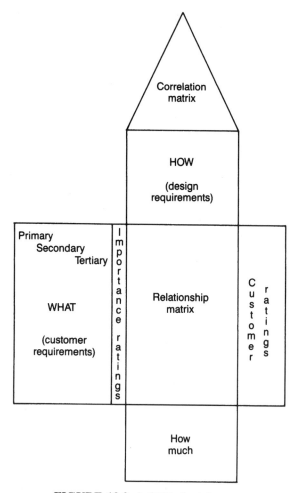

FIGURE 13.2 A QFD chart format.

2. The importance of each "what" item can similarly be determined from a survey using a rating scale (e.g., 1–5, where 5 is the most important). Care must be exercised when quantifying these values because the action of the customer may not accurately reflect their perceived importance. For example, a customer may purchase a product more because of packaging than because of characteristics of the product within the package.

3. Customer ratings should be obtained for both the competition and the existing design for each of the "what" items. It is important to identify and quantify the important "whats" in which a design of a competitor exceeds the current design so that design changes can focus upon these areas. The "whats" should be identified where the existing product is

preferred so that these items can be protected within future design considerations.

4. Engineering first compiles a list of design requirements that are necessary to achieve the market-driven "whats." The design team lists across the top of the matrix the design requirements ("hows") that affect one or more of the customer attributes. Each design requirement should describe the product in measurable terms and should directly affect customer perceptions. For example, within a design requirements matrix, the closing force of a car door may be noted, in contrast to the thickness of the metal within the door, which may be noted within a future parts characteristics matrix. The arrow at the top of the design requirements listing indicates the direction for improvement (e.g., a downward pointing error indicates that a lower value is better, while a zero indicates that a target is desired). Each "what" item is systematically assessed for specific measurement requirements. Vague and trivial characteristics should be avoided.

5. Cell strengths within the matrix are quantified to the importance of each "how" item relative to getting each "what" item. Symbols describing these relationships include the following: ⊙, which indicates much importance or a strong relationship; ○, which indicates some importance or relationship; △, which indicates a small importance or relationship, and no mark, which indicates no relationship or importance. The symbols are later replaced by weights (e.g., 9, 3 1, and 0) to give the relationship value needed to make the technical importance calculations. Initially, the symbols are used to clarify the degree of importance attributed to the relationships and weightings. From this visual representation, it is easier to determine where to place critical resources. If a current quality control measurement does not affect any customer attribute, this current quality control measurement is either not necessary or a "what" item is missing. "How" items may need to be added such that there is at least one "how" item for each "what" requirement.

6. From technical tests of both competitive products and our existing product design, objective measurements are added to the bottom of the house beneath each "how" item. Note that if the customer perception "what" of the competition does not correlate to the "how" engineering characteristic competition measurement, either the measurements are in error, the "how" measurement characteristic is not valid for this "what," or a product has an image perception problem.

7. The technical importance of each design requirement is determined by using the following equations. The two sets of calculations are made for each "how" consideration given a total of n "whats" affecting the relationship matrix. An equation to determine an absolute measurement for technical importance is

$$\text{Absolute} = \sum_{i=1}^{n} \text{relationship value} \times \text{customer importance}$$

To get a relative technical importance number, rank the responses from this equation, where 1 is the highest ranking. It should be noted that other equations and/or procedures found in textbooks or articles may be more appropriate for a given situation (e.g., for each "how" determine an overall percentage value of the total of all absolute technical importances).

8. The technical difficulty of each "how" design requirement is documented on the chart so focus can be given to important "hows" that may be difficult to achieve.

9. The correlation matrix is established to determine the technical interrelationships between the "hows." These relationships can be denoted by the following symbols: $\oplus$, high positive correlation; $+$, positive correlation; $\ominus$ high negative correlation; $-$, negative correlation, and a blank, no correlation (see Figure 13.3).

10. New target values are, in general, determined from the customer ratings and information within the correlation matrix. Trend charts and snapshots are very useful tools to determine target objective values for key items. DOE techniques are useful to determine targets that need to be compromised between "hows."

11. Areas that need concentrated effort are selected. Key elements are identified for follow-up matrix activity. The technical importance and technical difficulty areas are useful to identify these elements.

As previously noted, this discussion was written around a design requirement matrix. Information within the "how much" (see Figure 13.2) area can vary depending on the type of matrix. For example, the matrix may or may not have adjusted target specification values for the "hows," technical analyses of competitive products, and/or degree of technical difficulty.

13.3 EXAMPLE 13.1: CREATING A QFD CHART

A fraction of one QFD chart is directed toward determining the design requirements for a car door. The following describes the creation of a QFD chart for this design (Hauser and Clausing 1988).

Customer surveys and personal interviews led to the QFD chart inputs noted in items 1 to 3 in the previous section. The remaining items were the steps used to determine the technical aspects of achieving these "whats."

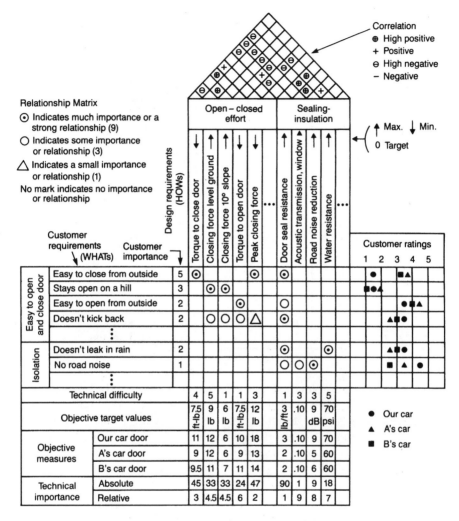

FIGURE 13.3 QFD chart example.

where lb = pounds   ft-lb = foot-pounds   dB = decibels   psi = pounds per square inch

1. A partial list of customer requirements ("whats") for the car door is noted in Table 13.2. A government impact resistance requirement was also a "what" item, but it is not shown in this list.

2. In Figure 13.3 an importance rating to the customer is noted for each "what" item. For example, the ease of closing the door from the outside was given an importance rating of 5.

3. A rating (1–5, where 5 is best) of two competitor products and the current design is noted in Figure 13.3 for each "what" item. For ex-

TABLE 13.2. List of "Whats" for Car Door Example

Primary	Secondary	Tertiary
Good operation and use	Easy to open and close door	Stays open on hill
		Easy to open from inside
		Easy to open from outside
		Easy to close from inside
		Easy to close from outside
		Doesn't kick back
	Isolation	Doesn't leak
		No road noise
		No wind noise
		Doesn't rattle
		Crash impact resistance
Good appearance	Arm rest	Soft
		Correct position
		Durable
	Interior trim	Material won't fade
		Attractive
	Clean	Easy to clean
		No grease from door

ample, the customer perceives our existing design to be the worst (i.e., 1.5) of the three evaluated in the area of "easy to close"; however, when making any design changes to change this rating, care must be given to protect the favorable opinion customers have about our current design in the area of road noise.

4. The engineering team addresses the design requirements ("hows") necessary to achieve the market-driven "whats" for the car door. For example, "Energy to close door" is a "how" to address the "what", "Easy to close from outside." The arrow indicates that a lower energy is better.

5. The relationship of the "hows" in meeting the customer's requirements ("whats") is noted. For example, an important measurement (⊙) to address the customer "what," "Easy to close from outside," is the "how," "Torque to close door."

6. Objective measurements are noted for both customer requirements and our existing product (i.e., a competitive survey). For example, our car door currently measures 11 ft-lb closing torque.

7. Absolute technical importance of the design requirements is then determined within the "how much" area. For example, the absolute technical importance (see Figure 13.3, second to last row) of door seal resistance would be $5(9) + 2(3) + 2(9) + 2(9) + 1(3) = 90$ (see Fig.

13.3, seventh column from left). Because this was the highest of those numbers shown, it had the highest ranking; hence, it is given a "1" relative ranking because it was the most import "how" in meeting the needs of the customer.

8. The technical difficulty requirements are determined. For example, the technical difficulty of water resistance is assessed the most difficult and is given a rating of 5.

9. The correlation matrix is established to determine the technical inter-relationships between the "hows." For example, the ⊖ symbol indicates that there is a high negative correlation between "Torque to close door" and "Closing force on level ground." The customer wants the door to be easy to close from outside along with being able to stay open on a hill (i.e., two opposite design requirement needs).

10. Because our car door had a relatively poor customer rating for the "what" "Easy to close from outside," a target value was set that was better than the measured values of the competition (i.e., 7.5 ft-lb). Tradeoffs may be necessary when determining targets to address relationships within the correlation matrix and relative importance ratings.

11. Important issues can be carried forward to "whats" of another "house" that is concerned with the detailed product design. For example, the engineering requirement of minimizing the torque (ft-lb) to close the door is important and can become a "what" for another matrix that leads to part characteristics such as weather stripping properties or hinge design.

13.4 A SIMPLIFIED METHODOLOGY TO ASSESS THE NEEDS OF CUSTOMERS

The mechanics of QFD can be very laborious and time-consuming. However, some situations do not necessarily require all the outputs from a formal QFD. (*Note:* A lengthy, accurate QFD investigation can be useless if it is not conducted and compiled in a timely fashion.)

This section describes an approach that utilizes brainstorming techniques along with surveys to quantify the needs of customers. The following steps describe an approach to first determine the questions to ask and then quantify and prioritize needs, as perceived by the customer.

1. Conduct brainstorming session(s) where a "wish list" of features, problem resolutions. and so forth are identified.

2. If there are many different brainstorming sessions that contain too many ideas to consider collectively in a single survey, it may be necessary to rank the individual brainstorming session items. A secret ballot rating

for each topic by the attendees could be done during or after the sessions. The items that have the highest rankings from each brainstorming session are then considered as a survey question consideration.

3. A set of questions is then determined and worded from a positive point of view. Obviously, care needs to be exercised with the wording of these questions so as not to interject bias. The respondent to the question is asked to give an importance statement and a satisfaction statement relative to the question. The question takes the form shown in Table 13.3. Note that this survey is soliciting the same type of information from customers as was solicited in a QFD. In Figure 13.3 the "customer satisfaction rating" and "customer importance" both were a numerical query issue for each "what" item.

4. The information from this type of survey can be plotted in a perceptual map (Urban and Hasser 1980) format.

A plot of this type can be created for each respondent to the survey, where the plot point that describes a particular question could be identified as its survey question number (see Figure 13.4). Areas that need work are those areas that are judged important with low satisfaction (i.e., questions 8 and 4).

The average question response could similarly be plotted; however, with any analysis approach of this type, care must be exercised not to lose individual response information that might be very important. An expert may rate something completely differently from the rest of the group because he or she has much more knowledge of an area.

Some effort needs to be given to identify these people so that they can be asked more questions individually for additional insight that could later prove to be very valuable (i.e., let's not miss the important issues by "playing games" with the numbers).

TABLE 13.3. Example Questionnaire Format That Can Give a Perceptual Map Response

The products produced by our company are reliable. (Please comment on any specific changes that you believe are needed.)

What is the importance of this requirement to you?	What is your level of satisfaction that this requirement is met?
5 Very important	5 Very satisfied
4 Important	4 Satisfied
3 Neither important nor unimportant	3 Neither satisfied nor unsatisfied
2 Unimportant	2 Unsatisfied
1 Very unimportant	1 Very unsatisfied
Response: _____	Response _____

Comments:

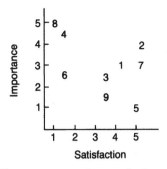

FIGURE 13.4 Coordinate system and example data for a perceptual map.

Determining the areas that need focus from such a plot would not be rigorous because the response has two-dimensional considerations (importance and satisfaction). To address a more rigorous approach, consider first the extreme situation where a question is thought to be very important (a 5) with low satisfaction (a 1). The difference between the importance and satisfaction numbers could be used to create a number that is used for the purpose of determining which areas have the largest opportunity for improvement. A large number difference (i.e., 4) indicates an area that has a large amount of potential for improvement, while lower numbers have less potential (a negative number is perhaps meaningless) (Wheeler 1990). These differences could then be ranked. From this ranking there can result a better understanding of where opportunities exist for improvement. Perhaps also from this ranking, important questions can be grouped to get a better idea of what areas should have the most focus for change.

This survey procedure is usually associated with determining the needs and wishes of the end users of a product. However, good customer–supplier relationships should exist within a company. Consider, for example, two steps of a process in a manufacturing line. People involved with the second step of the process are customers of the people who are involved with the first step of the process.

A customer–supplier relationship can also be considered to exist between the employees of an organization and the procedures that they use, for example, to develop a product. The methodology described in this section could be used to identify bureaucratic procedures that hamper productive activities of employees. After these areas are identified, additional brainstorming sessions could be conducted to improve the areas of processes that need to be changed.

13.5 CAUSE-AND-EFFECT MATRIX

The cause-and-effect matrix (or characteristic selection matrix) is a tool that can aid with the prioritization of importance of key process input variables.

This prioritization by a team can help with the selection of what will be monitored to determine if there is a cause and effect relationship and whether key process input controls are necessary. The results of a cause-and-effect matrix can lead to other activities such as FMEA, multi-vari charts correlation analysis, and DOE.

To construct a cause-and-effect matrix, do the following:

1. List horizontally the key process output variables that were identified when documenting the process (see Chapter 4). These variables are to represent what the customer of the process considers important and essential.

2. Assign a prioritization number for each key process output variable, where higher numbers have a larger priority (e.g., using values from 1 to 10). These values do not need to be sequential.

3. List vertically on the left side of the cause-and-effect matrix all key process input variables that may cause variability or nonconformance to one or more of the key process output variables.

4. Reach by consensus the amount of effect that each key process input variable has on each key process output variable. Rather than use values from 1 to 10 (where 10 indicates the largest effect), consider a scale using levels 0, 1, 3 and 5 or 0, 1, 3, and 9.

5. Determine the result for each process input variable by first multiplying the key process output priority (step 2) by the consensus of the effect for the key process input variable (step 4) and then summing these products.

6. The key process input variables can then be prioritized by the results from step 5 and/or a percentage of total calculation.

Table 13.4 exemplifies a cause-and-effect matrix, which indicates a consensus that focus should be given to key process input variables numbered 2 and 4. The results from a cause-and-effect matrix can give direction for

• The listing and evaluation of KPOV's in a capability summary.
• The listing and evaluation of KPIV's in a control plan summary.
• The listing and exploration of KPIV's in an FMEA.

13.6 DATA RELATIONSHIP MATRIX

A cause-and-effect matrix is a tool that helps quantify team consensus on relationships that are thought to be between key input and key output varia-

TABLE 13.4. Cause and Effect Matrix Example

		Key Process Output Variables (with Prioritization)							
		A	B	C	D	E	F		
		5	3	10	8	7	6	Results	Percentage
	1	4	3		3			53	7.85%
	2	10		4	6		6	138	20.44%
	3		4					12	1.78%
	4			9	5	9	8	130	19.26%
Key	5	4				6		20	2.96%
process	6		6		5		2	58	8.59%
input	7	5		4		5		65	9.63%
variables	8		3		4		5	41	6.07%
	9	6		3		2		60	8.89%
	10		2	4				46	6.81%
	11	4			4	2	5	52	7.70%

bles. This section describes a matrix that can be created to summarize how data are collected to assess these theorized relationships.

Key process input variables can be affected by

- Temporal variation (over time)—for example, shift-to-shift, day-to-day, week-to-week.
- Positional variation (on the same part)—for example, within-part variation, variation between departments, variation between operators.
- Cycling variation (between parts)—for example, part-to-part variation, lot-to-lot variation.

Key process input variables can be discrete (attribute) or continuous. Examples are

- Attribute—for example, machine A or machine B, batch 1 or batch 2, supplier 1 or supplier 2.
- Continuous—for example, pressure, temperature, time.

A data relationship then can be created for each key process in the example form:

				Data Relationship Matrix Key process variable: Flatness				
No.	Within Piece	Type (attribute or cont.)		Piece to Piece	Type (attribute or cont.)		Time to Time	Type (attribute or cont.)
1	Position on part	att		Inspector	att		shift to shift	att
2				Pressure	cont			
3				Operator	att			

A plan might then be created to collect flatness measurements as a function of the key process variables, which would be recorded in the following form:

Measurement	Position	Inspector	Pressure	Operator	Shift	Flatness
1	1	1	1148	1	1	0.005
2	2	2	1125	1	1	0.007
3	3	1	1102	2	2	0.009
4	1	2	1175	2	2	0.008
5	2	1	1128	1	3	0.010
6	3	2	1193	1	3	0.003

Once the data are collected, graphical or statistical analysis tools described in the following chapters can be used to determine which key process input variables affect the key process output variables the most. It should be noted that these data are collected under normal process operation and that at least 30 data points should be collected.

13.7 S⁴ ASSESSMENT

Organizations can spend a lot of time trying to make sense of data that originated under questionable circumstances. Often more time needs to be spent developing the best strategy for conducting brainstorming sessions (e.g., who should attend and how the session will be conducted) and/or how measured data are to be collected.

13.8 EXERCISES

1. *Catapult Exercise:* Create a cause-and-effect matrix and relationship matrix of key process input and key process output variables. Consider outputs of cycle time, projection distance from catapult base, and distance of projection from tape measure.

2. Document and/or research a process in work, school community, or personal life. List key process input variables, key process output variables, and appropriate metrics. Examples include the criminal conviction process, your investment strategy, a manufacturing process, and college admission process.

3. Describe how the techniques within this chapter are useful and can be applied to S^4 projects.

14

FAILURE MODE AND EFFECTS ANALYSIS (FMEA)

To be competitive, organizations must continually improve. Potential failure mode and effects analysis (FMEA) is a technique that offers a methodology to facilitate process improvement. Using FMEAs, organizations can identify and eliminate concerns early in the development of a process or design. The quality of procured parts or services can improve when organizations work with their suppliers to implement FMEAs within their organization. Properly executed FMEAs can improve internal and external customer satisfaction in addition to the bottom line of organizations.

Discussed in this chapter are design and process FMEAs. Design FMEA applications include component, subsystem, and main system. Process FMEA applications include assembly machines, work stations, gauges, procurement, training of operators, and tests.

Benefits of a properly executed FMEA include:

- Improved product functionality and robustness
- Reduced warranty costs
- Reduced day-to-day manufacturing problems
- Improved safety of products and implementation processes
- Reduced business process problems

14.1 IMPLEMENTATION

Timeliness and usefulness as a living document are important aspects of a successful FMEA. To achieve the maximum benefit, organizations need to

256

conduct FMEAs before a failure is unknowingly instituted into a process or design.

FMEA input is a team effort; however, one individual typically is responsible by necessity, for its preparation. It is the role of the responsible engineer to orchestrate the active involvement of representatives from all affected areas. FMEAs should be a part of design or process concept finalization that acts as a catalyst for the stimulation and interchange of ideas between functions. FMEAs should be a living document that is updated for design changes and the addition of new information.

Important FMEA implementation issues include the following:

- Use as a living document with periodic review and updates.
- Conduct early enough in development cycle to
  - design-out potential failure modes by eliminating root causes.
  - reduce seriousness of failure mode if elimination is not possible.
  - reduce the occurrence of the failure mode.

Implementation benefits of a FMEA include the following:

- Early actions in the design cycle save time and money.
- Thorough analysis with teams creates better designs and processes.
- Complete analysis provides possible legal evidence.
- Previous FMEAs provide knowledge leading to current design or product FMEAs.

Team interaction is important when executing an FMEA. Organizations should consider using outside suppliers within an FMEA and creating the team so that it consists of five to seven knowledgeable, active members. When executing an FMEA, teams work to identify potential failure modes for design functions or process requirements. They then assign a severity to the effect of this failure mode. They also assign a frequency of occurrence to the potential cause of failure and likelihood of detection. Organizations can differ in the their approach to assign magnitudes to these assigned numbers (i.e., Severity, frequency of Occurrence, and likelihood of Detection—sometimes called SOD values) with the restriction that higher numbers are worse. After these numbers are determined, teams calculate a risk priority number (RPN), which is the product of these three numbers. Teams use the ranking of RPNs to focus on process improvement efforts.

An effective road map to create FMEA entries is as follows:

- Note an input to a process or design (e.g., process step, key input identified in a cause-and-effect matrix, or design function).
- List two or three ways input/function can go wrong.

- List at least one effect of failure.
- For each failure mode list one or more causes of input going wrong.
- For each cause list at least one method of preventing or detecting cause.
- Enter SOD values.

14.2 DEVELOPMENT OF A DESIGN FMEA

Within a design FMEA, manufacturing and/or process engineering input is important to ensure that the process will produce to design specifications. A team should consider including knowledgeable representation from design, test, reliability, materials, service, and manufacturing/process organizations.

A design FMEA presumes the implementation of manufacturing/assembly needs and design intents. A design FMEA does not need to include potential failure modes, causes, and mechanisms originating from manufacturing/assembly when their identification, effect, and control is covered by a process FMEA. However, a design FMEA team may choose to include some process FMEA issues. Design FMEAs do not rely on process controls to overcome potential design weaknesses; however, it does consider technical and physical limits of the manufacturing/assembly process.

When beginning a design FMEA, the responsible design engineer compiles documents that give insight to the design intent. Design intent is expressed as a list of what the design is expected to do and what it is not expected to do. Quality function deployment (QFD) and manufacturing/assembly requirements are sources for determining the design wants and needs of customers. The identification of potential failure modes for corrective action is easiest when the design intent is clear and thorough.

A block diagram of the system, subsystem, and/or component at the beginning of a design FMEA is useful to improve the understanding of the flow of information and other characteristics for the FMEA. Blocks are the functions, while the deliverables are the inputs and outputs of the blocks. The block diagram shows the relationship between analysis items and establishes a logical order for analysis. The documentation for an FMEA should include its block diagram. Figure 14.1 exemplifies a relational block diagram; however, another type of block diagram may be more applicable to a team to clarify the items considered within their analysis.

Table 14.1 shows a blank FMEA form. A team determines the design FMEA tabular entries following guidelines as described in the next section.

14.3 DESIGN FMEA TABULAR ENTRIES

A design FMEA in the format of Table 14.1 contains the following:

- *Header Information.* Documents the system/subsystem/component (under project name/description) and supplies other information about when and who created the FMEA.

APPENDIX A
Design FMEA Block Diagram Example

FAILURE MODE AND EFFECTS ANALYSIS (FMEA)
BLOCK DIAGRAM/ENVIRONMENTAL EXTREMES

SYSTEM NAME: FLASHLIGHT
YEAR VEHICLE PLATFORM: 1994 NEW PRODUCT
FMEA I.D. NUMBER   XXXI10D001

OPERATIONAL ENVIRONMENTAL EXTREMES

TEMPERATURE: __-20 TO 160 F_____ CORROSIVE: __TEST SCHEDULE B__ VIBRATION: __NOT APPLICABLE____
SHOCK: __6 FOOT DROP_____ FOREIGN MATERIAL: __DUST_____ HUMIDITY: __0 - 100 % RH__
FLAMMABILITY: (WHAT COMPOINENT(S) ARE NEAR HEAT SOURCE(S)?_____
OTHER:_____

LETTERS = COMPONENTS   _____ = ATTACHED/JOINED   ------- = INTERFACING, NOT JOINED   □ = NOT INCLUDED IN
NUMBERS = ATTACHING METHODS   THIS FMEA

The example below is a relational block diagram. Other types of block diagrams may be used by the FMEA
Team to clarify the item(s) being considered in their analysis

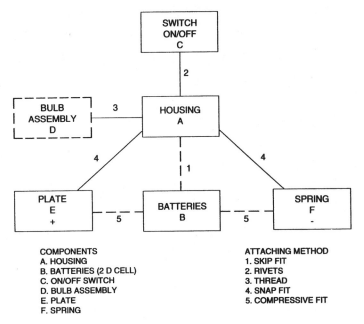

COMPONENTS	ATTACHING METHOD
A. HOUSING	1. SKIP FIT
B. BATTERIES (2 D CELL)	2. RIVETS
C. ON/OFF SWITCH	3. THREAD
D. BULB ASSEMBLY	4. SNAP FIT
E. PLATE	5. COMPRESSIVE FIT
F. SPRING	

FIGURE 14.1 Relational block diagram example. [From the *FMEA Manual* (Chrysler, Ford General Motors Supplier Quality Requirements Task Force), with permission.]

TABLE 14.1 Blank FMEA Form

FMEA Type (Design or Process):	Project Name/Description:		Date (Orig.):
Responsibility:	Prepared By:		Date (Rev.):
Core Team:			Date (Key):

Design FMEA (Item/ Function) Process FMEA (Function/ Requirements)	Potential Failure Mode	Potential Effect(s) of Failure	S e v	C l a s s	Potential Cause(s)/ Mechanism(s) of Failure	O c c u r	Current Controls	D e t e c	R P N	Recommended Actions	Responsibility & Target Completion Date	Actions Taken	S e v	O c c u r	D e t e c	R P N

- *Item/Function.* Contains the name and number of the analyzed item. Includes a concise, exact, and easy-to-understand explanation of a function of the item task or response that is analyzed to meet the intent of the design. Includes information regarding the temperature, pressure, and other pertinent system operating conditions. When there is more than one function, it lists each function separately with different potential failure modes.
- *Potential Failure Mode.* Describes ways a design could fail to perform its intended function. May include the cause of a potential failure mode in a higher level subsystem or process step. May also be the effect of one from a lower level component or process step. Contains for each item/function a list of each potential failure modes given the assumption that the failure could occur but may not necessarily occur. Items considered are previous problems and new issues from brainstorming sessions. Consideration is given to issues that could arise only under certain operation conditions such as high temperature and high humidity. Descriptions are in physical terms or technical terms, not as a symptom. Includes failure modes such as fractured, electrical short-circuited, oxidized, and circuit logic failed.
- *Potential Effect(s) of Failure.* Contains from an internal or external customer point of view the effects of the failure mode on the function. Highlights safety or noncompliance to regulation issues. Expressed in terms of the specific system, subsystem, or component hierarchical relationship that is analyzed. Includes failure effects such as intermittent operation, lost computer data, and poor performance.
- *Severity.* Assesses the seriousness of the effect of the potential failure mode to the next component, subsystem, or system, if it should occur. Reduction efforts for severity levels are through design change. Estimation is typically based on a 1 to 10 scale where the team agrees to a specific evaluation criteria for each ranking value. Table 14.2 shows example evaluation criteria for the automotive industry.
- *Classification.* Includes optional information such as critical characteristics that may require additional process controls. An appropriate character or symbol in this column indicates the need for an entry in the recommended action column and special process controls within the process FMEA.
- *Potential Causes(s) of Failure.* Indicates a design weakness that causes the potential failure mode. Contains a concise and descriptive list that is as complete as possible to describe all root causes (not symptom) of failure. Includes causes such as incorrect algorithm, hardness, porosity, and incorrect material specified. Includes failure mechanisms such as fatigue, wear, and corrosion.
- *Occurrence.* Estimates the likelihood that a specific cause will occur. Consideration of historical data of similar components/subsystems and

TABLE 14.2 Severity Evaluation Criteria Example for Design FMEA

Effect	Criteria: Severity of Effect	Ranking
Hazardous—without warning	Very high severity ranking when a potential failure mode affects safe vehicle operation and/or involves noncompliance with government regulations without warning.	10
Hazardous—with warning	Very high severity ranking when a potential failure mode affects safe vehicle operation and/or involves noncompliance with government regulation with warning.	9
Very high	Vehicle/item inoperable, with loss of primary function.	8
High	Vehicle/item operable, but at reduced level of performance. Customer dissatisfied.	7
Moderate	Vehicle/item operable, but comfort/convenience item(s) inoperable. Customer experiences discomfort.	6
Low	Vehicle/item operable, but comfort/convenience item(s) operable at reduced level of performance. Customer experiences some dissatisfaction.	5
Very low	Fit & finish/squeak & rattle item does not conform. Defect noticed by most customers.	4
Minor	Fit & finish/squeak & rattle item does not conform. Defect noticed by average customer.	3
Very minor	Fit & finish/squeak & rattle item does not conform. Defect noticed by discriminating customer.	2
None	No effect.	1

Source: FMEA Manual (Chrysler, Ford General Motors Supplier Quality Requirements Task Force), with permission.

differences to the new design help determine the ranking value. Teams need to agree on an evaluation criteria, where possible failure rates are anticipated values during design life. Table 14.3 shows example occurrence criteria.

- *Current Design Controls.* Lists activities (such as design verification tests, design reviews, DOEs, and tolerance analysis) that ensure adequacy of design control for the failure mode.
- *Detection.* Assessment of the ability of the current design control to detect the subsequence failure mode or potential cause of design weakness before releasing to production. Table 14.4 shows example detection criteria.
- *Risk Priority Number (RPN).* Product of severity, occurrence, and detection rankings. The ranking of RPN prioritizes design concerns; how-

TABLE 14.3 Occurrence Evaluation Criteria Example for Design FMEA

Probability of Failure	Possible Failure Rates	Ranking
Very high: Failure is almost inevitable	$\geq$1 in 2	10
	1 in 3	9
High: Repeated failures	1 in 8	8
	1 in 20	7
Moderate: Occasional failures	1 in 80	6
	1 in 400	5
	1 in 2,000	4
Low: Relatively few failures	1 in 15,000	3
	1 in 150,000	2
Remote: Failure is unlikely	$\leq$1 in 1,500,000	1

Source: FMEA Manual (Chrysler, Ford General Motors Supplier Quality Requirements Task Force), with permission.

ever, issues with a low RPN still deserve special attention if the severity ranking is high.

- *Recommended Action(s).* Intent of this entry is to institute actions that lower the occurrence, severity, and/or detection rankings of the highest RPN failure modes. Example actions include DOE, design revision, and test plan revision. "None" indicates there are no recommended actions.
- *Responsibility for Recommended Action.* Documents the organization and individual responsible for recommended action and target completion date.
- *Actions Taken.* Describes implementation action and effective date.
- *Resulting RPN.* Contains the recalculated RPN resulting from corrective actions that affected previous severity, occurrence. and detection rankings. Blanks indicate no action.

The responsible design engineer follows-up to ensure the adequate implementation of all recommended actions. An FMEA should include design changes and other relevant actions, even after the start of production. Table 14.5 exemplifies a completed process FMEA.

14.4 DEVELOPMENT OF A PROCESS FMEA

For a process or assembly FMEA, design engineering input is important to ensure the appropriate focus on important design needs. A team should consider including knowledgeable representation from design, manufacturing/process, quality, reliability, tooling, and operators.

A process FMEA presumes the product meets the intent of the design. A process FMEA does not need to include potential failure modes, causes, and

TABLE 14.4 Detection Evaluation Criteria Example for Design FMEA

Detection	Criteria: Likelihood of Detection by Design Control	Ranking
Absolute uncertainty	Design control will not and/or cannot detect a potential cause/mechanism and subsequent failure mode; or there is no design control.	10
Very remote	Very remote chance that the design control will detect a potential cause/mechanism and subsequent failure mode.	9
Remote	Remote chance that the design control will detect a potential cause/mechanism and subsequent failure mode.	8
Very low	Very low chance that the design control will detect a potential cause/mechanism and subsequent failure mode.	7
Low	Low chance that the design control will detect a potential cause/mechanism and subsequent failure mode.	6
Moderate	Moderate chance that the design control will detect a potential cause/mechanism and subsequent failure mode.	5
Moderately high	Moderately high chance that the design control will detect a potential cause/mechanism and subsequent failure mode.	4
High	High chance that the design control will detect a potential cause/mechanism and subsequent failure mode.	3
Very high	Very high chance that the design control will detect a potential cause/mechanism and subsequent failure mode.	2
Almost certain	Design control will almost certainly detect a potential cause/mechanism and subsequent failure mode.	1

Source: FMEA Manual (Chrysler, Ford General Motors Supplier Quality Requirements Task Force), with permission.

mechanisms originating from the design; however, a process FMEA team may choose to include some design issues. The design FMEA covers the effect and avoidance of these issues. A process FMEA can originate from a flowchart that identifies the characteristics of the product/process associated with each operation. Included are appropriate product effects from available design FMEA. The documentation for a FMEA should include its flowchart.

Table 14.1 shows a blank FMEA form. A team determines the process FMEA tabular entries following guidelines as described in the next section.

TABLE 14.5 Example: Potential Failure Mode and Effects Analysis (Design FMEA)

System ___
Subsystem ___
x Component 01.03/Body Closures
Model Year(s)/Vehicle(s) 199X/Lion 4 door/Wagon

Design Responsibility Body Engineering
Key Date 9X 03 01 ER

FMEA Number 1234
Page 1 of 1
Prepared By A. Tate—X6412—Body Engineer
FMEA Date (Orig.) 8X 03 22 (Rev.) 8X 07 14

Item Function	Potential Failure Mode	Potential Effect(s) of Failure	Sev	Class	Potential Cause(s)/Mechanism(s) of Failure	Occur	Current Design Controls	Detec	RPN	Recommended Action(s)	Responsibility and Target Completion Date	Actions Taken	Sev	Occ	Det	RPN
Front door L.H. H8HX-0000-A • Ingress to and egress from vehicle • Occupant protection from weather, noise, and side impact • Support anchorage for door hardware including mirror, hinges, latch and window regulator • Provide proper surface for appearance items • Paint and soft trim	Corroded interior lower door panels	Deteriorated life of door leading to: • Unsatisfactory appearance due to rust through paint over time • Impaired function of interior door hardware	7		Upper edge of protective wax application specified for inner door panels is too low	6	Vehicle general durability test vah. T-118 T-109 T-301	7	294	Add laboratory accelerated corrosion testing	A Tate-Body Engineering 8X 09 30	Based on test results (test no. 1481) upper edge spec raised 125 mm	7	2	2	28
					Insufficient wax thickness specified	4	Vehicle general durability testing (as above)	7	196	Add laboratory accelerated corrosion testing Conduct design of experiments (DOE) on wax thickness	Combine w/test for wax upper edge verification A Tate body engineering 9X 01 15	Test results (test no. 1481) show specified thickness is adequate. DOE shows 25% variation in specified thickness is acceptable.	7	2	2	28
					Inappropriate wax formulation specified	2	Physical and Chem Lab test: Report No. 1265	2	28	None						
					Entrapped air prevents wax from entering corner/edge access	5	Design aid investigation with nonfunctioning spray head	8	280	Add team evaluation using production spray equipment and specified wax	Body engineering and assembly operations 8X 11 15		7	1	3	21
					Wax application plugs door drain holes	3	Laboratory test using "worst-case" wax application and hole size	1	21	None						
					Insufficient room between panels for spray head access	4	Drawing evaluation of spray head access	4	112	Add team evaluation using design aid buck and spray head	Body engineering and assembly operations	Based on test, three additional vent holes provided in affected areas Evaluation showed adequate access	7	1	1	7

SAMPLE

Source: FMEA Manual (Chrysler, Ford General Motors Supplier Quality Requirements Task Force), with permission.

14.5 PROCESS FMEA TABULAR ENTRIES

A process FMEA in the format of Figure 14.1 contains the following:

- *Header Information.* Documents the process description and supplies other information about when and who created the FMEA.
- *Process Function/Requirements from a Process FMEA.* Contains a simple description of the analyzed process or operation. Example processes include assembling, soldering, and drilling. Concisely indicates the purpose of the analyzed process or operation. When numeric assembly operations exist with differing potential failure modes, the operations could be listed as separate processes.
- *Potential Failure Mode.* Describes how the process could potentially fail to conform to process requirements and/or design intent at a specific operation. Contains for each operation or item/function a list of each potential failure mode in terms of the component, subsystem, system, or process characteristic given the assumption that the failure could occur but may not necessarily occur. Gives consideration to how the process/ part fails to meet specifications and/or customer expectations. Subsequent or previous operations can cause these failure modes; however, teams should assume the correctness of incoming parts and materials. Items considered are previous problems and brainstorming for new issues. Includes failure modes such as broken, incorrect part placement, and electrical short-circuited.
- *Potential Effect(s) of Failure.* Contains from an internal or external customer point of view the effects of the failure mode on the function. Considers what the customer experiences or the ramifications of this failure mode either from the end-user point of view or from subsequent operation steps. Example end-user effects are poor performance, intermittent failure, and poor appearance. Example subsequent operation effects are "does not fit," "cannot mount," and "fails to open."
- *Severity.* Assesses the seriousness of the effect of the potential failure mode to the customer. Estimation is typically based on a 1 to 10 scale where the team agrees to a specific evaluation criteria for each ranking value. Table 14.6 shows example evaluation criteria for the automotive industry.
- *Classification.* Includes optional information that classifies special process characteristics that may require additional process controls. Applies when government regulations, safety, and engineering specification concerns exist for the product and/or process. An appropriate character or symbol in this column indicates the need for an entry in the recommended action column to address special controls in the control plan.
- *Potential Causes(s) of Failure.* Describes how failure could occur in terms of a correctable or controllable item. Contains a concise and de-

TABLE 14.6 Severity Evaluation Criteria Example for Process FMEA

Effect	Criteria: Severity of Effect	Ranking
Hazardous— without warning	May endanger machine or assembly operator. Very high severity ranking when a potential failure mode affects safe vehicle operation and/or involves noncompliance with government regulation. Failure will occur without warning.	10
Hazardous— with warning	May endanger machine or assembly operator. Very high severity ranking when a potential failure mode affects safe vehicle operation and/or involves noncompliance with government regulation. Failure will occur with warning.	9
Very high	Major disruption to production line. 100% of product may have to be scrapped. Vehicle/item inoperable, loss of primary function. Customer very dissatisfied.	8
High	Minor disruption to production line. Product may have to be sorted and a portion (less than 100%) scrapped. Vehicle operable, but at a reduced level of performance. Customer dissatisfied.	7
Moderate	Minor disruption to production line. A portion (less than 100%) of the product may have to be scrapped (no sorting). Vehicle/item operable, but some comfort/convenience item(s) inoperable. Customer experiences discomfort.	6
Low	Minor disruption to production line. 100% of product may have to be reworked. Vehicle/item operable, but some comfort/convenience item(s) operable at reduced level of performance. Customer experiences some dissatisfaction.	5
Very low	Minor disruption to production line. The product may have to be sorted and a portion (less than 100%) reworked. Fit & finish/squeak and rattle item does not conform. Defect noticed by most customers.	4
Minor	Minor disruption to production line. A portion (less than 100%) of the product may have to be reworked on-line but out-of-station. Fit & finish/squeak & rattle item does not conform. Defect noticed by average customers.	3
Very minor	Minor disruption to production line. A portion (less than 100%) of the product may have to be reworked on-line but in-station. Fit & finish/squeak & rattle item does not conform. Defect noticed by discriminating customers.	2
None	No effect.	1

Source: FMEA Manual (Chrysler, Ford General Motors Supplier Quality Requirements Task Force), with permission.

scriptive list that is as complete as possible to describe all root causes (not symptom) of failure. The resolution of some causes directly impacts the failure mode. In other situations a DOE determines the major and most easily controlled root causes. Includes causes such human error, improper cure time, and missing part.

- *Occurrence.* Estimates the frequency of occurrence without consideration to failure detecting measures. Described is the number of anticipated failures during the process execution. Consideration to statistical data from similar processes improves the accuracy of ranking values. Alternative subjective assessments use descriptive words to describe rankings. Table 14.7 shows example occurrence criteria.

- *Current Process Controls.* Describes controls that can prevent failure mode from occurring or detect occurrence of the failure mode. Includes control methods such as SPC and Poke-Yoke (fixture error proofing) at the subject or subsequent operations. The preferred method of control is prevention or reduction in the frequency of the cause/mechanism or the failure mode/effect. The next preferred method of control is detection of the cause/mechanism which leads to corrective actions. The least preferred method of control is detection of the failure mode.

- *Detection.* Assesses the probability to detect a potential cause/mechanism from process weakness or the subsequent failure mode before the

TABLE 14.7 Occurrence Evaluation Criteria Example for Process FMEA

Probability of Failure	Possible Failure Rates	C_{pk}	Ranking
Very high: Failure is almost inevitable.	≥ 1 in 2	<0.33	10
	1 in 3	≥ 0.33	9
High: Generally associated with processes similar to previous processes that have often failed.	1 in 8	≥ 0.51	8
	1 in 20	≥ 0.67	7
Moderate: Generally associated with processes similar to previous processes which have experienced occasional failures, but not in major proportions.	1 in 80	≥ 0.83	6
	1 in 400	≥ 1.00	5
	1 in 2000	≥ 1.17	4
Low: Isolated failures associated with similar processes.	1 in 15,000	≥ 1.33	3
Very low: Only isolated failures associated with almost identical processes.	1 in 150,000	≥ 1.50	2
Remote: Failure is unlikely. No failures ever associated with almost identical processes.	≤ 1 in 1,500,000	≥ 1.67	1

Source: FMEA Manual (Chrysler, Ford General Motors Supplier Quality Requirements Task Force), with permission.

part/component leaves the manufacturing operation. Ranking values consider the probability of detection when failure occurs. Table 14.8 shows example detection evaluation criteria.

- *Risk Priority Number* (*RPN*). Product of severity, occurrence, and detection rankings. The ranking of RPN prioritizes design concerns; however, issues with a low RPN still deserve special attention if the severity ranking is high.

- *Recommended Action(s)*. Intent of this entry is to institute actions that lower the occurrence, severity, and/or detection rankings of the highest RPN failure modes. Example actions include DOE to improve the understanding of causes and control charts to improve the focus of defect prevention/continuous improvement activities. Teams should focus on activities that lead to the prevention of defects (i.e., occurrence ranking reduction) rather than improvement of detection methodologies (i.e., detection ranking reduction). Teams should institute corrective action to

TABLE 14.8 Detection Evaluation Criteria Example for Process FMEA

Detection	Criteria: Likelihood that the Existence of a Defect will be Detected by Process Controls Before Next or Subsequent Process, or Before a Part or Component Leaves the Manufacturing or Assembly Location	Ranking
Almost impossible	No known control(s) available to detect failure mode.	10
Very remote	Very remote likelihood that current control(s) will detect failure mode.	9
Remote	Remote likelihood that current control(s) will detect failure mode.	8
Very low	Very low likelihood that current control(s) will detect failure mode.	7
Low	Low likelihood that current control(s) will detect failure mode.	6
Moderate	Moderate likelihood that current control(s) will detect failure mode.	5
Moderately high	Moderately high likelihood that current control(s) will detect failure mode.	4
High	High likelihood that current control(s) will detect failure mode.	3
Very high	Very high likelihood that current control(s) will detect failure mode.	2
Almost certain	Current control(s) is almost certain to detect the failure mode. Reliable detection controls are known with similar processes.	1

Source: FMEA Manual (Chrysler, Ford General Motors Supplier Quality Requirements Task Force), with permission.

identified potential failure modes where the effect is a hazard to manufacturing/assembly personnel. Severity reduction requires a revision in the design and/or process. "None" indicates there are no recommended actions.

- *Responsibility for Recommended Action.* Documents the organization and individual responsible for recommended action and target completion date.
- *Actions Taken.* Describes implementation action and effective date.
- *Resulting RPN.* Contains the recalculated RPN resulting from corrective actions that affected previous severity, occurrence, and detection rankings. Blanks indicate no action.

The responsible process engineer follows-up to ensure the adequate implementation of all recommended actions. An FMEA should include design changes and other relevant actions, even after the start of production. Table 14.9 exemplifies a completed process FMEA that has an RPN trigger number of 150, along with a trigger severity number of 7. Table 14.10 exemplifies another completed FMEA with a trigger action RPN number of 130.

14.6 EXERCISES

1. *Catapult Exercise:* Create an FMEA of the catapult shot process. Consider that an operator injury will occur if the ball drops out of the holder during loading, machine damage will occur if a rubber band breaks, and there is an additional specification of the right and left distance from the tape measure (e.g., ± 2 in.).

2. Conduct an FMEA of a pencil. Consider that the function is to make a black mark. Requirements could include that it is to make a mark, it marks a black color, and it does not mark intermittently. Failure mode would then be that it makes no mark at all, mark is not black in color, and it marks intermittently.

3. Conduct an FMEA on implementing Six Sigma within an organization.

4. Describe how the techniques within this chapter are useful and can be applied to S^4 projects.

TABLE 14.9 Example: Potential Failure Mode and Effects Analysis (Process FMEA)

FMEA Type (Design or Process): Process	Project Name/Description: Cheetah/Change surface finish of part		Date (Orig.): 4/14
Responsibility: Paula Hinkel	Prepared By: Paula Hinkel		Date (Rev.): 6/15
Core Team: Sam Smith, Harry Adams, Hilton Dean, Harry Hawkins, Sue Watkins			Date (Key):

Process Function/Requirements (Item/Function)	Potential Failure Mode	Potential Effect(s) of Failure	Sev	Class	Potential Cause(s)/Mechanism(s) of Failure	Occur	Current Controls	Detec	RPN	Recommended Actions	Responsibility and Target Completion Date	Actions Taken	Sev	Occur	Detec	RPN
Solder dipping	Excessive solder/solder wire protrusion	Short to shield cover	9		Flux wire termination	6	100% inspection	3	162	Automation/DOE/100% chk with go/no go gauge	Sam Smith 6/4	Done	9	4	2	72
	Interlock base damage	Visual defects	7		Long solder time	8	Automatic solder tool	3	168	Automation/DOE/define visual criteria	Harry Adams 5/15	Done	7	4	2	56
					High temp	8	Automatic solder tool/SPC	3	168	Automation/DOE	Hilton Dean 5/15	Done	7	4	2	56
	Delamination of interlock base	Visual defects	7		See interlock base damage	8	Automatic solder tool/SPC	3	168	Automation/DOE	Sue Watkins 5/15	Done	7	4	2	56
	Oxidization of golden plating pins	Contact problem/no signal	8		Moisture in interlock base	5	No	7	245	Inform supplier to control molding cond.	Harry Hawkins 5/15	Done	7	2	7	98
					Not being cleaned in time	7	Clean in 30 minutes after solder dip	5	280	Improve quality of plating define criteria with customer	Sam Smith 5/15	Done	8	2	5	80
Marking	Marking permanency test	Legible marking/customer unsatisfaction	6		Marking ink	4	SPC	2	48	None						
					Curing	5	UV energy and SPC	3	90	None						
					Smooth marking surface	8	None	6	288	Rough surface	Sam Smith 5/15	Change interlock texture surface	6	3	6	108

Source: Pulse, a Technitrol Company, San Diego, CA (Jim Fish and Mary McDonald).

TABLE 14.10 Example: Potential Failure Mode and Effects Analysis (Process FMEA)

FMEA Type (Design or Process):	Project Name/Description: Business operations of A to Z imports		Date (Orig.): 6/11
Responsibility:	Prepared By: KC		Date (Rev.): 7/31
Core Team: KC, JG, LM			Date (Key):

Design FMEA (Item/Function) Process FMEA (Function/Requirements)	Potential Failure Mode	Potential Effect(s) of Failure	Sev	Class	Potential Cause(s)/Mechanism(s) of Failure	Occur	Current Controls	Detec	RPN	Recommended Actions	Responsibility and Target Completion Date	Actions Taken	Sev	Occur	Detec	RPN
Business Operations	Shut down	Loss of income/bankruptcy	9		Tornado hits location	3	None	10	270	Install weather channel radio in store, and keep on during store hours	JG 7/8	Installed and tested	9	3	2	54
			9		Law suit by visitor hurt in store during visit	3	Insurance coverage against accidents in store	2	54	None						
			9		Law suit by visitor owing to faulty merchandise	5	Warning labels on merchandise	2	90	None						
			9		Electrical fire burns down store	2	Fire extinguishers and sprinklers	10	180	Install ground fault interruptors, and overload/thermal protection on all high wattage fixtures	LM 6/28	Installed GFIs and thermal protection	9	2	1	18
			9		IRS audit shows misreporting of finances	5	CPA audits accounts at tax time	4	180	Change procedure to allow closing of books every 6 months, and CPA to audit the same	KC 7/15	Procedure changed, accounting personnel and CPA informed	9	2	2	36
			9		Excessive competition	5	Agreement with property owners on limiting number of import stores	2	90	None						

Item	Failure Mode	Sev	Potential Cause	Occ	Current Controls	Det	RPN	Recommended Action	Resp / Date	Action Taken	Sev	Occ	Det	RPN
Earnings growth does not meet targets	Delayed loan repayments	9	Loss of lease	10	Rental agreement on month to month basis, automatically renews	10	900	Negotiate with leasing company to change lease agreement to yearly	KC 7/19	Talked matter over with property owners, obtained verbal assurance, but lease stays month to month	9	10	10	900
		6	Sales staff impolite	4	Job interview at time of hiring	5	120	Institute sales training of new hires for half day in addition to existing training. Do not assign to floor if candidate's performance in sales training is suspect	KC 8/2	Sales training module added to existing training package	6	2	2	24
		6	Excessive competition	5	Agreement with property owners on limiting number of import stores	2	60	None						
		6	Supplier delays owing to late payments	3	None	10	180	Conduct FMEA on this cause, treating it as a failure mode itself						
		6	Local economy slows	5	None	10	300	Monitor area growth thru quarterly checks with the local Chamber of Commerce	JG 7/15	Obtained population growth for city, and income statistics for quarter ending March 31st.	6	5	2	60
		6	Store untidy	9	Employees have standing orders to attend customers first; and upkeep of store second.	1	54	None						

TABLE 14.10 (Continued)

Design FMEA (Item/Function) Process FMEA (Function/Requirements)	Potential Failure Mode	Potential Effect(s) of Failure	Class	Sev	Potential Cause(s)/Mechanism(s) of Failure	Occur	Current Controls	Detec	RPN	Recommended Actions	Responsibility and Target Completion Date	Actions Taken	Sev	Occur	Detec	RPN
				6	Delayed or lost shipments from supplier	7	Freight forwarder faxes bill of lading when merchandise is loaded on ship/air. Next contact is when goods arrive at destination	10	420	Require freight forwarder to intimate status of shipment every 3 days	KC 7/28	Got agreement with freight forwarder; additional charge of 2.5% on freight agreed upon	6	7	3	126
				6	Defective merchandise	4	Inspection prior to putting merchandise on shelves	2	48	None						
				6	Theft of cash by employees from cash registers	7	Logs of employee names managing cash, by date and time	10	420	Supervisors to start accounting for cash with employees when they start work and at every changeover.	KC 8/3	Procedures put in place to accomplish cash management as recommended	6	2	2	24
				6	Theft of merchandise	5	Store attendants to monitor customers when feasible	8	240	Install magnetic theft prevention tags on merchandise and detectors at store entrance	LM 8/15	Completed on items with ticket prices over $20; rest will be completed by 8/15	6	5	1	30
				6	Wrong merchandise leading to slower inventory turns	5	Visit wholesale markets twice/year to keep up with current trends	3	90	None						
				6	Accounting errors	5	Books audited by CPA at tax time	4	120	None						

Source: Rai Chowdhary.

274

PART III

S⁴ ANALYSIS PHASE

This part (Chapters 15–26) addresses the analysis of data for the purpose of gaining knowledge about causal relationships. Information from this analysis can give insight to the sources of variability and unsatisfactory performance, which can be useful to improve processes. Tools included within this section include visualization of data inference testing, variance components, correlation analysis, and analysis of variance.

15

VISUALIZATION OF DATA

In previous chapters, graphical techniques were discussed to visually quantify information. These techniques included histograms, time series plots, scatter diagrams, probability plotting, control charts, cause-and-effect diagrams, and Pareto charts. Chapter 14 described techniques for determining by consensus key process input and output variables. Chapter 14 also discussed the collection of data to assess relationships between key process input variables and key process output variables.

This chapter describes additional graphical and charting techniques that expand upon these charting capabilities. These techniques can give insight to the relationships between key process input variables and key process output variables. Through the visualization offered by these techniques we can assess a lot of information about the process without modifying the process and gain insight to where we should focus our efforts for improvement opportunities.

We can look for differences between samples, interrelationships between variables, and change over time. When relationships are noted we can then test these hypothesis statistically. Knowledge gained from these tests can give us insight to what should be done differently in the process, key process input variable control needs, and DOE opportunities.

15.1 MULTI-VARI CHARTS

Within a discrete manufacturing environment, contributors to overall variability of a response include differences between time periods production tool differences, part-to-part variations, and within-part variability. Within a continuous flow manufacturing process, contributors to overall variability include difference within shifts, across shifts, and across days/weeks/months. Multi-vari charts allow the visual decomposition into components and the identification of the component that affects variability the most.

Considerations when constructing a multi-vari chart are as follows:

- If there are many measurements within a part, the average, highest, and lowest values could be used.
- Reconstruction of the chart using various arrangements for the axes can aid in the detection of patterns and relationships.
- Connecting mean values on the chart can aid the visual representation.

Visual observations can lead to the use of other analytical tools that test hypotheses. These techniques include variance components analysis and analysis of means, which are later discussed within this text. Information gained from these analyses can yield to effective targeting of process improvement efforts.

15.2   EXAMPLE 15.1: MULTI-VARI CHART OF INJECTION-MOLDING DATA

An injection-molding process made plastic cylindrical connectors (Taylor 1991). Every hour for three hours, two parts were selected from each of four mold cavities. Measurements were made at each end and the middle. The data are shown in Table 15.1, and the multi-vari chart is shown in Figure 15.1.

By observation from the multi-vari chart, it appears that:

- Time periods do not appear to be different.
- Differences occur between cavities for a given time period (largest variation source).

Cavities 2, 3, and 4 appear to have thicker ends, while cavity 1 has a slight taper. Sixteen of the 18 parts from cavities 2, 3, and 4 exhibit a "V" pattern.

Another option for presentation of multi-vari information is to use a mean effects plot of each variable source consideration.

These data will later be analyzed as a statistical hypothesis using Analysis of Means and Variance of Components techniques.

15.3   BOX PLOT

A box plot (or box and whisker plot) is useful to pictorially describe various aspects of data. Box plots can describe one set of data or visually show differences between characteristics of a data set.

TABLE 15.1 Multi-vari Chart Injection-Molding Data

Part	Location	Time 1 Cavity				Time 2 Cavity				Time 3 Cavity			
		1	2	3	4	1	2	3	4	1	2	3	4
1	Top	0.2522	0.2501	0.2510	0.2489	0.2518	0.2498	0.2516	0.2494	0.2524	0.2488	0.2511	0.2490
	Middle	0.2523	0.2497	0.2507	0.2481	0.2512	0.2484	0.2496	0.2485	0.2518	0.2486	0.2504	0.2479
	Bottom	0.2518	0.2501	0.2516	0.2485	0.2501	0.2492	0.2507	0.2492	0.2512	0.2497	0.2503	0.2488
2	Top	0.2514	0.2501	0.2508	0.2485	0.2520	0.2499	0.2503	0.2483	0.2517	0.2496	0.2503	0.2485
	Middle	0.2513	0.2494	0.2495	0.2478	0.2514	0.2495	0.2501	0.2482	0.2509	0.2487	0.2497	0.2483
	Bottom	0.2505	0.2495	0.2507	0.2484	0.2513	0.2501	0.2504	0.2491	0.2513	0.250	0.2492	0.2495

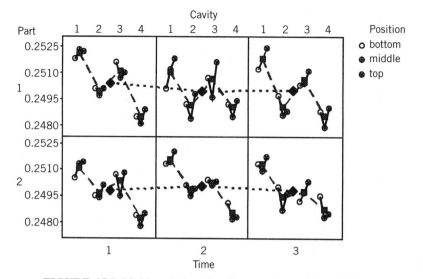

FIGURE 15.1 Multi-vari chart for diameter by position within part.

Figure 15.2 describes the common characteristics of a box plot. The box displays the lower and upper quartiles (the 25th and 75th percentiles) and the median (the 50th percentile) as a horizontal line within the box. The whiskers are then often extended to

Lower Limit: $Q_1 - 1.5(Q_3 - Q_1)$
Upper Limit: $Q_3 + 1.5(Q_3 - Q_1)$

For this case, points outside the lower and upper limits are considered to be outliers and are designated with asterisks (*).

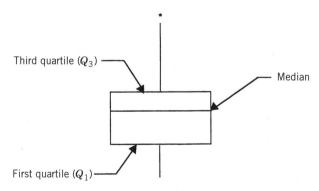

FIGURE 15.2 Box plot characteristics.

15.4   EXAMPLE 15.2: PLOTS OF INJECTION-MOLDING DATA

This example expands upon the previous multi-vari chart analysis of data in Table 15.1. Techniques applied are box plot, marginal plot main effects plot, and interaction plot.

The box plot in Figure 15.3 shows the differences in the sample by cavity. The marginal plot of the data shown in Figure 15.4 permits as an option, the visualization of the distribution of data in both the x and y direction. The main effects plot shown in Figure 15.5 quantifies the average difference noted between cavities.

From the multi-vari chart it appeared that parts from cavity 2, 3, and 4 were wider at the ends, while cavity number one had a taper. This observation basically indicates an interaction between cavity and position, which will be shown as out of parallel lines within an interaction plot (interaction is discussed in more depth later in this text). The interaction plot shown in Figure 15.6 is consistent with this multi-vari observation since the lines are slightly out of parallel and that the center dimension is lowest for cavities 2, 3, and 4, while the center measurement in cavity 1 is midway. From this plot we get a pictorial quantification of the average difference between these three cavities as a function of position.

15.5   S⁴ ASSESSMENT

Presenting information in the form of graphs and charts can be very enlightening. Visual representation of data can give insight to erroneous data points or why some statistical tests might not be valid. The techniques can give

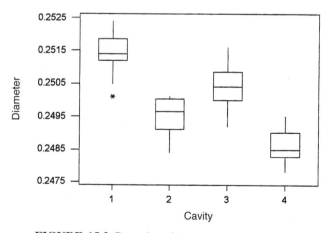

FIGURE 15.3 Box plot of diameter versus cavity.

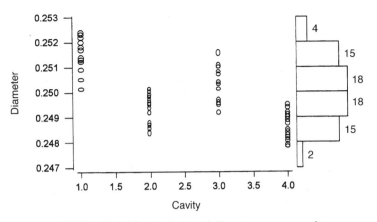

FIGURE 15.4 Marginal plot of diameter versus cavity.

information that leads to the discovery and implementation of very beneficial process improvements. In addition, visual representations can be used to present information in a form that can quickly be understood by others.

However, visual representations of data should not be used alone to formulate conclusions. What appears to be an important observation through a visual representation could simply be something occurring that has a relatively high probable chance of occurring. Hence, it is important to test observation theories using hypothesis techniques before formulating conclusions and action plans.

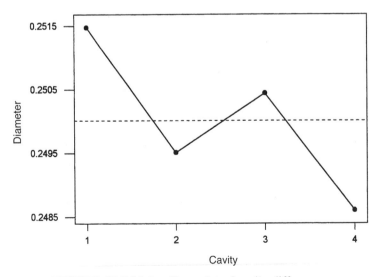

FIGURE 15.5 Main effects plot of cavity differences.

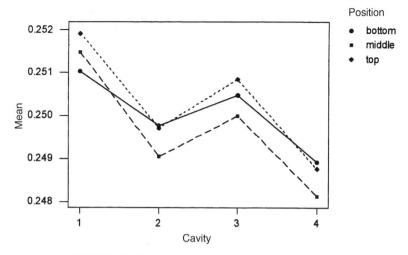

FIGURE 15.6 Interaction plot of cavity and position.

Another concern can arise when attempting to formulate conclusions from observed data. Consider the situation where temperature was monitored within a process and not found to be an important factor that affects a key process output variable. One might then disregard the possibility of changing the temperature of a process to improve the response of the key process output variable. We need to remember that the described visual and analytical tools typically consider only the current operating range of the key process input variables. In other words, changing the temperature of a process to a value either higher or lower than its current operating value could prove to be a very beneficial improvement. DOE techniques can complement the described techniques by offering a means to extend the knowledge gained to other factors and levels of factors beyond normal operating conditions.

The *wise* implementation of graphical. analytical hypothesis tests, DOE techniques, and other statistical tools can be a very powerful combination yielding very beneficial process measurement and improvement activities.

15.6   EXERCISES

1. *Catapult Exercise Data Analysis:* Using the catapult exercise data sets from Chapter 4, create a multi-vari chart and box plot of the two data sets. Consider operator as one of the factors.

2. An experiment was conducted where each student recorded his or her height, weight, gender, smoking preference, usual activity level, and resting pulse. Then they all flipped coins, and those whose coins came up heads ran in place for one minute. Then the entire class recorded their pulses

once more (Minitab 1998).

Create a multi-vari chart that gives insight to the affect of factors.

Column	Name	Count	Description
Cl	Pulse1	92	First pulse rate
C2	Pulse2	92	Second pulse rate
C3	Ran	92	1 = ran in place
			2 = did not run in place
C4	Smokes	92	1 = smokes regularly
			2 = does not smoke regularly
C5	Sex	92	1 = male 2 = female
C6	Height	92	Height in inches
C7	Weight	92	Weight in pounds
C8	Activity	92	Usual level of physical activity:
			1 = slight
			2 = moderate
			3 = a lot

Pulse1	Pulse2	Ran	Smokes	Sex	Height	Weight	Activity
64	88	1	2	1	66.00	140	2
58	70	1	2	1	72.00	145	2
62	76	1	1	1	73.50	160	3
66	78	1	1	1	73.00	190	1
64	80	1	2	1	69.00	155	2
74	84	1	2	1	73.00	165	1
84	84	1	2	1	72.00	150	3
68	72	1	2	1	74.00	190	2
62	75	1	2	1	72.00	195	2
76	118	1	2	1	71.00	138	2
90	94	1	1	1	74.00	160	1
80	96	1	2	1	72.00	155	2
92	84	1	1	1	70.00	153	3
68	76	1	2	1	67.00	145	2
60	76	1	2	1	71.00	170	3
62	58	1	2	1	72.00	175	3
66	82	1	1	1	69.00	175	2
70	72	1	1	1	73.00	170	3
68	76	1	1	1	74.00	180	2
72	80	1	2	1	66.00	135	3
70	106	1	2	1	71.00	170	2
74	76	1	2	1	70.00	157	2
66	102	1	2	1	70.00	130	2
70	94	1	1	1	75.00	185	2
96	140	1	2	2	61.00	140	2
62	100	1	2	2	66.00	120	2
78	104	1	1	2	68.00	130	2
82	100	1	2	2	68.00	138	2

100	115	1	1	2	63.00	121	2
68	112	1	2	2	70.00	125	2
96	116	1	2	2	68.00	116	2
78	118	1	2	2	69.00	145	2
88	110	1	1	2	69.00	150	2
62	98	1	1	2	62.75	112	2
80	128	1	2	2	68.00	125	2
62	62	2	2	1	74.00	190	1
60	62	2	2	1	71.00	155	2
72	74	2	1	1	69.00	170	2
62	66	2	2	1	70.00	155	2
76	76	2	2	1	72.00	215	2
68	66	2	1	1	67.00	150	2
54	56	2	1	1	69.00	145	2
74	70	2	2	1	73.00	155	3
74	74	2	2	1	73.00	155	2
68	68	2	2	1	71.00	150	3
72	74	2	1	1	68.00	155	3
68	64	2	2	1	69.50	150	3
82	84	2	1	1	73.00	180	2
64	62	2	2	1	75.00	160	3
58	58	2	2	1	66.00	135	3
54	50	2	2	1	69.00	160	2
70	62	2	1	1	66.00	130	2
62	68	2	1	1	73.00	155	2
48	54	2	1	1	68.00	150	0
76	76	2	2	1	74.00	148	3
88	84	2	2	1	73.50	155	2
70	70	2	2	1	70.00	150	2
90	88	2	1	1	67.00	140	2
78	76	2	2	1	72.00	180	3
70	66	2	1	1	75.00	190	2
90	90	2	2	1	68.00	145	1
92	94	2	1	1	69.00	150	2
60	70	2	1	1	71.50	164	2
72	70	2	2	1	71.00	140	2
68	68	2	2	1	72.00	142	3
84	84	2	2	1	69.00	136	2
74	76	2	2	1	67.00	123	2
68	66	2	2	1	68.00	155	2
84	84	2	2	2	66.00	130	2
61	70	2	2	2	65.50	120	2
64	60	2	2	2	66.00	130	3
94	92	2	1	2	62.00	131	2
60	66	2	2	2	62.00	120	2
72	70	2	2	2	63.00	118	2
58	56	2	2	2	67.00	125	2
88	74	2	1	2	65.00	135	2
66	72	2	2	2	66.00	125	2

84	80	2	2	2	65.00	118	1
62	66	2	2	2	65.00	122	3
66	76	2	2	2	65.00	115	2
80	74	2	2	2	64.00	102	2
78	78	2	2	2	67.00	115	2
68	68	2	2	2	69.00	150	2
72	68	2	2	2	68.00	110	2
82	80	2	2	2	63.00	116	1
76	76	2	1	2	62.00	108	3
87	84	2	2	2	63.00	95	3
90	92	2	1	2	64.00	125	1
78	80	2	2	2	68.00	133	1
68	68	2	2	2	62.00	110	2
86	84	2	2	2	67.00	150	3
76	76	2	2	2	61.75	108	2

3. Create a Box plot of the previous data set with pulse2 as the response and sex as the category.

4. Describe how the techniques within this chapter are useful and can be applied to S^4 projects.

16

CONFIDENCE INTERVALS AND HYPOTHESIS TESTS

From a random sample of a population we can estimate characteristics of the population. For example, earlier in this text we discussed how the mean of a sample $(\bar{x})$ is a point estimate of the population mean (μ). In this chapter we initiate discussion on confidence interval, which gives a probabilistic range of values for a true population characteristic from sampled data. Application of the central limit theorem to this situation will also be illustrated.

This chapter expands upon the previous discussion of hypothesis testing. Hypothesis tests address the situation where we need to make a selection between two choices from sampled data (or information). Because we are dealing with sampled data there is always the possibility (by the luck of the draw) that our sample was not an accurate representation of the population. Hypothesis tests address this risk.

16.1 CONFIDENCE INTERVAL STATEMENTS

As noted earlier, the mean of a sample does not normally equate exactly to the mean of the population from which the sample is taken. An experimenter has more "confidence" that a sample mean, for example, is close to the population mean whenever the sample size is large, as opposed to whenever a sample size is small. Statistical procedures quantify the uncertainty of a sample via a confidence interval statement.

A confidence interval can be single-sided or double-sided. Plus, a confidence interval statement can relate to other characteristics besides mean values (e.g., population variance). The following statements exemplify confidence interval statements on the mean that are single- and double-sided.

$$\mu \leq 8.0 \qquad \text{with 95\% confidence}$$
$$2.0 \leq \mu \leq 8.0 \qquad \text{with 90\% confidence}$$

Similar statements can be made about standard deviation and other population characteristics. Later sections in this text will describe the mechanics of determining confidence intervals for various situations.

16.2 CENTRAL LIMIT THEOREM

The Central Limit Theorem describes an important phenomenon that is a part of the theoretical basis for many procedures. The Central Limit Theorem states that a plot of *sampled mean values* from a population tends to be normally distributed. Figure 16.1 indicates that a plot of the 10 sample mean values from Table 3.3 has the shape of a normal distribution. The distribution shape of mean values taken from a population will tend to be normally distributed even though the underlying distribution is not normal. The standard deviation of this sampling distribution is $s/\sqrt{n}$, where s is the sample standard deviation and n is the sample size. From this relationship we can see that for a given standard deviation the spread of the sampling distribution decreases when sample size increases (i.e., we have more confidence in our results when there is a larger sample size).

The Central Limit Theorem is an important phenomenon that is a part of the theoretical basis to many procedures used in statistics (e.g., calculation of the confidence interval of a sample mean).

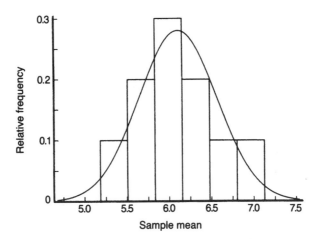

FIGURE 16.1 Plot of sample mean values.

16.3   HYPOTHESIS TESTING

In industrial situations we frequently want to decide whether the parameters of a distribution have particular values or relationships. That is, we may wish to test a hypothesis that the mean or standard deviation of a distribution has a certain value or that the difference between two means is zero. Hypothesis testing procedures are used for these tests. Practical examples include:

1. A manufacturer wishes to introduce a new product. In order to be profitable, they need to be able to manufacture 1200 items during the 200 hours available in the next five weeks. The product can be successfully manufactured if the mean time required to manufacture an item is no more than six hours. The manufacturer can evaluate manufacturability by testing the hypothesis that the mean time for manufacture is equal to six.
2. The same manufacturer is planning to modify the process to decrease the mean time required to manufacture another type of product. The manufacturer can evaluate the effectiveness of the change by testing the hypothesis that the mean manufacturing time is the same before and after the process change.

Both of these situations involve tests on the mean values of populations. Hypothesis tests may also involve the standard deviation or other parameters.
A statistical hypothesis has the following elements:

- A null hypothesis (H_0) that describes the value or relationship being tested
- An alternative hypothesis (H_a)
- A test statistic, or rule, used to decide whether to reject the null hypothesis
- A specified probability value (noted as α) that defines the maximum allowable probability that the null hypothesis will be rejected when it is true
- The power of the test, which is the probability (noted as $[1 - \beta]$) that a null hypothesis will be rejected when it is false
- A sample of observations to be used for testing the hypothesis

The null and alternate hypotheses arise from the problem being addressed. In example 1, the null hypothesis is that the mean time to manufacture an item is equal to six. The item cannot be successfully manufactured if the mean time is larger than six, so the alternate hypothesis is that the mean is greater than six. The mean time to manufacture is noted as μ, and the shorthand notation for the null and alternate hypotheses is

$$H_0: \quad \mu = \mu_0 \quad \text{and} \quad H_a: \quad \mu > \mu_0$$

where $\mu_0 = 6$. The hypothesis in the second example concerns the relationship between two mean values. The null hypothesis is that the mean time to manufacture the item is the same before and after the change. Because the manufacturer wishes to establish the effectiveness of the change, the alternative hypothesis is that the mean time is shorter after the change. If the mean time to manufacturer before the change is μ_1 and the mean time to manufacture after the change is μ_2. The shorthand notation is

$$H_0: \quad \mu_1 = \mu_2 \quad \text{and} \quad H_a: \quad \mu_1 > \mu_2$$

where no values need to be specified for μ_1 and μ_2. Table 16.1 exemplifies various hypothesis formats.

The rule used to test the hypothesis depends on the type of hypothesis being tested. Statisticians have developed good, or even optimal, rules for many situations. Most of these rules are intuitively appealing. To illustrate this, consider example 1, where the usual rule is to reject the null hypothesis if the average of an appropriate sample of manufacturing times is sufficiently larger than six. How much larger? Well, that depends on the allowable probability of making an error.

The result of hypothesis test is a decision to either reject or not reject the null hypothesis; that is, the hypothesis is either rejected or we reserve judgment about it. In practice, we may act as though the null hypothesis is accepted if it is not rejected. Because we do not know the truth, we can make one of the following two possible errors when running a hypothesis test:

1. We can reject a null hypothesis that is in fact true.
2. We can fail to reject a null hypothesis that is false.

The first error is called a type I error, and the second is called a type II error. This relationship is shown in Figure 16.2. Hypothesis tests are designed to control the probabilities of making either of these errors; we do not know

TABLE 16.1 Hypothesis Testing: Single- and Double-Sided Tests on Population Mean

Single-Sided		
$H_0: \mu = \mu_0$		$H_0: \mu = \mu_0$
	or	
$H_a: \mu > \mu_0$		$H_a: \mu < \mu_0$
Double-Sided		
$H_0: \mu = \mu_0$		$H_0: \mu_1 = \mu_2$
	or	
$H_a: \mu \neq \mu_0$		$H_a: \mu_1 \neq \mu_2$

| | | True state of nature | |
		H_0	H_a
Conclusion made	H_0	Correct conclusion	Type II error
	H_a	Type I error	Correct conclusion

FIGURE 16.2 Hypothesis testing error types.

that the result is correct, but we can be assured that the probability of making an error is within acceptable limits. The probability of making a type I error is controlled by establishing a maximum allowable value of the probability, called the level of the test, which is usually denoted by the letter α. The rule used to govern the decision to accept or reject the null hypothesis is selected using the selected value of α.

The probability of making a type II error is usually controlled by selecting an appropriate sample size. Consider example 1 again. If the true mean time to manufacture an item is not six, it can have one of any number of possible values. It could be 6.01, or 6.1 or 7 or 20 or 100 or whatever. To properly design the hypothesis test, the manufacturer selects a possible value that is to be protected against and specifies the probability that the hypothesis should be rejected if the true mean equals the selected value. For example, the manufacturer may decide that the hypothesis mean is 6 and should be rejected with probability 0.85 if the true mean time is 8 or with probability 0.98 if the true time is 9 hours. In common notation these differences of 2 (i.e., 8 − 6 = 2) and 3 (i.e., 9 − 6 = 3) correspond to values for δ. The probability of rejecting for a given vale of μ is called the Power of the Test at μ, and it is one minus the probability of making a type II error (β) at μ. The manufacturer designs the test by selecting a sample size that ensures the desired power at the specified alternative. Sample size selection is discussed in other sections.

Having selected a rule for rejecting the null hypothesis and a sample size, a random sample is selected and used to run the test. Statistical statements about the mean of a population are robust to the data not being normally distributed, while statistical evaluations about population standard deviations may not be robust to a lack of normality.

The parameters α, β, and δ are sometimes referred to as producer's risk, consumer's risk, and an acceptable amount of uncertainty, respectively.

16.4   EXAMPLE 16.1: HYPOTHESIS TESTING

Consider that someone is on trial in a court of law for murder. The person either committed the crime or did not commit the crime. This situation takes the form of a hypothesis test where the null hypothesis is that the person is innocent and the alternate hypothesis is that they are guilty.

Evidence (information) is presented to the jury. The jury then deliberates to make a decision whether the person is guilty or not. If the jury makes the decision that the person is innocent, there is β risk of error. If the jury makes the decision that the person is guilty, there is α risk of error.

To conceptually quantify these two risks within the current court of legal system of a country, consider the random selection of 10,000 murder cases where the suspect was found innocent and 10,000 murder cases where the suspect was found guilty. If we could determine the real truth (whether they did in fact commit murder or not), the risks associated with our current judicial system is estimated to be

$$\alpha = \frac{u}{10,000} \qquad \beta = \frac{v}{10,000}$$

where u is the number of people found guilty who were in fact innocent and v is the number of people not found guilty who were in fact guilty.

16.5 S⁴ ASSESSMENT

It is good practice to "look at the data" in conjunction with making mathematical computations. Probability plotting is a good tool to use when making such an observation. After "looking at the data" it might be determined that the wrong question was initially asked (e.g., a statement about the percentage of population would be more meaningful than a statement about the mean of a population).

Hoerl (1995) states that it is unfortunate that the vast majority of statistics texts and papers focus almost exclusively on deduction (i.e., testing hypothesis or an estimation of parameters in an assumed model). Very little exists in print on how to use induction to revise subject matter theory based on statistical analysis. Deductive reasoning begins with premises (theory) and analytically infers what should be seen in practice, where induction is reasoning from particulars to the general.

Both types of reasoning are required by scientific methodologies. However, statistical education primarily focuses on deduction because it lends more to mathematics. The implication of this is that most texts teach rigorous adherence to preset rules for decision making when covering hypothesis testing. For example, if the null hypothesis is rejected, no mention is even given to the possibility of questioning the original assumptions based on what is seen in the data. However, the primary needs of engineers and scientists is inductive. They need to use data to create generalities, which is an explanation of why statistical techniques are not more widely used within these disciplines.

This test suggests various approaches to create hypotheses. The S⁴ assessment sections at the end of many chapters can be viewed as a challenge to the underlying assumptions of many hypothesis tests. When analyzing data and integrating the statistical techniques described in this text, practitioner should not lose sight of the need to challenge the underlying assumptions of hypothesis tests. It is very important to answer the right question.

16.6 EXERCISES

1. *Catapult Exercise Data Analysis:* Describe the wording of various hypotheses that could be assessed relative to the data that were collected in Chapter 4.

2. *Dice Exercise:* Each person in an S⁴ workshop rolls a die 25 times, records the number of times each number appears, and calculates an average value. The instructor collects from attendees the total number of times each number is rolled and plots the information. Also, average values from all attendees are collected and plotted in a histogram format. Note the shape of each curve.

3. *Cards Exercise:* Each team is given a deck of 52 cards and told to remove the 8, 9, and 10's. The cards are shuffled. Five cards are removed. The face value of these cards are averaged (jack = 11, queen = 12, king = 13, and ace = 1). This is repeated 25 times by each team (removed cards are added to deck before reshuffling). Plot the distribution of mean values. Describe results and what would happen to the shape of the distribution if 10 card values would have been averaged instead of five cards.

4. From the curve of average rolls of the die (or averages of card draws), estimate the range of roll mean values expected for 25 rolls of the die 90% of the time. Describe how the distribution shape of mean values would change if there were 50 rolls of the die.

5. State if a null hypothesis is one-sided or two-sided when evaluating whether the product quality of two suppliers is equal.

6. Describe a decision that you make within your personal life that could be phrased as a hypothesis test.

7. Describe how the techniques within this chapter are useful and can be applied to S⁴ projects.

17

INFERENCES: CONTINUOUS RESPONSE

This chapter covers random sampling evaluations from a population that has a continuous response. An example of a continuous response is the amount of tire tread that exists after 40,000 kilometers (km) of automobile usage. One tire might, for example, have 6.0 millimeters (mm) of remaining tread while another tire might measure 5.5 mm.

In this chapter the estimation of population mean and standard deviation from sampled data is discussed in conjunction with probability plotting.

17.1 SUMMARIZING SAMPLED DATA

Classically, the analysis of sampled data taken from a continuous response population has focused on determining a sample mean $(\bar{x})$ and standard deviation (s), along with perhaps confidence interval statements that can relate both of these sampled characteristics to the actual population values (μ and σ, respectively). Experimental considerations of this type answer some basic questions about the sample and population. However, often a person responsible for either generating a criterion specification or making a pass/fail decision does not consider the other information that data analyses can convey. For example, an experiment might be able to indicate that 90% of the automobiles using a certain type of tire will have at least 4.9 mm of tire tread after 40,000 km. This type of statement can be more informative than a statement that only relates to the mean tire tread after 40,000 km.

17.2   SAMPLE SIZE: HYPOTHESIS TEST OF A MEAN CRITERION FOR CONTINUOUS RESPONSE DATA

One of the most traditional questions asked of a statistical consultant is, "What sample size do I need (to verity this mean criterion)?" The following equation (Diamond 1989) can be used to determine the sample size (n) to evaluate a hypothesis test criterion at given values for α, β, and δ (i.e., producer's risk. consumer's risk, and an acceptable amount of uncertainty, respectively). Sometimes the population standard deviation (σ) is known from previous test activity; however, this is not generally true. For this second situation, δ can be conveniently expressed in terms of σ:

$$n = (U_\alpha + U_\beta)^2 \frac{\sigma^2}{\delta^2}$$

In this equation, U_β is determined from the single-sided Table B in Appendix D. If the alternate hypothesis is single-sided (e.g., $\mu <$ criterion), U_α is also determined from Table B; however, if the alternate hypothesis is double-sided (e.g., $\mu <$ or $>$ criterion), U_α is determined from Table C.

If the standard deviation is not known, the sample size should be adjusted using (Diamond 1989)

$$n = (t_\alpha + t_\beta)^2 \frac{s^2}{\delta^2}$$

In this equation, t_β is determined from the single-sided Table D. If the alternate hypothesis is single-sided (e.g., $\mu <$ criterion), t_α is also determined from Table D; however, if the alternate hypothesis is double-sided (e.g., $\mu <$ or $>$ criterion), t_α is determined from Table E.

An alternative approach for sample size calculations is described later in this chapter.

17.3   EXAMPLE 17.1: SAMPLE SIZE DETERMINATION FOR A MEAN CRITERION TEST

A stereo amplifier output power level is to be on the average at least 100 watts (W) per channel. Determine the sample size that is needed to verify this criterion given the following:

$\alpha = 0.1$, which from Table B yields $U_\alpha = 1.282$.
$\beta = 0.05$, which from Table B yields $U_\beta = 1.645$.
$\delta = 0.5\sigma$.

Substitution yields

$$n = (1.282 + 1.645)^2 \frac{\sigma^2}{(0.5\sigma)^2} = 34.26$$

Rounding upward to a whole number yields a sample size of 35.

If the standard deviation is not known, this sample size needs to be adjusted, where the number of degrees of freedom for the t-table value equals 34 (i.e., $35 - 1$). Interpolation in Table D yields to $t_{0.1;34} = 1.307$ and $t_{0.05;34} = 1.692$; hence

$$n = (1.692 + 1.307)^2 \frac{s^2}{(0.5s)^2} = 35.95$$

Rounding upward to a whole number yields a sample of 36. This equation could be iterated again with this new sample size; however, this is not normally necessary.

Because individuals want to make sure that they are making the correct decision, they often specify very low α and β values, along with a low δ value. This can lead to a sample size that is unrealistically large with normal test time and resource constraints. When this happens, the experimenter may need to accept more risk than he or she was originally willing to tolerate. The sample size can then be recalculated permitting the larger risks (i.e., a higher α and/or β value) and/or an increase in uncertainty (i.e., a higher δ value).

17.4   CONFIDENCE INTERVALS ON THE MEAN AND HYPOTHESIS TEST CRITERIA ALTERNATIVES

After sample mean ($\bar{x}$) and standard deviation (s) are determined from the data. Table 17.1 summaries the equations used to determine from these population estimates the intervals that contain the true mean (μ) at a confidence level of $[(1 - \alpha)100]$. The equations in this table utilize the t tables (as opposed to the U tables) whenever the population standard deviation is not known. Because of the Central Limit Theorem, the equations noted in this table are robust to the data not being from a normal distribution.

If a sample size is calculated before conducting the experiment using desired values of α, β, and δ, the null hypothesis is not rejected if the criterion is contained within the appropriate confidence interval for μ. This decision is made with the β risk of error that was used in calculating the sample size (given the underlying δ input level of uncertainty). However, if the criterion

TABLE 17.1 Mean Confidence Interval Equations

	Single-Sided	Double-Sided
σ Known	$\mu \leq \bar{x} + \dfrac{U_\alpha \sigma}{\sqrt{n}}$ or $\mu \geq \bar{x} - \dfrac{U_\alpha \sigma}{\sqrt{n}}$	$\bar{x} - \dfrac{U_\alpha \sigma}{\sqrt{n}} \leq \mu \leq \bar{x} + \dfrac{U_\alpha \sigma}{\sqrt{n}}$
σ Unknown	$\mu \leq \bar{x} + \dfrac{t_\alpha s}{\sqrt{n}}$ or $\mu \geq \bar{x} - \dfrac{t_\alpha s}{\sqrt{n}}$	$\bar{x} - \dfrac{t_\alpha s}{\sqrt{n}} \leq \mu \leq \bar{x} + \dfrac{t_\alpha s}{\sqrt{n}}$
Using reference tables	U_α: Table B t_α: Table D[a]	U_α: Table C t_α: Table E[a]

[a] $v = n - 1$ (i.e., the number of degrees of freedom used in the t table is equal to one less than the sample size).

is not contained within the interval, then the null hypothesis is rejected. This decision is made with α risk of error.

Other methods can be used when setting up a hypothesis test criterion. Consider, for example, the alternative hypothesis (H_a) of $\mu > \mu_a$, where μ_a is a product specification criterion. From Table 17.1 it can be determined that

$$\bar{x}_{\text{criterion}} = \mu_a + \frac{t_\alpha s}{\sqrt{n}}$$

When $\bar{x}$ is greater than the test $\bar{x}_{\text{criterion}}$, the null hypothesis is rejected. When $\bar{x}$ is less than $\bar{x}_{\text{criterion}}$, the null hypothesis is not rejected. An alternative approach for this problem is to use the equation form

$$t_0 = \frac{(\bar{x} - \mu_a)\sqrt{n}}{s}$$

where the null hypothesis is rejected if $t_0 > t_\alpha$.

The above equations apply to planned statistical hypothesis testing where a decision was made prior to test start about α, β, and δ. However, in reality, data are often taken without making these pretest decisions. The described equations are still useful to make an assessment of the population, as described within the following example.

17.5   EXAMPLE 17.2: CONFIDENCE INTERVALS ON THE MEAN

Consider the 16 data points from sample 1 of Table 3.3, which had a sample mean of 5.77 and a sample standard deviation of 2.41. Determine the various 90% confidence statements that can be made relative to the true population mean given that the standard deviation is known to equal 2.0 and then as an unknown parameter.

Given that σ is known to equal 2.0 and the U_α values, the single-sided and double-sided 90% confidence (i.e., $\alpha = 0.1$) interval equations are as shown below. The U_α value of 1.282 is from the single-sided Table B, given $\alpha = 0.1$. The U_α value of 1.645 is from the double-sided Table C, given $\alpha = 0.1$.

Single-Sided Scenarios:

$$\mu \leq \bar{x} + \frac{U_\alpha \sigma}{\sqrt{n}} \qquad\qquad \mu \geq \bar{x} - \frac{U_\alpha \sigma}{\sqrt{n}}$$

$$\mu \leq 5.77 + \frac{1.282(2.0)}{\sqrt{16}} \qquad\qquad \mu \geq 5.77 - \frac{1.282(2.0)}{\sqrt{16}}$$

$$\mu \leq 5.77 + 0.64 \qquad\qquad \mu \geq 5.77 - 0.64$$

$$\mu \leq 6.41 \qquad\qquad \mu \geq 5.13$$

Double-Sided Scenario:

$$\bar{x} - \frac{U_\alpha \sigma}{\sqrt{n}} \leq \mu \leq \bar{x} + \frac{U_\alpha \sigma}{\sqrt{n}}$$

$$5.77 - \frac{1.645(2.0)}{\sqrt{16}} \leq \mu \leq 5.77 + \frac{1.645(2.0)}{\sqrt{16}}$$

$$5.77 - 0.82 \leq \mu \leq 5.77 + 0.82$$

$$4.95 \leq \mu \leq 6.59$$

If we consider that we do not know the standard deviation, the resulting equations for single- and double-sided 90% confidence intervals are the following. The t_α value of 1.341 is from the single-sided Table D, given $\alpha = 0.1$ and $v = 16 - 1 = 15$. The t_α value of 1.753 is from the double-sided Table E, given $\alpha = 0.1$ and $v = 16 - 1 = 15$.

Single-Sided Scenarios:

$$\mu \leq \bar{x} + \frac{t_\alpha s}{\sqrt{n}} \qquad\qquad \mu \geq \bar{x} - \frac{t_\alpha s}{\sqrt{n}}$$

$$\mu \leq 5.77 + \frac{(1.341)(2.41)}{\sqrt{16}} \qquad\qquad \mu \geq 5.77 - \frac{(1.341)(2.41)}{\sqrt{16}}$$

$$\mu \leq 5.77 + 0.81 \qquad\qquad \mu \geq 5.77 - 0.81$$

$$\mu \leq 6.58 \qquad\qquad \mu \geq 4.96$$

Double-Sided Scenario:

$$\bar{x} - \frac{t_\alpha s}{\sqrt{n}} \le \mu \le \bar{x} + \frac{t_\alpha s}{\sqrt{n}}$$

$$5.77 - \frac{1.753(2.41)}{\sqrt{16}} \le \mu \le 5.77 + \frac{1.753(2.41)}{\sqrt{16}}$$

$$5.77 - 1.06 \le \mu \le 5.77 + 1.06$$

$$4.71 \le \mu \le 6.83$$

The mean and standard deviation used in the preceding calculations were randomly created from a normal distribution where $\mu = 6.0$. Note that this true mean value is contained in these confidence intervals. When the confidence interval is 90%, we would expect the interval to contain the true value 90% of the time that we take random samples and analyze the data.

17.6   EXAMPLE 17.3: SAMPLE SIZE—AN ALTERNATIVE APPROACH

The previously described equation for sample size included the risk levels for both α and β. An alternative approach can be used if we want to determine a mean value within a certain $\pm$ value and level of confidence (e.g., ± 4 at 95% confidence). To determine the sample size for this situation, consider the relationship

$$\mu = \bar{x} \pm \frac{U_\alpha \sigma}{\sqrt{n}}$$

It then follows that

$$4 = \frac{U_\alpha \sigma}{\sqrt{n}} = \frac{1.96\sigma}{\sqrt{n}}$$

or

$$n = \frac{(1.96)^2 \sigma^2}{4^2} = 0.24\sigma^2$$

17.7 STANDARD DEVIATION CONFIDENCE INTERVAL

When a sample of size n is taken from a population that is normally distributed, the double-sided confidence interval equation for the population's standard deviation (σ) is

$$\left[\frac{(n-1)s^2}{\chi^2_{\alpha/2;\,v}}\right]^{1/2} \leq \sigma \leq \left[\frac{(n-1)s^2}{\chi^2_{(1-\alpha/2;\,v)}}\right]^{1/2}$$

where s is the standard deviation of the sample and the χ^2 values are taken from Table G with $\alpha/2$ risk and v degrees of freedom equal to the sample size minus 1. This relationship is not robust to data not being from a normal distribution.

17.8 EXAMPLE 17.4: STANDARD DEVIATION CONFIDENCE STATEMENT

Consider again the 16 data points from sample 1 of Table 3.3, which had a mean of 5.77 and a standard deviation of 2.41. Given that the standard deviation was not known, the 90% confidence interval for the standard deviation of the population would then be

$$\left[\frac{(16-1)(2.41)^2}{\chi^2_{(0.1/2;[16-1])}}\right]^{1/2} \leq \sigma \leq \left[\frac{(16-1)(2.41)^2}{\chi^2_{(1-[0.1/2];[16-1])}}\right]^{1/2}$$

$$\left[\frac{87.12}{25.00}\right]^{1/2} \leq \sigma \leq \left[\frac{87.12}{7.26}\right]^{1/2}$$

$$1.87 \leq \sigma \leq 3.46$$

The standard deviation used in this calculation was from a random sample taken from a normal distribution where $\sigma = 2.0$. Note that this true standard deviation value is contained in this confidence interval. When the confidence interval is 90%, we would expect the interval to contain the true value 90% of the time that we take random samples and analyze the data.

17.9 PERCENTAGE OF THE POPULATION ASSESSMENTS

Criteria are sometimes thought to apply to the mean response of the product's population, with no regard to the variability of the product response. Often what is really needed is that all of the product should have a response that is less than or greater than a criterion.

For example, a specification may exist that a product should be able to withstand an electrostatic discharge (ESD) level of 700 volts (V). Is the intent of this specification that the mean of the population (if tested to failure) should be above 700 V? Or perhaps all products built should be able to resist a voltage level of 700 V.

It is impossible to be 100% certain that every product will meet such a criterion without testing every product that is manufactured. For criteria that require much certainty and a 100% population requirement, 100% testing to a level that anticipates field performance degradation may be required. However, a reduced confidence level may be acceptable with a lower percent confidence requirement (e.g., 95% of the population). Depending on the situation, the initial criterion may need adjustment to reflect the basic test strategy.

There are approaches such as K factors (Natrella 1966) noted within other texts that address this situation using tables and equations that consider both the mean and standard deviation of the sample. However, with this approach the assumption of normality is very important and the sample size requirements may often be too large.

A "best estimate" probability plot is another approach consideration, which can give visual indications to population characteristics that may not otherwise be apparent. A probability plot may indicate, for example, that data outliers are present or that a normal distribution assumption is not appropriate. In addition, some computer software can include confidence intervals within their probability plots.

17.10   EXAMPLE 17.5: PERCENTAGE OF THE POPULATION STATEMENTS

Consider again the first sample from Table 3.3 that yielded a mean value of 5.77 and a standard deviation of 2.41. This time let's create a normal probability of the data. Table 17.2 has the ranked sample values matched with the percentage plot position taken from Table P for the sample size of 16. These coordinates can then be manually plotted on normal probability paper (see Table Q1). Figure 17.1 is a computer-generated normal probability plot of the data.

From this plot it is first noted that only evaluating the mean value for this sample may yield deceiving conclusions because the standard deviation is rather large compared to the reading values. It is also noted that the normal distribution can be used to represent the population, because the data tend to follow a straight line. If a criterion of 20 was specified for 95% of the population (given that a low number indicates goodness), an individual would probably feel comfortable that the specification was met because the "best estimate" plot estimates that 95% of the population is less than 9.5. However, if the criterion were 10 for this percentage of the population, we would probably conclude that too many of the machines might be beyond specification. To better meet this criterion of 10, perhaps the manufacturing process needs to be examined for ways that it could be improved. Regression and/or DOE

TABLE 17.2 Ranked Data and Plot Positions

Original Sample Number	Ranked Sample Value	Percentage Plot Position
7	2.17	3.1
3	2.65	9.4
1	2.99	15.6
8	4.13	21.9
15	4.74	28.1
16	5.19	34.4
10	5.20	40.6
5	5.31	46.9
12	5.39	53.1
11	5.80	59.4
6	5.84	65.6
2	6.29	71.9
9	7.29	78.1
14	9.29	84.4
13	10.00	90.6
4	10.11	96.9

might be appropriate to assess which of those parameters considered (from perhaps a brainstorming session) are significant in reducing the mean and/or standard deviation of the process.

Probability plots of data can often be enlightening. From these plots one may find, for example, that the data are not normally distributed. If there is a knee in the curve, this may indicate that there are two distributions within the process (i.e., a bimodal distribution). In this case it might be beneficial to

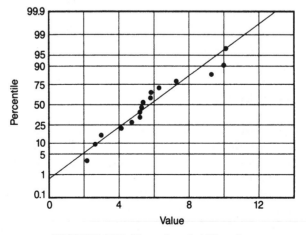

FIGURE 17.1 Normal probability plot.

try to determine why one sample is from one distribution while another sample is from another distribution. This phenomenon may happen, for example, because there are two suppliers where one supplier produces a better part than the other supplier. Or, another possibility is that the normal probability plot may have curvature and be better fitted to some other distribution (e.g., a three-parameter Weibull distribution).

As a minimum when choosing a sample size for making a decision about the percentage of population, extrapolation should be avoided to reach the desired percentage value. In this example it is noted from the tabulated values that the percentage plot position extremes are 3.1% and 9.6%. This means that a probability plot of the 16 data points has no extrapolation when single-sided (high value) statements are made about 95% of the population. The percentage plot positions in Table P indicate that 26 data points are needed to yield nonextrapolated single-sided statements about 98% of the population.

Another valid concern can emerge from this type of experiment. If the sample is drawn from a process over a short period of time, this sample does not necessarily represent what the process will do in the future. DOE techniques again can be used as a guide to adjust parameters used to manufacture the parts. The procedure described within this example could then still be applied to get a "big picture spatial representation" (i.e., the data are from the factorial trials and are not a true random sample of a population) of what could be expected of the process in the future (see Example 43.3). In addition, any significant parameters could then be focused upon, to perhaps improve the process mean and/or reduce the process van-ability. The process then could be continually monitored via control charts (discussed later in this text) for drifts of the process mean and standard deviation.

17.11   TOLERANCE ANALYSIS

When designing a product, the quality of the output (or whether the assembly will work or fail) can depend on the tolerances of the component parts used in the assembly process. A pencil-and-paper worst-case tolerance analysis is sometimes appropriate to make sure that tolerances do not "stack," causing an overall out-of-specification condition. However, if there are many components within the assembly process, it may be impossible to ensure that the completed product will perform satisfactorily if all the component tolerances were at worst-case conditions.

The overall effect of a component can sometimes be considered to follow a normal distribution with $\pm 3\sigma$ bounds equivalent to the tolerance limits (or some other tighter limits) of the component, and where the mean (μ) of the distribution is the midpoint between the tolerance limits.

Consider that measurements for n components that are each centered at mean (μ_i) of a normal distribution with plus or minus tolerances (T_i) around this mean value. The worst-case overall tolerance (T_w) for this situation is simply the addition of these tolerances.

$$T_w = \pm \sum_{i=1}^{n} T_i = \pm(T_1 + T_2 + \cdots + T_n)$$

The serial 3σ combination of the component tolerances yields an overall product 3σ tolerance $(T_{3\sigma})$ of

$$T_{3\sigma} = \pm \left[\sum_{i=1}^{n} T_i^2 \right]^{1/2} = \pm(T_1^2 + T_2^2 + \cdots + T_n^2)^{1/2}$$

Care must be exercised when using this equation. The accuracy of the assumption that each component follows a normal distribution is very important. There are situations where this assumption will not be valid. For example, a $\pm 10\%$ tolerance resistor may follow a bimodal distribution because the best parts can be sorted out and sold at a higher price with a $\pm 1\%$ or $\pm 5\%$ tolerance. Another situation where the normality assumption may be invalid is in the case where a manufacturer initially produces a part at one tolerance extreme, anticipating tool wear within the manufacturing process.

An alternative approach to use this equation is to estimate a distribution shape for each component. Then, via a computer, randomly choose a component characteristic from each distribution; then combine these values to yield an overall expected output. A computer can easily simulate thousands of assemblies to yield the expected overall distribution of the combined tolerances.

17.12   EXAMPLE 17.6: COMBINING ANALYTICAL DATA WITH A TOLERANCE ANALYSIS

An automatic sheet feed device is to load a sheet of paper into a printer such that the first character printed on the paper will be 1.26 ± 1.26 mm from the edge of the paper (Figure 17.2).

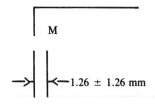

FIGURE 17.2 Diagram showing specification limits.

There are two variabilities that need consideration within this problem. First, the variability within machines and then the variability between machines. For some problem types, only variability between machines will be needed when there is only one output for the device. However, with this situation each machine will have multiple outputs because each printed page is basically an output.

Within industry, this type of question may need to be addressed early within a development cycle when there are only a few models available to test. The following will consider three alternatives given this physical test constraint. The first approach will be that all tolerances including some measurement data will be combined to yield a worst-case analysis (i.e., T_w). The second approach will consider the population to be all sheets of paper produced on all printers manufactured. The third consideration will be that the real intent of the question is to determine whether 99.7% ($\approx 3\sigma$) of the sheets printed on 99.7% of the printers will be within the tolerance limits.

The design group determined that there were 14 tolerances involved with either (a) the placement of the page within the printer or (b) the printing of the character on the page. The tolerance analyses also indicated a nominal character position of 1.26 mm. All the tolerances were plus or minus values; hence, the tolerances can be algebraically combined as later shown. The plus or minus tolerances (T_i) $(i = 1$ to 14) are

$$0.1, 0.2, 0.2, 0.03, 0.34, 0.15, 0.05, 0.08, 0.1, 0.1, 0.1, 0.1, 0.06, 0.1$$

When a machine is assembled, it takes on one of these values. However, for various reasons, the first print character will not always be positioned in the same position. Things that could affect this positioning are paper type, platen imperfections, initial loading of the paper tray, and so forth. The assessment of all these considerations suggests a DOE assessment. Assume that this experiment was performed and it was concluded from the test that a machine repeatability (σ_r) estimate of 0.103 mm would be used for any further calculations.

1. Considering a worst-case analysis approach, the worst-case machine tolerances (T_A) are then combined with the 3σ limits of machine repeatability to yield

$$T_A = \pm \sum_{i=1}^{n} T_i + 3\sigma_r$$

$$= \pm (0.1 + 0.2 \cdots 0.1) \pm 3(0.103)$$

$$= \pm 1.71 \pm 0.31 = \pm 2.02$$

Because ± 2.02 is greater than the specification ± 1.26 tolerance, the assembly is not expected to perform satisfactorily with this worst-case scenario.

2. Considering the specification as addressing 99.7% of all pages produced on the printers, it follows that

$$T_B = \pm \left\{ \left[\sum_{i=1}^{n} T_i^2 \right] \pm (3\sigma)^2 \right\}^{0.5}$$

$$= \pm \{ (0.1^2 + 0.2^2 \cdots 0.1^2) + [3(0.103)]^2 \}^{0.5}$$

$$= \pm 0.622$$

This combination yields a favorable result because ± 0.622 is less than the specification tolerance of ± 1.26. However, consider the person that has a printer with manufacturing tolerances at a 3σ limit. This individual will still experience the full effects of variations when loading the paper in addition to the adverse printer tolerance considerations. Hence, this approach may yield a conclusion that is too optimistic from a user perspective.

3. Considering that the specification should be met on 99.7% of the sheets produced on a "statistical worst-case" machine (i.e., 3σ combination), this yields

$$T_C = \pm \left[\sum_{i=1}^{n} T_i^2 \right]^{0.5} \pm (3\sigma)$$

$$= \pm (0.1^2 + 0.2^2 \cdots 0.1^2)^{0.5} \pm [3(0.103)]$$

$$= \pm 0.85$$

This approach yields a favorable result because ± 0.85 is less than the specification tolerance of ± 1.26.

This example illustrates an approach to combine experimental results with a tolerance analysis. Also, it was illustrated how the basic analysis strategy can change depending on the intent of the problem definition. Chapter 32 on Taguchi contributions will take this a step further. This chapter will challenge the historical logic of assuming that an assembly that just meets a criterion is good, while an assembly that just misses the criterion is bad (i.e., for this example, a ± 1.25 value around the criterion would be considered "good," while a ± 1.27 value around the criterion would be judged "bad").

17.13   S⁴ ASSESSMENT

This chapter illustrates techniques where a random sample is used for hypothesis testing or confidence interval statements. This type of assessment might be suggested during initial problem definition; however, one might consider the following questions to determine if there is an S^4 alternative:

1. Is the sample really taken from the population of interest? If, for example, a sample is taken from the start-up of a manufacturing process, the sample output will not necessarily represent future machine builds. Hence, a machine failure rate test during this early phase of production may not yield a failure rate that is similar to that which the customer will later be experiencing.
2. Is the process that is being sampled stable? If it is not, then the test methods and confidence statements cannot be interpreted with much precision. Process control charting techniques can be used to determine the stability of a process.
3. What is going to be done if the process does not meet a test criterion? Are the parts going to be shipped anyway, as long as the output is "reasonable"?
4. Would a DOE be more beneficial than a "random sample" taken at some point in time? A DOE test strategy can yield information as to where the process/design may be improved.

Let's not play games with the numbers. Future chapters will illustrate approaches that can be more beneficial in answering the real questions: How can we design, build, or test this product smarter to give the customer the best possible product at the lowest possible price?

17.14 EXERCISES

1. *Catapult Exercise Data Analysis:* Using the catapult exercise data sets from Chapter 4, determine the confidence intervals of the mean and standard deviation.

2. From sampled data, state the distribution used to calculate the confidence interval on the mean. Also, state the distribution that is used to calculate the confidence interval on the standard deviation.

3. The difference between the actual arrival time and the scheduled arrival time follows for the 12 monthly flights someone made into their resident city for the previous year (plus values indicate the number of minutes the flight was late). The traveler always is scheduled to arrive at the same time on the last Wednesday of the month.

June	July	Aug	Sep	Oct	Nov	Dec	Jan	Feb	Mar	Apr	May
0.1	3.2	18.4	2.5	15.6	90.9	102.1	0.8	20.2	31.3	1.4	21.9

(a) Determine the sample mean and standard deviation.

(b) Estimate the 95% confidence intervals for the population mean and standard deviation. Note any assumptions.

(c) Display data in a histogram format.

(d) Create a normal probability plot of the data.

(e) Estimate arrival time range for 90% of the flights (using normal probability plot and Z table—i.e., Table A). Comment on analysis.

(f) Interpret the plots and describe any further investigation.

(g) If someone was to make a general inference about the arrival times of all passengers into the airport, state a key underlying assumption that is violated.

(h) Describe the potential problem with making inferences about next year's arrival times from the current year's arrival times.

4. A random sample yielded the measurements 9.4, 10.6, 8.1, 12.2, 15.9, 9.0, 9.1, 10.0, 11.7, 11.0.

(a) Determine the sample mean and the 95% confidence interval for the population mean.

(b) Determine the sample standard deviation and the 95% confidence interval for the population standard deviation.

(c) Display the data using a histogram and normal probability plots.

(d) Estimate the response that is exceeded 10% of the time (using probability plot and Z table—i.e., Table A). Comment on the validity of the analysis and results.

(e) Estimate process capability/performance for a specification of 10.0 ±4.0. Comment on the validity of the analysis and results.

5. The following random sampled data was submitted for analysis: 33.4, 42.2, 37.1, 44.2, 46.0, 34.0, 32.6, 42.7, 32, 39.5.

(a) Determine the sample mean and the 95% confidence interval for the population mean.

(b) Determine the sample standard deviation and the 95% confidence interval for the population standard deviation.

(c) Display the data using a histogram and normal probability plots.

(d) Using the plots and Z table (i.e., Table A) estimate the range of responses expected 90% of the time. Comment on the validity of the analysis and results.

(e) Estimate process capability/performance for a specification of 40.0 ± 7.0. Comment on the validity of the analysis and results.

(f) Describe possible sources for this data.

6. A 10-random-sample evaluation of the specification 75 ± 3 yielded readings of 77.1, 76.8, 76.3, 75.9, 76.1, 77.7, 76.7, 75.7, 76.9, 77.4.

(a) Determine the sample mean and the 95% confidence interval for the population mean.

(b) Determine the sample standard deviation and the 95% confidence interval for the population standard deviation.

(c) Display the data using a histogram and normal probability plots.

(d) Using plots and Z table (i.e., Table A), estimate the proportion beyond the specification limits. Determine the process capability/performance. Comment on the validity of the analysis and results.

(e) Determine where emphasis should be given to make the process more capable of meeting specifications (reducing variability or shifting mean).

(f) Give an example from manufacturing, development, and service where these data might have originated.

7. A sample of 10 was taken from an in-control process. A variance of 4.2 and a mean of 23.2 was calculated. Determine the 95% confidence interval on the mean and standard deviation. Describe any potential problems with this analysis.

8. A sample from an in-control process had a variance of 4.2 and a mean of 23.2. Determine the 90% lower confidence bound on the mean and standard deviation? Describe any potential problems with this analysis.

9. To address some customer problem reports, management wants a random sample evaluation to assess the products currently produced. Determine the sample size needed to assess a mean response criterion of 75 if risks are at a level of 0.05. Describe the test hypothesis. Discuss how well the basic test strategy will probably assess the needs of the customer.

10. A product design consists of five components that collectively affected a response. Four of the component dimensions are 4.0 ± 0.1 mm, 3.0 ± 0.1 mm, 6.0 ± 0.1 mm, and 2.0 ± 0.1 mm. If the dimensions for each component follow a normal distribution, determine the dimension and specification needed for the fifth component given a final ±3σ sigma statistical dimension of 20.00 ± 0.25 mm. Describe practical difficulties with the results from this type of analysis.

11. A company designs and assembles the five components described in the previous exercise, which are manufactured by different suppliers. Create a strategy for meeting the overall specification requirement of the assembled product.

(a) Create a preproduction plan that assesses assumptions and how the process is producing relative to meeting specification requirements.

(b) Describe needs during production start-up.

(c) Describe alternatives for out-sourcing the component parts that could lead to improved quality.

12. Describe how the techniques within this chapter are useful and can be applied to S^4 projects.

18

INFERENCES: ATTRIBUTE (PASS/FAIL) RESPONSE

This chapter discusses the evaluation of defective count data (e.g., go/no-go attribute information). An example of an attribute (pass/fail or pass/noncon-formance) response situation would be that of a copier that fed or failed to feed individual sheets of paper satisfactorily (i.e., a copier may feed 999 sheets out of 1000 sheets of paper on the average without a jam). The purpose of these experiments may be to assess an attribute criterion or evaluate the proportion of parts beyond a continuous criterion value (e.g., 20% of the electrical measurements are less than 100,000 ohms).

Samples are evaluated to determine whether they will either pass or fail a requirement (a binary response). Experiments of this type can assess the proportion of a population that is defective through either a confidence interval statement or a hypothesis test of a criterion.

It will be illustrated later that tests of pass/fail attribute information can require a much larger sample size than tests of a continuous response. Because of this fact, this chapter also incudes suggestions on how an original attribute test approach could be changed to a continuous response test alternative. With this change more relevant information can often be obtained with a large reduction in sample size requirements.

The binomial distribution is used for this type of analyses given that the sample size is small relative to the size of the population (e.g., less than 10% of the population size). A hypergeometric distribution (see Appendix A) can be used when this assumption is not valid.

18.1 ATTRIBUTE RESPONSE SITUATIONS

The equation forms for the binomial and hypergeometric distributions shown in Appendix A might initially look complex; however, they are rather mathematically simple to apply. By simply knowing the sample size and the percentage of "good" parts, it is easy to determine the probability (chance) of getting a "bad" or "good" sample part.

However, a typical desired response is to determine whether a criterion is met with a manageable risk of making the wrong decision. For example, the experimenter may desire to state that at least 99% of the parts are satisfactory with only a risk of 0.10 of making the wrong decision. Or, an experimenter may desire the 90% confidence interval for the defective proportion of the population.

The binomial equation can be used to assess this situation using an iterative computer routine; however, care must be taken when writing the program to avoid computer number size limitation problems. The Poisson or the normal distribution can be used to approximate the binomial distribution under the situations noted within Table 7.2. Because failure rate typically found within industry are low, the Poisson distribution often is a viable alternative distribution to use for these attribute tests.

18.2   SAMPLE SIZE: HYPOTHESIS TEST OF AN ATTRIBUTE CRITERION

The following equation is a simple approximation for the sample size needed to make a hypothesis test using the binomial distribution with α and β risks (Diamond 1989), where the failure rate at which α applies ρ_α, while the failure rate at which β applies is ρ_β.

$$n = \left(\frac{(U_\alpha)[(\rho_\alpha)(1 - \rho_\alpha)]^{1/2} + (U_\beta)[(\rho_\beta)(1 - \rho_\beta)]^{1/2}}{\rho_\beta - \rho_\alpha} \right)^2$$

U_α is the value from Table B or C (depending on whether H_a is single- or double-sided) and U_β is from the single-sided Table B. After the test, if the failure rate is not shown to be outside the confidence bounds (described in a later section), the null hypothesis is not rejected with β risk of error.

For those readers who are interested, this sample size equation assumes that a normality approximation to the binomial equation is appropriate. In general, this is a valid approximation because the sample size required for typical α and β risk levels is high enough to approximate normality, even though the failure criterion is low. The example in the next section exemplifies this point. Alternative approaches for sample size calculations are described later in this chapter.

18.3   EXAMPLE 18.1: SAMPLE SIZE—A HYPOTHESIS TEST OF AN ATTRIBUTE CRITERION

A supplier manufactures a component that is not to have more than 1 defect every 1000 parts (i.e., a 0.001 failure rate criterion). They want to determine a test sample size for assessing this criterion.

The failure rate criterion is to be 1/1000 (i.e., 0.001); however, the sample size requires two failure rates (i.e., ρ_β and ρ_α). To determine values for ρ_β and ρ_α, assume that a shift of 200 was thought to be a minimal "important increment" from the above 1000-part criterion, along with $\alpha = \beta = 0.05$. The value for ρ_β would then be 0.00125 [i.e., $1/(1000 - 200)$], while the value for ρ_α would be 0.000833 [i.e., $1/(1000 + 200)$]. For this single-sided problem the values are determined from Table B. Substitution yields

$$n = \left(\frac{(1.645)[(0.000833)(1 - 0.000833)]^{1/2} + (1.645)[(0.00125)(1 - 0.00125)]^{1/2}}{0.00125 - 0.000833} \right)^2$$

$$n = 64,106$$

Ready to suggest this to your management? There goes your next raise! This is not an atypical type of sample size problem that is encountered when developing an attribute sampling plan. These calculations could be repeated for relaxed test considerations for α, β, ρ_β, and/or ρ_α. If these alternatives still do not appeal to you, consider the reduced sample size testing alternative and the S^4 assessment described later in this chapter.

It was stated that the origin of the sample size equation that we used involved a normal distribution approximation. To illustrate why this approximation is reasonable for this test situation, first note from Table 7.2 that normality is often assumed if $np > 5$ and $n(1 - p) > 5$. In the example, $p = 0.001$ and $N = 64,106$, which yields an np value of 64.106 [i.e., $64,106 \times 0.001$], which is greater than 5, and an $n(1 - p)$ value of 64,042 [i.e., $64,106 \times 0.999$], which is also greater than 5.

18.4 CONFIDENCE INTERVALS FOR ATTRIBUTE EVALUATIONS AND ALTERNATIVE SAMPLE SIZE CONSIDERATION

If there are r failures from a sample size of n, the simplest way to make a double-sided confidence interval statement for this pass/fail test situation is to use Clopper and Pearson (1934) charts (Figures 18.1 to 18.4). To use these charts, a sample failure rate is first determined (r/n). The confidence intervals are then read from the ordinate of the curve at the values of the intersection of the abscissa value and the sample size n.

For example, if we find 30 defectives out of a sample of 100, the sample failure rate would be 0.3 (i.e., 30/100). The intersection of this abscissa value with the sample size of 100 will yield from the ordinate an 80% confidence interval of 0.24–0.37.

However, these tables are difficult to read for low test failure rates, which often typify the tests of today's products. In lieu of using a computer algorithm to determine the confidence interval, the Poisson distribution can often

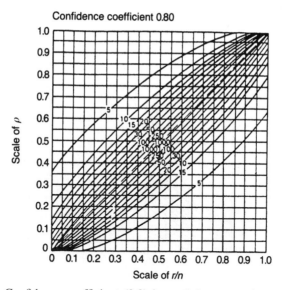

FIGURE 18.1 Confidence coefficient (0.8) interval for proportions. The axis labels r/n and ρ reflect the nomenclature used in this text. [From Clopper and Pearson (1934), with permission of *Biometrics* Trustees.]

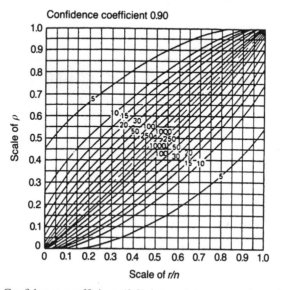

FIGURE 18.2 Confidence coefficient (0.9) interval for proportions. The axis labels r/n and ρ reflect the nomenclature used in this text. [From Clopper and Pearson (1934), with permission of *Biometrics* Trustees.]

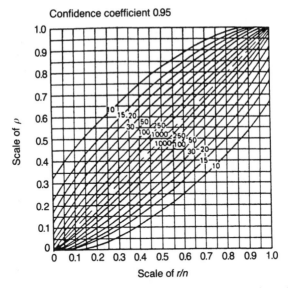

FIGURE 18.3 Confidence coefficient (0.95) interval for proportions. The axis labels r/n and ρ reflect the nomenclature used in this text. [From Clopper and Pearson (1934), with permission of *Biometrics* Trustees.]

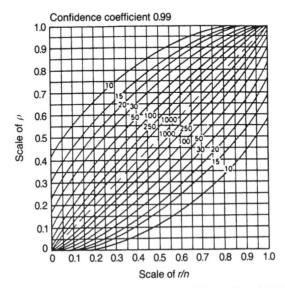

FIGURE 18.4 Confidence coefficient (0.99) interval for proportions. The axis labels r/n and ρ reflect the nomenclature used in this text. [From Clopper and Pearson (1934), with permission of *Biometrics* Trustees.]

be used to yield a satisfactory approximation. Given this assumption with a small number of failures, Table K can be used for a simplified approach to calculate a confidence interval for the population failure rate. A rule of thumb is that we would like to have a least five failures before determining attribute confidence intervals.

If a normal distribution approximation can be made (e.g., a large sample size), the confidence interval for the population proportion (ρ) can be determined from the relationship

$$p - U_\alpha \sqrt{\frac{pq}{n}} \leq \rho \leq p + U_\alpha \sqrt{\frac{pq}{n}}$$

where $p = r/n$, $q = 1 - p$, and U_α is taken from a two-sided U table (i.e., Table C). Similar to the approach described earlier for continuous data, a sample size could be determined from this relationship. To do this we can rearrange the above relationship to

$$\rho = p \pm U_\alpha \sqrt{\frac{pq}{n}}$$

For a desired $\pm$ confidence interval of Δp and a proportion rate of $\bar{p}$, we note

$$\Delta p = U_\alpha \sqrt{\frac{\bar{p}(1 - \bar{p})}{n}}$$

solving for n yields

$$n = \left(\frac{U_\alpha}{\Delta p}\right)^2 (\bar{p})(1 - \bar{p})$$

18.5   REDUCED SAMPLE SIZE TESTING FOR ATTRIBUTE SITUATIONS

The sample size calculation discussed originally within this chapter protects both the customer and the producer. A reduced sample size test is achievable for a criterion verification test when the test sample size is chosen such that the criterion is set to a bound of the confidence interval with a given number of allowed failures (i.e., the failure rate criterion will be equal to or less than the bound at the desired confidence level).

The example shown in the next section illustrates the simple procedure to use when designing such a test; this example also shows that in order to pass a test of this type the sample may be required to perform at a failure rate that is much better than the population criterion. This methodology is also applicable to the certification of a repairable system failure rate.

If the Poisson distribution is an appropriate approximation for this binomial test situation, sample size requirements can be determined from Table K. A tabular value (*B*) can be determined for the chosen number of permissible failures (*r*) and desired confidence value (*c*). This value is then substituted with the failure rate criterion (ρ_a) into the following equation to yield a value for *T*, the necessary test sample size (*T* is used in this equation so there will be consistency with the reliability application equation that is later discussed, where *T* symbolizes time):

$$T = B_{r,c}/\rho_a$$

18.6   EXAMPLE 18.2: REDUCED SAMPLE SIZE TESTING—ATTRIBUTE RESPONSE SITUATIONS

Given the failure rate criterion (ρ_a) of 0.001 (i.e., 1/1000) from the previous example, determine a zero failure test sample size such that a 95% confidence interval bound will be

$$\rho \leq 0.001$$

From Table 7.2 it is noted that the Poisson approximation seems to be a reasonable simplification because the failure rate criterion of 0.001 is much less than 0.05 and will surely require a sample size larger than 20.

From Table K, $B_{0;0.95}$ equals 2.996. The sample size is then

$$T = B_{0;0.95}/\rho_a = 2.996/0.001 = 2996$$

The sample size for this example is much less than that calculated in the previous example (i.e., 64,106); however, this example does not consider both α and β risks. With a zero failure test strategy, there is a good chance that the samples will not perform well enough to pass the test objectives, unless the actual failure rate (which is unknown to the experimenter) is much better than the criterion.

To illustrate this, consider, for example, that only one failure occurred while testing the sample of 2996. For this sample the failure rate is lower than the 0.001 criterion (i.e., 1/2996 = 0.00033). However, from Table K, $B_{1;0.95}$ equals 4.744 for one failure and a level equal to 0.95. The single-sided 95% confidence interval for the failure rate given information from this test using the relationship shown at the bottom of Table K is

$$\rho \leq B_{1;0.95}/T = 4.744/2996 = 0.00158 \qquad (\text{i.e., } \rho \leq 0.00158)$$

The 0.001 failure rate criterion value is contained in the above 95% confidence bounds. The original test objectives were not met (i.e., there was a failure that occurred during test); hence, from a technical point of view the "product did not pass the test." However, from a practical point of view, the experimenter may want to determine (for reference only) a lesser confidence interval (e.g., 80% confidence) that would have allowed the test to pass if this value were chosen initially.

From Table K the single-sided 80% confidence for the failure rate is

$$\rho \le B_{1;0.80}/T = 2.994/2996 = 0.0009993 \qquad (\text{i.e., } \rho \le 0.0009993)$$

The 0.001 criterion is now outside the single-sided 80% confidence interval. A major business decision may rest upon the outcome of this test. From a practical point of view, it seems wise for the experimenter to report this lower confidence interval information to management and others along with the cause of the failure and a corrective action strategy (i.e., don't we really want to have zero failures experienced by the customer?). The experimenter might also state that a DOE is being planned to determine the changes that should be made to improve the manufacturing process so that there is less chance that this type of failure will occur again. From this information, it may be decided that a limited shipment plan is appropriate for the current product. Note that the same general methodology could be used if more than one failure occurred during the test. Other confidence statements that might similarly be appropriate under certain situations are a double-sided confidence interval statement or a single-sided statement where ($\rho \ge$ a value) may be appropriate.

In the above situation the experimenter may have been surprised to find that one failure technically means that the test was not passed, even though the sample failure rate was much better than the criterion. To avoid this (perhaps) surprise when using this test strategy, Section 40.9 illustrates how a test performance ratio can be used to create pretest graphical information that can be an aid when choosing the number of permissible failures and test confidence interval level (a lower level than initially desired may be needed in order to create a reasonable test).

18.7   ATTRIBUTE SAMPLE PLAN ALTERNATIVES

The preceding discussion assumes that the sample size is small relative to the population size. If the sample size is greater than one-tenth of the population size, the hypergeometric distribution should be considered.

In addition, it is also important to reemphasize that the sample needs to be randomly taken from the population and that the outcome of the experiment only characterizes the population from which the sample is taken. For example, a sample taken from an initial production process may be very different from the characteristics of production parts manufactured in the future and sent to the customer.

Military standards could be used as an alternative approach to choosing an attribute sampling plan. For example,

- MIL-STD-105:   Sampling for attributes (US Department of Defense 1963)
- MIL-STD-414:   Sampling by variables for percent defective (US Department of Defense 1957)
- MIL-STD-1235:   Single- and multi-level continuous sampling procedures for attributes (US Department of Defense 1981b)

Still another approach is to consider sequential binomial test plans, which are similar in form to that shown in Section 40.2 for the Poisson distribution. Ireson (1966) discusses the equations necessary for the application of this approach, which was originally developed by Wald (1947). However, with the low failure rate criteria of today, I believe that this sequential test approach is not usually a realistic test alternative.

18.8   S⁴ ASSESSMENT

When determining a test strategy, the question of process stability needs to be addressed. If a process is not stable, the test methods and confidence statements cannot be interpreted with much precision. Process control charting techniques can be used to determine the stability of a process.

Consider also what actions will be taken when a failure occurs in a particular attribute sampling plan. Will the failure be "talked away"? Often no knowledge is obtained about the "good" parts. Are these "good parts" close to "failure"? What direction can be given to fixing the source of failure so that the failure will not occur with a customer environment? One should not "play games with numbers"! Tests need to be considered such that they can give useful information to continually improve the manufacturing process.

The examples in this chapter illustrate that a test sample size can become very large when verifying a low failure criterion. To make matters worse, large sample size requirements may actually be needed for each lot that is produced.

It is fortunate, however, that many problems that are initially defined as an attribute test can be redefined to a continuous response output. For example, a tester may reject an electronic panel if the electrical resistance of any circuit is below a certain resistance value. In this example, more benefits could be obtained from the test if actual resistance values are evaluated. With this information, percent of population projections for failure at the resistance threshold could then be made using probability plotting techniques. After an acceptable level of resistance is established within the process, resistance could then be monitored using control chart techniques for variables. These charts can then indicate when the resistance mean and standard deviation is decreasing/increasing, respectively, with time, which would be an expected indicator of an increase in the percentage builds that are beyond the threshold requirement.

Another test consideration is that DOE techniques could be used as a guide to manufacture the test samples such that they represent the limits of the process. This test could then perhaps yield parts that are more representative of future builds and future process variabilities. These samples will not be "random" from the process; however, this technique can potentially identify future process problems that a random sample from an initial "batch" lot would miss.

18.9 EXERCISES

1. *Catapult Exercise Data Analysis:* Using the catapult exercise data sets from Chapter 4, reassess the data using an attribute criterion described by the instructor (e.g., 75 ± 3 in. or ± 3 in. from the mean projection distance). Determine the confidence interval for the failure rate.

2. *M&M's Candy Data Analysis:* In the exercises at the end of Chapter 5 a bag of M&M's candy was to be opened. A count of each color was made. Determine from this count data the confidence interval of the true population percentage of brown.

3. Determine the 95% confidence interval for a population defective rate given a sample of 60 that had 5 defectives.

4. A 10-random-sample evaluation of the specification 75 ± 3 yielded readings of 77.1, 76.8, 76.3, 75.9, 76.1, 77.7, 76.7, 75.7, 76.9, 77.4. Make a best estimate attribute assessment of the population relative to the specification limits. Describe an S^4 analysis approach.

5. The following data is the difference between actual arrival times and the scheduled arrival time for the 12 monthly flights that someone made into their resident city (positive values indicate the number of minutes the flight was late). The traveler always used the same airline and was scheduled to arrive at the same time on the last Wednesday of the month.

June	July	Aug	Sep	Oct	Nov	Dec	Jan	Feb	Mar	Apr	May
0.1	3.2	18.4	2.5	15.6	90.9	102.1	0.8	20.2	31.3	1.4	21.9

   (a) Give conclusions if a flight were considered "on-time" if it is within 20 minutes.

   (b) Describe S^4 considerations.

6. A process is considered to have an unsatisfactory response whenever the output is greater than 100. A defective rate of 2% is considered tolerable; however a rate of 3% is not considered tolerable.

    (a) Calculate a sample size if all risk levels are 0.05.

    (b) Give an example from manufacturing, development, and service where this type of question might have originated.

    (c) Describe potential implementation problems and S^4 considerations.

7. A part is not to exceed a failure rate of one failure in 3.4 million.

    (a) Determine the sample size needed for a hypothesis test of the equality the failure rate to a 3.4 parts per million failure rate. Use risks of 0.05 and an uncertainty of $\pm 10\%$ of the failure rate target.

    (b) Determine the sample size if one failure were permitted with a 95% confidence statement (using a reduced sample size testing approach).

    (c) Determine the failure rate of the sample if two failures occurred during the test (using a reduced-sample-size testing approach).

    (d) Comment on your results and implementation challenges. List S^4 opportunities.

8. Earlier the results of an AQL = 4.0% sampling plan for lot size 75 and inspection level II yielded a sample size of 13 with acceptance number = 1 and rejection number = 2. If we considered the sample size to be small relative to the population, determine the confidence interval of the population failure rate if one failure occurred for this sample size. Repeat this calculation as if two failures occurred.

9. A random sample of 100 units was selected from a manufacturing process. These samples either passed or failed a tester within the manufacturing process. A record was kept so that each unit could later be identified as to whether it passed or failed the manufacturing test. Each sample was then thoroughly tested in the laboratory to determine whether the unit should have passed or failed the manufacturing test. The result of this laboratory evaluation was that a correct assessment was performed in manufacturing on 90 out of the 100 samples tested. Determine the 95% confidence interval for the test effectiveness.

10. Describe how the techniques within this chapter are useful and can be applied to S^4 projects.

19

COMPARISON TESTS: CONTINUOUS RESPONSE

This chapter focuses on continuous response situations (e.g., do two machines manufacture on the average the diameter of a shaft to the same dimension?). The next chapter focuses on attribute response situations (e.g. do the failure frequency of completing a purchase order differ between two departments?).

19.1 COMPARING CONTINUOUS DATA

The methods discussed in this chapter can be used, for example, to compare two production machines or suppliers. Both mean and standard deviation output can be compared between the samples to determine if a difference is large enough to be statistically significant. The comparison test of means is robust to the shape of the underlying distribution not being normal; however, this is not true when comparing standard deviation. Nonparametric statistical comparisons (described in other texts) when underlying distribution issues are of concern.

The null hypothesis for the comparison tests is that there is no difference, while the alternate hypothesis is that there is a difference. The basic comparison test equations apply also to the analysis of DOEs and the analysis of variance, which are described in more depth later within this text.

19.2 SAMPLE SIZE: COMPARING MEANS

Brush (1988) gives graphs that can be used to aid with the selection of sample sizes. Diamond (1989) multiplies the appropriate single sampled population equation by 2 to determine a sample size for each of the two populations.

19.3   COMPARING TWO MEANS

When comparing the means between two samples. the null hypothesis is that there is no difference between the population means, while the alternative hypothesis is that there is a difference between the population means. A difference between two means could be single-sided (i.e., $\mu_1 > \mu_2$ or $\mu_1 < \mu_2$) or double-sided (i.e., $\mu_1 \neq \mu_2$). Table 19.1 summarizes the equations and tables to use when making these comparisons to determine if there is a significant difference at the desired level of risk. The null hypothesis rejection criteria is noted for each of the tabulated scenarios.

TABLE 19.1   Significance Tests for the Difference Between the Means of Two Samples

$\sigma_1^2 = \sigma_2^2$	$\sigma_1^2 \neq \sigma_2^2$

σ Known

$$U_0 = \frac{|\bar{x}_1 - \bar{x}_2|}{\sigma \sqrt{\dfrac{1}{n_1} + \dfrac{1}{n_2}}}$$

$$U_0 = \frac{|\bar{x}_1 - \bar{x}_2|}{\sqrt{\dfrac{\sigma_1^2}{n_1} + \dfrac{\sigma_2^2}{n_2}}}$$

Reject H_0 if $U_0 > U_\alpha$ Reject H_0 if $U_0 > U_\alpha$

σ Unknown

$$t_0 = \frac{|\bar{x}_1 - \bar{x}_2|}{s \sqrt{\dfrac{1}{n_1} + \dfrac{1}{n_2}}}$$

$$t_0 = \frac{|\bar{x}_1 - \bar{x}_2|}{\sqrt{\dfrac{s_1^2}{n_1} + \dfrac{s_2^2}{n_2}}}$$

$$s = \sqrt{\frac{(n_1 - 1)s_1^2 + (n_2 - 1)s_2^2}{n_1 + n_2 - 2}}$$

Reject H_0 if $t_0 > t_\alpha$ where

$$v = \frac{[(s_1^2/n_1) + (s_2^2/n_2)]^2}{\dfrac{(s_1^2/n_1)^2}{n_1 + 1} + \dfrac{(s_2^2/n_2)^2}{n_2 + 1}} - 2$$

Reject H_0 if $t_0 > t_\alpha$ where
$v = n_1 + n_2 - 2$

Reference Tables

H_a	U_α	t_α
$\mu_1 \neq \mu_2$	Table C	Table E
$\mu_1 > \mu_2$ (if $\bar{x}_1 > \bar{x}_2$)		
or	Table B	Table D
$\mu_1 < \mu_2$ (if $\bar{x}_1 < \bar{x}_2$)		

19.4   EXAMPLE 19.1: COMPARING THE MEANS OF TWO SAMPLES

A problem existed within manufacturing where the voice quality of a portable dictating machine was unsatisfactory. It was decided to use off-line DOEs to assess the benefit of design and process change considerations before implementation rather than using the common strategy of implement changes and examine the results using a one-at-a-time strategy.

Over 20 changes were considered within these DOEs; however, only three design changes were found to be beneficial. A comparison experiment was conducted to confirm and quantity the benefit of these three design changes. The results from the test were as follows, where a lower number indicates that a machine has better voice quality:

Sample Number	Current Design (Voice Quality Measurement)	New Design (Voice Quality Measurement)
1	1.034	0.556
2	0.913	0.874
3	0.881	0.673
4	1.185	0.632
5	0.930	0.543
6	0.880	0.748
7	1.132	0.532
8	0.745	0.530
9	0.737	0.678
10	1.233	0.676
11	0.778	0.558
12	1.325	0.600
13	0.746	0.713
14	0.852	0.525

The mean $(\bar{x})$ and standard deviation (s) of the 14 samples are

Current Design	New Design
$\bar{x}_1 = 0.955$	$\bar{x}_2 = 0.631$
$s_1 = 0.915$	$s_2 = 0.102$

From the sample data the mean level from the new design is better than the current design; however, the question of concern is whether the difference is large enough to be considered significant. Because the standard deviations are unknown and are thought to be different, it follows that

$$t_0 = \frac{|\bar{x}_1 - \bar{x}_2|}{\sqrt{\dfrac{s_1^2}{n_1} + \dfrac{s_2^2}{n_2}}} = \frac{|0.955 - 0.631|}{\sqrt{\dfrac{(0.195)^2}{14} + \dfrac{(0.102)^2}{14}}} = 5.51$$

Reject H_0 if $t_0 > t_\alpha$, where the degrees of freedom for t_α is determined to be

$$v = \frac{[(s_1^2/n_1) + (s_2^2/n_2)]^2}{\dfrac{(s_1^2/n_1)^2}{n_1 + 1} + \dfrac{(s_2^2/n_2)^2}{n_2 + 1}} - 2$$

$$= \frac{[(0.195^2/14) + (0.102^2/14)]^2}{\dfrac{(0.195^2/14)^2}{14 + 1} + \dfrac{(0.102^2/14)^2}{14 + 1}} - 2 = 14.7$$

Assume that there is agreement to make the changes if this confirmation experiment shows significance at a level of 0.05. For 15 degrees of freedom, Table D yields a $t_\alpha = t_{0.05}$ value of 1.753.

The test question is single-sided (i.e., whether the new design is better than the old design). It does not make sense for this situation to address whether the samples are equal (double-sided scenario). Money should only be spent to make the change if the design changes show an improvement in voice quality. Because $5.51 > 1.753$ (i.e., $t_0 > t_\alpha$), the design changes should be made.

19.5 COMPARING VARIANCES OF TWO SAMPLES

A methodology to determine if a sample variance (s_1^2) is significantly larger than another sample variance (s_2^2) is to first determine

$$F_0 = \frac{s_1^2}{s_2^2} \qquad s_1^2 > s_2^2$$

For significance this ratio needs to be larger than the appropriate tabular value of the F distribution noted in Table F. From this one-sided table is taken $F_{\alpha; v_1; v_2}$, where v_1 is the number of degrees of freedom (sample size minus one) of the sample with the largest variance, while v_2 is the number of degrees of freedom of the smallest variance. A variance ratio that is larger than the tabular value for α indicates that there is a significant difference between the variances at the level of α.

Without prior reason to anticipate inequality of variance, the alternative to the null hypothesis is two-sided. The same equation applies. however. the value from Table F would now be $F_{\alpha/2;v_1;v_2}$ (Snedecor and Cochian 1980).

Unlike the test for differing means. this test is sensitive to the data being from a normal distribution. Care must be exercised when doing the following test because, for example, a "significant difference" may in reality be a violation of this underlying assumption. A probability plot of the data can yield information that can be used to make this assessment. Some statistical computer programs offer the Levene's test for the analysis if data are not normally distributed.

19.6   EXAMPLE 19.2: COMPARING THE VARIANCE OF TWO SAMPLES

The standard deviations from the two samples of 14 in Example 19.1 were 0.195 for the current design and 0.102 for the new design. The designers had hoped that the new design would have less variability. The question of concern is whether there is reason to believe (at the 0.05 significance level) that the variance of the new design is less.

$$F_0 = \frac{s_1^2}{s_2^2} = \frac{0.195^2}{0.102^2} = 3.633$$

The number of degrees of freedom are

$$v_1 = 14 - 1 = 13 \qquad v_2 = 14 - 1 = 13$$

With these degrees of freedom, interpolation in Table F yields

$$F_{\alpha;v_1;v_2} = F_{0.05;\,13;\,13} = 2.58$$

Because $3.633 > 2.58$ (i.e., $F_0 > F_{\alpha;v_1;v_2}$), it is concluded that the variability of the new design is less than the old design at a significance level of 0.05.

19.7   COMPARING POPULATIONS USING A PROBABILITY PLOT

Probability plots of experimental data can supplement the traditional comparison tests. These plots can show information that may yield a better basic understanding of the differences between the samples. Two probability plots on one set of axes can indicate graphically the differences in means, variances, and possible outliers (i.e., data points that are "different" from the other values; e.g., there may have been an error when recording some of the data). This type of understanding can often be used to help improve the manufacturing processes.

19.8   EXAMPLE 19.3: COMPARING SAMPLES USING A PROBABILITY PLOT

Consider the data presented in Example 19.1. The normal probability plots of these data in Figure 19.1 show graphically the improvement in mean and standard deviation (i.e., increased slope with new design). The data tends to follow a straight line on the normal probability paper; however, the experimenter in general should investigate any outlier points, slope changes (e.g., the highest "new design" value should probably be investigated), and other distribution possibilities.

Additional information can be obtained from the normal probability plot. If, for example, a final test criterion of 1.0 exists, the current design would experience a rejection rate of approximately 40%. while the new design would be close to zero.

The probability plot is a powerful tool; however, management may not be familiar with the interpretation of the graph. Because the data do seem to follow a normal distribution, perhaps a better understood final presentation

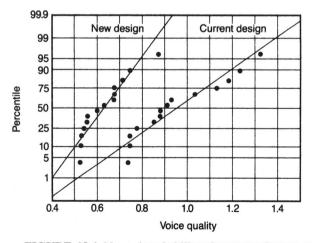

FIGURE 19.1 Normal probability plot comparison.

format would be to use the sample means and standard deviations to draw the estimated PDFs. These graphs can then be illustrated together as shown in Figure 19.2 for comparative purposes.

19.9   PAIRED COMPARISON TESTING

When possible, it is usually advantageous to pair samples during a comparison test. In a paired comparison test, a reduction in experimental variability can permit the detection of smaller data shifts, even though the total number of degrees of freedom is reduced because the sample size becomes now the number of comparisons.

An example of this type of test is the evaluation of two pieces of inspection equipment to determine if any significant difference exists between the equipment. With this technique, products could be inspected on each piece of equipment. The differences between the paired trials are statistically tested against a value of zero using the equations noted in Table 17.1. Note that the sample size now becomes the number of comparisons, and the degrees of freedom is one minus the number of comparisons.

19.10   EXAMPLE 19.4: PAIRED COMPARISON TESTING

The data in Example 19.1 were previously considered as two separate experiments. However the data were really collected in a paired comparison fashion. Fourteen existing drive mechanisms were labeled 1 through 14. The voice

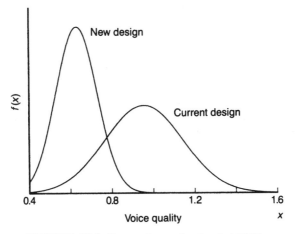

FIGURE 19.2 Comparison of estimated PDFs.

quality was measured in a machine using each of these drives. The drives were then rebuilt with the new design changes. The voice quality was noted again for each drive, as shown:

Sample Number	Current Design	New Design	Change (Current − New)
1	1.034	0.556	0.478
2	0.913	0.874	0.039
3	0.881	0.673	0.208
4	1.185	0.632	0.553
5	0.930	0.543	0.387
6	0.880	0.748	0.132
7	1.132	0.532	0.600
8	0.745	0.530	0.215
9	0.737	0.678	0.059
10	1.233	0.676	0.557
11	0.778	0.558	0.220
12	1.325	0.600	0.725
13	0.746	0.713	0.033
14	0.852	0.525	0.327
			$\bar{x} = 0.324$
			$s = 0.229$

For the alternate hypothesis that the new design is better than the existing design, we need to conduct a one-sided test. Noting that $t_{0.05} = 1.771$ in the single-sided Table D for $v = 13$ (i.e., $n - 1$) degrees of freedom. the change in voice quality for each drive sample is determined to be the following for this single-sided 95% confidence interval:

$$\mu \leq \bar{x} - \frac{t_\alpha s}{\sqrt{n}}$$

$$\mu \leq 0.324 - \frac{1.771(0.229)}{\sqrt{14}} = 0.216$$

The lower side of the single-sided 95% confidence interval is greater than zero, which indicates that the new design is better than the current design. Another way to determine if there is a significant difference is to consider

$$\text{Test criterion} = \frac{t_\alpha s}{\sqrt{n}} = \frac{1.771(0.216)}{\sqrt{14}} = 0.102$$

Because $0.324 > 0.102$, there is a significant difference in the population means (i.e., the new design is better than the old design) at the 0.05 level.

The normal probability plot of the change data, as shown in Figure 19.3, can be helpful to better understand the magnitude of improvement as it relates to percent of population. In addition, a best estimate of the PDF describing the expected change, as shown in Figure 19.4, can be a beneficial pictorial presentation to management. This PDF was created using the $\bar{x}$ and s estimates for change because the normal probability plot followed a straight line.

19.11   COMPARING MORE THAN TWO SAMPLES

Future chapters will discuss techniques where the means of more than two populations can be compared. One factor that analysis of variance techniques can assess is the overall differences between factor level or treatments. Analysis of means can test each factor level or treatment against an grand mean.

Some computer programs offer Bartlett's test when comparing multiple variances if the data are normal. If the data are not normal, a Levene's test can be used.

19.12   EXAMPLE 19.5: COMPARING MEANS TO DETERMINE IF PROCESS IMPROVED

Example 11.5 described a situation where I was the newly elected chair of an ASQ section and wanted to increase monthly meeting attendance during my term. The example illustrated what attendance should be expected if nothing were done differently. This example lists the process changes that were

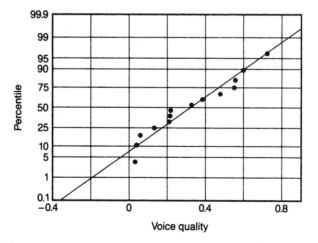

FIGURE 19.3 Normal probability plot indicating the expected difference between the new and old design.

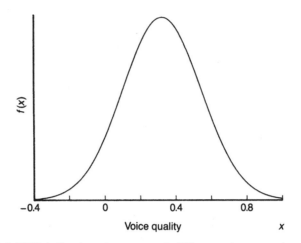

FIGURE 19.4 PDF indicating the expected difference between the new and old design.

made in an attempt to improve attendance. It also shows the resulting attendance and analyses to see if the objective was met.

I set a stretch goal to double attendance at our monthly meeting (but would have been happy with a *50%* increase in attendance). I knew that the stretch goal was going to be exceptionally difficult to meet because we had to reduce the frequency of our newsletter to every other month because of recent cash flow problems. My focus was not trying to drive improved attendance through the measurement (i.e., team go out and do better because our attendance is not up to my goal). Instead I worked with our executive committee on implementing the following process changes that were thought to improve attendance. Note that I had some control over the implementation of process changes, but I had no control over how many people would actually decide to attend the meeting. The process changes that I focused on implementing with the executive committee team were as follows:

- Personally work with program chair to define interesting programs and get commitments from all presenters before the September meeting.
- Create an email distribution list for ASQ members and others. Send notice out the weekend before the meeting.
- Create a website.
- Submit meeting notices to newspaper and other public media.
- Video tape programs for playing on cable TV.
- Add door prizes to meeting.
- Send welcome letters to visitors and new members.
- Post job openings on website, and email notices to those who might be interested.

- Timely submit "from the chair" article to the newsletter chair so newsletter could be mailed timely.

The term of a section chair is July 1 to June 30. There are no June, July, and August meetings. My term encompassed meetings from September 1997 to May 1998. The resulting attendance since September 1992 is shown Table 19.2.

Figure 19.5 shows an *XmR* plot of these data. For this control chart the control limits were calculated from data up to the beginning of my term (i.e., 9/9/93 to 5/8/97). This chart shows two out-of-control conditions during my term (to the better). The designation "1" indicated that one point was more than 3 sigma limits from the center line (this was the first meeting of my term as chair where we had a panel discussion—information for consideration when setting up future meetings). The designation "2" indicated nine points in a row on the same point of the center line (a zone test of the statistical software that was used).

Let's now compare the variance in attendance and mean attendance between 9/92–5/97 and 9/97–5/98 as a hypothesis test using statistical software. Figure 19.6 shows a test of the homogeneity of the two variances. The *F*-test shows a significant difference because the probability is less than 0.05: however, Levene's test does not. Levene's test is more appropriate for this situation because we did not remove the extreme data point (shown as an asterisk in the box plot) because we had no justification for removal. A test for mean difference yielded the following:

```
       Two Sample T-Test and Confidence Interval

Two sample T for attendi vs attend2

                       N     Mean     StDev    SE Mean
attend1 (9/92-5/97)    36    45.14     9.02       1.5
attend2 (9/97-5/98)     9    61.6     18.6        6.2

95% CI for mu attend1 - mu attend2: ( -31.1, -1.7)
T-Test mu attend1 = mu attend2 (vs <): T = -2.57
P = 0.017 DF = 8
```

For this test the null hypothesis was that the two means were equal, while the alternate hypothesis was that there was an improvement in attendance (i.e., one-sided *t*-test). Because the 95% confidence interval did not contain zero (also $P = 0.017$, which is less than 0.05), we can choose to reject the null hypothesis because α is less than 0.05.

From this output we are also 95% confident that our process changes improve mean attendance between 2 and 31 people per meeting. Our best estimate for percentage improvement is

TABLE 19.2 Attendance Data

9/9/93	10/14/93	11/11/93	12/9/93	1/13/94	2/17/94	3/10/94	4/14/94	5/12/94
66	45	61	36	42	41	46	44	47

9/8/94	10/13/94	11/10/94	12/8/94	1/12/95	2/16/95	3/9/95	4/3/95	5/16/95
46	51	42	42	61	57	47	46	28

9/14/95	10/12/95	11/9/95	12/14/95	1/11/96	2/8/96	3/14/96	4/11/96	5/9/96
45	37	45	42	58	49	39	53	58

9/12/96	10/10/96	11/14/96	12/12/96	1/9/97	2/13/97	3/13/97	4/10/95	5/8/97
44	37	52	33	43	45	35	29	33

9/11/97	10/16/97	11/13/97	12/11/97	1/8/97	2/12/98	3/12/98	4/9/98	5/13/98
108	59	51	49	68	60	51	48	60

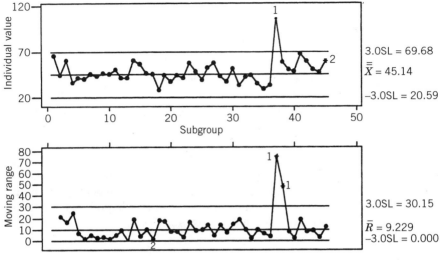

FIGURE 19.5 *XmR* plot of the data.

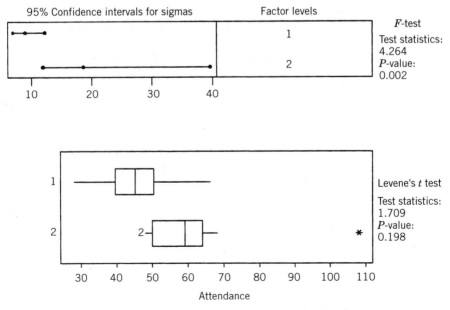

FIGURE 19.6 Homogeneity of combined variance.

$$\text{Best estimate for percent improvement in attendance} = \frac{61.6 - 45.14}{45.14}(100)$$

$$= 36.5\%$$

My stretch goal of doubling meeting attendance was not met; however, attendance was shown (at a significance level of 0.05) to improve during my term as chair with a best estimate of *36.5%*. I felt good about the results of the executive's teams effort to improve attendance. I am confident that the results would have been even better if we could have printed our newsletter at our previous frequency rate of once monthly.

An additional observation from the attendance plot is that it appears that attendance could have been on the decline immediately preceding my term. An exercise at the end of this chapter addresses the null hypothesis that there was no change between my term and the previous year.

19.13 S⁴ ASSESSMENT

Whenever conducting a comparison test, consider whether the test could be conducted using paired comparison techniques. Fewer samples, in general, are required if the test objective can be met using paired comparison techniques, as opposed to comparison tests between samples. In addition, probability plotting techniques can be very useful to better understand the data; a probability plot of the data may indicate that there is something worth investigating, which was not obvious when comparing mean or standard deviation values.

There are problems that can occur when making comparisons. For example, the quality of a part that is to be supplied by a supplier is compared from two sources. A problem with this type of test is that the samples that are drawn do not necessarily represent the type of parts manufactured in the future. Also, the samples need to be taken from processes that are stable. If the processes are not stable, the test conclusion may not be valid.

For this situation an S⁴ consideration might be to have the supplier manufacture (and label) specially made parts that reflect normal boundaries experienced within their processes. A DOE design structure can be used to describe how these specially built parts are to be manufactured, where one of the factors under consideration might be supplier A versus supplier B. Other factors to consider are new versus experienced operator, first shift versus second shift raw material supply source A versus B, high versus low machine tolerance limits manufacturing line A versus B, tester A versus B and so forth. This comparison test build strategy can also give indications on what factors are causing a degraded response (50 that these problems can get "fixed").

For some added insight to the range of variability that might be expected from the current process, a probability plot could be made of all the DOE trial data; note that care should be made interpreting this type of plot because the data are not random.

After a supplier is "qualified" using the preceding procedure, process control charts should be implemented for the purpose of tracking and stopping the process if degradation should later occur. A DOE strategy may again be needed in the future to better understand the source of any degradation.

19.14   EXERCISES

1. *Catapult Exercise Data Analysis:* Using the catapult exercise data sets from Chapter 4, conduct a hypothesis test of the equality of means (and variance) of the two different times the catapult was shot. Document the significance probabilities.

2. From sampled data, note the distribution used when
   (a) calculating the confidence interval on the mean
   (b) calculating the confidence interval on the standard deviation
   (c) comparing two sampled variances

3. In the example described within this section, compare the attendance of my term as ASQ chair to the previous year, as opposed to attendance since 1992.

4. The difference between the actual arrival time and the scheduled arrival time for 20 trips made into Dallas were noted. The flights were on the same airline at approximately the same time of day; however, half of the flights were from St. Louis (denoted as a "S"), while the other half were from New York (denoted as an "N"). Plus values indicate the number of minutes the flight was late. The times were 11.1(S), 8.7 (S), 14.3 (N), 11.1 (S), 10.4 (N), 6.4 (N), 11.2 (S), 6.3 (N), 13.3 (S), 8.9 (N), 11.0 (S), 8.5 (N), 9.4 (S), 10.2 (N), 10.0 (N), 8.7 (S), 9.1 (S), 13.2 (N), 16.5 (N), 9.6 (S).
   (a) Determine at a significance level of 0.05 if the variability in arrival times were longer for the New York flight.
   (b) Determine at a significance level of 0.05 if on the average the arrival time from New York was longer than that from St. Louis.
   (c) To save parking fees, estimate when a friend should meet the traveler at the pickup/drop-off area. Assume that the distribution of these arrival times is representative of future flights. Consider that it takes 10 minutes to walk from the gate to the load zone and that the friend should wait only 5% of the times.

5. It is important that the mean response from a manufacturing process be increased, however, any type of change to the process is expensive to implement. A team decided upon some changes that they thought would be beneficial. They conducted a test with the current process settings and

the new settings. They wanted to be very certain that the change would be beneficial before implementing changing in manufacturing. For this reason, they decided to keep the current process unless they could prove that the new process would be beneficial at a level of significance of 0.01. Discuss results and assess what should be done.

Current process readings: 98.1, 102.3, 98.5, 101.6, 97.7, 100.0, 103.1, 99.1, 97.7, 98.5

New process readings: 100.9, 101.1, 103.4, 85.0, 103.4, 103.6, 100.0, 99.7, 106.4, 101.2

6. In 1985 a manufacturing company produced televisions in both Japan and the United States. A very large random sample of products were taken to evaluate the quality of picture relative to a standard (which was a good measurement for picture quality). It was found that all the US-manufactured products had no defects, while the Japan-built products did have some defects. However, customers typically preferred the picture quality of Japanese-manufactured televisions. Explain this occurrence.

7. A manufacturer wants to determine if two testers yield a similar response. Ten parts were measured on machine A and another ten parts were measured on machine B.

Machine A: 147.3, 153.0, 140.3, 161.0, 145.1, 145.0, 150.1, 158.7, 154.9, 152.8

Machine B: 149.6, 155.5, 141.3, 162.1, 146.7, 145.5, 151.6, 159.3, 154.8, 152.7

(a) Determine if there is a significant difference in the mean response at a level of 0.05.

(b) If the data were collected such that 10 parts were evaluated on each of the two machines with the pairing as noted (e.g., the first part yielded a value of 147.3 on machine A, while it yielded 149.6 on machine B). determine if there is a significant difference in the mean.

(c) For the paired evaluation. use a normal probability plot to pictorially quantity the best estimate difference that would occur 80% of the time. Determine the value using a Z table (i.e. Table A).

8. Given the data sets:

Data set A: 35.8, 40.4, 30.3, 46.8, 34.1, 34.0, 38.1, 45.0, 41.9, 40.2

Data set B: 40.9, 35.7, 36.7, 37.3, 41.8, 39.9, 34.6, 38.8, 35.8, 35.6

(a) Determine if there is a difference in the means at a level of 0.05 for the data.

(b) Determine if the variability from data set A was larger.

(c) Describe a manufacturing. development, and service example where the data could have originated.

9. Describe how the techniques within this chapter are useful and can be applied to S^4 projects.

20

COMPARISON TESTS: ATTRIBUTE (PASS/FAIL) RESPONSE

The next chapter focuses on attribute response situations (e.g., do the failure frequency of completing a purchase order differ between departments?).

20.1 COMPARING ATTRIBUTE DATA

The methods discussed in this chapter can be used, for example, to compare the frequency of failure of two production machines or suppliers. The null hypothesis for the comparison tests is that there is no difference, while the alternate hypothesis is that there is a difference.

20.2 SAMPLE SIZE: COMPARING PROPORTIONS

Natrella (1966) gives tables for sample size selection when comparing the attribute response of two populations. Brush (1988) gives graphs that can be used to aid with the selection of sample sizes. Diamond (1989) multiplies the appropriate single-sampled population calculation by 2 to determine a sample size for each of the two populations. One rule of thumb that does not structurally assess α and β levels is that there should be at least five failures for each category.

20.3 COMPARING PROPORTIONS

The chi-square distribution can be used to compare the frequency of occurrence for discrete variables. An example application is that a company wants to determine if inspectors categorize failure similarly. Consider that inspectors are described as A_1, A_2, and so forth, while types of failures are B_1, B_2, and so forth. Basically the chi-square test is assessing the association (lack of independency) in a two-way classification. This procedure is used when testing to see if the probabilities of items or subjects being classified for one variable depends upon the classification of the other variable.

Data compilation and analysis is in the form of the following contingency table where observations are designated as O_{ij} and expected values are calculated to be E_{ij} (as described below):

	A_1	A_2	A_3	A_n	Total
B_1	O_{11}	O_{12}	O_{13}	O_{1t}	$T_{\text{row } 1} = O_{11} + O_{12} + O_{13} + \cdots + O_{1t}$
	E_{11}	E_{12}	E_{13}	E_{1t}	
B_2	O_{21}	O_{22}	O_{23}	O_{2t}	$T_{\text{row } 2} = O_{21} + O_{22} + O_{23} + \cdots + O_{2t}$
	E_{21}	E_{22}	E_{23}	E_{2t}	
B_3	O_{31}	O_{32}	O_{33}	O_{3t}	$T_{\text{row } 3} = O_{31} + O_{32} + O_{33} + \cdots + O_{3t}$
	E_{31}	E_{32}	E_{33}	E_{3t}	
B_s	O_{s1}	O_{s2}	O_{s3}	O_{st}	$T_{\text{row } s} = O_{31} + O_{32} + O_{33} + \cdots + O_{st}$
	E_{s1}	E_{s2}	E_{s3}	E_{st}	
Total	$T_{\text{col } 1}$	$T_{\text{col } 2}$	$T_{\text{col } 3}$	$T_{\text{col } t}$	$T = T_{\text{row } 1} + T_{\text{row } 2} + T_{\text{row } 3} + \cdots + T_{\text{row } s}$

Expected counts are printed below observed counts. The column totals are the sum of the observations in the columns, similar to the summations in the rows. The expected values are then calculated using the relationship

$$E_{st} = \frac{T_{\text{row } s} \times T_{\text{col } t}}{T} \quad \text{yielding, for example,} \quad E_{11} = \frac{T_{\text{row } 1} \times T_{\text{col } 1}}{T}$$

The null hypothesis might be worded that there is no difference between inspectors. The alternate hypothesis is that at least one of the proportions is different. The chi-square statistic (Table G) could be used when assessing this hypothesis, where the number of degrees of freedom (v) is the (number of rows $-$ 1)(number of columns $-$ 1) and α is the table value. If the following χ^2_{cal} is larger than this chi-square criteria ($\chi^2_{v,\,\alpha}$), the null hypothesis is rejected at α risk.

$$\chi^2_{\text{cal}} = \sum_{i=1}^{s} \sum_{j=1}^{t} \frac{(E_{ij} - O_{ij})^2}{O_{ij}}$$

20.4   EXAMPLE 20.1: COMPARING TWO PROPORTIONS

The ability of three x-ray inspectors at an airport were evaluated on the detection of key items. A test was devised where 90 pieces of luggage where "bugged" with a device that they should question. Each inspector was exposed to exactly 30 of the "bugged" items in random fashion. The null hypothesis is that there is no difference between inspectors. The alternate hypothesis is that at least one of the proportions is different (Wortman 1990).

	Insp 1	Insp 2	Insp 3	Treatment Total
Detected	27	25	22	74
Undetected	3	5	8	16
Sample total	30	30	30	90

A computer analysis of these data yielded the following:

```
Chi-Square Test

Expected counts are printed below observed counts

        Insp 1    Insp 2    Insp 3    Total
   1       27        25        22       74
         24.67     24.67     24.67

   2        3         5         8       16
          5.33      5.33      5.33

Total      30        30        30       90

Chi-Sq = 0.221 + 0.005 + 0.288 +
         1.021 + 0.021 + 1.333 = 2.889

DF = 2, P-Value = 0.236
```

The value for χ^2_{cal} was 2.889. which is not larger than $\chi^2_{v,\alpha} = \chi^2_{2,0.05} = 5.99$; hence, there is not sufficient evidence to reject the null hypothesis at $\alpha = 0.05$. Similarly, we can see from the computer output that the P-value of 0.236 is not less than an α criterion of 0.05.

20.5   COMPARING THE NONCONFORMANCE OF MORE THAN TWO PROPORTIONS

Consider the situation where an organization wants to evaluate the nonconformance rates of several suppliers to determine if there are differences. The previously described chi-square approach could assess this situation from an overall point of view; however, the methodology does not identify which supplier(s) is worse than the others.

A simple approach to address this problem is to plot the nonconformance data in a p-chart format where each supplier would be similar to a subgroup if the chart were a typical p chart. Obviously, no zone tests would be applicable because the order sequence of plotting the supplier information is arbitrary. The only test that is applicable is when a supplier exceeds either the upper or lower control limit.

20.6 S⁴ ASSESSMENT

The methods included within this chapter are traditionally used to compare suppliers, machines, and so forth, by taking samples from the populations. In general, when designing a test, attempts should be made to use a continuous response output, as opposed to an attribute response, whenever possible. For example, a particular part may be considered a failure when it tests beyond a certain level. Instead of analyzing what proportion of parts are beyond this level fewer samples are required if the actual measurement data are analyzed.

Let's revisit the example where a test was conducted to see if there was a difference between inspectors. If we only assessed the results of our hypothesis test deductively, we would stop our investigation because the null hypothesis could not be rejected. However, if we used inductive reasoning, we would learn from these data to perhaps challenge or create a new hypothesis. Using inductive reasoning, we probably should be concerned that the overall detection rate for the "bugs" we applied for the x-ray inspectors was only 82% (i.e., [74/90] × 100). From a practical point of view, it appears that the overall detection process needs to be investigated and improved. Perhaps a control chart program should be implemented as a means to track progress, where periodically over time "bugs" are applied and monitored for detection.

20.7 EXERCISES

1. *Catapult Exercise Data Analysis:* Using the catapult exercise data sets from Chapter 4, adjust the measurement response to consider the specification supplied by instructor (e.g., 75 ± in.). Conduct a hypothesis test of the equality of the attribute responses of the two different times the catapult was shot (e.g., 45 out of 100 failed first time against 10 out of 100 failed the second time). Document the probability level.

2. *M&M's Candy Data Analysis:* In an exercise at the end of Chapter 5 a bag of M&M's candy was opened. A count of each color was made. Attendees within the S⁴ workshop are to pair up with someone else in the class to compare data. Compare the proportion of browns counted in your bags of M&M's. Compare the proportion of browns in one bag to the

proportion of blues in another bag. Describe the applicability of this analysis approach to data you might encounter within your project (also any shortcomings because of the type of data).

3. *M&M's Candy Data Analysis:* In an exercise at the end of Chapter 5 a bag of M&M's candy was opened. A count of each color was made. Compare the proportions of browns that each person had with the bags (except for one person who is to submit their proportions of blue). Describe the applicability of this analysis approach to data you might encounter within your project (also any shortcomings because of the type of data).

4. A manufacturer wants to select only one supplier of a key part that is used within their manufacturing process. The cost for parts from supplier A is larger than that for supplier B. A random sample of 1000 parts was taken from each of the supplier's processes. The output from each sample was compared to the specification. Supplier A had 10 parts beyond the specification limits, while supplier B had 15.

   (a) Determine if there is a significance difference at a level of 0.1.

   (b) Comment on findings and make recommendations.

5. Describe how the techniques within this chapter are useful and can be applied to S^4 projects.

21

BOOTSTRAPPING

Bootstrapping is a resampling technique that provides a simple but effective methodology to describe the uncertainty associated with a summary statement without concern about details of complexity of the chosen summary or exact distribution from which data are calculated (Gunther 1991, 1992; Efron and Tibshirani 1993). This section will illustrate how bootstrapping can be used to determine the confidence interval for C_{pk}/P_{pk}.

21.1 DESCRIPTION

The basic methodology of bootstrapping involves the treatment of samples as though they were the underlying population of data. Consider, for example, selecting and making a measurement from 50 samples of a stable process. Now take many samples (1000 is typical) from these measurements where sampling is conducted with replacement. Compute the mean and other statistics of interest (e.g., median standard deviation, and percent of population) for each of the 1000 samples. Rank each statistic of interest. Determine the confidence interval for the statistic by choosing the value at the appropriate ranking level. For example, the 90% confidence interval for the ranking of 1000 mean values would be the values at the 100 and 900 ranking levels.

Bootstrapping frees practitioners from arbitrary assumptions and limiting procedures of classical methods that are based on normal theory. The methodology provides an intuitively appealing, statistically rigorous, and potentially automatic way for the assessment of uncertainty of estimates from sampled data that are taken from a variety of processes; however, a computer is needed to perform the random sampling. The technique can be used to determine a confidence interval for C_{pk} and/or P_{pk}.

The approach has meaning (like all confidence interval calculations) only when the process is stable. Without stability, the results from current sampling cannot give information about future sampling because we would not be able to determine whether value changes are caused by what is being measured or changes in the process. However, the technique can still be useful for two reasons. First, confidence intervals give us a snapshot of what should happen if current behavior continues. Second, these confidence intervals can discourage basing decisions on inadequate data.

Bootstrapping is easy to understand, is automatic, gives honest estimates (i.e., stringent assumptions are not required), and has good theoretical properties. Bootstrapping has potential for many applications beyond simple sampling statistics; however, sometimes these intervals are not quite right when the bootstrap distribution is biased. For these situations the estimate from the sample is not near enough to the median of the distribution of the bootstrap estimates. However. there is a simple bias correction procedure developed by Bradley Efron to fix this problem (Gunther 1991, 1992; Efron and Tibshirani 1993). The basic bias correction procedure of Efron is described in Example 21.2.

Bootstrapping can be a very useful tool; however, it does not give valid statistical inferences on everything. Dixon (1993), Hall (1992), Efron and Tibshirani (1993), and Shao and Tu (1995) describe limitations and other technical considerations of bootstrapping.

21.2 EXAMPLE 21.1: BOOTSTRAPPING TO DETERMINE CONFIDENCE INTERVAL FOR MEAN, STANDARD DEVIATION, P_p, AND P_{pk}

The data in Table 11.2 were used previously to illustrate procedures to determine P_p and P_{pk} (i.e., I am using this terminology instead of C_p and C_{pk} so that there is no confusion that we are taking a "long-term" view of variability). In this example we will calculate confidence intervals for these statistics along with confidence intervals for the mean and standard deviation using bootstrapping techniques. Comparison will be made to applicable formulas when appropriate.

Statistics determined from the sample were: $\bar{x} = 0.7375$, $s = 0.0817$, $P_p = 0.8159$, and $P_{pk} = 0.6629$. Bootstrap samples are then taken from the sample, where the 80 samples are resampled with replacement. My first bootstrap samples were

0.70 0.80 0.75 0.70 0.75 0.65 0.85 0.70 0.75 0.80 0.70 0.65 0.85
      0.80 0.50 0.85 0.80 0.65 0.60 0.75 0.80 0.65 0.85 0.70 0.85
      0.70 0.65 0.65 0.80 0.65 0.85 0.70 0.85 0.85 0.65 0.75 0.80
      0.75 0.85 0.75 0.80 0.75 0.60 0.90 0.85 0.80 0.75 0.75 0.70
      0.80 0.85 0.80 0.75 0.70 0.75 0.70 0.80 0.70 0.85 0.60 0.85
      0.50 0.65 0.65 0.75 0.65 0.80 0.70 0.60 0.90 0.65 0.85 0.85
      0.60 0.70 0.80 0.70 0.65 0.70 0.85

while the second bootstrap samples were

0.70 0.75 0.65 0.60 0.60 0.90 0.70 0.75 0.75 0.80 0.70 0.75 0.75
      0.85 0.75 0.85 0.70 0.75 0.75 0.80 0.65 0.70 0.80 0.65 0.65
      0.70 0.80 0.75 0.65 0.80 0.90 0.80 0.75 0.85 0.85 0.90 0.65
      0.75 0.80 0.75 0.70 0.75 0.65 0.65 0.65 0.75 0.70 0.75 0.65
      0.75 0.65 0.85 0.70 0.75 0.75 0.85 0.65 0.75 0.65 0.80 0.60
      0.85 0.75 0.85 0.60 0.80 0.80 0.70 0.80 0.85 0.75 0.80 0.85
      0.60 0.85 0.80 0.60 0.60 0.75 0.70

This resampling was repeated 1000 times using a computer program. For each example the mean, standard deviation, P_p, and P_{pk} were determined. Table 21.1 contains some of the ranked results for each of the four calculated statistics. Because there were 1000 bootstrap samples, the pertinent values from this table to determine the 95% confidence interval are as follows:

Ranked No.	Mean	SD	P_p	P_{pk}
50	0.722500	0.070641	0.729374	0.579831
500	0.737500	0.080975	0.822926	0.669102
950	0.752500	0.091368	0.943406	0.775125

The 95% confidence interval for the mean, for example, would be $0.7225 \le \mu \le 0.7525$.

We really do not need to use bootstrapping to determine a confidence interval for the mean, standard deviation, and P_p statistic, because these values can be determined through a direction equation relationship. However, it is not so easy to determine a confidence interval for P_{pk} and other statistics such as percent of population. The mean, standard deviation, and P_p statistic were included in this example so that comparisons could be made between bootstrap and calculated values.

The confidence interval for the mean calculation is

TABLE 21.1 A Selection of Ranked Bootstrap Results from 1000 Samples

Ranked No.	Mean	SD	P_p	P_{pk}	Ranked No.	Mean	SD	P_p	P_{pk}
1	0.706875	0.059521	0.656375	0.505541	504	0.737500	0.081043	0.823696	0.669264
2	0.709375	0.063367	0.665732	0.505798	505	0.737500	0.081043	0.823721	0.669647
40	0.721875	0.070079	0.724993	0.575695	506	0.737500	0.081043	0.823721	0.669697
41	0.722500	0.070236	0.724993	0.576120	940	0.751875	0.090699	0.938218	0.767487
42	0.722500	0.070250	0.725605	0.576358	941	0.751875	0.090699	0.938402	0.768494
43	0.722500	0.070250	0.725962	0.576936	942	0.751875	0.090914	0.939249	0.771415
44	0.722500	0.070304	0.726781	0.577194	943	0.751875	0.090977	0.939249	0.771843
45	0.722500	0.070416	0.727328	0.577194	944	0.751875	0.090977	0.939286	0.772424
46	0.722500	0.070442	0.727465	0.577340	945	0.751875	0.091001	0.940431	0.772769
47	0.722500	0.070442	0.728151	0.577631	946	0.751875	0.091001	0.940765	0.774240
48	0.722500	0.070461	0.728271	0.577813	947	0.751875	0.091123	0.941358	0.774660
49	0.722500	0.070461	0.728340	0.578178	948	0.751875	0.091140	0.941655	0.774743
50	0.722500	0.070641	0.729374	0.579831	949	0.752500	0.091325	0.942958	0.774743
51	0.722500	0.070666	0.729651	0.579891	950	0.752500	0.091368	0.943406	0.775125
52	0.722500	0.070699	0.729996	0.580076	951	0.752500	0.091403	0.943743	0.775330
53	0.723125	0.070797	0.731472	0.581249	952	0.752500	0.091532	0.946146	0.775777
54	0.723125	0.070820	0.731612	0.581556	953	0.752500	0.091541	0.946146	0.776451
55	0.723125	0.070864	0.732590	0.581646	954	0.752500	0.091556	0.946410	0.776982

TABLE 21.1 (*Continued*)

Ranked No.	Mean	SD	P_p	P_{pk}	Ranked No.	Mean	SD	P_p	P_{pk}
440	0.736250	0.079950	0.815103	0.658464	955	0.752500	0.091642	0.946410	0.777119
441	0.736250	0.079950	0.815465	0.659058	980	0.755625	0.094045	0.966055	0.800214
442	0.736250	0.079992	0.815465	0.659181	981	0.755625	0.094098	0.972540	0.800831
443	0.736250	0.080029	0.815489	0.659258	982	0.755625	0.094197	0.972540	0.802667
444	0.736250	0.080029	0.815851	0.659276	983	0.756250	0.094365	0.973524	0.803572
445	0.736250	0.080029	0.815851	0.659423	984	0.756250	0.094381	0.979156	0.805523
446	0.736250	0.080049	0.815876	0.659423	985	0.756250	0.094635	0.980119	0.811029
447	0.736250	0.080101	0.816069	0.659423	986	0.756875	0.094668	0.981168	0.812090
448	0.736250	0.080101	0.816238	0.659585	987	0.756875	0.094699	0.984548	0.817541
449	0.736250	0.080111	0.816335	0.659640	988	0.757500	0.094749	0.986892	0.817541
450	0.736250	0.080128	0.816335	0.659884	989	0.757500	0.094935	0.987749	0.819210
493	0.737500	0.080897	0.822604	0.667719	990	0.758125	0.095459	1.003200	0.823103
494	0.737500	0.080914	0.822604	0.667827	991	0.758750	0.095599	1.007404	0.826522
495	0.737500	0.080934	0.822604	0.667885	992	0.759375	0.095630	1.010467	0.827803
496	0.737500	0.080934	0.822604	0.667889	993	0.759375	0.096053	1.012909	0.831789
497	0.737500	0.080936	0.822604	0.667889	994	0.760000	0.096119	1.020391	0.832379
498	0.737500	0.080936	0.822604	0.669021	995	0.760625	0.096382	1.020911	0.839950
499	0.737500	0.080973	0.822728	0.669053	996	0.761250	0.096710	1.028573	0.844865
500	0.737500	0.080975	0.822926	0.669102	997	0.761250	0.096765	1.031540	0.847229
501	0.737500	0.081012	0.823299	0.669102	998	0.765000	0.099166	1.048303	0.867720
502	0.737500	0.081031	0.823323	0.669253	999	0.767500	0.100140	1.052066	0.917047
503	0.737500	0.081043	0.823696	0.669253	1000	0.768125	0.101568	1.120057	0.925201

$$\bar{x} - \frac{t_\alpha s}{\sqrt{n}} \leq \mu \leq \bar{x} + \frac{t_\alpha s}{\sqrt{n}}$$

$$0.7375 - \frac{1.99(0.0817)}{\sqrt{80}} \leq \mu \leq 0.7375 + \frac{1.99(0.0817)}{\sqrt{80}}$$

$$0.7375 - 0.0182 \leq \mu \leq 0.7375 + 0.0182$$

$$0.7193 \leq \mu \leq 0.7557$$

The results from the confidence interval are comparable to the bootstrap interval of $0.7225 \leq \mu \leq 0.7525$. If we ran another 1000 bootstrap samples, our confidence interval should differ by some small amount. Let's now compare the results for standard deviation using the relationship

$$\left[\frac{(n-1)s^2}{\chi^2_{\alpha/2;n-1}}\right]^{1/2} \leq \sigma \leq \left[\frac{(n-1)s^2}{\chi^2_{(1-\alpha/2;n-1)}}\right]^{1/2}$$

$$\left[\frac{(80-1)(0.0817)^2}{\chi^2_{(0.1/2;[80-1])}}\right]^{1/2} \leq \sigma \leq \left[\frac{(80-1)(0.0817)^2}{\chi^2_{(1-[0.1/2];[80-1])}}\right]^{1/2}$$

$$\left[\frac{0.5273}{105.4727}\right]^{1/2} \leq \sigma \leq \left[\frac{0.5273}{56.3089}\right]^{1/2}$$

$$0.0707 \leq \sigma \leq 0.0968$$

These confidence interval results are again comparable to the bootstrap interval of $0.0706 \leq \sigma \leq 0.0914$. Let's now compare the results for the confidence interval for P_p

$$\hat{P}_p \sqrt{\frac{\chi^2_{1-\alpha/2;n-1}}{n-1}} \leq P_p \leq \hat{P}_p \sqrt{\frac{\chi^2_{\alpha/2;n-1}}{n-1}}$$

$$0.8159 \sqrt{\frac{56.3089}{80-1}} \leq P_p \leq 0.8159 \sqrt{\frac{105.4727}{80-1}}$$

$$0.6888 \leq P_p \leq 0.9427$$

Because the results are comparable to the bootstrap interval for P_p of $0.7294 \leq P_p \leq 0.9434$, we would probably be fairly comfortable reporting also the P_{pk} 95% confidence bootstrap interval of $0.5798 \leq P_{pk} \leq 0.7751$, which we cannot determine through a simple mathematical relationship.

21.3   EXAMPLE 21.2: BOOTSTRAPPING WITH BIAS CORRECTION

This example illustrates application of Efron's bias correction methodology for the bootstrap interval estimate. In this example the 95% confidence interval of P_p will be determined and compared to the values determined in the previous example; however, other situations can have a higher need for this bias correction procedure.

To adjust for bias, we first note that we previously determined $P_p = 0.8159$ from the original data set. From Table 21.1 we determine a proportion of samples that are less than or equal to this sample value. From this table we note the following:

Ranked No.	Mean	SD	P_p	P_{pk}
445	0.736250	0.080029	0.815851	0.659423
446	0.736250	0.080049	0.815876	0.659423
447	0.736250	0.080101	0.816069	0.659423

The ranking number of 446 is used to determine this percentage because the value of P_p for this ranking number is 0.815876, which is less than or equal to 0.8159, and the P_p value of 0.816069 for ranking number 447 is greater than the P_p sample value of 0.8159. This proportion then equates to 0.446 (i.e., 446/1000).

The Z value (Z_0) for this proportion is then determined to be 0.1358 (from Table A or a computer program). For a 95% confidence interval, $\alpha = 0.025$ and $Z_\alpha = 1.96$. The upper and lower values are determined from the relationship of $2 \times Z_0 \pm z_\alpha$. These relationships yield lower and upper values of -1.6884 and 2.2315, which correspond to normal CDF values of 0.0457 and 0.98721. A lower bootstrap value is then determined such that its value is as close as possible but no larger than the 0.0457 value. An upper bootstrap value is also determined such that its value is as close as possible but no smaller than 0.9872. This relationship yields a lower bootstrap value of 45 (i.e., $1000 \times 0.0457 = 45.7$) and an upper bootstrap value of 988 (i.e., $1000 \times 0.09872 = 987.2$). From Table 21.1 for these bootstrap values we can determine an unbiased bootstrap estimate of $0.7273 \le P_p \le 0.9869$.

21.4   BOOTSTRAPPING APPLICATIONS

Bootstrapping can be applied to more situations beyond those described within this chapter (e.g., time series). However, let's consider in this section three extensions of the strategy described within this chapter.

For the first scenario a confidence interval for the median can be easily obtained using bootstrapping techniques, a statistic not readily available with standard theory. A median value can often give more insight to describe the characteristics of a population for a skewed distribution. For example, the median value of houses within an area typically gives more insight than the mean value of houses. A few high-valued houses can increase a mean a lot, giving a distorted perception of typical house values. This problem does not occur when a median value is reported.

For the second scenario consider calculating a mean and standard deviation for bootstraps and then combine these values to estimate a "percentage less than value," for example, three standard deviations from the sample mean. A confidence interval can then be obtained for this "percentage less than value." An extension to methodology is to transform non-normal data before applying the technique.

For the third situation consider a reliability test where the failure times of sample components are determined. It might be desired to determine the percentage expected to survive a particular amount of usage. From the data a maximum likelihood estimate for this percentage could be obtained for the sample using a computer program (or a manual estimate could be determined from a probability plot of the data). A confidence interval for this survival percentage can be determined using bootstrapping techniques by resampling the sample, determining the maximum likelihood (or manual) estimate of the desired value for each sample, and then determining a confidence interval using the same procedure described earlier.

21.5 EXERCISES

1. *Catapult Exercise Data Analysis:* Using the catapult exercise data sets from Chapter 4, use bootstrapping to determine the confidence intervals for mean, standard deviation, P_p, and P_{pk} (i.e., "long-term").

2. A previous exercise asked for the calculation of process capability from the following set of data. Determine now, using a computer, the bootstrap confidence interval for the mean, standard deviation (of all data combined), P_p, and P_{pk} (without and with bias correction). Compare bootstrap values to calculated values whenever possible. The origination of the data is as follows: An example $\bar{x}$ and R chart in the control chart chapter indicated that samples numbered 8, 9, 10, 12, 13, and 18 were out of control. The process specifications are 0.4037 ± 0.0013 (i.e., 0.4024 to 0.4050). Tabular and calculated values will be in units of 0.0001 (i.e., the specification limits will be considered 24 to 50). Assume that for each of these data points, circumstances for an out-of-control response were identified and will be avoided in future production.

1	36	35	34	33	32
2	31	31	34	32	30
3	30	30	32	30	32
4	32	33	33	32	35
5	32	34	37	37	35
6	32	32	31	33	33
7	33	33	36	32	31
8	34	38	35	34	38
9	36	35	37	34	33
10	30	37	33	34	35
11	28	31	33	33	33
12	33	30	34	33	35
13	35	36	29	27	32
14	33	35	35	39	36

3. Determine the confidence interval for P_{pk} for the data set in Table 21.1 using the bias correction procedure. Compare this interval to the non-corrected interval determined as an example within this chapter.

4. Describe how the techniques within this chapter are useful and can be applied to S^4 projects.

22

VARIANCE COMPONENTS

The methodology described within this chapter is a random effects model or components of variance model (as opposed to a fixed effects model as described within the analysis of variance chapter). The statistical model for the random effects or components of variance model is similar to that of the fixed effects model. The difference is that in the random effects model the levels (or treatments) could be a random sample from a larger population of levels. For this situation we would like to extend conclusions (which are based on sample of levels) to all population levels whether explicitly considered or not. In the situation the test hypothesis is about the variability from factor levels where we try to quantify this variability.

22.1 DESCRIPTION

Earlier we discussed the impact that key process input variables can have on the output of a process. A fixed effects model assesses how the level of key process input variables affects the mean response of key process outputs, while a random effects model assesses how the variability of key process input variables affect the variability of key process outputs.

A key process output of a manufacturing process could be the dimension or characteristic of a product. A key process output of a service or business process could be time from initiation to delivery. The total affect of n variance components on a key process output can be expressed as the sum of the variances of each of the components:

$$\sigma_{\text{total}}^2 = \sigma_1^2 + \sigma_2^2 + \sigma_3^2 + \cdots + \sigma_n^2$$

The components of variance within a manufacturing process could be material, machines, operators, and the measurement system. In service or business processes the variance components can be the day of the month the request was initiated, department-to-department variations when handling a request, and the quality of the input request. An important use of variance components is the isolation of different sources of variability that affect product or system variability. This problem of product variability frequently arises in quality assurance, where the isolation of the sources for this variability can often be very difficult.

Because of the nature of the situation, a test to determine these variance components often has the nesting structure as exemplified in Figure 22.1. Other texts describe the detail of the analysis of variance method to estimate variance components. In this procedure the expected mean squares of the analysis of variance table are equated to their observed value in the analysis of variance table and then solved for the variance components. In this text a statistical computer analysis program will be used for computations.

Occasionally, variance components analyses yield negative estimates. Negative estimates are viewed with concern because it is obvious that by definition, variance components cannot be negative. For these situations it has intuitive appeal to accept the negative estimate and use it as evidence that the true value is zero. This approach suffers from theoretical difficulties because using a zero in place of the negative estimates can affect the statistical properties of the other estimates. Another approach is to use an alternate calculating technique that yields a nonnegative estimate. Still another approach is to consider that this is evidence that the linear model is incorrect and the problem needs to be reexamined.

An output often included with a computer variance component analyses is the expected mean-square values. Although not described in this text, these values can be used to determine confidence intervals for variance components or percent contribution.

22.2   EXAMPLE 22.1: VARIANCE COMPONENTS OF PIGMENT PASTE

Consider that numerous batches of a pigment paste are sampled and tested once. We would like to understand the variation of the resulting moisture

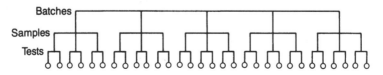

FIGURE 22.1 A $5 \times 3 \times 2$ hierarchical design. [From Box et al. (1978), with permission.]

content as a function of those components shown pictorially in Figure 22.2 (Box et al. 1978).

In this figure, η is shown to be the long-run process mean for moisture content. In this figure, process variation is shown to be the distribution of batch means about this process mean, sampling variation is shown to be the distribution of samples about the batch mean, and analytical variation is shown to be the distribution of analytical test results about the sample mean.

The overall error ($\varepsilon = y - \eta$) will contain the three separate error components (i.e., $\varepsilon = \varepsilon_t + \varepsilon_s + \varepsilon_b$), where ε_t is the analytical test error, ε_s is the error made in taking the samples, and ε_b is the batch-to-batch error. By these definitions the mean of the error components (i.e., ε_t, ε_s, and ε_b) have zero means. The assumption is made that the samples are random (independent) from normal distributions with fixed variances σ_t^2, σ_s^2, σ_b^2.

Consider now the following data that was collected using the hierarchical design shown in Figure 22.1:

		Batch														
Sample	Subsample	1	2	3	4	5	6	7	8	9	10	11	12	13	14	15
1	1	40	26	29	30	19	33	23	34	27	13	25	29	19	23	39
	2	39	28	28	31	20	32	24	34	27	16	23	29	20	24	37
2	1	30	25	14	24	17	26	32	29	31	27	25	31	29	25	26
	2	30	26	15	24	17	24	33	29	31	24	27	32	30	25	28

A variance components analysis for this set of experimental data is as follows:

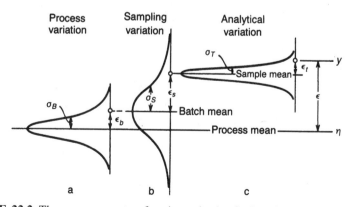

FIGURE 22.2 Three components of variance in the final moisture reading. (**a**) Distribution of batch means about the process mean η. (**b**) Distribution of sample means about the batch mean. (**c**) Distribution of analytical test results about sample mean. [From Box et al. (1978), with permission.]

Fully Nested Analysis of Variance

Analysis of Variance for Moisture

Source	DF	SS	MS	F	P
Batch	14	1210.9333	86.4952	1.492	0.226
Sample	15	869.7500	57.9833	63.255	0.000
Error	30	27.5000	0.9167		
Total	59	2108.1833			

Variance Components

Source	Var Comp.	% of Total	StDev
Batch	7.128	19.49	2.670
Sample	28.533	78.01	5.342
Error	0.917	2.51	0.957
Total	36.578		6.048

For this analysis the "sample" is nested in "batch." The variance components estimated in the model are

Analytical test variance = 0.92
Sample variance (within batches) = 28.5
Process variance (between batches) = 7.1

The square roots of these variances are estimates of the standard deviations that are pictorially compared in Figure 22.3. These results indicate that the largest individual source for variation was the error arising in chemical sampling. Investigators given this information then discovered and resolved the problem of operators not being aware of the correct sampling procedure.

22.3 EXAMPLE 22.2: VARIANCE COMPONENTS OF A MANUFACTURED DOOR INCLUDING MEASUREMENT SYSTEM COMPONENTS

When a door is closed, it needs to seal well with its mating service. Some twist of the manufactured door can be tolerated because of a seal that is attached to the door; however, a large degree of twist cannot be tolerated because the seal would not be effective, excessive force would be required to close the door, and excessive load on the door latching mechanism could in time cause failure.

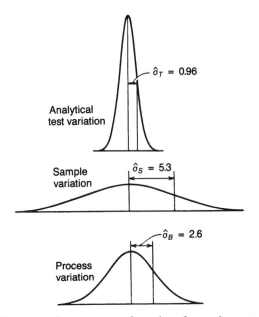

FIGURE 22.3 Diagrammatic summary of results of experiment to determine components of variance. [From Box et al. (1978), with permission.]

Let's consider this situation from the point of view of the supplier of the door. The burden of how well a door latches due to twist does not completely lie with the supplier of the door. If the mating door frame is twisted, no matter how well the door is manufactured, there can be a customer problem. The supplier of the door never sees the door frame; hence, they cannot check the quality of the overall assembly. Also, the doors are supposed to be interchangeable between frames.

Doors are often rejected by the customer of the door supplier. The supplier of the door can only manufacture to the specification. But the question then arises on how to measure the door twist. Drawing specifications indicate that the area where the door is to seal has a 0.031-in. tolerance. Currently, this dimension is measured within the fixture that manufacturers the door. However, it has been noticed that the door tends to spring into a different position after leaving the fixture. Because of this it was concluded that a measurement fixture needed to be built that would check the door similar to how the door is used by the customer (i.e., mount the door where it is hinged when taking the measurements that assess how the door seals).

A nested experiment was then planned where other issues of concern were also included (e.g., measurement system). There was only one manufacturing jig and one inspection jig. The following sources of variability were considered: week-to-week, shift-to-shift, operator-to-operator, within-part variability, inspector measurement repeatability, and inspector measurement reproducibility.

22.4 EXAMPLE 22.3: DETERMINING PROCESS CAPABILITY USING VARIANCE COMPONENTS

The following set of data (AIAG 1995b) was presented initially as Exercise 3 in Chapter 10 on control charts. Example 11.2 within the process capability/performance chapter described a procedure used to calculate process capability/performance for this in-control process. This chapter gives an additional calculation procedure for determining standard deviations from the process. Additional procedures for process capability/performance calculations are described within the single-factor analysis of variance chapter.

		\multicolumn{16}{c}{Subgroups}
		1	2	3	4	5	6	7	8	9	10	11	12	13	14	15	16
	1	0.65	0.75	0.75	0.60	0.70	0.60	0.75	0.60	0.65	0.60	0.80	0.85	0.70	0.65	0.90	0.75
	2	0.70	0.85	0.80	0.70	0.75	0.75	0.80	0.70	0.80	0.70	0.75	0.75	0.70	0.70	0.80	0.80
Samples	3	0.65	0.75	0.80	0.70	0.65	0.75	0.65	0.80	0.85	0.60	0.90	0.85	0.75	0.85	0.80	0.75
	4	0.65	0.85	0.70	0.75	0.85	0.85	0.75	0.75	0.85	0.80	0.50	0.65	0.75	0.75	0.75	0.80
	5	0.85	0.65	0.75	0.65	0.80	0.70	0.70	0.75	0.75	0.65	0.80	0.70	0.70	0.60	0.85	0.65

This control chart data has samples nested within the subgroups. A random-effects model would yield the following computer analysis results:

Fully Nested Analysis of Variance

```
Analysis of Variance for Data

Source  DF      SS       MS       F       P
Subgrp  15   0.1095   0.0073   1.118   0.360
Error   64   0.4180   0.0065
Total   79   0.5275


Variance Components

Source  Var Comp.  % of Total  StDev
Subgrp    0.000        2.30    0.012
Error     0.007       97.70    0.081
Total     0.007                0.082
```

An interpretation of this output is the "long-term" standard deviation would be the total component of 0.082, while the "short-term" standard deviation component would be the error component of 0.081. These values for standard deviation are very similar to the values determined using the approach described within the process capability chapter.

In general a variance components technique can be very beneficial to determine process capability when there is a hierarchical of sources affecting process variability. The strategy not only will describe the variability of the process for process capability/performance calculations, but will also give insight to where process improvement focus should be given to reduce the magnitude of component variabilities.

22.5   EXAMPLE 22.4: VARIANCE COMPONENTS ANALYSIS OF INJECTION-MOLDING DATA

From the multi-vari analysis in Example 15.1 of the injection molding data described in Table 15.1 it was thought that differences between cavities affected the diameter of parts. A variance components analysis of the factors yielded the following results, where the raw data was multiplied by 10,000 so that the magnitude of the variance components would be large enough to be quantified on the computer output.

Fully Nested Analysis of Variance

Analysis of Variance for Diameter

Source	DF	SS	MS	F	P
Time	2	56.4444	28.2222	0.030	0.970
Cavity	9	8437.3750	937.4861	17.957	0.000
Part	12	626.5000	52.2083	1.772	0.081
Position	48	1414.0000	29.4583		
Total	71	10534.3194			

Variance Components

Source	Var Comp.	% of Total	StDev
Time	-37.886*	0.00	0.000
Cavity	147.546	79.93	12.147
Part	7.583	4.11	2.754
Position	29.458	15.96	5.428
Total	184.588		13.586

Within this analysis, variability between position was used to estimate error. From this analysis we note that the probability value for cavity is the only factor less than 0.05 using position measurements to estimate error. From this analysis we estimate that the variability between cavities is the largest contributor (i.e., estimated to be most 80% of total variability). We also note that the percentage value for position has a fairly high percentage value relative to time. This could indicate that there are significant differences in measurements across the parts, which is consistent with our observation from the multi-vari chart. Variance component factors need to be adjusted by the 10,000 multiple initially made to the raw data.

22.6 S⁴ ASSESSMENT

Variability is often the elusive enemy of manufacturing processes. Variance components analysis can aid in the identification of the major contributors to this variability.

As noted earlier, variance components techniques can be used for process capability/performance assessments. When variability in a product or process is too large and the source for this variability is understood, perhaps only a few simple changes are necessary to reduce its magnitude and improve quality.

In other cases there may not be good insight on how a large detrimental variance component can be reduced. In this case it could be appropriate to next use a DOE strategy that considers various factors that could contribute to the largest amount of variability in the area of concern; output from this experiment could lead to better insight to what changes should be made to the process for the purpose of reducing variability. Perhaps this analysis can lead to the development of a process that is more robust to the variability of raw material.

Before conducting a gauge R&R study, as described within an earlier chapter, consider replacing the study with a variance components analysis, which can give more insight into the sources of variability for process improvement efforts. It may be found from this analysis that the measurement procedure is causing much variability and needs to be improved.

22.7 EXERCISES

1. *Catapult Exercise:* Conduct a variance components analysis of the catapult considering bands (3 bands) mount of bands (2 remounts of bands), repeatability of shots (2 replications), and reproducibility of measurements (2 people measuring the distance). There will be a total of 24 recordings for this experiment; however, there will be only 12 shots because two people will be making a shot measurement at the same time. The sequence of events is as follows:

   • Choose a rubber band, mount the band, take a shot, and measure the distance twice by two spotters.
   • Take another shot and measure the distance with two spotters.
   • Remount the rubber bands, take a shot, and measure the distance twice with two spotters.
   • Take another shot and measure the distance with two spotters.

- Select another rubber band, mount the band, take a shot, and measure the distance twice with two spotters.
- Repeat the above until a total of 24 readings (12 shots) are completed.

Estimate the variance components and assess the significance of the factors.

2. Fabric is woven on a large number of looms (Montgomery 1997). It is suspected that variation can occur both within samples from fabric from the same loom and between different looms. To investigate this, four looms were randomly selected and four strength determinations were made on the fabric that was produced. The data from this experiment were as follows:

Looms	Observations			
	1	2	3	4
1	98	97	99	96
2	91	90	93	92
3	96	95	97	95
4	95	96	99	98

3. Example 22.3 described a variance components strategy to measure the twist of a door. Build a plan to execute this strategy. Include the number of samples for each factor considered.

4. Describe how the techniques within this chapter are useful and can be applied to S^4 projects.

23

CORRELATION AND SIMPLE LINEAR REGRESSION

Within processes there is often a direct relationship between two variables. If a strong relationship between a process input variable is correlated with a key process output variable, the input variable could then be considered a key process input variable. The equation $Y = f(x)$ can express this relationship for continuous variables, where Y is the dependent variable and x is the independent variable. Parameters of this equation can be determined using regression techniques.

After the establishment of a relationship, an appropriate course of action would depend upon the particulars of the situation. If the overall process is not capable of consistently meeting the needs of the customer, it may be appropriate to initiate tighter specifications or to initiate control charts for this key process input variable. However, if the variability of a key process input variable describes the normal variability of raw material, an alternate course of action might be more appropriate. For this case it could be beneficial to conduct a DOE with the objective of determining other factor settings that would improve the process output robustness to normal variabilities of this key process input variable.

The mathematical relationships described within this chapter will focus on linear relationships. In general, correlation between two variables can be quadratic or even cubic. When investigating data it is important to plot the data. If there appears to be another relationship besides linear, other models can be investigated for a fit using a commercially available statistical analysis program.

23.1   SCATTER PLOT (DISPERSION GRAPH)

A scatter plot or dispersion graph pictorially describes the relationship between two variables. It gives a simple illustration of how one variable can influence the other. Care must be exercised when interpreting dispersion graphs. A plot that shows a relationship does not prove a true cause-and-effect relationship. Happenstance data can cause the appearance of a relationship. For example, the phase of the moon could appear to affect a process that has a monthly cycle.

When constructing a dispersion graph, first clearly define the variables that are to be evaluated. Next collect at least 30 data pairs (50 or 100 pairs is better). Plot data pairs using the horizontal axis for probable cause and using the vertical axis for probable effect.

23.2   CORRELATION

A statistic that can describe the strength of a linear relationship between two variables is the sample correlation coefficient (r). A correlation coefficient can take values between -1 and $+1$. A -1 indicates perfect negative correlation, while a $+1$ indicates perfect positive correlation. A zero indicates no correlation. The equation for the sample correlation coefficient (r) of two variables is

$$r = \frac{\sum (x_i - \bar{x})(y_i - \bar{y})}{\sqrt{\sum (x_i - \bar{x})^2 \sum (y_i - \bar{y})^2}}$$

where (x_i, y_i) are the coordinate pair of evaluated values and $\bar{x}$ and $\bar{y}$ are the averages of the x and y values, respectively. Figure 23.1 shows four plots with various correlation characteristics. It is important to plot the analyzed data. Two data variables may show no linear correlation but may still have a quadratic relationship. The hypothesis test for the correlation coefficient (ρ) to equal zero is

$$H_0: \rho = 0$$

$$H_A: \rho \neq 0$$

If the x and y relationships are jointly normally distributed, the test statistic for this hypothesis is

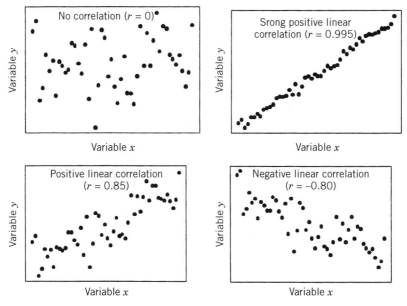

FIGURE 23.1 Correlation coefficients.

$$t_0 = \frac{r\sqrt{n-2}}{\sqrt{1-r^2}}$$

where the null hypothesis is rejected if $|t_0| > t_{\alpha/2, n-2}$ using a one-sided t-table value.

Coefficient of determination (R^2) is simply the square of the correlation coefficient. Values for R^2 describe the percentage of variability accounted for by the model. For example, $R^2 = 0.8$ indicates that 80% of the variability in the data is accounted for by the model.

23.3   EXAMPLE 23.1: CORRELATION

The times for 25 soft drink deliveries (y) monitored as a function of delivery volume (x) is shown in Table 23.1 (Montgomery and Peck 1982). The scatter diagram of these data shown in Figure 23.2 indicates that there probably is a strong correlation between the two variables. The sample correlation coefficient between delivery time and delivery volume is determined through use of a computer program or equation to be

TABLE 23.1 Delivery Time Data

Number of Cases (x)	Delivery Time (y)	Number of Cases (x)	Delivery Time (y)	Number of Cases (x)	Delivery Time (y)	Number of Cases (x)	Delivery Time (y)	Number of Cases (x)	Delivery Time (y)
7	16.68	7	18.11	16	40.33	10	29.00	10	17.90
3	11.50	2	8.00	10	21.00	6	15.35	26	52.32
3	12.03	7	17.83	4	13.50	7	19.00	9	18.75
4	14.88	30	79.24	6	19.75	3	9.50	8	19.83
6	13.75	5	21.50	9	24.00	17	35.10	4	10.75

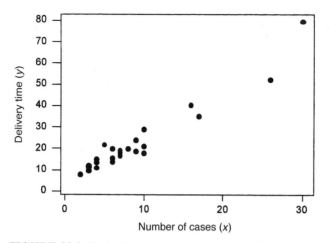

FIGURE 23.2 Plot of number of cases versus delivery time.

$$r = \frac{\sum (x_i - \bar{x})(y_i - \bar{y})}{\sqrt{\sum (x_i - \bar{x})^2 \sum (y_i - \bar{y})^2}} = \frac{2473.3440}{\sqrt{(1136.5700)(5784.5426)}} = 0.9646$$

Testing the null hypothesis that the correlation coefficient equals zero yields

$$t_0 = \frac{r\sqrt{n-2}}{\sqrt{1-r^2}} = \frac{0.9646\sqrt{25-2}}{\sqrt{1-0.9646^2}} = 17.56$$

Using a single-sided t-table (i.e., Table D) at $\alpha/2$, we can reject H_0 because $|t_0| > t_{\alpha/2,n-2}$, where $t_{0.05/2,23} = 2.069$. Or, we could use a two-sided t-table (i.e., Table E) at α. This data are discussed again in Exercise 23.2.

23.4 SIMPLE LINEAR REGRESSION

Correlation only measures association, while regression methods are useful to develop quantitative variable relationships that are useful for prediction. For this relationship the independent variable is variable x, while the dependent variable is y. This section gives focus to regression models that contain linear variables; however, regression models can also include quadratic and cubic terms.

The simple linear regression model (i.e., with a single regressor x) takes the form

$$Y = \beta_0 + \beta_1 x + \varepsilon \qquad i = 1, 2, \ldots, n$$

where β_0 is the intercept, β_1 is the slope, and ε is the error term. All data points do not typically fall exactly on the regression model line. The error term ε makes up for these differences from other variables such as measurement errors, material variations in a manufacturing operation, and personnel. Errors are assumed to have mean zero and unknown variance σ^2, and they are not correlated. When the magnitude of the coefficient of determination (R^2) is large, this indicates that the error term for this model is relatively small and the model fits good.

When a linear regression model contains only one independent (regressor or predictor) variable, it is called *simple linear regression*. When a regression model contains more than one independent variable, it is called a *multiple linear regression model*. The focus of this chapter is on simple linear regression.

A primary purpose of regression analysis is the determination of the unknown parameters in a regression model. We determine these regression coefficients through the method of least squares. Least squares minimizes the sum of squares of the residuals (which are described below). The fitted simple linear regression model that gives a point estimate of the mean of y for a particular x is

$$\hat{y} = \hat{\beta}_0 + \hat{\beta}_1 x$$

where the regression coefficients are

$$\hat{\beta}_1 = \frac{S_{xy}}{S_{xx}} = \frac{\sum_{i=1}^{n} y_i x_i - \dfrac{\left(\sum_{i=1}^{n} y_i\right)\left(\sum_{i=1}^{n} x_i\right)}{n}}{\sum_{i=1}^{n} x_i^2 - \dfrac{\left(\sum_{i=1}^{n} x_i\right)^2}{n}} = \frac{\sum_{i=1}^{n} y_i(x_i - \bar{x})}{\sum_{i=1}^{n} (x_i - \bar{x})^2}$$

$$\hat{\beta}_0 = \bar{y} - \hat{\beta}_1 \bar{x}$$

The difference between the observed value y_i and the corresponding fitted value $\hat{y}_i$ is a residual. The ith residual mathematically is

$$e_i = y_i - \hat{y}_i$$

Residuals are important in the investigation of the adequacy of the fitted model along with detecting the departure of underlying assumptions. Residual analysis techniques are described in the next section.

Statistical regression programs can calculate the model and plot the least-square estimates. Programs can also generate a table of coefficients and conduct an analysis of variance. Significance tests of the regression coefficients involve either the t-distribution for the table of coefficients or the F-distribution for analysis of variance. One null hypothesis is that β_0 is constant, and the alternate hypothesis is that it is not constant. Another null hypothesis is that β_1 is zero, and the alternate hypothesis is that it is not zero. In both cases $\alpha = 0.05$ corresponds to a computer probability p value of 0.05; practitioners often use this value as a level of significance to reject the null hypothesis.

For the analysis of variance table, total variation is broken down into the pieces described by the sum of squares (SS):

$$SS_{total} = SS_{regression} + SS_{error}$$

where

$$SS_{total} = \sum (y_i - \bar{y})^2$$

$$SS_{regression} = \sum (\hat{y}_i - \bar{y})^2$$

$$SS_{error} = \sum (y_i - \hat{y}_i)^2$$

Each sum of square has an associated number of degrees of freedom equal to

Sum of Squares	Degrees of Freedom
SS_{total}	$n - 1$
$SS_{regression}$	1
SS_{error}	$n - 2$

When divided by the appropriate number of degrees of freedom, the sums of squares give good estimates of the source of variability (i.e., total, regression, and error). This variability is analogous to a variance calculation and is called *mean square*. If there is no difference in treatment means, the two estimates are presumed to be similar. If there is a difference, we suspect that the observed difference is caused by the regressor. The null hypothesis that there is no difference because of the regressor is tested by calculating the F-test statistic:

$$F_0 = \frac{MS_{regression}}{MS_{error}}$$

Using an F-table, we should reject the null hypothesis and conclude there is a difference caused by the regressor if

$$F_0 > F_{\alpha,1,n-2}$$

Alternatively, a probability value could be calculated for F_0 and compared to a criterion (e.g., $\alpha = 0.05$). The null hypothesis is rejected if the calculated value is less than the criterion. This approach is most appropriate when a computer program makes the computations. This test procedure is summarized through an analysis of variance table, as shown in Table 23.2.

The coefficient of determination (R^2) is a ratio of the explained variation to total variation, which equates to

$$R^2 = \frac{SS_{regression}}{SS_{total}} = \frac{\sum (\hat{y}_i - \bar{y})^2}{\sum (y_i - \hat{y})^2} = 1 - \frac{SS_{error}}{SS_{total}}$$

The multiplication of this coefficient by 100 yields the percentage variation explained by the least-squares method. A higher percentage indicates a better least-squares predictor.

If a variable is added to a model equation, R^2 will increase even if the variable has no real value. A compensation for this is an adjusted value, R^2 (adj), which has an approximate unbiased estimate for the population R^2 of

$$R^2(\text{adj}) = 1 - \frac{\left(\dfrac{SS_{error}}{n - p}\right)}{\left(\dfrac{SS_{total}}{n - 1}\right)}$$

where p is the number of terms in the regression equation and n is the total number of degrees of freedom.

23.5 ANALYSIS OF RESIDUALS

An important method for testing the NID$(0, \sigma^2)$ assumption of an experiment is residual analysis (a residual is the difference between the observed value

TABLE 23.2 The Analysis of Variance Table for Simple Regression

Source of Variation	Sum of Squares	Degrees of Freedom	Mean Square	F_0
Regression	$SS_{regression}$	1	$MS_{regression}$	$F_0 = \dfrac{MS_{regression}}{MS_{error}}$
Error	SS_{error}	$n - 2$	MS_{error}	
Total	SS_{total}	$n - 1$		

and the corresponding fitted value). Residual analyses play an important role in investigating the adequacy of the fitted model and in detecting departures from the model.

Residual analysis techniques include the following:

- Check the normality assumption through a normal probability plot and/or histogram of the residuals.
- Check for correlation between residuals by plotting residuals in time sequence.
- Check for correctness of the model by plotting residuals versus fitted values.

23.6   ANALYSIS OF RESIDUALS: NORMALITY ASSESSMENT

If the NID(0, σ^2) assumption is valid, a histogram plot of the residuals should look like a sample from a normal distribution. Expect considerable departures from a normality appearance when the sample size is small. A normal probability plot of the residuals can similarly be conducted. If the underlying error distribution is normal, the plot will resemble a straight line.

Commonly a residual plot will show one point that is much larger or smaller than the others. This residual is typically called an *outlier*. One or more outliers can distort the analysis. Frequently, outliers are caused by the erroneous recording of information. If this is not the case, further analysis should be conducted. Perhaps this data point can give additional insight to what should be done to dramatically improve a process.

To perform a rough check for outliers, substitute residual error e_{ij} values into

$$dij = \frac{e_{ij}}{\sqrt{MS_E}}$$

and examine the standardized residuals values. About 68% of the standardized residuals should fall within a d_{ij} value of ± 1. Similarly about 95% of the standardized residuals should fall within a d_{ij} value of ± 2. Almost all (99%) of the standardized residuals should fall within a d_{ij} value of ± 3.

23.7   ANALYSIS OF RESIDUALS: TIME SEQUENCE

A plot of residuals in time order of data collection helps detect correlation between residuals. A tendency for positive or negative runs of residuals indicates positive correlation. This implies a violation of the independence assumption. An individuals chart of residuals in chronological order by observation number can verify the independence of errors. Positive autocorrelation occurs when residuals don't change signs as frequently as should be expected, while negative autocorrelation is indicated when the residuals frequently change signs. This problem can be very serious and difficult to correct. It is important to avoid the problem initially. An important step in obtaining independence is conducting proper randomization initially.

23.8 ANALYSIS OF RESIDUALS: FITTED VALUES

For a good model fit, this plot should show a random scatter and have no pattern. Common discrepancies include the following:

- Outliers, which appear as points that are either much higher or lower than normal residual values. These points should be investigated. Perhaps some recorded a number wrong or perhaps through an evaluation of this sample additional knowledge is gained that leads to a major process improvement breakthrough.
- Nonconstant variance, where the difference between the lowest and highest residual values either increases or decreases for an increase in the fitted values. This could be caused by a measurement instrument where error is proportional to the measured value.
- Poor model fit, where, for example, residual values seem to increase and then decrease with an increase in the fitted value. For the described situation, perhaps a quadratic model would be a better fit than a linear model.

Transformations, which are discussed in a later chapter, are sometimes very useful to address these above problems.

23.9 EXAMPLE 23.2: SIMPLE LINEAR REGRESSION

Consider the data shown in Table 23.1 that was used for the correlation Example 23.1. The output from a regression analysis computer program is as follows:

```
Regression Analysis

The regression equation is
Delivery Time (y) = 3.32 + 2.18 Cases
```

Predictor	Coef	StDev	T	P
Constant	3.321	1.371	2.42	0.024
Cases	2.1762	0.1240	17.55	0.000

```
S = 4.181      R-Sq = 93.0%      R-Sq(adj) = 92.7%
```

Analysis of Variance

Source	DF	SS	MS	F	P
Regression	1	5382.4	5382.4	307.85	0.000
Residual Error	23	402.1	17.5		
Total	24	5784.5			

Unusual Observations

Obs	Cases	Delivery	Fit	StDev Fit	Residual	St Resid
9	30.0	79.240	68.606	2.764	10.634	3.39RX
22	26.0	52.320	59.901	2.296	-7.581	-2.17RX

R denotes an observation with a large standardized residual.
X denotes an observation whose X value gives it large influence.

Figure 23.3 shows a plot of this model along with the 95% prediction bands and confidence bands. The confidence bands reflect the confidence intervals on the equation coefficients. The prediction bands reflect the confidence interval for responses at any given level of the independent variable. Figure 23.4 shows various residual analysis plots.

The tabular value of 92.7% for R^2 would initially give us a good feeling about our analysis. However, when we examine the data we notice that most readings were between 0 and 10 cases. The values beyond 10 could almost be considered an extrapolation to the majority of data used fitting this model. In addition, the plots indicate that these values are not fitting the general model very well. The residuals versus fitted plot indicates that there could also be an increase in the variability of delivery time with an increase in the number of cases.

At this point in time the practitioner needs to stop and reflect back on the real purpose of the analysis. The model does not fit real well, and Montgomery and Peck (1982) discuss further analysis such as the number of cases versus distance. This type of analysis may be appropriate, and there could be other additional factors to consider such as operator, time of day of delivery, and weather.

However, let's not forget that data collection and analysis takes time, and our time is valuable. If the general model response meets the needs of cus-

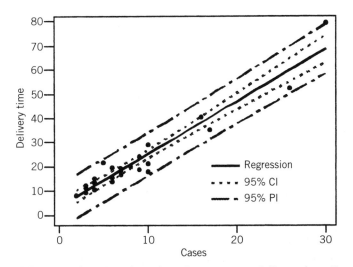

FIGURE 23.3 Regression plot of number of cases versus delivery time. $Y = 3.32078 + 2.17617X$; $R^2 = 93.0\%$.

tomers and is economically satisfactory, perhaps we should do no further analysis and move on to some other problem. However, if we need to reduce delivery time, then our actions need to reflect this objective.

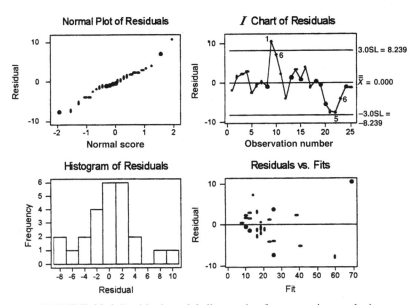

FIGURE 23.4 Residual model diagnostics for regression analysis.

23.10   S⁴ ASSESSMENT

Correlation and regression techniques can be very valuable; however, care needs to be exercised when using the methodologies. Some things to consider are the following:

- The regression model describes the region for which it models and may not be an accurate representation for extrapolated values.
- It is difficult to detect a cause-and-effect relationship if measurement error is large.
- A true cause-and-effect relationship does not necessarily exist when two variables are correlated.
- A process may have a third variable that affects the process such that the two variables vary simultaneously.
- Least-squares predictions are based on history data, which may not represent future relationships.
- An important independent variable to improve a process may be disregarded for further considerations because a study did not show correlation between this variable and the response that needed improvement. However, this variable might be shown to be important within a DOE if the variable were operated outside its normal operating range.

23.11   EXERCISES

1. *Catapult Exercise Data Analysis:* Conduct correlation and regression analyses of the catapult exercise data sets from Chapter 5.

2. Two variables within a process were thought to be correlated. Generate a scatter plot, determine the value of the coefficient of correlation, conduct a significance test on the coefficient of correlation, and estimate the variability in y thought to be caused by x.

x	Y	X	Y	X	y
27.02	50.17	43.09	50.09	57.07	49.80
30.01	49.84	43.96	49.77	59.07	49.91
33.10	50.00	46.14	49.61	59.96	50.20
34.04	49.79	46.99	49.86	61.05	49.97
35.09	49.99	48.20	50.18	61.88	50.16
35.99	49.97	49.87	49.90	63.08	49.97
36.86	49.93	51.92	49.84	63.87	50.12
37.83	49.94	53.97	49.89	66.10	50.05
39.13	50.10	55.02	50.02	67.17	50.20
39.98	50.09	55.97	49.81	68.01	50.19

3. The strength of a part was monitored as function of temperature within a process. Generate a scatter plot, determine the value of the coefficient of correlation, conduct a significance test on the coefficient of correlation, determine the regression equation, generate a residual diagnostic plot, and estimate the percentage of variability in strength caused by temperature.

Temp.	Strength	Temp.	Strength	Temp.	Strength
140.6	7.38	140.5	6.95	142.1	3.67
140.9	6.65	139.7	8.58	141.1	6.58
141.0	6.43	140.6	7.17	140.6	7.42
140.8	6.85	140.1	8.55	140.5	7.53
141.6	5.08	141.1	6.23	141.2	6.28
142.0	3.80	140.9	6.27	142.2	3.46
141.6	4.93	140.6	7.54	140.0	8.67
140.6	7.12	140.2	8.27	141.7	4.42
141.6	4.74	139.9	8.85	141.5	4.25
140.2	8.70	140.2	7.43	140.7	7.06

4. The dependent variable y was monitored as a function of an independent variable x. Conduct a regression analysis and comment.

x	y	x	y	x	y	x	y	x	y
2.19	47.17	10.45	48.93	47.17	10.45	31.2	52.8	40.46	55.2
0.73	47.43	11.38	49.14	47.43	11.38	28.83	52.95	44.29	55.39
3.95	47.16	10.72	49.50	47.16	10.72	35.64	53.31	36.68	55.44
6.85	47.44	13.42	49.69	47.44	13.42	34.5	53.8	50.75	55.61
1.81	47.83	12.35	49.78	47.83	12.35	29.35	53.77	37.99	55.77
4.49	47.94	13.91	49.92	47.94	13.91	33.87	54.16	49.02	56.03
3.71	48.20	9.43	50.29	48.20	9.43	40.08	54.17	45.66	56.14
11.21	48.19	21.76	50.17	48.19	21.76	38.72	54.52	43.55	56.25
6.02	48.59	19.92	50.78	48.59	19.92	34.86	54.88	48	56.53
8.42	48.77	19.45	50.41	48.77	19.45	38.47	54.85	49	57.01

5. Describe manufacturing and business process application of correlation and regression techniques.

6. Describe how the techniques within this chapter are useful and can be applied to S^4 projects.

24

SINGLE-FACTOR (ONE-WAY) ANALYSIS OF VARIANCE

Previously we discussed methods to compare two conditions or treatments. For example, the voice quality of a portable recording machine involved two different designs. Another analysis approach for this type of experiment is a single-factor analysis of variance experiment (or one-way analysis of variance) with two levels (or treatments), where the factor is machine design and the two levels are design 1 (old) and design 2 (new). Experiments of this type can involve more than two levels of the factor. This chapter describes single-factor analysis of variance experiments (completely randomized design) with two or more levels (or treatments).

This methodology is a fixed effects model (as opposed to a random-effects model or components of variance model) and tests the null hypothesis that the means that the different processes give an equal response. The statistical model for the fixed effects model is similar to that of the random effects model or components of variance model. The difference is that with the fixed-effects model the levels are specifically chosen by the experimenter. For this situation the test hypothesis is about the mean response effect between factor level effect, and conclusions apply only to the factor levels considered in the analysis. Conclusions cannot be extended to similar levels not explicitly considered. The term analysis of variance originates from a partitioning of total variability into its component part for the analysis; however, for a fixed effects model this partitioning of variability (or variance) is only a methodology to make an assessment about mean effects of the factor levels.

24.1 APPLICATION DEFINITION EXAMPLES

- Determine if there is a difference in the mean delivery time of five departments.

- Determine if there is a difference in the dimension of a part when a particular setting on a machine is changed to five different levels.

24.2 APPLICATION STEPS

Steps to consider when applying a single factor analysis of variance:

1. Describe the problem using a response variable that corresponds to the key process output variable or measured quality characteristic. Example applications include the following:
   a. Customer delivery time is sometimes too long.
   b. The dimension on a part is not meeting specification.
2. Describe the analysis. Example applications include the following:
   a. Determine if there is a difference in the mean delivery time of five departments.
   b. Determine if there is a difference in the dimension of a part when a particular setting on a machine is changed to five different levels.
3. State the null and alternate hypotheses. Example applications include the following:
   a. $H_0: \mu_1 = \mu_2 = \mu_3 = \mu_4 = \mu_5$ $H_A: \mu_1 \neq \mu_2 \neq \mu_3 \neq \mu_4 \neq \mu_5$, where μ_x is the mean delivery time of department x.
   b. $H_0: \mu_1 = \mu_2 = \mu_3 = \mu_4 = \mu_5$ $H_A: \mu_1 \neq \mu_2 \neq \mu_3 \neq \mu_4 \neq \mu_5$, where μ_x the mean part dimension from machine setting x.
4. Choose a large enough sample and conduct the experiment randomly.
5. Generate an analysis of variance table.
6. Test the data normality and equality of variances hypothesis.
7. Make hypothesis decisions about factors from analysis of variance table.
8. Calculate (if desired) epsilon squares (ε^2), as described in Section 24.14.
9. Conduct an analysis of means (ANOM).
10. Translate conclusions from the experiment into the needs of the problem or the process in question.

24.3 SINGLE-FACTOR ANALYSIS OF VARIANCE
HYPOTHESIS TEST

A single-factor analysis of variance problem can be represented graphical by a box plot, scatter diagram, and/or mean effects plot of the data. A plot might visually indicate differences between samples. An analysis of variance analysis assesses the differences between samples taken at different factor levels to determine if these differences are large enough relative to error to conclude that in general there is a significant different in response due to the level of the factor.

For a single-factor analysis of variance, a linear statistical model can describe the observations of a level, with j observations taken under level $i (i = 1, 2, \ldots, a; j = 1, 2, \ldots, n)$:

$$y_{ij} = \mu + \tau_i + \varepsilon_{ij}$$

where y_{ij} is the (ij) observation, μ is the overall mean, τ is the ith level effect, and ε_{ij} is random error.

For an analysis of variance hypothesis test, model errors are assumed to be normally and independently distributed random variables with mean zero and variance σ^2. This variance is assumed constant for all factor levels. Tests are later described to assess the validity of these assumptions.

An expression for the hypothesis test of means is

$$H_0: \quad \mu_1 = \mu_2 = \cdots = \mu_a$$

$$H_A: \quad \mu_1 \neq \mu_j \qquad \text{for at least one pair } (i, j)$$

When H_0 is true, all levels have a common mean μ, which leads to an equivalent expression in terms of τ:

$$H_0: \quad \tau_1 = \tau_2 = \cdots = \tau_a = 0$$

$$H_A: \quad \tau_i \neq 0 \qquad \text{(for at least one } i)$$

Hence, we can describe a single-factor analysis of variance test as assessing the equality of level means or whether the level effects (τ_i) are zero.

24.4   SINGLE-FACTOR ANALYSIS OF VARIANCE TABLE CALCULATIONS

The total sum of squares of deviations about the grand average $\bar{y}$ (sometimes referred to as the total corrected sum of squares) describes the overall variability of the data:

$$SS_{\text{total}} = \sum_{i=1}^{a} \sum_{j=1}^{n} (y_{ij} - \bar{y})^2$$

This equation is intuitively appealing because a division of SS_{total} by the appropriate number of degrees of freedom would yield a sample variance of y's. For this situation, the overall number of degrees of freedom is $an - 1 = N - 1$.

Total variability in data as measured by the total corrected sum of squares can be partitioned into a summation of two elements. The first element is a sum of squares for differences between factor level averages and the grand average. The second element is a sum of squares of the differences of observations within factor levels from the average of factorial levels. The first element is a measure of the differences between the means of the levels, whereas the second element is due to random error. Symbolically, this relationship is

$$SS_{\text{total}} = SS_{\text{factor levels}} + SS_{\text{error}}$$

where $SS_{\text{factor levels}}$ is called the sum of squares due to factor levels (i.e., between factor levels or treatments) and SS_{error} is called the sum of squares due to error (i.e., within factor levels or treatments):

$$SS_{\text{factor levels}} = n \sum_{i=1}^{a} (\bar{y}_i - \bar{y})^2$$

$$SS_{\text{error}} = \sum_{i=1}^{a} \sum_{j=1}^{n} (y_{ij} - \bar{y}_i)^2$$

When divided by the appropriate number of degrees of freedom, these sums of squares give good estimates of the total variability, the variability between factor levels, and the variability within factor levels (or error). Expressions for the mean square are

$$MS_{\text{factor levels}} = \frac{SS_{\text{factor levels}}}{a - 1}$$

$$MS_{\text{error}} = \frac{SS_{\text{error}}}{n - a}$$

If there is no difference in treatment means, the two estimates are presumed to be similar. If there is a difference, we suspect that the observed difference is caused by differences in the treatment factor levels. The null hypothesis that there is no difference in factor levels is tested by calculating the F-test statistic:

$$F_0 = \frac{MS_{\text{factor levels}}}{MS_{\text{error}}}$$

Using an F-table, we should reject the null hypothesis and conclude there are differences in treatment means if

$$F_0 > F_{\alpha, a-1, n-a}$$

Alternatively, a probability value could be calculated for F_0 and compared to a criterion (e.g., $\alpha = 0.05$). The null hypothesis is rejected if the calculated value is less than the criterion. This approach is most appropriate when a computer program makes the computations. This test procedure is summarized through an analysis of variance table, as shown in Table 24.1.

24.5 ESTIMATION OF MODEL PARAMETERS

In addition to factor-level significance, it can be useful to estimate the parameters of the single-factor model and the confidence intervals on the factor-level means. For the single-factor model

$$y_{ij} = \mu + \tau_i + \varepsilon_{ij}$$

estimates for the overall mean and factor-level effects are

$$\hat{\mu} = \bar{y}$$
$$\hat{\tau}_i = \bar{y}_i - \bar{y}, \qquad i = 1, 2, \ldots, a$$

These estimators have intuitive appeal. The grand average of observations estimates the overall mean and the difference between the factor levels and the overall mean estimates the factor-level effect.

A $100(1 - \alpha)$ percent confidence interval estimate on the ith factor level is

$$\bar{y}_i \pm t_{\alpha, N-a} \sqrt{MS_E / n}$$

where t-values for α are from a two-sided t-table.

TABLE 24.1 The Analysis of Variance Table for Single-Factor, Fixed Effects Model

Source of Variation	Sum of Squares	Degrees of Freedom	Mean Square	F_0
Between-factor levels	$SS_{\text{factor levels}}$	$a - 1$	$MS_{\text{factor levels}}$	$F_0 = \dfrac{MS_{\text{factor levels}}}{MS_{\text{error}}}$
Error (within-factor levels)	SS_{error}	$N - a$	MS_{error}	
Total	SS_{total}	$N - 1$		

24.6   UNBALANCED DATA

A design is considered unbalanced when the number of observations in the factor levels are different. For this situation, analysis of variance equations need only slight modifications. For an unbalanced design the formula for $SS_{\text{factor levels}}$ becomes

$$SS_{\text{factor levels}} = \sum_{i=1}^{a} n_i(\bar{y}_i - \bar{y})^2$$

A balanced design is preferable to an unbalanced design. With a balanced design the power of the test is maximized and the test statistic is robust to small departures from the assumption of equal variances. This is not the case for an unbalanced design.

24.7   MODEL ADEQUACY

As described within the correlation and simple regression chapters, valid analysis of variance results require the satisfying of certain assumptions. As experimenters we collect data and then statistically analyze the data. Whether we think about it or not, model building is often the center of a statistical analysis. The validity of an analysis also depends upon basic assumptions. One typical assumption is that errors are normally and independently distributed with mean zero and a constant but unknown variance NID(0, σ^2).

To help with meeting the independence and normal distribution requirement, an experimenter needs to select an adequate sample size and randomly conduct the trials. After data are collected, computer programs offer routines to test the assumptions. Generally in a fixed effects analysis of variance, moderate departures from normality of the residuals are of little concern. Because the F-test is only slighted affected, analysis of variance and related procedures of fixed effects is said to be robust to the normality assumption. Non-normality affects the random effects model more severely.

In addition to an analysis of residuals, there is also a direct statistical test for equality of variance. An expression for this hypothesis is

$$H_0: \quad \sigma_1^2 = \sigma_2^2 = \cdots = \sigma_a^2$$

$$H_A: \quad \text{above not true for at least one } \sigma_i^2$$

Bartlett's test is frequently used to test this hypothesis when the normality assumption is valid. Levene's test can be used when the normality assumption is questionable. An example later in this chapter illustrates a computer output using these test statistics.

24.8 ANALYSIS OF RESIDUALS: FITTED VALUE PLOTS AND DATA TRANSFORMATIONS

Residual plots should show no structure relative to any factor including the fitted response; however, trends within the data may occur for various reasons. One phenomenon that may occur is inconsistent variance. One example of this ∝ situation is that the error of an instrument may increase with larger readings because this error could be a percentage of the scale reading. If this were the case, the residuals would increase as a function of scale reading.

Fortunately, a balanced fixed effects model is robust to variance not being homogeneous. The problem does get more serious for unbalanced designs, situations where one variance is much larger than others and for the random effects model. A data transformation could then be used to reduce this phenomenon within the residuals, which would yield a more precise significance test.

Another situation occurs when the output is count data, where a square root transformation may be appropriate, while a log-normal transformation is often appropriate if the trial outputs are standard deviation values and a logit might be helpful when there are upper and lower limits. A summary of common transformations is noted in Table 24.2.

As an alternative approach to the tabular considerations, Box (1988) describes a method to eliminate unnecessary coupling of dispersion effects and location effects by determining an approximate transformation using a lambda plot. Montgomery (1997) and Box et al. (1978) discuss transformations in additional depth.

With transformations, one should note that the conclusions of the analysis apply to the transformed populations.

24.9 COMPARING PAIRS OF TREATMENT MEANS

The rejection of the null hypothesis in an analysis of variance indicates that there is a difference between the factor levels (treatments). However. there is

TABLE 24.2 Data Transformations

Data Characteristics	Data (x_i or p_i) Transformation
$\alpha \propto$ constant	None
$\sigma \propto \mu^2$	$1/x_i$
$\sigma \propto \mu^{3/2}$	$1/\sqrt{x_i}$
$\sigma \propto \mu$	Log x_i
$\sigma \propto \sqrt{\mu}$, Poisson (count) data	$\sqrt{x_i}$ or $\sqrt{x_i + 1}$
Binomial proportions	$\sin^{-1}(\sqrt{p_i})$
Upper- and lower-bounded data (e.g., 0–1 probability of failure) (logit transformation)	$\log \dfrac{x_i - \text{lower limit}}{\text{upper limit} - x_i}$

no information given to determine which means are different. Sometimes it is useful to make further comparisons and analysis among groups factor level means. Multiple comparison methods assess differences between treatment means in either the factor level totals or the factor level averages. Methodologies include Tukey's and Fisher's. Montgomery (1997) describes several methods of making these comparisons.

Later in this chapter the analysis of means (ANOM) approach is shown to compare individual means to a grand mean.

24.10   EXAMPLE 24.1: SINGLE-FACTOR ANALYSIS OF VARIANCE

The bursting strengths of diaphragms were determined in an experiment. Use analysis of variance techniques to determine if there is a difference at a level of 0.05.

Type 1	Type 2	Type 3	Type 4	Type 5	Type 6	Type 7
59.0	65.7	65.3	67.9	60.6	73.1	59.4
62.3	62.8	63.7	67.4	65.0	71.9	61.6
65.2	59.1	68.9	62.9	68.2	67.8	56.3
65.5	60.2	70.0	61.7	66.0	67.4	62.7

The origination of these data could similarly be measurements from

- Parts manufactured by 7 different operators
- Parts manufactured on 7 different machines
- Time for purchase order requests from 7 different sites
- Delivery time of 7 different suppliers

The box plot and dot plot shown in Figure 24.1 and Figure 24.2 indicate that there could be differences between the factor level (or treatments). However, these plots do not address the question statistically.

An analysis of variance tests the hypothesis for equality of treatment means, or it tests that the treatment effects are zero, which is expressed as

$$H_0: \quad \tau_1 = \tau_2 = \cdots \tau_a = 0$$

$$H_A: \quad \tau_i \neq 0 \qquad \text{(for at least one } i)$$

The resulting analysis of variance table is as follows:

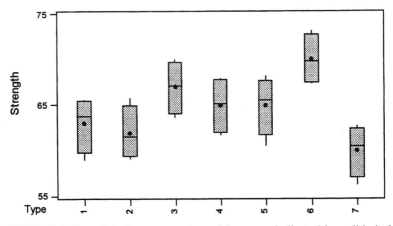

FIGURE 24.1 Box plots by response type. Means are indicated by solid circles.

One-Way Analysis of Variance

Analysis of Variance for Response

Source	DF	SS	MS	F	P
Type	6	265.34	44.22	4.92	0.003
Error	21	188.71	8.99		
Total	27	454.05			

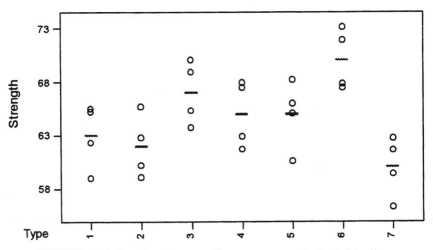

FIGURE 24.2 Dot plots by type. Group means are indicated by lines.

```
                              Individual 95% CIs for Mean

                              Based on Pooled StDev
Level  N   Mean    StDev    -------+-------+-------+-------
  1    4  63.000   3.032          (-----*-----)
  2    4  61.950   2.942          (-----*-----)
  3    4  66.975   2.966             (-----*-----)
  4    4  64.975   3.134           (-----*-----)
  5    4  64.950   3.193           (-----*-----)
  6    4  70.050   2.876                (-----*-----)
  7    4  60.000   2.823     (------*------)
                            -------+-------+-------+-------
Pooled StDev = 2.998            60.0    65.0    70.0
```

This analysis indicates that rejection of the null hypothesis is appropriate because the p-value is lower than 0.05. Figure 24.3 shows tests of the model assumptions. The probability values for the test of homogeneity of variances indicates that there is not enough information to reject the null hypothesis of equality of variances. No pattern or outlier data are apparent in either the "residuals versus order of the data" or "residuals versus fitted values." The normal probability plot and histogram indicate that the residuals may not be normally distributed. Perhaps a transformation of the data could improve this fit; however, it is doubtful that any difference would be large enough to be of practical importance. These data will be further analyzed as an analysis of means example.

24.11 ANALYSIS OF MEANS

Analysis of means (ANOM) is a graphical approach that can be used to compare k groups of size n. Consider the following x_{ij} data format where there are n observations within k groups.

		Groups		
1	2	3	$\cdots$	k
		Observations		
x_{11}	x_{21}	x_{31}	$\cdots$	x_{k1}
x_{12}	x_{22}	x_{32}	$\cdots$	x_{k2}
x_{13}	x_{23}	x_{33}	$\cdots$	x_{k3}
$\vdots$	$\vdots$	$\vdots$	$\vdots$	$\vdots$
x_{1j}	x_{2j}	x_{3j}	$\cdots$	x_{kj}
$\bar{x}_1$	$\bar{x}_2$	$\bar{x}_3$	$\cdots$	$\bar{x}_i$
s_1	s_2	s_3	$\cdots$	s_i

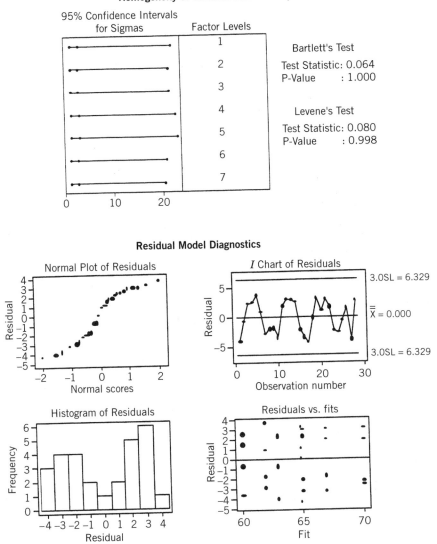

FIGURE 24.3 Single-factor analysis of variance: tests of the model.

The grand mean $\bar{\bar{x}}$ of the group means $(\bar{x}_i)$ is simply the average of these mean values, which is written

$$\bar{\bar{x}} = \frac{\displaystyle\sum_{i=1}^{k} \bar{x}_i}{k}$$

The pooled estimate for the standard deviation is the square root of the average of the variances for the individual observations.

$$s = \sqrt{\frac{\sum\limits_{i=1}^{k} s_i^2}{k}}$$

The lower and upper decision lines (LDL and UDL) are

$$\text{LDL} = \bar{\bar{x}} - h_\alpha s \sqrt{\frac{k-1}{kn}} \qquad \text{UDL} = \bar{\bar{x}} + h_\alpha s \sqrt{\frac{k-1}{kn}}$$

where h_α is from Table I for risk level α, number of means k, and degrees of freedom $[(n-1)k]$. The means are then plotted against the decision lines. If any mean falls outside the decision lines, there is a statistically significant difference for this mean from the grand mean.

If normality can be assumed, analysis of means is also directly applicable to attribute data. It is reasonable to consider a normality approximation if both np and $n(1-p)$ are at least 5. For a probability level p of 0.01, this would require a sample size of 500 [i.e., $500(0.01) = 5$].

24.12   EXAMPLE 24.2: ANALYSIS OF MEANS

The previous analysis of variance example indicated that there was a significant difference in the bursting strengths of seven different types of rubber diaphragms ($k = 7$). We will now determine which diaphragms differ from the grand mean. A data summary of the mean and variance for each rubber type, each having four observations ($n = 4$), is

				*i*th Sample Number			
	1	2	3	4	5	6	7
$\bar{x}_i$	63.0	62.0	67.0	65.0	65.0	70.0	60.0
s_i^2	9.2	8.7	8.8	9.8	10.2	8.3	8.0

The overall mean is

$$\bar{\bar{x}} = \frac{\sum_{i=1}^{k} \bar{x}_i}{k} = \frac{63 + 62 + 67 + 65 + 65 + 70 + 60}{7} = 64.57$$

The pooled estimate for the standard deviation is

$$s = \sqrt{\frac{\sum_{i=1}^{k} s_i^2}{k}}$$

$$= \left(\frac{9.2 + 8.7 + 8.8 + 9.8 + 10.2 + 8.3 + 8.0}{7}\right)^{1/2}$$

$$= 3.0$$

The number of degrees of freedom is $(n - 1)k = (4 - 1)(7) = 21$. For a significance level of 0.05 with 7 means and 21 degrees of freedom, it is determined by interpolation from Table I that $h_{0.05} = 2.94$. The upper and lower decision lines are then

$$\text{UDL} = \bar{\bar{x}} + h_\alpha s \sqrt{\frac{k-1}{kn}} = 64.57 + (2.94)(3.0)\sqrt{\frac{7-1}{7(4)}} = 68.65$$

$$\text{LDL} = \bar{\bar{x}} - h_\alpha s \sqrt{\frac{k-1}{kn}} = 64.57 - (2.94)(3.0)\sqrt{\frac{7-1}{7(4)}} = 60.49$$

An ANOM chart with the limits and measurements is shown in Figure 24.4. This plot illustrates graphically that $\bar{x}_6$ and $\bar{x}_7$ are significantly different from the grand mean.

24.13   EXAMPLE 24.3: ANALYSIS OF MEANS OF INJECTION-MOLDING DATA

From the Example 15.1 multi-vari analysis and the Example 22.4 variance components analysis of the injection molding data described in Table 15.1, it was concluded that differences between cavities affected the diameter of the part. However, the variance components analysis gave no insight to how the cavities differed. The computer analysis of means output shown in Figure 24.5 for cavities addresses these needs, where the level of significance for the decision lines is 0.05.

From this analysis we conclude that the differences between cavity 1 and 4 are the large contributors to this source of variability.

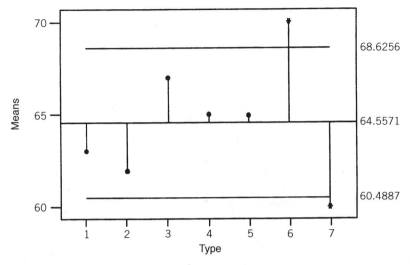

FIGURE 24.4 Analysis of means for diaphragm strength by type.

24.14 SIX SIGMA CONSIDERATIONS

This section describes some of the controversial metrics and methodologies of Six Sigma. The author is including these topics within this text to hopefully clarify some of the aspects of these methodologies. Even if an organization chooses not to use these techniques, the organization needs to be aware of the techniques because their suppliers or customers may be using the meth-

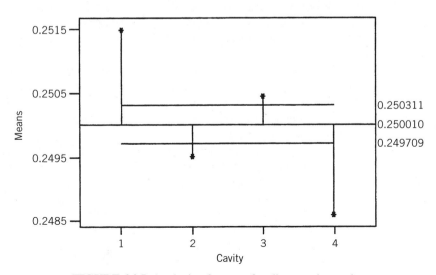

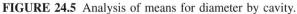
FIGURE 24.5 Analysis of means for diameter by cavity.

odologies for their metrics. Awareness of the techniques and alternatives can reduce the possibility of misunderstandings, which could be very expensive. The author emphasizes that the inclusion of these methodologies does not mean that he suggests that they all should be used within organizations.

Much controversy about Six Sigma revolves around whether there should be both a "short-term" and "long-term" process capability/performance metric. In addition, there is much controversy about the reporting of a Six Sigma metric that includes a 1.5 standard deviation shift. This section describes a methodology to calculate these metrics that is built upon the techniques described within this chapter.

A comparison of the proportion of total variability of the factor levels (or process) to the error term could be made in percentage units using a controversial epsilon square relationship:

$$\varepsilon_{\text{factor level}}^2 = 100 \times \frac{SS_{\text{factor}}}{SS_{\text{total}}}$$

$$\varepsilon_{\text{error}}^2 = 100 \times \frac{SS_{\text{error}}}{SS_{\text{total}}}$$

This relationship is sometimes presented in a pie chart format.

Consider the situation where a process was randomly sampled using conventionally rational sampling practices and there was a rational subgroup size between 4 and 6. Consider also that there were between 25 and 100 sets of samples taken over time. A commonly employed combination might be a subgroup size of 5 with 50 periodical samples yielding a total of 250 samples. Using the terms described within this chapter, this would equate to a factor of 50 levels having a within level sample size of 5. Note that this type of information could be generated to describe the common cause variability of data taken from an in-control control chart.

For this type of data the sums of squares from an analysis of variance table can be used to break down total variability into two parts. The division of these sum of squares by the correct number of degrees of freedom yields estimates for the different sources of variation. From these sources we can obtain an estimate of the total variation, the variation between subgroups, and the variation within subgroups. The estimator of total variability gives an estimate for "long-term" capability, while the estimator of within-group variability gives an estimate for "short-term" capability.

These concepts of variability can be used to reflect the influence of time on a process. The concepts could also be used to give understanding when calculating Six Sigma measurements for continuous data. The described "short-term" and "long-term" standard deviation estimates from an analysis of variance table are

$$\hat{\sigma}_{lt} = \sqrt{\frac{\sum\limits_{i=1}^{a}\sum\limits_{j=1}^{n}(y_{ij} - \bar{y})^2}{na - 1}}$$

$$\hat{\sigma}_{st} = \sqrt{\frac{\sum\limits_{i=1}^{a}\sum\limits_{j=1}^{n}(y_{ij} - \bar{y}_i)^2}{a(n - 1)}}$$

where the numerator terms are sum of squares and the denominator terms are appropriate degrees of freedom.

These two estimators are useful in calculating the "long-term" and "short-term" capability of the process. The variable used to measure this capability is the Z variable. Short-term Z values for the process are

$$Z_{LSL,st} = \frac{LSL - T}{\hat{\sigma}_{st}} \qquad Z_{USL,st} = \frac{USL - T}{\hat{\sigma}_{st}}$$

where LSL and USL are the lower and upper specification limit, respectively, and T is the target. The nominal specification T value is used in this relationship for Z_{st} because this represents the potential capability of the process, which implies that the process is considered to conform to the specification limits and is centered.

Long-term Z values for the process are

$$Z_{LSL,lt} = \frac{LSL - \hat{\mu}}{\hat{\sigma}_{lt}} \qquad Z_{USL,lt} = \frac{USL - \hat{\mu}}{\hat{\sigma}_{lt}}$$

where the estimated process average is $\hat{\mu}$. Z_{lt} describes the process over several time periods. The $\hat{\mu}$ estimator is used because the process is not assumed centered for this "long-term" case.

Probability values can then be obtained from the normal distribution table for the different values of Z. These probabilities correspond to the frequency of occurrence beyond specification limits or the probabilities of having a defect. The two probabilities for each situation are added together, resulting in the total probability of a defect for "short-term" and the total probability of a defect for "long-term." The multiplication of these two probabilities by one million gives DPMO (defects per million opportunities). From this information Z_{bench} could also be calculated. In addition, Z_{shift} could be estimated and then compared to the 1.5 value in the $Z_{st} = Z_{lt} + 1.5$ shift relationship.

24.15 EXAMPLE 24.4: DETERMINING PROCESS CAPABILITY USING ONE-FACTOR ANALYSIS OF VARIANCE

The following set of data (AIAG 1995b) was presented initially as Exercise 3 in Chapter 10 on control charts. Example 11.2 within the process capability/performance chapter described a procedure that AIAG (1995a) used to calculate process capability/performance for this in-control process. The chapter on variance components in Example 22.3 used a random effects model to determine standard deviation values to use within the process capability/performance equations. This example will describe a single-factor analysis of variance approach to quantity process capability/performance.

		Subgroups															
		1	2	3	4	5	6	7	8	9	10	11	12	13	14	15	16
	1	0.65	0.75	0.75	0.60	0.70	0.60	0.75	0.60	0.65	0.60	0.80	0.85	0.70	0.65	0.90	0.75
	2	0.70	0.85	0.80	0.70	0.75	0.75	0.80	0.70	0.80	0.70	0.75	0.75	0.70	0.70	0.80	0.80
Samples	3	0.65	0.75	0.80	0.70	0.65	0.75	0.65	0.80	0.85	0.60	0.90	0.85	0.75	0.85	0.80	0.75
	4	0.65	0.85	0.70	0.75	0.85	0.85	0.75	0.75	0.85	0.80	0.50	0.65	0.75	0.75	0.75	0.80
	5	0.85	0.65	0.75	0.65	0.80	0.70	0.70	0.75	0.75	0.65	0.80	0.70	0.70	0.60	0.85	0.65

For the single-factor analysis-of-variance approach we will consider that the subgroups are different factor levels. A computer-generated output for this consideration is as follows:

One-Way Analysis of Variance

```
Analysis of Variance for Data

Source     DF        SS          MS          F         P
subgrp     15        0.10950     0.00730     1.12      0.360
Error      64        0.41800     0.00653
Total      79        0.52750
```

From this analysis of variance table we can determine

$$\hat{\sigma}_{lt} = \sqrt{\frac{\sum_{i=1}^{a} \sum_{j=1}^{n} (y_{ij} - \bar{y})^2}{na - 1}} = \sqrt{\frac{0.52750}{(5)(16) - 1}} = 0.081714$$

$$\hat{\sigma}_{st} = \sqrt{\frac{\sum_{i=1}^{a} \sum_{j=1}^{n} (y_{ij} - \bar{y}_i)^2}{a(n - 1)}} = \sqrt{\frac{0.41800}{16(4)}} = 0.080816$$

These estimates for "long-term" and "short-term" are very similar to the results of previous calculations using different approaches. However, Section 24.14 offers additional alternatives to calculate process capability/performance. The methodologies from Section 24.14 yield

$$Z_{\mathrm{LSL,st}} = \frac{\mathrm{LSL} - T}{\hat{\sigma}_{\mathrm{st}}} = \frac{0.5 - 0.7}{0.080816} = -2.4747$$

$$Z_{\mathrm{USL,st}} = \frac{\mathrm{USL} - T}{\hat{\sigma}_{\mathrm{st}}} = \frac{0.9 - 0.7}{0.08016} = 2.4747$$

$$Z_{\mathrm{LSL,lt}} = \frac{\mathrm{LSL} - \hat{\mu}}{\hat{\sigma}_{\mathrm{lt}}} = \frac{0.5 - 0.7375}{0.081714} = -2.9065$$

$$Z_{\mathrm{USL,lt}} = \frac{\mathrm{USL} - \hat{\mu}}{\hat{\sigma}_{\mathrm{lt}}} = \frac{0.9 - 0.7375}{0.081714} = 1.9886$$

The probabilities for these Z values could then be determined using a statistical program or a standardized normal distribution curve (Table A). The combining and converting to a ppm defect rate yields the following "long-term" and "short-term" results:

Proportion out-of-spec calculations ("long-term") are

$$P(Z_{\mathrm{USL}})_{\text{"long-term"}} = P(1.9886) = 0.023373$$

$$P(Z_{\mathrm{LSL}})_{\text{"long-term"}} = P(2.9065) = 0.001828$$

$$P(\text{total})_{\text{"long-term"}} = 0.023373 + 0.001828 = 0.02520$$

(equates to a ppm rate of 25,201)

Proportion out-of-spec calculations ("short-term") are

$$P(Z_{\mathrm{USL}})_{\text{"short-term"}} = P(2.4747) = 0.006667$$

$$P(Z_{\mathrm{LSL}})_{\text{"short-term"}} = P(2.4747) = 0.006667$$

$$P(\text{total})_{\text{"short-term"}} = 0.006667 + 0.006667 = 0.013335$$

(equates to a ppm rate of 13,335)

24.16   OTHER CONSIDERATIONS

Variability within an experiment can be caused by nuisance factors in which we have no interest. These nuisance factors are sometimes unknown and not controlled. We use randomization to guard against this type of factor affecting our results. There are other situations where the nuisance factor is known but not controlled. When we can observe the value for a factor, it can be compensated for using analysis of covariance techniques. For still another situation where the nuisance factor is known and controllable, we can systematically eliminate the effect on comparisons among factor level considerations (i.e., treatments) by using a randomized block design.

Experiment results can often be dramatically improved through the wise management of nuisance factors. Statistical software can offer blocking and covariance analysis options. Statistical texts, such as Montgomery (1997), discuss the mechanics of these computations.

24.17 S^4 ASSESSMENT

Factors involved within a single-factor analysis of variance can be quantitative or qualitative. Quantitative factors are those whose levels can be associated with a numeric scale such as time or temperature. Qualitative factors such as machine and operator cannot be expressed in a numerical scale.

When there are several levels of a factor and the factors are quantitative, the experimenter is often interested in developing an empirical model equation for the response variable of the process that is being studied. When starting this investigation it is good practice to first create a scatter diagram of the data. This plot can give insight to the relationship between the response and factor levels. Perhaps this relationship is nonlinear. The fit of the model then could be conducted using regression analysis. This procedure makes no sense when the factor levels are qualitative.

It is unfortunate that an organization might choose not to embrace a Six Sigma methodology because of the controversial metrics. Many organizations use the basic approach of Six Sigma and not the controversial metrics. With S^4 the positive aspects of a basic Six Sigma approach is utilized to *wisely* integrate statistical techniques within their organization. This approach can lead to a dramatic bottom-line improvement.

One important aspect of determining the metrics of Six Sigma that is often not addressed is sample size and how the sample was selected. First, the sample must be a random sample of the population of interest. Second, the sample size must be large enough to give adequate confidence in the metric. Both these needs are not easy to achieve. Making supplier and other comparative decisions on magnitude of a metrics alone can cause problems. When an organization reports a Six Sigma metric or process capability/process index consider how they determined the value. Consider also asking them about the details of the process measurement and improvement program. This second inquiry may give more insight than any Six Sigma metric.

24.18   EXERCISES

1. *Catapult Exercise Data Analysis:* Using the catapult exercise data sets from Chapter 4, conduct single-factor analysis of variance and ANOM of the operator factor.

2. *Catapult Exercise Data Analysis:* Using the catapult exercise data sets from Chapter 4, determine using from subgroups of size 5 the "long-term" and "short-term" process capabilities/performances.

3. For the following data conduct an analysis of variance and ANOM. Assess significance levels at 0.05.

Machine Number	Samples									
1.0	35.8	40.4	30.3	46.8	34.1	34.0	38.1	45.0	41.9	40.2
2.0	40.9	35.7	36.7	37.3	41.8	39.9	34.6	38.8	35.8	35.6
3.0	36.0	38.3	47.9	35.9	38.1	35.8	31.5	37.4	40.3	44.0
4.0	44.8	40.0	43.9	43.3	38.8	44.9	42.3	51.8	44.1	45.2
5.0	37.5	40.4	37.6	34.6	38.9	37.4	35.9	41.0	39.4	28.9
6.0	33.1	43.4	43.4	43.3	44.3	38.4	33.9	34.5	40.1	33.7
7.0	37.5	41.9	43.7	38.6	33.2	42.7	40.5	36.1	38.3	38.0

4. The normal probability plot of residuals for the analysis of variance exercise within this chapter had some curvature. Repeat the analysis using a natural logarithm transformation of the data. Describe the results and whether the transformation leads to any change in conclusion.

5. When doing ANOM, what table and value would be used if a significance level of 0.05 is desired and there are 5 samples with sample sizes of 7?

6. Describe how the techniques within this chapter are useful and can be applied to S^4 projects.

25

TWO-FACTOR (TWO-WAY) ANALYSIS OF VARIANCE

Experiments often involve the study of more than one factor. Factorial designs are most efficient for this situation where the combinations of the levels of factors are investigated. These designs evaluate the change in response caused by different levels of factors and the interaction of factors.

This chapter focuses on two-factor analysis of variance or two-way analysis of variance of fixed effects. The following chapters describe factorial experiments where there are more than two factors.

25.1 TWO-FACTOR FACTORIAL DESIGN

The general two-factor factorial experiment takes the form shown in Table 25.1, where the design is considered a completely randomized design because observations are taken randomly. Within this table response, factor A has levels ranging from 1 to a, while factor B has levels ranging from 1 to b, and the replications have replicates 1 to n. Responses for the various combinations of factor A with factor B take the form y_{ijk}, where i describes the level of factor A, j describes the level of factor B, and k represents the replicate number. The total number of observations is then abn.

A description of the fixed linear two-factor model is then

$$y_{ijk} = \mu + \tau_i + \beta_j + (\tau\beta)_{ij} + \varepsilon_{ijk}$$

where μ is the overall mean effect. τ_i is the effect of the ith level of A (row

TABLE 25.1 General Arrangement for a Two-Factor Factorial Design

			Factor B		
		1	2	. . .	b
Factor A	1				
	2				
	.				
	a				

factor), β_j is the effect for the jth level of B (column factor), $(\tau\beta)_{ij}$ is the effect of the interaction, and ε_{ijk} is random error.

For a two-factor factorial, both row and column factors (or treatments) are of equal interest. The test hypothesis for row factor effects is

$$H_0: \quad \tau_1 = \tau_1 = \cdots = \tau_a = 0$$

$$H_A: \quad \text{at least one } \tau_i \neq 0$$

The test hypothesis for column factor effects is

$$H_0: \quad \beta_1 = \beta_1 = \cdots = \beta_b = 0$$

$$H_A: \quad \text{at least one } \beta_j \neq 0$$

The test hypothesis for the interaction of row and column factor effects is

$$H_0: \quad (\tau\beta)_{ij} = 0 \quad \text{for all values of } i, j$$

$$H_A: \quad \text{at least one } (\tau\beta)_{ij} \neq 0$$

Similar to one-factor analysis of variance the total variability can be partitioned into the summation of the sum of squares from the elements of the experiment, which can be represented as

$$SS_T = SS_A + SS_B + SS_{AB} + SS_e$$

where SS_T is the total sum of squares, SS_A is the sum of squares from factor A, SS_B is the sum of squares from factor B, SS_{AB} is the sum of squares from the interaction of factor A with factor B, and SS_e is the sum of squares from error. These sums of squares have the following degrees of freedom:

Effect	Degrees of Freedom
A	$a - 1$
B	$b - 1$
AB interaction	$(a - 1)(b - 1)$
Error	$ab(n - 1)$
Total	$abn - 1$

Mean square and F_0 calculations are also similar to one-factor analysis of variance. These relationships for the two-factor factorial are described in Table 25.2.

The difference between a two-factor analysis of variance approach and a randomized block design on one of the factors is that the randomized block design would not have the interaction consideration.

25.2   EXAMPLE 25.1: TWO-FACTOR FACTORIAL DESIGN

A battery is to be used within a device that is subjected to extreme temperature variations. At some point in time during development an engineer can only select one of three plate material types. After product shipment the engineer has no control over temperature; however, he/she believes that temperature could degrade the effective life of the battery. The engineer would like to determine if one of the material types is robust to temperature variations. Table 25.3 describes the observed effective life (hours) of this battery at controlled temperatures within a laboratory (Montgomery 1997).

The two-factor analysis of variance output is

TABLE 25.2   Two-Factor Factorial Analysis of Variance Table for Fixed Effects Model

Source	Sum of Squares	Degrees of Freedom	Mean Square	F_0
Factor A	SS_A	$a - 1$	$MS_A = \dfrac{SS_A}{a - 1}$	$F_0 = \dfrac{MS_A}{MS_E}$
Factor B	SS_B	$b - 1$	$MS_B = \dfrac{SS_B}{b - 1}$	$F_0 = \dfrac{MS_B}{MS_E}$
Interaction	SS_{AB}	$(a - 1)(b - 1)$	$MS_{AB} = \dfrac{SS_{AB}}{(a - 1)(b - 1)}$	$F_0 = \dfrac{MS_{AB}}{MS_E}$
Error	SS_E	$ab(n - 1)$	$MS_E = \dfrac{SS_E}{ab(n - 1)}$	
Total	SS_T	$abn - 1$		

TABLE 25.3 Life Data (in hours) for Battery Two-Factorial Design

Material Type	Temperature (°F)					
	15		70		125	
1	130	155	34	40	20	70
	74	180	80	75	82	58
2	150	188	136	122	25	70
	159	126	106	115	58	45
3	138	110	174	120	96	104
	168	160	150	139	82	60

Two-Way Analysis of Variance

Analysis of Variance for Response

```
Source         DF       SS      MS       F          P
Material        2    10684    5342    7.91      0.002
Temp            2    39119   19559   28.97      0.000
Interaction     4     9614    2403    3.56      0.019
Error          27    18231     675
Total          35    77647
```

Using an $\alpha = 0.05$ criterion, we conclude that there is a significant interaction between material types and temperature because its probability value is less than 0.05 [and $F_0 > (F_{0.05,4,27} = 2.73)$]. We also conclude that the main effects of material type and temperature are also significant because each of their probabilities is less than 0.05 [and $F_0 > (F_{0.05,2,27} = 3.35)$].

A plot of the average response at each factor level is shown in Figure 25.1, which aids the interpretation of experimental results. The significance of the interaction term in our model is shown as the lack of parallelism of these lines. From this plot we note a degradation in life with an increase in temperature regardless of material type. If it is desirable for this battery to experience less loss of life at elevated temperature, type 3 material seems to be the best choice of the three materials.

Whenever there is a difference in the rows' or columns' means, it can be beneficial to make additional comparisons. This analysis shows these differences; however, the significance of the interaction can obscure comparison tests. One approach to address this situation is to apply the test at only one level of a factor at a time.

Using this strategy, let us examine the data for significant differences at 70°F (i.e., level 2 of temperature). We can use ANOM techniques to gain insights to factor levels relative to the grand mean. The ANOM output shown in Figure 25.2 indicates that material types 1 and 3 are different from the grand mean.

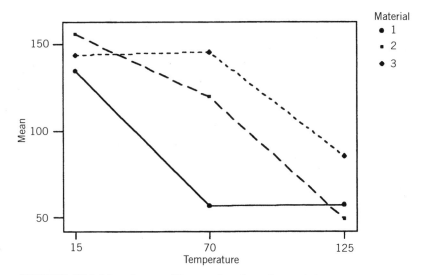

FIGURE 25.1 Mean battery life as a function of material and temperature.

Some statistical computer programs also offer options to make multiple comparisons of the means. Tukey's multiple comparison test shown below indicates that for a temperature level of 70°F the mean battery life between material types 2 and 3 cannot be shown different. In addition, the mean battery life for material type 1 is significantly lower than that of both battery types 2 and 3.

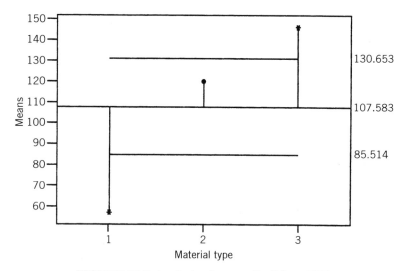

FIGURE 25.2 Analysis of means for life at 70°F.

```
Tukey Simultaneous Tests
Response Variable Response
All Pairwise Comparisons among Levels of Material

Material = 1 subtracted from:

    Level    Difference          SE of                   Adjusted
 Material     of Means      Difference    T-Value        P-Value
       2         62.50           14.29      4.373         0.0046
       3         88.50           14.29      6.193         0.0004

Material = 2 subtracted from:
    Level    Difference          SE of                   Adjusted
 Material     of Means      Difference    T-Value        P-Value
       3         26.00           14.29      1.819         0.2178
```

The coefficient of determination (R^2) can help describe the amount of variability in battery life explained by battery material, temperature, and the interaction of material with temperature. From the analysis of variance output we note

$$SS_{model} = SS_{material} + SS_{temperature} + SS_{interaction}$$

$$= 10{,}683 + 39{,}118 + 9613$$

$$= 59{,}414$$

which results in

$$R^2 = \frac{SS_{model}}{SS_{total}} = \frac{59{,}414}{77{,}647} = 0.77$$

From this we conclude that about 77% of the variability is described by our model factors.

The adequacy of the underlying model should be checked before the adoption of conclusions. Figure 25.3 gives a normal plot of the residuals and a plot of residuals versus the fitted values for the analysis of variance analysis.

The normal probability plot of the residuals does not reveal anything of particular concern. The residual plot of residuals versus fitted values seems to indicate a mild tendency for the variance of the residuals to increase as battery life increases. The residual plots of battery type and temperature seem to indicate that material type 1 and low temperature might have more variability. However, these problems, in general, do not appear to be large enough to have a dramatic impact on the analysis and conclusions.

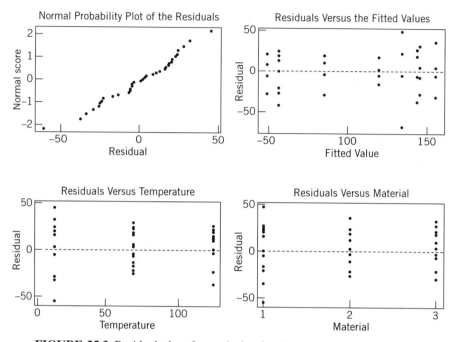

FIGURE 25.3 Residual plots for analysis of variance results of battery life.

25.3 S⁴ ASSESSMENT

Two-factor factorial experiments offer more information than one-factor experiments. The two-factor factorial experiment can be the best approach for a given situation. The methodology gives information about interactions and can apply to both manufacturing and business processes. However, in some situations the experiment can be very costly because the experiment can have a lot of test trials, plus the experiment does not address other factors that may significantly affect a process. The normal approach of dealing with these other process factors that are not considered within the experiment is to either hold them constant or let them exhibit "normal" variability. For many situations, both of these alternatives are not very desirable.

Before conducting a two-factor factorial, it is best to reflect on the objective of the experiment and important aspects of the situation. Often it is best to execute this reflection within a team setting where attendees have a different perspective on the situation. Initially the situation should be crisply defined, and what is desired from the experimental analysis should be determined. Next the group should use brainstorming techniques to create a list of all the factors that can affect the situation. The group could then prioritize these factors and list any test constraints.

If a two-factor factorial seems like the best approach after reflection of the issues within this team meeting, this approach is probably the best for the particular situation. However, if there are many factors, then perhaps a DOE approach is a better alternative. This approach is described in later chapters.

25.4 EXERCISES

1. *Catapult Exercise:* Each team is to select two factors to vary on the catapult (e.g., arm length and start angle). Three levels are chosen for each factor. Conduct a randomized experiment of projection distance where the level settings of the factors has one replication. There will be a total of 18 measurements. Conduct a two-factor analysis of variance.

2. The breaking strength of a fiber is studied as a function of four machines and three operators using fiber from one batch. Using computer software analyze the following data and draw conclusions. Comment on how these variables could be related to a transactional process (Montgomery 1997).

Operator	Machine			
	1	2	3	4
1	109	110	108	110
	110	115	109	108
2	110	110	111	114
	112	111	109	112
3	116	112	114	120
	114	115	119	117

3. Describe how the techniques within this chapter are useful and can be applied to S^4 projects.

26

MULTIPLE REGRESSION

Described earlier was a simple regression model where a model is built to estimate a response as a function of the magnitude of one regressor variable. This chapter describes the basic methodology of using multiple regressor variables to build a multiple regression model.

26.1 DESCRIPTION

A general model includes polynomial terms in one or more variables such as

$$Y = \beta_0 + \beta_1 x_1 + \beta_2 x_2 + \beta_3 x_1^2 + \beta_4 x_2^2 + \beta_5 x_1 x_2 + \varepsilon$$

where β's are unknown parameters and ε is random error. This full quadratic model of Y on x_1 and x_2 is of great use in DOE.

For the situation without polynomial terms where there are k predictor variables the general model reduces to the form

$$Y = \beta_0 + \beta_1 x_1 + \cdots + \beta_k x_k + \varepsilon$$

The object is to determine from data the least squares estimates ($b_0, b_1, \ldots, \beta_k$) of the unknown parameters ($\beta_0, \beta_1, \ldots, \beta_k$) for the prediction equation

$$\hat{Y} = b_0 + b_1 x_1 + \cdots + b_k x_k$$

where $\hat{Y}$ is the predicted value of Y for given values of $x_1 \ldots , x_k$. Many statistical software packages can conduct this analysis. The following example illustrates this type of analysis.

26.2   EXAMPLE 26.1: MULTIPLE REGRESSION

Investigation is desired to determine the relationship of a key process output variable (i.e., product strength) to two key process input variables (i.e., hydraulic pressure during a forming process and acid concentration). The data are given in Table 26.1 (Juran 1988), which resulted in the following analysis:

Regression Analysis

```
The regression equation is
strength = 16.3 + 1.57 pressure + 4.16 concent
```

TABLE 26.1 Data for Multiple Regression Model of Product Strength

Strength	Pressure	Concentration
665	110	116
618	119	104
620	138	94
578	130	86
682	143	110
594	133	87
722	147	114
700	142	106
681	125	107
695	135	106
664	152	98
548	118	86
620	155	87
595	128	96
740	146	120
670	132	108
640	130	104
590	112	91
570	113	92
640	120	100

```
Predictor          Coeff         StDev            T             P
Constant           16.28         44.30         0.37         0.718
Pressure           1.5718        0.2606        6.03         0.000
Concent            4.1629        0.3340       12.47         0.000


S = 15.10     R-Sq = 92.8%     R-Sq(adj) = 92.0%


Analysis of Variance

Source             DF        SS         MS          F           P
Regression          2     50101      25050      109.87      0.000
Residual Error     17      3876        228
Total              19     53977


Source        DF     Seq SS
Pressure       1      14673
Concent        1      35428
```

Some of the entries within this output are more important than others. I will now highlight some of the more important aspects of this table. The predictor and coefficient (i.e., coeff) describe the prediction model (i.e., strength = 16.3 + 1.57 pressure + 4.16 concent). The P columns give the significance level for each model term. Typically if a P value is less than or equal to 0.05, the variable is considered significant (i.e., null hypothesis is rejected). If a P value is greater than 0.10, the term is removed from the model. A practitioner might leave the term within the model if the P value is within the gray region between these two probability levels. Note that these probability values for the model parameters are determined from the t-statistic values that are shown in the output.

The coefficient of determination (R^2) is presented as R-Sq and R-Sq(adj) in the output. This value represents the proportion of the variability accounted for by the model. As noted in an earlier chapter, R^2(adj) adjusts for the degrees of freedom. When a variable is added to an equation, the coefficient of determination will get larger, even if the added variable has no real value. R^2(adj) is an approximate unbiased estimate that compensates for this. In this case the model describes a very large percentage of the variability because the R^2(adj) value is 92%.

In the analysis of variance portion of this output the F value is used to determine an overall P value for the model fit. In this case the resulting P value of 0.000 indicates a very high level of significance. The regression and residual sum of squares (SS) and mean square (MS) calculated values are interim steps to determine the F value. Standard error is the square root of mean square.

No unusual patterns were prevalent in the residual analysis plots. Also, no correlation was shown between hydraulic pressure and acid concentration.

26.3 OTHER CONSIDERATIONS

It should be noted that regressor variables should be independent within a model (i.e., they are completely uncorrelated). Multicollinearity describes the phenomenon when variables are dependent. A measure of the magnitude of multicollinearity, that is often available in statistical software, is the variance inflation factor (VIF). VIF quantifies how much the variance of an estimated regression coefficient increases if the predictors are correlated. Regression coefficients can be considered poorly estimated when VIF exceeds 5 or 10 (Montgomery and Peck 1982). Options to break up multicollinearity include collecting additional data or using different predictors.

Another approach to data analysis in general is the consideration of step-wise regression (Draper and Smith 1966) or taking all possible regressions of the data, when selecting the number of terms to include in a model. This approach can be most useful whenever data is from an experiment that does not have experiment structure. However, experimenters should be aware of the potential pitfalls from happenstance data (Box, et al. 1978).

Consider an analysis of all possible regressions for the data shown in Table 30.3. Table 26.2 illustrates a computer output with all possible regressions. This approach first considers only one factor within a model, then two, and so forth (Table 26.2, notes ① and ②). The R^2 value is then considered for each of the models (Table 26.2, note ③); only factor combinations containing the highest two R^2 values are shown in Table 26.2. For example, if one were to consider a model containing only one factor, the factor to consider would be algor. Likewise, if one were to consider a model containing only two factors, the factors to consider would be algor with mot_adj.

Mallow's C_p statistic [C(P) in Table 26.2, note ④] is useful to determine

TABLE 26.2 Summary from all Possible Regressions Analysis

N = 16			Regression Models for Dependent Variable: Timing Model: Model1
Number in Model ①	R-Square ③	C(P) ④	Variables in Model ②
1	0.33350061	75.246939	MOT_ADJ
1	0.57739025	43.320991	ALGOR
2	0.58342362	44.531203	ALGOR EXT_ADJ
2	0.91009086	1.664676	ALGOR MOT_ADJ
3	0.91500815	3.125709	ALGOR MOT_ADJ SUP_VOLT
3	0.91692423	2.874888	ALGOR MOT_ADJ EXT_ADJ
4	0.91949041	4.538967	ALGOR MOT_ADJ EXT_ADJ MOT_TEMP
4	0.92104153	4.335921	ALGOR MOT_ADJ EXT_ADJ SUP_VOLT
5	0.92360771	6.000000	ALGOR MOT_ADJ EXT_ADJ SUP_VOLT MOT_TEMP

the minimum number of parameters that best fits the model. Technically this statistic measures the sum of the squared biases plus the squared random errors in Y at all n data points (Daniel and Wood 1980).

The minimum number of factors needed in the model is when the Mallows' C_p statistic is a minimum. From this output the pertinent Mallows' C_p statistic values under consideration as a function of numbers of factors within this model are

Number in Model	Mallows' C_p [a]
1	43.32
2	1.67
3	2.87
4	4.33
5	6.00

[a] The Mallows' C_p is not related to the process index C_p.

From this summary it is noted that the Mallows' C_p statistic is minimized whenever there are two parameters in the model. The corresponding factors are algor and mot_adj. This conclusion is consistent with our analyses shown in Example 30.1.

26.4 EXERCISES

1. *Catapult Exercise Data Analysis:* Using the catapult exercise data sets from Chapter 25, conduct a multiple regression analysis.

2. Conduct a multiple regression analysis of the pulse data previously presented as Exercise 2 in Chapter 15. Summarize results.

3. Describe how the techniques within this chapter are useful and can be applied to S^4 projects.

PART IV

S⁴ IMPROVEMENT PHASE

This part (chapters 27–33) addresses the use of DOE to gain process knowledge by structurally changing the operating levels of several factors simultaneously within a process. This information can help identify the setting of key variables for process optimization and change opportunities.

27

BENEFITING FROM DESIGN OF EXPERIMENTS (DOE)

Analysis of variance and regression techniques are useful to determine if there is a statistically significant difference between treatments and levels of variables. Example analysis-of-variance assessments include tests for differences between departments, suppliers, or machines. Regression techniques are useful to describe the effects of temperature, pressure, delays, and other key process inputs on key process outputs such as cycle time and dimensions on a production part.

Analysis of variance and regression techniques help determine to the source of differences without making changes to the process. However, analysis of variance and regression results can sometimes not describe the most effective process improvement activities. For example, regression analysis might not indicate that temperature affects the output of a process. Because of this analysis a practitioner might choose not to further investigate a change in temperature setting to improve the response of a process. The deception can occur because the normal variability of temperature within the process is not large enough to be detected as a significant effect. This limitation is overcome with design of experiments (DOE).

George Box has a statement that is often quoted: "To find out what happens to a system when you interfere with it you have to interfere with it (not just passively observe it)" (Box 1966). DOE techniques are useful when a practitioner needs to "kick" a process so it can give us insight to how we can improve it. DOE techniques offer a structured approach to change many factor settings within a process at once and observe the data collectively for improvements/degradations. DOE analyses not only yield a significance test of the factor levels but also gives a prediction model for the response. These experiments can address all possible combinations of a set of inputs factor (i.e., a full factorial) or a subset of all combinations (i.e., a fractional factorial).

A Forbes article written by Koselka (1996) refers to the concepts as multivariable testing (MVT). DOE techniques yield an efficient strategy to a wide range of applications. In DOE the effects of several independent factors (variables) can be considered simultaneously in one experiment without evaluating all possible combinations of factor levels.

In the following chapters, various experiment design alternatives are illustrated with emphasis on two-level fractional factorial designs, as opposed to full factorial designs that consider all possible combinations of factor levels. Described also are (a) a simple illustration of why two-level fractional factorial experiments work and (b) the mechanics of setting up and conducting an experiment. Focus is given to continuous response designs; however, attribute data are also discussed.

DOE techniques offer an efficient, structured approach to assess the mean effects between factor levels for a response. However, often the real need is the reduction of variability. Chapter 32 addresses the use of DOE for variability reduction.

27.1 TERMINOLOGY AND BENEFITS

There are many benefits to DOE. Koselka (1996) lists the following benefits within a Forbes article:

- Reducing the rejection rate of a touch-sensitive computer screen from 25% to less then 1% within months.
- Maintaining paper quality at a mill while switching to a cheaper grade of wood.
- Reducing the risks of misusing a drug in a hospital by incorporating a standardized instruction sheet with patient–pharmacist discussion.
- Reducing the defect rate of the carbon-impregnated urethane foam used in bombs from 85% to zero.
- Improving the sales of shoes by using an inexpensive arrangement of shoes by color in a show chase, rather than an expensive flashy alternative.
- Reducing errors on service orders, while at the same time improving response time on service calls.
- Improving bearing durability by a factor of five.

27.2 EXAMPLE 27.1: TRADITIONAL EXPERIMENTATION

A one-at-a-time experiment was conducted when there was interest in reducing the photoconductor speed of a process. Bake temperature and percent additive were the factors under consideration, and each experimental trial was expensive.

The experimenter first chose to set bake temperature and percent additive to their lowest level setting because this was the cheapest manufacturing alternative. The percent additive was then increased while the bake temperature remained constant. Because the photoconductor speed degraded (i.e., a higher number resulted), the bake temperature was next increased while the percent additive was set to its original level. This combination yielded the lowest results; hence, the experimenter suggested this combination to management as the "optimum combination." A summary of this sequence is as follows:

Test Results as a Function of Factor Levels

Sequence Number	Bake Temperature (°C)	Percent Additive (%)	Speed of Photoconductor
1	45	1	1.1
2	45	3	1.2
3	55	1	1.0

From this summary of results it is obvious that one combination of bake temperature with additive percentage was not evaluated. Consider now that another trial was added to address this combination of parameters, and the resulting photoconductor speed was measured as 0.6. The two factors, bake temperature and percent additive, interact together to affect the output level. Figure 27.1 shows an interaction plot of these data where the lowest (best) speed of conductor is obtained by adjusting both parameters concurrently.

The straight line interconnecting the points assumes a linear relationship between the test point combinations, which may not be precise. However, this is surely a better initial test evaluation than using the original one-at-a-time approach.

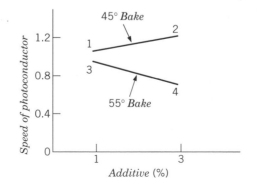

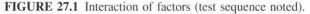

FIGURE 27.1 Interaction of factors (test sequence noted).

To exemplify a two-factor interaction, consider how copiers might have a higher failure rate when both temperature and humidity were high (moisture in air was high). The failure rate was not higher because of increased temperature or humidity levels alone. Temperature and humidity interacted to cause an increase in the failure rate. Failure rate models must consider temperature and humidity collectively. A one-at-a-time approach evaluating the failure of a copier could miss this scenario if the factors were not considered collectively.

27.3 THE NEED FOR DOE

To be competitive in today's markets, companies need to execute design, manufacturing, and business processes with aggressive cost and schedule constraints. To meet these challenges, organizations need efficient experimentation techniques that provide useful information. DOE techniques are tools that can help satisfy these needs.

Within manufacturing and design verification it is natural because of time constraints to focus experiment evaluations at nominal operating conditions. However, customers rarely either receive a "nominally" built machine or use a product under "nominal operating conditions." Similarly, a manufacturing process rarely produces products under nominal tolerance conditions. DOE techniques can aid in the development of quality products that meet the needs of customers even though they might have a variety of different applications. DOE techniques can also help manufacturing with their process parameters and other considerations so that they create quality products on a continuing basis.

Factors to consider in an experiment to determine whether a product will perform satisfactorily in a customer environment include such considerations as environmental conditions, external loads, product tolerances, and general human factor considerations. Factors for experimental consideration in the manufacturing process are part tolerances, process parameter tolerances, supplier sources, and manufacturing personnel. Factors to consider in a business process include departments, time of day, days of the week, and personnel.

If factors (e.g., part tolerances and environmental conditions) are assessed, it is natural to set up an experiment that monitors changes in an output as a function of factors when they are changed individually, while holding all other factors constant. However, experiments performed at nominal conditions and then at other conditions using a basic one-at-a-time assessment for factor levels are not only inefficient but can also lead to erroneous conclusions. It is important to understand the effect that factors have collectively on a product so that appropriate changes can be made to reduce variability and deliver a product that is price competitive.

In product development a test strategy needs to give early problem detection and isolation while promoting a reduced product development cycle time along with a low-cost basic design. In manufacturing, quick problem detection and resolution is most important. In addition, efficient techniques are needed to help maintain and continuously improve the manufacturing process. In transactional or business processes, the identification and quantification of process improvement opportunities can help weight the monetary tradeoffs between savings of implementation and cost of implementation. DOE techniques can give major benefits to both the development, manufacturing, and business/transactional processes.

Traditional one-at-a-time approach can miss interactions and are inefficient. However, much effort can be wasted if two-factor interactions are not investigated *wisely*. For example, consider the number of trials needed to assess all combination of seven two-level factors. There would be 128 trials (i.e., 2^7 = 128). Tests can become very expensive, and all combinations of many factor levels are considered during an experiment. Wisely applied DOE techniques can require only a very small subset of all combinations and still give information about two-factor interactions.

DOE techniques are often associated with manufacturing processes, as previously illustrated. For example, the setting of 15 knobs could be initially assessed in 16 trials. However, the techniques are also applicable to development tests. For example, an improved development test strategy could reduce the amount of no trouble found (NTF) encountered from field returns. The techniques are also applicable to services processes—for example, reducing absenteeism of students in high school.

27.4 EXERCISES

1. Create a two-factor interaction plot of the following data:

Temperature	Pressure	Response
100	250	275
100	300	285
120	250	270
120	300	325

(a) Determine what parameter settings yield the largest response.

(b) Determine what parameter settings of pressure would be best if it were important to reduce the variability of the response that results from frequent temperature variations between the two extremes.

2. Early in development, three prototype automobiles were tested to estimate the fuel consumption (i.e., average miles per gallon). The net average of the three vehicles over 20,000 miles was reported to management. Describe what could be done differently to the above test if we wanted to better understand characteristics that affect fuel consumption.

3. Describe how the techniques within this chapter are useful and can be applied to S^4 projects.

28

UNDERSTANDING THE CREATION OF FULL AND FRACTIONAL FACTORIAL 2^k DOEs

This chapter gives a conceptual explanation of two-level factorial experiments. It uses a nonmanufacturing example to illustrate the application of the techniques.

It should be noted that the DOE designs described in this text are not in "standard order." This was done to avoid possible confusion with the unique Tables M & N. Section C.6 illustrates the standard order format and compares a standard order design to that determined from Table M.

28.1 CONCEPTUAL EXPLANATION: TWO-LEVEL FULL FACTORIAL EXPERIMENTS AND TWO-FACTOR INTERACTIONS

This section discusses the basics of two-level full factorial experiment designs. The next section illustrates why fractional factorial design matrices "work."

When executing a full factorial experiment, a response is achieved for all combinations of the factor levels. The three-factor experiment design in Table 28.1 is a two-level full factorial experiment. For analyzing three factors, eight trials are needed (i.e., $2^3 = 8$) to address all assigned combinations of the factor levels. The plus/minus notation illustrates the high/low level of the factors. When a trial is performed, the factors are set to the noted plus/minus limits (levels) and a response value(s) is then noted for the trial.

Within this experiment design, each factor is executed at its high and low level an equal number of times. It can be noted that there are an equal number of plus and minus signs in each column. The best estimate factor effects can be assessed by noting the difference in the average outputs of the trials. The calculation of this relationship for the factor A effect is

TABLE 28.1 Two-Level Full Factorial Experiment Design

Trial No.	A	B	C	Experiment Response
1	+	+	+	x_1
2	+	+	−	x_2
3	+	−	+	x_3
4	+	−	−	x_4
5	−	+	+	x_5
6	−	+	−	x_6
7	−	−	+	x_7
8	−	−	−	x_8

Column headers span: Trial No. | Factor Designation (A, B, C) | Experiment Response

$$[(\bar{x}_{[A^+]}) - (\bar{x}_{[A^-]})] = \frac{x_1 + x_2 + x_3 + x_4}{4} - \frac{x_5 + x_6 + x_7 + x_8}{4}$$

The difference determined by the equation is an estimate of the average response change from the high to the low level of A. The other factor effects can similarly be calculated.

Interaction effects are a measurement of factor levels "working together" to affect a response (e.g., the product's performance degrades whenever temperature is high in conjunction with humidity being low). In addition to being able to calculate the main effects, all interaction effects can be assessed given these eight trials with three factors, as shown in Table 28.2. "Interaction columns" can be generated in the matrix by multiplying the appropriate columns together and noting the resultant sign using conventional algebraic rules. In this table the third trial sign, in the AB column, for example, is determined by multiplying the A sign (+) by the B sign (−) to achieve an AB sign (−).

Two-factor interaction effects are similarly noted. For the AB interaction, the best estimate of the effect can be determined from

TABLE 28.2 Full Factorial Experiment Design with Interaction Considerations

Trial No.	A	B	C	AB	BC	AC	ABC	Experiment Response
1	+	+	+	+	+	+	+	x_1
2	+	+	−	+	−	−	−	x_2
3	+	−	+	−	−	+	−	x_3
4	+	−	−	−	+	−	+	x_4
5	−	+	+	−	+	−	−	x_5
6	−	+	−	−	−	+	+	x_6
7	−	−	+	+	−	−	+	x_7
8	−	−	−	+	+	+	−	x_8

Column headers span: Trial No. | Factors and Interactions (A, B, C, AB, BC, AC, ABC) | Experiment Response

$$[(\overline{x}_{[AB^+]}) - (\overline{x}_{[AB^-]})] = \frac{x_1 + x_2 + x_7 + x_8}{4} - \frac{x_3 + x_4 + x_5 + x_6}{4}$$

A question of concern in a factorial experiment is whether the calculated effects are large enough to be considered "significant." In other words, we need to determine whether the resultant of the two previous calculations is a large number relative to differences caused by experimental error.

If a two-factor interaction is determined to be significant, more information is determined about the interaction through a plot such as that shown in Figure 28.1. From this plot it is noted that there are four combinations of the levels of the *AB* factors (*AB* levels: $++$, $+-$, $-+$, and $--$). To make the interaction plot, the average value for each of these combinations is first calculated [e.g., $AB = ++$ effect is $(x_1 + x_2)/2$]. The averages are then plotted. In this plot, A^-B^+ yields a high-output response while A^-B^- yields a low-output response; the levels of these factors interact to affect the output level.

If there is no interaction between factors, the lines on an interaction plot will be parallel. The overall effect initially determined for the interaction (i.e., $\overline{x}_{[AB^+]} - \overline{x}_{[AB^-]}$) was a measure for the lack of parallelism of the lines.

28.2   CONCEPTUAL EXPLANATION: SATURATED TWO-LEVEL DOE

When many factors are considered, full factorials can yield a very large test sample size, whereas a saturated fractional factorial can require a much reduced sample size. For example, an eight-trial saturated fractional factorial experiment can assess the seven two-level factors, while it would take 128 trials as a full factorial.

The basic concept of creating a saturated fractional factorial experiment design is illustrated in Table 28.3. In this table, the calculated interaction columns are used to describe the levels of four additional factors, which now

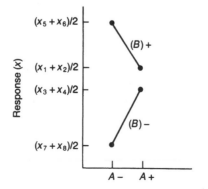

FIGURE 28.1 A two-factor interaction plot.

TABLE 28.3 Saturated Fractional Factorial Experiment: Eight Trials, Seven Factors

				D	E	F	G	Experiment
Trial No.	A	B	C	AB	BC	AC	ABC	Response
1	+	+	+	+	+	+	+	x_1
2	+	+	−	+	−	−	−	x_2
3	+	−	+	−	−	+	−	x_3
4	+	−	−	−	+	−	+	x_4
5	−	+	+	−	+	−	−	x_5
6	−	+	−	−	−	+	+	x_6
7	−	−	+	+	−	−	+	x_7
8	−	−	−	+	+	+	−	x_8

Factors and Interactions

makes the total number of two-level factor considerations seven in eight trials (i.e., a saturated fractional factorial design).

The disadvantage of this saturated fractional factorial experiment is the confounding of the two-factor interaction effects and the main effects. There is confounding of the AB interaction and the main effect D; however, there is also confounding of factor D and other two-factor interactions, because of the introduction of the additional factors D, E, F, and G.

Because each column can now have more than one meaning, each column is assigned a number, which in this text is referred to as a *contrast column number* (see Tables M1 to M5 and N1 to N3).

It may be hard for a reader to believe that all main effect information of seven two-level factors can be obtained in only eight trials. There may be a concern that the significance of one factor could affect the decision about another factor. To address this concern, assume that E is the only significant factor and there are no interactions. The question of concern, for example, is whether factor E can affect the decision of whether factor A is significant.

A subset of the matrix from Table 28.3 is shown in Table 28.4 with output that was designed to make factor E very significant.

The A and E factor mean effects are

$$\bar{x}_{[E^+]} - \bar{x}_{[E^+]} = \frac{x_1 + x_4 + x_5 + x_8}{4} - \frac{x_2 + x_3 + x_6 + x_7}{4}$$

$$= \frac{500 + 500 + 500 + 500}{4} - \frac{0 + 0 + 0 + 0}{4} = 500$$

$$\bar{x}_{[A^+]} - \bar{x}_{[A^+]} = \frac{x_1 + x_2 + x_3 + x_4}{4} - \frac{x_5 + x_6 + x_7 + x_8}{4}$$

$$= \frac{500 + 0 + 0 + 500}{4} - \frac{500 + 0 + 0 + 500}{4} = 0$$

TABLE 28.4 Example Output from Table 28.3. Design

Trial No.	A	E	Experiment Response
1	+	+	500
2	+	−	0
3	+	−	0
4	+	+	500
5	−	+	500
6	−	−	0
7	−	−	0
8	−	+	500

This example illustrates that even though factor E was "very significant," this significance did not affect our decision about the nonsignificance of factor A. Like factor A, factors B, C, D, F. and G can similarly be shown to be "not significant."

The purpose of this example is to illustrate that a main effect will not be confounded with another main effect in this seven-factor, eight-trial experiment design. However, the experimenter must be aware that it is possible that there is an interaction (e.g., BC) that could be making factor E appear significant even though factors B and C individually were not determined to be significant.

28.3   EXAMPLE 28.1: APPLYING DOE TECHNIQUES TO A NONMANUFACTURING PROCESS

This example gives an overview of the thought process when setting up a DOE experiment. To illustrate the application of the techniques, consider that a high-school administration wants to reduce absenteeism of students in high school.

Many factors can affect school absenteeism. These factors (identified perhaps from a brainstorming session) include the following:

- Student: age, sex, ethnic background . . .
- School: location, teacher, class . . .
- Time: day of week, class period . . .

Consider how you might approach the problem if you were a consultant commissioned to assist with this effort. A typical approach would be to regress factors on the response to determine which factors significantly affect the output. A regression approach might indicate that there was a difference in the amount of absenteeism depending upon the sex of the student. Consider what should now be done with the system to reduce absenteeism. Difficult isn't it? The information from this experiment might be interesting to report within the news media; however, determining what should be done differently to reduce absenteeism given this information is purely conjecture.

There are several problems with a purely regression approach. First, regression only observes the factors and levels of factors that occur naturally in the system (e.g., would not detect that an increase in pressure beyond normal operating conditions that could dramatically improve product quality). Second, it does not assess new factors (e.g., a call-back program). Third, the conclusion could be happenstance (e.g., the phase of the moon might look significant within a regression model because some other factor had a monthly cycle).

After an initial regression assessment, consider using a DOE approach with the following factor designations A–G:

A: Day of the week
B: Call back when absent
C: School
D: Class period
E: Mentor if missed a lot
F: Contract if already missed a lot of classes
G: Sex of the student

Consider what two fundamental differences exist between these factors. Some factors are observations, while other factors are improvement possibilities. Day of the week, school, class period, and sex of student are observations, while call back when absent, assignment of a mentor if missed a lot, and contract if already missed a lot of classes are improvement possibilities. (Normally a student would fail if they missed more than a certain number of days. This "contract" improvement possibility would offer the student a second chance if he or she agreed to attend all classes the remaining portion of the semester.)

Choose now how a brainstorming session addresses the levels for each factor. The tendency is to assign many levels to each factor. However, this can add much complexity to the experiment. We should always ask whether the additional level is helpful to address the initial problem—that is, gaining insight to what should be done to reduce absenteeism of students in school. Consider the number of trials that would be needed if there were the following levels assigned to each factor:

A: Day of the week: Mon. vs. Fri.
B: Call back when absent: Yes vs. No
C: School: Locations 1, 2, 3, 4
D: Class period: 1, 2, 3
E: Mentor if missed a lot: Yes vs. No
F: Contract if already missed a lot of classes: Yes vs. No
G: Sex of student: Male vs. Female

The total number of combinations for a full factorial is ($2 \times 2 \times 4 \times 3 \times 2 \times 2 \times 2 = 384$). This number of trials is impossible for many situations. To reduce the number of trials for the full factorial, consider altering the number of levels to two. To do this, consider the question at hand. Perhaps the question can be satisfactorily addressed, for example, by choosing only two schools where one had the best attendance record while the other had the worst attendance record. A two-level assessment would reduce the number of trials to $2^7 = 128$ trials for a full factorial design. This could be further reduced to 64, 32, 16, or 8 trials using a fractional factorial structure. For fractional DOEs, the alternatives of 64, 32, 16, or 8 trials gives varying resolution of factor information. Resolution describes the management of two-factor interactions. That is, two-factor interactions may or may not be confounded (aliased) with each other or main effects. To illustrate a two-factor interaction, consider that there was a difference between absenteeism caused by day of the week (Friday vs. Monday) and call-back program (yes vs. no), where the effectiveness of the call-back program was much more affective in reducing absenteeism Friday (perhaps because students would be corrected by parent after weekend calls).

When reducing the number of factors to two levels, quantitative factors such as pressure would be modeled as a linear relationship. For qualitative factors such as suppliers, schools, operators, or machines, consider choosing the sources that represent the extremes.

For the purpose of illustration, consider initially only three of the two-level factors:

- Day of Week: Mon. vs. Fri.
- Call back when absent: Yes vs. No
- School: 1 vs. 2

Eight trials can assess all possible combinations of the levels of three factors (i.e. $2^3 = 8$).

The factors and levels could have the following designation:

	Level	
Factor	−	+
A: Day of Week	Fri.	Mon.
B: Call back when absent	Yes	No
C: School	1	2

One experiment design and response approach could be to randomly select 800 students from two schools. Students are then randomly placed into one of the eight trial categories (i.e., there will be 100 students in each trial). The total number of days absent from each category for the 100 students is the response for the analysis.

This approach offers some advantages over a more traditional regression analysis approach. New factors are assessed that could improve the process (i.e., a call-back program). Effects from happenstance occurrences are lessened. The eight-trial combinations are as follows:

Trial No.	Factor Designation			Response
	A	B	C	
1	+	+	+	x_1
2	+	+	−	x_2
3	+	−	+	x_3
4	+	−	−	x_4
5	−	+	+	x_5
6	−	+	−	x_6
7	−	−	+	x_7
8	−	−	−	x_8

For the physical relationship of the design, consider trial 2. For this situation the response would be the total absenteeism of 100 students on Monday with no call back, for school 1. We also note from the initial design matrix that there are four levels for each factor for the experiment; that is, four trials had C at a "+" level and four trials had A at a "−" level. The effect for a factor would be the differences of the average for that factor at the "+" level minus the average for that factor at the "−" level.

Consider that this experiment yielded the following results (these data were created such that there was an interaction between factors A and B).

Trial No.	Factor Designation			Response
	A	B	C	
1	+	+	+	198
2	+	+	−	203

3	+	−	+	169
4	+	−	−	172
5	−	+	+	183
6	−	+	−	181
7	−	−	+	94
8	−	−	−	99

The estimated main effects are

A:	Day of week	+46.25
B:	Call back when absent	+57.75
C:	School	−2.75

By observation the magnitude of the school effect seems small. The sign of the other two factors indicates which level of the factor is best. In this case, lower numbers are best; hence Friday and call back is best. However, this model does not address the interaction.

As discussed earlier, a two-factor interaction causes out-of-parallelism of the two lines within a two-factor interaction plot. When sample data are plotted, the lines typically will not be exactly parallel. The question for a practitioner is whether the amount of out-of-parallelism of two lines from an interaction plot is large enough to be considered originating from a true interaction, as opposed to chance. This issue is addressed through the calculation of an interaction effect.

An interaction contrast column is created by multiplying the level designations of all main effect contrast columns to create new contrast columns of pluses and minuses:

	Factor Designation							
Trial No.	A	B	C	AB	BC	AC	ABC	Response
1	+	+	+	+	+	+	+	x_1
2	+	+	−	+	−	−	−	x_2
3	+	−	+	−	−	+	−	x_3
4	+	−	−	−	+	−	+	x_4
5	−	+	+	−	+	−	−	x_5
6	−	+	−	−	−	+	+	x_6
7	−	−	+	+	−	−	+	x_7
8	−	−	−	+	+	+	−	x_8

Again there are four pluses and four minuses in each contrast column. The magnitude of the effect from an interaction contrast column (e.g., AB) relative to other contract column effects could be used to assess the likelihood of an interaction. Hence, all possible two-factor interaction plots do not need to be plotted: Only those two-factor interactions that are thought to be large because of the magnitude of its effect need to be plotted.

Entering our trial responses in this format yields the following:

	Factor Designation							
Trial No.	A	B	C	AB	BC	AC	ABC	Response
1	+	+	+	+	+	+	+	198
2	+	+	−	+	−	−	−	203
3	+	−	+	−	−	+	−	169
4	+	−	−	−	+	−	+	172
5	−	+	+	−	+	−	−	183
6	−	+	−	−	−	+	+	181
7	−	−	+	+	−	−	+	94
8	−	−	−	+	+	+	−	99

The effects for interactions are determined similarly to main effects. For example, the *AB* interaction is determined from the equation $(198 + 203 + 94 + 99)/4 - (169 + 172 + 183 + 181)/4 = 27.75$. The following summarizes these results for all main effects and interactions:

A:	Day of week	46.25 (Fri. is best)
B:	Call back when absent	57.75 (call back is best)
C:	School	−2.75 (not significant)
AB:	Day*call back	27.75 (significant)
BC:	Call back*school	1.25 (not significant)
AC:	Call back*school	−1.25 (not significant)
ABC:	Day*call*school	−2.25 (not significant)

This summary indicates that the magnitude of the *A*, *B*, and *AB* effects are large relative to the other effects, which are presumed to be the result of experimental error. That is, the magnitude of the day*call back interaction looks significant. We cannot talk about "day of the week" and "call back" without talking about the two-factor interaction. A two-factor interaction plot shows which factor levels are most beneficial. A reduction of this table to create an *AB* interaction plot is

Trial No.	A	B	AB	Response
1	+	+	+	198
2	+	+	+	203
3	+	−	−	169
4	+	−	−	172
5	−	+	−	183

6	−	+	−	181
7	−	−	+	94
8	−	−	+	99

A plot of the average of the four response combinations for AB (i.e., $AB = ++$, $AB = -+$, $AB = +-$, and $AB = --$) shown in Figure 28.2 has out-of-parallelism of the two lines. The plot indicates that the call-back program helps more on Friday than on Monday. A call back when a student is absent on Friday indicates a reduction in absenteeism. The call-back program for absenteeism on Monday does not appear to reduce absenteeism.

To illustrate how the magnitude of an effect helps assesses the out-of-parallelism of a two-factor interaction plot, let's examine the appearance of an interaction that is not thought to be significant (e.g., AC). A subset of the contrast columns to combine for the plot are as follows:

Trial No.	A	C	AC	Response
1	+	+	+	198
2	+	−	−	203
3	+	+	+	169
4	+	−	−	172
5	−	+	−	183
6	−	−	+	181
7	−	+	−	94
8	−	−	+	99

	Experiment			Plot Positions		
	A	C		A	C	
1	+	+	198	$(198 + 169)/2 =$		
3	+	+	169	+	+	183
2	+	−	203	$(203 + 172)/2 =$		
4	+	−	172	+	−	187
5	−	+	183	$(183 + 94)/2 =$		
7	−	+	94	−	+	138
6	−	−	181	$(181 + 99)/2 =$		
8	−	−	99	−	−	140

Figure 28.3 shows a plot of these two lines where they are parallel (i.e., no interaction is apparently present).

Let's restate the strategy for two-factor interaction assessments. The effects of two-factor interaction column contrasts are used to determine if interactions are significant. Two-factor interaction plots are used to get a picture of what factor levels are best.

Reflecting again on the differences between this strategy and a regression approach, we were able to identify what should be done differently and quan-

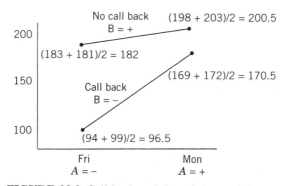

FIGURE 28.2 Call-back and day-of-the-week interaction.

tify the effects. Also, we might be able to theorize what we could do differently to the current "call-back methodology" to improve the effect on Mondays.

The number of trials can increase dramatically if we follow a similar procedure for an increase in the number of factors. For example, if we similarly assessed seven (not three) two-level factors, the resulting number of trials is 128 (2 = 128). Consider now the addition of four factors to our original design with the noted levels:

A: Day of the week: Fri. vs. Mon.
B: Call back when absent: Yes vs. No
C: School: Locations 1 vs. 2
D: Class period: 1 vs. 2
E: Mentor if missed a lot: Yes vs. No
F: Contract if already missed a lot of classes: Yes vs. No
G: Sex: Male vs. Female

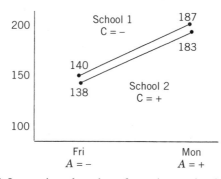

FIGURE 28.3 Interaction plot where factor interaction is not significant.

A 128-trial seven-factor experiment contains very-high-factor interactions. It contains other interactions: three-factor, four-factor, five-factor, six-factor, and seven-factor. Typically we assume that any interactions above two are small (if they would exist); hence, we don't need this many trials. A fractional DOE is an alternative to a full factorial DOE.

Consider again the eight-trial two-level full factorial design with all interactions. An assignment of the four additional factors to the interaction contrast columns yields the following:

Factor Designation

	A	B	C	D	E	F	G	Output
1	+	+	+	+	+	+	+	x_1
2	+	+	−	+	−	−	−	x_2
3	+	−	+	−	−	+	−	x_3
4	+	−	−	−	+	−	+	x_4
5	−	+	+	−	+	−	−	x_5
6	−	+	−	−	−	+	+	x_6
7	−	−	+	+	−	−	+	x_7
8	−	−	−	+	+	+	−	x_8

This seven-factor, eight-trial two-level factorial saturated design minimizes sample size, assesses main factor information, and confounds two-factor interactions with main effects. A summary of the main and two-factor interaction effects are as follows:

A:	Day of week (1 vs. 2)	46.25 (Fri. is best)
B:	Call back (yes vs. no)	57.75 (Call back is best)
C:	School (1 vs. 2)	−2.75 (not significant)
D:	Class period (1 vs. 2)	27.75 (significant)
E:	Mentor (yes vs. no)	1.25 (not significant)
F:	Contract (yes vs. no)	−1.25 (not significant)
G:	Sex (male vs. female)	−2.25 (not significant)

From the analysis of main effects the expectation now for factor D is that class period 2 has more absenteeism than class period 1 (about 27.75 days in a semester for 100 students). Strategies to address concerns that two-factor interaction confounding with main effects are distorting conclusions will be addressed in later chapters.

The above example illustrates a nonmanufacturing example of DOE techniques. For eight trials the discussed extremes are as follows:

- Three two-level factors (full factorial)
- Seven two-level factors (saturated factorial)

For eight trials, the confounding of two-factor interactions are as follows:

- Three two-level factors (full factorial)—all interactions are determined.
- Seven two-level factors (saturated factorial)—two-factor interactions are confounded with main effects.

For eight trials, the resolution designation is as follows:

- Three two-level factors (full factorial): V^+
- Seven two-level factors (saturated factorial): III

However, there are other choices for the number of factors in eight-trials instead of three or seven factors. There could be four, five, or six two-level factors examined in eight trials. This additional number of factors can lead to other alternatives besides resolution III and V^+. Resolution IV designs have two-factor interactions that are confounded with each other but not main effects. Resolution V designs have two-factor interactions are not confounded with other two-factor interactions or main effects. Table M shows various resolution alternatives, number of factors for 8, 16, 32, and 64 trials, and design matrices.

28.4 EXERCISES

1. *Catapult Exercise:* Teams are to create a two-level catapult DOE. The cause-and-effect diagram created within an exercise in Chapter 5 should be used to help determine the factors and level of factors that will be assessed during the experiment. Select at least six factors where ball type and arm length are two of the factors.

2. Create a 16-trial full factorial where the factors have two levels. Determine the contrast columns for all interactions and list them with the factorial design. Comment on the frequency of the $+$'s and $-$'s within each column.

3. Describe the setup of a DOE for a nonmanufacturing situation.

4. Describe how the techniques within this chapter are useful and can be applied to S^4 projects.

29

PLANNING 2^k DOEs

The mechanics of executing a DOE is not difficult. However, much time and resources can be wasted if the experiment is not set up *wisely*. This chapter discusses thoughts to consider when setting up a DOE.

29.1 INITIAL THOUGHTS WHEN SETTING UP A DOE

One major obstacle in implementing an efficient fractional factorial design test strategy is that the initial problem definition may not imply that fractional factorial design concepts are appropriate when in fact they are the best alternative.

A most effective blend is the combination of fractional factorial statistical methods with the skills of experts in a field of concern. Because of their structure, DOE techniques are conducive to evaluating in one experiment a collection of agreed-upon conditions determined by team brainstorming sessions. This "team management strategy tool" can be dramatically more efficient than many individuals independently making one-at-a-time experiments.

When designing an experiment, it is most important to first agree upon a clear set of objectives and criteria for the experiment. An S^4 practitioner would need to consider any history information and also ask many detailed questions before deciding upon the details of an experiment. Brainstorming and cause-and-effect diagram techniques can help with collecting this information.

The S^4 practitioner should strive to identify all relevant sources of information about factors, their levels, and ranges. Factors that are believed to be important need to be included in an experiment design such that there will be meaningful results. Factor effects that are not of primary interest for consideration in an experiment should be held constant or blocked (as described later). In addition, the sequence of experiment trials should be randomized in order to reduce the risk of an unknown/unexpected occurrence jeopardizing accurate conclusions. Care needs to also be exercised such that there is minimal error in the measurements for each trial.

After a proposed experiment is determined, the structure of the experiment is conducive to an individual or team presentation to management and other organizations. The proposed factors, levels of factors, and outputs in the experiment can be presented in a fashion such that individuals can quickly understand the test strategy. Perhaps from this presentation there will be a constructive critique that results in a better implementation strategy.

29.2 EXPERIMENT DESIGN CONSIDERATIONS

Examples in this text propose using unreplicated two-level fractional factorial design matrices in Tables M1 to M5. However, experiment design matrices are available in tabular form in other texts, journals, or computer programs. The basic experiment design strategy suggested in this text is also applicable to many of these design matrix alternatives.

For most people it seems appropriate to have factors with many levels, which can make an experiment become very cumbersome and "impossible" (or unreasonable) to conduct. Reducing the number of factor levels and listing associated assumptions can change the experiment feasibility dramatically.

The next question of concern is to determine what resolution should be considered. I often suggest a single replication of a 2^k design, which is sometimes called an *unreplicated factorial*. There is no internal estimate of error (i.e., pure error). An approach for the analysis of unreplicated factorial is to assume that high-order interactions are negligible and combine mean squares to estimate error. A justification for this is called the *sparsity of effects principle,* which states the following: Main effects dominate most systems and low-order interactions, and most high-order interactions are typically negligible.

In addition, I believe that many experiment design considerations fall into two general classifications. The first type needs to optimize a process (or help give direction toward a basic problem's resolution), while the second type needs to consider how a product will perform under various situations relative to meeting a specification.

Factor interaction consideration may be more important for the first type of classification than for the second type. In this second type a continuous response may have many factors that are significant; however, if the product is well within criterion, additional analysis may not be necessary. If the significant factor information will not lead to a cost reduction or a reduction in manufacturing variability, the experimenter should avoid analysis paralysis and move on to the next problem/investigation.

There may be a higher probability of having problems in a fractional factorial experiment from either unconscious experimental bias or data collection techniques that introduce large amounts of error, as opposed to an experiment that has "too small a sample size." Good techniques can reduce this exposure to experimental problems. First, the sequence in which the experimental trials are performed should be random to avoid the type of problem. Second, external experimentation factors should be blocked to avoid confusion between these external factors and experimental factor effects.

Note that for some factors, randomization may be a very difficult requirement to implement. Whenever the experiment is not randomized, care must be taken to consider that a bias (e.g., that may have been introduced in an experiment for convenience) could be the real reason that a factor is significant.

At the end of a fractional factorial experiment, a confirmation experiment should be performed to better quantify and confirm the magnitude of significant effects. A comparison test may, for example, be appropriate to compare an old design with new design considerations that were found significant within the experiment.

The following is a checklist of items to consider when designing a two-level DOE. Note that both a team brainstorming session and historical information should be considered when addressing these issues.

- List the objectives of the experiment (Consider whether the intent of the DOE is the understanding of factor mean effects or variability reduction).
- List the assumptions.
- List factors that might be considered in the experiment.
- Choose factors and their levels to consider in the experiment.
- List what "other factors" will not be evaluated in the experiment and will be held "constant."
- Reduce "many-level" factors to "two-level" factors.
- Choose the number of trials and resolution of the experiment.
- Determine if any of the factors will need to be blocked.
- Change, if possible, from an attribute response consideration to a continuous response consideration.
- Determine if any design center points will be used to check for curvature.
- Choose a fractional factorial design.
- Determine if trials will be replicated or repeated (see Chapter 32).
- Choose a sample size for the number of repetitions per trial and the number of replications needed (adjust number of trials and experiment resolution as needed).

- Determine a random order trial sequence to use.
- Determine what can be done to minimize the amount of experimental error.
- Plan a follow-up experiment strategy (e.g., a higher-resolution follow-up experiment or confirmation experiment).
- Plan the approach to be used for the analysis.

29.3 SAMPLE SIZE CONSIDERATIONS FOR A CONTINUOUS-RESPONSE OUTPUT DOE

Appendix C discusses a mathematical approach to determine a sample size to use when conducting a fractional factorial experiment. Through the years I have found the following procedure and rationale satisfactory for many industrial experiments that have a continuous response output where the DOE is to assess the significance of mean effects of a response. Note, this discussion does not address sample size issues when the focus of the experiment is to understand and reduce the variability of a response (see Chapter 32).

Many industry experiments can be structured such that they have either 16 or 32 trials, normally with no trial replication and only two-level factor considerations. (Obviously if trials are "cheap" and time is not an issue, more trials are better.)

The following discussion illustrates the logic for making this conclusion. With two-level experiment designs, advantages are achieved relative to two-factor interaction assessments when the number of trials are 2^n (i.e., those containing the number of trials in Tables M1 to M5), where n is a whole number. This will then yield 2, 4, 8, 16, 32, 64, 128, . . . trial experiment design alternatives. Experiments with 2, 4, and 8 trials are in general "too small" to give adequate confidence in the test results. Experiments with 64 and a higher number of trials are usually too expensive. Also, when larger experiments require much manual data collection, the person responsible for this work may become fatigued, causing sloppy data collection. Sloppy data collection can yield a high value for experimental error, which can mask factors that have a relatively small (but important) effect on the response. In addition, any individual trial mistake that goes undetected can jeopardize the accuracy of all conclusions. Sixteen- and 32-trial fractional factorial designs are a more manageable design size that can usually address the number of factors of interest with sufficient accuracy. Consider also that a series of shorter tests that give quick feedback can sometimes be more desirable than one long test.

It is perhaps more important than getting a "large sample size" to do everything that is possible to achieve the lowest possible measurement error. Often experimental error can be reduced by simple operator awareness. For an individual experiment, trade-off typically needs to be made between the number of factors, number of trials, experiment resolution, and number of possible follow-up experiments.

When someone is introduced to design experiment concepts, a 16-trial experiment may even appear to be "too much testing" to them. An eight-trial experiment can be a more viable alternative, which is still a much better approach than a one-at-a-time strategy.

29.4 EXPERIMENT DESIGN CONSIDERATIONS: CHOOSING FACTORS AND LEVELS

A DOE has application within a variety of situations. The specific situations can affect how factors and levels are chosen. Within a manufacturing environment, data analysis may give direction on the best factors and levels to use within an experiment to relate key process input variables with key process output variables. In development there may not be much data to give direction; hence, a DOE may be begun without much previous data analysis. However, in both cases a major benefit of the DOE structure is that it can easily give teams direct input to the selection of factors and the level of factors.

Factor levels also can take different forms. Levels can be quantitative or qualitative. A quantitative level is when the factor can take on one of many different values (e.g., the temperature input in a manufacturing process step), while qualitative levels take on discrete values (e.g., material x versus material y). The results obtained from the two-level manual fractional factorial analysis techniques discussed in this text are the same. However, the effect from two levels of a quantitative factor can be used to interpolate an output response for other magnitudes of the factor (assuming that a linear relationship exists between the two-level factors).

Within the implementation of a DOE there is often a very strong desire to conduct an initial DOE with factors that have more than two levels. Initial experiments that have more than two levels can add a lot of unnecessary time, expense, and complexity to an experiment. Before beginning a multilevel experiment the question should be asked why increase the levels of a factor beyond two. When analyzing the response to this question the initial reasons for having more than two levels often disappear.

In some situations this transition down from "many-level" to two-level considerations can require much thought. For example, instead of considering how a process operates at three temperatures, an experiment perhaps could first only be investigated at the tolerance extremes of temperature. If there were concern that the end condition levels of the factor have similar effects and the midpoint was significantly different, one tolerance extreme versus a nominal condition could be used in an initial experiment. If this factor is still considered important after the first experiment, the second tolerance extreme can be addressed in another experiment in conjunction with the nominal condition or another factor level setting. When the number of factors is not large, a response surface design may be an appropriate alternative.

If a factor has many levels (e.g., four supplier sources), perhaps previous knowledge can be used to choose the two extreme scenarios within the initial experiment considerations (realizing that there is a trade-off between the risk of making a wrong decision relative to the selection of suppliers and the implications of a larger sample size). If there appears to be a difference between these two levels, then additional investigation of the other levels may naturally be appropriate.

There can be concern about the possibility of nonlinearity when considering only two levels. I believe that it is generally best to initially consider a multiple experiment DOE approach and also utilize mathematical modeling during the analysis. Curvature can be checked by the addition of center points. If curvature exists within the region of concern, this can be quantified later through another experiment that is set up using response surface methods. The curvature relationship can then be described within a mathematical model. Also, it is sometimes more appropriate to reduce the magnitude of the differences between the levels within one experiment so that the response can be approximately modeled as a linear relationship between the factor levels.

Another issue can be that one factor is machine, and there is concern that there is a difference between three machines.. One of the main purposes for conducting a DOE is to make changes in a structured way within an experiment so that improvement opportunities can be identified. Other techniques described within this text are useful to determine and describe differences between such factors as machines, suppliers, and operators. To create a DOE, consider initially identifying the best and worst machine and use these as levels for the machine factor. This approach could lead to an interaction which could later be used to identify why the best machine is getting more desirable result.

Another situation is that one factor can either be performing at high tolerance, performing at low tolerance, or turned off. If we consider this factor within an experiment as initially described, we are forced to consider these levels as qualitative because one of the factor levels is "off." In addition to the added complexity of a three-level experiment, this initial experiment design does not permit us to directly model the expected response at different "on" settings within the tolerance extremes.

To better address this situation, consider that there are two experiment designs where each experiment considers each factor at two levels. Consider that the first experiment led to a 16-trial experiment where the two levels of the factor are the tolerance extremes when the factor is "on." The "off" factor condition is then considered by the addition of eight trials to the initial design. The other factor settings for a given trial in the "off" level setting are similar to those used at either the high or low factor setting for the "on" experiment design. This results in 24 total trials, which should be executed in random order.

After collecting the response from the 24 trials, the data can be analyzed using several approaches. Three simple techniques are as follows. First, the first 16 trials can be analyzed separately where the described factor level is quantitative. If the factor is significant for this case, the model equation can be used to predict the response at other settings besides tolerance extremes. Second, the eight trials for the "off" level can be analyzed in conjunction with the appropriate eight trials from the 16 trials that give a DOE matrix. This analysis will test the significance of the "on" versus "off" levels of this factor. Third, analyze the data collectively using multiple regression analysis techniques.

29.5   EXPERIMENT DESIGN CONSIDERATIONS: FACTOR SIGNIFICANCE

Continuous outputs (as opposed to attribute outputs) are normally desired for fractional factorial designed experiments. A typical fractional factorial conclusion could be that "voltage is significant at a level of 0.05." If voltage were a two-level factor consideration in the experiment, this statement means that a response is affected by changing the voltage from one level to another, and there is only an α risk of 0.05 that this statement is not true. Statements can also be made about the amount of change in output that is expected between the levels of factors. For example, a "best estimate" for a significant factor might be the following: A shift from the high tolerance level of the voltage factor to its low tolerance level will cause an average output timing change of 4 milliseconds (msec). The next chapter discusses methodologies to test for factor significance given an estimate for error. If a factor is "significant" (i.e., we reject the null hypothesis that the factor levels equally affect our response), the statement is made with an α risk of being wrong. However, the inverse is not true about factors not found to be significant. In other words, there is *not* an α risk of being wrong when these factors are *not* found to be significant. The reason for this is that the second statement relates to a β risk (i.e., not rejecting the null hypothesis, which is a function of the sample size and δ). Appendix C discusses an approach where the sample size of a factorial experiment is made large enough to address the β risk of not rejecting the null hypothesis when the null hypothesis is actually false.

29.6   EXPERIMENT DESIGN CONSIDERATIONS: EXPERIMENT RESOLUTION

Full factorial designs are used to assess all possible combination of the factor levels under consideration. Within these designs, information is contained about all possible interactions of the factor levels. For example, a full factorial experiment consisting of seven two-level factors will require 128 trials ($2^7 = 128$). There will be information in this experiment about all possible interactions, including whether all seven factors work in conjunction to affect the output (defined as a seven-factor interaction). Also, information is contained about lower factor interactions—that is, any combination of 6,5,4,3, and 2 factors.

In many situations, three-factor and higher interaction effects can be considered small relative to the main effects and two-factor interaction effects. Because of this, interactions higher than two in many situations can be ignored. When this can be done, a smaller number of trials are needed to assess the same number of factors. A fractional factorial design can assess the factors with various "resolutions" (see instruction on Table M1). A resolution V design evaluates the main effects and two-factor interactions independently. A resolution IV design evaluates the main effects and confounded (i.e., mixed up) two-factor interactions (i.e., there is aliasing of the two-factor interactions). A resolution III design evaluates the main effects, which are confounded with the two-factor interactions. Tables M1 to M5 will later be used to give test alternatives for each of these resolutions. Plackett and Burman (1946) have other resolution III design alternatives; however, the fashion in which two factor interactions are confounded with main effects is often complicated.

29.7 BLOCKING AND RANDOMIZATION

Many experiments can inadvertently give results that are biased. For example, error can occur in the analysis of experimental data if no consideration is given during the execution of an experiment toward the usage of more than one piece of equipment, operator, and/or test days. Blocking is a means to handle nuisance factors so that they do not distort the analysis of the factors that are of interest.

Consider, for example, that the experiment design in Table 28.3 as conducted sequentially in the numeric sequence shown over a two-day period (trials 1–4 on day 1 and trials 5–8 on day 2). Consider (unknown to the test designer) that humidity conditions affect the process results dramatically. As luck would have it, the weather conditions changed and it started raining very heavily on the second day. Results from the experiment would lead the experimenter to believe that factor A was very significant because this factor was $+$ on the first day and $-$ on the second day, when, in fact, the humidity conditions caused by the rain was the real source of significance.

There are two approaches to avoid this unplanned confounding: In the first approach the experimental trials are randomized (which should always be strive for). If this were done for the above scenario, the differences between days would not affect our decision about factor significance (the variability between day differences would show up as experimental error). Another approach is to block the experimental trials. This is a better approach for factors that we don't want to consider within our model but that could affect our results (e.g., operators, days, machines, ovens, etc.).

An application example for blocking in Table 28.3 is that "day" could have been blocked using the *ABC* interaction column. The trial numbers 1, 4, 6, and 7 could then be exercised in random sequence the first day, while the other four trials could be exercised in random sequence on the second day. If the block on "day" was shown to be significant, then the conclusion would be that something changed from day 1 to day 2; however, the specific cause of the difference may not be understood to the experimenter from a basic data analysis. More importantly, this confounding would not affect decisions made about the other factors of interest.

High-factor interaction contrast columns can be used for the assignment of blocks when there are only two-level blocks to consider, as noted earlier. However, care must be exercised when there are more than two levels in a block. Consider that four ovens were to be used in an experiment. Undesirable confounding can result if two high-factor interaction contrast columns are arbitrarily chosen to describe the trials that will use each of the ovens (i.e., $-- =$ oven 1, $-+ =$ oven 2, $+- =$ oven 3, and $++ =$ oven 4). Commercially available computer statistical packages often offer various blocking alternatives.

29.8   CURVATURE CHECK

In a two-level experiment design, linearity is assumed between the factor-level extremes. When factors are from a continuous scale (i.e., a quantitative factor) [e.g., factor *A* is an adjustment value that can take on any value from 1 to 10, as opposed to discrete levels (i.e., a qualitative factor) such as supplier 1 versus supplier 2], a curvature check can be made to evaluate the validity of this assumption by adding center points to the design matrix. To illustrate this procedure, the average of the four response trials for a 2^2 full factorial (i.e., $--$, $+-$, $-+$, and $++$) can be compared to the average of the trials that were taken separately at the average of levels of each of the factor extremes. The difference between these two numbers can then be compared to see if there is a significant difference in their magnitudes (i.e., curvature exists). In lieu of a manual approach when making this test, some computer programs can perform a statistical check for curvature. The examples discussed in this chapter do not have trials set up to make a curvature check; however, there is more discussion on this topic when response surface methodology is discussed.

29.9   S⁴ ASSESSMENT

Many "what ifs" can often be made about experimental designs proposed by "others." A good way to overcome challenges is to bring potential challenging parties and/or organization into a brainstorming session when planning DOEs. One of the main benefits of a DOE is that the selection of factors and levels of factors is ideal for a brainstorming session. Better designs typically result from this activity. In addition, there will be more buy-in to the basic strategy and results when they become available.

When planning a DOE, write down the options. For example, consider whether suppliers should be considered a controlled or noise factor within the design (see Chapter 32). Also, consider the cost of doing nothing; a DOE may not be the right thing to do.

When planning the execution of a DOE, where experimental trials are expensive, it might be advantageous to begin with trials that are the least expensive and evaluate the trial results as they occur. These findings might give direction to a solution before all trials are completed.

29.10 EXERCISES

1. The position of the leads on an electronic component is important to get a satisfactory solder mount of the component to an electronic printed circuit board. There is concern that with manufacturing an electronic tester of the component function is bending the component leads. To monitor physical changes from tester handling, the leads from a sample of components are noted before and after the tester.

   (a) Create a plan for implementing a DOE that assesses what should be done differently to reduce the amount of bending on each component. Consider the selection of measurement response, selection of factors, and results validation.

   (b) Create a plan that could be used in the future for a similar machine setup.

2. A machine measures the peel-back force necessary to remove the packaging for electrical components. The tester records an output force that changes as the packaging is separated. The process was found to be incapable of consistently meeting specification limits. The average peel back force needed to be reduced.

   (a) Create a DOE plan to determine what should be done to improve the capability of the process.

   (b) Create a plan that the company could use in the future to set up similar equipment to avoid this type of problem.

3. Half of the trials for an experiment need to be conducted on Monday, while the remaining need to be conducted on Tuesday. Describe what should be done to avoid potential changes from Monday to Tuesday affecting conclusions about the other factors.

4. Describe how the techniques within this chapter are useful and can be applied to S^4 projects.

30

DESIGN AND ANALYSIS OF 2^k DOEs

This chapter describes design alternatives and analysis techniques for conducting a DOE. A method is described where tables in the Appendix are used to easily create test trials. These test trials would be similar to those created by many statistical software packages (Appendix C exemplifies the equality of a test design from Table M to that of a statistical software package).

The advantage of explaining the creation of test cases using these tables is that the practitioner gains quick understanding of the concept of design resolution. With a good understanding of this concept the practitioner can create better experiment designs.

30.1 TWO-LEVEL DOE DESIGN ALTERNATIVES

It was previously illustrated how a saturated fractional factorial experiment design could be created from a full factorial design. However there are other two-level fractional factorial design alternatives between full and saturated fractional factorial designs, which can give differing "resolutions" to the experiment design. If this described procedure were used to create these test matrices the question of concern is how to make the matches of the factors to the interaction columns such that there is minimal confounding (e.g., of main effects and two-factor interactions).

Tables M1 to M5 manage this issue by making the column selections for the practitioner, while Tables N1 to N3 show the confounding with two-factor interaction. Another alternative to the manual creation of a test design using these tables is to create the design using a statistical software package. However, as described earlier, quick knowledge is gained by the novice to DOE techniques if these tables are used initially during their introduction to the techniques.

Table 30.1 (and Table M1) indicates test possibilities for 4, 8, 16, 32, and 64 two-level factor designs with resolution V+, V, IV, and III. To illustrate the use of this table, consider the eight-trial test alternatives that are shown. If an experiment has three two-level factors and is conducted in eight trials, all combinations are executed; hence, it is a full factorial. This test alternative is shown in the table as 3 (number of factors) at the intersection of the V+ column (full factorial) and the row designation 8 (number of trials).

Consider now an experiment where there are seven factors in eight trials. From Table 30.1 it is noted to be a resolution III design, which by definition describes designs that have the confounding of two-factor interactions and main effects. As noted earlier, there is confounding of the main effects of this design and the interaction effects, for example, the significance of a contrast could technically be caused by a main effect such as D or its aliased interaction AB (or other aliased interactions). In a resolution III (i.e., screening design), the experimenter normally initially assumes that the D level is significant and then confirms/rejects this theory via a confirmation experiment. This table shows that designs with five, six, or seven factors in eight trials produce a resolution III design.

It is also noted from Table 30.1 that a resolution IV design is possible where four two-level factors can be assessed in eight trials such that there is no confounding of the main effects and two-factor interaction effects, however, two-factor interaction effects are confounded with each other. This table also shows resolution V experiment alternatives where there is no confound-

TABLE 30.1 Number of Two-Level Factor Considerations Possible for Various Full and Fractional Factorial Design Alternatives in Table M

Number of Trials	Experiment Resolution			
	V+	V	IV	III
4	2			3
8	3		4	5–7
16	4	5	6–8	9–15
32	5	6	7–16	17–31
64	6	7–8	9–32	33–63

where resolution is defined as

V+: Full two-level factorial.
  V: All main effects and two-factor interactions are unconfounded with either main effects or two-factor interactions.
 IV: All main effects are unconfounded by two-factor interactions. Two-factor interactions are confounded with each other.
III: Main effects confounded with two-factor interactions.

ing of the main effects and two-factor interaction effects, plus the two-factor interaction effects are not confounded with each other (e.g., five factors in 16 trials).

The next section of this chapter will show how the experiment trials noted in Table 30.1 can be obtained from Table M.

30.2   DESIGNING A TWO-LEVEL FRACTIONAL EXPERIMENT USING TABLES M AND N

This section will describe the methodology used to create two-level full and fractional factorial design alternatives from the easy-to-use format of Tables M1 to M5 of this text. The confounding structure of these designs are shown in Tables N1 to N3. These designs may look different from the two-level design matrices suggested by other texts; however, they are very similar (if not exactly the same) to other two-level design matrices. Diamond (1989) describes the creation of these matrices from the Hadamard matrix. I have taken the 4, 8,16, 32, and 64 designs from this work and put the designs into the tabular format shown in Tables M1 to M5.

In Tables M1 to M5 the rows of the matrix define the trial configurations; hence, if 16 rows are defined, there will be 16 trials. The columns are used to define the two-level states of the factors for each trial, where the level designations are + or −. A step-by-step description of how to create an experiment design using these tables is summarized in Table M1.

After the number of factors. resolution, and number of trials are chosen, a design can then be determined from the tables where columns are chosen from left to right using those identified by an asterisk (*) and the numbers sequentially in the header, until the number of columns equals the number of factors in the experiment. The contrast column numbers are then assigned sequential alphabetic characters from left to right. These numbers from the original matrix are noted and cross-referenced to Tables N1 to N3, if information is desired about two-factor interactions and two-factor interaction confounding.

30.3   DETERMINING SIGNIFICANT EFFECTS AND PROBABILITY PLOTTING PROCEDURE

Analysis of variance techniques have traditionally been used to determine the significant effects in a factorial experiment. The t-test for assessing significance gives the same results as analysis of variance techniques but can be more appealing because the significance assessment is made against the magnitude of the effect, which has more physical meaning than a mcan square value, as would be done within an analysis of variance.

DOE techniques are often conducted with a small number of trials to save time and resources. Experimental trials are often not replicated, which leads to no knowledge about pure experimental error. When this occurs, other analysis methods are needed. One approach is to use nonsignificant interaction terms (or nonsignificant main effect terms) as an estimate error for these significance test. A methodology is then needed to identify these terms that can be combined to estimate experimental error.

This methodology is an alternative to a formal significance test where for this technique a probability plot of the contrast column effects is created. For the two-level factorial designs included in this text, a contrast column effect, Δ, can be determined from the relationship

$$\Delta = \left(\sum_{i=1}^{n_{\text{high}}} \frac{x_{\text{high } i}}{n_{\text{high}}} \right) - \left(\sum_{i=1}^{n_{\text{low}}} \frac{x_{\text{low } i}}{n_{\text{low}}} \right)$$

where $x_{\text{high}i}$ and $x_{\text{low}i}$ are the response values of each of the i responses from the total of n_{high} and n_{low} trials [for high $(+)$ and low $(-)$ factor-level conditions, respectively]. A plot of the absolute values of the contrast column effects is an alternative plotting approach (i.e., a half-normal probability plot).

An effect (i.e., main effect or interaction effect) is said to be "significant" if its magnitude is large relative to the other contrast column effects that can be determined from an experiment design. When the plot position of an effect is beyond the bounds of a "straight line" through the "nonsignificant" contrast column effects, this effect is thought to be "significant." Because this is not a rigorous approach, obviously there can be differences of opinions as to whether some effects are really significant.

Computer programs are available to create this probability plot of effects; however, the task can be executed manually by using the percentage plot positions from Table P and normal probability paper (Table Q1). The contrast columns that are not found to be significant can then be combined to give an estimate of experimental error for a significance test of the other factors.

30.4 MODELING EQUATION FORMAT FOR A TWO-LEVEL DOE

If an experimenter has a situation where "lower is always better" or "higher is always better," the choice of the significant factor levels to use either in a conformation or follow-up experiment may be obvious by some simple data analysis. However. in some situations a mathematical model is needed for the purpose of estimating the response as a function of the factor-level considerations.

For a seven-factor two-level model the modeling equation (without interaction terms) would initially take the form

$$y = b_0 + b_1 x_1 + b_2 x_2 + b_3 x_3 + b_4 x_4 + b_5 x_5 + b_6 x_6 + b_7 x_7$$

where y is the response and b_0 would be the average of all the trials. In this equation b_1 to b_7 are half of the calculated effects of the factors x_1 (factor A) to x_7 (factor G) noting that x_1 to x_7 would take on values of -1 or $+1$.

The reader should not confuse the x_1 to x_7 nomenclature used in the previous equation with the output response nomenclature shown previously (e.g., in Table 28.1).

The model resulting from the experimental responses shown in Table 28.4 would be

$$y = 250 + 0(x_1) + 0(x_2) + 0(x_3) + 0(x_4) + 250(x_5) + 0(x_6) + 0(x_7)$$

Because b_5 is the E factor (i.e., x_5 factor consideration) coefficient, it would have a value of 250. This equation would reduce to $y = 250 + 250(x_5)$. We then note that whenever factor E is high (i.e., $x_5 = 1$), the response y would be equal to 500 and when E is low (i.e., $x_5 = -1$) the response y is equal to zero.

This equation form considers that the factor levels have a linear relationship with the response. Center points may have been included in the basic experiment design to check this assumption. The results from one or more two-level fractional factorial experiments might lead a practitioner from having many factor considerations initially to a few factors that may need to be analyzed further using response surface techniques.

Interaction terms within a model are added as the product of the factors, as illustrated in the equation

$$y = b_0 + b_1 x_1 + b_2 x_2 + b_{12} x_1 x_2$$

If an interaction term is found significant from an analysis, the hierarchial rule states all main factors and lower interaction terms that are a part of the significant interaction should be included within the model.

30.5 EXAMPLE 30.1: A RESOLUTION V DOE

The settle-out time of a stepper motor was a critical item within the design of a document printer. The product development organization proposed a change to the stepping sequence algorithm that they believed would improve the settle-out characteristics of the motor. Note that the wording of this problem is very typical within industry. Both specification vagueness and engineering change evaluation exist. (*Note*: Appendix C describes an alternate analysis approach for the DOE experiment data that are later presented.)

One approach to this problem would be to manufacture several motors and monitor their settle-out time. If we assume that these motors are a random sample, a confidence interval on the average settle-out characteristics of the motor could then be determined. Another approach could also be to determine the percentage of population characters by using probability plotting techniques. However within the original problem description there was no mention of any specification. Also one could challenge that the sample would not necessarily be representative of future product builds.

What the development organization really was proposing was an improved design. This problem redirection could lead one to perform a comparison test between the old design and new design which might be conducted as a paired comparison test. Because there are several adjustments and environmental conditions that could effect this comparison, the next question is to determine test conditions for making this comparison. To address this question and perhaps get more information than just "between algorithm effects," a fractional factorial experiment design is useful.

Consider that a team brainstorming technique was conducted to determine what would be considered in the experiment when one evaluates the response (i.e., motor settle-out time). The resulting factor assignments and associated levels were as follows:

		Levels	
Factors and Their Designations		(−)	(+)
A: Motor temperature	(mot_temp)	Cold	Hot
B: Algorithm	(algor)	Current design	Proposed redesign
C: Motor adjustment	(mot_adj)	Low tolerance	High tolerance
D: External adjustment	(ext_adj)	Low tolerance	High tolerance
E: Supply voltage	(sup_volt)	Low tolerance	High tolerance

The development and test group team agreed to evaluate the five two-level factors in a resolution V design. Table 30.1 (or instructions on Table M1) shows that 16 test trials are needed to get this resolution with the 5 two-level factors. Table 30.2 illustrates the procedure to extract the design matrix trials from Table M3. Table 30.3 shows the resulting resolution V design matrix (with trial response outputs). From Table N1 it is noted for this design (and shown below) that all the contrast columns contain either a main or two-factor interaction effect; hence, there are no contrast columns that contain only three-factor and higher interactions which could have been used to estimate experimental error.

From this experimental design it is noted that trial 5, for example, would be exercised with

TABLE 30.2 Fractional Factorial Experiment Design Creation

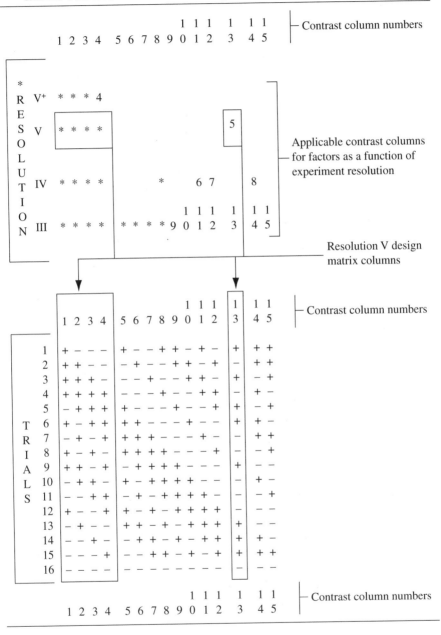

TABLE 30.3 Test Design with Trial Responses

	A	*B*	*C*	*D*	*E*	
	Number of Trail Input Factors					
	mot_temp	algor	mot_	ext_adj	sup_volt	Output timing (msec)
1	+	−	−	−	+	5.6
2	+	+	−	−	−	2.1
3	+	+	+	−	+	4.9
4	+	+	+	+	−	4.9
5	−	+	+	+	+	4.1
6	+	−	+	+	+	5.6
7	−	+	−	+	−	1.9
8	+	−	+	−	−	7.2
9	+	+	−	+	+	2.4
10	−	+	+	−	−	5.1
11	−	−	+	+	−	7.9
12	+	−	−	+	−	5.3
13	−	+	−	−	+	2.1
14	−	−	+	−	+	7.6
15	−	−	−	+	+	5.5
16	−	−	−	−	−	5.3
	1	2	3	4	13	Table M3 contrast column numbers

Mot_temp (−) = cold temperature

algor (+) = proposed redesign

mot_adj (+) = high tolerance

ext_adj (+) = high tolerance

sup_volt (+) = high tolerance

The interaction assignment that is associated with each contrast column number noted from Table N1 is

1	2	3	4	5	6	7	8	9	10	11	12	13	14	15
**A*	**B*	**C*	**D*	*AB*	*BC*	*CD*	*ABD* *CE*	*AC*	*BD*	*ABC* *DE*	*BCD* *AE*	*ABCD* **E*	*ACD* *BE*	*AD*

We note that all the contrast columns either have a two-factor interaction or main-effect consideration. It should also be noted that the factors are highlighted with an asterisk (*) and that the higher-order terms which were used to generate the design are also shown.

A probability plot of the effects from the contrast columns is shown in Figure 30.1. The normal score for each data point is shown in this plot, which can be related to percentage values through the Z Table (i.e., Table A). A Pareto chart of these contrast column effects (created from a computer program) is also shown in Figure 30.2, with an $\alpha = 0.05$ decision line. When the magnitude of an effect is beyond this line, then factor is thought to be significant. From these plots it is quite apparent that factors B and C are significant.

From this plot there is reason to now build a model using only factors B and C with no two-factor interaction terms. However, for this type of situation I prefer to first examine a model with all the main effects. The results of this analysis are as follows:

Fractional Factorial Fit

Estimated Effects and Coefficients for resp (coded units)

Term	Effect	Coef	StDev Coef	T	P
Constant		4.844	0.1618	29.95	0.000
mot_temp	−0.187	−0.094	0.1618	−0.58	0.575
algor	−2.812	−1.406	0.1618	−8.69	0.000
mot_adj	2.138	1.069	0.1618	6.61	0.000
ext_adj	−0.288	−0.144	0.1618	−0.89	0.395

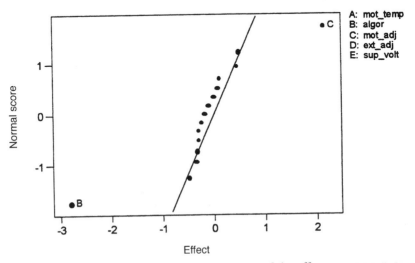

FIGURE 30.1 Normal score plot of the effects.

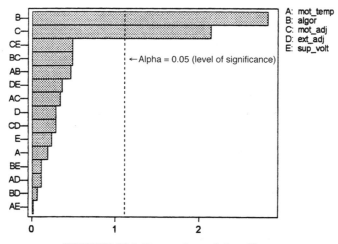

FIGURE 30.2 Pareto chart of the effects.

```
sup_volt    −0.238     −0.119        −0.1618    −0.73     0.480
```

Analysis of Variance for resp (coded units)

```
Source           DF  Seq SS  Adj SS   Adj MS      F       P
Main Effects      5  50.613  50.613  10.1226   24.18   0.000
Residual Error   10   4.186   4.186   0.4186
Total            15  54.799
```

Unusual Observations for resp

```
Obs      resp       Fit   StDev Fit   Residual   St Resid
  6   5.60000   6.96250     0.39621   −1.36250     −2.66R
```

R denotes an observation with a large standardized residual

The *P* value from this analysis again indicates how factors *B* and *C* are very significant (i.e., algor and mot_adj), and the other factors are not significant (because their *P* values are not equal to or less than 0.05). Let's now examine an analysis of the model where only the two significant terms are evaluated.

Fractional Factorial Fit

Estimated Effects and Coefficients for resp (coded units)

Term	Effect	Coef	StDev Coef	T	P
Constant		4.844	0.1532	31.61	0.000
algor	−2.812	−1.406	0.1532	−9.18	0.000
mot_adj	2.137	1.069	0.1532	6.98	0.000

Analysis of Variance for resp (coded units)

Source	DF	Seq SS	Adj SS	Adj MS	F	P
Main Effects	2	49.9163	49.9163	24.9581	66.44	0.000
Residual Error	13	4.8831	4.8831	0.3756		
Lack of Fit	1	0.9506	0.9506	0.9506	2.90	0.114
Pure Error	12	3.9325	3.9325	0.3277		
Total	15	54.7994				

Unusual Observations for resp

Obs	resp	Fit	StDev Fit	Residual	St Resid
6	5.60000	7.31875	0.26539	−1.71875	−−3.11R

R denotes an observation with a large standardized residual

The effect from this output describes the difference from going to two
levels of a factor. The sign indicates direction. For example, the effect −2.812
is an estimate that the proposed algorithm reduces the settle-out time of the
selection motor by 2.812 msec (on the average). Figure 30.3 graphically
shows these factor effects. If we accept this model and data, we could create
from the coefficients the estimated mean response model of

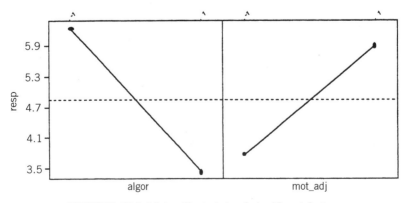

FIGURE 30.3 Main effect plots of significant factors.

$$\text{Motor settle-out time} = 4.844 - 1.406(\text{algorithm})$$
$$+ 1.069(\text{motor adjustment})$$

where the coded values used within the equation are algorithm = −1 (current design), algorithm = + (1 proposed redesign), motor adjustment = −1 (low tolerance), and motor adjustment = +1 (high tolerance).

The accuracy of these significance tests and best estimate assessments are dependent on the accuracy of the assumption that the errors are normal and independently distributed with mean zero and a constant but unknown variance. In reality, these assumptions are not generally exact; however, it is wise to ensure that there are not any large deviations from these assumptions. Violations of some basic assumptions can be investigated by examining the residuals of the model. The residual for each trial is the difference between the trial output and the model prediction value. If these assumptions are valid, the data have balanced scatter and no patterns. If there is much deviation from these assumptions, a data transformation may be necessary to get a more accurate significance test.

The statistical software package output of the data indicates that there is an unusual observation. Table 30.4 shows the residuals and predicted values for each trial. The residual plots of these data in Figure 30.4 and Figure 30.5 are consistent with this computer software package analysis in showing that observation 6 does not fit the model well. Consider now that we examined our data and concluded that there was something wrong with observation 6. Computer analysis of the data without this data point yields

TABLE 30.4 Experimental Data with Model Predictions and Residuals

Trial No.	mot_temp	algor	mot_adj	ext_adj	sup_volt	resp	Fits	Residuals
1	1	−1	−1	−1	1	5.6	5.18125	0.41875
2	1	1	−1	−1	−1	2.1	2.36875	−0.26875
3	1	1	1	−1	1	4.9	4.50625	0.39375
4	1	1	1	1	−1	4.9	4.50625	0.39375
5	−1	1	1	1	1	4.1	4.50625	−0.40625
6	1	−1	1	1	1	5.6	7.31875	−1.71875
7	−1	1	−1	1	−1	1.9	2.36875	−0.46875
8	1	−1	1	−1	−1	7.2	7.31875	−0.11875
9	1	1	−1	1	1	2.4	2.36875	0.03125
10	−1	1	1	−1	−1	5.1	4.50625	0.59375
11	−1	−1	1	1	−1	7.9	7.31875	0.58125
12	1	−1	−1	1	−1	5.3	5.18125	0.11875
13	−1	1	−1	−1	1	2.1	2.36875	−0.26875
14	−1	−1	1	−1	1	7.6	7.31875	0.28125
15	−1	−1	−1	1	1	5.5	5.18125	0.31875
16	−1	−1	−1	−1	−1	5.3	5.18125	0.11875

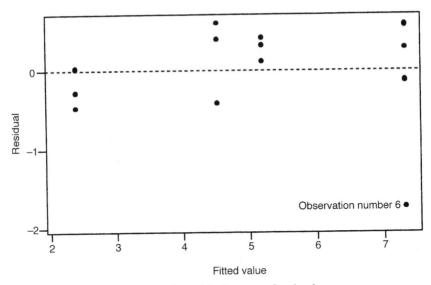

FIGURE 30.4 Residuals versus fitted values.

Fractional Factorial Fit

Estimated Effects and Coefficients for resp (coded units)

Term	Effect	Coef	StDev Coef	T	P
Constant		4.976	0.08364	59.49	0.000
algor	−3.077	−1.538	0.08364	−18.39	0.000

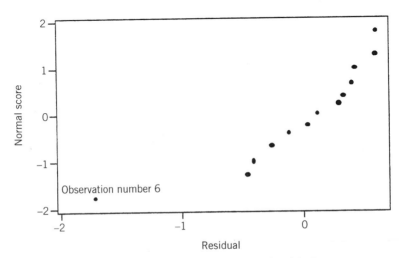

FIGURE 30.5 Normal score plot of residuals.

```
mot_adj     2.402    1.201       0.08364    14.36  0.000
```

Analysis of Variance for resp (coded units)

```
Source            DF  Seq SS  Adj SS  Adj MS       F       P
Main Effects       2 52.9420 52.9420 26.4710 254.67 0.000
Residual Error    12  1.2473  1.2473  0.1039
  Lack of Fit      1  0.2156  0.2156  0.2156    2.30 0.158
  Pure Error      11  1.0317  1.0317  0.0938
Total             14 54.1893
```

This model does not indicate any unusual observations, which is consistent with the residual plots shown in Figures 30.6 and 30.7. For this model and data we could create from the coefficients the estimated mean response model of

$$\text{Motor settle-out time} = 4.976 - 1.538(\text{algorithm})$$
$$+ 1.201(\text{motor adjustment})$$

which has coefficients that are slightly different from those of the previous model.

The initial purpose of the experiment was to determine whether a new algorithm should be used to move a stepper motor. The answer to this question is yes; the new algorithm can be expected to improve the motor settle-out time by approximately 2.81 msec. However, we have also learned that the motor adjustment can also affect settle-out time.

A couple of additional steps can be useful to address questions beyond the initial problem definition and put the data in better presentation form. Dissecting and presenting the data in a clear form can have hidden benefits. These

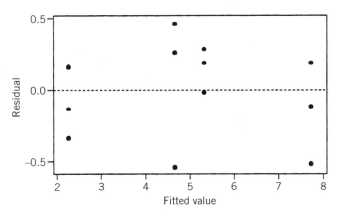

FIGURE 30.6 Residuals versus fitted values (second analysis).

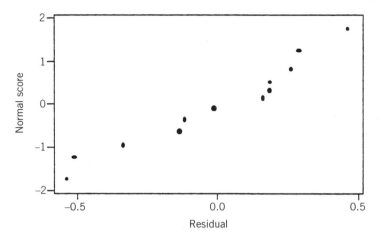

FIGURE 30.7 Normal score plot of the residuals (second analysis).

additional considerations can be useful in reducing overall product costs. With these additional considerations, perhaps a tolerance is discovered that should be tightened to reduce overall manufacturing variability, resulting in fewer customer failures and/or complaints. Another possibility is that a noncritical tolerance may be increased, causing another form of cost reduction.

Within this experiment the settle-out time was shown to be affected by motor adjustment (in addition to algorithm level); a +1 level of motor adjustment on the average increases the settle-out time by 2.1 msec. To better understand this physical effect determine from the raw data (all data 16 data points were considered) the mean values for the four combinations of algorithm (algor) and motor adjustment (mot_adj):

New algorithm	Motor adjustment low tolerance	2.125
New algorithm	Motor adjustment high tolerance	4.75
Old algorithm	Motor adjustment low tolerance	5.425
Old algorithm	Motor adjustment high tolerance	7.075

Assuming that the decision is made to convert to the new algorithm, a settle-out time of about 4.75 msec with the +1 level of the motor adjustment is expected, while this time should be about 2.125 msec with the −1 level of the factor (a settle-out time difference of 2.625 msec).

Obviously, it is expected that it would be better if the motor adjustment factor could always be adjusted near the low tolerance. However the cost to achieve this could be large. The probability plot shown in Figure 30.8 gives a picture of the four scenario possibilities that can give a better understanding of alternatives. This plot clearly indicates that combination 4 is superior. The outlier data point from the previous analysis (lowest value for

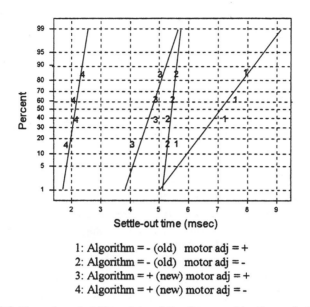

1: Algorithm = - (old) motor adj = +
2: Algorithm = - (old) motor adj = -
3: Algorithm = + (new) motor adj = +
4: Algorithm = + (new) motor adj = -

FIGURE 30.8 Normal probability plots of the four combinations of algorithm and motor adjustment.

situation 1) again does not appear to fit the model as well as the other data points.

Similarly, using the means and standard deviation values from each of the four combinations, the probability density function shown in Figure 30.9

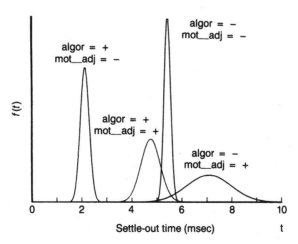

FIGURE 30.9 PDF "sizing" of the four combinations of algorithm and motor adjustment.

gives a graphical sizing that illustrates the potential effects in another format. Care needs to be exercised when drawing specific conclusions from these graphs because the graphs only indicate trends from the calculated estimates and do not represent a random sample of a population with such characteristics.

The next action step of the experimenter depends on the settle-out time requirements for the product design. If a settle-out time less than 15 msec, for example, presents no chance of causing a machine failure, the best decision may be to simply accept the new algorithm with no special considerations about the motor adjustment. However, to obtain additional safety factors for unknown variabilities (e.g., motor-to-motor differences) a tightening of the motor adjustment tolerance toward the low tolerance perhaps should be considered. If, however the settle-out time requirement were less than 6 msec, for example, then another experiment seems appropriate to further assess other factors along with the other significant factor, motor adjustment, to reduce this variability. Perhaps a further extremity below the current low tolerance level could be considered.

A confirmation experiment should be considered before using fractional factorial information in the manufacturing process. For the previous example a comparison experiment might be appropriate using several motors (e.g., 10) where the settle-out time characteristics of old algorithm/motor adj = +1 is compared to new algorithm/motor adj = −1. In addition to statistically comparing mean and variance of the two situations, probability plots of the timings for the 10 "new" and "old" motors could be very enlightening.

Example 35.2 continues the discussion on what could be done in the manufacturing environment to track the settle-out time of motors that are being built. In this example a CUSUM control chart is used to monitor for degradation of the motor's performance.

30.6 DOE ALTERNATIVES

The purpose of this section is to exemplify DOE experiment alternatives that are available in 16 trials. Three examples will be illustrated that have differing resolutions for 16 trials. The confounding of main effects and interactions will be discussed. Situation X will be a five-factor 16-trial experiment, situation Y will be an eight-factor 16-trial experiment and situation Z will be a 15-factor 16-trial experiment. Table 30.5 shows how these designs can be determined from Table M3.

Situation X, which has five factors in 16 trials, is a resolution V design. From Table 30.5 we note that the design uses contrast columns 1, 2, 3, 4 and 13. From Table N1 we can determine the aliasing structure of the 15 contrast columns for this design to be

TABLE 30.5 DOE Matrix Alternatives

		1	2	3	4	5	6	7	8	9	10	11	12	13	14	15	
V+		*	*	*	4												X
V		*	*	*	*										5		Y
IV		*	*	*	*				*			6	7		8		Z
III		*	*	*	*	*	*	*	*	9	10	11	12	13	14	15	

		1	2	3	4	5	6	7	8	9	10	11	12	13	14	15
T R I A L S	1	+	–	–	–	+	–	–	+	+	–	+	–	+	+	+
	2	+	+	–	–	–	+	–	–	+	+	–	+	–	+	+
	15	–	–	–	+	–	–	+	+	–	+	–	+	+	+	+
	16	–	–	–	–	–	–	–	–	–	–	–	–	–	–	–

1	2	3	4	5	6	7	8
A	B	C	D	AB	BC	CD	ABD CE

9	10	11	12	13	14	15
AC	BD	ABC DE	BCD AE	ABCD E	ACD BE	AD

We note from this summary that all contrast columns either have no more than one main effect or one two-factor interaction. This is a characteristic of a resolution V design. The first row of the contrast column describes how it was created. Because this is a 16-trial design, four columns are needed to create the 15 contrast columns (i.e., the first columns A, B, C and D). Each of the remaining contrast columns is a multiple of these first four contrast columns (may include a minus one multiple). For example, contrast column 13 is the multiple of $A \times B \times C \times D$. For this design the fifth factor E was placed in the 13 contrast column. The result of this is the other two-factor interaction combinations that contain E (e.g., contrast column 12 has a pattern which is the multiple of A times E).

When conducting an analysis (probability plot or t-test) we are assessing the magnitude of each contrast column relative to error. If a two-factor interaction contrast column is large relative to error, our conclusion is that an interaction exists. We would then create a two-factor interaction plot to determine which set of conditions is most advantageous for our particular situation. In the model equation for a balanced design, one-half of the effect would be the coefficient of the multiple of the two factor levels.

Situation *Y*, which has eight factors in 16 trials, is a resolution IV design. From Table 30.5 we note that the design uses contrast columns 1, 2, 3, 4, 8, 11, 12, and 14. From Table N2 we can determine the aliasing structure of the 15 contrast columns for this design to be

1	2	3	4	5	6	7	8
*A	*B	*C	*D	AB	BC	CD	ABD
				DE	AF	EF	*E
				CF	DG	BG	
				GH	EH	AH	

9	10	11	12	13	14	15
AC	BD	ABC	BCD	ABCD	ACD	AD
BF	AE	*F	*G	CE	*H	BE
EG	CG			DF		FG
DH	FH			AG		CH
				BH		

We note from this summary that all contrast columns either have one main effect or two-factor interactions. This is a characteristic of a resolution IV design. If the design has less than eight factors, the inappropriate two-factor interactions are not considered part of the aliasing structure. If, for example, there were only seven factors (i.e., *A, B, C, D, E, F,* and *G*). two-factor interactions with *H* would make no sense (e.g., *CH* in contrast column 15).

Situation *Z*, which has five factors in 16 trials is a resolution V design. From Table 30.5 we note that the design uses all the contrast columns. From Table N3 we can determine the aliasing structure of the 15 contrast columns for this design to be

1	2	3	4	5	6	7	8
*A	*B	*C	*D	AB	BC	CD	ABD
BE	AE	BF	CG	*E	*F	*G	DE
CI	CF	DG	EH	DH	EI	FJ	*H
HJ	DJ	AI	BJ	FI	GJ	HK	AJ
FK	IK	EK	FL	CK	AK	BL	GK
LM	GL	JL	KM	GM	DL	EM	IL
GN	MN	HM	IN	LN	HN	AN	CM
DO	HO	NO	AO	JO	MO	IO	FN
							BO

9	10	11	12	13	14	15
AC	BD	ABC	BCD	ABCD	ACD	AD
EF	FG	CE	DF	EG	AG	BH
*I	AH	AF	BG	CH	FH	GI
BK	*J	GH	HI	IJ	DI	EJ
HL	CL	BI	CJ	DK	JK	KL
JM	IM	*K	*L	AL	EL	FM
DN	KN	DM	AM	*M	BM	CN
GO	EO	JN	EN	BN	*N	*O
BO			LO	KO	FO	CO

We note from this summary that these contrast columns have main effects confounded with two-factor interactions. This is a characteristic of a resolution III design. This particular design is a saturated design because it has 15 factors in 16 trials.

An experiment with enough trials to address all interaction concerns is desirable; however, the economics to perform such a test may be prohibitive. Instead, experimenters may consider fewer factors. This would lead to less confounding of interactions. but yields no information about the factors not considered within the experiment.

The concerns and issues of missing significant factors during an initial experiment of reasonable size are addressed when using a basic multiexperiment test strategy. A screening experiment (perhaps 25% of the resource allotment for the total experimental effort) should "weed out" small effects so that more detailed information can be obtained about the large effects and their interactions via a higher-resolution experiment. A resolution III or IV design can be used for a screening experiment.

There are situations where an experimenter would like a resolution III or IV design but yet manage a "few" two-factor interactions. This is achievable by using Tables M1 to M5 and N1 to N3 collectively when designing an experiment. When using Tables M1 to M5, if there are columns remaining above the number of main effect assignments, these columns can be used for interaction assignments. This is done by using Tables N1 to N3 to assign the factor designations such that these interactions appear within these columns. It should be noted that in Tables N1 to N3 the lower tabular interaction considerations are dropped if they are not possible in the experiment (e.g., an AO interaction should be dropped from the list of confounded items if there is no "O" main effect in the design).

Much care needs to be exercised when using this pretest interaction assignment approach because erroneous conclusions can result if there was, in fact, a significant interaction that was overlooked when setting up the experiment (especially with resolution III experiment designs). When interaction information is needed, it is best to increase the number of trials to capture this information. The descriptive insert to Table M1 is useful, for example to determine the resolution that is obtainable for six two-level factors when the test size is increased to 32 or 64 trials.

Even though there is much confounding in a resolution III design, interaction information can sometimes be assessed when technical information is blended with experimental results. For example, if factors *A, B,* and *E* are significant, one might suspect that there is a two-factor interaction prevalent. It is possible that a two-factor interaction does not contain main effects that are significant (an "X" pattern on a two-factor interaction plot); however, this does not often occur. From the above aliasing pattern we note that factor *E* is confounded with the *AB* interaction, factor *A* is confounded with *BE* and factor *B* is confounded with *AE*. For this situation we might plot all three interactions during the analysis to see if any of the three make any technical sense. This could give us additional insight during a follow-up experiment.

30.7   EXAMPLE 30.2: A DOE DEVELOPMENT TEST

Often the techniques of DOE are related to what can be done to improve a process. Described within this example is a methodology that can be used within the development process to assess how well a design performs.

Consider that a computer manufacturer determines that "no trouble found (NTF)" is the largest category of returns that they get from their customers. For this category of problem a customer had a problem and returned the system; however, the manufacturer could not duplicate the problem (hence the category description NTF). This manufacturer did some further investigation to determine that there was a heat problem within the system. Whenever a system would heat up, circuit timing would start to change and eventually cause a failure. When the system cooled down, the failure mode disappeared.

A fix for the problem in manufacturing would be very difficult because the problem was design-related. Because of this it was thought that emphasis should be given to this potential problem within the design process so new products do not exhibit similar problems. A test was desired that could check the current design before first customer shipment.

As a result, the problem description is a new computer design that can fail whenever a module temperature exceeds a value that frequently occurs in a customer environment with certain hardware configurations and software applications. The objective is to develop a strategy that identifies both the problem and risk of failure early in the product development cycle.

Computers can have different configurations depending upon customer preferences. Some configurations are probably more likely to cause failure than other configurations. Our direction will be to first identify the worst-case configuration using DOE techniques and then stress a sample of these configured machines to failure to determine the temperature guardband.

From a brainstorming session the following factors and levels were chosen:

	Level	
Factor	−1	1
System type	New	Old
Processor speed	Fast	Slow
Hard-drive size	Large	Small
Card	No card	1 card
Memory module	2 extra	0 extra
Test case	Test case 1	Test case 2
Battery state	Full charge	Charging

Table 30.6 shows the selected design. Temperature was measured at three different positions within the product. An analysis of the data for processor temperature yielded the following mean temperature model:

$$\text{Processor temp. (est.)} = 73.9 + 3.3(\text{system type}) - 3.5(\text{processor speed})$$
$$- 0.9(\text{memory module}) - 0.8(\text{test case})$$

Consider that we want to determine the configuration that causes the highest temperature and estimate the mean component temperature at this configuration. From the modeling equation for the processor the mean overall temperature is 73.9 °F. Temperature is higher for some configurations. For example the processor module temperature would increase 3.3° if system type were at the +1 level (i.e., old system type). The worst-case levels and temperatures are

Average	73.9
System type = 1 (old)	3.3
Processor speed = −1 (fast)	3.5
Memory module = −1(2 extra)	0.9
Test_case = −1 (test case 1)	0.8
Total	82.4

In this model we need to note that mean temperature is modeled as a function of various configurations. Product-to-product variability has a distribution around an overall mean. If the mean temperature of a configuration is close to an expected failure temperature, additional product-to-product evaluation is needed.

We now have to select a worst-case configuration to evaluate further. In this model we note that the new system type has a lower temperature than the old system type. Because we are most interested in new products, we would probably limit additional evaluations to this area. We need to also

TABLE 30.6 Design of Experiment Results

Trial	System Type	Processor Speed	Hard-Drive Size	Card	Memory Module	Test Case	Battery State	Temperature Processor	Temperature Hard-Drive Case	Temp. Video Chip
1	-1	-1	-1	-1	-1	-1	-1	76	58.5	72.8
2	1	1	-1	-1	-1	1	-1	73.7	63.3	71.3
3	-1	-1	1	-1	-1	1	1	73.8	67.2	75.2
4	1	1	1	-1	-1	-1	1	74.8	58.3	73.2
5	1	-1	-1	1	-1	-1	1	81.3	66.2	70.9
6	-1	1	-1	1	-1	1	1	67	56.1	69.1
7	1	-1	1	1	-1	1	-1	84.1	61.1	69.7
8	-1	1	1	1	-1	-1	-1	67.5	63.6	71.7
9	1	-1	-1	-1	1	1	1	79.4	58.2	65.5
10	-1	1	-1	-1	1	-1	1	65.6	62.3	69.6
11	1	-1	1	-1	1	-1	-1	78.7	59.2	68.1
12	-1	1	1	-1	1	1	-1	68.6	61.3	71.5
13	-1	-1	-1	1	1	1	-1	71.6	64.6	74.5
14	1	1	-1	1	1	-1	-1	73.7	56.8	69.8
15	-1	-1	1	1	1	-1	1	74.4	64.2	74.2
16	1	1	1	1	1	1	1	72.3	57.4	69.5

consider that failure from temperature might be more sensitive in other areas of the product (e.g., hard drive).

The model(s) created from the DOE experiment is a mean temperature model. For any configuration we would expect product-to-product temperature variability as exemplified in Figure 30.10. However, we would not expect all products to fail at a particular temperature because of the variability of electrical characteristics between assemblies and other factors. Hence there would be another distribution that describes temperature at failure because of this variability of product parameters. The difference between these distributions would be the margin of safety for a machine, as exemplified in Figure 30.11 (where the zero value for temperature is an expected customer ambient temperature). This figure indicates that roughly 5% of the products would fail when the internal operating temperatures of the worst-case configured machines reaches a steady-state temperature (i.e., approximately 5% of the area of the curve is below the zero value, which is ambient temperature).

We need to next build a plan that estimates this margin of safety for temperature. One approach would be to randomly select a sample of machines that have a worst-case configuration. This sample could then placed within a temperature chamber. The chamber could be initially set below the normal ambient temperature chosen. All machines would then be exercised continually with an appropriate test case. After the machines reach their normal internal operating temperature, the chamber temperature would then be gradually increased. Chamber temperature is then documented when each machine fails. Ambient temperature is subtracted from these temperatures at failure for

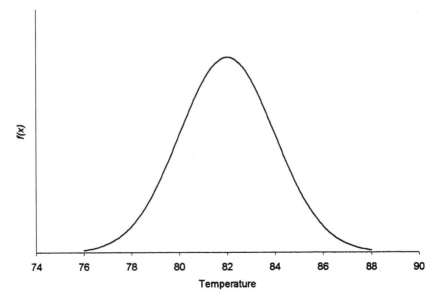

FIGURE 30.10 Potential product-to-product processor temperature variability.

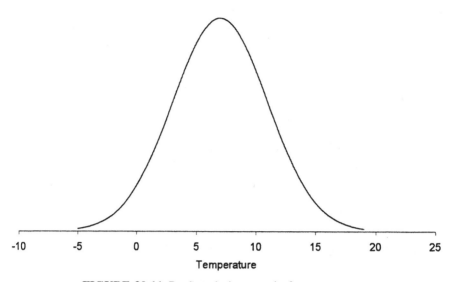

FIGURE 30.11 Product design margin for temperature.

each of the products under test. A normal probability plot of these data can yield the percentage value described conceptually in Figure 30.11. The resulting percentage is an estimate of the margin of safety for temperature. This information can give insight into whether changes are needed.

30.8   S⁴ ASSESSMENT

I have found that sorting fractional factorial experiment trials by the level of a response can be an effective tool when "looking at the data" for the purpose of gaining additional insight into that given by traditional statistical analyses. Diamond (1989) refers to this basic analysis approach as "analysis of goodness." This informal approach can lead to the identification of factors or combination of factors that could affect the response and may not show significance in a formal analysis. In addition, this approach can lead to the identification of a "bad data" point that distorted the formal statistical analysis. Obviously, conclusions from this type of evaluation usually need further consideration in a follow-up confirmation experiment.

Practitioners sometimes do not consider the "hidden" amount of information that might be prevalent from the data obtained when running a fractional factorial experiment, even when no factors are found to be significant. It is obvious that if no factors are found to be significant and a problem still exists, it may be helpful to consider having another brainstorming session to determine other factors to consider and/or how the measurement technique might be improved to give a more consistent response in another experiment. There are situations where looking at the trial response data can be very enlightening. Consider the following:

- If all the response data are "good," then perhaps the experimenter is done with the specific task at hand.
- A ranking of the fractional factorial trials according to the level of a response can sometimes yield additional insight into other interaction possibilities that may be prevalent.
- If much of the response data are "bad" but a few trials were especially "good," unusual setup or other conditions should be investigated for these good trials so that these conditions might be mimicked.
- If factors with levels consistent to that in the manufacturing process were not found significant, these factor tolerances could possibly be relaxed as part of a cost reduction effort.
- A probability plot of the raw experiment data could be useful to pictorially describe the variability of the overall response when the factors are varied within the levels described by the fractional factorial experiment.
- A "sizing" for the process capability could be made from the raw data information.

Often the output from a DOE is only considered at one point in time. However, there are applications where a DOE can be considered a part of a process improvement effort. This was illustrated in Example 30.2 where a DOE was part of a process to estimate temperature design margin for a product design. If we consider the creation of product as an output to a development and test process, we could track the design margin over time for similar product vintages. This tracking could give us insight to whether (and what) changes might be needed within the development process. Example metrics that could be tracked in this matter are electromagnetic emission levels. acoustic emissions, and electrostatic discharge levels.

It should be noted that it is not only important to decide upon an efficient test strategy, it is also important for the experimenter (and team) to become involved in the data collection. If this is not done, the data might be faulty because of a misunderstanding, which can lead to erroneous conclusions and/or a waste of resources.

Confirmation experiments should be used to assess the validity and quantify the benefits of changes resulting from DOE activities. It is always good practice to document the results of a experimental work and present the benefits in monetary terms so that others (including all levels of management) can appreciate the results. This work will make the justification of similar efforts in the future much easier.

30.9 EXERCISES

1. *Catapult Exercise*: For the factors and levels from the catapult DOE experiment that was set up in Chapter 28, create a 16-trial randomized design.

2. *Catapult Exercise*: Execute the catapult two-level DOE trials that was designed within the previous exercise. Analyze the data, build a model of significant factors, and create a set of factor levels that are estimated to give a projection distance specified by instructor (e.g., 75 inches). Set up catapult to these settings and take five shots. Make refinement adjustments using the model, if necessary. Execute 20 shots at this setting. Make process capbaility/performance assessments relative to a specification given by the instructor (e.g., 75 ± 3 inches). Work with the team to create a list of what they would do differently if they had the opportunity to redo the experiment.

3. A five-factor two-level 16-trial fractional factorial design is needed.
    (a) List the experimental trials in nonrandom order.
    (b) List the main and two-factor interaction effects in each contrast column.
    (c) Note the experiment resolution and describe what this level of resolution means.
    (d) Describe a possible application of this experiment to both a manufacturing problem and a service problem. Include potential responses and factors.

4. A seven-factor two-level, 16-trial fractional factorial design is needed.
    (a) List the experimental trials in nonrandom order.
    (b) List the main and two-factor interaction effects in each contrast column.
    (c) Note the experiment resolution and describe what this level of resolution means.

5. An 11-factor two-level, 16-trial fractional factorial design is needed.
    (a) List the experimental trials in non-random order.
    (b) List the main and two-factor interaction effects in each contrast column.
    (c) Note the experiment resolution and describe what this level of resolution means.

6. A factorial design is needed to assess 10 factors.
    (a) Create a two-level, 16-trail factorial design matrix.
    (b) Note the experiment resolution and describe what this level of resolution means.

(c) Describe any main or two-factor interaction aliasing with the AB interaction.

(d) If this were the first experiment to fix a problem, note the suggested percentage of resources that is often suggested for this type of experiment.

(e) Describe a procedure to determine the factors and levels of factors to use within the experiment.

(f) Consider that the analysis indicated the likelihood of a $C*D$ interaction. Draw a conceptual two-factor interaction plot where $C = +$ and $D = -$ yielded a high value while the other combinations yielded a low number.

7. The resources for an experiment are limited to 16 trials. There are 14 factors (factor designations are A–N): however, there is concern about the interaction of the temperature and humidity factors. Describe an appropriate assignment of the temperature and humidity factors.

8. Create an eight-trial unreplicated two-level fractional factorial experiment. List the trials in the sequence planned for the investigation.

(a) Include the effects of four factors: $A = 150$–300; $B = 0.2$–0.8; $C = 22$–26; $D = 1200$–1800.

(b) Add five center points.

(c) Your manager insists that the best combination is when $A = 150$, $B = 0.7$, $C = 26$, and $D = 1800$. If the above design does not contain this combination, make adjustments so that this combination will occur during the experiment.

9. Conduct a DOE analysis of the processor temperature data within Example 30.2. Recreate the model and describe any assumptions.

10. Conduct an analysis of the hard-drive case temperature response shown within Table 30.6. Create a model. Describe any assumptions or further investigation needs.

11. Conduct an analysis of the video chip temperature response shown within Table 30.6. Create a model. Describe any assumptions or further investigation needs.

12. Analyze the following DOE data:

A	B	C	D	E	Response
−1	−1	−1	−1	1	38.9
1	−1	−1	−1	−1	35.3
−1	1	−1	−1	−1	36.7
1	1	−1	−1	1	45.5
−1	−1	1	−1	−1	35.3

1	−1	1	−1	1	37.8
−1	1	1	−1	1	44.3
1	1	1	−1	−1	34.8
−1	−1	−1	1	−1	34.4
1	−1	−1	1	1	38.4
−1	1	−1	1	1	43.5
1	1	−1	1	−1	35.6
−1	−1	1	1	1	37.1
1	−1	1	1	−1	33.8
−1	1	1	1	−1	36.0
1	1	1	1	1	44.9

(a) Determine if there are any outlier data points. Comment on the techniques used to make the assessment.

(b) Determine what factors (if any) are significant and to what significance level.

(c) Determine if there are any two-factor interactions. Determine and illustrate the combinations from any interactions that give the largest results.

(d) Write a model equation with the significant terms.

(e) If B high (i.e., +) were 30 volts and B low (i.e., −) were 40 volts, determine from the model equation the expected output at 32 volts if all other factors are set to nominal conditions.

13. Describe how the techniques within this chapter are useful and can be applied to S^4 projects.

31

OTHER DOE CONSIDERATIONS

31.1 EVOLUTIONARY OPERATIONS (EVOP)

Evolutionary operation (EVOP) is an analytical approach targeted at securing data from a manufacturing process where process conditions are varied in a planned factorial structure from one lot to another without jeopardizing the manufactured product. Analytical techniques are then used to determine what process changes to make for product improvement (Box et al. 1978).

31.2 FOLD-OVER DESIGNS

Consider the situation where a resolution III experiment is conducted. After looking at the results, an experiment wished they had conducted a resolution IV experiment initially because they are concern about the confounding of two-factor interactions with the main effect.

A technique called fold-over can be used to create a resolution IV design from a resolution III design. To create a fold-over design, simply include with the original resolution III design a second fractional factorial design with all the signs reversed. This fold-over process can be useful in the situation where the experimenter has performed a resolution III design initially and now wishes to remove the confounding of the main effects and the two-factor interaction effects.

31.3 DOE EXPERIMENT: ATTRIBUTE RESPONSE

The previous chapter described DOEs that have continuous response outputs. In some situations the appropriate response for a trial may be, for example, that there were two failures out of 300,000 tested solder joints.

If the sample size is the same for each trial, the attribute data can be analyzed using the proportion defect rate as a response for each trial; however a data transformation may be needed when doing this analysis. The accuracy of such an analysis approach can become questionable whenever the sample size is such that many trials have no failures.

An alternative approach is to use a computer categorical data modeling routine that is offered by some statistical software packages. In some cases, additional insight may be achieved by "looking at the data" after they are ranked; however, an attribute test that should evaluate the proportion of failures for each trial should not begin with the intent of relying solely on such an analysis strategy.

31.4 DOE EXPERIMENT: RELIABILITY EVALUATIONS

In some situations, when doing a reliability evaluation it is beneficial to build and test devices/systems using a DOE structure. This strategy can be beneficial when deciding on what design changes should be implemented to fix a problem. This strategy could also be used to describe how systems are built/configured when running a generic reliability test during early stages of production. In this type of test if all trials experience failures, a failure rate (or time of failure) could be the response that is used when doing the DOE analysis, with the transformation considerations.

31.5 FACTORIAL DESIGNS THAT HAVE MORE THAN TWO LEVELS

A multiple experiment strategy that builds upon two-level fractional factorials can be a very useful approach to gain insight into what is needed to better understand and improve a process. Usually nonlinear conditions can be addressed by not being too bold when choosing factorial levels. If a description of a region is necessary, a response surface design such as Box–Behnken or central composite design can be beneficial (see Chapter 33). Statistical software packages can offer other alternatives.

Tables M1 to M5 can be used to create designs that can be used for these test considerations. To do this the contrast columns of the designs in Tables M1 to M5 are combined for these test considerations (e.g., $--$ = source W, $-+$ = source X, $+-$ = source Y, $++$ = source Z). However, an additional contrast column needs to be preserved in the case of four levels, because there are three degrees of freedom with 4 levels (4 levels $-$ 1 = 3 degrees of freedom). The contrast column to preserve is the contrast column that normally contains the two-factor interaction effect of the two contrast columns selected to represent the four levels. For example, if the A and B contrast columns were combined to define the levels, the AB contrast column should not be assigned a factor. These three contrast columns contain the four-level main effect information.

Again, I believe that for test efficiency most factor-level considerations above the level of 2 should be reduced to the value of 2 during an initial DOE experiment. Higher-level considerations that cannot be eliminated from consideration can still be evaluated in a test strategy that consists of multiple experiments. When the number of factors that significantly affect a response is reduced to a manageable number through two-level experiments, response surface analysis techniques can be useful to find the factor levels that optimize a response.

31.6 EXAMPLE 31.1: CREATING A TWO-LEVEL DOE STRATEGY FROM A "MANY-LEVEL" FULL FACTORIAL INITIAL PROPOSAL

Consider two-level factorial experiments wherever possible. However, how to make the change from an experiment design of "many-level" considerations to two-level considerations is sometimes not very obvious. The purpose of this example is to illustrate a basic thought process that can be used when addressing this transition.

An experiment is proposed that considers an output as a function of the following factors with various level considerations.

Factors	Number of Levels
A	4
B	3
C	2
D	2
E	2
F	2

where the A factor may be temperature at four temperature levels, and B to F may consider the effects from other process or design factor tolerances.

To use an experiment design that considers all possible combinations of the factors (i.e., a full factorial experiment), there would need to be 192 experiment trials ($4 \times 3 \times 2 \times 2 \times 2 \times 2 = 192$). In reality, this experiment would probably never be performed because the number of trials would make the experiment too expensive and time-consuming to perform for most industrial situations.

Again an experiment that considers all possible combinations of the factors typically contains more information than is needed for engineering decisions. By changing all factors to two levels and reducing the amount of interaction output information, a design alternative can be determined by using Tables M1 to M5. This experiment could then be performed in 8, 16, or 32 trials depending on the desired experimental resolution.

The first of two basic arguments against restructuring this example is that the factor levels cannot be changed to two levels. In some cases a reduction to a two-level experiment is not possible; however, in many situations an experiment can be reduced to two-level considerations. For example, perhaps only two temperatures are initially assessed, and then if significance is found, perhaps more investigation is appropriate for other temperature effects via another experiment. The specific temperature values to use in an experiment can be dependent on the test objectives. If the test is to determine whether a product is to have a satisfactory output within a temperature range, the levels of temperature may be the two tolerance extremes. However, if a test is to determine the sensitivity of a process to a temperature input, a smaller difference in temperature range may be appropriate. Even factors that appear impossible to change to a two-level consideration can often initially be made two levels with the understanding that if factor significance is found, additional investigation of the other levels will be made via another experiment.

The second argument is the what-if doldrums. These questions can take numerous basic forms. Limiting assumptions should be listed and critiqued before performing experiments so appropriate modifications suggested by others can be incorporated into the initial experiment strategy.

If reasonable limiting assumptions are not made, a "test-all-combinations" strategy will probably prove to be "too large" and will not be done. A one-at-a-time test strategy can then occur, which is inefficient and may in the end require more test time than a fractional factorial experiment. In addition, a one-at-a-time strategy will, in general, have a higher risk of not yielding the desired information.

A strategy using a series of two-level experiments (with perhaps a screening experiment) is in general a more efficient basic test strategy, where in this strategy an experiment resolution is chosen such that two-factor interactions may be confounded but are managed. After the significant parameters are identified, a follow-up experiment is made at a resolution that better assesses main effects and the two-factor interactions of these factors.

31.7   EXAMPLE 31.2: RESOLUTION III DOE WITH INTERACTION CONSIDERATION

An experimenter wants to assess the effects of 14 two-level factors ($A–N$) on an output. Two of these factors are temperature and humidity. Each test trial is very expensive; hence, only a 16-trial resolution III screening experiment is planned. However, the experimenter is concerned that temperature and humidity may interact.

From Table M3 it is noted that for a 14-factor experiment, the 15th contrast column is not needed for any main effect consideration. This column could be used to estimate experimental error or the temperature-humidity interaction that is of concern. To make the temperature–humidity interaction term appear within this column, the factor assignments must be managed such that the temperature and humidity assignments are consistent with an interaction noted within this column. From Table N3 it is noted that there are several assignment alternatives (i.e., *AD*, *BH*, *GI*, *EJ*, *KL*, *FM*, and *CN*). For example, temperature could be assigned an *A* while humidity is assigned a *D*, or humidity could be assigned a *B* while temperature is assigned an *H*.

This basic methodology could be extended to address more than one interaction consideration for both resolution III and IV designs, as long as the total number of two-level factors and interaction contrast column considerations does not exceed one less than the number of trials.

31.8 EXAMPLE 31.3: ANALYSIS OF A RESOLUTION III EXPERIMENT WITH TWO-FACTOR INTERACTION ASSESSMENT

A resolution III experiment was conducted to determine if a product would give a desirable response under various design tolerance extremes and operating conditions. The experiment had 64 trials with 52 two-level factors (*A–Z*, *a–z*). The experiment design format from Table M5 is shown in Table 31.1.

Consider that an analysis was conducted that indicated that the only factors found significant were contrast columns 6, 8, and 18, which implies that factors *F*, *H*, and *R* are significant. However, if Table N3 is examined, it is noted that contrast column 6 (i.e., factor *F*) also contains the *HR* interaction, while contrast column 8 (i.e., factor *H*) also contains the *FR* interaction and contrast column 18 (i.e., factor *R*) also contains the *FH* interaction. Hence, it could be that instead of the three factors each being significant, one of three two-factor interactions might be making the third contrast column significant. To assess which of these scenarios is most likely from a technical point of view, interaction plots can be made of the possibilities assuming that each of them are true. Engineering judgment could possibly then be used to assess which interaction is most likely or whether the three factors individually is the most probable cause for significance.

It is important to note that this example only illustrates a procedure that can be used to give additional insight to possible sources of significance. A confirmation experiment is necessary to confirm or dispute any theories. There are many circumstances that can cause contrast column significance within a resolution III experiment. For example, any of the interaction considerations within a contrast column could be the sources for significance, without the

TABLE 31.1 DOE Experimental Trials

	Factors
	$A\ B\ C\ D\ E\ F\ G\ H\ I\ J\ K\ L\ M\ N\ O\ P\ Q\ R\ S\ T\ U\ V\ W\ X\ Y\ Z\ a\ b\ c\ d\ e\ f\ g\ h\ i\ j\ k\ l\ m\ n\ o\ p\ q\ r\ s\ t\ u\ v\ w\ x\ y\ z$

Contrast column →

```
              1 1 1 1 1 1 1 1 1 1 2 2 2 2 2 2 2 2 2 2 3 3 3 3 3 3 3 3 3 3 4 4 4 4 4 4 4 4 4 4 5 5 5 5
  1 2 3 4 5 6 7 8 9 0 1 2 3 4 5 6 7 8 9 0 1 2 3 4 5 6 7 8 9 0 1 2 3 4 5 6 7 8 9 0 1 2 3 4 5 6 7 8 9 0 1 2

 1  + - - - - - - + - - - - - + + - - + + + + + - + + - - + - + - + + + + + - - + + - - + + + - - + + - - +
 2  + + - - - - + - - + + - + - + + + + - - + - - - + - + + - + - + - + + + - + - + + + + - + + - - + + - - -
 3  + + + - - + - - - + - - - + + - + + + + + + + + - + + - + - + - + + - + + + + + - + + + + - - + - + - + -
 4
 ...                                                    *
                                                          *
                                                            *

63  - - - - - + - - + + - - - - - - - + + - + + - - + + - + + + + - + + - - + + - - + + - - - - - - + + - +
64  - - - - - - - - - - - - - - - - - - - - - - - - - - - - - - - - - - - - - - - - - - - - - - - - - - - -
```

main effect being significant. However, with the initial problem definition, if all the trial responses are well within a desirable output range, then it may not be important to have a precise analysis to determine which factor(s) are significant.

31.9 EXAMPLE 31.4: DOE WITH ATTRIBUTE RESPONSE

A manufacturing surface mount processes and assembles electrical components onto a printed circuit board. A visual quality assessment at several locations on the printed circuit board assesses residual flux and tin (Sn) residual. A lower value for these responses is most desirable. A DOE was conducted with the following factors:

	Level	
Factor	-1	$+1$
A Paste age	Fresh	"Old"
B Humidity	Ambient	High
C Print-reflow time	Short	Long
D IR temperature	Low	High
E Cleaning temperature	Low	High
F Is component present?	No	Yes

Inspectors were not blocked within the experiment (however, they should have been). Table 31.2 shows the result of the experiment along with the experimental trials.

Consider first an analysis of the flux response. There are a lot of zeros for this response which makes a traditional DOE analysis impossible. However, when we rank the responses as shown in Table 31.3, it is noted that there are seven nonzero values. The largest six of these values are with $C = +1$ (i.e., long print-reflow time). However, there is concern that all of these assessments were made by the same inspector. From this result, one might inquire whether a gauge R&R study had been conducted, and one may also inquire about the results the study. Also, these boards should be reassessed to make sure that the documented results are valid. If there is agreement that the results are valid, one would conclude that the -1 level for C is best (i.e., short print-reflow time).

Consider next an analysis of the tin (Sn) response. This response does not have as many zeros and lends itself to regular DOE analysis techniques. Because the response is count data, a transformation should be considered. Analysis of these data is an exercise at the end of this chapter.

TABLE 31.2 Experimental Trials from Attribute Experiment

No.	A	B	C	D	E	F	Insp	Flux	Sn
1	−1	−1	+1	−1	−1	−1	+1	0	3
2	+1	+1	+1	−1	−1	−1	+1	0	0
3	−1	+1	+1	−1	−1	+1	+1	0	0
4	+1	−1	+1	−1	−1	+1	+1	0	25
5	−1	+1	+1	+1	−1	−1	+1	7	25
6	+1	−1	+1	+1	−1	−1	+1	5	3
7	−1	−1	+1	+1	−1	+1	+1	11	78
8	+1	+1	+1	+1	−1	+1	+1	13	67
9	−1	+1	−1	−1	+1	−1	−1	0	0
10	+1	−1	−1	−1	+1	−1	−1	0	12
11	−1	+1	−1	−1	+1	+1	−1	0	150
12	+1	−1	−1	−1	+1	+1	−1	0	94
13	−1	−1	−1	+1	+1	−1	−1	0	424
14	+1	+1	−1	+1	+1	−1	−1	0	500
15	−1	−1	−1	+1	+1	+1	−1	0	1060
16	+1	+1	−1	+1	+1	+1	−1	0	280
17	+1	−1	+1	+1	+1	+1	+1	0	1176
18	−1	+1	+1	−1	+1	−1	+1	24	17
19	+1	−1	+1	−1	+1	−1	+1	5	14
20	−1	−1	+1	−1	+1	+1	+1	0	839
21	+1	+1	+1	−1	+1	+1	+1	0	376
22	−1	−1	+1	+1	+1	−1	+1	0	366
23	+1	+1	+1	+1	+1	−1	+1	0	690
24	−1	+1	+1	+1	+1	+1	+1	0	722
25	−1	+1	−1	+1	−1	−1	−1	0	50
26	−1	−1	−1	−1	−1	−1	−1	0	12
27	+1	+1	−1	−1	−1	−1	−1	0	50
28	−1	+1	−1	+1	−1	+1	−1	0	207
29	+1	−1	−1	+1	−1	+1	−1	0	172
30	+1	−1	−1	+1	−1	−1	−1	2	54
31	−1	−1	−1	−1	−1	+1	+1	0	0
32	+1	+1	−1	−1	−1	+1	+1	0	2

31.10   EXAMPLE 31.5: A SYSTEM DOE STRESS TO FAIL TEST

During the development of a new computer a limited amount of test hardware is available to evaluate the overall design of the product. Four test systems are available along with three different card/adapter types (designated as card A, card B, and adapter) that are interchangeable between the systems.

A "quick and dirty" fractional factorial test approach is desired to evaluate the different combinations of the hardware along with the temperature and humidity extremes typically encountered in a customer's office. One obvious response for the experimental trial configurations is whether the combination of hardware "worked" or "did not work" satisfactorily. However, more in-

TABLE 31.3 Ranking Experimental Trials from Attribute Experiment by Flux Response

No.	A	B	C	D	E	F	Insp	Flux	Sn
1	−1	−1	+1	−1	−1	−1	+1	0	3
2	+1	+1	+1	−1	−1	−1	+1	0	0
3	−1	+1	+1	−1	−1	+1	+1	0	0
4	+1	−1	+1	−1	−1	+1	+1	0	25
9	−1	+1	−1	−1	+1	−1	−1	0	0
10	+1	−1	−1	−1	+1	−1	−1	0	12
11	−1	+1	−1	−1	+1	+1	−1	0	150
12	+1	−1	−1	−1	+1	+1	−1	0	94
13	−1	−1	−1	+1	+1	−1	−1	0	424
14	+1	+1	−1	+1	+1	−1	−1	0	500
15	−1	−1	−1	+1	+1	+1	−1	0	1060
16	+1	+1	−1	+1	+1	+1	−1	0	280
17	+1	−1	+1	+1	+1	+1	+1	0	1176
20	−1	−1	+1	−1	+1	+1	+1	0	839
21	+1	+1	+1	−1	+1	+1	+1	0	376
22	−1	−1	+1	+1	+1	−1	+1	0	366
23	+1	+1	+1	+1	+1	−1	+1	0	690
24	−1	+1	+1	+1	+1	+1	+1	0	722
25	−1	+1	−1	+1	−1	−1	−1	0	50
26	−1	−1	−1	−1	−1	−1	−1	0	12
27	+1	+1	−1	−1	−1	−1	−1	0	50
28	−1	+1	−1	+1	−1	+1	−1	0	207
29	+1	−1	−1	+1	−1	+1	−1	0	172
31	−1	−1	−1	−1	−1	+1	+1	0	0
32	+1	+1	−1	−1	−1	+1	+1	0	2
30	+1	−1	−1	+1	−1	−1	−1	2	54
6	+1	−1	+1	+1	−1	−1	+1	5	3
19	+1	−1	+1	−1	+1	−1	+1	5	14
5	−1	+1	+1	+1	−1	−1	+1	7	25
7	−1	−1	+1	+1	−1	+1	+1	11	78
8	+1	+1	+1	+1	−1	+1	+1	13	67
18	−1	+1	+1	−1	+1	−1	+1	24	17

formation was desired from the experiment than just a binary response. In the past it was shown that the "system design safety factor" can be quantified by noting the 5-V power supply output level values (both upward and downward) at which the system begins to perform unsatisfactorily. A probability plot is then made of these voltage values to estimate the number of systems from the population that would not perform satisfactorily outside the 4.7 to 5.3 tolerance range of the 5-V power supply.

Determining a "low-voltage" failure value could easily be accomplished for this test procedure because this type of system failure was not catastrophic (i.e., the system would still perform satisfactorily again if the voltage level were increased). However, if a failure did not occur at 6.00, previous experience indicates that additional stressing might destroy one or more components. Because of this nonrecoverable scenario, it was decided that the system voltage stressing would be suspended at 6.00 V.

A 16-trial test matrix is shown in Table 31.4 along with measured voltage levels. Note that the trial fractional factorial levels of this type can be created from Tables M1 to M5 where four levels of the factors are created by combining contrast columns (e.g., $-- = 1$, $-+ = 2$, $+- = 3$, and $++ = 4$). It should be noted that the intent of the experiment was to do "a quick and dirty test" at the boundaries of the conditions to assess the range of response that might be expected when parts are assembled in different patterns. Because of this, no special care was taken when picking the contrast columns to create the four levels of factors; hence, there will be some confounding of the effects. Obviously a practitioner would need to take more care when choosing a design matrix if he or she wishes to make an analysis that addresses these effect considerations.

From Table 31.4 it is noted that the system 3 planar board was changed during the experiment (denoted by a postscript a). Changes of this type should

TABLE 31.4 Experimental System Data

Temperature (°F)	Humidity (%)	System (#)	Card A (#)	Card B (#)	Adapter (#)	5 V (error types[a], voltages) Elevated Voltage	Lowered Voltage
95	50	1	4	1**	4	E1 5.92	E2 4.41
95	50	3*	3	3	2	sus 6.00	E3 4.60
95	50	4	1	2	1	sus 6.00	E2 4.50
95	50	2	2	4	3	sus 6.00	E2 4.41
55	20	1	4	1**	1	sus 6.00	E2 4.34
55	20	2	1	4	2	sus 6.00	E2 4.41
55	20	3a***	2	3	3	sus 6.00	E2 4.45
55	20	4	3	2	4	sus 6.00	E2 4.51
55	85	1	1	2	2	sus 6.00	E2 4.52
55	85	2	4	3	1	sus 6.00	E2 4.45
55	85	3*	2	4	4	sus 6.00	E3 4.62
55	85	4	3	1**	3	E1 5.88	E2 4.58
95	20	1	1	2	3	sus 6.00	E2 4.51
95	20	2	3	3	4	sus 6.00	E2 4.44
95	20	3a***	4	4	1	sus 6.00	E2 4.41
95	20	4	2	1**	2	E1 5.98	E2 4.41

[a] sus = suspended test at noted voltage.
*   Lowering 5 V caused an E3 error.
** Lowering 5 V caused a different error type (i.e., E1) three out of four times when card B = 1.
*** 3a = new system planar board installed.

be avoided during a test; however, if an unexpected event mandates a change, the change should be documented. It is also noted that the trials containing system 3 with the original system planar resulted in a different error message when the 5-V power supply was lowered to failure. It is also noted that the only "elevated voltage" failures occurred (three out of four times) when card B number I was installed. Generalities made from observations of this type must be made with extreme caution because aliasing and experimental measurement errors can lead to erroneous conclusions. Additional investigation beyond the original experiment needs to be performed for the purpose of either confirming or rejecting such theories.

Since the failures only occurred whenever the voltage was varied outside its limits, some people might conclude that there is "no problem." It is true that these observations and failure voltage levels may not be indicative of future production problems. However, the basic strategy behind this type of experiment is to assess the amount of "safety factor" before failure with a limited amount of hardware. A design that has a small margin of safety may experience problems in the future if the manufacturing process experiences any slight change. In addition, it is good general practice to make other appropriate evaluations on any cards and devices that have peculiar failures for the purpose of assessing whether there is a potential design problem.

A probability plot of the trial responses in Figure 31.1 gives some idea of the amount of safety factor that is prevalent in the design (note that this is not a probability plot of random data). From this plot a best estimate projection is that about 99.9% of the systems will perform at the low-voltage tolerance value of 4.7.

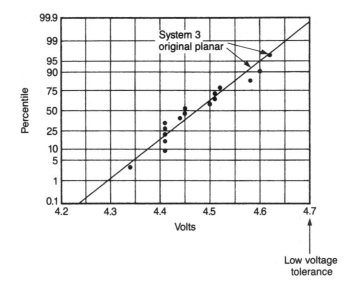

FIGURE 31.1 Normal probability plot of the 5-V stress to fail responses (first design test).

Consider next that another similar experiment is performed with a new level of hardware. The results from this experiment are shown in Table 31.5. From this table it is noted that abnormalities from the previous test did not occur. A probability plot of the low-voltage stress values is again made and is shown in Figure 31.2. One of the points in this probability plot could be an outlier. This data measurement should be investigated for abnormalities. Another observation from this plot is that there is a larger percentage projection at the 4.7-V specification limit than from the earlier set of data; hence, this later design appears to have a larger safety factor.

Figure 31.3 gives a pictorial presentation of this comparison using the estimated normal probability density functions (PDFs) from each set of data. From this figure it is noted that the average value of the density functions are approximately the same; however, there was a reduction in measurement variability in the later design level. This is "goodness"; however, if the situation were reversed and the newer design had greater variability, then there might be concern that things could degrade more in the future.

In manufacturing it is feasible that the preceding basic test strategy could be repeated periodically. Data could then be monitored on $\bar{x}$ and R control charts for degradation/improvement as a function of time.

TABLE 31.5 Experiment Data with New Hardware

Temperature (°F)	Humidity (%)	System (#)	Card A (#)	Card B (#)	Adapter (#)	5 V (error types[a], voltages) Elevated Voltage	5 V (error types[a], voltages) Lowered Voltage
95	50	1	4	1	1	sus 6.00	E2 4.48
95	20	2	1	4	2	sus 6.00	E2 4.48
95	20	3	2	3	3	sus 6.00	E2 4.45
95	20	4	3	2	4	sus 6.00	E2 4.42
55	85	1	1	2	2	sus 6.00	E2 4.56
55	85	2	4	3	1	sus 6.00	E2 4.46
55	85	3	2	4	4	sus 6.00	E2 4.45
55	85	4	3	1	3	sus 6.00	E2 4.43
55	20	1	1	2	3	sus 6.00	E2 4.45
55	20	2	3	3	4	sus 6.00	E2 4.46
55	20	3	4	4	1	sus 6.00	E3 4.42
55	20	4	2	1	2	sus 6.00	E2 4.48
95	50	1	4	1	4	sus 6.00	E2 4.45
95	50	3	2	4	3	sus 6.00	E2 4.49
95	50	4	3	3	2	sus 6.00	E2 4.45
95	50	2	1	2	1	sus 6.00	E2 4.49

[a] sus = suspended test at noted voltage.

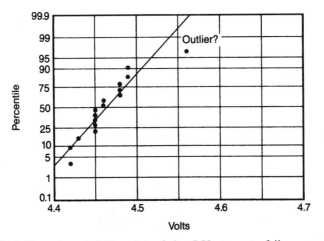

FIGURE 31.2 Normal probability plot of the 5-V stress to fail responses (second design test).

31.11 S⁴ ASSESSMENT

In some situations, effort should be given to understanding the magnitude of the effects from significant factors. With this understanding, follow-up experiments can be designed to yield additional insight toward an optimal solution. Understanding the levels of factors that did not affect the output significantly is also important because this knowledge can lead to relaxed tolerances that can be easier to achieve.

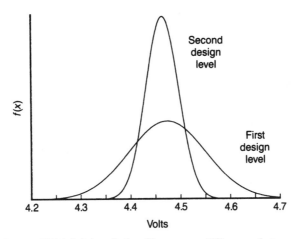

FIGURE 31.3 Two PDF "sizings" that illustrate a difference between the first and second design.

In many instances the overall understanding of the process through fractional factorial experiments can be combined with general cost considerations in order to determine the changes that are "best" in order to supply the customer with a high-quality/low-cost product. In other instances, fractional factorial experiments can be used to structure a test strategy so that the test efficiently evaluates a product relative to meeting the needs of the customer.

When deciding what should be done next, consider the real purpose of the experiment. If the primary objective was to determine whether a satisfactory output is achieved within the operational extremes of environmental and tolerance conditions and all the responses are "very good," the significance of effects may be of little practical importance. A probability plot of the experimental outputs for each trial can be a "picture" to assess variabilities in this "operational space"—perhaps with only one prototype system. It should be noted, however, that this would not be a random sample (of future production); hence, the percentage of population values are not necessarily representative of the true population. However, this procedure can often give a more meaningful "picture" of how well a specification criterion will be met in future systems/devices than will a "random" sample of a single lot of early production assemblies.

31.12 EXERCISES

1. Analyze the tin (Sn) degree count response within Table 31.2 as a function of the described factors and levels. Compare an analysis where the trial responses are transformed to one where there is no transformation.

2. A 16-trial experiment is conducted with 15 factors. There is now concern that some two-factor interactions could have distorted the results. Some additional trials are added.
   (a) Describe the design technique used to choose the additional trial settings when converting from a resolution III to resolution IV design.
   (b) From Table M document the level settings for the first trial factors for both the initial and additional trial test.

3. Discuss how DOE techniques might be used within development to reduce cycle times.

4. Describe how the techniques within this chapter are useful and can be applied to S^4 projects.

32

VARIABILITY REDUCTION THROUGH DOE AND TAGUCHI CONSIDERATIONS

The experimentation procedures proposed by Genichi Taguchi (Taguchi and Konishi 1987, Ross 1988) have experienced both acclaim and criticism. Some nonstatisticians like the practicality of the techniques, while statisticians have noted problems that can lead to erroneous conclusions. However, most statisticians will agree that Taguchi has increased visibility to the area of DOE. In addition, most statisticians and engineers will probably agree with Taguchi that more direct emphasis should have been given in the past to the reduction of process variability and the reduction of cost within product design and manufacturing processes.

This chapter gives a brief overview of the basic Taguchi philosophy as it relates to the concepts discussed in this text. The loss function also is discussed along with an approach that can be used to reduce variability in the manufacturing process. In addition, the analysis of 2^k residuals is discussed for assessing the potential sources to variability reduction.

32.1 TEST STRATEGIES

Published Taguchi (Taguchi and Konishi 1987) "orthogonal arrays and linear graphs" contain both two- and three-level experiment design matrices. I, in general, prefer a basic two-level factor strategy for most experiments with follow-up experiments that could address additional levels of a factor or factors. The response surface techniques described in a later chapter could also be used, in some cases, as part of that follow-up effort.

The basic two-level Taguchi design matrices are equivalent to those in Table M (Breyfogle, 1989e), where these basic matrices have n trials with

$n - 1$ contrast column considerations. For the two-level designs of 4, 8, 16, 32, and 64 trials. Table N contains the two-factor interaction confounding for the design matrices found in Table M.

One suggested Taguchi test strategy consists of implementing one experiment (which could be rather large) with a confirmation experiment. Taguchi experiment analysis techniques do not normally dwell upon interaction considerations that are not anticipated before the start of test. If care is not taken during contrast column selection when choosing the experiment design matrix, an unnecessary or a messy interaction confounding structure may result, which can lead the experimenter to an erroneous conclusion (Box et al. 1988).

This text suggests first considering what initial experiment resolution is needed and manageable with the number of two-level factors that are present. If a resolution is chosen that does not directly consider interactions, some interaction concerns can be managed by using the techniques described earlier in this text. After this first experiment analysis, one of several actions may next be appropriate, depending on the analysis results. First, the test may yield dramatic conclusions that could answer the question of concern. For this situation a simple confirmation experiment may then be appropriate. The results from another experiment may lead testers to plan a follow-up experiment that considers other factors in conjunction with those factors that appear significant. Still another situation may suggest a follow-up experiment of significant factors at a higher resolution for interaction considerations.

Again, if interactions are not managed properly within an experiment, confusion and erroneous action plans can result. In addition, the management of these interactions is much more plausible when three-level factors are not involved in the fractional factorial experiment design.

32.2 LOSS FUNCTION

The loss function is a contribution of Genichi Taguchi (Taguchi 1978). This concept can bridge the language barrier between upper management and those involved in the technical details. Upper management best understands money, while those involved within the technical arena better understand product variability. Classical experiment design concepts traditionally do not directly emphasize the reduction of process variability and translate this need to economical considerations understood by all management.

The loss function describes the loss that occurs when a process does not produce a product that meets a target value. Loss is minimized when there is "no variability," and the "best" response is achieved in all areas of the product design.

Traditionally, manufacturing has considered all parts that are outside specification limits to be equally nonconforming, while all parts within specification are equally conforming. The loss function associated with this way of thinking is noted in Figure 32.1.

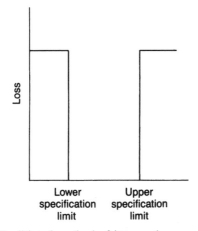

FIGURE 32.1 Traditional method of interpreting manufacturing limits.

With the Taguchi approach it is not believed that loss relative to the specification limit is a step function. To understand this point, consider whether it is realistic, for example, to believe that there is no exposure of having any problems (i.e., loss) when a part is barely within the specification limit and if the maximum loss level is appropriate whenever the part is barely outside these limits. Most people would agree that this is not normally true.

Taguchi addresses variability within the process using a loss function. The loss function can take many forms. A common form is the quadratic loss function

$$L = k(y - m)^2$$

where L is the loss associated with a particular value of the independent variable y. The specification nominal value is m, while k is a constant depending on the cost and width of the specification limits. Figure 32.2 illustrates this loss function graphically. When this loss function is applied to a situation, more emphasis will be given toward achieving target as opposed to just meeting specification limits. This type of philosophy encourages, for example, a television manufacturer to continually strive to routinely manufacture products that have a very high quality picture (i.e., a nominal specification value), as opposed to accepting and distributing a quality level that is "good enough."

32.3   EXAMPLE 32.1: LOSS FUNCTION

Given that the cost of scrapping a part is $10.00 when it deteriorates from a target by ± 0.50 mm, the quadratic loss function given m (the nominal value) of 0.0 is

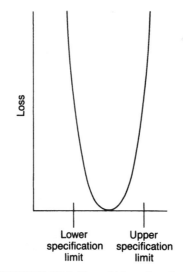

FIGURE 32.2 Taguchi loss function.

$$\$10.00 = k(0.5 - 0.0)^2$$

Hence

$$k = 10.00/0.25 = \$40.00 \text{ per mm}^2 \text{ (i.e., } \$25,806 \text{ per in.}^2)$$

This loss function then becomes

$$L = 40(y - 0)^2$$

The loss function can yield different conclusions from decisions based on classical "goal post" specification limits. For example, a different decision can result relative to frequency of maintenance for a tool that wears within a manufacturing process. In addition, with this loss function economic decisions can now be made to determine whether expense should be incurred to implement a new process that can yield a tighter tolerance.

32.4   STANDARD DEVIATION AS A RESPONSE

Again, most practitioners of statistical techniques agree with Taguchi that it is important to reduce variability within the manufacturing process. To do this, Taguchi suggests using an inner and outer array (i.e., fractional factorial design structure) to address the issue. The inner array addresses the items that can be controlled (e.g., part tolerances), while the outer array addresses factors that cannot necessarily be controlled (e.g., ambient temperature and humidity). To analyze the data, he devised a signal-to-noise ratio technique, which Box et al. (1988) show can yield debatable results. However, Box (1988) states that it can be shown that use of the signal-to-noise ratio concept is equivalent to an analysis that uses the logarithm of the data.

The included fractional factorial designs in this text can be used to address the basic strategy of reducing manufacturing variability using the inner/outer array experimentation strategy. To do this, simply categorize the factor listing into controllable and non-controllable factors. The controllable factors would contain a design structure similar to that illustrated with the previous chapters on DOE, while the non-controllable factors would be set to levels denoted by another fractional factorial design. All the noncontrollable factor experimental design trials would be performed for each trial of the controllable factor experimentation design. Note, however, that in using this inner/outer experimentation strategy a traditional design of 16 trials might now contain a total of 64 trials, if there is an outer experiment design containing 4 test trials.

Now, both a mean and standard deviation value can be obtained for each trial and analyzed independently. The trial mean value could be directly analyzed using the previously described DOE procedures. The standard deviation (or variance) for each trial may need to have a logarithm transformation within the analysis procedure (the transformation commonly used to normalize standard deviation data).

If the Taguchi experiment philosophy of using an inner and outer array were followed in the design of the stepper motor fractional factorial experiment, the temperature factor in the experiment would probably be considered within an outer array matrix. This could be done along with perhaps other parameters, remembering that the mean value needs to be optimized (minimized to meet this particular test objective) in addition to minimizing variability considerations.

Obviously a practitioner is not required to use the inner/outer array experiment design approach when investigating the source of variability. It may be appropriate, for example, to construct an experiment design where each trial is repeated and (in addition to a mean trial response) the variance (or standard deviation) between repetitions is considered a trial response (data may need a log transformation). The sample size for each trial repetition needs to be large enough so detection of the magnitude of variability differences desired is possible.

32.5   ANALYZING 2^k RESIDUALS FOR SOURCES OF VARIABILITY REDUCTION

A study of residuals from a single replicate of a 2^k design can give insight into process variability, because residuals can be viewed as observed values of noise or error (Montgomery 1997, Box and Meyer 1986). When the level of a factor affects variability, a plot of residuals versus the factor levels will indicate more variability of the residuals at one factor level than at the other level of the factor.

The magnitude of contrast column dispersion effects in the experiment can be tested by calculating

$$F_i^* = \ln \frac{s^2(i^+)}{s^2(i^-)} \qquad i = 1, 2, \ldots, n$$

where n is the number of contrast columns for an experiment. Also, the standard deviation of the residuals for each group of signs in each contrast column is designated as $s^2(i^-)$ and $s^2(i^+)$. This statistic is approximately normally distributed if the two variances are equal. A normal probability plot of the dispersion effects for the contrast columns can be used to assess the significance of a dispersion effect.

32.6 EXAMPLE 32.2: ANALYZING 2^k RESIDUALS FOR SOURCES OF VARIABILITY REDUCTION

The present defect rate of a process producing internal panels for commercial aircraft is too high (5.5 defects per panel). A four-factor, 16-trial, 2^k single replicate design was conducted and yielded the results shown in Table 32.1 for a single press load (Montgomery 1997).

A normal probability plot of the factor effects shown in Figure 32.3 indicates clearly that factors A and C are significant. From this analysis we conclude that lower temperature (A) and higher resin flow (C) would decrease the frequency of panel defects.

However, careful analysis of the residuals gives other insight. For a model containing factors A and C, no abnormalities were shown from a normal probability plot of the residuals, but a plot of the residuals versus each of factors (A, B, C, and D) yielded the pattern shown in Figure 32.4 for B. The B factor was not shown to affect the average number of defects per panel, but appears to very important in its effect on process variability. It appears that a low clamp time results in less variability in the average number of defects per panel.

The magnitude of the B contrast column dispersion effect in the experiment is

$$F_B^* = \ln \frac{s^2(B^+)}{s^2(B^-)} = \frac{(2.72)^2}{(0.82)^2} = 2.39$$

Table 32.2 shows the result of this dispersion effect calculation for all contrast columns. The normal probability plot of these contrast column dispersion

TABLE 32.1 Experiment Design and Results

Trial	A	B	C	D	Response		Factors	Level −	+
1	−1	−1	−1	−1	5	A	Temperature	295	325
2	1	−1	−1	−1	11	B	Clamp time	7	9
3	−1	1	−1	−1	3.5	C	Resin flow	10	20
4	1	1	−1	−1	9	D	Closing time	15	30
5	−1	−1	1	−1	0.5				
6	1	−1	1	−1	8				
7	−1	1	1	−1	1.5				
8	1	1	1	−1	9.5				
9	−1	−1	−1	1	6				
10	1	−1	−1	1	12.5				
11	−1	1	−1	1	8				
12	1	1	−1	1	15.5				
13	−1	−1	1	1	1				
14	1	−1	1	1	6				
15	−1	1	1	1	5				
16	1	1	1	1	5				

effects shown in Figure 32.5 clearly confirms our early observation of the importance of the B factor with respect process dispersion.

32.7 S⁴ ASSESSMENT

The mechanics of implementing some of the Taguchi concepts discussed in other texts is questionable. However, Taguchi has gotten management's attention on the importance of using DOE techniques. He has also shown the importance of reducing variability. The process index C_p addresses the effects that variability can have on the consistency of a process toward meeting specification objectives. Fractional factorial experiment concepts with standard deviation as a response can be used to improve C_p. In addition, an assessment of residuals within a 2^k design can give us insight to sources for the reduction of variability.

32.8 EXERCISES

1. *Catapult Exercise*: Set up, conduct, and analyze a DOE experiment similar to the one which was executed in Chapter 30. However, this time repeat each trial three times. Analyze the mean and standard deviation of each trial response. Evaluate the residuals of the standard deviation to determine if a data transformation is needed. Consider factors that not only adjust

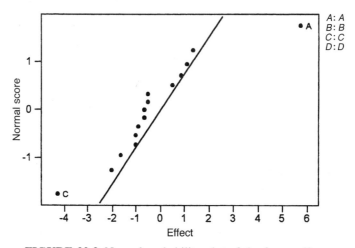

FIGURE 32.3 Normal probability plot of the factor effects.

the mean response (e.g., arm length) but also could affect the variability of the response. Include a measurement method factor, where one level of the factor is a visual recording of the distance with no marking (i.e., no carbon paper or talcum powder to mark ball impact point) and the other is using some method to mark the ball position at impact. Consider how the factor levels will be chosen (e.g., high ball projection arc or flat projection arc). Consider also whether the factor levels are going to be chosen so that there is much variability between all the throw distances or so that

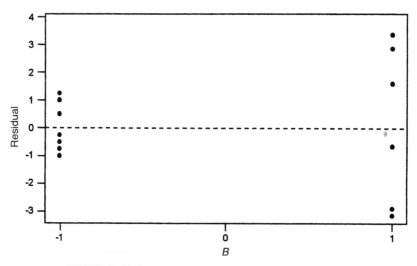

FIGURE 32.4 Plot of residuals versus clamp time (B).

TABLE 32.2 Calculation of Dispersion Effects

Trial	A	B	C	D	AB	AC	BC	ABC	AD	BD	$-ABD$	CD	ACD	BCD	ABCD	Residual
1	−	−	−	−	+	+	+	−	+	+	−	+	−	−	+	−0.94
2	+	−	−	−	−	−	+	+	−	+	+	+	+	−	−	−0.69
3	−	+	−	−	−	+	−	+	+	−	+	+	−	+	−	−2.44
4	+	+	−	−	+	−	−	−	−	−	−	+	+	+	+	−2.69
5	−	−	+	−	+	−	−	+	+	+	−	−	+	+	−	−1.19
6	+	−	+	−	−	+	−	−	−	+	+	−	−	+	+	0.56
7	−	+	+	−	−	−	+	−	+	−	+	−	+	−	+	−0.19
8	+	+	+	−	+	+	+	+	−	−	−	−	−	−	−	2.06
9	−	−	−	+	+	+	+	−	−	−	+	−	+	+	−	0.06
10	+	−	−	+	−	−	+	+	+	−	−	−	−	+	+	0.81
11	−	+	−	+	−	+	−	+	−	+	−	−	+	−	+	2.06
12	+	+	−	+	+	−	−	−	+	+	+	−	−	−	−	3.81
13	−	−	+	+	+	−	−	+	−	−	+	+	−	−	+	−0.69
14	+	−	+	+	−	+	−	−	+	−	−	+	+	−	−	−1.44
15	−	+	+	+	−	−	+	−	−	+	−	+	−	+	−	3.31
16	+	+	+	+	+	+	+	+	+	+	+	+	+	+	+	−2.44
$s(i^+)$	2.25	2.72	1.91	2.24	2.21	1.81	1.80	1.80	2.05	2.28	1.97	1.93	1.52	2.09	1.61	
$s(i^-)$	1.85	0.82	2.20	1.55	1.86	2.24	2.26	2.24	1.93	1.61	2.11	1.58	2.16	1.89	2.33	
F_i^*	0.39	2.39	−0.29	0.74	0.35	−0.43	−0.45	−0.44	0.13	0.69	−0.14	0.40	−0.71	0.20	−0.74	

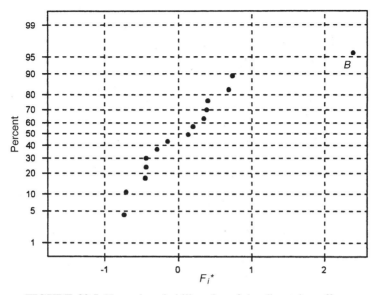

FIGURE 32.5 Normal probability plot of the dispersion effects.

the throw distances will be more clustered around the target (i.e.. very bold or not so bold selection of factor levels).

2. A study had the objective to study the effects of four factors on airflow through a valve that is used in an automobile air pollution control device. The factors and levels are noted below along with the response for test trials. Analyze all responses and summarize conclusions (Moen et al. 1991, and Bisgaard and Fuller 1995):

Factors				−1				1
Length of armature				0.595 in.				0.605 in.
Spring load				70 g				100 g
Bobbin length				1.095 in.				1.105 in.
Tube length				0.500 in.				0.510 in.

Trial	Arm Length	Spring Load	Bobbin Depth	Tube Length	$\bar{y}$	s	s^2	$\ln(s^2)$
1	−1	−1	−1	−1	0.46	0.04	0.0016	−6.44
2	1	−1	−1	−1	0.42	0.16	0.0256	−3.67
3	−1	1	−1	−1	0.57	0.02	0.0004	−7.82
4	1	1	−1	−1	0.45	0.1	0.0100	−4.61
5	−1	−1	1	−1	0.73	0.02	0.0004	−7.82
6	1	−1	1	−1	0.71	0.01	0.0001	−9.21
7	−1	1	1	−1	0.7	0.05	0.0025	−5.99
8	1	1	1	−1	0.7	0.01	0.0001	−9.21

9	−1	−1	−1	1	0.42	0.04	0.0016	−6.44
10	1	−1	−1	1	0.28	0.15	0.0225	−3.79
11	−1	1	−1	1	0.6	0.07	0.0049	−5.32
12	1	1	−1	1	0.29	0.06	0.0036	−5.63
13	−1	−1	1	1	0.7	0.02	0.0004	−7.82
14	1	−1	1	1	0.71	0.02	0.0004	−7.82
15	−1	1	1	1	0.71	0.02	0.0004	−7.82
16	1	1	1	1	0.72	0.01	0.0001	−9.21

3. Reconsider how the following situation initially described as an exercise in Chapter 29 could be conducted using a DOE philosophy centered around the reduction of variability: The position of the leads on an electronic component is important to get a satisfactory solder mount of the component to an electronic printed circuit board. There is concern that with manufacturing, an electronic tester of the component function is bending the component leads. To monitor physical changes from tester handling, the leads from a sample of components are noted before and after the tester.

(a) Create a plan for implementing a DOE that assesses what should be done different to reduce the amount of bending on each component. Consider the selection of measurement response, selection of factors, and results validation.

(b) Create a plan that could be used in the future for a similar machine setup.

4. Reconsider how the following situation initially described as an exercise in Chapter 29 could be conducted using a DOE philosophy centered around the reduction of variability: A machine measures the peel back force necessary to remove the packaging for electrical components. The tester records an output force that changes as the packaging is separated. The process was found not capable of consistently meeting specification limits. The average peel-back force needed to be reduced.

(a) Create a DOE plan to determine what should be done to improve the capability of the process.

(b) Create a plan that the company could use in the future to set up similar equipment to avoid this type of problem.

5. A manufacturing process has 15 controllable and three uncontrollable factors that could affect the output of a process.

(a) Create an inner/outer array test plan if the three uncontrollable factors were ambient temperature humidity, and barometric pressure.

(b) Describe difficulties that would probably be encountered when conducting the experiment.

6. Early in development, three prototype automobiles were used to estimate average miles per gallon. The net average of the three vehicles over 20,000 miles was reported to management. Describe what might be done differently if the objective of the work was to better understand the characteristics of the vehicles relative to sensitivity of different operators.

7. Describe how the techniques within this chapter are useful and can be applied to S^4 projects.

33

RESPONSE SURFACE METHODOLOGY

Response surface methodology (RSM) is used to determine how a response is affected by a set of quantitative variables/factors over some specified region. This information can be used to optimize the settings of a process to give, for example, a maximum or minimum response. With knowledge of the response surface, settings can possibly be chosen for a process such that day-to-day variations typically found in a manufacturing environment will have a minimum affect on the degradation of product quality.

For a given number of variables, response surface analysis techniques require more trials than the two-level fractional factorial design techniques; hence, the number of variables to consider within an experiment may first need to be reduced through either technical considerations or fractional factorial experiments.

This chapter shows the application of the central composite rotatable and Box–Behnken designs for determining the response surface analysis of variables. This chapter also discusses extreme vertices and simplex lattice designs along with computer algorithm designs for mixtures.

33.1 MODELING EQUATIONS

Previous DOE chapters covering two-level fractional factorial experimentation considered main effects and interaction effects. For these designs the response was assumed to be linear between the level considerations for the factors. In these chapters the general philosophy is that several factor extremes are investigated to address many types of different problems expediently with a minimal number of test trials. This form of experimentation is adequate in itself to solve many types of problems. However, there are situations where a response needs to be optimized as a function of the levels of a few input factors/variables. This chapter focuses on such a situation.

The prediction equation for a two-factor linear main-effect model without the consideration of interactions takes the form

$$y = b_0 + b_1 x_1 + b_2 x_2$$

where y is the response, b_0 is the y-axis intercept, and (b_1, b_2) are the coefficients of the factors. For a balanced experiment design that had factor-level considerations for x_1 and x_2, respectively equal to -1 and $+1$, the b_1 and b_2 coefficients equate to one-half of the effect and b_0 is the overall average of all the responses. For a given set of experimental data, computer programs can determine these coefficients by such techniques as least squares regression.

If there were an interaction consideration in a model, the equation would then take the form

$$y = b_0 + b_1 x_1 + b_2 x_2 + b_{12} x_1 x_2$$

The number of terms in the equation describes the minimum number of experimental trials that are needed to determine the model. For example, the above equation has four terms; hence, a minimum of four experimental design trials are needed to calculate the coefficients. The two-level DOE significance tests described in previous chapters were to determine which of the coefficient estimates were "large enough" to affect the response (y) "significantly" when changed from a low (-1) level to a high ($+1$) level.

Center points can be added to the two-level fractional factorial design to determine the validity of the linearity assumption of the model. When using a regression program on the coded effects, the fractional factorial levels should take on symmetry values around zero (i.e., -1 and $+1$). To determine if the linearity assumption is valid, the average response of the center points can be compared to the overall average of the two-level fractional factorial experiment trials.

If the first-degree polynomial approximation does not fit the data when describing the process, a second-degree polynomial model may adequately describe the curvature of the response surface as a function of the input factors. For two factor consideration, this model takes the form

$$y = b_0 + b_1 x_1 + b_2 x_2 + b_{11} x_1^2 + b_{22} x_2^2 + b_{12} x_1 x_2$$

33.2 CENTRAL COMPOSITE DESIGN

To determine the additional coefficients of a second-degree polynomial, additional levels of the variables are needed between the end-point levels. An efficient test approach to determine the coefficients of a second-degree polynomial is to use a central composite design. Figure 33.1 shows this design for the two-factor situation.

An experiment design is said to be rotatable if the variance of the predicted response at some point is a function of only the distance of the point from the center. The central composite design is made rotatable when $[a = (F)^{1/4}]$, where F is the number of points used in the factorial part of the design. For two factors $F = 2^2 = 4$; hence $a = (4)^{1/4} = 1.414$. A useful property of the central composite design is that the additional axial points can be added to a two-level fractional factorial design as additional trials after the curvature is detected from the initial experimental data.

With a proper number of center points, the central composite design can be made such that the variance of the response at the origin is equal to the variance of the response at unit distance from the origin (i.e., a uniform precision design). This characteristic in the uniform precision design is important because it gives more protection against bias in the regression coefficients (because of the presence of third-degree and higher terms in the true surface) than does the orthogonal design. Table 33.1 shows the parameters needed to achieve a uniform precision design as a function of the number of variables within the experiment. From this table a design, for example, assessing five variables along with all two-factor interactions plus the curvature of all variables would be that shown in Table 33.2. Data are then analyzed using regression analysis techniques to determine the output response surface as a function of the input variables.

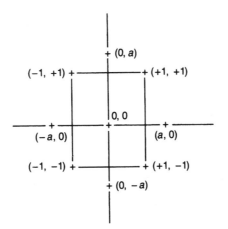

FIGURE 33.1 Central composite design for two factors.

TABLE 33.1 Uniform Precision Central Composite Rotatable Designs

Number of Variables	Number of Factorial Trials	Number of Axial Trials	Number of Center Trials	a	Total Number of Trials
2	4	4	5	1.4142	13
3	8	6	6	1.6820	20
4	16	8	7	2.0000	31
5	16	10	6	2.0000	32
6	32	12	9	2.3780	53
7	64	14	14	2.8280	92

TABLE 33.2 Response Surface Design Matrix for Five Variables

A	B	C	D	E	
+1	−1	−1	−1	+1	
+1	+1	−1	−1	−1	
+1	+1	+1	−1	+1	
+1	+1	+1	+1	−1	
−1	+1	+1	+1	+1	
+1	−1	+1	+1	+1	
−1	+1	−1	+1	−1	Fractional factorial design from
+1	−1	+1	−1	−1	Table M3
+1	+1	−1	+1	+1	
−1	+1	+1	−1	−1	
−1	−1	+1	+1	−1	
+1	−1	−1	+1	−1	
−1	+1	−1	−1	+1	
−1	−1	+1	−1	+1	
−1	−1	−1	+1	+1	
−1	−1	−1	−1	−1	
−2	0	0	0	0	
+2	0	0	0	0	
0	−2	0	0	0	
0	+2	0	0	0	
0	0	−2	0	0	Axial trials
0	0	+2	0	0	with levels
0	0	0	−2	0	consistent
0	0	0	+2	0	with
0	0	0	0	−2	Table 33.1
0	0	0	0	+2	
0	0	0	0	0	
0	0	0	0	0	
0	0	0	0	0	Center point trials
0	0	0	0	0	consistent with
0	0	0	0	0	Table 33.1
0	0	0	0	0	

Cornell (1984), Montgomery (1997), and Box et al. (1978) discuss analytical methods to then determine maximum points on the response surface using the canonical form of the equation. The coefficients of this equation can be used to describe the shape of the surface (ellipsoid, hyperboloid, etc.). An alternative approach is to understand the response surface by using a computer contour plotting program, as illustrated in the next example. From the understanding of a particular contour plot, perhaps. for example, process factors can be determined/changed to yield a desirable/improved response output that has minimal expected day-to-day variation.

33.3 EXAMPLE 33.1: RESPONSE SURFACE DESIGN

A chemical engineer desires to determine the operating conditions that maximize the yield of a process. A previous two-level factorial experiment of many considerations indicated that reaction time and reaction temperature were the parameters that should be optimized. A central composite design was chosen and yielded the responses shown in Table 33.3 (Montgomery 1997). A second-degree model can be fitted using the natural levels of the variables (e.g., time = 80) or the coded levels (e.g., time = −1). A statistical analysis of yield in terms of the coded variables is as follows:

Response Surface Regression

The analysis was done using coded variables.

TABLE 33.3 Responses in Central Composite Design

Natural Variables		Coded Variables		Responses		
				Yield	Viscosity	Molecular weight
u_1	u_2	v_1	v_2	y_1	y_2	y_3
80	170	−1	−1	76.5	62	2940
80	180	−1	1	77.0	60	3470
90	170	1	−1	78.0	66	3680
90	180	1	1	79.5	59	3890
85	175	0	0	79.9	72	3480
85	175	0	0	80.3	69	3200
85	175	0	0	80.0	68	3410
85	175	0	0	79.7	70	3290
85	175	0	0	79.8	71	3500
92.07	175	1.414	0	78.4	68	3360
77.93	175	−1.414	0	75.6	71	3020
85	182.07	0	1.414	78.5	58	3630
85	167.93	0	−1.414	77.0	57	3150

```
Estimated Regression Coefficients for y1 (yield)
```

Term	Coef	StDev	T	P
Constant	79.940	0.11909	671.264	0.000
v1 (time)	0.995	0.09415	10.568	0.000
v2 (temperature)	0.515	0.09415	5.472	0.001
v1*v1	-1.376	0.10098	-13.630	0.000
v2*v2	-1.001	0.10098	-9.916	0.000
v1*v2	0.250	0.13315	1.878	0.103

```
S = 0.2663        R-Sq = 98.3%        R-Sq(adj) = 97.0%
```

```
Analysis of Variance for y1
```

Source	DF	Seq SS	Adj SS	Adj MS	F	P
Regression	5	28.2467	28.2467	5.64934	79.67	0.000
Linear	2	10.0430	10.0430	5.02148	70.81	0.000
Square	2	17.9537	17.9537	8.97687	126.59	0.000
Interaction	1	0.2500	0.2500	0.25000	3.53	0.103
Residual Error	7	0.4964	0.4964	0.07091		
Lack-of-Fit	3	0.2844	0.2844	0.09479	1.79	0.289
Pure Error	4	0.2120	0.2120	0.05300		
Total	12	28.7431				

A statistical analysis of yield in terms of natural variables is as follows:

Response Surface Regression

```
The analysis was done using natural variables.
Estimated Regression Coefficients for y1 (yield)
```

Term	Coef	StDev	T	P
Constant	-1430.69	152.851	-9.360	0.000
u1 (time)	7.81	1.158	6.744	0.000
u2 (temperature)	13.27	1.485	8.940	0.000
u1*u1	-0.06	0.004	-13.630	0.000
u2*u2	-0.04	0.004	-9.916	0.000
u1*u2	0.01	0.005	1.878	0.103

```
S = 0.2663        R-Sq = 98.3%        R-Sq(adj) = 97.0%
```

```
Analysis of Variance for y1
```

Source	DF	Seq SS	Adj SS	Adj MS	F	P
Regression	5	28.2467	28.2467	5.64934	79.67	0.000
Linear	2	10.0430	6.8629	3.43147	48.39	0.000
Square	2	17.9537	17.9537	8.97687	126.59	0.000
Interaction	1	0.2500	0.2500	0.25000	3.53	0.103
Residual Error	7	0.4964	0.4964	0.07091		
Lack-of-Fit	3	0.2844	0.2844	0.09479	1.79	0.289
Pure Error	4	0.2120	0.2120	0.05300		
Total	12	28.7431				

From this analysis the second-degree model in terms of the coded levels of the variables is

$$\hat{y} = 79.940 + 0.995v_1 + 0.515v_2 - 1.376v_1^2 + 0.250v_1v_2 - 1.001v_2^2$$

This equates to an equation for the natural levels of

$$\hat{y} = -1430.69 + 7.81u_1 + 13.27u_2 - 0.06u_1^2 + 0.01u_1u_2 - 0.04u_2^2$$

These equations will yield the same response value for a given input data state. The advantage of using the coded levels is that the importance of each term can be compared somewhat by looking at the magnitude of the coefficients because the relative magnitude of the variable levels are brought to a single unit of measure.

When projections are made off a response surface, it is obviously important that the model fit the initial data satisfactorily. Erroneous conclusions can result where there is lack of fit. The computer analysis did not indicate that there was lack of fit; hence, the second-degree polynomial model is accepted. The natural form of this polynomial equation is shown as a contour plot in Figure 33.2 and a response surface plot in Figure 33.3.

33.4 BOX–BEHNKEN DESIGNS

When estimating the first- and second-order terms of a response surface, Box and Behnken (1960) give an alternative to a central composite design approach. In their paper the authors present a list of 10 second-order rotatable designs covering 3, 4, 5, 6, 7, 9, 10, 11, 12, and 16 variables. However, in general Box-Behnken designs are not always rotatable nor are they block orthogonal.

One reason that an experimenter may choose to use this design over a central composite design is because of physical test constraints. This design requires only three levels of each variable, as opposed to five for the central

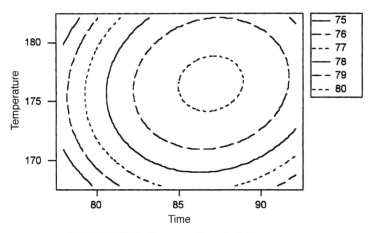

FIGURE 33.2 Contour plot of yield response.

composite design. Figure 33.4 shows the test points for this design approach given three design variables.

33.5 MIXTURE DESIGNS

The experimenter designs discussed previously in this text were for discrete and/or continuous factors, where the levels of each factor was completely independent from the other factors. However, consider a chemist who mixes three ingredients together. If the chemist wishes to increase the content of one ingredient, the percentage of another ingredient must be adjusted accord-

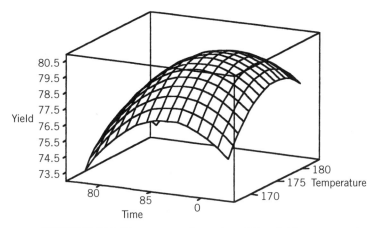

FIGURE 33.3 Response surface plot of the yield response.

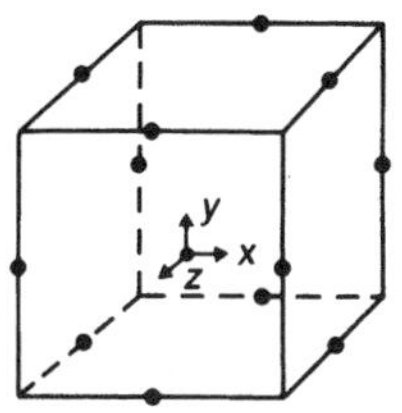

Experiment Trials		
x	y	z
+1	+1	0
+1	−1	0
−1	+1	0
−1	−1	0
+1	0	+1
+1	0	−1
−1	0	+1
−1	0	−1
0	+1	−1
0	+1	+1
0	−1	−1
0	−1	+1
0	0	0
0	0	0
0	0	0

FIGURE 33.4 Box–Behnken design space for three factors.

ingly. Mixture experiment designs are used for this situation, where the components (factors/variables) under consideration take levels that are a proportion of the whole.

For the practitioner of mixture designs, the discussion in the next few sections of this chapter explains the concepts. In practice a textbook experiment design approach to this type of problem is often not practical. Computer-generated designs and analyses are usually better for most realistic mixture problems.

In the general mixture problem the measured response depends only on the proportions of the components present in the mixture and does not depend on the total amount of the mixture. For three components this can be expressed as

$$x_1 + x_2 + x_3 = 1$$

To illustrate the application of this equation, consider that a mixture consisted of three components: A, B, and C. If component A was 20% and B was 50%, C would have to be 30% to give a total of 100% (i.e., 0.2 + 0.5 + 0.3 = 1).

When three factors were considered in a two-level full factorial experiment (2^3), the factor space of interest is a cube. However, a three-component mixture experiment is represented by an equilateral triangle. The coordinate system for these problems is called a *simplex coordinate system*. Figure 33.5 shows the triangle for three components whose proportions are x_1, x_2, and x_3. A four-component would similarly take on the space of a tetrahedron.

With three components, coordinates are plotted on equilateral triangular graph paper that has lines parallel to the three sides of the triangle. Each

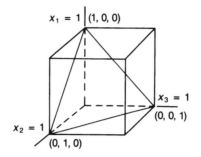

FIGURE 33.5 Three-component simplex factor space. [From Cornell (1983), with permission.]

vertex of the triangle represents 100% of one of the components in the mixture. The lines away from a vertex represent decreasing amounts of the component described by that vertex. The center of the equilateral triangle represents, for example, a mixture with equal proportions (i.e., 1/3, 1/3, 1/3) from each of the components.

In a designed mixture experiment, several combinations of components are chosen within the spatial extremes defined by the number of components (e.g., an equilateral triangle for three components). Within one experiment all possible combinations of the components can be considered as viable candidates to determine an "optimal" response. However, in many situations some combinations of the components are not reasonable or may even cause a dangerous response (e.g., an explosion).

Within this chapter, simplex lattice designs will be used when all combinations of the components are under consideration, while extreme vertices designs will be used for the situation when there are restrictions placed in the test on the proportions of the components.

33.6 SIMPLEX LATTICE DESIGNS FOR EXPLORING THE WHOLE SIMPLEX REGION

The simplex lattice designs (Scheffé 1958) in this section address problems where there are no restrictions on the limits of the percentages when determining the total 100% composition.

A simplex lattice designs for q components consists of points defined by the coordinates (q, m), where the proportions assumed by each component take $m + 1$ equally spaced values from 0 to 1 and all possible combinations of the components are considered. Figure 33.6 illustrates pictorially the spatial test consideration of several lattice design alternatives for three and four components. Cornell (1983) notes that a general form of regression function that can be fitted easily to data collected at the points of a (q, m) simplex lattice

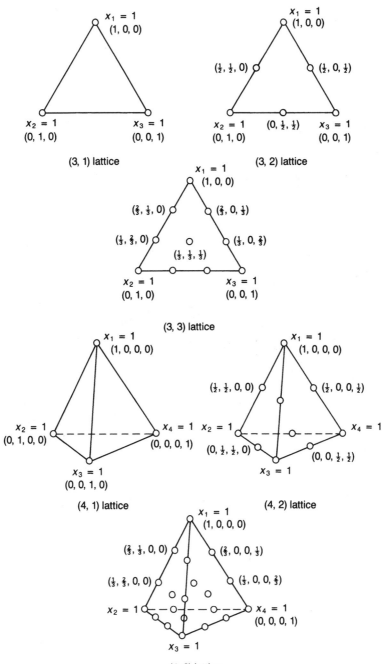

FIGURE 33.6 Some simplex lattice designs for three and four components. [From Cornell (1983), with permission.]

is the canonical form of the polynomial. This form is then derived by applying the restriction that the terms in a standard polynomial of a mixture design sum to 1. The simplified expression yields for three components the first-degree model form

$$y = b_1 x_1 + b_2 x_2 + b_3 x_3$$

The second-degree model form is

$$y = b_1 x_1 + b_2 x_2 + b_3 x_3 + b_{12} x_1 x_2 + b_{13} x_{13} + b_{23} x_2 x_3$$

The special cubic polynomial form is

$$y = b_1 x_1 + b_2 x_2 + b_3 x_3 + b_{12} x_1 x_2 + b_{13} x_1 x_3 + b_{23} x_2 x_3 + b_{123} x_1 x_2 x_3$$

33.7   EXAMPLE 33.2: SIMPLEX-LATTICE DESIGNED MIXTURE EXPERIMENT

Any one combination of three solvents could be most effective in the solvent rinse of a contaminating by-product (Diamond 1989). A (3, 2) simplex lattice with a center point was chosen for the initial evaluation. The design proportions with the by-product responses are shown in Table 33.4.

A plot of the results is shown in Figure 33.7. A regression analysis for mixtures, which is available on some statistical software packages, could be conducted; however, in some cases, such as this example, the conclusions are obvious. For this example the best result is the center point composition; however, there is curvature and a still better response is likely in the vicinity of this point.

To reduce the by-product content amount of 2.2%, more experimental trials are needed near this point to determine a better process optimum. Diamond (1989) chose to consider adding the following additional trials using the noted rationale. These points are spatially shown in Figure 33.8, where the lines

TABLE 33.4 Design of Proportions of Solvents, and By-product Response

Trial	Methanol	Acetone	Trichloroethylene	By-product (%)
1	1	0	0	6.2
2	0	1	0	8.4
3	0	0	1	3.9
4	½	½	0	7.4
5	½	0	½	2.8
6	0	½	½	6.1
7[a]	⅓	⅓	⅓	2.2

[a] Center point

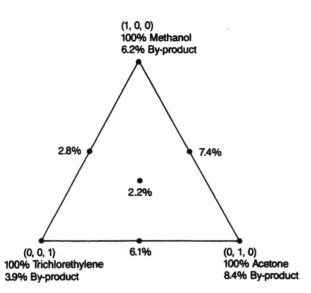

FIGURE 33.7 Plot of initial test results. [From Diamond (1989), with permission.]

decrease in magnitude of 0.05 for a variable from an initial proportion value of 1.0 at the apex. Table 33.5 illustrates these trials and their rationales.

The results from these experimental trials are seen in Table 33.6. A plot of the data and an estimate of the response surface is shown in Figure 33.9. The apparent minimum (shown as the point with no number in Figure 33.9) along with the results from an additional trial setting at this value is as follows:

Trial	Methonal	Acetone	Trichloroethylene	By-product (%)
13	0.33	0.15	0.52	0.45

Additional simplex design trials around this point could yield a smaller amount of by-product. However, if the by-product percentage is "low enough," additional experimental trials might not serve any economic purpose.

33.8   MIXTURE DESIGNS WITH PROCESS VARIABLES

Consider the situation where a response is not only a function of a mixture but also a function of its process variables (e.g., cooking temperature and cooking time). For the situation where there are three components to a mixture and there are three process variables, the complex simplex-centroid design takes the form shown in Figure 33.10.

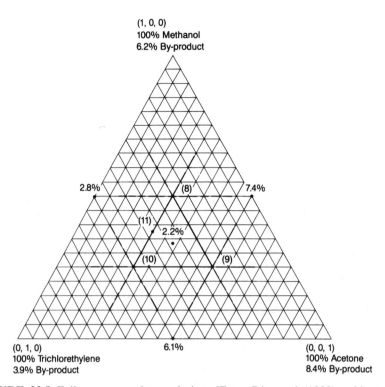

FIGURE 33.8 Follow-up experiment design. [From Diamond (1989), with permission.]

In general, the number of experimental trial possibilities can get very large when there are many variable considerations. Cornell and Gorman (1984) discuss fractional factorial design alternatives. Cornell (1990) discusses the embedding of mixture experiments inside factorial experiments. Algorithm designs, which are discussed in a later section of this chapter, are another test alternative which can reduce the number of test trials.

TABLE 33.5 Experimental Points and Their Rationales

Experimental Point Number	Rationale
8, 9, 10	(3,1) simplex lattice design vertices around the best response with the noted diagonal relationship to the original data points.
11	Because point 5 is the second best result, another data point was added in that direction.
12	Repeat of the treatment combination that was the best in the previous experiment and is now the centroid of this follow-up experiment.

TABLE 33.6 Results of Experimental Trials

Trial	Methanol	Acetone	Trichloroethylene	By-product (%)
8	½	¼	¼	3.3
9	¼	½	¼	4.8
10	¼	¼	½	1.4
11	⅜	¼	⅜	1.2
12	⅓	⅓	⅓	2.4

33.9 EXAMPLE 33.3: MIXTURE EXPERIMENT WITH PROCESS VARIABLES

The data in Table 33.7 is the average of replicated texture reading in kilogram force required to puncture fish patty surfaces (Cornell 1981, Cornell and Gorman 1984, Gorman and Cornell 1982) that were prepared under process conditions that had code values of -1 and $+1$ for

z_1: cooking temperature ($-1 = 375°F$, $+1 = 425°F$)

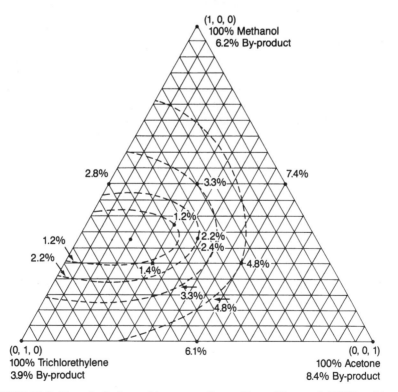

FIGURE 33.9 Plot of all data with contour lines. [From Diamond (1989), with permission.]

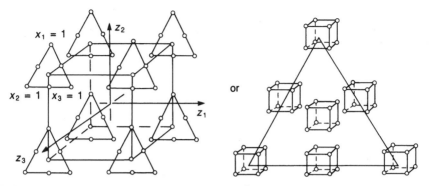

FIGURE 33.10 Complete simplex Centroid $\times$ 2^3 factorial design. [From Cornell and Gorman (1984), with permission.]

z_2: cooking time (-1 = 25 min, $+1$ = 40 min)
z_3: deep fat frying time (-1 = 25 sec, $+1$ = 40 sec)

The patty was composed of three types of fish that took on composition ratios of 0, 1/3, 1/2, or 1. The fish designations are

x_1: mullet
x_2: sheepshead
x_3: croaker

The desired range of fish texture (in the noted scaled units) for customer satisfaction is between 2.0 and 3.5; however, other characteristics (not discussed here) were also considered as responses within the actual experiment.

TABLE 33.7 Results of Mixture Experiment with Process Variables

						Texture Readings			
Coded Process Variables						Mixture Composition (x_1, x_2, x_3)			
z_1	z_2	z_3	(1,0,0)	(0,1,0)	(0,0,1)	($\frac{1}{2}$,$\frac{1}{2}$,0)	($\frac{1}{2}$,0,$\frac{1}{2}$)	(0,$\frac{1}{2}$,$\frac{1}{2}$)	($\frac{1}{3}$,$\frac{1}{3}$,$\frac{1}{3}$)
-1	-1	-1	1.84	0.67	1.51	1.29	1.42	1.16	1.59
1	-1	-1	2.86	1.10	1.60	1.53	1.81	1.50	1.68
-1	1	-1	3.01	1.21	2.32	1.93	2.57	1.83	1.94
1	1	-1	4.13	1.67	2.57	2.26	3.15	2.22	2.60
-1	-1	1	1.65	0.58	1.21	1.18	1.45	1.07	1.41
1	-1	1	2.32	0.97	2.12	1.45	1.93	1.28	1.54
-1	1	1	3.04	1.16	2.00	1.85	2.39	1.60	2.05
1	1	1	4.13	1.30	2.75	2.06	2.82	2.10	2.32

A computer analysis of these data yielded the coefficient estimates shown in Table 33.8. The standard error (SE) for this example was determined using all the original data and was taken from Cornell (1981).

In the data analysis of the averages, there were 54 data inputs and the same number of estimates; hence, a regression analysis cannot give any significance test on the variables. A half-normal probability plot of the effects is not mathematically helpful because the SE is not consistent between the estimates.

However, using the standard error terms (where the number of degrees of freedom for error is 56; i.e., $v_{error} = 56$) that were noted in Cornell (1981), the asterisk shows those items that are thought to be different from zero. To illustrate this, the effect level for significance for a variable with an SE of 0.05 is as shown below (see Table E for interpolated t value):

Effect level criterion $= (SE)(t_{\alpha;v}) = (SE) (t_{0.01;56}) = 0.05 (2.667) = 0.13$

Any of the effects noted in the table that have an SE of 0.05 are significant at the 0.01 level if their magnitude is greater that 0.13. A highly significant probability level of 0.01 for this problem is appropriate because the parameter effect estimates are not independent; hence, the individual t tests are not independent.

Various characteristics of fish patty hardness can be determined by evaluating the main effect and interaction considerations in the preceding table; however, another alternative to evaluate the characteristics is to isolate the individual blend characteristics at each of the eight process variable treatments.

The equation to consider, for example, is where $z_1 = -1$, $z_2 = -1$, and $z_3 = -1$ is

$$y = a_1 x_1 + a_2 x_1 z_1 + \cdots = 2.87 x_1 + 0.49 x_1 (-1) \cdots$$

Various x_1, x_2, and x_3 values are then substituted to create a contour plot in a simplex coordinate system for each of the eight variable treatments, as

TABLE 33.8 Coefficient Estimates from Computer Analysis

	Mean	z_1	z_2	z_3	$z_1 z_2$	$z_1 z_3$	$z_2 z_3$	$z_1 z_2 z_3$	SE
x_1	2.87[a]	0.49[a]	0.71[a]	−0.09	0.07	−0.05	0.10	0.04	0.05
x_2	1.08[a]	0.18[a]	0.25[a]	−0.08	−0.03	−0.05	−0.03	−0.04	0.05
x_3	2.01[a]	0.25[a]	0.40[a]	0.01	0.00	0.17*	−0.05	−0.04	0.05
$x_1 x_2$	−1.14[a]	−0.81[a]	−0.59	0.10	−0.06	0.14	−0.19	−0.09	0.23
$x_1 x_3$	−1.00[a]	−0.54	−0.05	−0.03	−0.06	−0.27	−0.43	−0.12	0.23
$x_2 x_3$	0.20	−0.14	0.07	−0.19	0.23	−0.25	0.12	0.27	0.23
$x_1 x_2 x_3$	3.18	0.07	−1.41	0.11	1.74	−0.71	1.77	−1.33	1.65

[a] Individual estimates thought to be significant.

noted in Figure 33.11. The shaded area in this figure shows when the desirable response range of 2.0 to 3.5 (nominal = 2.75) was achieved. This figure illustrates that a $z_2 = 1$ level (i.e., 40 mm cooking time) is desirable; however, there are many other combinations of the other parameters at $z_2 = 1$ that can yield a satisfactory texture reading. However, to maximize customer satisfaction, effort should be directed toward achieving the nominal criterion on the average with minimum variability between batches.

At this point in the analysis, perhaps other issues should be considered. For example, it may be desirable to make the composition of the fish patty so that its sensitivity is minimized relative to deep fat frying time. In the "real world" it may be relatively easy to control the cooking temperature; however, a person frying patties in a fast-food restaurant may be too busy to remove the patties immediately when the timer sounds. To address this concern, it appears that a $z_1 = -1$ level (i.e., 375°F cooking temperature) is most desirable with a relative high concentration of mullet in the fish patty composition.

Other considerations to make, for example, when determining the "best" composition and variable levels are economics (e.g., cost of each type of fish) and other experimental output response surface plots (e.g., taste evaluation of fish patties). To aid in the decision-making process, a similar output to that

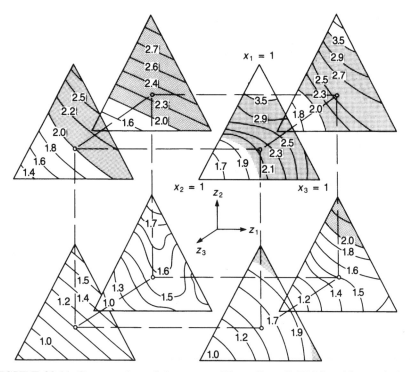

FIGURE 33.11 Contour plots of the texture. [From Cornell (1981), with permission.]

of Figure 33.11 could be made for a weighted (by importance) mathematical combination of the several responses.

33.10   EXTREME VERTICES MIXTURE DESIGNS

Extreme vertices designs can take on most of the nice properties of the previously discussed matrix designs (Diamond 1989). This design is explained in the following example.

33.11   EXAMPLE 33.4: EXTREME VERTICES MIXTURE EXPERIMENT

A chemist wishes to develop a floor wax product. The following range of proportions of three ingredients are under consideration along with the noted proportion percentage limitations. The response to this experiment takes on several values: level of shine, scuff resistance, and so forth.

Wax: 0–0.25 (i.e., 0%–25%)
Resin: 0–0.20 (i.e., 0%–20%)
Polymer: 0.70–0.90 (i.e., 70%–90%)

Again, mixture experiment trial combinations are determined by using a simplex coordinate system. This relationship is noted in Figure 33.12, where the lines leaving a vertex decrease in magnitude of 0.05 proportion from an initial proportion value of 1.

The space of interest is noted by the polygon shown in the figure. Table 33.9 shows test trials for the vertices along with a center point. The logic used in Example 33.1 for follow-up experiments can similarly be applied to this problem in an attempt to better optimize the process using additional trials.

33.12   COMPUTER-GENERATED MIXTURE DESIGNS/ANALYSES

The concepts behind algorithm design were introduced by Wynn (1970) and Fedorov (1972). With these designs a computer program creates a list of possible trials to fit the model, calculates the standard deviation of the value predicted by the polynomial for each trial, and picks the trial with the largest standard deviation as the next trial to include in the design. The coefficients of the polynomial are then recalculated using this new trial and the process is repeated. The designs that are best are those having the largest variance proportional to the number of terms in the polynomial (B. Wheeler 1989).

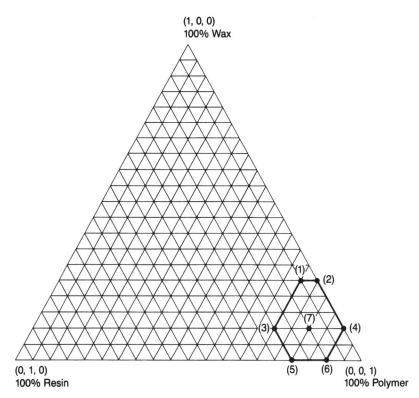

FIGURE 33.12 Extreme vertices design.

Mixture design problems typically have physical constraints that make "textbook designs" impractical. Algorithm designs are particularly helpful for mixture design problems. A practitioner that needs to perform a mixture experiment should consider utilizing a commercially available computer program that both creates an algorithm design and can analyze the results.

TABLE 33.9 Test Trial Combinations

Trial	Wax (x_1)	Resin (x_2)	Polymer (x_3)	Response (Y)
1	0.25	0.05	0.70	y_1
2	0.25	0	0.75	y_2
3	0.10	0.20	0.70	y_3
4	0.10	0	0.90	y_4
5	0	0.20	0.80	y_5
6	0	0.10	0.90	y_6
7^a	0.10	0.10	0.80	y_7

[a] Center point.

The following example illustrates the application of a computer program to generate a design matrix and then analyze the results.

33.13   EXAMPLE 33.5: COMPUTER-GENERATED MIXTURE DESIGN/ANALYSIS

An improvement is needed in the paste used to attach electronic components when manufacturing surface-mounted printed circuit cards. Viscosity of the paste was one response that was desired as a function of the proportion composition of the five mixture components that had the following ranges:

Component	Proportion
Comp1	0.57–0.68
Comp2	0.15–0.21
Comp3	0.03–0.08
Comp4	0.05–0.10
Comp5	0.04–0.06

ECHIP, a computer program (B. Wheeler 1989), was used to create an algorithm design, given the above constraints. The mixture proportions for this resulting design along with the experimental viscosity measurement responses (in units of pascal-seconds) for the trials are shown in Table 33.10.

From the analysis, three variables were found to be significant (Comp1, Comp2, and Comp3). Figure 33.13 shows three pictorial views that were then generated to better understand the relationship of these variables, where Comp4 was set to a proportion of 0.077 and Comp5 was set to a proportion of 0.050. It should be noted that the program highlights the bounds of the levels of the variables used in the experiment so that the interpreter of the plots will know when to exercise caution because the predictions are extrapolated.

33.14   ADDITIONAL RESPONSE SURFACE DESIGN CONSIDERATIONS

When no linear relationship exists between the regressors, they are said to be orthogonal. For these situations the following inferences can be made relatively easily:

- Estimation and/or prediction.
- Identification of relative effects of regressor variables.
- Selection of a set of variables for the model.

TABLE 33.10 Input Variable Levels and Viscosity Response

	Comp1	Comp2	Comp3	Comp4	Comp5	Viscosity
1[a]	0.5700	0.2100	0.0800	0.1000	0.0400	7.6
2	0.6800	0.1500	0.0600	0.0500	0.0600	32.6
3	0.6700	0.2100	0.0300	0.0500	0.0400	20.5
4	0.6800	0.1500	0.0300	0.1000	0.0400	13.9
5	0.6000	0.2100	0.0300	0.1000	0.0600	12.2
6	0.6000	0.2100	0.0800	0.0500	0.0600	13.6
7	0.6100	0.1500	0.0800	0.1000	0.0600	15.8
8	0.6800	0.1500	0.0800	0.0500	0.0400	21.4
9	0.6200	0.2100	0.0300	0.1000	0.0400	12.5
10	0.6200	0.2100	0.0800	0.0500	0.0400	14.8
11	0.6300	0.1500	0.0800	0.1000	0.0400	7.0
12	0.6650	0.1800	0.0300	0.0650	0.0600	19.3
13	0.6750	0.1800	0.0550	0.0500	0.0400	15.2
14	0.6200	0.2100	0.0550	0.0750	0.0400	11.6
15	0.6600	0.2100	0.0300	0.0500	0.0500	16.4
16	0.5700	0.2100	0.0800	0.0800	0.0600	7.8
17	0.6600	0.1500	0.0300	0.1000	0.0600	19.3
18	0.5700	0.2100	0.0600	0.1000	0.0600	9.6
19	0.5900	0.1800	0.0800	0.1000	0.0500	6.8
20	0.6800	0.1500	0.0450	0.0750	0.0500	20.5
1[a]	0.5700	0.2100	0.0800	0.1000	0.0400	7.8
2	0.6800	0.1500	0.0600	0.0500	0.0600	35.5
3	0.6700	0.2100	0.0300	0.0500	0.0400	20.7
4	0.6800	0.1500	0.0300	0.1000	0.0400	12.6
5	0.6000	0.2100	0.0300	0.1000	0.0600	11.0

[a]NOTE: Some variable level combinations are repeated.

However, inferences from the analysis of response surface designs can yield conclusions that may be misleading because of dependencies between the regressors. When near-linear dependencies exist between the regressors, multicollinearity is said to be prevalent. Other texts [e.g., Montgomery and Peck (1982)] discuss diagnostic procedures for this problem (e.g., variance inflation factor) along with other procedures that are used to better understand the output from regression analyses (e.g., detecting influential observations).

Additional "textbook" design alternatives to that of the central composite and Box–Behnken designs are discussed in Cornell (1984), Montgomery (1997), and Khuri and Cornell (1987). "Algorithm" designs can also be applied to nonmixture designs, as discussed in B. Wheeler (1989), where, as previously noted, algorithm designs are "optimized" to fit a particular model (e.g., linear or quadratic) with a given set of factor considerations.

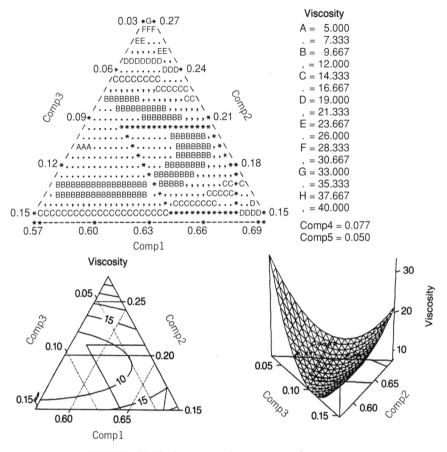

FIGURE 33.13 Contour and response surface outputs.

33.15 S⁴ ASSESSMENT

If there are several response outputs to the trials, it may be necessary to compromise the optimum solution for each response to get an overall optimization. Several response outputs can be collectively weighted to yield a combined response output for consideration within the analyses.

An overall experiment implementation strategy for continuous-response variables can be to first implement a linear model design (i.e., a two-level fractional factorial design for a nonmixture design) with center points. The center points are used to determine if there is adequate fit. If the model does not fit well and an "optimum" response is needed, then additional trials can be added in consideration of higher-order model terms (e.g., second-order polynomial). After the initial test, factor considerations that were found not important can be removed to make the response surface experiment more manageable in size.

B. Wheeler (1989) notes that "boldness" should be used when choosing the levels of the variables so either the desired maximum or minimum is likely to be contained within the response surface design. When building a response surface, a basic strategy is first to choose bold factor levels that are consistent with a simple model and then make lack-of-fit tests. If the model does not fit, additional trials can then be added to the original design consistent with the variable levels needed to add higher-order terms to the model.

Perhaps an evaluation of the magnitude of the center points relative to the fractional factorial end points indicate that the initial selection of the magnitude of the variables did not have enough "boldness" to contain the optimum value. The surface outside these bounds can be quite different than the extrapolated value. A multiexperiment response surface test strategy may be needed to evaluate possible process improvements outside the bounds initially considered within the experiment. The variable levels to consider in the next experiment can be determined by evaluating the direction for improvement [i.e., the path of steepest ascent of the response curve, assuming that higher numbers are better (Box et al. 1978, Cornell 1984, Montgomery 1997)].

33.16   EXERCISES

1. *Catapult exercise:* Create, conduct, and analyze a central composite design of the catapult process using three factors. Discuss and document what was learned from the experiment relative to the catapult process and execution of the experiment.

2. Create a three-factor central composite response surface design.

3. Create a three-factor Box–Behnken response surface design.

4. Conduct a response surface analysis of the viscosity response shown in Table 33.3.

5. Conduct a response surface analysis of the molecular weight response shown in Table 33.3.

6. Describe how the techniques within this chapter are useful and can be applied to S^4 projects.

PART V

S⁴ CONTROL PHASE

This part (Chapters 34–44) addresses process control. Some of the chapters within this part expand upon the control charting techniques described earlier. The reason for splitting the control chart chapters into two different portions of the book is that the control charts described within this section are not used as frequently as the previously described control charts and also could be covered during the fourth week of a four-week S⁴ training session.

In addition this part also describes engineering process control along with pre-control and error-proofing (poka-yoke). Other tools and techniques described within this part are often not associated with a Six Sigma program. The chapters on reliability, pass/fail functional testing and application examples have broader implementation possibilities than often initially perceived. However, as with any training, the instructor needs to determine the needs of attendees when selecting what should be covered within an S⁴ workshop.

34

SHORT-RUN AND TARGET CONTROL CHARTS

Often a control chart is thought to be a technique to control the characteristics or dimensions of products, the thought being that a controlled process would yield products that are more consistent. However the dimension of a part, for example is the end result of a process. It is typically more useful to focus on key product characteristics and their related process parameters rather than focus on a single product characteristic. Brainstorming techniques can help with this selection activity. The most effective statistical process control (SPC) program utilizes the minimum number of charts that at the same time maximizes the usefulness of the charts.

General application categories for short run include the following:

- Insufficient parts in a single production run
- Small lot sizes of many different parts
- Completion time that is too short for the collection and analysis of data, even though the production size is large

However, someone might initially think that control charting techniques are *not* useful to their situation for one or more of these categories. If we examine the wording of these three application scenarios, we note that focus is given to product measurements. Thoughts about the applicability of control charting to these situations changes when we use a methodology that bridges these product scenarios to process measurements. The described control charting techniques within this chapter can help us make this transition. Future part numbers from a process can benefit from the work of today on that process (in the area of *wisely* applied control charting and process improvement activity). The *wise* application of SPC techniques to the above categories can reduce future "fire fighting" through the "fire prevention" activities of today.

Manufacturing and business process applications for short run charts include the following:

- Solder thickness for circuit boards
- Inside diameter of extrusion parts
- Cycle time for purchase orders
- Delivery time for parts

The following should be considered during the initial phases of a process. If standard control limits are used when there are only a small number of subgroups, there is a greater likelihood of erroneously rejecting a process that is actually in control. Pyzdek (1993) includes tables that can be used to adjust control limits when there are a small number of subgroups. The illustrative examples included within this text do not consider this adjustment.

34.1 DIFFERENCE CHART (TARGET CHART AND NOMINAL CHART)

Difference charts (also known as target chart and nominal chart) permit the visualization of underlying process even though it has short runs of differing products. The nominal value that is to be subtracted from each value that is observed is specific to each product. This value can either be a historic grand mean for each product or a product target value.

Specification targets depend upon the type of specification. Symmetrical bilateral tolerances such as 1.250 ± 0.005 would have the nominal value as the target. Unilateral tolerances such as 1.000 maximum could have any desired value—for example, 0.750.

Historical targets focus on the actual target value of the process with less emphasis on specifications. The definition of historical target is the average output of the process. Applications include situations where the target value is preferred over the specification or there is a single specification (maximum or minimum) limit.

General application rules of the difference chart are as follows:

- Constant subgroup size
- Twenty data points for control limits
- Same type of measurement
- Similar part-to-part range

If the average ranges for the products are dramatically different or the types of measurements are different, it is better to use a Z chart.

34.2   EXAMPLE 34.1: TARGET CHART

Possible sources for the following set of data are as follows: the length of three part types after a machining operation, the number of days late for differing order types, and the thickness of solder paste on a printed circuit board. Table 34.1 shows the measurements from three parts designated as "a," "b," and "c" that have differing targets. The subgroup measurements for each part is designated as *M1*, *M2*, and *M3*. Measurement shifts from the target are designated as *M1* shift, *M2* shift, and *M3* shift. The methods to calculate these control chart is similar to typical $\bar{x}$ and R charts.

The control chart in Figure 34.1 indicates that the process is in control. Process capability assessments could also be made from this data.

34.3   Z CHART (STANDARDIZED VARIABLES CONTROL CHART)

A plot of the standard values (Z) can be a useful control chart for some situations. With this chart, multiple processes can be examined on the same chart. For example, the hardness, profile, and surface finish can all be tracked on the same chart. A chart can even be set up to track a part as it goes through its manufacturing operation. This charting technique can be used to monitor the same chart measurements that have different units of measure and standard deviations. The control limits are also fixed so they never need recomputing (the plot points are standardized to the limits, typically ± 3).

However, caution should be used when applying these charts because more calculations are required for each point, they require frequent updating of historical values from the processes, the value that is tracked on the chart (Z value) is not the unit of measure (e.g., dimension of a part), and the user can become distant from individual processes.

This charting technique are based on the transformation

$$Z = \frac{\text{Sample statistic} - \text{Process average}}{\text{Process standard deviation}}$$

The methodology can apply to both attribute and continuous data; however, only the *ZmR* chart will be exemplified here.

Short-run charts can pool and standardize data in various ways. The most general way assumes that each part or batch produced by a process has a unique average and standard deviation. If the average and standard deviation

TABLE 34.1 Target Control Chart Data and Calculations

Sequence	Part	Target	M1	M2	M3	M1 Shift	M2 Shift	M3 Shift	$\bar{x}$	Range
1	a	3.250	3.493	3.496	3.533	0.243	0.246	0.283	0.257	0.040
2	a	3.250	3.450	3.431	3.533	0.200	0.181	0.283	0.221	0.102
3	b	5.500	6.028	5.668	5.922	0.528	0.168	0.422	0.373	0.360
4	b	5.500	5.639	5.690	5.634	0.139	0.190	0.134	0.154	0.056
5	b	5.500	5.790	5.757	5.735	0.290	0.257	0.235	0.261	0.055
6	b	5.500	5.709	5.743	5.661	0.209	0.243	0.161	0.204	0.082
7	c	7.750	8.115	7.992	7.956	0.365	0.242	0.206	0.271	0.159
8	c	7.750	7.885	8.023	8.077	0.135	0.273	0.327	0.245	0.192
9	c	7.750	7.932	8.078	7.958	0.182	0.328	0.208	0.239	0.146
10	c	7.750	8.142	7.860	7.934	0.392	0.110	0.184	0.229	0.282
11	c	7.750	7.907	7.951	7.947	0.157	0.201	0.197	0.185	0.044
12	c	7.750	7.905	7.943	8.091	0.155	0.193	0.341	0.230	0.186

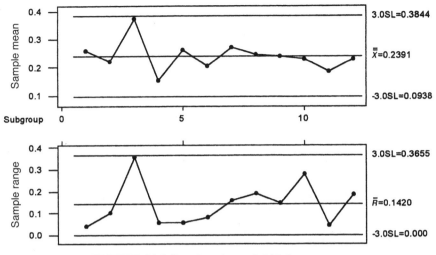

FIGURE 34.1 $\bar{x}$ and R chart of shift from target.

can be obtained, the process data can be standardized by subtracting the mean and dividing the result by the standard deviation. When using a *ZmR* chart consider the following when determining standard deviation:

- When all output has the same variance regardless of size of measurement, consider using a pooled estimate of the standard deviation across all runs and parts to obtain a common standard deviation estimate.
- When the variance increases fairly constantly as the measurement size increases, consider using a natural log transformation to stabilize variation.
- When runs of a particular part or product have the same variance, consider using an estimate that combines all runs of the same part or product to estimate standard deviation.
- When you cannot assume all runs for a particular product or part have the same variance, consider using an estimate for standard deviation from each run independently.

34.4   EXAMPLE 34.2: *ZmR* CHART

The following individual observations were taken in a paper mill for different grades of paper which are made in short runs (Minitab 1998):

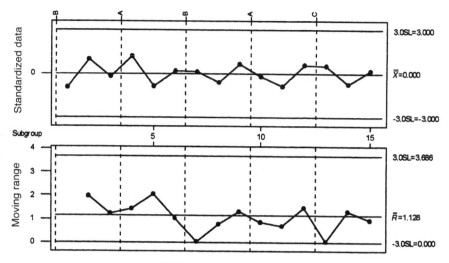

FIGURE 34.2 *ZmR* chart.

Sequence	Grade	Thickness
1	B	1.435
2	B	1.572
3	B	1.486
4	A	1.883
5	A	1.715
6	A	1.799
7	B	1.511
8	B	1.457
9	B	1.548
10	A	1.768
11	A	1.711
12	A	1.832
13	C	1.427
14	C	1.344
15	C	1.404

The *ZmR* chart shown in Figure 34.2 was calculated where standard deviation was determine by pooling all runs of same part. This chart shows no out of control condition.

34.5 EXERCISES

1. Create a difference chart for the following set of data (Wheeler 1991):

Sample	Product	Target	Value	Sample	Product	Target	Value	Sample	Product	Target	Value
1	A	35	33	18	B	22	22	35	B	24	24
2	A	35	37	19	A	33	33	36	B	23	23
3	B	24	24	20	A	36	36	37	A	34	34
4	A	35	35	21	A	38	38	38	A	34	34
5	B	24	22	22	B	22	22	39	A	34	34
6	B	24	23	23	B	21	21	40	B	21	21
7	B	24	25	24	B	23	23	41	B	23	23
8	B	24	23	25	A	35	35	42	A	34	34
9	A	35	32	26	B	26	26	43	A	30	30
10	A	35	34	27	A	35	35	44	B	22	22
11	A	35	33	28	B	24	24	45	B	25	25
12	A	35	37	29	A	33	33	46	A	35	35
13	B	24	26	30	B	21	21	47	A	36	36
14	A	35	36	31	A	35	35	48	A	37	37
15	A	35	35	32	B	27	27	49	A	35	35
16	B	24	23	33	B	26	26	50	B	25	25
17	B	24	26	34	B	25	25				

2. Create a *ZmR* chart for the data in Example 34.2 with the additional knowledge that variation in the process is proportional to thickness of paper produced.

3. Describe how the techniques within this chapter are useful and can be applied to S^4 projects.

35

OTHER CONTROL
CHARTING ALTERNATIVES

Described within this chapter are the three-way control chart and cumulative sum (CUSUM) control chart.

The three-way control chart is useful to track both within and between part variability. One application example is that an electrical component has many leads. An important criterion to the customer is that the leads should not be bent. Variability for bent leads has both within and between part variability. Another application is the flatness readings that are made when manufacturing an aircraft cargo door. Flatness measurements that are taken at several points across a door has both within part and between part variability.

An alternative to Shewhart control charts is the CUSUM control chart. CUSUM charts can detect small process shifts faster than Shewhart control charts.

35.1 THREE-WAY CONTROL CHART (MONITORING WITHIN AND BETWEEN PART VARIABILITY)

Consider that a part is sampled once every hour and that five readings are made at specific locations within the part. Not only can there be hour-to-hour part variability, but also the measurements at the five locations within a part can be consistently different in all parts. One particular location, for example, might consistently produce either the largest or smallest measurement.

For this situation the within-sample standard deviation no longer estimates random error. Instead this standard deviation is estimating both random error and location effect. The result from this is an inflated standard deviation which causes control limits that are too wide, and the plot position of most points are very close to the centerline. An XmR–R(between/within) chart can solve this problem through the creation of three separate evaluations of process variation:

The first two charts are an individuals chart and a moving-range chart of the mean from each sample. Moving ranges between the consecutive means are used to determine the control limits. The distribution of the sample means will be related to random error. The moving range will estimate the standard distribution of the sample means, which is similar to estimating just the random error component. Using only the between-sample component of variation, these two charts in conjunction track both process location and process variation. The third chart is an R chart of the original measurements. This chart tracks the within-sample component of variation.

The combination of the three charts provides a methodology of assessing the stability of process location, between-sample component of variation, and within-sample component of variation.

35.2   EXAMPLE 35.1: THREE-WAY CONTROL CHART

Plastic film is coated onto paper. A set of three samples are taken at the end of each roll. The coating weight for each of these samples is shown in Table 35.1 (Wheeler 1995a).

Figure 35.1 shows the three-way control chart. The individuals chart for subgroup means shows roll-to-roll coating weights to be out of control. Something happening within this process is allowing film thickness to vary excessively. The sawtooth pattern within the moving-range chart is suggesting that larger changes in film thickness tend to occur every other roll. The sample-range chart is indicating stability between rolls; however, the magnitude of this positional variation is larger than the average moving range between rolls (an opportunity for improvement).

35.3   CUSUM CHART (CUMULATIVE SUM OF MEASUREMENTS)

An alternative to Shewhart control charts is the CUSUM control chart. CUSUM charts can detect small process shifts faster than Shewhart control charts. The form of a CUSUM charts can be "V mask" or "decision intervals." The decision intervals approach will be discussed in this text.

The following scenario is for the consideration where smaller numbers are better (single-sided case). For a double-sided situation, two single-sided intervals are run concurrently. The three parameters considered in CUSUM analyses are n, k, and h, where n is the sample size of the subgroup, k is the reference value, and h is the decision interval.

TABLE 35.1 Three-Way Control Chart Data of Film Coating Weights

								Roll Number							
Position	1	2	3	4	5	6	7	8	9	10	11	12	13	14	15
Near side	269	274	268	280	288	278	306	303	306	283	279	285	274	265	269
Middle	306	275	291	277	288	288	284	292	292	303	300	279	278	278	276
Far side	279	302	308	306	298	313	308	307	307	297	299	293	297	282	286

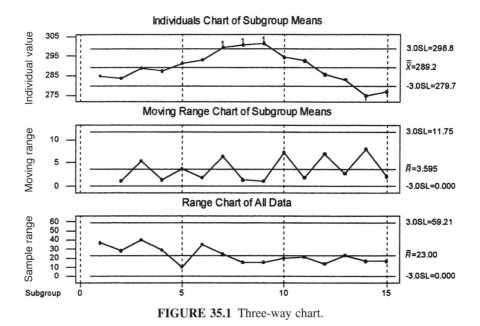

FIGURE 35.1 Three-way chart.

Consider a situation where it is desirable for a process to operate at a target value μ [an acceptable quality level (AQL)] with desired protection against an upper shift of the mean to a reject quality level (RQL). The chart is obtained by plotting s_m, the CUSUM value for the mth subgroup:

$$s_m = \sum_{i=1}^{m} (\bar{x}_i - k)$$

where $\bar{x}_i$ the average of the ith subgroup of a total m subgroups and k is the reference value, which is usually chosen to be halfway between the AQL and RQL values.

This equation is written in a one-sided form where only high numbers can cause problems, the process is assumed to be in control, and no chart even needs to be generated if the values for $\bar{x}_i$ are less than k. However, whenever s_m exceeds h, the process should be investigated to determine if a problem exists within the process. The procedure to determine h is discussed later in this section. Note that for a two-sided decision interval two single-sided intervals are examined concurrently (one for the upper limit and one for the lower limit).

CUSUM charting is not in general a direct substitute for Shewhart charting because this procedure often tests the process to a quantifiable shift in the process mean or directly to acceptable/rejectable limits determined from specifications or from a pre-production DOE test. Because of this direct comparison to limits, the CUSUM chart setup procedure differs from that of a Shewhart chart.

When samples are taken frequently within a process and tested against a criterion, there are two types of sampling problems. First, when the threshold to detect problems is large, small process perturbations and shifts can take a "long" time to detect. Second when many samples are taken within a process, eventually false alarms will occur because of chance. The design of a CUSUM chart addresses these problems directly using average run length (ARL) as a design input. where L_r is the ARL at the reject quality level (RQL) and L_a is the ARL at the accept quality level (AQL).

When first considering a CUSUM test procedure, the selection of L_a and L_r values can appear to be difficult. Items to consider when selecting these parameters are as follows:

1. High frequency of sampling. (For example, L_r should usually be higher with a high-volume process that is checked hourly than with a process that is checked monthly.)
2. Low frequency of sampling. (For example, L_a should usually be lower for a sampling plan that has infrequent sampling than that which has frequent sampling.)
3. Other process charting. (For example, L_r should usually be higher when a product has many process control charts that have frequent test intervals because the overall chance of false alarms can increase dramatically.)
4. Importance of specification. (For example, L_a should usually be lower when the specification limit is important to product safety and reliability.)

The final input requirement to the design of a CUSUM chart is the process standard deviation (σ). The output from a pre-production designed experiment is a possible source for this information. Note that after the CUSUM test is begun, it may be necessary to readjust the sampling plan because of an erroneous assumption or an improvement (hopefully), with time, of the parameter of concern.

The nomogram in Figure 35.2 can now be used to design the sampling plan. By placing a ruler across the nomogram corresponding to L_a and L_r, values for the following can be determined:

$$|\mu - k| \frac{\sqrt{n}}{\sigma}$$

$$\frac{h\sqrt{n}}{\sigma}$$

At the reject quality level, $\mu - k$ is a known parameter; hence, n can then

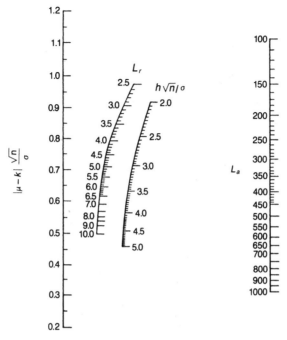

FIGURE 35.2 Nomogram for designing CUSUM control charts. (The labeling reflects the nomenclature used in this text.) [From Kemp (1962), with permission.]

be determined from the first of these two equations. With this n value the second of these two equations can then be used to yield the value of h. The data are then plotted with the control limit h using the previously described equation:

$$s_m = \sum_{i=1}^{m} (\bar{x}_i - k)$$

35.4   EXAMPLE 35.2: CUSUM CHART

An earlier example described a pre-production DOE of the settle-out time of a selection motor. Within this experimentation it was determined that an algorithm change was important (which had no base machine implementation costs), along with an inexpensive reduction in a motor adjustment tolerance. Because of this work and other analyses it was determined that there would be no functional problems if the motors did not experience a settle-out time greater than 8 msec. A CUSUM control charting scheme was desired to monitor the production process to assess this criterion on a continuing basis.

If we consider the 8-msec tolerance to be a single-sided 3σ upper limit, we need to subtract the expected 3σ variability from 8 to get an upper mean limit for our CUSUM chart. Hence, given an expected production 3σ value of 2 (i.e. $\sigma = \frac{2}{3}$) the upper accepted mean criterion could be assigned a value of 6 ($8 - 2 = 6$). However, because of the importance of this machine criterion and the previous test results, the designers decided to set the upper AQL to 5 along with an RQL set to 4. The value for k is then determined to be 4.5, which is the midpoint between these extremes.

Given an L_r of 3 and a L_a of 800, from Figure 35.2 this leads to

$$|\mu - k| \frac{\sqrt{n}}{\sigma} = 1.11$$

Substitution yields

$$|5.0 - 4.5| \frac{\sqrt{n}}{2/3} = 1.11 \qquad \text{so} \quad n = 2.19$$

Being conservative, n should be rounded up to give a sample size of 3. In addition, from Figure 35.2 we can determine

$$\frac{h\sqrt{n}}{\sigma} = 2.3$$

Substitution then yields

$$\frac{h\sqrt{3}}{2/3} = 2.3 \qquad \text{so} \quad h = 0.89$$

In summary, the overall design is as follows. The inputs were an RQL of 4.0 with an associated L_r (ARL) of 3, an AQL of 4.0 with an associated L_a (ARL) of 800, and a process standard deviation of $\frac{2}{3}$. Rationale subgroup samples of size 3 should be taken where a change in the process is declared whenever the cumulative sum above 4.5 exceeds 0.89. That is, whenever

$$S_m = \left[\sum_{i=1}^{m} (\bar{x}_i - 4.5) \right] > 0.89$$

A typical conceptual plot of this information is shown in Figure 35.3. In time, enough data can be collected to yield a more precise estimate for the standard deviation, which can be used to adjust the preceding procedural computations. In addition, it may be appropriate to adjust the k value to the mean of the sample that is being assessed, which can yield an earlier indicator to determine when there is a process change occurring.

Other supplemental tests can be useful when the process in stable to better understand the data and yield earlier problem detection. For example, a prob-

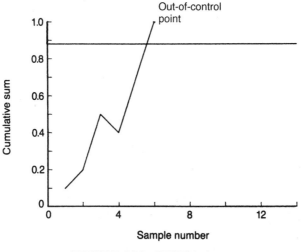

FIGURE 35.3 CUSUM chart.

ability plot of data by lots could be used to visually assess whether there appears to be a percentage of population differences that can be detrimental. If no differences are noted, one probability plot might be made of all collected data over time to better determine the percentage of population as a function of a control parameter.

35.5 S⁴ ASSESSMENT

CUSUM charting has some basic differences from Shewhart charts. Additional considerations for Shewhart versus CUSUM chart selection are as follows: (1) When choosing a control chart strategy using Shewhart techniques, variable sample sizes can be difficult to manage when calculating control limits, while this is not a concern with CUSUM techniques. (2) Shewhart charts handle a number of nonconforming items via *p* charts, while CUSUM can consider this a continuous variable (e.g., number of "good" samples selected before a "bad" sample is found). (3) CUSUM charting does not use many rules to define an out-of-control condition, which can, in the case of Shewhart charting, lead to an increase in false alarms (Yashchin 1989).

35.6 EXERCISES

1. *Catapult Exercise:* Set up a catapult in the middle of a classroom where student tables are placed in a U-shape. Adjust the catapult (quickly taking no more than 1 minute) to project a ball a mean distance as provided by the instructor (e.g., 75 in.). As one group, collect data in the form of a

control chart. Two people are inspectors that rotate after two subgroups are completed. The rest of the class are operators. The catapult is shot from a position on the floor with a tape measurer. No adhesive tape is allowed, and there are no aids to help the location of the ball position when it impacts the floor. Each person shoots the catapult five times and then rotates to the next person. This is repeated until 15 subgroups of data are collected. Record the operator and inspector for each shot. The catapult and tape measurer is now taped to the floor. In addition, people can help hold the catapult so that it does not move when a shot is conducted. In addition, some method is added to help aid the spotting of ball impact (e.g., carbon paper with blank paper under the sheet, talcum powder, or aluminum foil). Measurements are made to the center of ball impact with the best measurement resolution possible (e.g., 0.1 in.). Add additional standard operating procedures as desired by the class. Repeat the above inspection process until an additional 15 subgroups of data are collected (some operators may shoot more than once). Plot data as an $\bar{x}$ and R chart. Also, plot the first reading of each subgroup as an XmR chart. Calculate process capability/performance using specifications provided by instructor (e.g. 75 ± 3 inches). Consider all the analysis tools described within this text when describing the data. Describe a plan to make improvements.

2. To monitor physical changes from tester handling, the leads of 21 electronic chips in a tray are scanned for bent leads. The average and standard deviation of the worst dimensions on the 21 parts are noted. The parts are then placed in position by a test handler; good parts are placed in one tray, and bad parts are placed in another. The lead scanner test is repeated. Twenty lots are evaluated per day and reported on the following worksheets (Spec. max. delta is 0.3).

(a) Create a control charting plan.

(b) The delta (before to after test) for average and standard deviation of worst dimension on the 21 parts is determined for bent lead and recorded in the table format noted below. Create a plan to determine if the process is capable of meeting the maximum allowed specification limit of 0.3.

(c) Describe S^4 possibilities.

	Post-test	Pre-test	Delta
Average of bent leads			
Standard deviation of bent leads			

3. Describe how the techniques within this chapter are useful and can be applied to S^4 projects.

36

EXPONENTIALLY WEIGHTED MOVING AVERAGE (EWMA) AND ENGINEERING PROCESS CONTROL (EPC)

Under the Shewhart model for control charting, the assumption is made that the mean is constant. Also, errors are to be normal, independent with zero mean, and constant variance σ^2. In many applications this assumption is not true. Exponentially weighted average moving (EWMA) techniques offer an alternative that is based on exponential smoothing (sometimes called geometric smoothing).

The computation of EWMA as a filter is done by taking the weighted average of past observations with progressively smaller weights over time. EWMA has flexibility of computation through the selection of a weight factor and can use this factor to achieve balance between older data and more recent observations.

EWMA techniques can be combined with engineering process control (EPC) to give insight into when a process should be adjusted. Application examples for EWMA with EPC include the monitoring of parts produced by a tool that wears and needs periodic sharpening, adjustment, or replacement.

Much of the discussion in this chapter is a summary of the description given by Hunter (1995, 1996).

36.1 DESCRIPTION

Consider a sequence of observations $Y_1, Y_2, Y_3, \ldots, Y_t$. We could examine these data using any of the following procedures with noted differences:

- Shewhart—no weighting of previous data
- CUSUM—equal weights for previous data
- Moving average—weight, for example, the five most recent responses equally as an average
- EWMA—weight the most recent reading the highest and decrease weights exponentially for previous readings.

A Shewhart, CUSUM, or EWMA control chart for these variable data would all be based on the model

$$Y_t = \eta + m_t$$

where the expected value of the observations $E(Y_t)$ is a constant η and m_t is NID$(0, \sigma_m^2)$. For the Shewhart model the mean and variance are both constant with independent errors. Also with the Shewhart model the forecast for the next observation or average of observations is the centerline of the chart (η_0).

An EWMA is retrospective when plotted under Shewhart model conditions. It smoothes the time trace, thereby reducing the role of noise which can offer insight into what the level of the process might have been, which can be helpful when identifying special causes. Mathematically, for $0 < \lambda < 1$ this can be expressed as

$$\text{EWMA} = \hat{Y}_{s,t} = \lambda Y_t + \theta \hat{Y}_{s,t-1} \qquad \text{where } \theta = (1 - \lambda)$$

This equation can be described as follows: At time t the smoothed value of the response equals the multiple of lambda times today's observation plus theta times yesterday's smoothed value. A more typical plotting expression for this relationship is

$$\text{EWMA} = \hat{Y}_{t+1} = \hat{Y}_t + \lambda e_t \qquad \text{where } e_t = Y_t - \hat{Y}_t$$

This equation can be described as follows: The predicted value for tomorrow equals the predicted value of today plus a "depth of memory parameter" (lambda) times the difference between the observation and the current day's prediction. For plotting convenience, EWMA is often put one unit ahead of Y_t. Under certain conditions, as described later, EWMA can be used as a forecast.

The three sigma limits for an EWMA control chart is

$$\pm 3\sigma_{\text{EWMA}} = \sqrt{\lambda/(2 - \lambda)}[\pm 3\sigma_{\text{Shewhart}}]$$

When there are independent events, an EWMA chart with $\lambda = 0.4$ yields results almost identically to the combination of Western Electric rules, where control limits are exactly half of those from a Shewhart chart (Hunter 1989).

The underlying assumptions for a Shewhart model are often not true in reality. Expected values are not necessarily constant, and data values are not necessarily independent. An EWMA model does not have this limitation. An EWMA can be used to model processes that have linear or low-order time trends, cyclic behavior, a response that is a function of an external factor, nonconstant variance, and autocorrelated patterns.

The following example illustrates the application of EWMA and EPC.

36.2 EXAMPLE 36.1: EWMA WITH ENGINEERING PROCESS CONTROL

The data shown in Table 36.1 (Wheeler 1995b, Hunter 1995) are the bearing diameters of 50 camshafts collected over time. A traditional *XmR* chart of these data that is shown in Figure 36.1 indicates there are many out-of-control conditions. However, this example illustrates how underlying assumptions for application of the *XmR* chart to this data set are probably violated. EWMA and EPC alternatives are then applied.

First we will check for nonindependence. To do this we will use time series analysis techniques. If data meander, each observation tends to be close to the previous observation and there is no correlation between successive observations. That is, there is no autocorrelation (i.e., correlation with itself).

If observations are independent of time, their autocorrelation should equal zero. A test for autocorrelation involves regressing the current value on previous values of the time series to determine if there is correlation. The term *lag* quantifies how far back comparisons are made. Independence of data across time can be checked by the estimation of lag autocorrelation coeffi-

TABLE 36.1 Camshaft Bearing Diameters

Sequence	1	2	3	4	5	6	7	8	9	10
Diameter	50	51	50.5	49	50	43	42	45	47	49
Sequence	11	12	13	14	15	16	17	18	19	20
Diameter	46	50	52	52.5	51	52	50	49	54	51
Sequence	21	22	23	24	25	26	27	28	29	30
Diameter	52	46	42	43	45	46	42	44	43	46
Sequence	31	32	33	34	35	36	37	38	39	40
Diameter	42	43	42	45	49	50	51	52	54	51
Sequence	41	42	43	44	45	46	47	48	49	50
Diameter	49	50	49.5	51	50	52	50	48	49.5	49

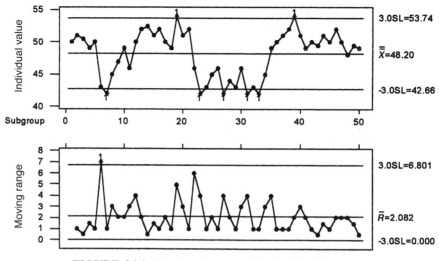

FIGURE 36.1 *XmR* chart of camshaft bearing diameters.

cients ρ_k, where $k = 1, 2, \ldots$. Statistical software packages can perform these calculations. Lag values are exemplified as

Data	Lag 1	Lag 2	Lag 3	Lag 4	Lag 5	Lag 6	Lag 7	Lag 8	Lag 9	Lag 10
50	·	·	·	·	·	·	·	·	·	·
51	50	·	·	·	·	·	·	·	·	·
50.5	51	50	·	·	·	·	·	·	·	·
49	50.5	51	50	·	·	·	·	·	·	·
50	49	50.5	51	50	·	·	·	·	·	·
43	50	49	50.5	51	50	·	·	·	·	·
42	43	50	49	50.5	51	50	·	·	·	·
45	42	43	50	49	50.5	51	50	·	·	·
47	45	42	43	50	49	50.5	51	50	·	·
49	47	45	42	43	50	49	50.5	51	50	·
46	49	47	45	42	43	50	49	50.5	51	50
50	46	49	47	45	42	43	50	49	50.5	51
52	50	46	49	47	45	42	43	50	49	50.5
52.5	52	50	46	49	47	45	42	43	50	49
·	·	·	·	·	·	·	·	·	·	·
·	·	·	·	·	·	·	·	·	·	·
·	·	·	·	·	·	·	·	·	·	·

For example, the correlation coefficient between the original and the lag 1 data is 0.74. The estimates of the autocorrelation coefficients are then

$$
\begin{array}{ll}
r_1 = 0.74 & r_6 = -0.02 \\
r_2 = 0.55 & r_7 = -0.09 \\
r_3 = 0.34 & r_8 = -0.23 \\
r_4 = 0.24 & r_9 = -0.23 \\
r_5 = 0.13 & r_{10} = -0.34
\end{array}
$$

For the hypothesis that all $\rho_k = 0$ the approximate standard error of r_k is $1/\sqrt{n}$, which leads to an approximate 95% confidence interval for ρ_1 of $r_1 + 2/\sqrt{n}$, which results in 0.74 ± 0.28. Because zero is not contained within this interval, we reject the null hypothesis. The implication of correlation is that the moving-range statistic does not provide a good estimate of standard deviation to calculate the control limits.

George Box (Hunter 1995, Box and Luceno 1997) suggests using a variogram to check adequacy of the assumptions of constant mean, independence, and constant variance. It checks the assumption of data being from a stationary process. A variogram does this by taking pairs of observations 1, 2, or m apart to produce alternative time series. When the assumptions are valid, there should be no difference in the expectation of statistics obtained from these differences. For the standardized variogram

$$
G_m = [\mathrm{Var}(Y_{t+m} - Y_t)]/[\mathrm{Var}(Y_{t+1} - Y_t)]
$$

the ratio G_m equals 1 for all values of m, if the data have a constant mean, independence, and constant variance. For processes that have an ultimate constant variance (i.e., stationary process) G_m will increase at first but soon become constant. For processes where the level and variance can grow without limit (i.e., nonstationary process), G_m will continually increase. For processes that increase as a straight line, an EWMA gives a unique model.

A simple method to compute G_m would be to use the moving-range computations for standard deviations. Table 36.2 shows the computations for moving range, while Table 36.3 shows the results of the calculations for each of the separation steps m. The plot of G_m versus the interval m shown in Figure 36.2 is an increasing straight line which suggests that an EWMA model is reasonable. An estimate for λ can be obtained from the slope of the line. Because the line must pass through $G(m) = 1$ and $m = 1$ the slope can be obtained from the relationship

$$
b = \frac{\Sigma\, xy}{\Sigma\, x^2} = \frac{\Sigma[m - 1][G(m) - 1]}{[m - 1]^2}
$$

$$
= \frac{0(1) + 1(1.552) + 2(2.445) + \cdots + 9(6.330)}{0^2 + 1^2 + 2^2 + \cdots + 9^2}
$$

$$
= \frac{155.913}{285} = 0.547
$$

An interactive solution of the relationship

TABLE 36.2 Moving-Range Calculations

Sequence	Bearing Diameter	MR $m=1$	MR $m=2$	MR $m=3$	MR $m=4$	MR $m=5$	MR $m=6$	MR $m=7$	MR $m=8$	MR $m=9$	MR $m=10$
1	50										
2	51	1									
3	50.5	0.5	0.5								
4	49	1.5	2	1							
5	50	1	0.5	1	0						
6	43	7	6	7.5	8	7					
7	42	1	8	7	8.5	9	8				
8	45	3	2	5	4	5.5	6	5			
9	47	2	5	4	3	2	3.5	4	3		
10	49	2	4	7	6	1	0	1.5	2	1	
11	46	3	1	1	4	3	4	3	4.5	5	4
12	50	4	1	3	5	8	7	0	1	0.5	1
13	52	2	6	3	5	7	10	9	2	3	1.5
14	52.5	0.5	2.5	6.5	3.5	5.5	7.5	10.5	9.5	2.5	3.5
·	·	·	·	·	·	·	·	·	·	·	·
·	·	·	·	·	·	·	·	·	·	·	·
·	·	$\overline{MR}$	$\overline{MR}$	$\overline{MR}$	$\overline{MR}$	$\overline{MR}$	$\overline{MR}$	$\overline{MR}$	$\overline{MR}$	$\overline{MR}$	$\overline{MR}$
		2.082	2.594	3.255	3.391	3.689	4.045	4.209	4.393	4.793	5.238

TABLE 36.3 Variogram Computations

m	Moving Range $(\overline{MR})$	d_2	$\sigma_{Y_m} = \overline{MR}/d_2$	$\sigma^2_{Y_m}$	$G(m) = \dfrac{\sigma^2_{Y_m}}{\sigma^2_{Y_1}}$
1	2.082	1.128	1.845	3.406	1.000
2	2.594	1.128	2.299	5.287	1.553
3	3.255	1.128	2.886	8.329	2.446
4	3.391	1.128	3.006	9.039	2.654
5	3.689	1.128	3.270	10.695	3.140
6	4.045	1.128	3.586	12.862	3.777
7	4.209	1.128	3.732	13.925	4.089
8	4.393	1.128	3.894	15.166	4.453
9	4.793	1.128	4.249	18.053	5.301
10	5.238	1.128	4.643	21.559	6.331

$$b = \frac{\lambda^2}{1 + (1 - \lambda)^2}$$

where $b = 0.547$ yields $\lambda = 0.76$. The limits of the EWMA control chart are adjusted by the relationship

$$\pm 3\sigma_{\text{EWMA}} = \sqrt{\lambda/(2 - \lambda)}[\pm 3\sigma_{\text{shewhart}}] = \sqrt{0.76/(2 - 0.76)}(53.74 - 48.20)$$

$$= 0.783 \times 5.54 = 4.33$$

The resulting control limits are then 52.53 and 43.87 (i.e., 48.20 + 4.33 and

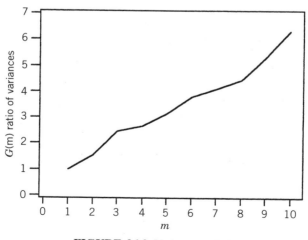

FIGURE 36.2 Variogram plot.

48.20 − 4.33). The EWMA control chart in Figure 36.3 shows these adjusted control limits from λ.

The resulting fitted EWMA model is

$$\hat{Y}_{t+1} = \hat{Y}_t + 0.76(Y_t - \hat{Y}_t) = 0.76Y_t + 0.24\hat{Y}_t = 0.76Y_t + 0.24\hat{Y}_t$$

Let us now consider employing the fitted EWMA model. If we let the target value for the camshaft diameters be τ = 50 and let the first prediction be $\hat{Y}_1$ = 50, an employment of the fitted EWMA gives the prediction values and errors in Table 36.4. From this table we can determine

$$\bar{Y}_{t+1} = 48.2$$

$$\sum(Y_t - \tau)^2 = 775.00 \qquad \text{hence} \quad s_\tau = \sqrt{\frac{775}{50 - 1}} = 3.98$$

$$\sum(Y_t - \bar{Y})^2 = 613.000 \qquad \text{hence} \quad s_Y = \sqrt{\frac{775}{50 - 1}} = 3.54$$

$$\sum(Y_t - \hat{Y}_t)^2 = \sum e_t^2 = 312.47 \qquad \text{hence} \quad s_e = \sqrt{\frac{312.47}{50 - 1}} = 2.53$$

From this we conclude that it seems possible that use of the EWMA as a forecast to control the process could result in a very large reduction in variability (i.e., sum of squares from 775.00 to 312.47).

A comparison of the autocorrelation coefficients of the original observations with the residuals e_t after fitting the EWMA model is as follows:

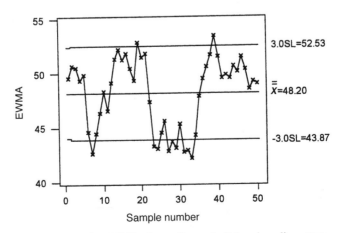

FIGURE 36.3 EWMA chart of camshaft bearing diameters.

TABLE 36.4 Observations, Predictions, and Errors

t	Y_t	$\hat{Y}_{t+1}$	e_t	t	Y_t	$\hat{Y}_{t+1}$	e_t
1	50.0	50.000	0.000	26	46.0	44.537	1.463
2	51.0	50.000	1.000	27	42.0	45.649	-3.649
3	50.5	50.760	-0.260	28	44.0	42.876	1.124
4	49.0	50.562	-1.562	29	43.0	43.730	-0.730
5	50.0	49.375	0.625	30	46.0	43.175	2.825
6	43.0	49.850	-6.850	31	42.0	45.322	-3.322
7	42.0	44.644	-2.644	32	43.0	42.797	0.203
8	45.0	42.635	2.365	33	42.0	42.951	-0.951
9	47.0	44.432	2.568	34	45.0	42.228	2.772
10	49.0	46.384	2.616	35	49.0	44.335	4.665
11	46.0	48.372	-2.372	36	50.0	47.880	2.120
12	50.0	46.569	3.431	37	51.0	49.491	1.509
13	52.0	49.177	2.823	38	52.0	50.638	1.362
14	52.5	51.322	1.178	39	54.0	51.673	2.327
15	51.0	52.217	-1.217	40	51.0	53.442	-2.442
16	52.0	51.292	0.708	41	49.0	51.586	-2.586
17	50.0	51.830	-1.830	42	50.0	49.621	0.379
18	49.0	50.439	-1.439	43	49.5	49.909	-0.409
19	54.0	49.345	4.655	44	51.0	49.598	1.402
20	51.0	52.883	-1.833	45	50.0	50.664	-0.664
21	52.0	51.452	0.548	46	52.0	50.159	1.841
22	46.0	51.868	-5.868	47	50.0	51.558	-1.558
23	42.0	47.408	-5.408	48	48.0	50.374	-2.374
24	43.0	43.298	-0.298	49	49.5	48.570	0.930
25	45.0	43.072	1.928	50	49.0	49.277	-0.277

Original Observations Y_t		EWMA Residuals e_t	
$r_1 = 0.74$	$r_6 = -0.02$	$r_1 = 0.11$	$r_6 = -0.15$
$r_2 = 0.55$	$r_7 = -0.09$	$r_2 = -0.01$	$r_7 = 0.02$
$r_3 = 0.34$	$r_8 = -0.23$	$r_3 = -0.19$	$r_8 = -0.24$
$r_4 = 0.24$	$r_9 = -0.23$	$r_4 = -0.03$	$r_9 = 0.13$
$r_5 = 0.13$	$r_{10} = -0.34$	$r_5 = 0.09$	$r_{10} = -0.10$

The residuals suggest independence and supports our use of EWMA as a reasonable model that can give useful forecast information of process performance.

Consider now what could be done to take active control. To do this we must be willing to accept a forecast for where a process will be in the next instant of time. When a forecast falls too distant from a target τ, an operator can then change some influential external factor X_t to force the forecast to equal target τ. This differs from the previously discussed Shewhart model in that the statistical approach is now not hypothesis testing but instead estimation.

The application of process controls from an external factor can be conducted periodically when the response reaches a certain level relative to the specification. However, for this example we will consider that adjustments are made after each reading and that full consequences of taking corrective action can be accomplished within the next time interval. Table 36.5 summarizes the calculations, which are described as follows. Let us consider that X_t is the current setting of a control factor where $\hat{Y}_{t+1}$ is the forecast. Also, we can exactly compensate for a discrepancy of $z_t = \hat{Y}_{t+i} - \tau$ by making the change $x_t = X_{t+1} - X_t$. When bringing a process back to its target, we would set $gx_t = -z_t$, where g is the adjuster gain.

The controlling factor is initially set to zero and the first forecast is 50, the target. The table contains the original observations and new observations, which differ from original observations by the amount shown. The difference between the new observation and the target of 50 is shown as $e(t)$, while 0.76 $e(t)$ quantifies the new amount of adjustment needed. EWMA is determined from the relationship $\hat{Y}_{t+1} = 0.76Y_t + 0.24\hat{Y}_t$.

We can see that the XmR chart of the new observations shown in Figure 36.4 is now in control. The estimated implications of control to the process are as follows:

	Mean	Standard Deviation
No control	48.20	3.54
Every observation control	49.98	2.53

It should be noted that for this situation a chart could be created from the EWMA relationship that describes how an operator in manufacturing should adjust a machine depending upon its current output.

36.3 EXERCISES

1. *Catapult Exercise Data Analysis:* Using the catapult exercise data sets from Chapter 4, conduct EWMA analyses. Assess whether there appears to be any value of using an EWMA chart and whether an EPC plan should be considered.

2. Repeat the example with process control such that the operator leaves the process alone whenever the forecast $\hat{Y}_{t+1}$ is within the interval $47.5 \leq \hat{Y}_{t+1} \leq 52.5$. If the forecast falls beyond these limits, the process is to be adjusted back to a target of 50.

3. Describe how the techniques within this chapter are useful and can be applied to S^4 projects.

TABLE 36.5 Engineering Process Control Results

t	Original Observation	Adjustment to Original Observation	New Observation	EWMA	e(t)	0.76 × e(t)
1	50	0.00	50.00	50.00	0.00	0.00
2	51	0.00	51.00	50.76	1.00	0.76
3	50.5	-0.76	49.74	49.98	-0.26	-0.20
4	49	-0.56	48.44	48.81	-1.56	-1.19
5	50	0.63	50.63	50.19	0.63	0.48
6	43	0.15	43.15	44.84	-6.85	-5.21
7	42	5.36	47.36	46.75	-2.64	-2.01
8	45	7.37	52.37	51.02	2.37	1.80
9	47	5.57	52.57	52.20	2.57	1.95
10	49	3.62	52.62	52.52	2.62	1.99
11	46	1.63	47.63	48.80	-2.37	-1.80
12	50	3.43	53.43	52.32	3.43	2.61
13	52	0.82	52.82	52.70	2.82	2.15
14	52.5	-1.32	51.18	51.54	1.18	0.89
15	51	-2.22	48.78	49.45	-1.22	-0.93
16	52	-1.29	50.71	50.40	0.71	0.54
17	50	-1.83	48.17	48.71	-1.83	-1.39
18	49	-0.44	48.56	48.60	-1.44	-1.09
19	54	0.65	54.65	53.20	4.65	3.54
20	51	-2.88	48.12	49.34	-1.88	-1.43
21	52	-1.45	50.55	50.26	0.55	0.42
22	46	-1.87	44.13	45.60	-5.87	-4.46
23	42	2.59	44.59	44.83	-5.41	-4.11
24	43	6.70	49.70	48.53	-0.30	-0.23
25	45	6.93	51.93	51.11	1.93	1.47
26	46	5.46	51.46	51.38	1.46	1.11
27	42	4.35	46.35	47.56	-3.65	-2.77
28	44	7.12	51.12	50.27	1.12	0.85
29	43	6.27	49.27	49.51	-0.73	-0.55
30	46	6.82	52.82	52.03	2.82	2.15
31	42	4.68	46.68	47.96	-3.32	-2.52
32	43	7.20	50.20	49.66	0.20	0.15
33	42	7.05	49.05	49.20	-0.95	-0.72
34	45	7.77	52.77	51.91	2.77	2.11
35	49	5.67	54.67	54.00	4.67	3.55
36	50	2.12	52.12	52.57	2.12	1.61
37	51	0.51	51.51	51.76	1.51	1.15
38	52	-0.64	51.36	51.46	1.36	1.04
39	54	-1.67	52.33	52.12	2.33	1.77
40	51	-3.44	47.56	48.65	-2.44	-1.86
41	49	-1.59	47.41	47.71	-2.59	-1.97
42	50	0.38	50.38	49.74	-0.38	0.29
43	49.5	0.09	49.59	49.63	-0.41	-0.31
44	51	0.40	51.40	50.98	1.40	1.07
45	50	-0.66	49.34	49.73	-0.66	-0.50
46	52	-0.16	51.84	51.33	1.84	1.40
47	50	-1.56	48.44	49.14	-1.56	-1.18
48	48	-0.37	47.63	47.99	-2.37	-1.80
49	49.5	1.43	50.93	50.22	0.93	0.71
50	49	0.72	49.72	49.84	-0.28	-0.21

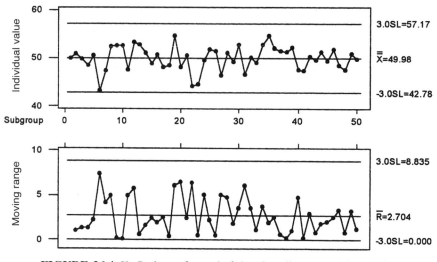

FIGURE 36.4 *XmR* chart of camshaft bearing diameters (after EPC).

37

PRE-CONTROL CHARTS

A team in 1953 from Rath & Strong, Inc., developed pre-control as an easier alternative to Shewhart control charts. Pre-control (sometimes called stoplight control) monitors test units within manufacturing by classifying them into one of three groups (green, yellow, or red). From a small sample the number of green, yellow, and red units observed determines when to stop and adjust the process. Since its initial proposal, at least three different versions of pre-control have been suggested. This chapter will discuss the classical, two-stage, and modified versions.

37.1 DESCRIPTION

Classical pre-control refers to the original described methodology. Two-stage pre-control is a method that takes an additional sample if the initial sample results are ambiguous. Modified pre-control attempts to compromise between the type of philosophy of the Shewhart control chart and the simplicity of applying Pre-control.

The schemes of pre-control are defined by their group classification, decision, and qualification procedures. The setup or qualification procedure defines the required results of an initial sampling scheme that is used to determine if pre-control is appropriate for the situation. For all three of these options a process passes qualification if five consecutive green units are observed. Differences between the three versions of pre-control are most substantial in their method of group classification. Classical and two-stage pre-control base the classification of units on specification limits, while modified pre-control classifies units use control limits, as defined by Shewhart control charts.

After qualification or setup. a unit is classified as green if its quality characteristic is within the central half of the tolerance range (for classical or two-stage pre-control) or control chart limits (for modified pre-control). A yellow unit has a quality characteristic within the remaining tolerance range (for classical or two-stage pre-control) or control chart limits (for modified pre-control). A red unit has a quality characteristic that is outside the tolerance range (for classical or two-stage pre-control) or control chart limits (for modified pre-control).

37.2   PRE-CONTROL SETUP (QUALIFICATION PROCEDURE)

Before conducting classical, two-stage, or modified pre-control in a "running" basis, a setup needs to be passed. A unit is classified as green if its quality characteristic is within the central half of the tolerance range. A yellow unit has a quality characteristic within the remaining tolerance. A red unit has a quality characteristic that is outside the tolerance range. The setup rules are as follows (Shainin and Shainin 1989):

Setup. OK to run when five pieces in a row are green:
   A. If one yellow, restart count.
   B. If two yellows in a row, adjust.
   C. Return to setup after adjustment, tool change, new operator, or material.

37.3   CLASSICAL PRE-CONTROL

With classical pre-control a unit is classified as green if its quality characteristic is within the central half of the tolerance range. A yellow unit has a quality characteristic within the remaining tolerance range. A red unit has a quality characteristic that is outside the tolerance range.

When the setup or qualification rules are satisfied, the following rules are applied (Shainin and Shainin 1989):

Running. Sample two consecutive pieces, A and B:
   A. If A is green. continue to run.
   B. If A is yellow, check B.
   C. If A and B are yellow, stop.
   D. If A or B are red, stop.

Average six sample pairs between consecutive adjustment:

Average Time Between Process Adjustments	Sampling Interval
8 hours	Every 80 minutes
4 hours	Every 40 minutes
2 hours	Every 20 minutes
1 hour	Every 10 minutes

37.4   TWO-STAGE PRE-CONTROL

With two-stage pre-control a unit is classified as green if its quality characteristic is within the central half of the tolerance range. A yellow unit has a quality characteristic within the remaining tolerance range. A red unit has a quality characteristic that is outside the tolerance range. When the setup or qualification rules are satisfied, the following rules are applied (Steiner 1997):

Sample two consecutive parts.

- If either part is red, stop process and adjust.
- If both parts are green, continue operation.
- If either or both of the parts are yellow, continue to sample up to three more units. Continue operation if the combined sample contains three green units, and stop the process if three yellow units or a single red unit are observed.

37.5   MODIFIED PRE-CONTROL

With modified pre-control a unit is classified as green if its quality characteristic is within the central half of the ±three standard control limits defined by Shewhart control charts. A yellow unit has a quality characteristic within the remaining control chart bounds. A red unit has a quality characteristic that is outside the control chart limits. When the setup or qualification rules are satisfied, the following rules are applied (Steiner 1997):

Sample two consecutive parts.

- If either part is red, stop process and adjust.
- If both parts are green, continue operation.
- If either or both of the parts are yellow, continue to sample up to three more units. Continue operation if the combined sample contains three green units, and stop the process if three yellow units or a single red unit are observed.

37.6 APPLICATION CONSIDERATIONS

Classical and two-stage pre-control do not require estimates of the current process mean and standard deviation; hence, they are easier to set up than a modified pre-control chart. It has been suggested that pre-control and two-stage pre-control are only applicable if the current process spread of six standard deviations covers less than 88% of the tolerance range (Traver 1985). Modified pre-control has the same goal as an $\bar{x}$ chart but has an excessively large false alarm rate and is not recommended (Steiner 1997).

The advantage of the more complicated decision procedure for two-stage and modified pre-control over classical pre-control is that decision errors are less likely. However, the disadvantage is that, on the average, large sample sizes are needed to make decisions about the state of the process.

37.7 S⁴ ASSESSMENT

Pre-control charting is a technique that causes much debate. Some companies specifically state that pre-control charting should not be used. As with all tools (statistical or not), there are applications where a particular tool is best for an application, OK for an application, or not right for an application. I believe that pre-control charting is a tool that can complement a strategy that *wisely* integrates Shewhart control charts, gauge R&R studies, DOE experimentation, FMEA, and so on.

37.8 EXERCISE

1. Describe how the techniques within this chapter are useful and can be applied to S⁴ projects.

38

CONTROL PLAN AND OTHER STRATEGIES

This chapter discusses realistic tolerances and a control plan in addition to a very brief discussion of some common industry methodologies that can give insight to directions that can be considered a part of an S^4 measurement and improvement strategy.

38.1 POKA-YOKE

A *poka-yoke* (pronounced POH-kah YOH-kay) device is a mechanism that either prevents a mistake from occurring or makes a mistake obvious at a glance. Shigeo Shingo at Tokya was one of the industrial engineers who has been credited for creating and formalizing zero quality control (ZQC), an approach that relies heavily on poka-yoke (or mistake-proofing).

To illustrate a poka-yoke application, consider an operator who creates customized assemblies from small bins that are in front of them. One approach to accomplish the task would be to give the operator a list of parts to assemble, where they are to take the parts as needed from the bins. This approach can lead to assembly errors by the operator. They might either forget to include a part or add parts that are not specified. A poka-yoke solution might be to include lights on all bins. When the operator is to create a new assembly, the bins that contain the specified parts for the assembly light up. The operator then systematically removes one part from each bin and places it in front of them. They do it until one part has been removed from each bin. They later know that their assembly is complete when no parts remain in front of them.

Poke-yoke can offer solutions to organizations that often have frequent discrepancies in the packaging of their products (e.g., someone forgot to include the instructions or a mounting screw). Poke-yoke devices can be much more effective than alternative demands of workers to "be more careful."

38.2 KAIZEN

In its literal translation from Japanese, *kaizen* means continuous improvement. The hallmark of kaizen is its empowerment given to people that fosters their creativity. Through the work of Taiichi Ohno, the Toyota Production System (TPS) has become synonymous with kaizen by embodying the philosophy and applying the principles.

Kaizen and the TPS is centered around quantitative analysis. Ohno said "At our factory, we start our kaizen efforts by looking at the way our people do their work, because it doesn't cost anything." A starting point for the identification of waste can be the study of the motion. In the late 19th and early 20th century, Frederick W. Taylor set the foundation for industrial engineering. The initial objectives were to set work standards by quantifying times and motions of the routine tasks performed by workers, which gave a basis for compensation. This resulted in a method where work could be analyzed and wasted motion eliminated. The scientific management approach was broadly adopted but was perceived by many as inhumane, although he did admire the worker and undoubtedly intended the system to benefit both the employer and employee.

Taylor's primary tool of time study remains a basis tool for kaizen. The difference between Taylor's original implementation and the implementation of today is the source of inputs to work methods (i.e., process). Previously, Taylor's work standards were set by the standards department with no worker input. Now kaizen provides the worker both the opportunity and means to find better ways to do his or her job.

The implementation of S^4 not only involves good quantitative measurements but also involves humanism. Abraham Maslow describes self-actualization as an individual developing to the fullest or the process of growth that unfolds and frees what is already within the individual. This is the highest level of Maslow's hierarchy of needs [i.e., physiological (lowest), safety, belongingness and love, esteem, self-actualization (highest)]. Kaizen has been described as a new manifestation of achievement motivation.

The once-thought opposite management styles of Taylor and Maslow can have common ground with a kaizen approach (Cheser 1994).

38.3 THEORY OF CONSTRAINTS (TOC)

The implementation of TQM often has taken on the approach of dividing the system into processes and then optimizing the quality of each process. This approach is preferable to chasing symptoms, but it can create new problems if the role of individual processes is not considered along with other processes. However, new problems can be created if the individual process is not considered in concert with other processes that it affects.

The theory of constraints described by Goldratt (1992) presents a system thinking process where focus is given to reducing system bottlenecks resulting in continual improvement of the performance of the entire system. Rather than viewing the system in terms of discrete processes, TOC addresses the larger systematic picture as a chain or grid of interlinked chains. The performance of the whole chain determines the performance of the weakest link. Few constraints are physical according to Goldratt. A vast majority of constraints are caused by policies (e.g., rules, training, and other measures), while few constraints are physical (e.g., machines, facilities, people, and other tangible resources). For example, a large portion of the highway road repair seems initially to be a physical constraint to traffic flow. But the physical constraint is that government acquisition policy often mandates the award of contracts to the lowest bidder, which drives contractors to the use of low-quality materials that have less life in an effort to keep costs down and remain competitive.

Three dimensions of system performance are considered by TOC in the following order: throughput (total sales revenues minus the total variable costs for producing a product or service), inventory (all the money a company invests in items it sells), and operating expense (money a company spends transforming inventory into throughput). Focus on these dimensions can lead a company to the invalidation of traditional management cost accounting and a simultaneous improvement in competitive price advantage.

38.4 KANBAN

The Japanese word *kanban* refers to the pulling of product through a production process (i.e., a pull system). The intent of kanban is to signal to a former process that the next process needs parts/material. Because a bottleneck is the slowest operation in a chain of operations, it will pace the output of the entire line. Buffers in high-volume manufacturing serves to affect line balance among bottlenecks and product specific operations. It is very important that bottleneck operations be supplied with the necessary work-in-process (WIP) at the appropriate time and that poorly sequenced work not interfere with the work that is to be accomplished at these operations.

Rules to consider when operating an effective kanban are as follows: No withdrawal of parts are to occur without a kanban; subsequent processes are to withdraw only what is needed; defective parts are not to be sent to subsequent processes; preceding processes are to produce only the exact quantity of parts withdrawn by subsequent processes; varability in the demand process should be minimized as much as possible; and if production requirements drop off, the process must be stopped (overtime and process improvements are to be applied with the increase in production requirements).

38.5   LEAN MANUFACTURING AND WASTE PREVENTION

If we consider that waste is being generated anywhere work is accomplished, we can create a vehicle through which organizations can identify and reduce waste. The goal is total elimination of waste through the process of defining waste, identifying the source, planning for the elimination of waste, and establishing permanent control to prevent reoccurrence.

Seven elements to consider for the elimination of "muda" or waste are correction, overproduction, processing, conveyance, inventory, motion, and waiting. Initiative considerations to resolve these wastes can involve the "5S": sorting (cleaning up), storage (organizing), shining (cleaning), standardize (standardizing), and sustaining (training and discipline).

38.6   REALISTIC TOLERANCES

Consider that the previous S^4 methodologies identified the criticality and then characterized KPIVs. Consider also that mistake-proofing methods were not found effective. We would like to create an SPC method to control the process inputs, where the inputs are continuous.

We can track process inputs through automation or manual techniques. This tracking can involve monitoring or control. Often we only monitor KPOVs because we are unable to control process inputs. When we can control KPIV characteristics it indicates that we have prediction capability for the process output; hence, we can control the process through these inputs.

When the KPIV to KPOV relationship is understood, the establishment of optimum levels for KPIVs can be accomplished through the following approach:

1. Identify the target and specification for a critical KPOV.
2. Select from previous S^4 activities KPIVs that have been shown to affect the KPOV.
3. Describe what has been learned from previous S^4 activities (e.g., the DOE activities) about the levels of each KPIV that is thought to yield an optimum KPOV response.
4. Plot the relationship between each KPIV and the KPOV on an $x-y$ plot describing not only the best-fit line but also the 95% prediction interval bounds. An approach to do this is to create 30 samples over the range of the KPIVs that is thought to optimize the KPOV. Plot then the re-

lationship of each KPIV to the KPOV using statistical software to determine the 95% prediction bounds for individual points. Consider not only the effect from each KPIV when creating these relationships but also the impact of other KPIVs that can occur at the same time.

5. Draw two parallel lines horizontally from the specification bounds of the KPOV to the upper and lower prediction limits.

6. Draw two parallel lines vertically from the intersection of the previous drawn lines and the prediction limits.

7. Determine the maximum tolerance permitted for each KPIV by observing the x-axis intersection points of the two vertical lines.

8. Compare the determined KPIV tolerance to existing operating levels.

9. Implement changes to the standard operating procedure, as required, while documenting changes in the FMEA and control plan.

38.7   CONTROL PLAN

A control plan is created to ensure that processes are operated so that products meet or exceed customer requirements all the time. A control plan is an extension of the current control column of an FMEA. The FMEA should be an important source for the identification of KPIVs that are included within a control plan. Other sources for the identification of KPIVs are process map, cause-and-effect matrix, multi-vari studies, regression analysis, and DOE.

A control plan offers a systematic approach to finding and resolving out-of-control conditions. It offers a troubleshooting guide for operators through its documented reaction plan. A good control plan strategy should reduce process tampering, provide a vehicle for the initiation/implementation of process improvement activities, describe the training needs for standard operating procedures, and document maintenance schedule requirements. Control plans should reduce the amount of "fire fighting" and save money through "fire prevention" activities.

A summary of a control plan can include, in spreadsheet format, the following items: process, process step, input, output, process specification (lower limit, target, and upper limit), C_{pk}/P_{pk} (describe sample size and methodology to obtain), MSA (include system, %R&R, and % of tolerance), current control method (include sample size and sample frequency), and reaction plan. Control plans should be created from the knowledge gained from other S^4 phases and utilize not only control charts but also error proofing. Key process input variable considerations should include monitoring procedures, frequency of verification, and selection of optimum targets/specifications. Uncontrollable noise input considerations should include their identification, control procedures, and robustness of the system to the noise. Standard operating procedures issues include documentation, ease-of-use, applicability, utilization, up-to-date, and training. Maintenance procedures issues include identification of critical components, scheduling frequency, responsibility, training, and availability of instructions.

38.8 S⁴ ASSESSMENT

Peter Senge (1990) writes that "Learning disabilities are tragic in children, but they are fatal in organizations. Because of them, few corporations live even half as long as a person—most die before they reach the age of forty." "Learning organizations" defy these odds and overcome learning disabilities to understand threats and recognize new opportunities. The methodologies of S⁴ offer a roadmap for changing data into knowledge that leads to new opportunities.

People often lose the sight that the purpose of measurements is to gather data from which information can be derived. The methodologies described within this chapter can be used to help determine the best way of viewing the system and processes. This view can give a better methodology of determining what questions to ask, what important factors or constraints should be measured to answer them, and what can be done to improve a methodology by integrating techniques.

Relative to this third issue, consider Kanban. Kanban can be a great improvement to a process that produces few defects within workstations. However, if workstations have high defect rates (i.e., a hidden factory), the system can become "starved" for parts. This problem could be avoided by integrating Kanban and S⁴ methodologies.

38.9 EXERCISE

1. Describe how the techniques within this chapter are useful and can be applied to S⁴ projects.

39

RELIABILITY TESTING/ ASSESSMENT: OVERVIEW

This chapter is an introduction to the following two chapters, which discuss the reliability testing of repairable systems and nonrepairable devices, respectively. In this text the Weibull and log-normal distributions are used for nonrepairable device analyses, while the Poisson distribution and nonhomogeneous Poisson process (NHPP) are used for repairable system analyses.

A test that evaluates the frequency of failure for systems (or the time of failure for devices) can take a long time to complete when the failure rate criterion is low (or the average life is high). To complete a test in a reasonable period of time, considerations may need to be made to have the sample tested in an environment that accelerates usage. Alternatives to achieve this acceleration within the electronic industries include tests at high temperature, high humidity, thermal cycling, vibration, corrosive environments, and increased duty cycle. This chapter covers some accelerated testing models and a general accelerated reliability test strategy.

39.1 PRODUCT LIFE CYCLE

The "bathtub" curve shown in Figure 39.1 describes the general life cycle of a product. The downward sloping portion of the curve is considered to be the "early-life" portion where the chance of a given product failing during a unit of time decreases with usage. The flat portion is the portion of the cycle where the failure rate does not change with additional usage. Finally, the increasing slope portion is the "wear-out" region where the chance of failure in a unit of time increases as the product's usage increases.

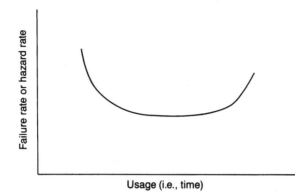

FIGURE 39.1 Bathtub curve.

An automobile is a repairable system that can experience a bathtub life cycle. New car owners may have to return the vehicle several times to the dealer to remove the "bugs." Failures during this time are typically due to manufacturing workmanship problems; a customer may experience problems with a wheel alignment adjustment, a door not closing properly, or a rattle in the dashboard. During this early-life period, the frequency of returning the vehicle decreases with vehicle age. After these initial bugs are removed, usually the car will start to approach a relative constant failure rate. When the constant failure rate portion of life is reached, the vehicle may experience, for example, a mean time between failure (MTBF) rate of 6 months or 10.000 miles. Failures during this period will normally differ from early-life failures for an automobile; problems may occur with the water pump bearings, wheel bearings. brake linings, and exhaust systems. Note that at the device level the parts may be wearing out; however, at the system level the overall failure rate may be constant as a function of usage of the vehicle. However, with usage an automobile then may start to experience an overall increasing failure rate. During this period, the frequency of component wear-out and required adjustments increases with time. This period of time may contain many of the same failures as the constant failure rate period; however, now the frequency of repair will be increasing with the addition of wear-out from other components. Wear-out might now involve such components as the steering linkage, differential, suspension, and valve lifters.

As discussed earlier. there are repairable systems and nonrepairable devices. The automobile is obviously a repairable system because we don't throw the vehicle away after its first failure. Other items are not so obvious. For example, a water pump may be repairable or nonrepairable. The most frequent failure mode for a water pump may be its bearings. If a water pump is repaired (rebuilt) because of a bearing failure, then that water pump could be considered a repairable system. If a water pump that has never been rebuilt is discarded after a failure, then this device would be considered a nonrepairable device.

There are other devices that are easier to classify as a nonrepairable device. These devices include brake pads, headlights. wheel bearings, exhaust pipe, muffler, and the bearings of the water pump. These devices are discarded after failure.

39.2   UNITS

Even though a failure rate is not constant over time, often a single average number is reported to describe an average failure rate (AFR) over an interval (T_1, T_2). Because the failure rates of electronic components are so small, failures are often expressed in failure rates per thousand hours (%/K) instead of failures per hour. Another scale that is popular is the expression of the reliability of components in parts per million (ppm) per thousand hours (ppm/K); ppm/K is often expressed as FIT (failures in time). A summary of conversions for a failure rate $r(t)$ and AFR are (Tobias and Trindade 1995)

$$\text{Failure rate in } \%/\text{K} = 10^5 \times r(t)$$

$$\text{AFR in } \%/\text{K} = 10^5 \times \text{AFR } (T_1, T_2)$$

$$\text{Failure rate in FITs} = 10^9 \times r(t)$$

$$\text{AFR in FITs} = 10^9 \times \text{AFR } (T_1, T_2)$$

39.3   REPAIRABLE VERSUS NONREPAIRABLE TESTING

Consider first a nonrepairable device. Assume that 10 tires were randomly selected from a warehouse and were tested to wear-out or failure. With this situation, input to an analysis may simply be 10 customer equivalent mileage numbers reflecting when the tire treads decreased to 2.0 mm. From this information an "average life" (e.g., 60,000 km) and other characteristics could be determined (e.g., 90% of the tires are not expected to fail by 40,000 km). Chapter 41 addresses this problem type (reliability of nonrepairable devices) using Weibull or log-normal analysis techniques.

Consider now a repairable system such as an overall automobile failure rate. The data from this test analysis might be in the following form:

2000 km: repaired electronic ignition, idling problems
8000 km: pollution device replacement, acceleration problems
18,000 km: dashboard brake light repair
30,000 km: water pump bearing failure
40,000 km: test terminated

This above information may apply to one of 10 cars that were monitored that had similar information. Because multiple failures can occur on each test device, a Weibull probability plot, for example, is not an appropriate direct analysis tool. For this situation we are not interested in the percentage of population that fails at a given test time or an average life number; we are interested in the failure rate of the car (or the time between failures).

Extending this conceptual automobile failure example further, the following is then considered. If the failure rate is believed not to be dependent on the age of the automobile, then in the above example we may estimate that the failure rate for the vehicle during a 20,000-km test would be on the average 0.0001 failures/km (4 failures/40,000 km = 0.0001) or 10,000 km MTBF (40,000 km/4 failures = 10,000) [note that this is a biased estimate for MTBF]. However, the logic behind the "constant failure rate" assumption seems questionable because the time between each succeeding failure seems to be increasing. Chapter 40 addresses this type of problem (reliability of repairable systems with constant and decreasing/increasing failure rates) using the Poisson distribution or the NHPP with Weibull intensity.

39.4   NONREPAIRABLE DEVICE TESTING

The two-parameter Weibull distribution is often used for the analysis of nonrepairable device failure times because it can model any one of the three situations commonly encountered as a function of device age: reducing chance of failure, constant chance of failure, and increasing chance of failure for a time increment.

The Weibull cumulative distribution function takes the form (where t is used to represent time)

$$F(t) = 1 - \exp[-(t/k)^b]$$

where the b is the shape parameter and k is the scale parameter (or characteristic life). If both k and b are known, a cumulative failure value [$F(t)$] can be determined for any value of time (t). For example, $F(100,000 \text{ hr}) = 0.9$ indicates that 90% of the population is expected to fail before a usage of 100,000 hr. The purpose of a test and corresponding data analyses then becomes a means to estimate the unknown parameters of the equation.

Much can be understood about a device failure mode if the shape parameter b is known. The probability density function (PDF) for differing shape parameters is shown in Figure 39.2. Numerically, this shape parameter b indicates the following relative to Figure 39.1:

$b < 1$: early life, decreasing failure rate with usage

$b = 1$: random or intrinsic failures, constant failure rate with usage

$b > 1$: wear-out mode, increasing failure rate with usage

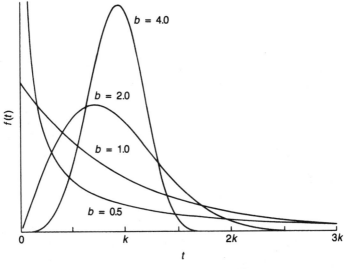

FIGURE 39.2 Weibull PDF.

The log-normal distribution is another alternative often found suitable to describe the underlying failure distribution of electrical/mechanical components (e.g., resistors and journal bearings). This distribution is applicable when the logarithms of the failure time data are normally distributed. With this distribution the model parameters take the form of a mean and standard deviation; hence, the mathematical tools of the normal distribution are applicable to the log-normal distribution. Figures 7.12 and 7.13 show PDFs and cumulative distribution functions (CDFs) for this distribution.

39.5   REPAIRABLE SYSTEM TESTING

The Poisson distribution is commonly used when determining the details of a repairable system test. The underlying assumption when using this distribution is that the system failure rate will be constant as a function of usage (i.e., follows an exponential distribution). Conceptually, this means that systems will have the same mean time between failure during their first year of service as they will have in their tenth year of service. In reality this may not often be true. However, the ease of using this type of test strategy makes it very popular; it can be satisfactory for many situations, if care is taken when designing and implementing the test (even though the test is not technically robust relative to the validity of this underlying assumption).

A reasonable basic overall reliability test strategy for repairable systems can be to first select a satisfactory sample size and test interval using the Poisson distribution. Then, if enough failures occur during a test, analyze the data to determine if a better fit could be made using the NHPP model, which can consider failure rate change as a function of usage.

When designing a test to certify a criterion (failures/unit time or MTBF) using the Poisson distribution, the design consideration to determine is the total test time. For example, a test criterion for an automobile might be 7000 km MTBF or 1/7000 failures/km. From Table K (using the concepts illustrated in Section 40.7) it can be determined that a proposed test to verify that the 90% confidence interval (i.e., for $\rho < 1/7000$ failures/km), while permitting eight failures would require a total test time of about 90,965 km.

Because the underlying assumption is that the failure rate does not change as a function of usage on the system, two extremes for the physical test are to either test one automobile for 90,965 km or to test 90,965 automobiles for 1 km. The first test alternative is perhaps physically achievable; however, by the time the test is completed, knowledge gained from the test relative to its criterion may be too late to impact the design. These test results may then be used for information only. The 90,963 sample size alternative extreme is not realistic because this sample size is typically too large for a complex system test. It should be noted that both these test extremes would be very sensitive to the accuracy of the underlying assumption of there being a constant failure rate.

The next chapter discusses realistic compromises that can be made between the sample size and the test duration for individual systems. This chapter also discusses analyzing the results to consider the failure rate changing as a function of usage.

Another test consideration that might be applicable and advantageous to consider is the modeling of the positive improvement displayed during reliability tests over a period of time due to changes in product design or the manufacturing process. US Department of Defense (1980, 1981a), Crow (1975), and Dwaine (1964) discuss the modeling of "reliability growth."

39.6   ACCELERATED TESTING: DISCUSSION

Reliability certification of electronic assemblies can be difficult because often the failure rate criterion is low and there are usually aggressive time and resource constraints. Accelerated testing techniques are often essential to complete certification within a reasonable period of time and with reasonable resources. However, care must be exercised when choosing an accelerated test strategy. A model that does not closely follow the characteristics of a device can result in an invalid conclusion. The following sections give a general overview of some accelerated test models.

Product technology, design, application, and performance objectives need to be considered when choosing stress tests for a product. After the stress tests are chosen, stress levels must not change the normal product failure modes. Without extensive model validation within the proposed experiment, an acceleration model should technically be known and implemented to contain both sample size and test duration limitations. Unfortunately, because of test constraints, model applicability may only be speculative. In addition, the results from a lack-of-fit analysis might not be very decisive because of test sample size constraints.

Often a simple form of acceleration is implemented without any awareness that the test is being accelerated. For example, a device under test may be subjected to a reliability test 24 hr per day, 7 days a week (i.e., 168 hr per week). If we believe that a customer will only use the device 8 hr a day, 5 days a week (i.e., 40 hr per week), we could consider that our test has a customer usage time acceleration of 4.2 (i.e., 168/40). Even with this simple form of acceleration, traps can be encountered. With this test the assumption is made that the sample is tested exactly as a customer uses the product. This assumption may not be valid; for example, on/off cycling may be ignored during the test. This cycling might contribute to thermal or electrical changes that may result in a big contribution to failures within the customer environment. Or, perhaps even no run time within the customer's facility causes a significant number of failures due to large corrosive or high-humidity conditions. Again, care must be exercised to protect against performing an accelerated test that either ignores an underlying phenomenon that can cause a significant number of failures or has an erroneous acceleration factor. Perhaps too much emphasis is often given to the question of the confidence level that the product will be equal to or better than the criterion, as opposed to the basic assumptions that are made in the test design.

Accelerated tests can use one or more of many stress test environments (e.g., high temperature, thermal cycling, power cycling, voltage, high current, vibration, high humidity, and mechanical stress). The following discussion includes model considerations for elevated temperature and thermal cycling tests.

39.7 HIGH-TEMPERATURE ACCELERATION

A common acceleration model used in the electronics industry is the Arrhenius equation. This model suggests that degradation leading to component failure is governed by a chemical and physical process reaction rate. This high-temperature model yields a temperature acceleration factor (A_t) of

$$A_t = \exp[(E_a/k)(1/T_u - 1/T_s)]$$

where

E_a = activation energy (eV), function of device type/technology/mechanism

k = Boltzmann's constant, 8.617×10^5 (eV/K)

T_u = unstress temperature (K)
T_s = Stress temperature (K)
K = 273.16 + °C

This equation was originally generated to predict the rate of chemical reactions. It is applied often to electronic component testing because many failure mechanisms are dependent on such reactions. A key parameter within this equation is the activation energy, which commonly ranges from 0.3 to 0.7 eV, depending on the device. Jensen and Petersen (1982) summarize activation energies that have been found applicable for certain device types, while Figure 39.3 illustrates the sensitivity of the equation to any activation energy constant assumption.

Multiple temperature stress cells can be used to determine the activation energy using the following equation, which is in a form conducive to a simple analysis of a two-cell temperature test T_1 and T_2. To use this equation, first determine the 50% failure point for each cell (T_{50_1} and T_{50_2}) using Weibull or other analysis techniques discussed in this text (note that it is not required that 50% of the sample fail to make a T_{50} estimate). The ratio of T_{50_1}/T_{50_2} is the best estimate for the acceleration factor (A_t). The activation energy (E_a) can then be determined using the equation (Tobias and Trindad 1995)

$$E_a = k \left[\ln\left(\frac{T_{50_1}}{T_{50_2}} \right) \right] \left(\frac{1}{T_1} - \frac{1}{T_2} \right)^{-1} \quad T_2 > T_1$$

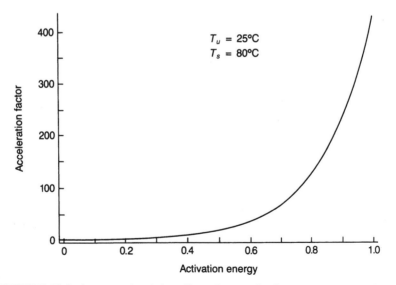

FIGURE 39.3 An example of the effects from activation energy assumptions.

Assembly testing offers the additional challenge of having multiple component types that have various activation energies. When addressing this issue, one approach for a test is to determine an overall activation energy for the assembly. Jensen and Petersen suggest that "at the present time, and lacking further information, we would, for integrated circuits, be inclined to follow Peck and Trapp (1978) and suggest a value of 0.4 eV for an otherwise unspecified freak population failure," where a freak population is produced by random occurrences in the manufacturing process as it describes a population of substandard products. To add more uncertainty to the number, Jensen and Petersen state that activation is not necessarily constant as a function of test temperature.

In addition to an activation energy constant, the Arrhenius equation needs temperature inputs. In component tests these inputs should be measured on the component in degrees Kelvin where the failure process is taking place. Within an assembly, temperature varies as a function of component position, type, and usage; hence, for practical considerations, some test designers use the module ambient temperature.

Additional discussion on the application of the Arrhenius equation is found in Nelson (1990), Tobias and Trindade (1995), Jensen and Petersen (1982), and Sutterland and Videlo (1985).

39.8   EXAMPLE 39.1: HIGH-TEMPERATURE ACCELERATION TESTING

The life criterion of an electronic component needs verification using a high-temperature test. Given an ambient operating temperature of 35°C, a stress temperature of 85°C, and an activation energy of 0.6, determine the test acceleration (A_t).

Converting the centigrade temperatures to units of Kelvin yields

$$T_0 = 35 + 273 = 308$$

$$T_s = 85 + 273 = 358$$

Substitution yields

$$A_t = \exp[(E_a/k)(1/T_u - 1/T_s)]$$
$$= \exp[(0.6/8.617 \times 10^{-5})(1/308 - 1/358)]$$
$$= \exp[6963(1/308 - 1/358)] = 23.5$$

39.9   EYRING MODEL

Most of the well-known acceleration functions can be considered to be a special case of the general Eyring acceleration function. This model also offers a general solution to the problem of combining additional stresses.

The Arrhenius model is an empirical equation that justifies its use by the fact that it "works" in many situations. The Eyring model has the added strength of having a theoretical derivation based on chemical reaction rate theory and quantum mechanics. For the time to fail of 50% of the population (T_{50}), the generalized form of the Eyring model equation is

$$T_{50} = AT^Z[\exp(E_a/kT)]\{\exp[B + (C/T)]S_1\}$$

where temperature (T) is one stress and S_1 is a second stress; A, B, C, and Z are constants. Several notes should be made about this equation:

1. The Eyring model equation describes failures at one condition. A test acceleration factor can be calculated by taking the ratio of two of these equations with differing input conditions. When this mathematical operation is performed, the A constant will cancel.
2. Many expressions may not initially appear to originate from an Eyring model, but in fact have this origination there. For example, the temperature/voltage stress model in the following equation may be thought to be applicable under a certain situation:

$$T_{50} = A[\exp(E_a/kT)](V^B)$$

The generalized two-stress Eyring equation reduces to this form by substituting $Z = 0$, $C = 0$, and S_1 in V (where V is in volts).
3. T_{50} describes the time when 50% of the test units will fail. However, other percentiles can likewise be determined.
4. The term $T^Z[\exp(E_a/kT)]$ models the effect of temperature and compares with the Arrhenius model if Z is close to 0.
5. Additional stresses (e.g., S_2) can be added as factors in the following form:

$$T_{50} = AT^Z[\exp(E_a/kT)]\{\exp[B + (C/T)]S_1\}\{\exp[D + (E/T)]S_2\}$$

Each additional set of factors adds two more unknown constants (e.g., D and E), making the model more difficult to work with in a general state. Considering all the constants as unknowns requires at least as many separate experimental stress cells as there are unknown constants in the model.

6. Choosing the units to use in a model equation can be a problem. Temperature is in degrees Kelvin. But, for example, how should voltage or humidity be input? The theoretical model derivation does not specify; hence, the experimenter must either (a) work it out by trial and error or (b) derive an applicable model using arguments from physics and statistics.

39.10   THERMAL CYCLING: COFFIN–MANSON RELATIONSHIP

The inverse power law is used to model fatigue failure of metals that are subjected to thermal cycling. For the purpose of accelerated testing, this model relationship is called the Coffin–Manson relationship (Coffin 1954, 1974: Manson 1953, 1966) and can be expressed in the form

$$A_t = (\Delta T_s / \Delta T_u)^B$$

where A_t is the acceleration factor and B is a constant characteristic of the metal and test method and cycle. ΔT_u is the temperature change under normal operation, while ΔT_s is the temperature change under stress operation. The constant B is near 2 for metals, while Nelson (1990) states that for plastic encapsulates for microelectronics, B is near 5.

An application of this equation is in the electronic industry. Heating/cooling conditions can often occur within the covers of a product because of simple on/off cycling. Thermal changes cause expansion/contraction processes to occur within a product. If solder joints are weak and the thermal change is sufficiently large, stresses can then occur within solder joints, thus causing fractures, which can lead to product failure.

In the electronics industry, modifications are sometimes needed to the basic Coffin–Manson equation. For example, Norris and Landzberg (1969) noted that for tin–lead solders used in C-4 (controlled collapse chip connections), joints at room temperature are at about 50% of their absolute melting temperature. They state: "the Coffin–Manson equation was found to be inadequate for projecting the thermal failure of solder interconnections; in laboratory experiments it was found to yield very pessimistic estimates of fatigue lifetimes." They added a frequency-dependent term and an Arrhenius temperature-dependent term to form a "modified Coffin–Manson" equation.

Tummala and Rymaszewski (1989) show a modified Coffin–Manson relationship of

$$A_t = \exp[0.123/k)(1/T_u - 1/T_s)] \left(\frac{f_u}{f_s}\right)^{0.3} \left(\frac{\Delta T_s}{\Delta T_u}\right)^{1.9}$$

where the added terms f_u and f_s reflect the frequency of cyclic changes in use and stress conditions, respectively. T_u and T_s represent the maximum use and stress temperature in the cycles in degrees Kelvin; k is Boltzmann's constant.

Other sources for information about the Coffin–Manson relationship are Engelmaier (1985), Goldmann (1969), Tobias and Trindade (1995), Nachlas (1986), and Nishimura et al. (1987). Saari et al. (1982) has an additional discussion on thermal cycle screening strengths in a manufacturing environment.

39.11   MODEL SELECTION: ACCELERATED TESTING

Previous sections within this chapter included only a few of the test alternatives suggested within the literature to accelerate certain types of failure modes. In addition, there are other stress alternatives such as humidity, voltage, current, corrosive gas, and vibration that are sometimes used in industry for accelerated tests.

Whenever one must choose an accelerated test strategy to address reliability certification, it becomes immediately obvious that model selection and test strategy can dramatically affect a product pass-versus-fail test position. For the model to be valid, the accelerated test methodology must not change the failure mode of the component. Care must be exercised when making a confidence interval assessment after using an accelerated test model because, in reality, much unknown error can exist within the "acceleration factor number."

Each model is most appropriate for a specific component failure mechanism. Assemblies can contain many components with different failure mechanisms, which makes the selection of test models even more difficult. There is additional discussion on the application of acceleration models in Nelson (1990) and in Tobias and Trindade (1995). These references also discuss step stress testing where, for example, the temperature stress on a set of test components is increased periodically and the times to failure are noted at each temperature level.

39.12   S⁴ ASSESSMENT

When choosing a basic test strategy for a given situation, one should consider the following:

1. Determine whether the units under test are repairable or nonrepairable.
2. Determine through consultation and literature searching the most accurate accelerated test modeling strategy that will suffice for the test constraints yet capture the failure modes that the customer might ex-

perience. Note, for example, that a test that constantly exercises a component only at an accelerated high-temperature environment is not evaluating possible failure modes caused by thermal cycling.

3. Determine a sample size, test duration (per unit), and number of permissible failures using detailed test strategies discussed within one of the two following chapters.
4. List all the test assumptions.

Reliability tests are often performed to "ensure" that the frequency of failures of a component or assembly is below a criterion. Often this test is performed during initial model builds or initial production.

One of the major assumptions that is often compromised in a typical reliability test is that the sample is randomly taken from the population of interest. Often with qualification tests the population of interest is really future product production. For this situation a perhaps better strategy is to test a product that has been specially manufactured to represent the variability "space" of a production process. Special test samples could be manufactured according to DOE considerations. With this strategy there is the added advantage that a major process problem could be detected before mass production is begun (e.g., when a manufacturing factor is at its low tolerance setting, the product failure rate is significantly increased). This advantage can outweigh the sacrifice in a loss of randomization when it is considered that a "random" sample from an early manufacturing process may be far from representing product that the customer will actually receive.

DOE can also have reliability test output considerations for each trial. For example, consider that the failure rate of a system needs to be reduced in order to increase customer satisfaction. A fractional factorial experiment could be used to evaluate proposed design changes, where special systems would be built according to the trial factor considerations. If all test units were operated to failure, the time of failure or a failure rate for the test units could be analyzed as a response for each trial. (Note that a data transformation may be required.)

However, it may be difficult to test long enough for all test units to fail. Because of this, it would be advantageous to monitor periodically during test some response that typically degrades in unison with the life characteristics of the device. The factors that appear to be significant for this response would then be presumed to significantly affect the system failure rate. The factor levels that are found to be best from this experiment should then be considered important when making changes to the design if appropriate.

In some system situations it might erroneously be assumed that the major source of customer problems is component failures. It is common for situations to occur where the customer would have experienced a problem that was dependent on how he or she used the product. When the inherent failure rate of components is very low, it is very difficult to quantify a reliability failure rate. Because of this, perhaps more effort should be given toward ensuring that the product meets the real needs of the customer, in lieu of a simple "build them and test them" strategy.

Within manufacturing in the electronics industry, systems or components are often run-in or burned-in (i.e., screened) to capture early-life failures before the product reaches the customer's office. However, it is not reasonable to expect that this test will capture all problem escapes of the manufacturing process before a product reaches the customer, although if the product does experience an early/life failure mode, it is reasonable to expect that the quality experienced by the customer will be better because of the burn-in/run-in test.

After a burn-in/run-in test time is determined, a failure rate tracking chart can be beneficial to monitor over time the proportion that fails during the test. When special causes are identified in the chart, it is reasonable to expect that the customer will also have an increased failure rate because, as noted earlier, all individual machine problems will not normally be captured during this test. In a stable process over some period of time, a list of failure causes can be generated and presented in a Pareto chart. Reduction of the vital few causes could then be addressed using fractional factorial experiment techniques or perhaps by making some obvious changes to the process. Significant improvements that reduce the number of the causes in the manufacturing process should later be detected as an out-of-control condition (for the better) in the overall failure rate control chart of the burn-in station. This procedure could then be repeated for further improvements.

In time it would be desirable to get enough improvement in the basic manufacturing process such that a dramatic, consistent reduction in the control chart overall failure rate is shown. If this happens, it might be appropriate to change the 100% burn-in/run-in procedure to a sampling plan for the detection of special causes. It should be noted, however, that even though the burn-in/run-in (i.e., screen) test may experience no failures, a customer may be having many difficulties. A Pareto chart of the cause of field problems can be illuminating. Perhaps the burn-in/run-in test is evaluating the wrong things and missing many of the problems experienced by customers. The tester function may, for example, need to be changed to capture these types of problems.

39.13 EXERCISE

1. Describe how the techniques within this chapter are useful and can be applied to S^4 projects.

40

RELIABILITY TESTING/ASSESSMENT: REPAIRABLE SYSTEM

This chapter explores the problem of "certifying" the failure rate criterion (failures per unit of time, ρ_a) or mean time between failures (MTBF) criterion of a system, where a system is defined as a collection of components, and components are replaced or repaired whenever a failure occurs.

Both constant and changing failure rate situations are considered. The Poisson distribution can be used when the system failure rate is constant as a function of the age of a system. The nonhomogeneous Poisson process (NHPP) with Weibull intensity can often be used when the failure rate is considered to change as a function of system usage.

40.1 CONSIDERATIONS WHEN DESIGNING A TEST OF A REPAIRABLE SYSTEM FAILURE CRITERION

One of several test design alternatives could be chosen when "certifying" a repairable system failure rate criterion. In this chapter, classical test design alternatives are discussed along with some extensions and S⁴ assessments.

The techniques discussed within this chapter address the rate at which systems experience failures as a function of time. Criteria that are expressed in units of MTBF will need to be transformed by a simple reciprocal conversion. For example, an MTBF rate of 10,000 hr can be converted to a failure rate criterion of 0.0001 failures/hour (i.e., 1/10,000 = 0.0001).

Reliability tests can be either sequential or fixed length. With the sequential approach, test termination is generally after either the product has exhibited few enough failures at some point in time during test for a "pass" decision (with β risk of error) or enough failures have occurred to make a "fail" decision (with α risk of error). The other alternative is either fixed length or fixed failure tests. Because fixed failure tests are not terminated until a predetermined number of failures have occurred and most test situations have schedule/time constraints, time-terminated tests are the normal choice for fixed-length test strategies.

System failure rate test designs often initially assume that the failure rate is constant as a function of system age. This limiting assumption can lead to the selection of the Poisson distribution for these test designs and analyses. With the Poisson distribution, total usage on all systems is the parameter of concern; it theoretically does not matter how many units are on the test to achieve this total test usage value. For example, with a 15,000-hr fixed-length test, it does not technically matter if one unit is exercised for 15,000 hr or 15,000 units are exercised for 1 hr.

Theoretically, these scenarios may be the same; however, in reality the two test extremes may yield quite different results. If one of these two extremes were chosen, dramatic differences can be expected if the "constant failure rate" assumption is invalid. That is, this type of test evaluation is not robust to the underlying assumption not being valid. The following discussion considers test strategies that can be used to reduce the risk of getting an answer that has minimal value.

Technically, before using the Poisson distribution for test design, the failure rate of the system should be a known constant (flat part of a bathtub curve) for the time of concern (e.g., product warranty or product useful life). However, process problems can cause more early-life failures, while wear-out phenomena can cause the instantaneous system failure rate to increase as a function of usage on the product. In reality, the experimenter does not know for sure that this response will be constant. However, if care is exercised when making initial decisions relative to sample size versus individual sample usage, error due to unknown information about the shape of this intensity function can be minimized.

When a test is being designed, consideration must be given to the real objective or concern. If concerns are about capturing wear-out problems, a small number of systems need to be tested for a long period of time. If concern is whether manufacturing or early-life problems exist, a larger number of samples should be tested for a shorter period of time. If there are concerns about early life and wear-out, it may be the best economics to exercise a large sample for a "short" period and then continue the test for a subset of machines to "product life" usage to assess system wear-out exposures.

If a warranty or maintenance criterion needs to be assessed to ensure that failures will not exceed targets, then it may be best that the test duration per unit equals the warranty or maintenance agreement period. If a sufficient number of failures occurs during this test, then the NHPP can be used to determine if (and how) failure rates are changing as a function of usage on individual systems.

Failure rate tests during product development are sometimes expected to give an accurate confidence interval assessment of what the failure rate will be when the product is built within production. If there is concern about design and manufacturing problems, does it make sense to take a "random" sample of the first parts that are produced to certify a criterion? A "random" sample of future products is needed to test for design and manufacturing problems. Assemblies produced within a short time period tend to be similar; these samples do not necessarily represent the product "space" (i.e., boundary limits) of design tolerances and manufacturing variability.

In lieu of classical reliability testing, there are other economical alternatives that may capture these problems that can haunt a manufacturer later during production. Initial lot sampling may not expose design and process problems that in fact exist, because the sample is representative of only the current lot population. Example 43.2 discusses alternatives that may be appropriate to replace or supplement this classical test approach in capturing these elusive problems earlier within the development of the product design and manufacturing processes.

Again, fixed-length and sequential test plans (US Department of Defense 1986, 1987) are the two general types of test strategies applicable to system failure rate "certification." Fixed-length test plans are perhaps more commonly used; however, sequential test plan alternatives are also discussed. The results from these tests could also be used to give a confidence interval for the failure rate of the product population from which the sample is drawn. It is assumed with this test that the manufacturing process is stable and that there will be no design changes to the product during test. In addition, it is also assumed for the described tests that the sample size is small relative to the population size. For this last assumption to be true, it is best that the ratio of sample size to population size does not exceed 10%.

A sequential test plan is considered the best test alternative when it is a requirement to either accept or reject predetermined failure rate values (ρ_0 and ρ_1) with predetermined risks of error (α and β). With sequential testing, uncertainty must be expected with regard to total test time.

A fixed-length test plan is appropriate when the total test time must be known in advance. In this chapter, two test alternatives for this type of test are discussed. In one section, sample size for a hypothesis test is discussed where both α and β risks are considered, while another section offers a reduced sample size testing strategy option. This second test approach can be used to "certify" system criteria, with the understanding that the real test purpose is to obtain a confidence interval for the true failure rate and then compare the single-sided bound to the criterion.

40.2   SEQUENTIAL TESTING: POISSON DISTRIBUTION

For sequential plans, in addition to both α and β risks, two failure rates (ρ_0 and ρ_1) are needed as input to this model. If a system has only one criterion

(ρ_a) and this criterion is be "certified" with a consumer risk β, the highest failure rate ρ_1 should probably be set equal to the criterion. Perhaps the easiest way to select a ρ_0 which relates to α risk, is to select first a discrimination ratio (d), which relates the two failure rate test extremes (US Department of Defense 1987). This ratio can be defined as the ratio of a higher failure rate (ρ_1) to a lower failure rate (ρ_0):

$$d = \frac{\rho_1}{\rho_0} \qquad \rho_1 > \rho_0$$

The discrimination ratio input is a key parameter, along with α and β, when determining the specifics of the test. Before the test, all concerned groups need to agree to all parameter inputs.

A sequential probability ratio plan for repairable systems can then be expressed as two straight lines with coordinates of failures (r) and total test time (T):

$$\frac{\ln[\beta/(1 - \alpha)]}{\ln(\rho_1/\rho_0)} + \frac{(\rho_1 - \rho_0)}{\ln(\rho_1/\rho_0)} T < r < \frac{\ln[C(1 - \beta)/\alpha]}{\ln(\rho_1/\rho_0)} + \frac{(\rho_1 - \rho_0)}{\ln(\rho_1/\rho_0)} T$$

where $C = 1$ when there is no test truncation time. The actual test failures are then plotted versus test time. The test is terminated whenever this plot intersects either the pass or fail line determined from the equation.

The factor C in this equation takes on the value of ($[1 + d]/2d$) when the following test truncation procedure is used (US Department of Defense 1987). In this procedure, the parallel lines from the equation have truncation lines added at T_0 and r_0. To determine r_0, an appropriate value of r is first determined to be the smallest integer such that

$$\frac{\chi^2_{(1-\alpha);2r}}{\chi^2_{\beta;2r}} \geq \frac{\rho_0}{\rho_1}$$

In this equation, values are then determined for the numerator and denominator by simultaneously searching the Chi-square tables (see Table G) until the ratio of the variables is equal to or greater than ρ_0/ρ_1. The number of degrees of freedom r_0 will be half of this value that is determined; values for r_0 are rounded to the next higher integer. The test truncation time T_0 is then determined to be

$$T_0 = \frac{\chi^2_{(1-\alpha);2r_0}}{2\rho_0}$$

40.3   EXAMPLE 40.1: SEQUENTIAL RELIABILITY TEST

1. A sequential test is to assess whether a criterion of 1000 hr MTBF (i.e., 0.001 failures/hr) is met on a system given the following:
   a. $\beta = 0.1$ for $\rho_1 =$ criterion $= 0.001$
   b. Discrimination ratio $= d = 1.6$
   c. $\alpha = 0.05$
   Hence, $\rho_0 = \rho_1/d = 0.001/1.6 = 0.000625$
   $C = (1 + 1.6)/(2[1.6]) = 0.8125$
2. The test was then conducted. The accumulated usages on the systems when there was a system failure was 2006, 3020, 6008, 8030, and 9010. With a given total test time of 12,268 hr it was necessary to determine what action should be taken (i.e., continue test, pass test, or fail test).

Substitution yields the following sequential decision lines:

$$\frac{\ln[0.1/(1 - 0.05)]}{\ln(0.001/0.000625)} + \frac{(0.001 - 0.000625)}{\ln(0.001/0.000625)} T < r$$

$$-4.790 + 0.000798T < r$$

$$r < \frac{\ln[0.8125(1 - 0.1)/0.05]}{\ln(0.001/0.000625)} + \frac{(0.001 - 0.000625)}{\ln(0.001/0.000625)} T$$

$$r < 5.708 + 0.000798T$$

Using the previously described procedure for termination time, Table G yields the following since $\rho_0/\rho_1 = 0.000625/0.001 = 0.625$:

$$\frac{\chi^2_{[(1-0.05);80]}}{\chi^2_{[0.1;80]}} = \frac{60.39}{96.58} = 0.6253 \geq 0.625$$

It then follows that $r_0 = 40$ failures (i.e., 80/2) and

$$T_0 = \frac{\chi^2_{(1-\alpha);2r_0}}{2\rho_0} = \frac{60.39}{0.00125} = 48,312$$

Figure 40.1 illustrates the plotting of these sequential test boundary conditions with the failure data to determine that the test indicates that the systems in test "passed" at the test usage of 12,268 hr; that is, from the first equation above, $T = [(5 + 4.79)/0.000798] = 12,268$.

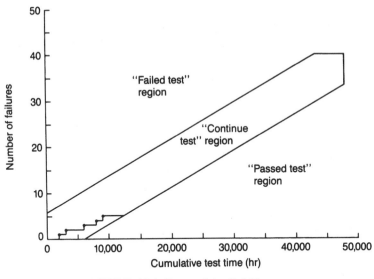

FIGURE 40.1 Sequential reliability test.

At the "passed test" time of 12,268 hr for this example, the product sample was performing at a failure rate of 0.00041 (i.e., 5/12,268 = 0.00041), which is 41% of the 0.001 criterion. If the test system actually performed close to the specification limit, the test duration time could be much larger.

In general, a sequential test strategy will yield a shorter test duration than a fixed test strategy with the same α and β. However, planning termination times before the "truncation time" can make accurate scheduling difficult.

40.4 TOTAL TEST TIME: HYPOTHESIS TEST OF A FAILURE RATE CRITERION

When the underlying distribution is Poisson, the total run time (in the case of a reliability test) for a hypothesis test about one population can be determined to be

$$T = \left[\frac{(U_\alpha)(\rho_\alpha)^{1/2} + (U_\beta)(\rho_\beta)^{1/2}}{\rho_\beta - \rho_\alpha} \right]^2$$

where T is the total test time given the failure rates ρ_β and ρ_α that relate to the null (H_0) and alternate (H_a) hypotheses, respectively. U_α is the value from Table B or C, depending on whether H_a is single or double-sided, and U_β is from Table B. Note that T represents the sample size in the situation where the Poisson distribution is used as an approximation for the binomial distribution in an attribute hypothesis test. To illustrate this point, consider the units of these two types of failure rates. A reliability failure rate criterion could be 0.0001 failures/hour, while an attribute criterion could be 0.0001 jams/sheet of paper loaded. In the second example the experimenter is interested in determining the total number of sheets of paper to load into devices.

40.5 CONFIDENCE INTERVAL FOR FAILURE RATE EVALUATIONS

The following confidence interval equation is for time-terminated tests where the failure rate is constant. For a failure-terminated test the lower confidence interval remains the same; however, the number of degrees of freedom for the upper confidence interval changes from $(2r + 2)$ to $2r$:

$$\frac{\chi^2_{2r;(1+c)/2}}{2T} \le \rho \le \frac{\chi^2_{2r+2;(1-c)/2}}{2T}$$

where

T = total cumulative usage

r = number of failures

χ^2 = chi-square value from Table G for $2r + 2$ or $2r$ degrees of freedom

c = level of confidence selected expressed in decimal form

For a time-terminated test an alternative approach is to use Table K with the equation

$$\frac{A_{r;(1+c)/2}}{T} \le \rho \le \frac{B_{r;(1+c)/2}}{T}$$

where

B = factor from Table K with r failures and $[(1 + c)/2]$ decimal confidence value

A = factor from Table K with r failures and $[(1 + c)/2]$ decimal confidence value

The single-sided confidence statement takes a similar form using the decimal confidence value directly. If $r = 0$ at the test termination time, only a single-sided confidence interval is possible.

40.6 EXAMPLE 40.2: TIME-TERMINATED RELIABILITY TESTING CONFIDENCE STATEMENT

Ten systems are tested for 1000 equivalent customer usage hours each. When a failure occurs, the system is repaired and placed back on the test. Ten failures occurred during the time-terminated test. The 90% confidence interval for the failure rate can be determined using either of the following two procedures:

Substitution yields

$$\frac{\chi^2_{[(2)(10)];[(1+0.9)/2]}}{2[(10)(1000)]} \leq \rho \leq \frac{\chi^2_{[(2)(10)+2];[(1-0.9)/2]}}{2[(10)(1000)]}$$

from the chi-square distribution (Table G)

$$\chi^2_{20;0.95} = 10.85 \qquad \chi^2_{22;0.05} = 33.92$$

Substitution yields

$$0.0005425 \leq \rho \leq 0.001696$$

Similarly, Table K could be used to get the same answer:

$$\frac{A_{10;(1+0.9)/2}}{(10)(1000)} \leq \rho \leq \frac{B_{10;(1+0.9)/2}}{(10)(1000)}$$

$$\frac{5.424}{10,000} \leq \rho \leq \frac{16.962}{10,000}$$

$$0.0005425 \leq \rho \leq 0.0016962$$

Since concerns are usually about ensuring the upper limits of the failure rate, the preceding double-sided 90% confidence interval could be expressed as a single-sided 95% confidence level of

$$\rho \leq 0.001696$$

40.7 REDUCED SAMPLE SIZE TESTING: POISSON DISTRIBUTION

The sample size procedure illustrated previously protects both the customer (with β risk) and the producer (with α risk). The test objective of the plan described in this section is to only "certify" that the product does not exceed a criterion ρ_a. This single-sided test strategy will yield a test plan similar to those proposed by commercially available "reliability slide rules." In this strategy, fewer than r failures must occur within a total test time T for "certification."

This reduced sample size testing strategy is applicable to a criterion certification test when the total test time is chosen such that the criterion is set to a bound of the confidence interval with a given number of allowed failures (i.e., the failure rate of the population is equal to or less than the criterion failure rate at the desired confidence level).

To get the total test duration that is required for such an evaluation, $B_{r;c}$ can be determined using Table K for the chosen number of permissible failures and desired confidence interval value. $B_{r;c}$ is then substituted with the failure rate criterion (ρ_a) to yield a value for T, the total test time:

$$T = \frac{B_{r;c}}{\rho_a}$$

The following example illustrates the simple procedure to use when designing such a test. In order to pass a test of this type, the sample may be required to perform at a failure rate that is much better than the population criterion.

40.8   EXAMPLE 40.3: REDUCED SAMPLE SIZE TESTING—POISSON DISTRIBUTION

Product planning states that a computer system is to have a failure rate (i.e., a failure rate criterion) that is not to exceed 0.001 failures/hour (i.e., $\rho_a = 0.001$). The projected annual customer usage of the system is 1330 hr. A test duration is desired such that two failures are acceptable and a 90% confidence interval bound on the failure rate will be

$$\rho \leq 0.001$$

Table K is used to determine that $B_{2;0.90} = 5.322$. It then follows that

$$T = \frac{B_{r;c}}{\rho_a} = \frac{B_{2;0.90}}{0.001} = \frac{5.322}{0.001} = 5322 \text{ hr}$$

As previously noted for this type of test, one system could be tested for 5322 hr or 5322 systems for 1 hr. A compromise approach (although a potentially very expensive test) is to test 4 units 1330 hr each [i.e., (4)(1330)

≈ 5322 total hr]. With this scenario each unit would experience usage equal to the annual warranty usage of 1330 hr. If a total of two or less failures occur on the test machines, the test is "passed."

40.9   RELIABILITY TEST DESIGN WITH TEST PERFORMANCE CONSIDERATIONS

The test strategy discussed in the previous section does not consider how difficult it might be for a product to pass a given test design. To illustrate this, consider what position should be taken if a zero failure, 99% confidence bound test plan had 1 failure? 2 failures? 10 failures? Technically, in all these cases the test was failed because the zero failure objective was not met. However, care needs to be exercised with this "failed test" position. It seems unreasonable to take an equal failed test position with the three posttest scenarios. With a 99% confidence bound test plan and one or two failures at test completion, the sample failure rate (i.e., number of failures divided by total test time) would be found to be better than criterion. However, if 10 failures occurred during the test, the sample failure rate would be much worse than the criterion. The following discussion proposes a methodology to guide the experimenter in making better test input decisions.

Within corporations, test groups could have an adversary relationship with the manufacturing and development communities. Testers want certainty that criteria objectives are met, while other groups may have the primary emphasis of meeting schedule and production volume requirements. Posttest confrontation between testers and others can be expected when certifying aggressive failure criteria with a fixed-length test design that permits only a small number of failures and a high amount of confidence that the criterion will be met. If the product had one too many failures, the development or manufacturing organizations may take the position that the product should be considered satisfactory because the test failure rate was better than specification. There is some merit to this position, because with this type of test strategy the development/manufacturing organizations are taking the full impact of test uncertainty resulting from the test requirements of a high "pass test" confidence level and a small number of permissible failures.

One alternative to this uncertainty dilemma is to design a test that will address both α and β risks collectively. The disadvantage to this strategy is that the test sample size and test duration are normally "too large."

A compromise to this approach is to address what-if scenarios "up front" with possible outcomes before the test is begun. To aid this pretest scenario process, I suggest considering the "test performance ratio" (P) factor of various test alternatives before the test starts.

To explain this factor, consider a test alternative that permits r failures with T total test time. The sample failure ρ_t rate for this test design would then be

$$\rho_t = \frac{r}{T}$$

This test design failure rate (ρ_t) is then a function of both the number of allowable failures and desired percent confidence interval consideration for the chosen scenario. The test performance ratio (P) is then used to compare this test design failure rate (ρ_t) to the criterion (ρ_a) by the relationship

$$P = \frac{\rho_t}{\rho_a}$$

Note that low values for P indicate that the product will need to perform at a failure rate much better than the criterion to achieve a "pass test" position. For example, if P were equal to 0.25, this means that for a pass test position to occur the product will need to perform four times better than specification during the test. If this ratio is assessed before the test, perhaps tests that are doomed to failure can be avoided. In this example the development organization may state that this proposed test is not feasible because it is highly unlikely that the product sample will perform four times better than the criterion.

The following example illustrates the application of the test performance ratio to help achieve test design inputs that are agreeable to all concerned organizations before test initiation.

40.10   EXAMPLE 40.4: TIME-TERMINATED RELIABILITY TEST DESIGN—WITH TEST PERFORMANCE CONSIDERATIONS

A test performance ratio graph can aid in the selection of the number of permissible test failures to allow when verifying a criterion. The failure criterion in this example was 0.001 failures/hour with a test 90% confidence interval bound.

From Table K the following B values for 90% confidence given the 0, 1, 2, and 3 failure(s) scenarios are

r:	0	1	2	3
B:	2.303	3.890	5.322	6.681

These tabular values yield a total test time (T) [e.g., 5.322/0.001 = 5322] for the differing failure scenarios of

r:	0	1	2	3
T:	2303	3890	5322	6681

For these scenarios, ρ_t is determined by dividing the number of failures by the total test time (e.g., $2/5322 = 0.0003758$) to achieve

r:	0	1	2	3
ρ_r:	0	0.0002571	0.0003758	0.0004490

For the failure criterion of 0.001, the test performance ratio (P) for each test possibility becomes (e.g., $0.0002571/0.001 = 0.2571$)

r:	0	1	2	3
P:	0	0.2571	0.3758	0.4490

This table gives an indication how much better than criterion the sample needs to perform for the 90% confidence interval bounded tests. For example, a one-failure test requires that the sample failure rate be at least 3.89 times (i.e., $1/0.2571 = 3.89$) better than criterion for passage, while a three-failure test needs to be a multiple of 2.23 ($1/0.4490 = 2.23$). Obviously a product will have a better chance of passing a three-failure test; however, the price to pay is additional testing. To get a better idea of the test alternatives, test performance ratio (P) can be plotted versus the corresponding test times for each failure, as shown in Figure 40.2.

Each of these points on the graph represents a test plan alternative. This plot is not "half" of a sequential test plot. It is noted that a zero-failure test requires usage of 2303 hr, while the previous sequential test plan in the example requires 6003. This difference exists because with a fixed-length test a decision is to be made after test time (T), while normally a sequential test

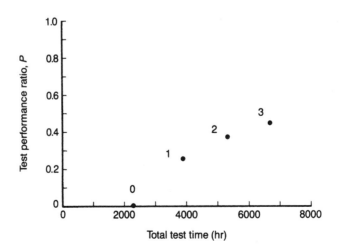

FIGURE 40.2 Test performance ratio versus total test time for various test scenarios.

plan will be continued for a much longer test time until a decision can be made with either an α or β risk.

Figure 40.2 addresses a test performance ratio that relates a "pass test" failure rate to a criterion. The plot shown in Figure 40.3 indicates, in addition to the preceding curve, a test performance ratio curve that is appropriate if each possible test failure objective is exceeded by one, which is the minimal number of failures that is considered for a "failed test" decision.

The plot form shown in Figure 40.4 is useful to assess the effects of various input confidence level alternatives on the test performance ratio (P). With this information a more realistic pass/fail test can often be chosen that better considers the general economics of the test situation.

40.11   POSTTEST ASSESSMENTS

More failures than originally permitted may occur within a reliability test. However, management may not be willing to stop the production build process purely on the test position that the targeted failure rate cannot be "passed" with the desired confidence level. Management may want to better understand what future failure rate can be expected with minimal process changes. Management may even be willing to accept the risk of a higher customer failure rate exposure for some period of time until long-term "fixes"

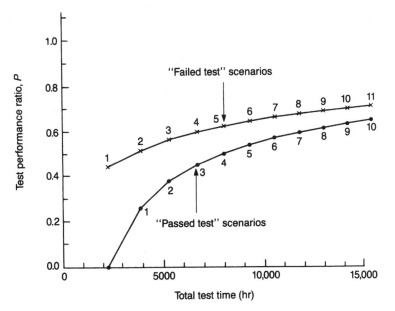

FIGURE 40.3 Test performance ratio versus total test time for various test scenarios.

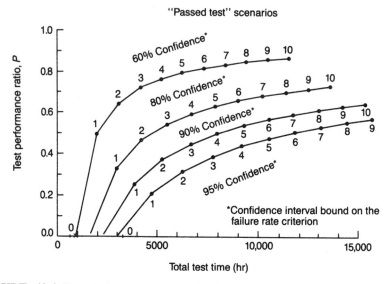

FIGURE 40.4 Test design alternatives (60%, 80%, 90%, and 95% confidence-criterion-bounded interval).

can be incorporated within the design or manufacturing process. The question of concern to make this decision becomes: What customer failure rate can be expected with the given test data, given minor product alterations?

To address this question, each failure within the test should be evaluated to determine whether a fix was made to eliminate future occurrences of this failure. Many of the problems experienced may be "talked away" by either future design change proposals or process changes. Care must be exercised with this strategy because a "retest" may experience additional process or design problems that did not happen to occur with the initial test sample, resulting in an overall failure rate that did not decrease to the extent that was expected.

However, a confidence interval could be calculated to illustrate the probabilistic range of failure rate for the population with a given test failure scenario. However, often two problems can exist with this strategy. First, differing organizations within a corporation do not often agree on the number of failures that "should be counted" from the test data. Also, the confidence level to be reported may not be in general agreement.

40.12   EXAMPLE 40.5: POSTRELIABILITY TEST CONFIDENCE STATEMENTS

Consider that from the earlier example the three-failure test of the 0.001 failures/hr criterion was chosen. A total test time of 6681 was planned to verify the criterion; however, the test did not actually stop until a total customer equivalent usage time of 7000 hr was achieved. This time-terminated test experienced a total of eight failures.

The eight failures were analyzed to determine what would be necessary to prevent future occurrences of each failure type. Representatives from all concerned organizations agreed that three of the failure types could happen again because the cost to alter the manufacturing process to eliminate these differing failure types would currently be cost prohibitive. These representatives also agreed that two of the failures would be transparent to a customer and should not be considered a failure. The manufacturing and development organizations believed that the other three would be fixed by an engineering change to either the process or the design; they believed that if this test were performed again with these changes, there would "probably be" three failures. The test organization was not so optimistic about these fixes, and they believed that some other type of failures might surface if the test were repeated. They wanted to consider six failures until proven otherwise.

To better assess the business risk relative to the 0.001 criterion, the following failure rate table was created for various confidence levels using Table K:

	Three Failures	Six Failures
Sample failure rate	3/7000 = 0.00043	6/7000 = 0.00086
70% upper limit	4.762/7000 = 0.00068	8.111/7000 = 0.00116
90% upper limit	6.681/7000 = 0.00095	10.532/7000 = 0.0015

Cost factors can be an appropriate extension to this table to aid with the business decision process.

The preceding discussion was relative to the goal of meeting a criterion. However, neither testers nor management should "play games with the numbers." A customer wants no failures to occur. Emphasis should be given to continually improve the process by eliminating first the source for the large problems and then smaller problems, with the target in mind of eventually improving the process so that no failures will occur. Brainstorming, Pareto charts, DOE, and other S^4 tools can be very beneficial tools to help improve processes.

40.13 REPAIRABLE SYSTEMS WITH CHANGING FAILURE RATE

A Weibull probability plot yields an estimate for the percent of population failed as a function of device usage. For a system a question of concern is whether the "instantaneous" failure rate (e.g., failures/hr) changes as a function of usage, not percentage of population failures as a function of usage. The NHPP model is often applicable to this situation, which can be expressed as

$$r(t) = \lambda b(t)^{b-1}$$

If λ and b in this equation were known, then the system failure rate, $r(t)$, is described as a function of time.

Consider that time-of-failure data were available either from a test or from a data base containing information about system failures in a customer's office. If we consider that these systems had multiple start times, iterative solutions are needed to determine the estimators to this model. However, the equations are in closed form in the special case when the systems are considered to have the same start time (see Crow 1974); hence, this scenario does not require an iterative solution.

For a time-truncated scenario the conditional maximum-likelihood estimates $\hat{b}$ and $\hat{\lambda}$ when all the systems start at the same time are given by the following equations. These equations can be used to estimate the unknown quantities b and λ.

$$\hat{b} = \frac{\displaystyle\sum_{q=1}^{K} N_q}{\displaystyle\sum_{q=1}^{K} \sum_{i=1}^{Nq} \ln \frac{T_q}{X_{iq}}}$$

$$\hat{\lambda} = \frac{\displaystyle\sum_{q=1}^{K} N_q}{\displaystyle\sum_{q=1}^{K} T_q^b}$$

where

K = total number of systems on test
q = system number $(1, 2, \ldots, K)$
N_q = the number of failures exhibited by qth system
T_q = the termination time for qth system
X_{iq} = age of the q system for the ith occurrence of failure

The following example illustrates how the NHPP can be used to assess a system failure rate as a function of usage on the system. The type of data in this example could have been collected either from a failure criterion test, from field tracking information, or from an "in-house" stress screen test, if we assume that the systems have the same "start time."

40.14   EXAMPLE 40.6: REPAIRABLE SYSTEMS WITH CHANGING FAILURE RATE

A manufacturing process is to produce systems that are to be tested before shipment within an accelerated test environment. This screen is to be long enough to capture most quality problems. Twenty systems were tested to a duration that was longer than the "planned" normal stress screen duration. This test yielded the results shown in Table 40.1, where the accelerated test usage was converted to expected "customer usage" values. Figure 40.5 pictorially illustrates these failures on the individual systems. Note that the following discussion assumes that multiple failures occur on a system by chance. In general, an experimenter should try to determine if (and then try to understand why) some systems perform significantly better/worse than the other systems.

Substitution yields

$$\hat{b} = \frac{\sum\limits_{q=1}^{K} N_q}{\sum\limits_{q=1}^{K} \sum\limits_{i=1}^{Nq} \ln \dfrac{T_q}{X_{iq}}} = \frac{1 + 2 + 1 + 3 + \cdots}{\ln \dfrac{58}{0.3} + \ln \dfrac{61}{14} + \ln \dfrac{61}{42} + \ln \dfrac{27}{20} + \cdots} = 0.54$$

$$\hat{\lambda} = \frac{\sum\limits_{q=1}^{K} N_q}{\sum\limits_{q=1}^{K} T_q^{\hat{b}}} = \frac{1 + 2 + 1 + 3 + \cdots}{58^{0.54} + 61^{0.54} + 27^{0.54} + 54^{0.54} + \cdots} = 0.15$$

The expected individual system failure rate is then

$$r(t) = \lambda b(t)^{b-1} = (0.15)(0.54)t^{0.54-1} = 0.081t^{-0.46}$$

This intensity function is pictorially illustrated in Figure 40.6, where, for example, the failure rate at 10 days was determined to be

$$r(10) = 0.081\,(10)^{-0.46} = 0.028 \text{ failures/day}$$

One visual representation of the model fit to the data is to determine and then plot for each of the 22 failures the average system cumulative failure rate as a function of usage. Figure 40.7 shows the fitted equation along with these data points.

To determine the raw data plot positions in this figure, consider, for example, the plot position for the eighth ascending ranked data point. From the original data set, the failure time for both the eighth and ninth data point was 6 days, which would be the abscissa value for both these points. The ordinate value for the eighth data point would be the average failure rate of the systems under test at this point in time. For the eighth data point the ordinate value is

$$\frac{8 \text{ total failures}}{20 \text{ systems in test}} = 0.4 \text{ failures/system}$$

TABLE 40.1 System Failure Times

System Number	Failure Times ("Customer Days")	Termination Time ("Customer Days")
1	0.3	58
2	14, 42	61
3	20	27
4	1, 7, 15	54
5	12, 25	27
6	0.3, 6, 30	35
7	6	40
8	24	31
9	1	42
10	26	54
11	0.3, 12, 31	46
12	10	25
13	3	35
14	5	25
15	None	67
16	None	40
17	None	43
18	None	55
19	None	46
20	None	31

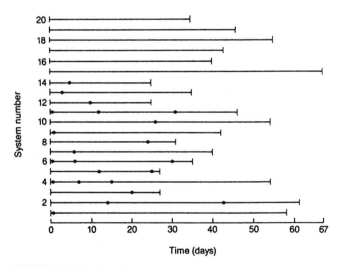

FIGURE 40.5 Pictorial representation of system failure times.

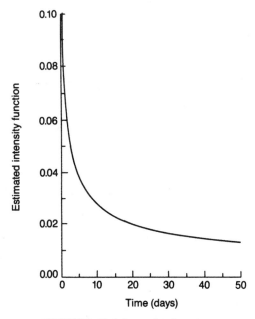

FIGURE 40.6 Intensity function.

The rapidly decreasing intensity function curve shown in the previous fig-ure indicates a decreasing failure rate and that the test is detecting early-life problems, which are often production quality issues. There does not appear to be a knee in the curve of the average failures per system plot, which leads

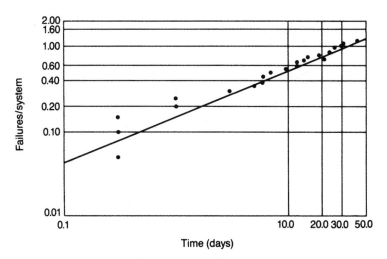

FIGURE 40.7 Average failures per system.

us to believe that our test duration is not getting past any initial early-life problem mode that could exist with the population.

From Figure 40.6 it appears that a 10-day "customer usage test" screen reduces the initial failure rate from approximately 0.10 failures/day to 0.02 failures/day. Additional test time does not have as much benefit as this initial test period; hence, a 10-day customer equivalent usage test may initially seem to be a reasonable starting point for a production screen. Other economic factors could be added to this decision process; however, it should be noted that a "10-day screen" would not have captured all the failures from the original data set. Hence, it might be appropriate to critique the screening procedure to determine if a better scheme can be found to get failures to occur sooner. Perhaps a vibration screen should be considered for use in conjunction with a thermal cycling screen.

After the specifics and duration of a screen test are established, a process control chart could then be used to monitor this manufacturing process step for future changes in failure rate characteristics. An increase in the failure rate detected by the screen might be an indicator that the process has degraded (i.e., a special cause situation) and that customers might also be expected to begin experiencing an increase in the failure rate. Because of early problem identification using a control chart, action can be taken to "fix" this degradation before it impacts the customer appreciably.

However, in reality it seems that for most products the noted failure rate would be too high to tolerate on a continuing basis (i.e., a common cause situation). A problem determination program should be used to find the cause of the failures. If the process is changed to minimize the number of problems that occur in this test, there is less risk of these problems occurring in a customer's office.

Pareto charts along with DOE and other Six Sigma tools can be a valuable combination of tools to understand and give direction in reducing the number of problems. The control charts noted earlier could be used as a tool to determine when the process is creating fewer failures, which would be an indicator that the fixes are beneficial.

A significant reduction (or increase) in the process control chart mean value might also be considered as a trigger to repeat the above test to "reoptimize" the screening procedure. It may be later determined, for example, that our stress screen duration can be reduced appreciably, thus reducing costs.

40.15   EXAMPLE 40.7: AN ONGOING RELIABILITY TEST (ORT) PLAN

Consider that the customer of a company requires an ongoing reliability test (ORT) of an electronic assembly that they produce. If care is not exercised when developing this plan, much resource can be spent without much value add.

Typically, ORT plans are exercised at elevated temperatures; however, when developing this plan it was thought that elevated temperatures was not worth the expense (also, this supplying company had no available temperature chamber). The reasoning behind this decision was that a plan was desired that would stress the conditions that could be controlled. Elevated temperatures typically address intrinsic failure rates of components, which were not under the control of the company. It was thought that a power cycle test would be more valuable to identify marginal design issues and solder joint problems.

The strategy behind the described ORT plan is to timely identify manufacturing and supplier issues that could adversely degrade product mean time between failure (MTBF) performance from initial projections determined from a bottoms-up analysis, where reported component failure rates are combined using computer software. If any failures occur during ORT, the process will be evaluated for improvements that could reduce the possibility of reoccurrence of similar failures.

The ORT will stress the system through power cycling at ambient conditions. Within a customer environment, units are typically under constant power. The increased frequency of heating and cooling of units under test will mechanically stress solder joints created by the manufacturing process. Similarly, frequent power cycling of the units under test will stress circuit timings. The likelihood of failures increases during power cycling when component parameters are either initially unsatisfactory or degrade with usage.

If production volumes exceed 100 per week, sampling for the ORT will consist of randomly choosing one unit per week. If production volumes are less than 100 per week, a sample will be drawn for every 100 produced. Sampling and putting a new unit in ORT will occur according to the above plan until there are 10 units on test. Whenever a new sample makes the ORT sample size 11, the unit under test that has been running the longest will be removed from test.

Units under test will experience a power-on cycle that lasts for one hour. Units will then be powered down and remain off for 20 minutes. A tester will control the powering cycles and monitor the units under test for failures. The tester will record any failure times. Logs will be maintained showing the serial numbers of units tested along with their test performance. Total time of the units under test will be tracked weekly.

The frequency of failures, if any, will be tracked over time using control charts that monitor rare events. *XmR* and charts will track the total time of all units tested since the last failure of any one unit. The average of the *X* chart will be used as an MTBF type estimate for the units under test. Individual ORT failures will be evaluated to estimate the acceleration factor for that failure. This information will be used to assist process improvement.

If more than one failure occurs, the nonhomogeneous Poisson process with Weibull intensity will be used to estimate the intensity function of the repairable device. The information from the intensity function can give insight into whether the problem is early-life, intrinsic, or wear-out. This information can assist process improvement efforts to reduce the likelihood of new products having a similar occurrence.

In addition to ORT, 10 other units will be immediately placed on life test. These units will be tested for failure under long-term usage. The total usage from all units will be recorded weekly. Failures, if any, will be investigated for root cause and process improvement opportunities. If more than one failure occurs, the intensity function of the units under test will be estimated using the nonhomogeneous Poisson process.

40.16   S⁴ ASSESSMENT

The reliability tests discussed in this chapter can be a useful portion of the process to get a quality product to the customer. However, these tests should only be a portion of this total process to develop/manufacture a quality product. A false sense of security can result from a favorable reliability test at the beginning of production. Future production units may be quite different, and the customer may use the system much differently than simulated by the test driver, which could cause a higher field failure rate than anticipated. In addition, results from this test are typically late in the process; hence, problems that are discovered because of this test can be very difficult and expensive to fix. Reliability tests often can only be used as a sanity check, not as a means to "inspect in quality" (Deming's point 3 of his 14 points). DOEs early within the development and manufacturing process are usually a more effective means of creating an atmosphere in which quality can be designed within the product and its manufacturing process. Statistical process control charts are then an effective tool to monitor the manufacturing process for sporadic problems that could degrade product quality.

Determining the changing failure rate of a repairable system within tests in a manufacturing facility can be difficult because there may not be enough failures in the amount of test time to fit a model. However, the NHPP can be a useful tool to track a product within the customer environment if there is an accurate method of determining time to failure. With this information perhaps, for example, a better screen could be determined to use within the process to capture similar problems before units leave the manufacturing facility.

40.17   EXERCISES

1. You are told to certify a 500,000-hr MTBF failure rate criteria.
   (a) Determine the total test time if two failures are allowed and a 90% confidence level is desired.
   (b) If the true MTBF of the population were 600,000 hr, determine and justify whether the product will most likely pass or fail test.

(c) Create a test performance ratio chart that lists various test alternatives.

(d) Select one of the following regions where the product failure rate is presumed for the above analysis to be valid (early life, flat part of bath tub curve, or wear-out).

2. An automobile manufacturer randomly chose 10 vehicles to monitor the number of service calls in one year. There was a total number of 22 service calls.

(a) Estimate the MTBF.

(b) Calculate the MTBF 90% confidence interval.

(c) List issues that need clarification for a better assessment of what should be done differently to reduce the frequency of defects.

3. A test is needed to verify a 300,000-hr MTBF product criterion. The product is typically utilized 24 hr per day by customers.

(a) If five failures are allowed and a 90% confidence interval statement is desired, determine the total number of test hours.

(b) Create a test performance ratio chart that lists various test alternatives.

(c) Consider test alternatives (e.g., a DOE strategy).

4. Describe how the techniques within this chapter are useful and can be applied to S^4 projects.

41

RELIABILITY TESTING/ASSESSMENT: NONREPAIRABLE DEVICES

This chapter is an extension of the concepts described in Chapter 39 relative to reliability tests that are performed on nonrepairable devices. The techniques discussed within this chapter are directed toward the situation where a random sample of a product is monitored for failure times during a reliability test assessment, given that samples that fail are *not* placed back on test after failure (i.e., a nonrepairable test plan). These techniques are applicable to the reliability testing of such devices as electronic modules, television displays, and automobile tires. In the test situations described there are no accelerated stress conditions on the devices under test or there is a known acceleration factor.

41.1 RELIABILITY TEST CONSIDERATIONS FOR A NONREPAIRABLE DEVICE

In this chapter the Weibull distribution is most often used when assessing the reliability of nonrepairable devices: however, many of the concepts apply similarly to the log-normal distribution, which is also discussed. The Weibull distribution is often appropriate to analyze this type of problem because this distribution can model the three usage-sensitive characteristics commonly encountered for a nonrepairable device: improving failure rate, constant failure rate and degrading failure rate. As also noted, the log-normal distribution is an alternative approach to modeling these characteristics.

The unit of time considered in the data analysis can be chosen after acceleration factor adjustments are made to the test times on the devices. For example, a 1-hr test with an acceleration factor of 20 can yield a test time input to the Weibull model of 20 hr.

In the previous chapter the Poisson distribution was used to design tests for repairable systems that were assumed to experience a constant failure rate. For a given set of test requirements, Table K was used to determine the total test time, which would be spread between several test machines. However, for a nonrepairable device following the Weibull distribution, the constant failure rate assumption often is not appropriate; hence, the test time cannot be spread "arbitrarily" between the devices under test. The test time for each unit needs to be considered in conjunction with the sample size. To illustrate this point, consider that a wear-out problem would occur at 10,000 hr. Ten units tested to 1000 hr would not detect this problem; however, one unit tested to 10,000 hr would experience the problem.

From an analysis point of view, it is best to test long enough to have a failure time for each device under test. When this is done, the data can be analyzed using probability plotting techniques. However, often in this type of test, all devices do not experience a failure before test termination. Data from this type of test can be analyzed manually using hazard plotting techniques (if no computer program is available to analyze this type of data using probability plotting techniques).

However, both of these test alternatives can involve a lot of test time. A test alternative, described later in this chapter, can be used when the shape of the underlying Weibull distribution is known (or can be assumed). With this approach, probability plots are not anticipated because the test often would be planned to permit no failures. This section also illustrates how trade-off can be made between the sample size and test duration for the individual samples.

41.2 WEIBULL PROBABILITY PLOTTING AND HAZARD PLOTTING

When planning a reliability test for a nonrepairable device, a sample size and test duration need to be considered along with a methodology that will be used to determine the time of failures during test. An accelerated test environment may be needed so that the test can be completed in a reasonable period of time. The failure time data from such a test can be plotted on Weibull probability paper (see Table Q3) or Weibull hazard paper (see Table R3) for the data analysis.

When making a trade-off between sample size and test duration, the real test objective should be considered. If wear-out is of concern, perhaps a "smaller" number of units will then suffice; however, the test time for these devices could be very lengthy (e.g., the expected average life of the device or expected life usage in a customer's office). However, if early-life failures are of concern, more production parts need to be tested for a shorter period of time (e.g., 1 to 6 months equivalent "customer's usage").

Again, it is desirable from an analysis point of view to have a long enough test such that all test samples fail. The mechanics of this analysis was described within the chapter on probability and hazard plotting, while the following example illustrates the probability plot procedure for a reliability test. However, this type of test is often not realistic, and test analyses may often need to be done on data that have a mixture of failure and no failure (censored data) times.

If all the test samples have not failed, it is best that they have a consistent test termination time beyond the last failure point; however, other censoring times can be accommodated. The mechanics of the manual hazard plotting analysis was described initially within the chapter on probability and hazard plotting and given further description in Example 43.2.

A probability plot of the data from a Weibull distribution yields a slope equating to the shape parameter (*b*), and the 63.2% cumulative failure point equates to the characteristic life (*k*) (see Appendix A for more mathematical relationships). The cumulative frequency distribution is then described by the following, where *t* is used to represent time:

$$F(t) = 1 - \exp[-(t/k)^b]$$

The following examples illustrate how the two unknown parameters of the Weibull distribution equation can be estimated using a probability plot or hazard plot approach. Manual analysis techniques were used in these examples; however, computer programs are available that can give more accuracy to both the graphical illustration and parameter computations.

For a manual plot of the data, Appendix B describes an approach that can be used to determine a best-fit line. Computer-generated probability plots are an alternative that can have additional accuracy because the estimates are determined mathematically (e.g., maximum-likelihood estimators).

41.3   EXAMPLE 41.1: WEIBULL PROBABILITY PLOT FOR FAILURE DATA

Seven printwheel components were tested and failed with the following number of months of usage: 8.5, 12.54, 13.75, 19.75, 21.46, 26.34, and 28.45.

The ranked data along with the Table P percentage plot positions for a sample size of seven yields the following:

Ranked Life Data	Percentage Plot Position
8.5	7.1
12.54	21.4
13.75	35.7
19.75	50.0
21.46	64.3
26.34	78.6
28.45	92.9

The ranked life data values are then plotted with the corresponding percentage plot position values on Weibull probability paper to create a best-fit line as noted by the solid line shown in Figure 41.1.

The shape parameter (b) is determined from the slope of the curve to be 3.1 by drawing a line parallel to the best-fit line to a key that is found on the Weibull probability paper. The characteristic life (k) is determined by noting the usage value corresponding to a 63.2% percentage point, which yields an approximate value of 21.0. These values for b and k are considered the best estimates for the unknown parameters.

Other information that can be noted from the graph is, for example, that the best estimate for B_{25} is approximately 14.0 (i.e., 75% of the components are expected to survive a usage of 14.0 without failure) and the best estimate for the median life B_{50} is approximately 18.6.

Because the output Weibull distribution is not generally symmetrical, the average life of a Weibull plot is not normally the 50% failure point. Table L is useful to determine the percentage value that relates to the average life as a function of Weibull shape parameters (Lipson and Sheth 1973). This table yields a value of 50.7%, which is only slightly larger than the median value for this particular shape parameter. Note that when all the data fail, an average (mean) life and confidence interval could be determined using the techniques described earlier in this text; however, this approach is not appropriate with censored data, and it cannot give information about the tails of the distribution.

41.4   EXAMPLE 41.2: WEIBULL HAZARD PLOT WITH CENSORED DATA

Assume that the printwheel life failure times from the previous example also contained four censored times of 13.00, 20.00, 29.00, and 29.00 (i.e., they were taken off the test at these times). These times are noted in the following table by a plus sign.

For ease of manual calculations, this text uses hazard plot techniques for censored data. Application of the probability and hazard plotting procedure

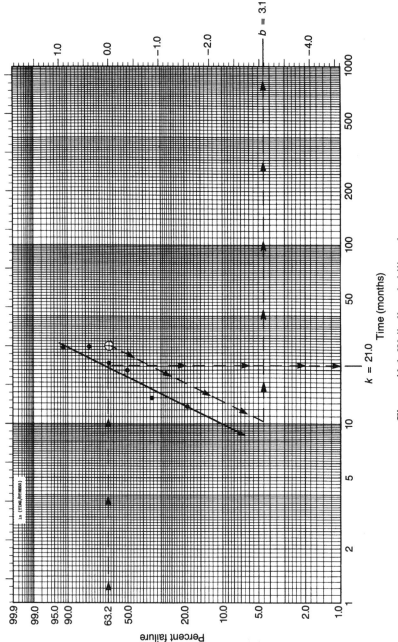

Figure 41.1 Weibull probability plot.

described earlier within this text yields the following cumulative hazard plot percentage values:

Time of Failure	Reverse Rank (1)	Hazard (100/j)	Cumulative Hazard
8.50	11	9.1	9.1
12.54	10	10.0	19.1
13.00+	9		
13.75	8	12.5	31.6
19.75	7	14.3	45.9
20.00+	6		
21.46	5	20.0	65.9
26.34	4	25.0	90.9
28.45	3	33.3	124.2
29.00+	2		
29.00+	1		

The time-to-failure values are then plotted with the corresponding cumulative hazard values on Weibull hazard paper to create the plot shown in Figure 41.2. The percentage probability value readings can then be noted and interpreted. A comparison of the results from this manual analyses with censored data to noncensored data yields the following:

Data	b	k	B_{50}	B_{25}
7 failures + 4 censored points	2.3	26.0	22.0	15.0
7 failures	3.1	21.0	18.6	14.0

The characteristic life (k) is noted to be obviously larger (as it should be) with the censored data set (which is also reflected in the values for B_{50} and B_{25}).

41.5 NONLINEAR DATA PLOTS

When the data do not follow a "straight line" on a Weibull probability or hazard plot, the data are not from a Weibull distribution. In this case the probability or hazard plot may be telling us a story; the appearance of data plotted on probability or hazard paper can give insight to better understanding the device failure modes. For example, when the data plot has a knee in the curve, this could be indicating that the data are from two different distributions. A knee may be prevalent in a plot when, for example, a device experiences a definite transition between early-life failures to a constant failure rate.

To better describe the overall frequency of cumulative failures as a function of usage when multiple distributions are present, the data can be split into

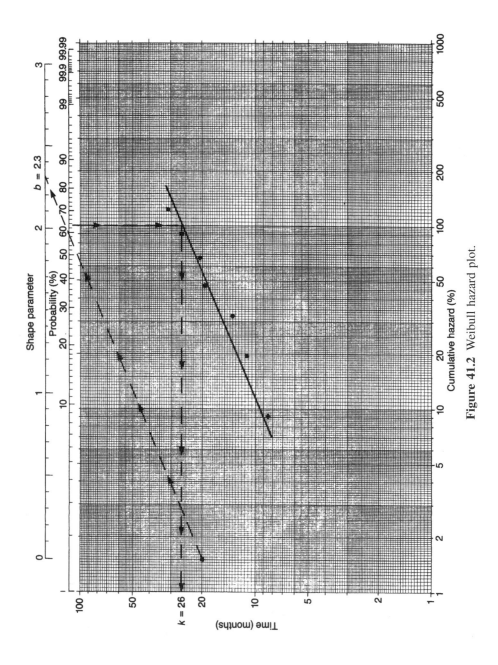

Figure 41.2 Weibull hazard plot.

groups of data from the differing distributions. The data are then analyzed in these groups and combined mathematically using the equation.

$$F(t) = 1 - \{[1 - F_1(t)] \times [1 - F_2(t)] \times \cdots \times [1 - F_n(t)]\}$$

Note that this equation does not require $F_1(t)$, $F_2(t)$, and so on, to all be from a Weibull distribution. Data should be split into groups of various distributions that make physical sense; however, in reality it is often difficult to have a large enough test effort to be able to get to this level of detail in the analysis.

The above-described "knee characteristic" of a Weibull plot from two different distributions can be used in a basic test strategy. For example, a test can be designed to optimize the duration of a screen that is going to be installed in a manufacturing process (Navy 1979). It is desirable that the screen duration is at a point where a knee occurs in the curve such that the early-life problems are detected and fixed in the manufacturing plant, as opposed to the customer's office. This situation can take the form described by Jensen and Petersen (1982) and illustrated by the situation where a small number of poor parts could be considered to be from a freak distribution, while a larger portion of parts is from the main distribution (see Figure 41.3). It should be noted that the parts in the freak distribution could have a Weibull slope that indicates wear-out tendencies.

Another situation where one overall Weibull distribution may not be applicable is when analysis of test data indicates that a mechanism experienced several distinctly different failure modes. In this situation the data might again be split up, analyzed separately, and then combined via this equation.

Still another common occurrence is for the data to have a convex shape. Often with this scenario the data can be fitted by transforming the data into a three-parameter Weibull model. This can be done by subtracting from all the data points a constant (i.e., location parameter, t_0) of such a magnitude that a two-parameter Weibull plot of the adjusted data follows a straight line. Mathematically, this relationship is

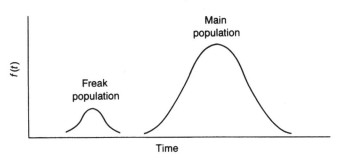

FIGURE 41.3 Freak and main distribution.

$$F(t) = 1 - \exp\left[-\left(\frac{t - t_0}{k - t_0}\right)^b\right]$$

Data transformation to a three-parameter Weibull distribution can make sense if the data are to describe a physical phenomena where the probability of failing at any value from zero up to the shift value is zero. This is not usually a reasonable physical restriction to make in the case of a reliability test because the device always has a chance of failing the instant after it has begun to perform its intended function (without considering dead on arrival devices).

However, there are situations where a three-parameter Weibull distribution may be applicable; for example, when considering the tensile strength of a material, it is reasonable to assume that there is zero chance for a steel bar to break until some axial force much larger than zero is applied. This physical value of shift for the expected zero probability point is the location parameter (i.e., t_0) within the three-parameter Weibull distribution.

41.6 REDUCED SAMPLE SIZE TESTING: WEIBULL DISTRIBUTION

It is best to have a test where many components are tested long enough such that there are many failure points to plot using Weibull analysis considerations. However, because of economic constraints, it is not often possible to have a large number of devices under test for a long period of time.

This section describes a test strategy that can be used to assess the feasibility of a mean life criterion if the failure distribution is Weibull and the practitioner is able (and willing) to assume a value for the shape parameter (b).

For data t_i the transformed values $U_i = t_i^b$ come from the exponential distribution with mean $\theta = k^b$ (Nelson 1982), where k is the characteristic life constant. From these relationships the methodologies for exponential data can be used to obtain estimates, confidence limits, and predictions, noting that the precision of this approach is dependent on the accuracy of b.

To use this relationship, consider a test that is to have no failures and the resultant mean life T_d confidence interval is to have the form $T_d \geq$ criterion. T_d can then be translated to a characteristic life criterion by using the relationship

$$k = \frac{T_d}{\Gamma(1 + 1/b)}$$

where the gamma function value $\Gamma(1 + 1/b)$ is determined from Table H. From the exponential distribution that has a mean (θ) of

$$\theta = k^b$$

the individual transformed test times are

$$t_i = U_i^{1/b}$$

From Table K it is noted that the total test time (T) to obtain a confidence interval for θ (i.e., $1/\rho$ in Table K) is

$$T = (B_{r;c})\theta$$

For a zero failure test strategy it then follows that when n units are on test for an equal time period, U_i would be

$$U_i = [(B_{r;c})(\theta)]/n$$

Substitution then yields

$$t_i = \{[(B_{r;c})(k^b)]/n\}^{1/b}$$

Reducing this equation results in the following equation, which can be used to determine the amount of individual test time (t_i) that (n) devices need to experience during a "zero failure permissible" test:

$$t_i = k[(B_{r;c})/n]^{1/b}$$

41.7   EXAMPLE 41.3: A ZERO FAILURE WEIBULL TEST STRATEGY

A previous reliability test indicated that the Weibull shape parameter was 2.18 for an automobile clutch. How long should a test consisting of 1, 2, 3, or 10 samples be tested to yield an 80% confidence bound that the mean life (T_d) is greater than or equal to 100,000 km of automobile usage, given that no failures occur?

The Γ function in Table H can be used to determine k from the relationship

$$k = \frac{T_d}{\Gamma(1 + 1/b)}$$

The 100,000-km mean life criterion then equates to a characteristic life criterion of

$$k = \frac{T_d}{\Gamma(1 + 1/b)} = \frac{100,000}{\Gamma(1 + 1/2.18)} = \frac{100,000}{\Gamma(1.459)} = \frac{100,000}{0.8856} = 112,918$$

For an 80% confidence interval with no permissible failures, Table K yields $B_{0;0.8} = 1.609$. If there were only one device on the test, it follows that

$$t_i = k \left[\frac{B_{r;c}}{n}\right]^{1/b} = 112,918 \left[\frac{(1.609)}{1}\right]^{1/2.18} = 140,447$$

A summary of the individual test time requirements with no device failures for 1, 2, 3, and 10 sample size alternatives is as follows:

Sample Size	Individual Device Test Time
1	140,447
2	102,194
3	84,850
10	48,843

In general, the shape parameter estimate needs to be accurate so that the unit test times will be accurate. However, this accuracy requirement decreases as the test time for each unit approaches the average life criterion. Hence, when assessing wear-out concerns, it is normally better to test a smaller number of units to the approximate mean life usage than to test a large number to only a portion of this usage. When there is uncertainty about the accuracy of the shape parameter estimate, the sample size can be calculated for several differing shape parameters. This information can yield better understanding of the sensitivity of this underlying assumption when choosing a sample size.

The objective of this test approach is that no failures occur; however, at the completion of a test, many more failures may occur than originally anticipated. Times-of-failure data from a test could then be analyzed using probability or hazard plotting techniques to determine an experimental value for the shape parameter, and so forth.

41.8   LOG-NORMAL DISTRIBUTION

The log-normal distribution can be a good analysis alternative to the Weibull distribution. If this distribution is applicable, the equations for the normal distribution are appropriate through a log transformation. Data can also be plotted on log-normal probability paper (see Table Q2) or hazard paper (see Table R2) using the plot positions noted in Table P.

41.9   EXAMPLE 41.4: LOG-NORMAL PROBABILITY PLOT ANALYSIS

The noncensored printwheel failure times (i.e., 8.5, 12.54, 13.75, 19.75, 21.46, 26.34, and 28.45) described earlier will now be analyzed using log-normal probability plotting techniques.

Table P is used to yield the same percentage plot position values as those from the previous example; however, this time the data are plotted on log-normal probability paper to create Figure 41.4. It may be difficult from a manual plot to determine whether the Weibull or log-normal distribution fits the data better. With computer programs, lack-of-fit output parameters could be compared to choose the best distribution. A comparison of conclusions from the two manual Weibull and log-normal plots yields the following:

Analysis	B_{50}	B_{25}
Log-normal	17.0	13.0
Weibull	18.6	14.0

41.10   S⁴ ASSESSMENT

When planning a reliability test for a device, the practitioner needs to remember that in order to plot a point on Weibull or log-normal probability paper a failure must occur. With the reliability of components improving with technology, the task of quantifying the reliability of these components during test is becoming increasingly difficult. To address this issue, acceleration models can be used to accelerate failure modes. Step stress testing is another test alternative that can be considered.

However, even with accelerated testing methods, test durations can be very long. Another approach to address this problem is to consider monitoring another response in conjunction with noting when the device fails completely. From experience it might be "known" for a type of device that whenever a particular output signal degrades 10%, the device has reached 20% of its life expectancy. To project the expected device failure usage, the practitioner could then multiply five by the amount of usage that the device had experienced whenever the signal degraded 10%.

If there are wear-out exposures, testing a small number of samples for a long period of time is more effective than testing a large number of samples for a short period. The test duration for the components should be at least to the usage of concern (e.g., life of the assembly that will contain the device). If early-life problems are anticipated, a large number of parts from a manufacturing process should be tested for a relatively "short" period of time to capture these failures. In some situations it may be best to conduct both types

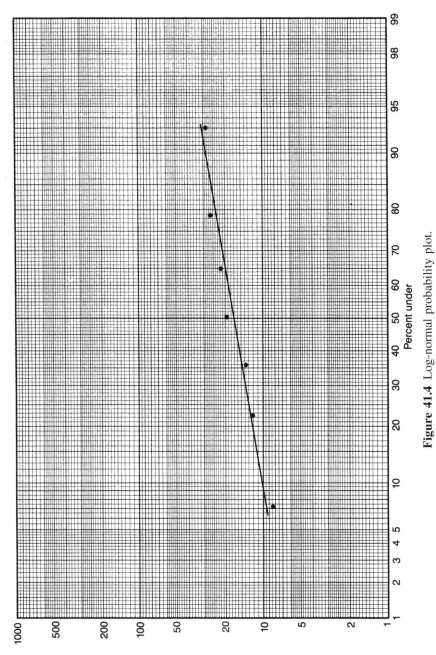

Figure 41.4 Log-normal probability plot.

of tests (possibly concurrently) to evaluate the characteristics of both failure modes.

Time-to-failure data from a screen test of components on the manufacturing line could be tracked using control charting techniques. Information from a Weibull analysis of the failure data (from a stable screen test) can be used to optimize the duration of a manufacturer's in-house burn-in test that is used to capture early-life failures before customer shipment. It should be noted, however, that a burn-in of all manufactured components does not preclude effort that should be taken to improve the manufacturing process so that the number of defects found during the screen test is lower in the future.

41.11 EXERCISES

1. A sample of 10 electronic components were tested to a customer usage value of 110 months. Seven failed at times 89.6, 109.2, 79.2, 54.6, 83.0, 86.5, and 29.1 months. Use the Weibull distribution to estimate the usage where 75% of the population have not experienced failure.

2. A computer component life test of four randomly selected computer modems had failure times of 1.2, 2.7, 3.4, and 5.1 years.
   (a) Create a Weibull probability plot.
   (b) Estimate when 25% of the population will fail.
   (c) Estimate the parameters of the distribution.
   (d) State the most likely failure mode (i.e., early-life, intrinsic, wear-out).

3. A computer component life test of 10 assemblies tested to 6 years equivalent customer usage exhibited failures of five units at 1.2, 2.7, 3.4, and 5.1 years.
   (a) Create a Weibull probability plot.
   (b) Estimate when 25% of the population will fail.
   (c) Estimate the parameters of the distribution.
   (d) State the most likely failure mode (i.e., early-life, intrinsic, wear-out).

4. A sample of 10 electronic components were tested to a customer usage of 110 months. Seven failed at times 89.6, 109.2, 79.2, 54.6, 83.0, 86.5, and 29.1 months.
   (a) Create a Weibull probability plot.
   (b) Estimate when 30% of the population will not have fail.
   (c) Estimate the parameters of the distribution.
   (d) State the most likely failure mode (i.e., early-life, intrinsic, wear-out).

5. A tire design had a Weibull shape parameter of 3.2. Fifty percent of the failures are estimated to occur on or before 27,000 miles.
   (a) Estimate when 90% of the tires will fail.
   (b) Determine the failure mode (i.e., early-life, intrinsic, wear-out).

6. All electronic subassembly is known to have a failure rate that follows a Weibull distribution where the slope of the Weibull probability plot was 2.2 and the usage when 63.2% failed was 67 months. Determine the percentage expected to fail at an annual usage of 12 months.

7. Parts are to experience an accelerated test before customer shipment. Create a plan to determine an effective test that captures typical customer problems before shipment.

8. Describe how the techniques within this chapter are useful and can be applied to S^4 projects.

42

PASS/FAIL FUNCTIONAL TESTING

In many instances it is impossible to test all possible combinations of input parameters when trying to ensure that there is no combination that can cause a failure. This chapter illustrates an efficient test strategy where fractional factorial design matrices are used to design an efficient test of a *pass/fail logic* response for multiple combinational considerations. The strategy suggests that a small carefully selected subset of possible factor combinations can yield a satisfactory test of combinational effects (not to be confused with interaction effects). In addition, an expected "test coverage" is quantifiable for a given test matrix and factor considerations.

42.1   THE CONCEPT OF PASS/FAIL FUNCTIONAL TESTING

Consider the situation where a product will be "put together" (i.e., configured) in many different ways by a customer. Because of possible design flaws, it is of interest to discover when things will not work together during an in-house test (i.e., a "logic" failure situation). If the number of configuration possibilities is not large, a test person should simply evaluate all possible combinations to assess whether there are any design problems. However, in some situations the number of combinational possibilities can be very large (e.g., tens of thousands). For these situations it becomes very difficult (if not impossible) to test all possible combinations.

This chapter describes a test strategy for the situation where the number of test scenarios needs to be much less than all possible combinations. This approach is used to identify a small subset of test configurations that will identify the types of problems that are found in many situations.

Consider, for example, the electromagnetic interference (EMI) emissions of a product. Compliance to government specifications is important because noncompliance can result in legal actions by the Federal Communications Commission (FCC). However each EMI test setup and measurement can be very time-consuming; hence, to test all possible configurations of a complex system can be a virtually impossible task.

To illustrate the type of EMI problem that this approach will capture, consider that (unknown to the experimenter) a new computer design only emits unacceptable high EMI levels whenever a certain type of display monitor is used in conjunction with a power supply that was manufactured by a certain supplier that had an optional "long size" cable.

In lieu of testing all possible combinations, an EMI test strategy that evaluates factors one at a time would probably not detect this type of combinational problem. A nonstructural test alternative that evaluates a few common "typical configurations" might miss important factor considerations because they are "not typical." In addition, with this second approach, there is typically no mention of test coverage at the completion of the test.

The test strategy discussed in this chapter is directed toward efficiently identifying circumstances where combinational problems exists. This identification focuses on how problems are often defined. In this problem a "group size" of three factor levels caused a combinational problem (a typical manner in which problems are often identified). A later example illustrates a simple basic test design strategy for evaluating this "logic pass/fail situation" using only a minimal number of test scenarios. The example also addresses a measurement for the "test coverage" that is achieved when using such a test strategy.

42.2   EXAMPLE 42.1: AUTOMOTIVE TEST—PASS/FAIL FUNCTIONAL TESTING CONSIDERATIONS

To illustrate the concept of pass/fail functional testing, consider the fictitious example where there is a catastrophic failure situation involving the combination of three factor levels. The test described in Table 42.1 was designed from Table M2.

Assume that it is a fact that elderly drivers always caused accidents when driving a new automotive vehicle on curved roads. The question of concern is whether this experiment would detect this fact. The answer is yes, because this combination is covered in trial 6 (elderly driver: $D = +$; new vehicle: $E = +$; road curved; $F = +$).

Most of the three-factor combinations of any of the factor levels (i.e., group size equaling three) are covered in this experiment. This level of "test coverage" is illustrated conceptually where all combinations of DEF are included in the design matrix in Table 42.2. The following section and example discuss test coverage further.

TABLE 42.1 Experimental Design for Automotive Test

Trial Number	A B C D E F			
1	+ − − + − +	where		
2	+ + − − + −		(−)	(+)
3	+ + + − − +	A = weather	Wet	Dry
4	− + + + − −	B = alcohol	None	Legal limit
5	+ − + + + −	C = speed	40 mph	70 mph
6	− + − + + +	D = age of driver	20–30	60–70
7	− − + − + +	E = vehicle	Current	New
8	− − − − − −	F = road curvature	None	Curved

42.3 A TEST APPROACH FOR PASS/FAIL FUNCTIONAL TESTING

Fractional factorial designs classically are used to assess continuous response outputs as a function of factor-level considerations. However, there are instances where a more appropriate experimental task is to determine a *logic pass/fail* (binary) result that will *always* occur relative to machine function or configuration. This section illustrates how the structure of fractional factorial designs can also be used to give an efficient test strategy for this type of evaluation.

With pass/fail functional testing, test trials from a fractional factorial design are used to define configurations and/or experimental conditions, while test coverage is used to describe the percentage of all possible combinations of the factor levels (C) tested for various group sizes (G). In the EMI problem noted earlier, the levels from a group size of three factors were identified (i.e., display type, power supply manufacturer, and power supply cable length). Using the strategy described in this chapter, the following example shows how a test coverage of 90% can be expected for a group of size three given a logic pass/fail output consideration of seven two-level factors in only eight test trials.

TABLE 42.2 Illustration of Three-Factor Coverage

D E F	Trial Number
− − −	8
− − +	3
− + −	2
− + +	7
+ − −	4
+ − +	1
+ + −	5
+ + +	6

The desired output from a fractional factorial design matrix using this test strategy is that all experimental trial conditions pass. The percent coverage as a function of the group size and the number of test trials can be determined from Table O. It should be noted, however, that whenever a trial fails there may be no statistical analysis technique that indicates the source of the problem. If additional engineering analyses do not identify the problem source, additional trials can be added to assist the experimenter in determining the cause of failure.

The percentage test coverage C that is possible from a fractional factorial designed experiment, where F two-level factors are assessed in T trials, is

$$C(F) = \frac{T}{2^F} \times 100 \qquad C(F) \leq 100\%$$

This means, for example, that if $T = 32$, the maximum number of factors yielding complete coverage (i.e., $C = 100\%$) is $F = 5$.

Besides the total coverage of the experiment, it would be interesting to know the coverage of a particular subclass (or group) of G factors chosen out of the total F factors that comprise the experiment under consideration. Theoretically, the equation is still valid if G replaced F, but actually for a generic group of G factors the fractional factorial design is not guaranteed against pattern repetitions. Therefore we expect to have

$$C(G) \leq \frac{T}{2^G} \times 100 \qquad G \leq T - 1$$

This relation gives us a theoretical maximum coverage value in a very general case. The mean percent coverage of all the possible G groups from F factors was calculated using a computer for a representative sample of resolution III fractional factorial design matrices for 2^n trials, where $n = 3, 4, 5,$ and 6 (see Tables M1 to M5). Results from this study indicate that there is only a slight variation in the value of coverage (C) as a function of the number of factors (F), which, when ignored, graphically yields the percentage coverage noted in Table O. Note that in lieu of using a computer program to manually observe and calculate the observed coverage, the aliasing structure could have been examined to determine this coverage.

The number of P possible G groups of factors is determined from the binomial coefficient formula

$$P = \binom{F}{G} = \frac{F!}{G!(F - G)!}$$

The N total number of possible combinations of the two-level factors then becomes

$$N = 2^G \binom{F}{G}$$

The value C determined from Table O is the test percent coverage of the N possible combinations of the factor levels for a group size G.

A step-by-step implementation approach to this procedure for two-level factor considerations is as follows:

1. List the number of two-level factors (F).
2. Determine the minimum number of trials (T) (i.e., 8, 16, 32, or 64 trials) that is at least one larger than the number of factors. Higher test coverage can be obtained by using a fractional factorial design that has more trials.
3. Choose a fractional factorial design from Tables M1 to M5 (or some other source). Use Table O to determine the test percent coverage (C) for 3, 4, 5, 6, . . . two-level group sizes (G) with the number of trials (T).
4. Determine the number of possible combinations (N) for each group size (G) considered (e.g., 1, 2, and 3).
5. Tabulate the percent coverage with possible combinational effects to understand better the effectiveness of the test.

Often determining the "right problem to solve" is more difficult than performing the mechanics of solving the problem. The next three examples have two purposes. The first purpose is to illustrate more applications of pass/fail functional testing. The second purpose is to illustrate some typical discussions that could be encountered when choosing factors and their levels. Even though the reader may not directly relate to a specific example for his or her job, it is hoped that this discussion will stimulate additional insight into how the technique may be applied.

42.4   EXAMPLE 42.2: A PASS/FAIL SYSTEM FUNCTIONAL TEST

A computer is to be tested where a *logic pass/fail* response is thought to be a function of the two-level considerations of seven factors shown in Table 42.3. A minimal number of test trials is needed while achieving high test coverage. (*Note*: A similar approach can be applied to the test situation where many more factors are involved. For example, 63 two-level factors could be assessed in a 64-trial design.)

Using the preceding procedure this test can be performed using the following eight trials, taken from Table M2, shown in Table 42.4. From Table O and the previously described relationship for N the information in Table 42.5 can be determined.

TABLE 42.3 Factors and Levels of Computer Test

Factor	Contrast Column Level	
Designation	(−)	(+)
A	Display type X	Display type Y
B	Memory size, small	Memory size, large
C	Power supply vendor X	Power supply vendor Y
D	Power cable length, short	Power cable length, long
E	Printer type X	Printer type Y
F	Hardfile size, small	Hardfile size, large
G	Modem, yes	Modem, no

Note that with only eight trials there is 90% coverage for the number of groups of size three, which contains 280 possibilities! If this is not considered to be satisfactory test coverage Table O can be referenced to determine the increase in coverage that will be obtained if the number of fractional factorial experimental trials is doubled, for example, to 16.

To illustrate the type of problem that this test would be able to detect, consider that the following failure condition exists (unknown to the test person):

Display type X: $A = -$

Power supply supplier Y: $C = +$

Power supply cable length, long: $D = +$

This combination of factor levels is noted to be contained in trial 4; hence, trial 4 (in this case) would be the only test trial to "fail." As noted earlier, an experimenter would not know from the pass/fail information of the trials (i.e., trial 4 was the only trial that failed) what specifically caused the failure (i.e. the *ACD* combination of $-++$ caused the failure). This information cannot be deduced because many combinations of factor levels could have

TABLE 42.4 Test Matrix from Table M2

Trial Number	A B C D E F G
1	+ − − + − + +
2	+ + − − + − +
3	+ + + − − + −
4	− + + + − − +
5	+ − + + + − −
6	− + − + + + −
7	− − + − + + +
8	− − − − − − −

TABLE 42.5 Percent Coverage and Number of Possible Combinations

	Number of Groups					
	2	3	4	5	6	7
Percentage coverage	100[a]	90	50	25	12	6
Number of possible combinations	84	280[b]	560	672	448	128

[a]Example coverage statement: 100% coverage of two combinations of the seven two-level factors.
[b]Example calculation: When the number of groups = 3 and the number of factors = 7, it follows

$$\binom{7}{3} = \frac{7!}{3!(7-3)!} = 35$$

which yields

$$\text{Number of possible combinations} = 2^3 \binom{7}{3} = 8(35) = 280$$

caused the problem; however, with this test strategy, the tester was able to identify that a problem exists with a minimal number of test case scenarios. For the experimenter to determine the root cause of failure a simple technical investigation may be the only additional work that is necessary. If the cause cannot be determined from such an investigation additional trial patterns may need to be added to search for the root cause.

42.5 EXAMPLE 42.3: A PASS/FAIL HARDWARE/SOFTWARE SYSTEM FUNCTIONAL TEST

A company is considering buying several new personal computers to replace its existing equipment. The company has some atypical configurations for its computers; hence, the company wishes to have a "quick and dirty" test to verify that the product will work with its existing peripheral equipment and software.

The company believes that there will probably be no future problems if it can find no combination of the levels of three factors that cause a failure. The following discussion describes their test concerns.

Four different types of printers are used; however, it was believed that two of the four "special" printers could assess the "space" of the printer applications. Some of the companies users had an application where two displays were concurrently used on one computer. Two different word processor packages were often used with two different database managers and two different spreadsheet programs. Some individuals used a plotter, while others did not. In addition, the company had two basic network systems interconnecting the computers.

The seven factors and associated levels can take the form shown in Table 42.6. Because $2^3 = 8$, an eight-trial experiment can then be used to test most of the combinational possibilities of group size three. From Tables Ml to M5. this test matrix is as shown in Table 42.7.

One approach to executing this experiment is to first build various "configurations" and applications and then perform test cases that exercise command sequences that "stress" the product application. As an addition to a pass/fail output scenario. one may include "performance" test cases that can realistically assess the amount of performance improvement that can be expected via the new computer.

The percentage test coverage of the factor levels for the test would be similar to that shown in the previous example; if no failures are noted, the company will probably feel more secure with the purchase. A later example illustrates a search methodology for determining the cause, if failures occur during the test.

42.6   GENERAL CONSIDERATIONS WHEN ASSIGNING FACTORS

For a given test, some groups of G factors can have 100% coverage while others have 50% coverage for the 2^n trial designs in Tables M1 to M5. Instead of arbitrarily assigning factors, an experimenter may wish to make assignments so that factor combinational considerations that are thought to be important will have 100% test coverage. Combinational considerations to avoid for these factors are those that are identity elements (Diamond 1989; Box et al. 1978. Montgomery 1997) or a multiple of identity elements of the design matrix.

42.7   FACTOR LEVELS GREATER THAN TWO

Two-level factors are generally desirable in a fractional factorial experiment; however, fractional factorial design matrices that contain more than two levels

TABLE 42.6 Factors and Levels in Computer Assessment

Factor	$(-)$	$(+)$
A	Printer X	Printer Y
B	One display	Two displays
C	Word processor X	Word processor Y
D	Database manager X	Database manager Y
E	Spreadsheet X	Spreadsheet Y
F	No plotter	Plotter
G	Network X	Network Y

TABLE 42.7 Test Matrix from Table M2

Trial Number	$A\ B\ C\ D\ E\ F\ G$
1	$+ - - + - + +$
2	$+ + - - + - +$
3	$+ + + - - + -$
4	$- + + + - - +$
5	$+ - + + + - -$
6	$- + - + + + -$
7	$- - + - + + +$
8	$- - - - - - -$

can still be used to efficiently detect the type of functional problems discussed in this chapter. If there are no design matrices available to describe the desired number of factor levels of interest, a two-level fractional factorial matrix design can be used to create a design matrix. For pass/fail functional testing I believe that contrast column selection is not as important as it is whenever the response is continuous (relative to addressing the problem of confounded effects). Because of this, sometimes (e.g., when test resources are limited) I do not "preserve additional contrast columns" when creating these greater-than-two-level designs from Tables M1 to M5.

For this test situation the previous procedure using Tables M1 to M5 could be used with some modification to determine test coverage. However, in general, when there are several factors of differing multiple levels, it seems more applicable to randomly choose many differing configurations of a group size and examine whether these configurations were tested. The test percentage coverage (C) could then be calculated and plotted versus group size (G) to give a generalized pictorial representation of the coverage for the particular test.

Readers can contact the author about a computer program that creates test cases for any number of factors that have any number of levels.

42.8   EXAMPLE 42.4: A SOFTWARE INTERFACE PASS/FAIL FUNCTIONAL TEST

A program was written so that a computer terminal could interface with a link that is attached to a computer network. A structured test strategy was desired to directly assess combinational problems with only a relatively small number of test cases and hardware configurations. The test cases need to check for combinational problems and abnormal situations that could occur and cause a problem in a situation that customers may encounter.

The following assumptions were made when creating the test cases. A basic test case scenario will be defined using a fractional factorial matrix design from Tables Ml to M5. The test case will be written to stress the level combinations of the factors.

- If two extreme levels of factors pass, the levels between these extremes will be assumed to pass.
- If an abnormal situation causes a failure, the trial will be reassessed without the abnormal situation.

The factors and factor levels considered within the experiment design are shown in Table 42.8. From Table M3 the experimental design matrix is shown in Table 42.9.

TABLE 42.8 Factors and Levels in Software Interface Test

	Levels	
Factors	(−)	(+)
A Send data	Large data block (32K)	Small control message (8 bytes)
B Receive data	Large data block (32K)	Small control message (8 bytes)
C Interrupt	No	Yes
D Link type	Switched circuit	Leased line
E Type of cable interface between the terminal and modem	Slow Minimum baud rate	Fast Maximum baud rate
F Throughput negotiations	No: use default baud rate	Yes: different baud rate then default rate
G Loading/ utilization of system	Multiple sessions	Single session
H Personal computer processor type	Fast type	Slow type
I Personal computer internal clock speed	Fastest	Slowest
J Abnormal situations	None	Connection broken
M Upstream link to mainframe computer	No	Yes
K and L Network adapters	−− Only one type X network adapter −+ Two type X network adapters +− One type X and one type Y network adapter ++ One type X and one type Z network adapter	

TABLE 42.9 Test Matrix from Table M3

Trial Number	A B C D E F G H I J K L M
1	+ − − − + − − + + − + − +
2	+ + − − − + − − + + − + −
3	+ + + − − − + − − + + − +
4	+ + + + − − − + − − + + −
5	− + + + + − − − + − − + +
6	+ − + + + + − − − + − − +
7	− + − + + + + − − − + − −
8	+ − + − + + + + − − − + −
9	+ + − + − + + + + − − − +
10	− + + − + − + + + + − − −
11	− − + + − + − + + + + − −
12	+ − − + + − + − + + + + −
13	− + − − + + − + − + + + +
14	− − + − − + + − + − + + +
15	− − − + − − + + − + − + +
16	− − − − − − − − − − − − −

42.9 A SEARCH PATTERN STRATEGY TO DETERMINE THE SOURCE OF FAILURE

When a failure occurs when using the preceding matrix test strategy, sometimes the problem source is obvious, from a physical point of view. However, sometimes a cause cannot be determined and a search pattern is needed to better understand the failure mode.

A diagnostic search pattern strategy can begin with first noting the trials that had a common failure mode. Next, factors that obviously do not affect the output are removed from consideration. A logical assessment of the previous combinational pass/fail conditions is done to determine additional test trials that should be conducted, or a good starting point for additional trials can be the reversal of the level states in the original matrix design (i.e., a fold-over design). These two techniques are illustrated in the following example.

42.10 EXAMPLE 42.5: A SEARCH PATTERN STRATEGY TO DETERMINE THE SOURCE OF FAILURE

If there were no failures found in Example 42.3, the company would probably be comfortable in purchasing the product, because most three-factor combinations are considered in the test and there was no reason to expect any failure.

However, if a trial or trials did fall for an unknown reason, the experimenter in general, may not understand the cause. The following illustrates, using three different scenarios, a logic search pattern procedure to diagnose a *single-source combinational problem* of factor levels that results in a failure condition for certain trials.

Consider first that the experiment design had failures with trials 2, 3, 4, and 6, as noted by the x's:

Trial Number	A B C D E F G
1	+ − − + − + +
2	+ + − − + − + x
3	+ + + − − + − x
4	− + + + − − + x
5	+ − + + + − −
6	− + − + + + − x
7	− − + − + + +
8	− − − − − − −

The trials with failures are noted to be as follows:

Trial Number	A B C D E F G
2	+ + − − + − + x
3	+ + + − − + − x
4	− + + + − − + x
6	− + − + + + − x

Assuming that problems originate from a single source, this pass/fail pattern leads us to conclude that the failure is caused by $B = +$, because the level of $B = -$ had no failures (i.e., the computer does not work with two displays).

Consider now that trials 2 and 3 were the only two that had failures:

Trial Number	A B C D E F G
1	+ − − + − + +
2	+ + − − + − + x
3	+ + + − − + − x
4	− + + + − − +
5	+ − + + + − −
6	− + − + + + −
7	− − + − + + +
8	− − − − − − −

The trials with failure are then noted to be as follows:

Trial Number	$A\,B\,C\,D\,E\,F\,G$
2	$+\,+\,-\,-\,+\,-\,+$ x
3	$+\,+\,+\,-\,-\,+\,-$ x

This pass/fail pattern leads us to conclude initially that the failure could be caused by $ABD = ++-$. However, consider the subset of all possible combinations of ABD that were exercised in this test:

$A\,B\,D$	Trial Numbers
$-\,-\,-$	7, 8
$-\,-\,+$	
* $-\,+\,-$	
$-\,+\,+$	4, 6
$+\,-\,-$	
$+\,-\,+$	1, 5
$+\,+\,-$	2, 3
* $+\,+\,+$	

As noted earlier, not all combinations of three factors are covered within $2^3 = 8$ test trials. Approximately 90% of the all possible combinations are covered when there are seven two-level factors in eight trials. For this particular combination of factors (ABD), there is 50% coverage. Hence, to determine the cause of the failure, the other subset combinations of ABD need to be considered.

To determine whether the problem is from an $ABD = ++-$ effect or a combinational consideration that has one less factor consider a test of the combinations that contain a "single-factor-level" change from the state of $++-$ to levels not previously tested. The two combinational considerations not previously tested that meet this "single-factor-level change" are noted by an *. If; for example, the problem was really caused by $AB = ++$, then the $ABD = +++$ trial would fail while the $ABD = -+-$ combination would pass. Further step reductions in the number of factors would not be necessary because these combinations have previously passed.

Consider now that trial 3 was the only trial that failed. The failure pattern for this trial is as follows:

Trial Number	$A\,B\,C\,D\,E\,F\,G$
3	$+\,+\,+\,-\,-\,+\,-$

There are many reasons why this one trial could have failed; hence, several test trials are needed to further assess the failure source.

Consider that the real cause was from the combinational effect BCD of $++-$ (i.e., two displays with word processor Y and database manager X).

However, the experimenter did not know the cause and wanted to determine the reason for failure.

Sometimes there are obvious factors that can be removed from further consideration, which can lead to a significant reduction in test effort. However, let's assume in this example that there was no engineering/programming knowledge that could eliminate some of the factor considerations. A good beginning strategy to consider is using a fold-over design. In this approach, all the levels are changed to the opposite level condition. These trials are then tested. The additional trials to execute then would be as follows:

Trial Number	$ABCDEFG$
9	$-++-+--$ x
10	$--++-+-$
11	$---++-+$
12	$+---++-$
13	$-+---++$
14	$+-+---+$
15	$++-+---$
16	$+++++++$

Trial 9 would now be the only failure because it is the only trial with $BCD = ++-$. The trials that failed collectively are now as follows:

Trial Number	$ABCDEFG$
3	$+++--+-$ x
9	$-++-+--$ x

From the information obtained at this point of the experiment process, effects A, E, and F can be removed from consideration because these factors occurred at both high and low levels for the failure conditions. The reduced combinational factor effect considerations are then as follows:

Trial Number	$BCDG$
3	$++--$ x
9	$++--$ x

At this point it is not known where there is a $BCDG$ combinational relationship or a subset of these effects causing the failure. These trials can then be listed to determine which combinations were/were not exercised. By examination, the combinations of $BCDG$ shown in Table 42.10 were exercised by the noted trial(s) in the preceding two experiments.

To determine whether the problem is from an $BCDG = ++--$ effect or a subset that has one less factor-level consideration, note the combinations

TABLE 42.10 Listing of *BCDG* Combinations and Trials

B C D G	Trial Numbers
$----$	8, 12
$---+$	
$--+-$	
$--++$	1, 11
* $-+--$	
$-+-+$	7, 14
$-++-$	5, 10
$-+++$	
* $+---$	
$+--+$	2, 13
$+-+-$	6, 15
$+-++$	
$++--$	3, 9[a]
* $++-+$	
* $+++-$	
$++++$	4, 16

[a] 9 was the previously failed scenario.

that contain a single-factor-level change from the *BCDG* state of $++--$ to those levels not previously tested. The four preceding combinational considerations not previously tested that meet this single-factor-level change are again noted by an *. Since *BCD* = $++-$ is the "real" problem, the *BCDG* = $++-+$ combination would fail, while the other combinations would pass. Because all smaller "group sizes" of these factor levels were already tested without failure, the experimenter would then correctly conclude that the problem was originated by *BCD* = $++-$ (i.e., two displays, word processor Y, and database manager X).

Note that for this last single failure scenario, this procedure was able to structurally identify a three-level combinational problem in eight trials and then isolate the source of the problem in only 12 more trials, given the combinational possibilities of seven two-level factors.

It should be noted, in general, that it is good experimental practice to run a confirmation experiment because there are situations where multiple combinational effects or other experimental problems could cause an erroneous conclusion.

42.11 ADDITIONAL APPLICATIONS

Pass/fail functional testing procedures can also apply to the situation where a problem is noted within an assembly; suspected "bad" part components can be exchanged in a structured fashion with an assembly that has "good parts." The objective of this test then is to determine a particular part type or combination of part types that cause a problem. For this situation each part type becomes a factor with a level that indicates whether it was from either a "good" or "bad" assembly. However, with this type of situation, trial replication may be necessary to determine whether, for example, a consistent pass/fail response occurs for the combination consideration. This is important because the assembly process may be a major source of the problem.

Pass/fail search patterns can also be useful to get some insight to why some attribute fractional factorial trials are very good and others are not very good, even when attribute fractional factorial testing procedures showed nothing to be significant in terms of the "mean" effect analysis. Insight can sometimes be achieved by ranking the trials from goodness to badness. Sometimes there is an obvious change in the failure rate between the ranked trials. For example, trials 7 and 9 may have had no failures, while all the other trials had between 6 and 10 failures. Perhaps something unique can then be identified for these trials (e.g., a pass/ fail logic condition) by looking at the patterns of +'s and −'s. Obviously any theories that are developed would need further evaluation in a confirmation experiment.

42.12   A PROCESS TO STRUCTURALLY USE DOES WITH PRODUCT DEVELOPMENT

Competitive pressures within many industries are driving for improved quality and reduced costs while requiring state-of-the-art technology with a shorter development cycle time. Historical product development processes are not adequate to create a product that is competitive.

Consider a product development strategy where a product is to be conceived by developers and then tested by a "design test" organization. After the test is complete, the product design is then given to the manufacturing organization that will mass produce the product under the supervision of a quality department. Information flow with this approach is graphically depicted in Figure 42.1.

This review approach may be satisfactory with small projects that are not on aggressive development and build programs. However. it is impractical for a test organization of a complex product to know as much detail about the

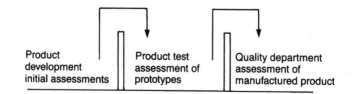

FIGURE 42.1 Typical information flow in a product development cycle.

product as the developers and to choose a reasonable test approach without the aid of the developers. However, each developer cannot define a thorough test strategy alone because he or she can become "too close" to the design and may not have insight to potential problems that can exist when the design interfaces with the designs of other developers.

Organizations might state that Figure 42.1 does not represent their situation because the testing and manufacturing organizations review the work plans of the previous group. I do not believe that the review of plans is often as effective as one would like to believe. Let's consider the question: How might a review/test process structure be improved upon so as to increase its effectiveness between organizations such that a higher-quality product will be produced more expediently?

A common language to aid communication between all organizations should be used to remove any walls between both test activities and organization function. To yield the best overall test strategy, all organizations might need to input (e.g. brainstorming) to a basic test strategy and limiting assumptions that assess the product performance relative to needs of the customer. This language needs be at a "high enough" level for effective communication and still "low enough" to give adequate test details within the experiment(s).

The analysis techniques illustrated earlier in this text are useful after the basic problem is defined; however, determining the best test strategy is often both more important and difficult then "analyzing the data." This challenge increases when developing a complex product because consideration should be made of how to institute a multiple experimental test strategy that promotes both test efficiency and early problem detection.

This text has often encouraged the use of fractional factorial experiment design matrices, when possible, to address questions that may initially take a different form, because this powerful approach to problem solving assesses several factors (i.e., variables) within one experiment. In addition, these designs have a format that can aid in bridging the communication barriers that can exist between departments within an organization.

The experimental strategy that is illustrated in the following example contains a layering of planned fractional factorial experiments within the product development cycle. The fractional factorial experiments can have structural inputs from other organizations (via brainstorming and cause-and-effect diagrams) to improve the effectiveness of the experiment and to achieve maximum coverage and early problem detection within the product development cycle.

42.13 EXAMPLE 42.6: MANAGING PRODUCT DEVELOPMENT USING DOES

Consider the design cycle and integration testing of a complex computer system. Figure 42.2 pictorially illustrates an approach where example con-

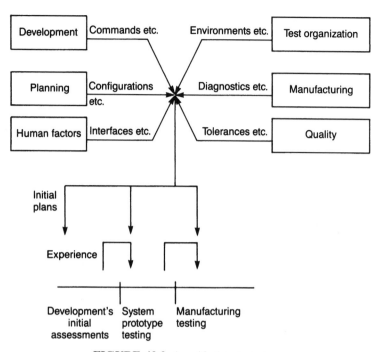

FIGURE 42.2 A unified test strategy.

cerns are expressed from each organization to yield a collaborative general test strategy that can utilize brainstorming concepts to evaluate the development of a computer.

This unified test strategy can reduce a products development cycle time, resource requirements, and solution costs while achieving improved test effectiveness. Product cycles and resource requirements can be reduced by eliminating redundant testing and by improved test efficiency, while solution costs are reduced by earlier problem detection and minimizing the chance of problem escapes.

Inputs for test consideration should place emphasis on directing efforts toward meeting the needs of the customer with less emphasis on criterion validation of noncritical areas (that are currently being performed because "that is the way it has been done in the past"). For this to be a reality, the original test objective may need reassessment and redefinition.

Figure 42.3 illustrates a basic experiment design building process for this product development cycle. The product is first broken down into functional areas that will have individual fractional factorial experiments. Also at this time, plans should be made for pyramiding functional area experiments to assess the interrelationships between areas. Initial "rough" factor plans should be made at this time for experimental designs at all levels of the pyramid. Factor selection for higher-level pyramid designs should consider those factors and levels that can cause interrelationship problems because lower-level

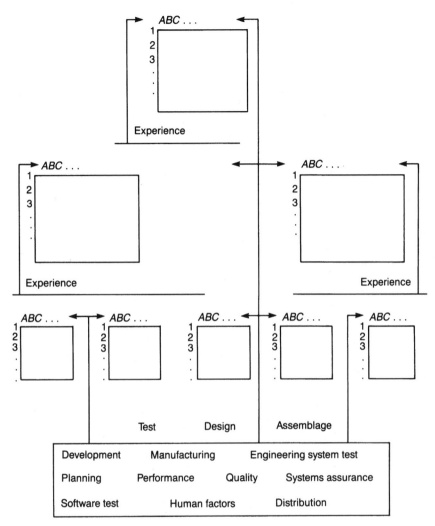

FIGURE 42.3 A structured test strategy.

designs should have previously considered the factors as independent entities. However, the higher-level design factors and levels will be subject to change because information from earlier experiments can be combined with initial thoughts on these selections.

The following steps should be considered for this process flow:

1. Assemble representatives of affected areas to determine the functional area and hierarchical structure, as noted in Figure 42.3.
2. Use brainstorming techniques to determine for each functional area the
   a. Test objective

    b. Limiting assumptions

    c. Outputs

    d. Factors with respective levels

3. Perform experiments and analyze results.

4. Draw conclusions with assemblage and then publish results.

5. Adjust other higher hierarchical structure experimental plans which may change depending on previous experiments.

6. Repeat the process as needed throughout the hierarchy of experiments.

42.14   S⁴ ASSESSMENT

Obviously, when using a fractional factorial design strategy, it is important not to exclude factors or factor levels that are important relative to the response of interest. One major advantage to the test strategy discussed in this chapter is that this risk can be minimized if brainstorming techniques are used to choose the test factors and factor levels. In addition, the concepts lend themselves to a structured pyramid test strategy that can be used in the development of products.

It is often impossible to test all combinations of factor levels because of the potentially staggering number of combinational possibilities. However by determining the number of factor groupings that realistically should be assessed and then testing the combinations of factor levels within a fractional factorial design structure, an "impossible" situation can become quite manageable, plus, the test coverage effectiveness can be reported. It should also be remembered that fractional factorial design matrices can have more than one response. A pass/fail functional response in addition to multiple continuous response outputs can be a very powerful basic test strategy.

The basic test strategy described in this chapter can also be used to assess software and microcode effectiveness where the number of factors and desired trials could exceed the matrix designs given in this text. Larger 2^n trial design matrices could be generated for this situation by combining the $+/-$ patterns of columns (via a computer program). The methodology described in Section 42.7 could then be used to determine test coverage (Breyfogle 1991).

It should be remembered fractional factorial design matrices can have more than one response. A pass/fail functional response in addition to multiple continuous response outputs can be a very powerful basic test strategy.

42.15   EXERCISES

1. One system (call it A) is having failures that will occur within 1 hr, while another system (call it B) is experiencing no problems. It was thought that a combinational problem of two things might cause a problem to occur.

A "big picture" of the assessment was needed for the investigation because many one-at-a-time changes gave no indication of the origin of the problem. A brainstorming session yielded the following six possible causal factors: hard file hardware, processor card (a difference between component tolerances could affect a critical clock speed), network interface card, system software (was thought to be the same but there might be some internal setup differences that were unknown), a software internal address of the system, and the other remaining portions of the system hardware.

(a) Design a two-level test such that 100% of all two-factor level combinations would be evaluated.

(b) Determine the test coverage for three-factor combinations, for four-factor combinations.

2. Several new software levels (i.e. wordprocessor, spread sheet, and fax) offer better functionality than existing software. A customer should be able to use these levels in any combination. It is desired to evaluate whether the programs work satisfactorily when the levels are combined in any fashion and also work with other software.

(a) List 15 factors and their levels in a 16-trial test plan that assesses combinational problems. Choose the factors and levels according to how you would use a particular wordprocessor package. Note the specific hardware and software that will not be changed during the test. (e.g., model and speed of computer).

(b) Determine the percent coverage of two and three factor combinations.

3. Describe how the techniques within this chapter are useful and can be applied to S^4 projects.

43

APPLICATION EXAMPLES

This chapter gives examples that combine the techniques of several chapters and/or illustrate a nontraditional application of a Six Sigma tool.

43.1 EXAMPLE 43.1: IMPROVING PRODUCT DEVELOPMENT

This section was presented originally within the first edition of *Statistical Methods for Testing, Development, and Manufacturing* (Breyfogle 1992) as a possible road map for the Six Sigma implementation within product development (Lorenzen 1990). I am again presenting the methodology, but with a different intent. Within this edition my intent is to stimulate thoughts on how to create a project within the development process (this is where Six Sigma benefits can be the greatest).

The following suggests that statistical techniques could be a more integral part of the product development process, not just used to identify what should be done different to improve the process:

1. *Provide education in statistical methodologies.* The fundamental methodologies of statistical process control design of experiments (DOE), brainstorming, and quality function deployment (QFD)-type activity must be used by large numbers of individuals to develop, manufacture, and deliver the best possible products to customers at competitive prices.
2. *Identify and optimize key process and product parameters.* Defining all processes and creating flowcharts that describe the steps of the process

can give enlightening insight that may not be otherwise apparent. The list of processes needs to include existing basic internal processes in the development process. Brainstorming and Pareto chart techniques can be helpful to determine which processes need to be changed and how these processes can be improved. For example, a brainstorming session may identify a source as "simple" as the current procurement procedure for standard components as the major contributor to "long" development cycles. Another brainstorming session that bridges departmental barriers may then indicate the changes that are needed to improve this process so that it better meets the overall needs of the business. It is also important to establish processes that can identify the parameters that affect product performance and quality early in the design and development phase. DOE response surface experiments, and pass/fail functional testing are tools that need to be considered as an integral part of these processes.

3. *Define tolerances on key parameters.* QFD is a tool that can be helpful when defining limits relative to meeting the needs of the customer. DOE and statistical tolerancing techniques can also be useful tools to determine tolerance levels. For example, a DOE on one prototype early in the development cycle could indicate that the tolerancing of only one of four areas under consideration needed to be closely monitored in the manufacturing process.

4. *Construct control charts, establish control limits, and determine process capability indices.* The initial identification and tracking procedures for key parameters need to begin in development. Continuous response outputs should be used wherever possible. The initial data collection should begin as part of the development process.

5. *Implement statistical process controls in the development line with a management system to assure compliance.* Functional statistical process control (SPC, not just the existence of control charts) is a tool that can monitor the key product parameters as a function of time. An implementation process is needed to address both sporadic/special (i.e., out-of control) conditions and chronic/common conditions (e.g., the number of defects is consistent from day-to-day; however, the amount of defects is too high). An implementation process must be created that encourages continual process improvement, as opposed to "fixing all the problems" via "fire-fighting" techniques.

6. *Demonstrate process capability indices for key processes.* For an accurate quantification of common-cause variability, the process capability indices need to be calculated from data that were taken from a stable process over time. However, it is beneficial to make an estimate of the process capabilities for key parameters and their tolerances with early data. Results from this activity can yield a priority list of work that needs to be done with a starting point where robust designed experi-

ments (i.e., DOE strategy) are used for optimization and the reduction of product variability. To meet variability reduction needs, it may be necessary in some cases to change the design or process. Additional key parameters can be identified from the knowledge gained from this work. Periodic review and updates need to be made for the parameters and their tolerances.

7. *Transfer the responsibility for continuing process improvement to manufacturing.* Note, the manufacturing organization should be involved within development activities; however, in most organizations there is some point in time when the ownership of these processes needs to be transferred to a manufacturing organization. Care must be given to avoid hand-off problems. SPC charting needs to be conducted on all key parameters with an emphasis on making continual process improvements where required.

43.2   EXAMPLE 43.2: A QFD EVALUATION WITH DOE

A company (the customer) purchased metalized glass plates from a supplier for additional processing in an assembly (Lorenzen 1989). The quality of these parts was unsatisfactory. The current supplier process of sputtering chrome/copper/chrome thin films onto these glass substrates caused yields that were too low and costs that were too high. It should be noted that the information for this example was taken from an experiment that was conducted in the early 1980s before QFD and Taguchi concepts became popular; hence, some of the analyses cannot be recreated with the procedural rigor suggested within the procedure.

There are many trade-offs to consider when attempting to improve this process. For this example a QFD approach is used to address this type of situation. The discussion that follows addresses how some of the information that is contained in Figure 43.1 was determined.

The primary QFD "what" of the customer was first determined to be high yield/low cost. The secondary customer "whats" addressed the type of problems encountered in meeting these primary desires. These secondary "what" considerations were then determined to be superior adhesion to eliminate peeling lines, uniform line widths to improve electrical operating margins, and no electrical open circuit paths. Tertiary "whats" then follow, addressing these desires along with an importance rating. The process/design requirements thought necessary to meet these tertiary "what" items are then listed as the "hows" across the top of this matrix. The following discussion will give the thought process used to determine the other parameters of this "house of quality."

The next step that can be taken is to define the relationship between the "whats" and "hows." One option is to assign a value from a known or

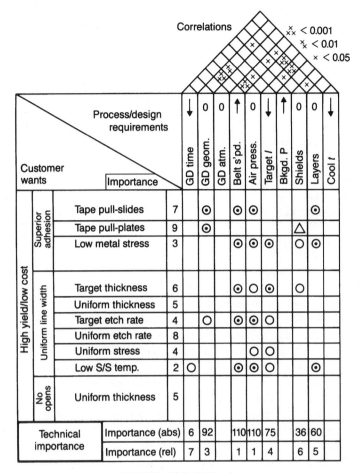

FIGURE 43.1 QFD chart.

assumed relationship of fundamental principles; however, this relationship may be invalid. Another approach is to use a fractional factorial experiment. When taking this second approach, consider a "what" (e.g., "target thickness") as output to a fractional factorial experiment with the 10 "how" factors and levels, as shown in Table 43.1.

One glass substrate would be manufactured according to a fractional factorial design matrix that sets the 10 factor levels for each sample that is produced. The 64-trial experiment design shown in Table 43.2 (which was created from Table M5) gives unconfounded information about the main effects with two-factor interactions; however, the two-factor interactions are confounded with each other (i.e., a resolution IV design).

For the purpose of illustration, consider the target thickness "what" that had a value of 1600 angstroms, with a customer tolerance of 300 angstroms.

TABLE 43.1 "How's" for Glass Plates

Factor	Level	
	(−)	(+)
A: Belt speed	2.2 rpm	1.1 rpm
B: Argon sputter pressure	4 mtorr	14 mtorr
C: Glow discharge atmosphere	Dry	Wet
D: Target current	4 amperes	8 amperes
E: Glow discharge plate geometry	Flat	Edge
F: Background pressure	8×10^{-6} torr	5×10^{-5} torr
G: Plate cool-down time	2 min	10 min
H: Shields	With	Without
I: Number of layers	1	3
J: Glow discharge time	10 min	20 min

This thickness measurement response is noted in Table 43.2 for each of the 64 trials. The other "whats" can similarly have an output level for each trial.

The results from a computer analysis are shown in Table 43.3, where the factors and interactions are noted as contrasts columns (i.e., cont1–cont63). It should be noted that this nomenclature is consistent with Table N2 and that the contrast columns not noted in the computer output were used by the program to estimate experimental error (because only factors A–J and their two-factor interaction contrast columns were defined in this resolution IV experiment design model).

For this design the interaction effects are confounded. Table 43.3 includes the results of the engineering judgment that was used to determine which of the interactions noted from Table N2 probably caused the contrast column to be significant. A confirmation experiment will later be needed to assess the validity of these assumptions.

Results from this data analysis provide quantitative information on the nature of the relationships between the customer "wants" and the "hows" for the process/design requirements noted in Figure 43.1. When computing importance for the QFD chart, a 5 (⊙) was used to indicate a very strong relationship ($P < 0.001$), a 3 (○) represented a strong relationship ($P < 0.01$), and a 1 (△) indicated a weak relationship ($P < 0.05$). A ↑ indicated from the range of factor levels used in this experiment that the value of the customer "want" improves as the process requirement increased, while ↓ indicated lower values are better and ○ indicated that there was a preferred target value. Significant interactions are indicated in the correlation matrix with the noted significance levels (the "roof of the house" in QFD chart).

A strategy could now be taken to evaluate parameter and tolerance design considerations from a "target thickness" point of view. In general, the model parameter coefficients could be used to determine target parameters for each design requirement. However, in lieu of this procedure, consider the summary

TABLE 43.2 A "What" Output Versus "How" Factors

Trial Number	"Hows" Factors A B C D E F G H I J	("What") Thickness	Trial Number	"Hows" Factors A B C D E F G H I J	("What") Thickness
1	+ − − − − − + + − +	1405	33	+ + − − + − − + + +	1300
2	+ + − − − − − − + −	1122	34	+ + + − − + + − + +	1074
3	+ + + − − − − − − −	895	35	− + + + − − + + − −	1070
4	+ + + + − − − − − +	1915	36	− − + + + − − + + −	1360
5	+ + + + + − − + − −	2060	37	− − − + + + + + + +	1340
6	+ + + + + + + + + +	1985	38	+ − − − + + − − + +	1530
7	− + + + + + − − + −	1050	39	− + − − − + − + − −	870
8	+ − + + + + − − − −	2440	40	+ − + − − − + + + +	1480
9	− + − + + + − − − −	960	41	+ + − + − − − − + +	1920
10	+ − + − + + − − − +	1260	42	+ + + − + − − + − +	975
11	− + − + − + − + − +	1110	43	+ + + + − + + − + −	2130
12	+ − + − + − + − + −	1495	44	− + + + + − + − − +	770
13	+ + − + − + + − − −	1810	45	− − + + + + + + − +	1210
14	− + + − + − + − − −	482	46	+ − − + + + − − + −	1800
15	− − + + − + + − − −	1040	47	− + − − + + − − − +	450
16	+ − − + + − + − − +	2620	48	+ − + − − + − + − −	1380
17	+ + − − + + + + − −	910	49	− + − + − − + + + −	1360
18	− + + − − + − + + −	545	50	− − + − + − − + + +	840
19	+ − + + − − + + + −	3650	51	− − − + − + + − + −	1020
20	+ + − + + − − + + −	2430	52	+ − − − + − + − − −	1180
21	+ + + − + + + + + −	1065	53	+ + − − − + + − − +	980
22	− + + + − + − + + +	1260	54	− + + − − − + + − +	470
23	+ − + + + − + − + +	1976	55	− − + + − − − − + +	770
24	+ + − + + + + + − +	2000	56	− − − + + − − + − −	1320
25	− + + − + + − − + +	430	57	− − − − + + + + + −	820
26	+ − + + − + − + − +	2070	58	+ − − − − + − + + −	1424
27	− + − + + − + − + +	780	59	− + − − − − + + + +	620
28	− − + − + + + + + − −	570	60	− − + − − − − − + −	500
29	+ − − + − + − + + +	3600	61	− − − + − − − − − +	1010
30	− + − − + − + − + −	495	62	− − − − + − − + − +	545
31	− − + − − + + − − +	620	63	− − − − − + + − + +	600
32	+ − − + − − + + − −	2520	64	− − − − − − − − − −	590

of significant interacting factors shown in Table 43.4. When significant main effects are involved in interactions, the main effects must be discussed in terms of other factors (e.g., the average of all the 16 thickness responses where $A = 1$ and $B = 1$ was 1535.68750).

Of the interactions noted in this table, first consider the $A*B$ interaction. Given the target objective of 1300 to 1900 (i.e., 1600 ± 300), it is inferred that the process should have A and B both near the $+1$ level. From the $A*D$ interaction, A should be near the $+1$ level with D approximately halfway

TABLE 43.3 Computer Output (Significance Calculations)

ANALYSIS OF VARIANCE PROCEDURE

DEPENDENT VARIABLE: THICKNESS

SOURCE	DF	SUM OF SQUARES	MEAN SQUARE	F VALUE	PR > F	R-SQUARE	C.V.
MODEL	41	30235649.12500000	737454.85670732	11.12	0.0001	0.953963	19.7919
ERROR	22	1459141.81250000	66324.62784091			ROOT MSE	THICKNESS MEAN
CORRECTED TOTAL	63	31694790.93750000				257.53568266	1301.21875000

SOURCE	DF	ANOVA SS	F VALUE	PR > F	
CONT1	1	13619790.25000000	205.35	0.0001	← A: Belt Speed
CONT2	1	1180482.25000000	17.80	0.0004	← B: Argon Sputter Pressure
CONT3	1	40200.25000000	0.61	0.4445	
CONT4	1	10107630.56250000	152.40	0.0001	← D: Target Current
CONT5	1	88655.06250000	1.34	0.2600	
CONT6	1	5112.25000000	0.08	0.7839	
CONT7	1	530348.06250000	8.00	0.0098	← A*B: Belt Speed * Argon Pressure
CONT8	1	1207.56250000	0.02	0.8939	
CONT9	1	110.25000000	0.00	0.9678	
CONT10	1	57960.56250000	0.87	0.3600	
CONT11	1	17030.25000000	0.26	0.6174	
CONT12	1	529.00000000	0.01	0.9296	
CONT13	1	637.56250000	0.01	0.9228	
CONT14	1	39006.25000000	0.59	0.4513	
CONT15	1	5256.25000000	0.08	0.7809	
CONT16	1	11025.00000000	0.17	0.6874	
CONT17	1	962851.56250000	14.52	0.0010	← H: Target Shields
CONT18	1	284089.00000000	4.28	0.0504	← I: Number of Metal Layers
CONT19	1	6.25000000	0.00	0.9923	
CONT20	1	25680.06250000	0.39	0.5402	
CONT21	1	249750.06250000	3.77	0.0652	
CONT22	1	32761.00000000	0.49	0.4895	
CONT23	1	378840.25000000	5.71	0.0258	← H*I: Target Shields * Number of Layers
CONT25	1	83810.25000000	1.26	0.2731	
CONT26	1	3937.56250000	0.06	0.8098	
CONT31	1	57600.00000000	0.87	0.3615	
CONT33	1	1400672.25000000	21.12	0.0001	← A*D: Belt Speed * Target Current
CONT34	1	2070.25000000	0.03	0.8614	
CONT35	1	5365.56250000	0.08	0.7787	
CONT39	1	362705.06250000	5.47	0.0289	← D*H: Target Current * Target Shields
CONT40	1	88209.00000000	1.33	0.2612	
CONT42	1	85.56250000	0.00	0.9717	
CONT43	1	15813.06250000	0.24	0.6302	
CONT45	1	65025.00000000	0.98	0.3329	
CONT48	1	127627.56250000	1.92	0.1793	
CONT52	1	5550.25000000	0.08	0.7751	
CONT55	1	38220.25000000	0.58	0.4558	
CONT56	1	8742.25000000	0.13	0.7200	
CONT59	1	226338.06250000	3.41	0.0782	
CONT61	1	15067.56250000	0.23	0.6383	
CONT63	1	89850.06250000	1.35	0.2569	

TABLE 43.4 Result from Computer Output (Mean Interaction Effects from Data)

Note 1: A*B Interaction

A	B	N^a	Thickness	
1	1	16	1535.68750	* Conclude that A and B should be near
1	−1	16	1989.37500	+1 level.
−1	1	16	795.12500	
−1	−1	16	884.68750	

Note 2: A*D Interaction

A	D	N	Thickness	
1	1	16	2307.87500	* Conclude that D should be near
1	−1	16	1217.18750	halfway point between −1 and +1
−1	1	16	1089.37500	levels given A = +1.
−1	−1	16	590.43750	

Note 3: H*I Interaction

H	I	N	Thickness	
1	1	16	1567.43750	* Conclude that H and I should be near
1	−1	16	1280.31250	+1 level.
−1	1	16	1168.25000	
−1	−1	16	1188.87500	

Note 4: D*H Interaction

D	H	N	Thickness	
1	1	16	1896.56250	* Conclude that previous D and H
1	−1	16	1500.68750	levels look reasonable.
−1	1	16	951.18750	
−1	−1	16	856.43750	

^{a}N is the number of trials that were averaged to get the thickness response.

between its two test extremes. From the H*I interaction, H should be at a level near the +1 level with I also at a +1 level. Finally, the D*H interaction information does not dispute the conclusions for our previously selected factor levels.

A summary of the conclusions is as follows: A = +, B = +, D = halfway between high and low, H = +, and I = +. From the raw data consider now the thickness output for the trials that had the preceding combination levels:

Trial	A	B	D	H	I				
6	+	+	+	+	+	1985			We would
20	+	+	+	+	+	2430	↦ average 2007.5	if D	expect an
								↦ were halfway	↦ output of
21	+	+	−	+	+	1065	↦ average 1183		approx.
33	+	+	−	+	+	1300			1595.25

The expected value of 1595.25 is close to the desired target value of 1600. A confirmation experiment should be performed to verify this conclusion. A response surface design could also be used to gain more information about the sensitivity of the factor levels to the output response.

Note that these are the target considerations given that thickness tolerance is the only output. There may be conflict between "what" items, causing a compromise for these levels.

The preceding thought process parallels the intent of what some other texts on Tagnchi techniques call parameter design. When using a Taguchi strategy the next step would be a tolerance design (i.e., an experiment design that is to determine the tolerance of the parameters). It can be easy to assign a tolerance value to the nonsignificant factors. From the previous analysis for thickness and other "what" analyses not discussed, the cooling time from 2 mm (the experimental low level) to 10 mm (the high level) had no affect on the "what" items. Hence, it is probably safe to use the test extremes as tolerance extremes. Likewise, the background pressure can vary from its experimental level settings of 8 to 5×10^{-5} torr, and the glow discharge atmosphere can be wet or dry. However, to speculate about a reasonable tolerance for these other critical parameters from the given data could yield questionable conclusions. Hence, more information would be needed to determine satisfactory tolerance limits for these factors.

We believe that the five parameters noted earlier affect thickness individually and through two-factor interaction considerations. Let's consider economics first. I suggest first determining what tolerance can be maintained without any additional expenditures to the process. An experiment can then be conducted similar to that shown around the "new" nominal values. From Table M3 we can get a 16-trial experiment that can be used to assess all two-factor interactions of five factors. A 16-trial test where the two factors are evaluated at their tolerance extremes represent the "space" (i.e., assessment of boundary conditions) of the tolerances expected. If these data are plotted on probability paper, a picture of the extreme operating range can be determined. If this plot is centered and the 0.1%–99.9% probability plot positions are well within the tolerance extremes, then it would be reasonable to conclude that the tolerances are adequate. If this is not true, then the fractional factorial information needs to be analyzed again using the preceding logic so that the tolerance of critical factors can be tightened while less important factors maintain their loose tolerance limits. A response surface design approach can be used to optimize complex process parameters.

After the process parameters are determined, control charting techniques should be used to monitor the important process factors noted in the manufacturing process. In addition, sampling should be performed as necessary along with control charting to monitor all the other primary and secondary "what" factors.

43.3   EXAMPLE 43.3: A RELIABILITY AND FUNCTIONAL TEST OF AN ASSEMBLY

A power supply has sophisticated design requirements. In addition, the specification indicates an aggressive MTBF (mean time between failures) criterion of 10×10^6 hr. A test organization is to evaluate the reliability and function of the nonrepairable power supply.

Tests of this type seem to be directed toward emphasizing testing the failure rate criterion by exercising enough units long enough to verify the criterion. Considering that the failure rate of the units is constant with age, as the criterion implies. Table K can yield a factor that is used to determine the total number of test hours needed. If we desire 90% confidence with a test design that allows no failures, then the factor would be 2.303, which would yield a total test time of

$$T = 2.303 \ (10 \times 10^6) = 23.03 \times 10^6 \text{ hr}$$

The number of units could range from 23.03×10^6 units for 1 hr or one unit for 23.03×10^6 hr. Relative to the single-unit test length, it may be unlikely that many products would survive this much usage without failure because of some type of wear-out mechanism. And, in reality, it is not very important that a single product would last this long, because for continual customer usage it would require 114 years to accumulate 1×10^6 hr of usage. Hence, for this test a single product would need to survive 2636 years without failure before "passing" the test. This test approach is a "little" ridiculous.

In addition, the wording of this criterion is deceptive from another point of view. Whenever a nonrepairable device fails, it needs to be replaced. The wording for the above criterion implies a repairable device (mean time between failures). What is probably intended by the criterion is that the failure rate for each hour should not exceed 0.0000001 failures/hr (i.e., $1/[10 \times 10^6$ hr/failure]). From a customer point of view, where the annual usage is expected to be 5000 hr and there is a 5-year expected life, this would equate to 0.05% of the assemblies failing after 1 year's usage and 0.25% of the assemblies after 5 year's usage. If the criterion were quoted with percentages of this type, there would be no confusion about the reliability objectives of the product.

In general, it seems that two percentage values, for example, are often adequate for this type criterion, where the first percentage value is directed toward a maximum fail percentage value within a warranty period, while the second percentage value is directed toward a maximum fail percentage value during the expected product life.

Consider that the expected annual number of power-on hours for the power supply is 5000 hr, and each unit is tested to this expected usage. This test would require 4605 (i.e., $23.026 \times 10^6/5000 = 4605$) units, while a 5-year test would require 921 units [i.e., $23.026 \times 10^6/(5000)(5) = 921$]). For most scenarios involving complex assemblies, neither of these two test alternatives are reasonable because the unit costs would be prohibitive, the test facilities would be very large, the test would be too long, and information obtained late in the test would probably be "too late" for any "value added." Accelerated test alternatives can be helpful to reduce test duration; however, the same basic problems still exist with less magnitude.

Even if the time and resources are spent to do this test and no failure occurs, customer reliability problems can still exist. Two basic assumptions are often overlooked with the preceding test strategy. The first assumption is that the sample is a random sample of the population. If this test were performed early in the manufacturing process, the "sample" may be the first units built, which is not a random sample of future builds that will go to the customer. Problems can occur later in the manufacturing process and cause field problems, which this test will not detect because test samples were from an earlier production vintage. The second assumption is that the test replicates customer usage. If a test does not closely replicate customer situations, real problems may not be detected. For example, if the customer turns off a system unit that contains the power supply each evening and our test units are just exercised continuously, the test may miss some thermal cycling component fatigue failures. Or, another example could be that the customer puts more electrical load on the system than was done on the test system. The test may again miss a failure mode caused by this additional loading. Perhaps a fractional factorial test strategy could better define how the power supplies should be loaded and exercised when trying to identify customer reliability problems.

It is easy to get in the trap of "playing games" when testing to verify a failure rate criterion. Let's consider S^4 alternatives. Let's reflect on problems of other products that were found during previous tests or in the user environment. Tests should be designed to give the *customer* the best possible product.

Single-lot testing that gives primary emphasis to initial production testing where the product is considered as a "black box" can yield a large test effort where important problems are not detected. To maximize test efforts, consider the following: Should more emphasis be placed on monitoring the component selection/design considerations as opposed to "running them and counting the number of failures?" Should more emphasis be given to the monitoring of the manufacturing process (i.e., control charting, process capability, etc.)? Should more fractional factorial experiments be used within the internal design process of the mechanism, with stress to failure considerations as an output?

Consider also the real purpose of a reliability test. For the product test criterion, what should really happen if a zero failure test plan had one, two, three, . . . failures? It is hoped that the process or design would be "fixed" so that the failures did not occur again. It is doubtful that time would permit another sample of the "new design/process" every time a failure was detected. Hence, typically the test-stated objective may be to verify a criterion; however, the real intent of the test may be to determine and then fix problems.

Now, if the real objective is to identify and fix problems (instead of playing games with numbers), test efforts should be directed to do this *efficiently*. An efficient test would not probably be to turn on 4605 units for a 5000-hr test and once a week monitor them to see if any failures occur. An efficient approach, for example, can include querying the experts for the types of failure expected and monitoring historical field data so that test efforts can be directed toward these considerations and new technology risks. For example, a test without power on/off switching and heating/cooling effects does not make sense if previous power supplies experience 70% of their field failures during the power-on cycling (i.e., a light-bulb failure mode) or if 10% of the time the power supply does not start the first time it is used because handling during shipment caused "out-of-box" failures.

Using S^4 considerations, it may be found to be appropriate to use more fractional factorial experiments within the development process. Then, for a pre-production test, the experimenter may decide to test only three units at an elevated temperature for as long as possible to determine if there are any wear-out "surprises." The person who conducts the test may also plan to exercise some units within a thermal cycle chamber and thermal shock chamber. Plans may also consider a shipping test and an out-of-box vibration stress to failure test for some units.

In addition, the experimenter should work with the manufacturing group to obtain time-of-failure information during the production preshipment run-in tests. Data from this test could be used to determine early-life characteristics of the product, which could possibly be projected into the customer environment. The experimenter also would like to ensure that any run-in test time focus on in manufacturing is optimized.

A good reliability test strategy has a blend of test considerations that focus on efficiently capturing the types of failures that would be experienced by the customer. It is not a massive test effort that "plays games with numbers." In addition to the reliability considerations, the experimenter needs to also address functional considerations within the customer environment. Fractional factorial testing is an efficient method to meet these needs.

For the preceding test, one pre-production unit could be functionally tested at the extremes of its operating environment using a fractional factorial test strategy. The following is such a strategy where input factors are evaluated for their effect on the various important output characteristic requirements of the power supply; it is summarized in Table 43.5.

TABLE 43.5 Summary of Test Strategy

	Inputs	
	Levels	
Factors	$(-)$	$(+)$
A: Ambient temperature	47°C	25°C
B: Input ac voltage range	110 V	220 V
C: Mode on programmable output	3.4 V	5.1 V
D: ac line voltage (within range in B)	Min	Max
E: Frequency at ac input	Min	Max
F: Load on -12 V output	Min	Max
G: Load on -5 V output	Min	Max
H: Load on 12 V output	Min	Max
I: Load on 5.1 V output	Min	Max
J: Load on 3.4 V output	Min	Max
K: Load on programmable output	Min	Max

Outputs

Output voltage on each output (-12 V, -5 V, 12 V, 5.1 V, 3.4 V, programmable volt output)
Ripple/noise
Noise
Input (power factor)
Efficiency
Line current
Line power

From Table M4 a 32-trial resolution IV design was chosen. With this design the main effects would not be confounded with two-factor interactions; however, there would be confounding of two-factor interactions with each other. The 11 contrast columns from Table M4 were assigned alphabetical factor designations from left to right (A–K). These test trials along with two of the experimental trial outputs (-12- and 3.4-V output levels) are noted in Table 43.6.

The effect of the -12-V loading (factor F), for example, on the -12-V output level is simply the difference in average output response for the trials at the high load to those at low load, which is

Average effect on -12-V output by -12-V load (F effect)

$$= \frac{(-11.755 - 11.702, \cdots)}{16} - \frac{(12.202 - 12.200, \cdots)}{16}$$

$$= -0.43 \text{ V}$$

TABLE 43.6 Design Factors and Levels

Factors	Levels	
	(−)	(+)
A: Polymer brand	Original source	New source
B: Wax brand	Original source	New source
C: Wax proportion amount	0.08	0.12
D: Resin brand	New source	Original source
E: Resin proportion amount	0.14	0.10

The main effect and interaction considerations (given the confounding that is noted in Table N2) plotted on normal probability paper is shown in Figure 43.2. The −0.43-V effect is a large outlier from any linear relationships; hence, it is concluded that the loading of the −12-V output significantly affects the −12-V output (best estimate value of 0.43 V). Other less significant effects are similarly noted.

The results of statistical analyses are commonly presented as significance statements. However, a practitioner may be interested in the overall affects relative to specification limits. One approach to size this consideration is to make a probability plot of the outputs of the 32 trials and include the specification limits on the plot (note that this plot is not a true random sample plot of a population). Figure 43.3 illustrates such a plot for the −12-V source, where the magnitude of the loading effect is noticeable as a discontinuity in the line. This plot reflects the variability of one machine given various worst-

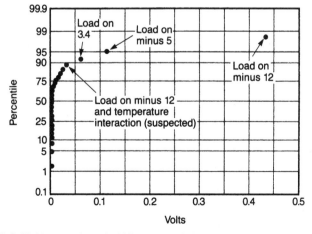

FIGURE 43.2 Half-normal probability plot of the contrast column effects (−12-V output).

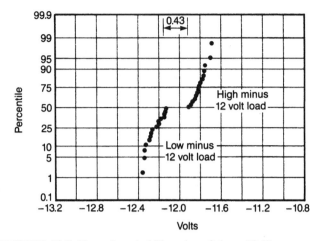

FIGURE 43.3 Normal probability plot of the -12-V responses.

case loading scenarios. Because the distribution tails are within the noted specification limits, it might be concluded that there are no major problems (if the variability from machine to machine is not large and there is not a degradation with usage).

Consider now the 3.4-V output. A probability plot of the 3.4-V effects is shown in Figure 43.4. The 3.4-V loading effect appears to be most significant when followed by the temperature effect. The third most significant effect is noted to be a suspicion of an interaction between this loading and temperature.

This interaction effect is suspected because two-factor interactions are confounded with this resolution IV experiment design. This probability point is

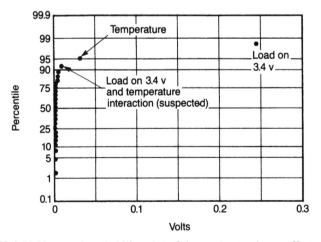

FIGURE 43.4 Half-normal probability plot of the contrast column effects (3.4-V output).

in reality contrast column 15 (see the design matrix in Table M4). Table N2 indicates that contrast 15, in general, has many interactions that are confounded. However, the number of interaction possibilities is reduced because this experiment had only 11 factors (designated *A* through *K*); hence, the number of possibilities is reduced to *EF*, *GH*, *AJ*, and *BK*. Engineering then technically considered which of these interaction possibilities [frequency at ac input/load on −12-V output (*EF*), load on −5-V output/load on 12-V output (*GH*), ambient temperature/load on 3.4-V output (*AJ*), and input ac voltage range/load on programmable output (*BK*)] would be the most likely to affect the −12-V output level. Engineering concluded that the most likely interaction was temperature/load on −12-V output (*AJ*). Obviously, if it is important to be certain about this contrast column effect, then a confirmation experiment would later need to be conducted.

Similarly to the −12-V analyses, a probability plot of the 32 trial outputs is shown in Figure 43.5. This plot illustrates the previously suspected two-factor interaction by the grouping of the data. However, some of the data points fall below the lower specification limit. It appears that the supplier is adjusting the power supply to a 3.4-V output under a low-load condition. However, with additional load, the output decreases to a value that is close to the specification limit. It is apparent from the out-of-specification condition that the voltage adjustment procedure at the supplier should be changed to "center" the high/low loading conditions within the specification limits.

Figure 43.6 shows an estimate for the PDFs that describe the four different scenarios. With this format the findings from the experiment might possibly be more easily presented to others who are not familiar with probability plots (noting that this is a very rough estimate because the data were not a random sample consisting of many units).

The next question of concern is whether there are any other parameters that should be considered. One possible addition to the variability conditions

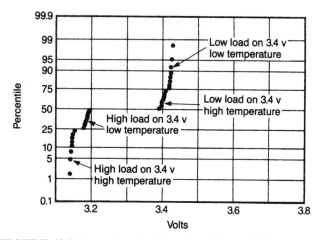

FIGURE 43.5 Normal probability plot of the 3.4-V responses.

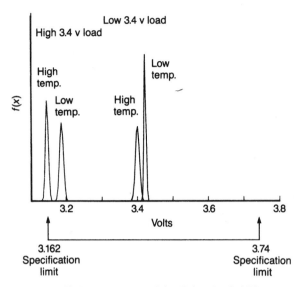

FIGURE 43.6 Four PDF "sizing" for the 3.4-V output.

is circuitry drift with component age. Another is variability between power supply assembly units.

To address the between-assemblies condition, multiple units could have been used for these analyses. However, the test duration and resource requirements could be much larger. An alternative is to consider an addition derived from historical information; however, this information is not often available. Another alternative is to evaluate a sample of parts held at constant conditions to assess the magnitude of this variability. This effort can also serve as a confirmation experiment to assess whether the conclusions that were drawn from the fractional factorial experiment are valid.

In Figure 43.7 the test data for 10 power supply assemblies are plotted. The test data consist of two points for each assembly (taken at low and high load on the 3.4-V output and at low temperature). The plot indicates that approximately 99.8% of the population variability is within a 0.1-V range. Therefore, if we assume the same machine-to-machine variability at high temperatures, allowance should be made for this 0.1-V variation in the 3.4-V analyses. Note that this type of plot should be constructed for each level of voltage because the variation probably will be different for these other outputs.

After the power supply qualification test process is completed satisfactorily, information from this test can be used to determine which parameters need to be monitored within the manufacturing process using process control chart techniques. Also, it should be noted that if this problem escaped development tests, manufacturing would probably be reporting this issue as a "no trouble found" when failing units were returned by the customer ("no trouble" issues are very expensive within many organizations).

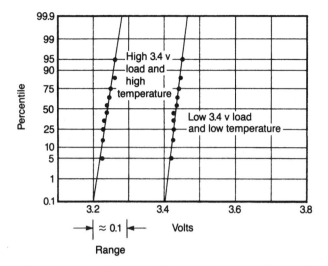

FIGURE 43.7 Normal probability plot of the 3.4-V output on 10 machines under two different conditions.

43.4   EXAMPLE 43.4: A DEVELOPMENT STRATEGY FOR A CHEMICAL PRODUCT

A chemist needs to develop a floor polish that is equal to or better than the competitions' floor polish in 20 areas of measurement (e.g., slip resistance, scuff resistance, visual gloss, and buffability).

A previous example illustrated an extreme vertices design approach that used response surface design techniques to "optimize" the amount of mixture components of wax, resin, and polymer to create a quality floor polish. Consider from this experiment that the conclusion was that a good-quality floor finish would be obtained with the mixture proportions of wax (0.08–0.12) and resin (0.10–0.14), where polymer was the remaining proportion.

Consider now that this previous experiment was performed with only one source for each of the mixture components. Consider that there is now another source for the materials that claims higher quality with reduced costs. A fractional factorial test is now desired to compare the alternate sources for the mixture components.

It was believed that the range of mixture proportions previously determined needed consideration as factor level effects. The factors and levels were assigned as noted in the following for consideration in a 16-trial, resolution V design, where the amount of polymer used within a mixture trial would be the amount necessary to achieve a total proportion of 1.0 with the given proportions of resin and wax specified for each trial shown in Table 43.6.

From Table M3 the design matrix for five factors would be as shown in Table 43.7. From this design, two-factor interaction effects can be determined. After the 16 formulations are prepared, the test environment and trial re-

TABLE 43.7 Design Matrix for 16-Trial Test

Trial Number	$A\ B\ C\ D\ E$
1	+ − − − +
2	+ + − − −
3	+ + + − +
4	+ + + + −
5	− + + + +
6	+ − + + +
7	− + − + −
8	+ − + − −
9	+ + − + +
10	− + + − −
11	− − + + −
12	+ − − + −
13	− + − − +
14	− − + − +
15	− − − + +
16	− − − − −

sponses could also be considered. Do we expect the response to vary as a function of the weather (temperature and humidity), application equipment, application techniques, and/or type of flooring? If so, we could choose a Taguchi strategy of using these factors within an outer array. This inner/outer array test strategy would require more trials; however, it can help us avoid developing a product that works well in a laboratory environment but not well in a customer situation. Or, as an alternative to an inner/outer array strategy, these considerations can be managed as factors within the experiment design considerations.

Another concern that can be addressed is the relationship of our new product composition to that of the competition. To make a competitive assessment, competitive products could be evaluated in a similar "outer array" test environment during initial testing. From this information, comparisons can be made during and after the selection of the final chemical composition.

After the chemical composition is determined, stability is needed within the manufacturing process so that a quality product is produced on a continuing basis. An *XmR* chart is a tool that is useful to monitor key parameters within a batch chemical manufacturing process.

43.5 EXAMPLE 43.5: TRACKING ONGOING PRODUCT COMPLIANCE FROM A PROCESS POINT OF VIEW

An organization is periodically required to sample product from manufacturing to assess ongoing compliance per government requirements. The test is time-consuming and is known to have much test error (but has not been quantified). There are many products produced by the company that are to undergo this test. These products are similar in nature but have different design requirements and suppliers. To address these government requirements the organization periodically samples the manufacturing process and tests to specifications. If the product does not meet requirements, corrective action is taken within the manufacturing organization. The organization notes that when manufacturing needs to be notified for issue resolution, the frequency is higher than desired.

Current tests are attribute (pass or fail) and measurements focus on the product. Also, when samples are outside of specification the reaction to the situation is that the problem is special cause (i.e., go to the manufacturing and fix the problem). Let's look at the situation from a higher viewpoint and examine the data as continuous from process. All products basically go through the same process of design, design qualification test, and manufacturing. From this point of view we can assess if the failures are special-cause or common-cause. If the failures are common-cause, we might be able to get insight to what should be done different within the process to reduce the overall frequency of failure. The variable data of measurements relative to specification limits are the following, where zero is the specification and positive values indicate that the amount the measurement is beyond specification:

```
-9.4   -9.4   -6.4   -7.7   -9.7   -8.6   -4.7   -4.7   -6.2   -0.3    3     0.6   -8.8
       -9.5   -2.6   -6.9   11.2   -9.5   -9.3   -7.8  -12.4   -3.2   -4.9  -16.3  -3.5
       -6.7  -10     3.6    -0.2   -7.6    1.9
```

The *XmR* control chart of the variable shown in Figure 43.8 indicates only one special cause, while Figure 43.9 shows a normal probability plot of all

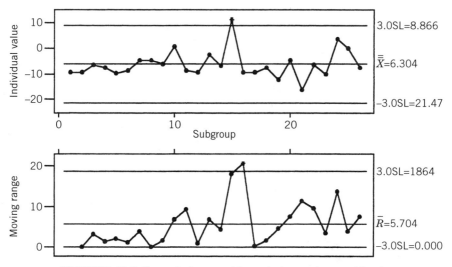

FIGURE 43.8 Control chart tracking relative to the specification.

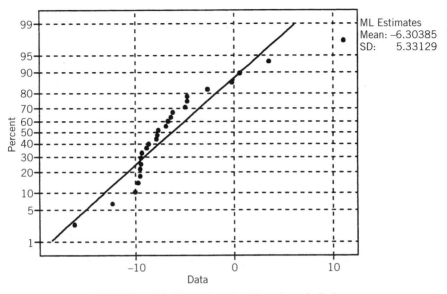

FIGURE 43.9 Normal probability plot of all data.

data. (This plot is to be recreated without the special cause data point as part of an exercise.) From this plot it indicates that our overall process is not very capable of consistently meeting the test requirements. The plot indicates that we might expect a 10%–20% failure rate unless we do something differently (the mathematical estimation of this rate and other statistical calculations is given later as an exercise).

From a process improvement point of view, we would next like to assess what should be done differently within our process. With existing data we could create a Pareto chart of what was done to bring the previous out-of-specification product back into compliance. Perhaps there is some "common thread" between the different product types that are being measured. This information could be passed on to development and manufacturing with emphasis on improving the robustness of the design in the future and poka-yoke.

So far we have only looked at data differently (i.e., no additional measurements have been made). The next process improvement effort that seems to be appropriate is to better understand our measurement system (i.e., conduct a gauge R&R). After this is complete, a DOE might be appropriate to give insight into what could be done differently within the process.

43.6   EXAMPLE 43.6: TRACKING AND IMPROVING TIMES FOR CHANGE ORDERS

An organization would like engineering change orders to be resolved quickly. Collected time series data showing the number of days to complete change orders were as follows:

18	2	0	0	0	0	0	0	0	0	0	0	0
	0	0	0	0	0	14	0	0	7	3	0	41
	0	0	0	0	0	0	0	0	17	0	0	0
	0	0	0	0	0	0	0	0	0	0	0	0
	0	1	0	0	0	0	0	0	11	0	0	17
	26	0	0	0	0	0	0	21	0	0	0	0
	6	0	0	17	0	0	0	0	0	0	0	0

The *XmR* chart of these data shown in Figure 43.10 does not give much insight to the process because there are so many zeros. A histogram of these data indicates that it might be better to consider the situation bimodal—that is, less than one day (i.e., 0) as one distribution and one day or more as another distribution. An estimate of the proportion of instances it takes one day or more is $14/85 = 0.16$. The control chart of the one or greater values shown in Figure 43.11 does not indicate any trends or special causes when duration takes longer than one day. The normal probability plot shown in Figure 43.12 indicates the variability that can be expected when a change order takes one day or longer. We can combine these two distributions to give an estimate of the percentage of change orders beyond a criterion. To illustrate this, consider a criterion of 10 days. The estimated percentage of engineering change orders taking longer than 10 days is $100(0.16)(0.65) = 11\%$ (where 0.65 is the estimate proportion $[1 - 0.35 = 0.65]$ from the figure). With this information we could categorize the characteristics of change orders that take a long period of time. From this information we could create a Pareto chart that would give us a visual representation that leads to focus areas for process improvement efforts.

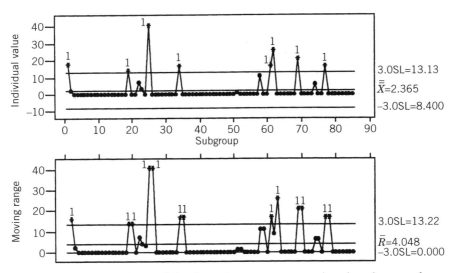

FIGURE 43.10 *XmR* Chart of the time taken to process engineering change orders.

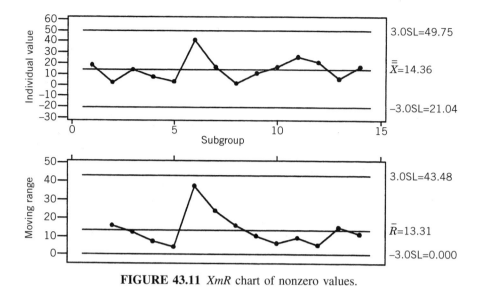

FIGURE 43.11 *XmR* chart of nonzero values.

43.7   EXAMPLE 43.7: IMPROVING THE EFFECTIVENESS OF EMPLOYEE OPINION SURVEYS

The described methodology was developed for a company employee opinion survey; however, the approach can be applied in other situations.

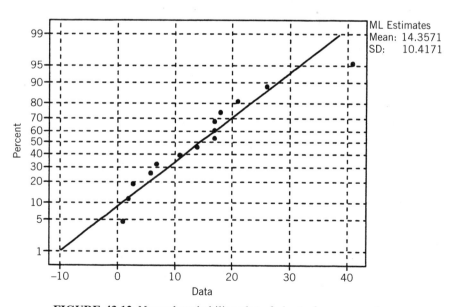

FIGURE 43.12 Normal probability plot of chart of nonzero values.

Many employee opinion surveys are conducted periodically (e.g., annually). These surveys can use a Likert scale with the associated numerical responses of: strongly agree (5), agree (4), uncertain (3), disagree (2), and strongly disagree (1). Much time and effort can be given to interpreting the results. After all this effort we might question the value of the survey. When interpreting these results, one might ask several questions:

1. Are these response levels okay?
2. Are there any improvement trends?
3. Might the results be different if the survey were taken a month later (e.g., a gloomy time of year might yield a less favorable response than a bright time of year.)
4. What should be done differently?

Let's examine what might be done different with the survey approach to address these issues. This survey strategy will focus on giving insight to company internal "processes," as opposed, for example, to the ranking of departmental results and taking "corrective action" as required.

Because the absolute number of a 1–5 Likert response has bounds, it is difficult to determine if opinions have changed (e.g., if one were to get all 5's for a year in a category, how could improvement be measured for future years?). To address this issue, consider phrasing the questions relative to changes from last year with response levels of: a lot of improvements (5), some improvements (4), no change (3), some worse (2), and a lot worse (1). Much more flexibility is offered with this approach because there is no upper bounds. For example, management could set a stretch goal (that is consistent from year-to-year) of an average response of 0.5 with 80% of those surveyed believing improvement has been made. Because of the phrasing of the question, people would obviously need to be employed for one year or more within the area before they take the survey.

To address the issue of both trends in the response levels and biases in results because of "noise considerations" (e.g., weather, fear of layoffs, etc., when survey was taken), consider having surveys conducted monthly using a sampling strategy where each person is to give input once annually. A control chart then could be used to evaluate overall and specific question responses. Other Six Sigma tools such as normal probability plotting and ANOM can give other insights to variability and areas that need focus.

The organization that is conducting the survey would like to get an assessment of what should be done differently. Good information for improvement opportunities is often contained with the comment section of surveys, but this information is often very hard to quantify relative to perceived value. To address this, consider adding a section that lists "improvement ideas." Each person can "vote" on a certain number of ideas. This information can then be presented in a Pareto chart format. The origination of the "improvement ideas" list can come from previous write-in comments and an off-line committee who evaluates these comments and other ideas to create a list that will be used during the upcoming year (*note:* different areas could have different lists).

43.8   EXAMPLE 43.8: TRACKING AND REDUCING THE TIME OF CUSTOMER PAYMENT

A histogram of the number of days a sample of invoices were overdue is shown in Figure 43.13 (negative number indicate payment was made before due date). The data are not normally distributed. A three-parameter Weibull distribution or Box-Cox transformation (Box et al. 1978) might be useful to better describe the data. It should be noted that for this study the measurement was changed from attribute (i.e., the invoice was paid on time or not) to a continuous measurement relative to due date.

When collecting the data, other characteristics were recorded at the same time (e.g., company that was invoiced, amount of invoice, whether invoice had errors upon submittal, and whether any payment incentives were given to the customer). From these data the cost of delinquency could be determined for the existing process of invoicing and collection (i.e., the baseline for an S^4 project).

Analysis of variance and analysis of means (ANOM) studies indicated that the size of invoice did not significantly affect the delinquency; however, some companies were more delinquent in payment. Also, often invoices were rejected because of errors, which caused payment delays. In addition, a costly payment incentive given to some customers had no value add. With this in-

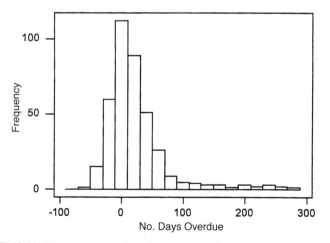

FIGURE 43.13 Histogram showing the number of days invoices are delinquent.

formation the team started documenting the current process and then determined what should be done differently to address these problems areas.

43.9 EXAMPLE 43.9: AUTOMOBILE TEST—ANSWERING THE RIGHT QUESTION

Consider the hypothetical situation in which the insurance industry and automotive industry want to work together to determine whether the average accident rate of an automobile that has an innovative steering and braking mechanism will occur no more frequently than with the previous design (one accident every 5 years). This initial question form is similar to a mean time between failure (MTBF) criterion test of a product. [*Note:* This is only a conceptual example that illustrates how a problem can be redefined for the purpose of S^4 considerations. All "results" and "conclusions" from this "experiment" were fabricated for illustration purposes only.]

One can use the techniques discussed earlier in this text to determine the number of prototype vehicles to build and then the number of miles to test drive a "random sample." For these test vehicles the desired accident rate must be achieved with some level of belief that the criterion will not be exceeded by the customer after shipment begins. The test would surely require a rather large random sample of automobiles, "typical drivers," and test time. The experimenter would probably also require that the cause of accidents be investigated to note if there was a design problem that caused the accident. However, with the current definition, this "problem diagnosis" is not a formal requirement of the experiment.

When reassessing the problem definition, it seems that the "real question of concern" may not be addressed by the test. Perhaps the test should directly assess whether this new design is going to increase the chance of accidents under varying road and driver situations. For example, if the initial test were performed in a locality during dry months, design problems that can cause accidents on wet pavements may not be detected. Other concerns may also be expressed. For example, speed, driver's age, sex of driver, alcohol content in driver, traffic conditions, and road curvature are not formally considered individually or in combination. Care needs to be given to create driving scenarios that match the frequency of customer situations during such a "random" test strategy. Often it is not practical to consider a random sampling plan where all infrequent situations are covered during test; however, in such situations a very serious problem could be overlooked because it was considered a "rare event" and was not tested. When such a rare event occurs later to a customer, the situation might result in a very serious problem. In lieu of verifying an overall failure criterion, a test alternative is to structurally force various situations, to assess whether a problem exists with the design. A fractional factorial experiment design offers such a structure.

Next, alternative responses should be considered because the sole output of "accidents" is expensive and can be catastrophic. In this example, two possible output alternatives to the experiment are operator and vehicle response time to a simulated adverse condition. These outputs can be assessed relative to each other for a simulated obstacle to determine if an accident would have occurred. If the accident was avoided, the "safety factor" time could also then be determined for each adverse condition.

Reflecting back to the original problem definition, it is noted that the failure rate criterion validation question was changed to a test that focused directly on meeting the needs of the customer. A test strategy that attempted to answer the original question would not focus on the different customer situations that might cause a basic problem (or very hazardous situation) for some users. The redefined question would also save moneys in that the test could be conducted earlier in the development cycle with fewer test systems. This earlier test strategy would permit more expedient (and less costly) fixes to those problems that are identified during the test.

So far this automobile test description contained the logic that was used to change test considerations from a failure rate criterion test to a fractional factorial experiment approach (i.e., to answer the right question). Consider now how brainstorming and cause-and-effect techniques can aid with the selection of factors and their levels.

A group of people initially might choose the factors and factor levels along with the test assumptions as noted in Table 43.8 for the fractional factorial experiment, where the factor levels are indicated by a + or − designation in this table. Next, a meeting of peers from all affected areas was conducted to consider expansion/deletion of selected factors, outputs, and limiting assumptions for the experiment.

In the meeting, inputs to the basic test design will depend on the experience and perspective of each individual. Probably everyone would not agree to the initial proposal. The following scenario could typify such a meeting:

> Someone indicates that historically there has been no difference in driving capabilities between men and women; he suggests using men for the test because there was a shortage of women workers in the area. The group agreed to this change along with other suggestions that both automobile performance on curves and operator age should be included. The group thought that operator age should be considered because they did not want to jeopardize the safety of elderly people who might have trouble adapting to the new design. Also, the excellent suggestion was made that a comparison be made between the new design and the existing vehicle design within the same experiment to determine whether the new vehicle caused a difference in response under similar conditions. Also, it was agreed that operators should have one hour to get experience operating the new vehicle design before experiencing any simulated hazards. The revised test design shown in Table 43.9 was created, where each factor will be tested at either a − or + factor level condition, as described later.

TABLE 43.8 Initial Proposal

Objective
> Test operators under simulated road hazards to assess their reaction time along with automobile performance to determine if the new design will perform satisfactorily in various customer driving situations.

Limiting Assumptions
> No passing
> Flat terrain
> No traffic

Outputs
> Operator response time to adverse condition
> Automobile response characteristics to operator input
> Pass/fail expectation

Factor Consideration	Factor-Level Conditons	
	(−)	(+)
Weather	Wet	Dry
Alcohol	None	Legal limit
Speed	40 mph	70 mph
Sex	Male	Female

Note that this example is a conceptual example to illustrate the power of using factorial tests versus a "random" test strategy. In reality, for this particular situation there would be other statistical concerns for the factor levels. For example, it would be unreasonable to assume that one elderly driver could accurately represent the complete population of elderly drivers. Several drivers, for example, may be needed for each trial to determine whether they all would respond favorably to the test situation.

Let us consider what has happened so far. Initially a failure rate criterion test was changed to a fractional factorial test strategy because this strategy would better meet the needs of the customer. Next the brainstorming process was used to choose the experiment factors and their levels. This example discusses the creation of a fractional factorial experiment design.

An eight-trial resolution III design alternative was chosen from Table M2 and is noted in Table 43.10 with the experiment factors and their levels. In this conceptual example the two-factor interactions would then be confounded with the main effects.

The output to each trial (response) could be one or more measurement considerations. For example, it could be the electronically measured response times of the vehicle and the driver to various obstacles placed in the path of

TABLE 43.9 Revised Proposal

Objective

Test operators under simulated road hazards to assess their reaction time along with automobile performance to determine if the new design will perform satisfactorily within customer driving situations.

Limiting assumptions

No passing

Flat terrain

No traffic

Operators will have one hour to get accustomed to the car before experiencing any hazards

Only male drivers will be used since previous testing indicates that there is no difference between male and female drivers.

Outputs

Operator response time to adverse condition

Automobile response characteristics to operator input

Pass/fail expectation

Factor	Factor Level Conditions	
Consideration	(−)	(+)
Weather	Wet	Dry
Alcohol	None	Legal limit
Speed	40 mph	70 mph
Age of driver	20–30 years	70–80 years
Car design	Current	New
Road curvature	None	Curved

TABLE 43.10 An Eight-Trial Test Design

Trial Number	$A\,B\,C\,D\,E\,F$	Where	(−)	(+)
1	+ − − + − +	A = Weather	Wet	Dry
2	+ + − − + −	B = Alcohol	None	Legal limit
3	+ + + − − +	C = Speed	40 mph	70 mph
4	− + + + − −	D = Age of driver	20–30 years	70–80 years
5	+ − + + + −	E = Vehicle	Current	New
6	− + − + + +	F = Road curvature	None	Curved
7	− − + − + +			
8	− − − − − −			

the operator in a simulated test environment (similar to that given to airline pilots during training).

Instead of having a "random" sample of people driving automobiles under their "normal" operating conditions (as proposed in the original problem definition), this test philosophy considers the range of operator types along with a range of operating conditions—the thought being that if there is satisfactory performance under extreme conditions (i.e., factor levels are set to "boundary" conditions), then there would probably be satisfactory performance under less extreme conditions.

Consider the hypothetical situation shown in Figure 43.14, where, unknown to the experimenter, the "age of driver" interacts with "vehicle design." Experiments are performed for the purpose of finding useful information that is true so that actions can be taken, as needed, in either the design or the manufacturing process. This plot indicates that elderly drivers have a high reaction time when operating the new vehicle design. Because of this type of information, a design change may then need to be made that improves the safety of this vehicle for elderly people. Detection of this type of problem is most important early in the development cycle, not after the new automobile design is in production.

The resolution III designs, such as the one shown in Table 43.10, are not normally used to determine two-factor interactions; however, Table N3 can be used to show how the two-level factors are confounded with two-factor interactions. This confounding in the contrast columns for this design is noted in Table 43.11.

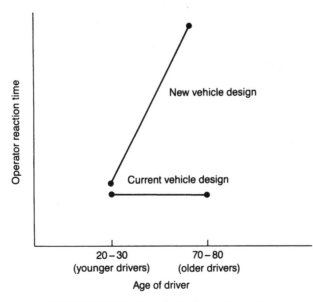

FIGURE 43.14 Two-factor interaction plot.

TABLE 43.11 Two-Factor Interaction Confounding from Table N3

			Contrast Column Number			
1	2	3	4	5	6	7
A	*B*	*C*	AB	BC	ABC	AC
BD	AD	BE	*D*	*E*	CD	DE
EF	CE	DF	CF	AF	AE	BF
CG	FG	AG	EG	DG	*F*	*G*
					BG	

^{a}Main effects are denoted by an asterisk.

In this experiment the age of the driver was factor D and the vehicle design was E. The preceding DE interaction effect would be described in contrast column 7. Consider that a probability plot of contrast column effects noted that absolute value effect from contrast column 7 was "significant" compared to the other effects. Because in this experiment there were only six factors (i.e., there was no G factor), there was no confounding of this interaction effect with any main effects. If there were considerations that were (in fact) important, the experimenter at test completion might speculate that this interaction (or one of the other interactions in this column) was significant. Obviously any of the chosen theories would need to be verified in a confirmation experiment.

A fractional factorial tests strategy can have much power over a "random" test strategy. As noted previously, there are other practical concerns for this experiment design. For example, it would be unreasonable to assume that one elderly driver would accurately represent the complete population of elderly drivers. Generally, several drivers should be considered for each trial assessment. An alternate response for this type of test would be an attribute response (i.e., a certain portion of drivers did not respond satisfactory. To illustrate this situation, consider 3 out of 10 people having a reaction time that was not quick enough to avoid a simulated obstacle; hence, these people are classified as having an accident for this trial. Example 42.1 illustrates another conceptual analysis possibility for this example. In this analysis the trials are considered to yield a "logic pass/fail" response.

The purpose of the automobile example in this text is to illustrate the importance of "answering the right question." Within the initial test strategy of verifying a criterion, someone could easily end up as a test where individuals might "play games with the numbers" to certify one accident in 5 years as the failure criterion before "shipment" (e.g., what do you expect would be done if the day before shipment it is discovered that the automobile does not "meet" its failure criterion?). Next a "customer-driven" test strategy combined the knowledge that exists within organizations toward a similar goal that can be achieved early in the development cycle.

These examples illustrate how a few early development models (or a simulator) could be used to evaluate a product design. This test could be better than a larger "random" sample that was simply exercised against a failure rate criterion. With this approach, multiple applications are assessed concurrently to assess interaction or combinational affects, which are very difficult, if not impossible, to detect when assessing each factor individually (i.e., a one-at-a-time test strategy). Problems detected early in product development with this strategy can be resolved with less cost and schedule impacts. However, it must be reemphasized that often the original question needs redefinition.

From this hypothetical example, early detection of a high accident risk for "elderly drivers" could lead to a redesign resulting in increased safety for these drivers.

43.10   EXERCISES

1. For the data in Example 43.5, assume the special-cause data point was identified. Remove this data point and create an XmR and normal probability plot of the data. Determine if the data appear normal. Use the Z distribution to a better estimate the percentage of time an out-of-specification condition will occur. Use the Z distribution to determine the expected range of values 80% of the time. Show this range on the probability plot. Calculate C_{pk} and P_{pk}.

2. Recalculate the probability of failure in Example 43.6 for a criterion of 15 days. Rather than estimating the probability value from a normal probability plot, use the Z distribution to determine the estimate.

3. A mail-in customer survey identified the following responses: 500 favorable, 300 neutral, 300 unfavorable. The only written comment that occurred more than once was that the price of the product should be reduced.
   (a) Describe how this information could be reported.
   (b) Describe what might be done differently to get better feedback.

4. Describe how the techniques within this chapter are useful and can be applied to S^4 projects.

APPENDIX A

EQUATIONS FOR THE DISTRIBUTIONS

This appendix contains equations associated with many of the distributions discussed in this text. In this text, t replaces x when the independent variable considered is time. In the following equations, $f(x)$ is used to describe the PDF, $F(x)$ is used to describe the CDF, and the $P(X = x)$ format is used to describe probability. The relationship of $F(x)$ and $P(x)$ to $f(x)$ is

$$F(x) = P(X \leq x) = \int_{-\infty}^{x} f(x)\, dx$$

where the capital letter X denotes the distribution, which is can be called a random variable.

A.1 NORMAL DISTRIBUTION

The normal PDF is

$$f(x) = \frac{1}{\sigma\sqrt{2\pi}} \exp\left[-\frac{(x - \mu)^2}{2\sigma^2} \right] \qquad -\infty \leq x \leq +\infty$$

where μ = mean and σ = standard deviation. The CDF is

$$F(x) = \int_{-\infty}^{x} \frac{1}{\sigma\sqrt{2\pi}} \exp\left[-\frac{(x - \mu)^2}{2\sigma^2} \right] dx$$

A.2   BINOMIAL DISTRIBUTION

The probability of exactly x defects in n binomial trials with probability of defect equal to p is

$$P(X = x) = \binom{n}{x} p^x(1 - p)^{n-x} \qquad x = 0, 1, 2, \ldots, n$$

where

$$\binom{n}{x} = \frac{n!}{x!(n - x)!}$$

The mean (μ) and standard deviation (σ) of the distribution are

$$\mu = np$$
$$\sigma = \sqrt{np(1 - p)}$$

The probability of observing a or fewer defects is

$$P(X \leq a) = \sum_{x=0}^{a} P(X = x)$$

A.3   HYPERGEOMETRIC DISTRIBUTION

The probability of observing exactly x defects when n items are sampled without replacement from a population of N items containing D defects is given by the hypergeometric distribution

$$P(X = x) = \frac{\binom{D}{x}\binom{N - D}{n - x}}{\binom{N}{n}} \qquad x = 0, 1, 2, \ldots, n$$

The probability of observing a or fewer defects is

$$P(X \leq a) = \sum_{x=0}^{a} P(X = x)$$

A.4 POISSON DISTRIBUTION

The probability of observing exactly x events in the Poisson situation is given by the Poisson PDF:

$$P(X = x) = \frac{e^{-\lambda}\lambda^x}{x!} \qquad x = 0, 1, 2, 3, \ldots$$

The mean and standard deviation are, respectively,

$$\mu = \lambda$$
$$\sigma = \sqrt{\lambda}$$

The probability of observing a or fewer events is

$$P(X \leq a) = \sum_{x=0}^{a} P(X = x)$$

A.5 EXPONENTIAL DISTRIBUTION

The PDF of the exponential distribution is

$$f(x) = \left(\frac{1}{\theta}\right) e^{-x/\theta}$$

The exponential distribution has only one parameter (θ), which is also the mean and equates to the standard deviation. The exponential CDF is

$$F(x) = \int_0^x \left(\frac{1}{\theta}\right) e^{-x/\theta} \, dx$$
$$= 1 - e^{-x/\theta}$$

For the exponential distribution, substitution into the earlier described hazard rate equation (t is replaced by an x) yields a constant hazard rate of

$$\lambda = \frac{f(x)}{1 - F(x)} = \frac{(1/\theta)e^{-x/\theta}}{1 - (1 - e^{-x/\theta})} = \frac{1}{\theta}$$

A.6 WEIBULL DISTRIBUTIONS

The PDF of the three-parameter Weibull is

$$f(x) = \left[\frac{b}{k - x_0} \left(\frac{x - x_0}{k - x_0} \right)^{b-1} \right] \left\{ \exp \left[-\left(\frac{x - x_0}{k - x_0} \right)^{b} \right] \right\}$$

and the CDF is

$$F(x) = 1 - \exp \left[-\left(\frac{x - x_0}{k - x_0} \right)^{b} \right]$$

The three-parameter Weibull distribution reduces to the two-parameter distribution when x_0 (i.e., location parameter) equals zero, as is commonly done in reliability analysis. The PDF of the two-parameter Weibull is

$$f(x) = \left[\frac{b}{k} \left(\frac{x}{k} \right)^{b-1} \right] \left\{ \exp \left[-\left(\frac{x}{k} \right)^{b} \right] \right\}$$

and the CDF is

$$F(x) = 1 - \exp \left[-\left(\frac{x}{k} \right)^{b} \right]$$

For the two-parameter Weibull distribution the probability that a device will fail at the characteristic life k or less is 0.632, as illustrated when making the following substitution:

$$F(k) = 1 - \exp \left[-\left(\frac{k}{k} \right)^{b} \right] = 1 - \frac{1}{e} = 0.632$$

Another way of stating this phenomenon is that the characteristic life (k) of a device is the usage probability plot coordinate value that corresponds to the percentage less than the value of 63.2%.

The characteristic life (k) is also related to the median life (B_{50}) since the CDF at $B_{50} = 0.5$ is

$$F(B_{50}) = 0.50 = 1 - \exp \left[-\left(\frac{B_{50}}{k} \right)^{b} \right]$$

or

$$0.5 = \exp\left[-\left(\frac{B_{50}}{k}\right)^b\right]$$

which gives

$$\ln 2 = \left(\frac{B_{50}}{k}\right)^b$$

and finally

$$k = \frac{B_{50}}{(0.693)^{1/b}}$$

It can also be shown that the characteristic life k relates to the Weibull mean (T_d) by the equation (Nelson 1982)

$$k = \frac{T_d}{\Gamma(1 + 1/b)}$$

where the gamma function value $\Gamma(1 + 1/b)$ is determined from Table H.

The hazard rate of the two-parameter Weibull distribution is

$$\lambda = \frac{f(x)}{1 - F(x)} = \frac{b}{k^b}(x)^{b-1}$$

When the shape parameter b equals 1, this reduces to a constant failure rate $\lambda = 1/k$. Because the Weibull with $b = 1$ is an exponential distribution, it can be shown that $\lambda = 1/k = 1/\theta$ for the exponential distribution. The values of b less than 1 are noted to have a hazard rate that decreases with x (early-life failures), while b values greater than 1 have a hazard rate that increases with x (wear-out failures). The classical reliability bathtub curve describes this characteristic.

APPENDIX B

DESCRIPTIVE INFORMATION

This appendix extends the discussion found earlier on histogram and probability plotting. Included is a discussion on the details of manual histogram plotting. The theoretical concept of probability plotting is also discussed along with alternative probability plotting positions to that described earlier.

Probability plots can be determined either manually or by using a computer package. Relative to each of these approaches, this appendix also discusses how to determine the best-fit probability line and how to determine if this line (i.e., the estimated PDF) adequately represents the data.

B.1 FLOWCHARTS: MOTOROLA'S SIX SIGMA TEN STEPS

As discussed in Section 1.5, Figures B.1–B.4 show a set of steps and methodologies that Motorola used for continuous improvement toward Six Sigma quality level.

B.2 AGENDAS FOR MANAGEMENT AND EMPLOYEE S⁴ TRAINING

A one-day S^4 executive (S^4 leadership) training program could use as a foundation selected topics from Chapters 1–3. Other considerations are as follows:

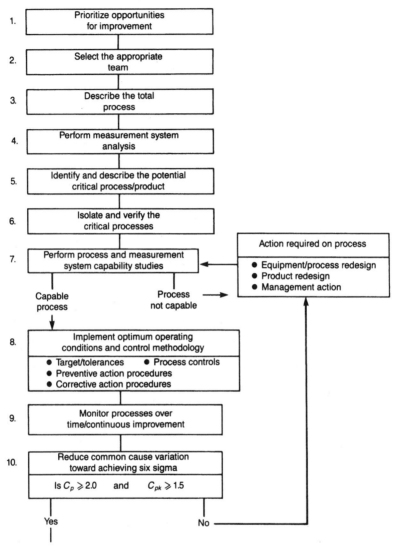

FIGURE B.1 Product/process improvement flow diagram (Copyright of Motorola, Inc., used with permission.)

- Exercises
  - The first exercise in Chapter 1 can be a good start for the session. In this exercise, catapults are used to simulate a production environment where production is driven "through the numbers." The discussion that follows the short session can give insight to the advantage of the *wise* implementation of many Six Sigma tools.

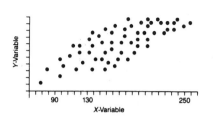

Scatter Diagrams

- These diagrams are used to study the relationship between one variable and another.
- A measure of the strength of the relationship may be obtained.
- Used to determine a cause and effect relationship between the input and output parameters of a process.
- These are individual data points, not averages.

Scatter Diagram. Used to Study the Relationship Between Variables

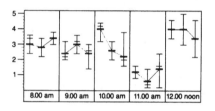

Multi-vari Charts

This type of chart allows insight into the component parts of the variations. The chart is useful for the following:
- Monitor the product variation.
- View and analyze the relationship between two variables.
- View and assess the variations that occur within part, between parts, and across time.
- Simultaneously analyze multiple parameters.
- Study natural or artificially induced variations.
- Study a process without any alterations or interruptions to it.

Multi-vari Chart. Allows Insight into the Nature of Variations

Control Charts

TYPE	USAGE
X bar & R	Variables Data
X bar & S	Variables Data
"P"	Binary Data
'C'	Count Data
X & R_M	Batch Processes

- Illustrates when special cause variation is present (process needs attention.)
- Illustrates when only common cause variation is present (predictable & stable).
- For use on critical process parameters
- May be used to determine process capability.

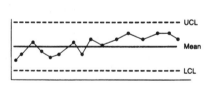

Control Chart. Used as a Continuous Indicator of Process Control and Capability

FIGURE B.2 Graphical tools for continuous improvement. (Copyright of Motorola, Inc., used with permission.)

- The card exercise at the end of Chapter 9 is very beneficial to describe throughput yield and the cost of the hidden factory.
- Have attendees choose from a list of potential S⁴ application examples (see Section 1.9) those that they would like to see. Discuss these chosen examples and then describe how the technique can be applied to project candidates that they bring to the S⁴ workshop.

Pareto Diagrams

- 80 % of the costs are associated with approximately 20 % of the defect types.
- These diagrams are used to indicate which problems we should solve first.

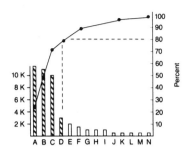

Pareto Diagram. Represents the Basis for Project Improvement Studies

Cause and Effect Diagrams

- This diagram is most effectively used for brainstorming using the " six M's ".
- Rank order (prioritize) potential problems and/or group them for investigation or experimentation.
- This type of diagram may be combined with a process flow diagram to form a process cause and effects problem-solving flow diagram.
- This is a powerful tool in the early stages of problem-solving.

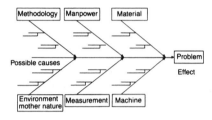

Cause and Effect Diagram. Powerful Tool for Early Stages of Problem Solving (Brainstorming)

Process Flow Charts

This type of diagram graphically illustrates:
- Sequential process steps
- Relationship between process steps
- Problem areas
- Unnecessary loops and complexity
- Where simplification is possible
- May be used in conjunction with a cause and effect diagram for problem-solving.
- Material Flow

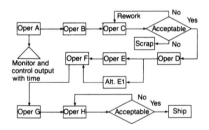

Process Flow Chart. Shows Sequential Process Steps for Isolation of Problem Areas

FIGURE B.3 Graphical tools for continuous improvement. (Copyright of Motorola, Inc., used with permission.)

The following describes a four-week training program following the themes of S^4 measurement, analysis, improvement, and control. In a four-week S^4 black-belt workshop program it is difficult to include an amount of material within each week that can exactly match these themes. Within this noted four-week program the material from weeks one and two could flow over into later weeks. Topics such as reliability and pass/fail functional testing are optional. The program could be reduced to two or three weeks if measurement

Flow

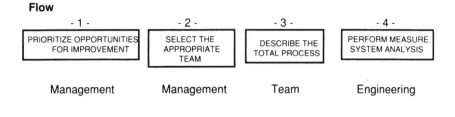

- 1 -	- 2 -	- 3 -	- 4 -
PRIORITIZE OPPORTUNITIES FOR IMPROVEMENT	SELECT THE APPROPRIATE TEAM	DESCRIBE THE TOTAL PROCESS	PERFORM MEASURE. SYSTEM ANALYSIS
Management	Management	Team	Engineering

Description

Quantify any known or perceived opportunities for improvement. Specify the problems in quantifiable terms such as how much, when, where, and how. Indicate which impact the customer, reliability, product quality and yields. Identify potential cost savings to the customer and Motorola.	Select a small group of people with the product / process knowledge, experience, technical discipline, authority, time and skill in the specific area of concern. Establish and identify the role of the team and each member. Identify a "Champion" (in addition to the team leader) who can assist the team and can ensure that the teams recommendations are carried out. The team must decide what and how much it can accomplish.	Utilize a process flow diagram to illustrate the possible variations and alternatives of the process. Include all equipment, manpower, methods, tools, piece parts and measurement instruments in the process description. **Identify all of the known** input / output relationships. Highlight any of the alternative work procedures and flows.	Determine precision, accuracy, repeatability and reproducibility of each instrument or gauge used in order to ensure that they are capable. Ensure that the measurement precision is at least ten times better than the magnitude that is to be discerned

Tools

• Pareto Analysis • Reliability Reports • Yield Loss Reports • Cost of Quality • Graphic Illustrations	• Select Champion Leader Advisors • Identify Correct Number of Participants • Ensure Cross-functional Membership	• Flow Diagram • Pareto Analysis • Historical Data • Process Definitions • C & E Diagrams • Trend Charts	• Calibration • Measurement System Error Study

(a)

FIGURE B.4a The Motorola guide to implementation of SPC. (Copyright of Motorola, Inc., used with permission.) Figure is continued on next page.

systems analysis, DOE, and some other tools are not considered applicable to the processes of attendees (e.g., some transactional processes).

- Week 1 (S⁴ Measurement): Chapters 1–14
- Week 2 (S⁴ Analysis): Chapters 15–26

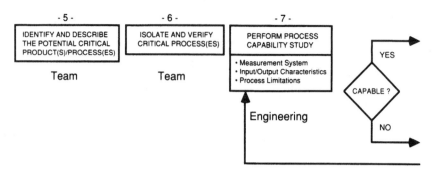

- 5 -	- 6 -	- 7 -	
IDENTIFY AND DESCRIBE THE POTENTIAL CRITICAL PRODUCT(S)/PROCESS(ES)	ISOLATE AND VERIFY CRITICAL PROCESS(ES)	PERFORM PROCESS CAPABILITY STUDY	
Team	Team	• Measurement System • Input/Output Characteristics • Process Limitations	YES CAPABLE ? NO
		Engineering	

List and describe all of the potential critical processes obtained from brainstorming sessions, historical data, yield reports, failure analysis reports, analysis of line fall-out and model the potential problems using graphical illustrations.	Narrow the potential list of problems to the vital few." Identify the input / output relationship which directly affects specific problems. Verify potential causes of process variability and product problems through engineering experiments, scatter diagrams, and multi-vari charts. Ensure that the data is clear and stratified.	Identify and define the limitations of the processes. Ensure that the processes are capable of achieving their maximum potential. Identify and remove all variation due to special causes. Determine what the realistic specifications are.	A process is to be considered capable when it is in control, (predictable and stable) and with minimum Indices of: Cp≥ Cpk ≥ 1.0 However, a process at this point in time may not meet these conditions.

• Analyze Line Fallout • C & E Diagram • Multi-vari Chart • Scatter Diagram • Failure Analysis Reports • Trend Charts • Time Line Charts • Randomized Sequencing • Model the Problem	• Factorial Experiments • Graphs • Brainstorming C & E Diagrams • Response Surface Methodology • Trend Charts	• Factorial Experiments • Multi-vari Chart • Appropriate Control Charts • Test for Normality • Data Transformation • Response Surface Methodology • Rational Sample Plan

(*b*)

FIGURE B.4b The Motorola guide to implementation of SPC (continued). (Copyright of Motorola, Inc., used with permission.)

• Week 3 (S^4 Improvement): Chapters 27–33
• Week 4 (S^4 Control): Chapters 34–43

A three-day S^4 champion training course should give a shortened overview of all the topics covered within the four-week S^4 black-belt training. Emphasis can be given to the management and selection of projects, along with the process of S^4 black-belt candidate selection. It is best that someone from

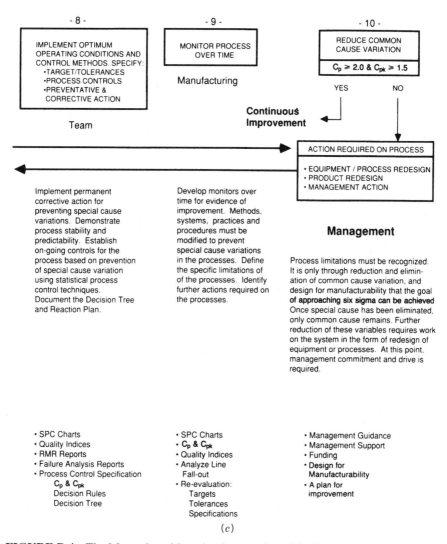

FIGURE B.4c The Motorola guide to implementation of SPC (continued). (Copyright of Motorola, Inc., used with permission.)

finance get involved with these sessions. Consider including Examples 5.1, 5.2, and 5.3, along with appropriate examples from those noted in Section 1.9. Consider also including the catapult exercise in Chapter 4 on process flowcharting.

Shorter training sessions that are one or two weeks long (e.g., S⁴ green-belt training sessions) can include topics and exercises as desired from the four-week training sessions. S⁴ master black-belt training sessions can involve the expansion of topics or addition of other related topics not included in the normal S^4 black-belt training. The training of S^4 master black belts can involve the critique of their training of S^4 black belts.

B.3   CREATING HISTOGRAMS MANUALLY

When making a histogram of response data that are not continuous, the data need first to be placed into groups (i.e., cells). Many computer programs internally handle this grouping; however, a practitioner may have to manually create this grouping if no program is available.

For manual data plotting, it should be noted that the group size or class width is an important detail to give meaningful results to the plot. King (1981) suggests grouping data according to Sturges's rule (Freund 1960). This rule gives a method of determining the number of groups, cells (K), and cell width (W) to use when tallying the results for a graphical summary. Using this rule, the "optimum" number of cells for sample size N is first calculated to be

$$K = 1 + 3.3 \log N$$

From the range of data (R) the class width to be assigned each cell is then determined to be

$$W = \frac{R}{K}$$

Example B.1 illustrates the application of this approach. There is another common alternative approach where the number of classes is the square root of the sample size (i.e., $K = \sqrt{N}$), with upward rounding, and the class width is also the range divided by the number of classes.

B.4   EXAMPLE B.1: HISTOGRAM PLOT

A earlier example had samples that yielded the following 24 ranked (low to high value) data points:

2.2   2.6   3.0   4.3   4.7   5.2   5.2   5.3   5.4   5.7   5.8   5.8   5.9   6.3   6.7
7.1   7.3   7.6   7.6   7.8   7.9   9.3   10.0   10.1

To create a histogram, a starting point for the grouping can be determined to be

$$K = 1 + 3.3 \log N = 1 + 3.3 \log (24) = 5.55$$

Hence, for a sample of 24, the number of cells falls between 5 and 6. The range of data is 7.9(10.1 − 2.2 = 7.9). With a basic unit size of 0.1, this range is 79 units. Consequently, we have the following:

Using 5 cells:

$$W = \frac{79}{5} = 15.8 \qquad \text{(16 rounded off)}$$

Using 6 cells:

$$W = \frac{79}{6} = 13.2 \qquad \text{(13 rounded off)}$$

Either number of units is acceptable. After this rounding-off, the number of cells calculates to be the following:

Using 16 units:

$$\text{Number of cells} = \frac{79}{16} = 4^+$$

Using 13 units:

$$\text{Number of cells} = \frac{79}{13} = 6^+$$

Consider now positioning the cell boundaries by balancing the end points. The number of units required to display the range is 80 units (i.e., 79 + 1). If we choose 13 units per cell, then 7 cells would take 91 units (i.e., 7 × 13 = 91). There would be 11 units (i.e., 91 − 80 = 11) that need to be split between the two end points. Five or 6 units could then be subtracted from the lowest value to begin the increment sequencing. If we subtracted 6 units from the lowest point to get the first minimum cell value (i.e., 2.2 − 0.6 = 1.6), the increments would then be

Minimum cell values = 1.6, 2.9, 4.2, 5.5, 6.8, 8.1, 9.4

Because the cell size is 1.3 (i.e., 13 units per cell with a basic unit size of 0.1), it then follows from these values that

Maximum cell values = 2.9, 4.2, 5.5, 6.8, 8.1, 9.4, 10.7

A histogram of these data is shown in Figure 3.2. Even with the rigorous procedure used within this example, the practitioner should note that another increment could yield a better histogram pictorial representation of the data. This procedure should perhaps be considered when determining a "starting point" before doing a more traditional "select and view" procedure.

B.5   THEORETICAL CONCEPT OF PROBABILITY PLOTTING

Consider the Weibull CDF equation

$$F(x) = 1 - \exp[-(x/k)^b]$$

The rearrangement and transformation of this equation yields

$$\frac{1}{1 - F(x)} = \exp\left(\frac{x}{k}\right)^b$$

$$\ln\left(\frac{1}{1 - F(x)}\right) = \left(\frac{x}{k}\right)^b$$

$$\ln\ln\left(\frac{1}{1 - F(x)}\right) = b\ln x - b\ln k$$

This equation is in the form of a straight line $[Y = mX + c]$ where

$$Y = \ln\ln\frac{1}{1 - F(x)}$$

$$m = b$$

$$X = \ln x$$

$$c = -b\ln k$$

Weibull probability paper has incorporated these X and Y transformations. Hence, data plotted on Weibull probability paper that follow a straight line can be assumed to be from a unimodal Weibull density function.

The unknown parameters for the population *(k and b* for the Weibull distribution) can also be estimated from the plot. Because of the resulting transformation formats, the slope of the line yields an estimate for b (Weibull shape parameter). Given the Y-axis intercept (c) and shape parameter (b), the other unknown parameter k (characteristic life) can be determined.

Similar transformations are made to create the scale for the probability axes for other functions such as the normal and log-normal distributions.

B.6 PLOTTING POSITIONS

An equation to determine the "midpoint" plotting position on probability paper for an ith-ranked data point is

$$F_i = \frac{100(i - 0.5)}{n} \qquad i = 1, 2, \ldots, n$$

Nelson (1982) describes the motivation for using the equation; however, he also notes that different plotting positions have been zealously advanced. Some of these alternative plotting positions are as follows:

The "mean" plotting position is a popular alternative, which is

$$F_i = \frac{100i}{n + 1} \qquad i = 1, 2, \ldots, n$$

King (1981) suggests using the equation noted by Cunnane (1978):

$$F_i = \frac{100(i - a)}{n + 1 - 2a} \qquad i = 1, 2, \ldots, n$$

where a is a distribution-related constant with values of

0.375 for the normal and logarithmic normal distributions
0.44   for the type I extreme value distributions
0.5   for types II and III (Weibull) extreme value distributions
0.4   as a compromise for other non-normal distributions

Johnson (1964) advocates and tabulates median plotting positions that are well approximated by

$$F_i \approx \frac{100(i - 0.3)}{n + 0.4} \qquad i = 1, 2, \ldots, n$$

Nelson (1982) states that plotting positions differ little compared with the randomness of the data. For convenience, I chose to use and tabulate (i.e., Table P) the plotting positions, which are consistent with Nelson. However, a reader may choose to use another set of plotting positions and still apply the concepts described in this text.

B.7   MANUAL ESTIMATION OF A BEST-FIT PROBABILITY PLOT LINE

There are inconsistencies when determining the best-fit line when manually plotting data. To obtain consistent results for a given set of data, King (1981) promotes the following technique. [This section is reproduced from King (1981) with permission of the author.]

Ferrell (1958) proposed the use of a "median regression line" to be fitted to a set of data points plotted on probability paper in order to characterize the data in a manner that allows subsequent estimation of the distribution parameters directly from the probability plot. The Ferrell best-fit line divides the data plot into two halves in which half of the data points are above the fitted line and half are below the line, which is a classical definition of a median. It is obtained as follows:

1. Divide the data set into two parts to obtain a "lower half" and an "upper half," as indicated in Figure B.5. If the number of points is even, then each half is unique and distinct such that no overlap occurs. When the number of points is odd, the middle point is plotted on the 50% vertical line and it is not clear to which half the odd point belongs. There are two choices: (a) Ignore the odd point or (b) treat the odd point as though it belongs to each half until a preference can be determined. We recommend choice (b).

2. Place a sharp pencil on the lowest point of the plot, as shown in Figure B.5. Then, place a transparent straightedge against the pencil point and rotate the straightedge until the upper half of the data points are subdivided into two equal parts. This is accomplished simply by counting until 50% of the upper points are above the edge of the straightedge.

3. Mark a second reference point on the graph somewhere beyond the highest plotted point. Transfer the pencil to this point and, again, rotating the straightedge against the pencil, divide the lower half of the data points into two equal halves.

4. Make another reference point toward the lower left corner of the plot and repeat steps 2 and 3 until both the upper and lower halves of the data points are equally divided by the same position of the straightedge. Using this final split, draw in the best-fit line.

Lack of fit of the line to the data can then be assessed by the following technique (King 1981): After a Ferrell median regression line is obtained, the fit of this line is checked by two simple tests. The first test is to check the accuracy with which the lower and upper halves of the data set were divided by counting the number of points above the median regression line and the number of points below it. The difference in the number of points on either side of the line should not exceed $|2|$, otherwise the line should be redrawn.

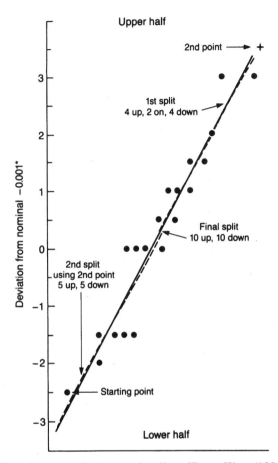

FIGURE B.5 Drawing a median regression line. [From King (1981), with permission.]

If the count difference is satisfactory, the second test is to count the number of runs above and below the line. A "run" is any group of consecutive points on the same side of the line. Any point which lies on the fitted line counts as the end of a run. After the number of runs is determined, refer to Table B.1. This table gives the approximate 95% confidence limits for the number of runs to be expected from different sample sizes, assuming that only random sampling variation occurs in the sample. Limits for sample sizes not given may be approximated by simple linear interpolation.

When the number of runs above and below the fitted line are too few, there is good evidence that the data are not homogeneous—that is, that they did not come from a stable or consistent process when it is known that the data are plotted on an appropriate probability paper. Such knowledge usually comes from prior experience or from technical considerations. If one is not

TABLE B.1 Approximate 95% Critical Values for the Number of Runs Above and Below the Median Regression Line[a]

Sample Size	Limits	Sample Size	Limits	Sample Size	Limits
4	2–4	28	4–14	48	6–19
8	3–7	30	4–14		
12	3–9	32	5–15		
16	3–11	36	5–16		
20	4–12	40	5–17		
24	4–13	44	5–18		

[a] Created by Stan Wheeler. Based on simulation with 3000 trials per sample size.

sure that the appropriate probability paper is being used, a simple test of the data is to place a straightedge across the lowest and highest points on the plot. If all remaining data points fall on either side of the straightedge, then it is likely that the wrong probability paper has been used. When this occurs, also place the straightedge across the second lowest and the second highest points. If all the remaining points are still on the same side of the straightedge, then it is highly likely that the wrong paper was used.

On a second check, if some points now fall on either side of the straightedge, there may be a problem due to the incomplete data caused by such activities as inspection, sorting, and/or test used to remove certain portions of the original or intrinsic population for special uses or for failure to conform to a governing specification.

Finally, if there are too many runs above and below the line, then there is evidence that the sample was not randomly selected and that the sampling procedures should be reviewed to prevent similar results in the future.

B.8   COMPUTER-GENERATED PLOTS AND LACK OF FIT

As part of a computer-generated plot, a best-fit line can be determined by using approaches that can be computationally intensive (e.g., maximum likelihood). In these programs, lack-of-fit calculations of the line fit to the data may be available on the program package. The program could use statistical tests such as chi-square goodness of fit (Duncan 1986, Tobias and Trindade 1995), Kolmogorov–Smirnov (KS) [Massey 1951; Jensen and Petersen 1982, constant hazard rate test], Cramer–Von Misses (Crow 1974), and Shapiro–Wilk (Shapiro and Wilk 1965). More information is contained in D'Agostino and Stephens (1986).

When determining if a model is adequate using these techniques, the data are presumed to fit the model until proven otherwise by a lack-of-fit significance test. When making a "nonfit" statement, risks have type I error (e.g., α risk at a level of 0.05).

If the distribution test is for data normality, a "skewness" calculation can be made to measure the "sidedness" of the distribution, while a kurtosis calculation can be used to measure heaviness of tails (Duncan 1986; Ramsey and Ramsey 1990).

Much discussion has been made over the years about lack-of-fit tests. Each test has benefits under certain situations; however, there is no one universal "best test." In addition, some tests can require more than 30 to 50 data points to be "valid" and can be quite conservative.

B.9   MATHEMATICALLY DETERMINING THE C_4 CONSTANT

The c_4 constant (Table J) is sometimes used to remove bias from standard deviation estimates. Values for c_4 are listed in Table J; however, frequently there is a need for values not listed in the table. The purpose of this section is to illustrate a mathematical computation procedure for this constant using a function often found in statistical computer packages. Using the Γ function, the c_4 constant for a value of d can be determined from the relationship

$$c_4(d) = \sqrt{\frac{2}{d-1}} \left(\frac{\Gamma(d/2)}{\Gamma((d-1)/2)} \right)$$

When d becomes large, direct computations for this equation can result in computer overflow conditions because of the nature of the Γ function. To avoid this problem, computer programs might offer the natural log of the Γ function. The difference between these two natural log values raised to the power of e (i.e., 2.718282) yields the same result as the above ratio of two Γ functions. To illustrate this procedure, consider

$$c_4(6) = \sqrt{\frac{2}{6-1}} \exp[(\ln(\Gamma(6/2))) - (\ln \Gamma((6-1)/2))]$$

$$= (0.6325) \exp[0.6931 - 0.2847] = 0.9515$$

This value is consistent with the Table J value for c_4.

APPENDIX C

DOE SUPPLEMENT

This appendix discusses other considerations when conducting a DOE. Included are sample size calculations methodologies and alternative analysis methodologies.

C.1 DOE: SAMPLE SIZE FOR MEAN FACTOR EFFECTS

A 16- or 32-trial DOE experiment that is used to evaluate mean effects can be satisfactory for many situations. However, for some situations a more rigorous approach that assesses the power $(1 - \beta)$ of the test is needed to determine sample size. Note, this section does not address sample size needs relative to assessing the impact of the factor levels on the variability of a response (see Chapter 32).

Sample size is a common question encountered when designing a fractional factorial experiment. Unfortunately, there is no general agreed-upon approach to address the question. Even though there is no procedure to determine the "right" sample size for a given situation, the question is still a real issue for the practitioner. The following methodology and discussion are based on an approach discussed in Diamond (1989).

Previously, methodologies were described to test for factor significance when there is an estimate for error. If a factor were found significant (i.e., the decision was to reject the null hypothesis), the statement was made with an α risk of error. However, the inverse is not true about factors not found to be significant. In other words, there is not an α risk of being wrong when these factors are not shown to be significant. The reason for this is that the second statement relates to a β risk (i.e., the decision was not to reject the null hypothesis, which is a function of the sample size and δ).

To make a statement relative to the risk of being in error when it is stated that there is no significant difference (between the levels of factors), consider e, which is defined as the ratio of an acceptable amount of uncertainty to the standard deviation.

$$e = \delta/\sigma$$

where δ is an amount that may be of importance in making β-risk statements and σ is the standard deviation of error (s_e). If the parameter (e) is "too large," then additional trials should be considered for the experiment design.

The total number of trials to use in a two-level fractional factorial experiment at each level can be determined by the relationship (Diamond 1989)

$$n = 2(t_\alpha + t_\beta)^2 \frac{\sigma^2}{\delta^2} = 2(t_\alpha + t_\beta)^2 \frac{\sigma^2}{(e\delta)^2}$$

Solving for e yields

$$e = \frac{[2(t_\alpha + t_\beta)^2]^{1/2}}{\sqrt{n}}$$

which reduces to

$$e = \frac{1.414(t_\alpha + t_\beta)}{\sqrt{n}}$$

Consider the situation where $\alpha = 0.1$, $\beta = 0.1$, and $n_{high} = n_{low} = 8$ (i.e., 8 trials are conduced at the high level and 8 trials at the low level of the factors). For 7 degrees of freedom, $t_\beta = 1.415$ (from Table D) and $t_\alpha = 1.895$ (from Table E), respectively, then yields

$$e = \frac{1.414(1.415 + 1.895)}{\sqrt{8}} = 1.65$$

Because of the given assumptions and analyses, the risk is 0.10 that the nonsignificant factor levels do not alter the response by 1.65 times the standard deviation (s_e). For comparison, consider the amount that e would decrease if there were 32 trials instead of 16 (i.e., 16 at each factor level). Then e would become

$$e = \frac{1.414(1.341 + 1.753)}{\sqrt{16}} = 1.09$$

It could then be stated that doubling the number of trials from 16 to 32 improves the nonsignificance statements by about 34% {i.e., 100 [(1.65 − 1.09)/1.65]}. Increasing the sample size may be necessary to get better resolution when setting up an experiment to evaluate interactions; however, the cost to double the sample size from 16 to 32 using trial replications to get a more accurate response is often not justifiable. Instead of striving to get a larger sample size, it may be more feasible, in some cases, for a practitioner to work at getting a measurement scheme that yields a smaller amount error relative to the amount of change considered important. As noted earlier in this text a test strategy of several information-building "small" factorial experiments is often more advantageous than a "large" factorial experiment that may technically have a "better" sample size.

C.2 DOE: ESTIMATING EXPERIMENTAL ERROR

Given a set of continuous trial outputs, statistics is used to determine whether the differences between the levels of the factors on the response (i.e., factor effect) is large enough to be significant (e.g., was the difference between the mean response of factor A at the plus level and the minus level large enough to be considered significant). To make this determination, an estimate of the error is needed.

Sometimes trials are replicated to give an estimate for this error. Unfortunately, this is often not a practical approach because the total number of experimental trials would double for one replication. Another alternative is to design the experiment with a resolution such that there are extra contrast columns that contain interactions higher than those the design is to capture. The information contained in these contrast columns can then be used to estimate the amount of experimental error. Still another alternative is to replicate one or more trials several times within the sequence of random trial selection. These approaches to experimental error can be handled directly via the data input by some computer programs. An alternative is to use historical information and combine the error estimates from the different sources. A methodology that can use this estimate for error to assess factor significance is described within the following sections.

C.3 DOE: DERIVATION OF EQUATION TO DETERMINE CONTRAST COLUMN SUM OF SQUARES

This section describes a technique to manually determine the sum of squares of the column contrasts for the two-level fractional factorial unreplicated designs originating from Tables M1–M5. The following discussion illustrates how a more typical format found in other texts reduces to the simplified format in this equation (for the fractional factorial test design approach proposed in this text). This significance test methodology illustrated in the included example could also be used if knowledge exists about experimental error outside the experimental trials.

Sometimes the contrast column sum of squares (SS) that is used when creating an analysis of variance table is described as having a crude treatment SS that is adjusted by a correction factor to yield a desired between-treatment SS. This can be expressed as

$$SS \text{ (between-treatment)} = \sum_{t=1}^{k} \frac{T_t^2}{n_t} - \frac{(\Sigma x)^2}{n}$$

where T_t is the total for each treatment (i.e., factor level), n_t is the number of observations (i.e., responses) comprising this total, x is the observations, n is the total number of observations, and k is the number of treatment classifications (i.e., number of levels).

For a two-level fractional factorial consideration where half of the trials are at a "high" level and the other half are at a "low" level, this equation can be rewritten as

$$SS \text{ (contract column)} = \left(\frac{T_{high}^2}{n/2} + \frac{T_{low}^2}{n/2} \right) - \frac{(T_{high} + T_{low})^2}{n}$$

where for a contrast column T_{high} and T_{low} are the totals of the responses at the high and low levels, respectively, and n is the total number of trials. This equation then can be rearranged to

$$SS \text{ (contrast column)} = \frac{2T_{high}^2 + 2T_{low}^2 - T_{high}^2 - 2T_{low}T_{high} - T_{low}^2}{n}$$

which reduces to

$$SS \text{ (contrast column)} = \frac{(T_{high} - T_{low})^2}{n}$$

This equation equates to

$$(SS)_j = \frac{\left[\sum_{i=1}^{n} w_i \right]^2}{n}$$

given that w_i is the trial response values preceded by either a + or − sign, depending on the level designation that is in the contrast column j (i.e., a high + or a low − level).

C.4   DOE: A SIGNIFICANCE TEST PROCEDURE FOR TWO-LEVEL EXPERIMENTS

As noted earlier, if there is an estimate for the standard deviation of experimental error, t tests can be used to determine if the change from a high to low level of a factor significantly affects a response. As was previously noted, contrast columns for high-factor interaction considerations can be used to determine an estimate for the experimental error.

To perform this significance test for the two-level factor designs in this text, the equation derived in the previous section can be used to determine a sum of squares (SS) contribution for a contrast column (Diamond 1989):

$$(SS)_j = \frac{\left[\sum\limits_{i=1}^{n} w_i\right]^2}{n}$$

where w_i is a trial response preceded by either a + or − sign for contrast column j, and n denotes the number of trials.

Next the sum of squares for the contrast columns that are being used to estimate error (SS_e) are combined to yield a mean square (MS) value:

$$MS = \frac{\sum\limits_{j=1}^{q} (SS_e)_j}{q}$$

where q is the number of contrast columns combined.

It then follows that the standard deviation estimate for the error s_e (i.e., root mean square error) is

$$s_e = \sqrt{MS}$$

Contrast column effects are then considered significant if the magnitude of the effect from a high to low level is greater than the value determined from

$$|\bar{x}_{\text{high}} - \bar{x}_{\text{low}}|_{\text{criterion}} = t_\alpha s_e \sqrt{1/n_{\text{high}} + 1/n_{\text{low}}}$$

where the t_α is taken from the double-sided Table E with the number of degrees of freedom equal to the number of contrast columns that were combined.

C.5 DOE: APPLICATION EXAMPLE

An application of the methodology described in the previous section will now be applied to the data from Example 30.1. In this example the following factors and level assignments were made for an experiment that was to give understanding of (with an intent to minimize) the settle-out time of a stepper motor when it was stopped.

Factors and Their Designations		Levels (−)	Levels (+)
A: Motor temperature	(mot_temp)	Cold	Hot
B: Algorithm	(algor)	Current Design	Proposed redesign
C: Motor adjustment	(mot_adj)	Low tolerance	High tolerance
D: External adjustment	(ext_adj)	Low tolerance	High tolerance
E: Supply voltage	(sup_volt)	Low tolerance	High tolerance

The experiment yielded the trial responses shown in Table C.1 along with the noted input factors levels. In general, standard analysis of variance or

TABLE C.1 Design Matrix with Outputs

	A	*B*	*C*	*D*	*E*	
	Number of Trial Input Factors					Output Timing (msec)
	mot_temp	algor	mot_adj	ext_adj	sup_volt	
1	+	−	−	−	+	5.6
2	+	+	−	−	−	2.1
3	+	+	+	−	+	4.9
4	+	+	+	+	−	4.9
5	−	+	+	+	+	4.1
6	+	−	+	+	+	5.6
7	−	+	−	+	−	1.9
8	+	−	+	−	−	7.2
9	+	+	−	+	+	2.4
10	−	+	+	−	−	5.1
11	−	−	+	+	−	7.9
12	+	−	−	+	−	5.3
13	−	+	−	−	+	2.1
14	−	−	+	−	+	7.6
15	−	−	−	+	+	5.5
16	−	−	−	−	−	5.3
	1	2	3	4	13	Table M3 contrast column numbers

t-test techniques could be used to determine the factors that are significant. However, if two-factor interactions are considered within the model, there are no columns remaining to assess experimental error.

An alternative analysis approach to a formal significance test is to create a probability plot of the mean contrast column effects. A probability plot of the main and interaction effects (i.e., all the contrast column effects from Table M3) can be used to pictorially determine the "significant" effects. For this resolution V design, the interaction considerations for each contrast column are noted from Table N1.

Computer programs are available to perform this task; however, this example describes a manual procedure utilizes normal probability paper (Table Q1) with percentage plot points (F_i) determined from Table P. The following discussion illustrates the mechanics of a procedure that can be used to manage the numbers when creating such a probability plot.

Table C.2 is first created when the plus/minus signs of the experiment design are combined with the response value for each trial. The mean contrast column effect for factor A (contrast column 1) is then, for example,

$$\frac{5.6 + 2.1 + 4.9 + \cdots}{8} - \frac{4.1 + 1.9 + 5.1}{8} + \cdots = -0.188$$

When using the two-level fractional factorial designs in Table M, an alternative approach is to simply divide the contrast column summation from by half the total sample size. For factor A this would be

$$-1.5/8 = -0.188$$

Similarly, the mean effects for all 15 factors can be determined. These results are shown in Table C.3. Next, the absolute values of these effects can be ranked and plotted with the percent plot positions noted from Table P to make a half normal probability plot. These ranked effects and corresponding plot coordinates are shown in Table C.4.

A computer generated normal probability plot of these absolute values (half normal probability plot) is shown in Figure C.1. The conclusion from this plot is that factors B and C (contrast column numbers 2 and 3) are significant. The "best estimates" for the magnitude of the difference (with no regard to sign) from a high level to low level for these factors are 2.813 for B and 2.138 for C. Because of the procedure used to calculate the estimates, the $+2.138$ mean effect for mot_adj indicates that the low tolerance value [(−) level for C] yields a smaller settle-out time for the motor by approximately 2.138 msec, while the -2.812 mean effect for the algorithm [(+) level for B] indicates that the proposed algorithm redesign yields a smaller settle-out time by approximately 2.812 msec. No other main effects or interactions were considered to be significant.

TABLE C.2 Experiment Response Values with Level Considerations and Contrast Column Totals

Contrast Column Number/Factor Designation

1 A	2 B	3 C	4 D	5 AB	6 BC	7 CD	8 CE	9 AC	10 BD	11 DE	12 AE	13 E	14 BE	15 ND
+5.6	−5.6	−5.6	−5.6	+5.6	−5.6	−5.6	+5.6	+5.6	−5.6	+5.6	−5.6	+5.6	+5.6	+5.6
+2.1	+2.1	−2.1	−2.1	−2.1	+2.1	−2.1	−2.1	+2.1	+2.1	−2.1	+2.1	−2.1	+2.1	+2.1
+4.9	+4.9	+4.9	−4.9	−4.9	−4.9	+4.9	−4.9	−4.9	+4.9	+4.9	−4.9	+4.9	−4.9	+4.9
+4.9	+4.9	+4.9	+4.9	−4.9	−4.9	−4.9	+4.9	−4.9	−4.9	+4.9	+4.9	−4.9	+4.9	−4.9
−4.1	+4.1	+4.1	+4.1	+4.1	−4.1	−4.1	−4.1	+4.1	−4.1	−4.1	+4.1	+4.1	−4.1	+4.1
+5.6	−5.6	+5.6	+5.6	+5.6	+5.6	−5.6	−5.6	−5.6	+5.6	−5.6	−5.6	+5.6	+5.6	−5.6
−1.9	+1.9	−1.9	+1.9	+1.9	+1.9	+1.9	−1.9	−1.9	−1.9	+1.9	−1.9	−1.9	+1.9	+1.9
+7.2	−7.2	+7.2	−7.2	+7.2	+7.2	+7.2	+7.2	−7.2	−7.2	−7.2	+7.2	−7.2	−7.2	+7.2
+2.4	+2.4	−2.4	+2.4	−2.4	+2.4	+2.4	+2.4	+2.4	−2.4	−2.4	−2.4	+2.4	−2.4	−2.4
−5.1	+5.1	+5.1	−5.1	+5.1	−5.1	+5.1	+5.1	+5.1	+5.1	−5.1	−5.1	−5.1	+5.1	−5.1
−7.9	−7.9	+7.9	+7.9	−7.9	+7.9	−7.9	+7.9	+7.9	+7.9	+7.9	−7.9	−7.9	−7.9	+7.9
+5.3	−5.3	−5.3	+5.3	+5.3	−5.3	+5.3	−5.3	+5.3	+5.3	+5.3	+5.3	−5.3	−5.3	−5.3
−2.1	+2.1	−2.1	−2.1	+2.1	+2.1	−2.1	+2.1	−2.1	+2.1	+2.1	+2.1	+2.1	−2.1	−2.1
−7.6	−7.6	+7.6	−7.6	−7.6	+7.6	+7.6	−7.6	+7.6	−7.6	+7.6	+7.6	+7.6	+7.6	−7.6
−5.5	−5.5	−5.5	+5.5	−5.5	−5.5	+5.5	+5.5	−5.5	+5.5	−5.5	+5.5	+5.5	+5.5	+5.5
−5.3	−5.3	−5.3	−5.3	−5.3	−5.3	−5.3	−5.3	−5.3	−5.3	−5.3	−5.3	−5.3	−5.3	−5.3
Totals −1.5	−22.5	+17.1	−2.3	−3.7	−3.9	+2.3	+3.9	+2.7	−0.5	+2.9	+0.1	−1.9	−0.9	+0.9

TABLE C.3 Mean Effects of Contrasts Columns

			Column Contrast Number, Factor Designation, and Mean Effect				
1	2	3	4	5	6	7	8
A	B	C	D	AB	BC	CD	CD
−0.188	−2.813	+2.138	−0.288	−0.463	−0.488	+0.288	+0.488
9	10	11	12	13	14	15	
AC	BD	DE	AE	E	BC	AD	
+0.338	−0.063	+0.363	+0.013	−0.238	−0.113	+0.113	

Because there appears to be no interaction terms, let's, for the purpose of illustration, leave all the main effects in the model and use the contrast columns to make an estimate of error. To do this manually, Table C.2 is referenced. The SS value for each contrast column that is used to estimate error can then be determined (i.e., all contrast columns except 1, 2 3, 4, and 13). For example, the SS for contrast column 5 is

$$SS = \frac{(\Sigma w_i)^2}{16} = \frac{(-3.7)^2}{16} = 0.8556$$

TABLE C.4 Ranking of Absolute Value of Mean Effects with Plot Positions

Contrast Column	Factor Designation	Mean Effect	Percentage Plot Position
12	AE	0.013	3.3
10	BD	0.063	10.0
14	BE	0.113	16.7
15	AD	0.113	23.3
1	A	0.188	30.0
13	E	0.238	36.7
4	D	0.288	43.3
7	CD	0.288	50.0
9	AC	0.338	56.7
11	DE	0.363	63.3
5	AB	0.463	70.0
6	BC	0.488	76.7
8	CE	0.488	83.3
3	C	2.138	90.0
2	B	2.813	96.7

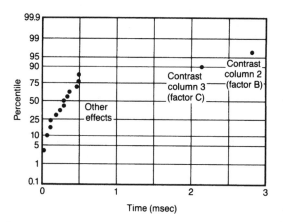

FIGURE C.1 Half normal probability plot of the contrast column effects.

The results of the *SS* calculations for the contrast columns that will be used to estimate experimental error (i.e., two factor interaction contrast columns) are

5	6	7	8	9	10	11	12	14	15
0.8556	0.9506	0.3306	0.9506	0.4556	0.0156	0.5256	0.0006	0.0506	0.0506

It follows that *MS* is then

$$MS = \frac{0.8556 + 0.9506 + \cdots + 0.0506 + 0.0506}{10}$$

$$= 0.4186$$

The standard deviation estimate for experimental error (s_e) is (with 10 degrees of freedom)

$$s_e = \sqrt{0.4186} = 0.647$$

The factors are then considered to be significant if the output effect from high to low is greater than that determined from the following. From the double-sided *t* table (Table E), the t_α values for various α values with 10 degrees of freedom are as follows, with the noted significance criteria calculations:

α	t_α	$|\bar{x}_{\text{high}} - \bar{x}_{\text{low}}|_{\text{criterion}}$
0.10	1.812	0.586^a
0.05	2.228	0.721
0.01	3.169	1.025

$^a|\bar{x}_{\text{high}} - \bar{x}_{\text{low}}|_{\text{criterion}} = t_\alpha s_e \sqrt{1/n_{\text{high}} + 1/n_{\text{low}}} = 1.812(0.647)\sqrt{1/8 + 1/8} = 0.586$

A comparison of the absolute values for the A, B, C, D, and E mean effects from Table C.3 (-0.188, -2.813, 2.138, -0.288, and 0.238, respectively) to the preceding tabular values yields B (algor) and C (mot_adj) significant at the 0.01 level, while the other three main effects cannot be shown significant at the 0.10 level.

C.6 ILLUSTRATION THAT A STANDARD ORDER DOE DESIGN MATRIX FROM STATISTICAL SOFTWARE IS EQUIVALENT TO A TABLE M DESIGN

The DOE designs shown in Table M are similar to the designs generated by computers. Table C.5 is an illustrative example where the only difference is the change in sign.

TABLE C.5 Comparison of Table M Design to a Computer-Generated Standard Order Design

	Standard Order Design from Computer						Table M3 Design					
Tr#	A	B	C	D	E	Tr#	A1	A2	A3	A4	A5	Resp
1	−1	−1	−1	−1	1	4	1	1	−1	−1	1	4.9
2	1	−1	−1	−1	−1	5	−1	−1	1	−1	1	4.1
3	−1	1	−1	−1	−1	6	1	−1	1	−1	−1	5.6
4	1	1	−1	−1	1	11	−1	1	−1	1	1	7.9
5	−1	−1	1	−1	1	9	−1	−1	−1	1	−1	2.4
6	1	−1	1	−1	−1	7	−1	1	1	−1	−1	1.9
7	−1	1	1	−1	−1	12	1	1	−1	1	−1	5.3
8	1	1	1	−1	1	15	−1	1	1	1	−1	5.5
9	−1	−1	−1	1	−1	3	−1	1	−1	−1	−1	4.9
10	1	−1	−1	1	1	10	1	−1	−1	1	1	5.1
11	−1	1	−1	1	1	8	1	1	1	−1	1	7.2
12	1	1	−1	1	−1	14	1	−1	1	1	−1	7.6
13	−1	−1	1	1	1	2	1	−1	−1	−1	−1	2.1
14	1	−1	1	1	−1	13	−1	−1	1	1	1	2.1
15	−1	1	1	1	−1	1	−1	−1	−1	−1	1	5.6
16	1	1	1	1	1	16	1	1	1	1	−1	5.3

APPENDIX D

REFERENCE TABLES

TABLE A Area Under the Standardized Normal Curve

z_α	.00	.01	.02	.03	.04	.05	.06	.07	.08	.09
0.0	.5000	.4960	.4920	.4880	.4840	.4801	.4761	.4721	.4681	.4641
0.1	.4602	.4562	.4522	.4483	.4443	.4404	.4364	.4325	.4286	.4247
0.2	.4207	.4168	.4129	.4090	.4052	.4013	.3974	.3936	.3897	.3859
0.3	.3821	.3783	.3745	.3707	.3669	.3632	.3594	.3557	.3520	.3483
0.4	.3446	.3409	.3372	.3336	.3300	.3264	.3228	.3192	.3156	.3121
0.5	.3085	.3050	.3015	.2981	.2946	.2912	.2877	.2843	.2810	.2776
0.6	.2743	.2709	.2676	.2643	.2611	.2578	.2546	.2514	.2483	.2451
0.7	.2420	.2389	.2358	.2327	.2296	.2266	.2236	.2206	.2177	.2146
0.8	.2119	.2090	.2061	.2033	.2005	.1977	.1949	.1922	.1894	.1867
0.9	.1841	.1814	.1788	.1762	.1736	.1711	.1685	.1660	.1635	.1611
1.0	.1587	.1562	.1539	.1515	.1492	.1469	.1446	.1243	.1401	.1379
1.1	.1357	.1335	.1314	.1292	.1271	.1251	.1230	.1210	.1190	.1170
1.2	.1151	.1131	.1112	.1093	.1075	.1056	.1038	.1020	.1003	.0985
1.3	.0968	.0951	.0934	.0918	.0901	.0885	.0869	.0853	.0838	.0823
1.4	.0808	.0793	.0778	.0764	.0749	.0735	.0721	.0708	.0694	.0681
1.5	.0668	.0655	.0643	.0630	.0618	.0606	.0594	.0582	.0571	.0559
1.6	.0548	.0537	.0526	.0516	.0505	.0495	.0485	.0475	.0465	.0455
1.7	.0446	.0436	.0427	.0418	.0409	.0401	.0392	.0384	.0375	.0367
1.8	.0359	.0351	.0344	.0336	.0329	.0322	.0314	.0307	.0301	.0294
1.9	.0287	.0281	.0274	.0268	.0262	.0256	.0250	.0244	.0239	.0233

TABLE A (*Continued*)

z_α	.0	.1	.2	.3	.4	.5	.6	.7	.8	.9
2.0	.0228	.0222	.0217	.0212	.0207	.0202	.0197	.0192	.0188	.0183
2.1	.0179	.0174	.0170	.0166	.0162	.0158	.0154	.0150	.0146	.0143
2.2	.0139	.0136	.0132	.0129	.0125	.0122	.0119	.0116	.0113	.0110
2.3	.0107	.0104	.0102	.00990	.00964	.00939	.00914	.00889	.00866	.00842
2.4	.00820	.00798	.00776	.00755	.00734	.00714	.00695	.00676	.00657	.00639
2.5	.00621	.00604	.00587	.00570	.00554	.00539	.00523	.00508	.00494	.00480
2.6	.00466	.00453	.00440	.00427	.00415	.00402	.00391	.00379	.00368	.00357
2.7	.00347	.00336	.00326	.00317	.00307	.00298	.00289	.00280	.00272	.00264
2.8	.00256	.00248	.00240	.00233	.00226	.00219	.00212	.00205	.00199	.00193
2.9	.00187	.00181	.00175	.00169	.00164	.00159	.00154	.00149	.00144	.00139
3	.00135	$.0^3988$	$.0^3687$	$.0^3483$	$.0^3337$	$.0^3233$	$.0^3159$	$.0^3108$	$.0^4723$	$.0^4481$
4	$.0^4317$	$.0^4207$	$.0^4133$	$.0^5854$	$.0^5541^a$	$.0^5340$	$.0^5211$	$.0^5130$	$.0^6793$	$.0^6479$
5	$.0^6287$	$.0^6170$	$.0^7996$	$.0^7579$	$.0^7333$	$.0^7190$	$.0^7107$	$.0^8599$	$.0^8332$	$.0^8182$
6	$.0^9987$	$.0^9530$	$.0^9282$	$.0^9149$	$.0^{10}777$	$.0^{10}402$	$.0^{10}206$	$.0^{10}104$	$.0^{11}523$	$.0^{11}260$

[a] $.0^5541$ means .00000541.

Note 1: The same information can be obtained from Tables B and C; however, this table format is different.

Note 2: In this text the tabular value corresponds to Z_α, where α is the value of probability associated with the distribution area pictorially represented as

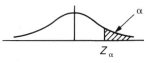

Source: Croxton (1953).

TABLE B Probability Points of the Normal Distribution: Single-Sided (Variance Known)

α or β	U	α or β	U
0.001	3.090	0.100	1.282
0.005	2.576	0.150	1.036
0.010	2.326	0.200	0.842
0.015	2.170	0.300	0.524
0.020	2.054	0.400	0.253
0.025	1.960	0.500	0.000
0.050	1.645	0.600	−0.253

Note 1: The same information can be obtained from Table A; however, this table format is different.

Note 2: In this text the tabular value corresponds to U_α, where α is the value of probability associated with the distribution area pictorially represented as

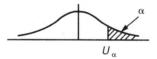

Source: Diamond (1989), with permission.

TABLE C Probability Points of the Normal Distribution: Double-Sided (Variance Known)

α only	U	α only	U
0.001	3.291	0.100	1.645
0.005	2.807	0.150	1.440
0.010	2.576	0.200	1.282
0.015	2.432	0.300	1.036
0.020	2.326	0.400	0.842
0.025	2.241	0.500	0.675
0.050	1.960	0.600	0.524

Note 1: The same information can be obtained from Table A; however, this table format is different.

Note 2: In this text the tabular value corresponds to U_α, where α is the value of probability associated with the distribution area pictorially represented as

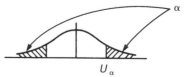

Source: Diamond (1989), with permission.

TABLE D Probability Points of the *t* Distribution: Single-Sided

					α					
v	.40	.30	.20	.10	.050	.025	.010	.005	.001	.0005
1	.325	.727	1.376	3.078	6.314	12.71	31.82	63.66	318.3	636.6
2	.289	.617	1.061	1.886	2.920	4.303	6.965	9.925	22.33	31.60
3	.277	.584	.978	1.638	2.353	3.182	4.541	5.841	10.22	12.94
4	.271	.569	.941	1.533	2.132	2.776	3.747	4.604	7.173	8.610
5	.267	.559	.920	1.476	2.015	2.571	3.365	4.032	5.893	6.859
6	.265	.553	.906	1.440	1.943	2.447	3.143	3.707	5.208	5.959
7	.263	.549	.896	1.415	1.895	2.365	2.998	3.499	4.785	5.405
8	.262	.546	.889	1.397	1.860	2.306	2.896	3.355	4.501	5.041
9	.261	.543	.883	1.383	1.833	2.262	2.821	3.250	4.297	4.781
10	.260	.542	.879	1.372	1.812	2.228	2.764	3.169	4.144	4.587
11	.260	.540	.876	1.363	1.796	2.201	2.718	3.106	4.025	4.437
12	.259	.539	.873	1.356	1.782	2.179	2.681	3.055	3.930	4.318
13	.259	.538	.870	1.350	1.771	2.160	2.650	3.012	3.852	4.221
14	.258	.537	.868	1.345	1.761	2.145	2.624	2.977	3.787	4.140
15	.258	.536	.866	1.341	1.753	2.131	2.602	2.947	3.733	4.073
16	.258	.535	.865	1.337	1.746	2.120	2.583	2.921	3.686	4.015
17	.257	.534	.863	1.333	1.740	2.110	2.567	2.898	3.646	3.965
18	.257	.534	.862	1.330	1.734	2.101	2.552	2.878	3.611	3.922
19	.257	.533	.861	1.328	1.729	2.093	2.539	2.861	3.579	3.883
20	.257	.533	.860	1.325	1.725	2.086	2.528	2.845	3.552	3.850
21	.257	.532	.859	1.323	1.721	2.080	2.518	2.831	3.527	3.819
22	.256	.532	.858	1.321	1.717	2.074	2.508	2.819	3.505	3.792
23	.256	.532	.858	1.319	1.714	2.069	2.500	2.807	3.485	3.767
24	.256	.531	.857	1.318	1.711	2.064	2.492	2.797	3.467	3.745
25	.256	.531	.856	1.316	1.708	2.060	2.485	2.787	3.450	3.725
26	.256	.531	.856	1.315	1.706	2.056	2.479	2.779	3.435	3.707
27	.256	.531	.855	1.314	1.703	2.052	2.473	2.771	3.421	3.690
28	.256	.530	.855	1.313	1.701	2.048	2.467	2.763	3.408	3.674
29	.256	.530	.854	1.311	1.699	2.045	2.462	2.756	3.396	3.659
30	.256	.530	.854	1.310	1.697	2.042	2.457	2.750	3.385	3.646
40	.255	.529	.851	1.303	1.684	2.021	2.423	2.704	3.307	3.551
50	.255	.528	.849	1.298	1.676	2.009	2.403	2.678	3.262	3.495
60	.254	.527	.848	1.296	1.671	2.000	2.390	2.660	3.232	3.460
80	.254	.527	.846	1.292	1.664	1.990	2.374	2.639	3.195	3.415
100	.254	.526	.845	1.290	1.660	1.984	2.365	2.626	3.174	3.389
200	.254	.525	.843	1.286	1.653	1.972	2.345	2.601	3.131	3.339
500	.253	.525	.842	1.283	1.648	1.965	2.334	2.586	3.106	3.310
∞	.253	.524	.842	1.282	1.645	1.960	2.326	2.576	3.090	3.291

Note: In this text the tabular value corresponds to $t_{\alpha;v}$, where v is the number of degrees of freedom and α is the value of probability associated with the distribution area pictorially represented as

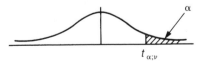

Source: Pearson and Hartley (1958), with permission. Parts of the table are also taken from Table III of Fisher and Yates (1953), with permission.

TABLE E Probability Points of the *t* Distribution: Double-Sided

Degrees of Freedom	Probability of a Larger Value, Sign Ignored								
	0.500	0.400	0.200	0.100	0.050	0.025	0.010	0.005	0.001
1	1.000	1.376	3.078	6.314	12.706	25.452	63.657		
2	.816	1.061	1.886	2.920	4.303	6.205	9.925	14.089	31.598
3	.765	.978	1.638	2.353	3.182	4.176	5.841	7.453	12.941
4	.741	.941	1.533	2.132	2.776	3.495	4.604	5.598	8.610
5	.727	.920	1.476	2.015	2.571	3.163	4.032	4.773	6.859
6	.718	.906	1.440	1.943	2.447	2.969	3.707	4.317	5.959
7	.711	.896	1.415	1.895	2.365	2.841	3.499	4.029	5.405
8	.706	.889	1.397	1.860	2.306	2.752	3.355	3.832	5.041
9	.703	.883	1.383	1.833	2.262	2.685	3.250	3.690	4.781
10	.700	.879	1.372	1.812	2.228	2.634	3.169	3.581	4.587
11	.697	.876	1.363	1.796	2.201	2.593	3.106	3.497	4.437
12	.695	.873	1.356	1.782	2.179	2.560	3.055	3.428	4.318
13	.694	.870	1.350	1.771	2.160	2.533	3.012	3.372	4.221
14	.692	.868	1.345	1.761	2.145	2.510	2.977	3.326	4.140
15	.691	.866	1.341	1.753	2.131	2.490	2.947	3.286	4.073
16	.690	.865	1.337	1.746	2.120	2.473	2.921	3.252	4.015
17	.689	.863	1.333	1.740	2.110	2.458	2.898	3.222	3.965
18	.688	.862	1.330	1.734	2.101	2.445	2.878	3.197	3.922
19	.688	.861	1.328	1.729	2.093	2.433	2.861	3.174	3.883
20	.687	.860	1.325	1.725	2.086	2.423	2.845	3.153	3.850
21	.686	.859	1.323	1.721	2.080	2.414	2.831	3.135	3.819
22	.686	.858	1.321	1.717	2.074	2.406	2.819	3.119	3.792
23	.685	.858	1.319	1.714	2.069	2.398	2.807	3.104	3.767
24	.685	.857	1.318	1.711	2.064	2.391	2.797	3.090	3.745
25	.684	.856	1.316	1.708	2.060	2.385	2.787	3.078	3.725
26	.684	.856	1.315	1.706	2.056	2.379	2.779	3.067	3.707
27	.684	.855	1.314	1.703	2.052	2.373	2.771	3.056	3.690
28	.683	.855	1.313	1.701	2.048	2.368	2.763	3.047	3.674
29	.683	.854	1.311	1.699	2.045	2.364	2.756	3.038	3.659
30	.683	.854	1.310	1.697	2.042	2.360	2.750	3.030	3.646
35	.682	.852	1.306	1.690	2.030	2.342	2.724	2.996	3.591
40	.681	.851	1.303	1.684	2.021	2.329	2.704	2.971	3.551
45	.680	.850	1.301	1.680	2.014	2.319	2.690	2.952	3.520
50	.680	.849	1.299	1.676	2.008	2.310	2.678	2.937	3.496
55	.679	.849	1.297	1.673	2.004	2.304	2.669	2.925	3.476

TABLE E (*Continued*)

Degrees of Freedom	Probability of a Larger Value, Sign Ignored								
	0.500	0.400	0.200	0.100	0.050	0.025	0.010	0.005	0.001
60	.679	.848	1.296	1.671	2.000	2.299	2.660	2.915	3.460
70	.678	.847	1.294	1.667	1.994	2.290	2.648	2.899	3.435
80	.678	.847	1.293	1.665	1.989	2.284	2.638	2.887	3.416
90	.678	.846	1.291	1.662	1.986	2.279	2.631	2.878	3.402
100	.677	.846	1.290	1.661	1.982	2.276	2.625	2.871	3.390
120	.677	.845	1.289	1.658	1.980	2.270	2.617	2.860	3.373
∞	.6745	.8416	1.2816	1.6448	1.9600	2.2414	2.5758	2.8070	3.2905

Note: In this text the tabular value corresponds to $t_{\alpha;\nu}$, where ν is the number of degrees of freedom and α is the value of probability associated with the distribution area, pictorially represented as

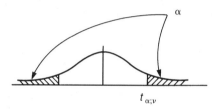

Source: Snedecor and Cochran (1989), with permission.

TABLE F Probability Points of the Variance Ratio (F Distribution)

Probability Point	ν_2	Numerator (ν_1)																		
		1	2	3	4	5	6	7	8	9	10	12	15	20	24	30	40	60	120	α
0.1	1	39.9	49.5	53.6	55.8	57.2	58.2	58.9	59.4	59.9	60.2	60.7	61.2	61.7	62.0	62.3	62.5	62.8	63.1	63.3
0.05		161	199	216	225	230	234	237	239	241	242	244	246	248	249	250	251	252	253	254
0.01		4052	4999	5403	5625	5764	5859	5928	5982	6022	6056	6106	6157	6209	6235	6261	6287	6313	6339	6366
0.1	2	8.53	9.00	9.16	9.24	9.29	9.33	9.35	9.37	9.38	9.39	9.41	9.42	9.44	9.45	9.46	9.47	9.47	9.48	9.49
0.05		18.5	19.0	19.2	19.2	19.3	19.3	19.4	19.4	19.4	19.4	19.4	19.4	19.4	19.5	19.5	19.5	19.5	19.5	19.5
0.01		98.5	99.0	99.2	99.2	99.3	99.3	99.4	99.4	99.4	99.4	99.4	99.4	99.4	99.5	99.5	99.5	99.5	99.5	99.5
0.1	3	5.54	5.46	5.39	5.34	5.31	5.28	5.27	5.25	5.24	5.23	5.22	5.20	5.18	5.18	5.17	5.16	5.15	5.14	5.13
0.05		10.1	9.55	9.28	9.12	9.01	8.94	8.89	8.85	8.81	8.79	8.74	8.70	8.66	8.64	8.62	8.59	8.57	8.55	8.53
0.01		34.1	30.8	29.5	28.7	28.2	27.9	27.7	27.5	27.3	27.2	27.1	26.9	26.7	26.6	26.5	26.4	26.3	26.2	26.1
0.1	4	4.54	4.32	4.19	4.11	4.05	4.01	3.98	3.95	3.94	3.92	3.90	3.87	3.84	3.83	3.82	3.80	3.79	3.78	3.76
0.05		7.71	6.94	6.59	6.39	6.26	6.16	6.09	6.04	6.00	5.96	5.91	5.86	5.80	5.77	5.75	5.72	5.69	5.66	5.63
0.01		21.2	18.0	16.7	16.0	15.5	15.2	15.0	14.8	14.7	14.5	14.4	14.2	14.0	13.9	13.8	13.7	13.7	13.6	13.5
0.1	5	4.06	3.78	3.62	3.52	3.45	3.40	3.37	3.34	3.32	3.30	3.27	3.24	3.21	3.19	3.17	3.16	3.14	3.12	3.10
0.05		6.61	5.79	5.41	5.19	5.05	4.95	4.88	4.82	4.77	4.74	4.68	4.62	4.56	4.53	4.50	4.46	4.43	4.40	4.36
0.01		16.3	13.3	12.1	11.4	11.0	10.7	10.5	10.3	10.2	10.1	9.89	9.72	9.55	9.47	9.38	9.29	9.20	9.11	9.02
0.1	6	3.78	3.46	3.29	3.18	3.11	3.05	3.01	2.98	2.96	2.94	2.90	2.87	2.84	2.82	2.80	2.78	2.76	2.74	2.72
0.05		5.99	5.14	4.76	4.53	4.39	4.28	4.21	4.15	4.10	4.06	4.00	3.94	3.87	3.84	3.81	3.77	3.74	3.70	3.67
0.01		13.7	10.9	9.78	9.15	8.75	8.47	8.26	8.10	7.98	7.87	7.72	7.56	7.40	7.31	7.23	7.14	7.06	6.97	6.88
0.1	7	3.59	3.26	3.07	2.96	2.88	2.83	2.78	2.75	2.72	2.70	2.67	2.63	2.59	2.58	2.56	2.54	2.51	2.49	2.47
0.05		5.59	4.74	4.35	4.12	3.97	3.87	3.79	3.73	3.68	3.64	3.57	3.51	3.44	3.41	3.38	3.34	3.30	3.27	3.23
0.01		12.2	9.55	8.45	7.85	7.46	7.19	6.99	6.84	6.72	6.62	6.47	6.31	6.16	6.07	5.99	5.91	5.82	5.74	5.65
0.1	8	3.46	3.11	2.92	2.81	2.73	2.67	2.62	2.59	2.56	2.54	2.50	2.46	2.42	2.40	2.38	2.36	2.34	2.32	2.29
0.05		5.32	4.46	4.07	3.84	3.69	3.58	3.50	3.44	3.39	3.35	3.28	3.22	3.15	3.12	3.08	3.04	3.01	2.97	2.93
0.01		11.3	8.65	7.59	7.01	6.63	6.37	6.18	6.03	5.91	5.81	5.67	5.52	5.36	5.28	5.20	5.12	5.03	4.95	4.86
0.1	9	3.36	3.01	2.81	2.69	2.61	2.55	2.51	2.47	2.44	2.42	2.38	2.34	2.30	2.28	2.25	2.23	2.21	2.18	2.16
0.05		5.12	4.26	3.86	3.63	3.48	3.37	3.29	3.23	3.18	3.14	3.07	3.01	2.94	2.90	2.86	2.83	2.79	2.75	2.71
0.01		10.6	8.02	6.99	6.42	6.06	5.80	5.61	5.47	5.35	5.26	5.11	4.96	4.81	4.73	4.65	4.57	4.48	4.40	4.31

ν	α																			
10	0.1	2.06	2.08	2.11	2.13	2.16	2.18	2.20	2.24	2.28	2.32	2.35	2.38	2.41	2.46	2.52	2.61	2.73	2.92	3.28
	0.05	2.54	2.58	2.62	2.66	2.70	2.74	2.77	2.84	2.91	2.98	3.02	3.07	3.14	3.22	3.33	3.48	3.71	4.10	4.96
	0.01	3.91	4.00	4.08	4.17	4.25	4.33	4.41	4.56	4.71	4.85	4.94	5.06	5.20	5.39	5.64	5.99	6.55	7.56	10.0
11	0.1	1.97	2.00	2.03	2.05	2.08	2.10	2.12	2.17	2.21	2.25	2.27	2.30	2.34	2.39	2.45	2.54	2.66	2.86	3.23
	0.05	2.40	2.45	2.49	2.53	2.57	2.61	2.65	2.72	2.79	2.85	2.90	2.95	3.01	3.09	3.20	3.36	3.59	3.98	4.84
	0.01	3.60	3.69	3.78	3.86	3.94	4.02	4.10	4.25	4.40	4.54	4.63	4.74	4.89	5.07	5.32	5.67	6.22	7.21	9.65
12	0.1	1.90	1.93	1.96	1.99	2.01	2.04	2.06	2.10	2.15	2.19	2.21	2.24	2.28	2.33	2.39	2.48	2.61	2.81	3.18
	0.05	2.30	2.34	2.38	2.43	2.47	2.51	2.54	2.62	2.69	2.75	2.80	2.85	2.91	3.00	3.11	3.26	3.49	3.89	4.75
	0.01	3.36	3.45	3.54	3.62	3.70	3.78	3.86	4.01	4.16	4.30	4.39	4.50	4.64	4.82	5.06	5.41	5.95	6.93	9.33
13	0.1	1.85	1.88	1.90	1.93	1.96	1.98	2.01	2.05	2.10	2.14	2.16	2.20	2.23	2.28	2.35	2.43	2.56	2.76	3.14
	0.05	2.21	2.25	2.30	2.34	2.38	2.42	2.46	2.53	2.60	2.67	2.71	2.77	2.83	2.92	3.03	3.18	3.41	3.81	4.67
	0.01	3.17	3.25	3.34	3.43	3.51	3.59	3.66	3.82	3.96	4.10	4.19	4.30	4.44	4.62	4.86	5.21	5.74	6.70	9.07
14	0.1	1.80	1.83	1.86	1.89	1.91	1.94	1.96	2.01	2.05	2.10	2.12	2.15	2.19	2.24	2.31	2.39	2.52	2.73	3.10
	0.05	2.13	2.18	2.22	2.27	2.31	2.35	2.39	2.46	2.53	2.60	2.65	2.70	2.76	2.85	2.96	3.11	3.34	3.74	4.60
	0.01	3.00	3.09	3.18	3.27	3.35	3.43	3.51	3.66	3.80	3.94	4.03	4.14	4.28	4.46	4.69	5.04	5.56	6.51	8.86
15	0.1	1.76	1.79	1.82	1.85	1.87	1.90	1.92	1.97	2.02	2.06	2.09	2.12	2.16	2.21	2.27	2.36	2.49	2.70	3.07
	0.05	2.07	2.11	2.16	2.20	2.25	2.29	2.33	2.40	2.48	2.54	2.59	2.64	2.71	2.79	2.90	3.06	3.29	3.68	4.54
	0.01	2.87	2.96	3.05	3.13	3.21	3.29	3.37	3.52	3.67	3.80	3.89	4.00	4.14	4.32	4.56	4.89	5.42	6.36	8.68
16	0.1	1.72	1.75	1.78	1.81	1.84	1.87	1.89	1.94	1.99	2.03	2.06	2.09	2.13	2.18	2.24	2.33	2.46	2.67	3.05
	0.05	2.01	2.06	2.11	2.15	2.19	2.24	2.28	2.35	2.42	2.49	2.54	2.59	2.66	2.74	2.85	3.01	3.24	3.63	4.49
	0.01	2.75	2.84	2.93	3.02	3.10	3.18	3.26	3.41	3.55	3.69	3.78	3.89	4.03	4.20	4.44	4.77	5.29	6.23	8.53
17	0.1	1.69	1.72	1.75	1.78	1.81	1.84	1.86	1.91	1.96	2.00	2.03	2.06	2.10	2.15	2.22	2.31	2.44	2.64	3.03
	0.05	1.96	2.01	2.06	2.10	2.15	2.19	2.23	2.31	2.38	2.45	2.49	2.55	2.61	2.70	2.81	2.96	3.20	3.59	4.45
	0.01	2.65	2.75	2.83	2.92	3.00	3.08	3.16	3.31	3.46	3.59	3.68	3.79	3.93	4.10	4.34	4.67	5.18	6.11	8.40
18	0.1	1.66	1.69	1.72	1.75	1.78	1.81	1.84	1.89	1.93	1.98	2.00	2.04	2.08	2.13	2.20	2.29	2.42	2.62	3.01
	0.05	1.92	1.97	2.02	2.06	2.11	2.15	2.19	2.27	2.34	2.41	2.46	2.51	2.58	2.66	2.77	2.93	3.16	3.55	4.41
	0.01	2.57	2.66	2.75	2.84	2.92	3.00	3.08	3.23	3.37	3.51	3.60	3.71	3.84	4.01	4.25	4.58	5.09	6.01	8.29
19	0.1	1.63	1.67	1.70	1.73	1.76	1.79	1.81	1.86	1.91	1.96	1.98	2.02	2.06	2.11	2.18	2.27	2.40	2.61	2.99
	0.05	1.88	1.93	1.98	2.03	2.07	2.11	2.16	2.23	2.31	2.38	2.42	2.48	2.54	2.63	2.74	2.90	3.13	3.52	4.38
	0.01	2.49	2.58	2.67	2.76	2.84	2.92	3.00	3.15	3.30	3.43	3.52	3.63	3.77	3.94	4.17	4.50	5.01	5.93	8.18

TABLE F (Continued)

Probability Point	v_2	\multicolumn{19}{c}{Numerator (v_1)}

Probability Point	v_2	1	2	3	4	5	6	7	8	9	10	12	15	20	24	30	40	60	120	α
0.1	20	2.97	2.59	2.38	2.25	2.16	2.09	2.04	2.00	1.96	1.94	1.89	1.84	1.79	1.77	1.74	1.71	1.68	1.64	1.61
0.05		4.35	3.49	3.10	2.87	2.71	2.60	2.51	2.45	2.39	2.35	2.28	2.20	2.12	2.08	2.04	1.99	1.95	1.90	1.84
0.01		8.10	5.85	4.94	4.43	4.10	3.87	3.70	3.56	3.46	3.37	3.23	3.09	2.94	2.86	2.78	2.69	2.61	2.52	2.42
0.1	21	2.96	2.57	2.36	2.23	2.14	2.08	2.02	1.98	1.95	1.92	1.87	1.83	1.78	1.75	1.72	1.69	1.66	1.62	1.59
0.05		4.32	3.47	3.07	2.84	2.68	2.57	2.49	2.42	2.37	2.32	2.25	2.18	2.10	2.05	2.01	1.96	1.92	1.87	1.81
0.01		8.02	5.78	4.87	4.37	4.04	3.81	3.64	3.51	3.40	3.31	3.17	3.03	2.88	2.80	2.72	2.64	2.55	2.46	2.36
0.1	22	2.95	2.56	2.35	2.22	2.13	2.06	2.01	1.97	1.93	1.90	1.86	1.81	1.76	1.73	1.70	1.67	1.64	1.60	1.57
0.05		4.30	3.44	3.05	2.82	2.66	2.55	2.46	2.40	2.34	2.30	2.23	2.15	2.07	2.03	1.98	1.94	1.89	1.84	1.78
0.01		7.95	5.72	4.82	4.31	3.99	3.76	3.59	3.45	3.35	3.26	3.12	2.98	2.83	2.75	2.67	2.58	2.50	2.40	2.31
0.1	23	2.94	2.55	2.34	2.21	2.11	2.05	1.99	1.95	1.92	1.89	1.85	1.80	1.74	1.72	1.69	1.66	1.62	1.59	1.55
0.05		4.28	3.42	3.03	2.80	2.64	2.53	2.44	2.37	2.32	2.27	2.20	2.13	2.05	2.00	1.96	1.91	1.86	1.81	1.76
0.01		7.88	5.66	4.76	4.26	3.94	3.71	3.54	3.41	3.30	3.21	3.07	2.93	2.78	2.70	2.62	2.54	2.45	2.35	2.26
0.1	24	2.93	2.54	2.33	2.19	2.10	2.04	1.98	1.94	1.91	1.88	1.83	1.78	1.73	1.70	1.67	1.64	1.61	1.57	1.53
0.05		4.26	3.40	3.01	2.78	2.62	2.51	2.42	2.36	2.30	2.25	2.18	2.11	2.03	1.98	1.94	1.89	1.84	1.79	1.73
0.01		7.82	5.61	4.72	4.22	3.90	3.67	3.50	3.36	3.26	3.17	3.03	2.89	2.74	2.66	2.58	2.49	2.40	2.31	2.21
0.1	25	2.92	2.53	2.32	2.18	2.09	2.02	1.97	1.93	1.89	1.87	1.82	1.77	1.72	1.69	1.66	1.63	1.59	1.56	1.52
0.05		4.24	3.39	2.99	2.76	2.60	2.49	2.40	2.34	2.28	2.24	2.16	2.09	2.01	1.96	1.92	1.87	1.82	1.77	1.71
0.01		7.77	5.57	4.68	4.18	3.86	3.63	3.46	3.32	3.22	3.13	2.99	2.85	2.70	2.62	2.54	2.45	2.36	2.27	2.17
0.1	26	2.91	2.52	2.31	2.17	2.08	2.01	1.96	1.92	1.88	1.86	1.81	1.76	1.71	1.68	1.65	1.61	1.58	1.54	1.50
0.05		4.23	3.37	2.98	2.74	2.59	2.47	2.39	2.32	2.27	2.22	2.15	2.07	1.99	1.95	1.90	1.85	1.80	1.75	1.69
0.01		7.72	5.53	4.64	4.14	3.82	3.59	3.42	3.29	3.18	3.09	2.96	2.82	2.66	2.58	2.50	2.42	2.33	2.23	2.13
0.1	27	2.90	2.51	2.30	2.17	2.07	2.00	1.95	1.91	1.87	1.85	1.80	1.75	1.70	1.67	1.64	1.60	1.57	1.53	1.49
0.05		4.21	3.35	2.96	2.73	2.57	2.46	2.37	2.31	2.25	2.20	2.13	2.06	1.97	1.93	1.88	1.84	1.79	1.73	1.67
0.01		7.68	5.49	4.60	4.11	3.78	3.56	3.39	3.26	3.15	3.06	2.93	2.78	2.63	2.55	2.47	2.38	2.29	2.20	2.10
0.1	28	2.89	2.50	2.29	2.16	2.06	2.00	1.94	1.90	1.87	1.84	1.79	1.74	1.69	1.66	1.63	1.59	1.56	1.52	1.48
0.05		4.20	3.34	2.95	2.71	2.56	2.45	2.36	2.29	2.24	2.19	2.12	2.04	1.96	1.91	1.87	1.82	1.77	1.71	1.65
0.01		7.64	5.45	4.57	4.07	3.75	3.53	3.36	3.23	3.12	3.03	2.90	2.75	2.60	2.52	2.44	2.35	2.26	2.17	2.06

v_2	α	1	2	3	4	5	6	7	8	9	10	12	15	20	24	30	40	60	120	∞
29	0.1	2.89	2.50	2.28	2.15	2.06	1.99	1.93	1.89	1.86	1.83	1.78	1.73	1.68	1.65	1.62	1.58	1.55	1.51	1.47
	0.05	4.18	3.33	2.93	2.70	2.55	2.43	2.35	2.28	2.22	2.18	2.10	2.03	1.94	1.90	1.85	1.81	1.75	1.70	1.64
	0.01	7.60	5.42	4.54	4.04	3.73	3.50	3.33	3.20	3.09	3.00	2.87	2.73	2.57	2.49	2.41	2.33	2.23	2.14	2.03
30	0.1	2.88	2.49	2.28	2.14	2.05	1.98	1.93	1.88	1.85	1.82	1.77	1.72	1.67	1.64	1.61	1.57	1.54	1.50	1.46
	0.05	4.17	3.32	2.92	2.69	2.53	2.42	2.33	2.27	2.21	2.16	2.09	2.01	1.93	1.89	1.84	1.79	1.74	1.68	1.62
	0.01	7.56	5.39	4.51	4.02	3.70	3.47	3.30	3.17	3.07	2.98	2.84	2.70	2.55	2.47	2.39	2.30	2.21	2.11	2.01
40	0.1	2.84	2.44	2.23	2.09	2.00	1.93	1.87	1.83	1.79	1.76	1.71	1.66	1.61	1.57	1.54	1.51	1.47	1.42	1.38
	0.05	4.08	3.23	2.84	2.61	2.45	2.34	2.25	2.18	2.12	2.08	2.00	1.92	1.84	1.79	1.74	1.69	1.64	1.58	1.51
	0.01	7.31	5.18	4.31	3.83	3.51	3.29	3.12	2.99	2.89	2.80	2.66	2.52	2.37	2.29	2.20	2.11	2.02	1.92	1.80
60	0.1	2.79	2.39	2.18	2.04	1.95	1.87	1.82	1.77	1.74	1.71	1.66	1.60	1.54	1.51	1.48	1.44	1.40	1.35	1.29
	0.05	4.00	3.15	2.76	2.53	2.37	2.25	2.17	2.10	2.04	1.99	1.92	1.84	1.75	1.70	1.65	1.59	1.53	1.47	1.39
	0.01	7.08	4.98	4.13	3.65	3.34	3.12	2.95	2.82	2.72	2.63	2.50	2.35	2.20	2.12	2.03	1.94	1.84	1.73	1.60
120	0.1	2.75	2.35	2.13	1.99	1.90	1.82	1.77	1.72	1.68	1.65	1.60	1.54	1.48	1.45	1.41	1.37	1.32	1.26	1.19
	0.05	3.92	3.07	2.68	2.45	2.29	2.18	2.09	2.02	1.96	1.91	1.83	1.75	1.66	1.61	1.55	1.50	1.43	1.35	1.25
	0.01	6.85	4.79	3.95	3.48	3.17	2.96	2.79	2.66	2.56	2.47	2.34	2.19	2.03	1.95	1.86	1.76	1.66	1.53	1.38
∞	0.1	2.71	2.30	2.08	1.94	1.85	1.77	1.72	1.67	1.63	1.60	1.55	1.49	1.42	1.38	1.34	1.30	1.24	1.17	1.00
	0.05	3.84	3.00	2.60	2.37	2.21	2.10	2.01	1.94	1.88	1.83	1.75	1.67	1.57	1.52	1.46	1.39	1.32	1.22	1.00
	0.01	6.63	4.61	3.78	3.32	3.02	2.80	2.64	2.51	2.41	2.32	2.18	2.04	1.88	1.79	1.70	1.59	1.47	1.32	1.00

Note: The tabular value corresponds to $F_{\alpha; v_1; v_2}$, where v_1 is the number of degrees of freedom of the larger value in the numerator, v_2 is the number of degrees of freedom of the smaller value in the denominator, and α is the value of probability associated with the distribution area pictorially represented as

$F_{\alpha; v_1; v_2}$

Source: Table V of Fisher and Yates (1953), with permission. (The labeling reflects the nomenclature used in this text.)

TABLE G Cumulative Distribution of Chi-Square

Degrees of Freedom	Probability of a Greater Value													
	0.995	0.990	0.975	0.950	0.900	0.750	0.500	0.250	0.100	0.050	0.025	0.010	0.005
1	...	...	...	...	0.02	0.10	0.45	1.32	2.71	3.84	5.02	6.63	7.88
2	0.01	0.02	0.05	0.10	0.21	0.58	1.39	2.77	4.61	5.99	7.38	9.21	10.60
3	0.07	0.11	0.22	0.35	0.58	1.21	2.37	4.11	6.25	7.81	9.35	11.34	12.84
4	0.21	0.30	0.48	0.71	1.06	1.92	3.36	5.39	7.78	9.49	11.14	13.28	14.86
5	0.41	0.55	0.83	1.15	1.61	2.67	4.35	6.63	9.24	11.07	12.83	15.09	16.75
6	0.68	0.87	1.24	1.64	2.20	3.45	5.35	7.84	10.64	12.59	14.45	16.81	18.55
7	0.99	1.24	1.69	2.17	2.83	4.25	6.35	9.04	12.02	14.07	16.01	18.48	20.28
8	1.34	1.65	2.18	2.73	3.49	5.07	7.34	10.22	13.36	15.51	17.53	20.09	21.96
9	1.73	2.09	2.70	3.33	4.17	5.90	8.34	11.39	14.68	16.92	19.02	21.67	23.59
10	2.16	2.56	3.25	3.94	4.87	6.74	9.34	12.55	15.99	18.31	20.48	23.21	25.19
11	2.60	3.05	3.82	4.57	5.58	7.58	10.34	13.70	17.28	19.68	21.92	24.72	26.76
12	3.07	3.57	4.40	5.23	6.30	8.44	11.34	14.85	18.55	21.03	23.34	26.22	28.30
13	3.57	4.11	5.01	5.89	7.04	9.30	12.34	15.98	19.81	22.36	24.74	27.69	29.82
14	4.07	4.66	5.63	6.57	7.79	10.17	13.34	17.12	21.06	23.68	26.12	29.14	31.32
15	4.60	5.23	6.27	7.26	8.55	11.04	14.34	18.25	22.31	25.00	27.49	30.58	32.80
16	5.14	5.81	6.91	7.96	9.31	11.91	15.34	19.37	23.54	26.30	28.85	32.00	34.27
17	5.70	6.41	7.56	8.67	10.09	12.79	16.34	20.49	24.77	27.59	30.19	33.41	35.72
18	6.26	7.01	8.23	9.39	10.86	13.68	17.34	21.60	25.99	28.87	31.53	34.81	37.16
19	6.84	7.63	8.91	10.12	11.65	14.56	18.34	22.72	27.20	30.14	32.85	36.19	38.58
20	7.43	8.26	9.59	10.85	12.44	15.45	19.34	23.83	28.41	31.41	34.17	37.57	40.00

ν													
21	8.03	8.90	10.28	11.59	13.24	16.34	20.34	24.93	29.62	32.67	35.48	38.93	41.40
22	8.64	9.54	10.98	12.34	14.04	17.24	21.34	26.04	30.81	33.92	36.78	40.29	42.80
23	9.26	10.20	11.69	13.09	14.85	18.14	22.34	27.14	32.01	35.17	38.08	41.64	44.18
24	9.89	10.86	12.40	13.85	15.66	19.04	23.34	28.24	33.20	36.42	39.36	42.98	45.56
25	10.52	11.52	13.12	14.61	16.47	19.94	24.34	29.34	34.38	37.65	40.65	44.31	46.93
26	11.16	12.20	13.84	15.38	17.29	20.84	25.34	30.43	35.56	38.89	41.92	45.64	48.29
27	11.81	12.88	14.57	16.15	18.11	21.75	26.34	31.53	36.74	40.11	43.19	46.96	49.64
28	12.46	13.56	15.31	16.93	18.94	22.66	27.34	32.62	37.92	41.34	44.46	48.28	50.99
29	13.12	14.26	16.05	17.71	19.77	23.57	28.34	33.71	39.09	42.56	45.72	49.59	52.34
30	13.79	14.95	16.79	18.49	20.60	24.48	29.34	34.80	40.26	43.77	46.98	50.89	53.67
40	20.71	22.16	24.43	26.51	29.05	33.66	39.34	45.62	51.80	55.76	59.34	63.69	66.77
50	27.99	29.71	32.36	34.76	37.69	42.94	49.33	56.33	63.17	67.50	71.42	76.15	79.49
60	35.53	37.48	40.48	43.19	46.46	52.29	59.33	66.98	74.40	79.08	83.30	88.38	91.95
70	43.28	45.44	48.76	51.74	55.33	61.70	69.33	77.58	85.53	90.53	95.02	100.42	104.22
80	51.17	53.54	57.15	60.39	64.28	71.14	79.33	88.13	96.58	101.88	106.63	112.33	116.32
90	59.20	61.75	65.65	69.13	73.29	80.62	89.33	98.64	107.56	113.14	118.14	124.12	128.30
100	67.33	70.06	74.22	77.93	82.36	90.13	99.33	109.14	118.50	124.34	129.56	135.81	140.17

Note: In this text the tabular value corresponds to $\chi^2_{\alpha;\nu}$, where ν is the number of degrees of freedom and α is the value of probability associated with the distribution area pictorially represented as

Source: Snedecor and Cochran (1989), with permission.

TABLE H   Gamma Function

Tabulation of Value of $\Gamma(n)$ versus n

n	$\Gamma(n)$	n	$\Gamma(n)$	n	$\Gamma(n)$	n	$\Gamma(n)$
1.00	1.00000	1.25	.90640	1.50	.88623	1.75	.91906
1.01	.99433	1.26	.90440	1.51	.88659	1.76	.92137
1.02	.98884	1.27	.90250	1.52	.88704	1.77	.92376
1.03	.98355	1.28	.90072	1.53	.88757	1.78	.92623
1.04	.97844	1.29	.89904	1.54	.88818	1.79	.92877
1.05	.97350	1.30	.89747	1.55	.88887	1.80	.93138
1.06	.96874	1.31	.89600	1.56	.88964	1.81	.93408
1.07	.96415	1.32	.89464	1.57	.89049	1.82	.93685
1.08	.95973	1.33	.89338	1.58	.89142	1.83	.93969
1.09	.95546	1.34	.89222	1.59	.89243	1.84	.94261
1.10	.95135	1.35	.89115	1.60	.89352	1.85	.94561
1.11	.94739	1.36	.89018	1.61	.89468	1.86	.94869
1.12	.94359	1.37	.88931	1.62	.89592	1.87	.95184
1.13	.93993	1.38	.88854	1.63	.89724	1.88	.95507
1.14	.93642	1.39	.88785	1.64	.89864	1.89	.95838
1.15	.93304	1.40	.88726	1.65	.90012	1.90	.96177
1.16	.92980	1.41	.88676	1.66	.90167	1.91	.96523
1.17	.92670	1.42	.88636	1.67	.90330	1.92	.96878
1.18	.92373	1.43	.88604	1.68	.90500	1.93	.97240
1.19	.92088	1.44	.88580	1.69	.90678	1.94	.97610
1.20	.91817	1.45	.88565	1.70	.90864	1.95	.97988
1.21	.91558	1.46	.88560	1.71	.91057	1.96	.98374
1.22	.91311	1.47	.88563	1.72	.91258	1.97	.98768
1.23	.91075	1.48	.88575	1.73	.91466	1.98	.99171
1.24	.90852	1.49	.88595	1.74	.91683	1.99	.99581
						2.00	1.00000

$$\Gamma(n) = \int_0^\infty e^{-x} x^{n-1} \, dx$$

$$\Gamma(n + 1) = n\Gamma(n)$$

$$\Gamma(1) = 1$$

$$\Gamma\left(\frac{1}{2}\right) = \sqrt{\pi}$$

$$\Gamma\left(\frac{n}{2}\right) = \left(\frac{n}{2} - 1\right)! = \begin{cases} \left(\frac{n}{2} - 1\right)\left(\frac{n}{2} - 2\right) \cdots (3) \cdot (2) \cdot (1) & \text{for } n \text{ even and } n > 2 \\ \left(\frac{n}{2} - 1\right)\left(\frac{n}{2} - 2\right) \cdots \left(\frac{3}{2}\right)\left(\frac{1}{2}\right)\sqrt{\pi} & \text{for } n \text{ odd and } n > 2 \end{cases}$$

Source: Lipson and Sheth (1973), with permission.

TABLE I Exact Critical Values for Use of the Analysis of Means

Exact Critical Values $h_{0.10}$ for the Analysis of Means
Significance Level = 0.10
Number of Means, k

DF	3	4	5	6	7	8	9	10	11	12	13	14	15	16	17	18	19	20	DF
3	3.16																		3
4	2.81	3.10																	4
5	2.63	2.88	3.05																5
6	2.52	2.74	2.91	3.03															6
7	2.44	2.65	2.81	2.92	3.02														7
8	2.39	2.59	2.73	2.85	2.94	3.02													8
9	2.34	2.54	2.68	2.79	2.88	2.95	3.01												9
10	2.31	2.50	2.64	2.74	2.83	2.90	2.96	3.02											10
11	2.29	2.47	2.60	2.70	2.79	2.86	2.92	2.97	3.02										11
12	2.27	2.45	2.57	2.67	2.75	2.82	2.88	2.93	2.98	3.02									12

TABLE I (*Continued*)

Exact Critical Values $h_{0.10}$ for the Analysis of Means

Significance Level = 0.10

Number of Means, k

DF	3	4	5	6	7	8	9	10	11	12	13	14	15	16	17	18	19	20	DF
13	2.25	2.43	2.55	2.65	2.73	2.79	2.85	2.90	2.95	2.99	3.03								13
14	2.23	2.41	2.53	2.63	2.70	2.77	2.83	2.88	2.92	2.96	3.00	3.03							14
15	2.22	2.39	2.51	2.61	2.68	2.75	2.80	2.85	2.90	2.94	2.97	3.01	3.04						15
16	2.21	2.38	2.50	2.59	2.67	2.73	2.79	2.83	2.88	2.92	2.95	2.99	3.02	3.05					16
17	2.20	2.37	2.49	2.58	2.65	2.72	2.77	2.82	2.86	2.90	2.93	2.97	3.00	3.03	3.05				17
18	2.19	2.36	2.47	2.56	2.64	2.70	2.75	2.80	2.84	2.88	2.92	2.95	2.98	3.01	3.03	3.06			18
19	2.18	2.35	2.46	2.55	2.63	2.69	2.74	2.79	2.83	2.87	2.90	2.94	2.96	2.99	3.02	3.04	3.06		19
20	2.18	2.34	2.45	2.54	2.62	2.68	2.73	2.78	2.82	2.86	2.89	2.92	2.95	2.98	3.00	3.03	3.05	3.07	20
24	2.15	2.32	2.43	2.51	2.58	2.64	2.69	2.74	2.78	2.82	2.85	2.88	2.91	2.93	2.96	2.98	3.00	3.02	24
30	2.13	2.29	2.40	2.48	2.55	2.61	2.66	2.70	2.74	2.77	2.81	2.84	2.86	2.89	2.91	2.93	2.96	2.98	30
40	2.11	2.27	2.37	2.45	2.52	2.57	2.62	2.66	2.70	2.73	2.77	2.79	2.82	2.85	2.87	2.89	2.91	2.93	40
60	2.09	2.24	2.34	2.42	2.49	2.54	2.59	2.63	2.66	2.70	2.73	2.75	2.78	2.80	2.82	2.84	2.86	2.88	60
120	2.07	2.22	2.32	2.39	2.45	2.51	2.55	2.59	2.62	2.66	2.69	2.71	2.74	2.76	2.78	2.80	2.82	2.84	120
∞	2.05	2.19	2.29	2.36	2.42	2.47	2.52	2.55	2.59	2.62	2.65	2.67	2.69	2.72	2.74	2.76	2.77	2.79	∞

Exact Critical Values $h_{0.05}$ for the Analysis of Means
Significance Level = 0.05
Number of Means, k

DF	3	4	5	6	7	8	9	10	11	12	13	14	15	16	17	18	19	20	DF
3	4.18																		3
4	3.56	3.89																	4
5	3.25	3.53	3.72																5
6	3.07	3.31	3.49	3.62															6
7	2.94	3.17	3.33	3.45	3.56														7
8	2.86	3.07	3.21	3.33	3.43	3.51													8
9	2.79	2.99	3.13	3.24	3.33	3.41	3.48												9
10	2.74	2.93	3.07	3.17	3.26	3.33	3.40	3.45											10
11	2.70	2.88	3.01	3.12	3.20	3.27	3.33	3.39	3.44										11
12	2.67	2.85	2.97	3.07	3.15	3.22	3.28	3.33	3.38	3.42									12
13	2.64	2.81	2.94	3.03	3.11	3.18	3.24	3.29	3.34	3.38	3.42								13
14	2.62	2.79	2.91	3.00	3.08	3.14	3.20	3.25	3.30	3.34	3.37	3.41							14
15	2.60	2.76	2.88	2.97	3.05	3.11	3.17	3.22	3.26	3.30	3.34	3.37	3.40						15

TABLE I (Continued)

Exact Critical Values $h_{0.05}$ for the Analysis of Means
Significance Level = 0.05
Number of Means, k

DF	3	4	5	6	7	8	9	10	11	12	13	14	15	16	17	18	19	20	DF
16	2.58	2.74	2.86	2.95	3.02	3.09	3.14	3.19	3.23	3.27	3.31	3.34	3.37	3.40					16
17	2.57	2.73	2.84	2.93	3.00	3.06	3.12	3.16	3.21	3.25	3.28	3.31	3.34	3.37	3.40				17
18	2.55	2.71	2.82	2.91	2.98	3.04	3.10	3.14	3.18	3.22	3.26	3.29	3.32	3.35	3.37	3.40			18
19	2.54	2.70	2.81	2.89	2.96	3.02	3.08	3.12	3.16	3.20	3.24	3.27	3.30	3.32	3.35	3.37	3.40		19
20	2.53	2.68	2.79	2.88	2.95	3.01	3.06	3.11	3.15	3.18	3.22	3.25	3.28	3.30	3.33	3.35	3.37	3.40	20
24	2.50	2.65	2.75	2.83	2.90	2.96	3.01	3.05	3.09	3.13	3.16	3.19	3.22	3.24	3.27	3.29	3.31	3.33	24
30	2.47	2.61	2.71	2.79	2.85	2.91	2.96	3.00	3.04	3.07	3.10	3.13	3.16	3.18	3.20	3.22	3.25	3.27	30
40	2.43	2.57	2.67	2.75	2.81	2.86	2.91	2.95	2.98	3.01	3.04	3.07	3.10	3.12	3.14	3.16	3.18	3.20	40
60	2.40	2.54	2.63	2.70	2.76	2.81	2.86	2.90	2.93	2.96	2.99	3.02	3.04	3.06	3.08	3.10	3.12	3.14	60
120	2.37	2.50	2.59	2.66	2.72	2.77	2.81	2.84	2.88	2.91	2.93	2.96	2.98	3.00	3.02	3.04	3.06	3.08	120
∞	2.34	2.47	2.56	2.62	2.68	2.72	2.76	2.80	2.83	2.86	2.88	2.90	2.93	2.95	2.97	2.98	3.00	3.02	∞

Exact Critical Values $h_{0.01}$ for the Analysis of Means

Significance Level = 0.01

Number of Means, k

DF	3	4	5	6	7	8	9	10	11	12	13	14	15	16	17	18	19	20	DF
3	7.51																		3
4	5.74	6.21																	4
5	4.93	5.29	5.55																5
6	4.48	4.77	4.98	5.16															6
7	4.18	4.44	4.63	4.78	4.90														7
8	3.98	4.21	4.38	4.52	4.63	4.72													8
9	3.84	4.05	4.20	4.33	4.43	4.51	4.59												9
10	3.73	3.92	4.07	4.18	4.28	4.36	4.43	4.49											10
11	3.64	3.82	3.96	4.07	4.16	4.23	4.30	4.36	4.41										11
12	3.57	3.74	3.87	3.98	4.06	4.13	4.20	4.25	4.31	4.35									12
13	3.51	3.68	3.80	3.90	3.98	4.05	4.11	4.17	4.22	4.26	4.30								13
14	3.46	3.63	3.74	3.84	3.92	3.98	4.04	4.09	4.14	4.18	4.22	4.26							14
15	3.42	3.58	3.69	3.79	3.86	3.92	3.98	4.03	4.08	4.12	4.16	4.19	4.22						15
16	3.38	3.54	3.65	3.74	3.81	3.87	3.93	3.98	4.02	4.06	4.10	4.14	4.17	4.20					16
17	3.35	3.50	3.61	3.70	3.77	3.83	3.89	3.93	3.98	4.02	4.05	4.09	4.12	4.14	4.17				17
18	3.33	3.47	3.58	3.66	3.73	3.79	3.85	3.89	3.94	3.97	4.01	4.04	4.07	4.10	4.12	4.15			18
19	3.30	3.45	3.55	3.63	3.70	3.76	3.81	3.86	3.90	3.94	3.97	4.00	4.03	4.06	4.08	4.11	4.13		19
20	3.28	3.42	3.53	3.61	3.67	3.73	3.78	3.83	3.87	3.90	3.94	3.97	4.00	4.02	4.05	4.07	4.09	4.12	20
24	3.21	3.35	3.45	3.52	3.58	3.64	3.69	3.73	3.77	3.80	3.83	3.86	3.89	3.91	3.94	3.96	3.98	4.00	24
30	3.15	3.28	3.37	3.44	3.50	3.55	3.59	3.63	3.67	3.70	3.73	3.76	3.78	3.81	3.83	3.85	3.87	3.89	30
40	3.09	3.21	3.29	3.36	3.42	3.46	3.50	3.54	3.58	3.60	3.63	3.66	3.68	3.70	3.72	3.74	3.76	3.78	40
60	3.03	3.14	3.22	3.29	3.34	3.38	3.42	3.46	3.49	3.51	3.54	3.56	3.59	3.61	3.63	3.64	3.66	3.68	60
120	2.97	3.07	3.15	3.21	3.26	3.30	3.34	3.37	3.40	3.42	3.45	3.47	3.49	3.51	3.53	3.55	3.56	3.58	120
∞	2.91	3.01	3.08	3.14	3.18	3.22	3.26	3.29	3.32	3.34	3.36	3.38	3.40	3.42	3.44	3.45	3.47	3.48	∞

TABLE I (*Continued*)

Exact Critical Values $h_{0.001}$ for the Analysis of Means

Significance Level = 0.001

Number of Means, k

DF	3	4	5	6	7	8	9	10	11	12	13	14	15	16	17	18	19	20	DF
3	16.4																		3
4	10.6	11.4																	4
5	8.25	8.79	9.19																5
6	7.04	7.45	7.76	8.00															6
7	6.31	6.65	6.89	7.09	7.25														7
8	5.83	6.12	6.32	6.49	6.63	6.75													8
9	5.49	5.74	5.92	6.07	6.20	6.30	6.40												9
10	5.24	5.46	5.63	5.76	5.87	5.97	6.05	6.13											10
11	5.05	5.25	5.40	5.52	5.63	5.71	5.79	5.86	5.92										11
12	4.89	5.08	5.22	5.33	5.43	5.51	5.58	5.65	5.71	5.76									12
13	4.77	4.95	5.08	5.18	5.27	5.35	5.42	5.48	5.53	5.58	5.63								13
14	4.66	4.83	4.96	5.06	5.14	5.21	5.28	5.33	5.38	5.43	5.48	5.51							14
15	4.57	4.74	4.86	4.95	5.03	5.10	5.16	5.21	5.26	5.31	5.35	5.39	5.42						15
16	4.50	4.66	4.77	4.86	4.94	5.00	5.06	5.11	5.16	5.20	5.24	5.28	5.31	5.34					16
17	4.44	4.59	4.70	4.78	4.86	4.92	4.98	5.03	5.07	5.11	5.15	5.18	5.22	5.25	5.28				17
18	4.38	4.53	4.63	4.72	4.79	4.85	4.90	4.95	4.99	5.03	5.07	5.10	5.14	5.16	5.19	5.22			18
19	4.33	4.47	4.58	4.66	4.73	4.79	4.84	4.88	4.93	4.96	5.00	5.03	5.06	5.09	5.12	5.14	5.17		19
20	4.29	4.42	4.53	4.61	4.67	4.73	4.78	4.83	4.87	4.90	4.94	4.97	5.00	5.03	5.05	5.08	5.10	5.12	20
24	4.16	4.28	4.37	4.45	4.51	4.56	4.61	4.65	4.69	4.72	4.75	4.78	4.81	4.83	4.86	4.88	4.90	4.92	24
30	4.03	4.14	4.23	4.30	4.35	4.40	4.44	4.48	4.51	4.54	4.57	4.60	4.62	4.64	4.67	4.69	4.71	4.72	30
40	3.91	4.01	4.09	4.15	4.20	4.25	4.29	4.32	4.35	4.38	4.40	4.43	4.45	4.47	4.49	4.50	4.52	4.54	40
60	3.80	3.89	3.96	4.02	4.06	4.10	4.14	4.17	4.19	4.22	4.24	4.27	4.29	4.30	4.32	4.33	4.35	4.37	60
120	3.69	3.77	3.84	3.89	3.93	3.96	4.00	4.03	4.05	4.07	4.09	4.11	4.13	4.15	4.16	4.17	4.19	4.21	120
∞	3.58	3.66	3.72	3.76	3.80	3.84	3.87	3.89	3.91	3.93	3.95	3.97	3.99	4.00	4.02	4.03	4.04	4.06	∞

Source: Nelson (1983), with permission of the American Society for Quality Control.

TABLE J Factors for Constructing Variables Control Charts

Observations in Sample n	Chart for Averages — Factors for Control Limits			Factors for Central Line		Chart for Standard Deviations — Factors for Control Limits				Chart for Ranges — Factors for Central Line			Factors for Control Limits			
	A	A_2	A_3	c_4	$1/c_4$	B_3	B_4	B_5	B_6	d_2	$1/d_2$	d_3	D_1	D_2	D_3	D_4
2	2.121	1.880	2.659	0.7979	1.2533	0	3.267	0	2.606	1.128	0.8865	0.853	0	3.686	0	3.267
3	1.732	1.023	1.954	0.8862	1.1284	0	2.568	0	2.276	1.693	0.5907	0.888	0	4.358	0	2.574
4	1.500	0.729	1.628	0.9213	1.0854	0	2.266	0	2.088	2.059	0.4857	0.880	0	4.698	0	2.282
5	1.342	0.577	1.427	0.9400	1.0638	0	2.089	0	1.964	2.326	0.4299	0.864	0	4.918	0	2.114
6	1.225	0.483	1.287	0.9515	1.0510	0.030	1.970	0.029	1.874	2.534	0.3946	0.848	0	5.078	0	2.004
7	1.134	0.419	1.182	0.9594	1.0423	0.118	1.882	0.113	1.806	2.704	0.3698	0.833	0.204	5.204	0.076	1.924
8	1.061	0.373	1.099	0.9650	1.0363	0.185	1.815	0.179	1.751	2.847	0.3512	0.820	0.388	5.306	0.136	1.864
9	1.000	0.337	1.032	0.9693	1.0317	0.239	1.761	0.232	1.707	2.970	0.3367	0.808	0.547	5.393	0.184	1.816
10	0.949	0.308	0.975	0.9727	1.0281	0.284	1.716	0.276	1.669	3.078	0.3249	0.797	0.687	5.469	0.223	1.777
11	0.905	0.285	0.927	0.9754	1.0252	0.321	1.679	0.313	1.637	3.173	0.3152	0.787	0.811	5.535	0.256	1.744
12	0.866	0.266	0.886	0.9776	1.0229	0.354	1.646	0.346	1.610	3.258	0.3069	0.778	0.922	5.594	0.283	1.717
13	0.832	0.249	0.850	0.9794	1.0210	0.382	1.618	0.374	1.585	3.336	0.2998	0.770	1.025	5.647	0.307	1.693
14	0.802	0.235	0.817	0.9810	1.0194	0.406	1.594	0.399	1.563	3.407	0.2935	0.763	1.118	5.696	0.328	1.672
15	0.775	0.223	0.789	0.9823	1.0180	0.428	1.572	0.421	1.544	3.472	0.2880	0.756	1.203	5.741	0.347	1.653
16	0.750	0.212	0.763	0.9835	1.0168	0.448	1.552	0.440	1.526	3.532	0.2831	0.750	1.282	5.782	0.363	1.637
17	0.728	0.203	0.739	0.9845	1.0157	0.466	1.534	0.458	1.511	3.588	0.2787	0.744	1.356	5.820	0.378	1.622
18	0.707	0.194	0.718	0.9854	1.0148	0.482	1.518	0.475	1.496	3.640	0.2747	0.739	1.424	5.856	0.391	1.608
19	0.688	0.187	0.698	0.9862	1.0140	0.497	1.503	0.490	1.483	3.689	0.2711	0.734	1.487	5.891	0.403	1.597
20	0.671	0.180	0.680	0.9869	1.0133	0.510	1.490	0.504	1.470	3.735	0.2677	0.729	1.549	5.921	0.415	1.585
21	0.655	0.173	0.663	0.9876	1.0126	0.523	1.477	0.516	1.459	3.778	0.2647	0.724	1.605	5.951	0.425	1.575
22	0.640	0.167	0.647	0.9882	1.0119	0.534	1.466	0.528	1.448	3.819	0.2618	0.720	1.659	5.979	0.434	1.566
23	0.626	0.162	0.633	0.9887	1.0114	0.545	1.455	0.539	1.438	3.858	0.2592	0.716	1.710	6.006	0.443	1.557
24	0.612	0.157	0.619	0.9892	1.0109	0.555	1.445	0.549	1.429	3.895	0.2567	0.712	1.759	6.031	0.451	1.548
25	0.600	0.153	0.606	0.9896	1.0105	0.565	1.435	0.559	1.420	3.931	0.2544	0.708	1.806	6.056	0.459	1.541

For $n > 25$

$$A = \frac{3}{\sqrt{n}}, \quad A_3 = \frac{3}{c_4\sqrt{n}}, \quad c_4 \approx \frac{4(n-1)}{4n-3},$$

$$B_3 = 1 - \frac{3}{c_4\sqrt{2(n-1)}}, \quad B_4 = 1 + \frac{3}{c_4\sqrt{2(n-1)}}, \quad B_5 = c_4 - \frac{3}{\sqrt{2(n-1)}}, \quad B_6 = c_4 + \frac{3}{\sqrt{2(n-1)}}$$

Source: Montgomery (1985), with permission.

TABLE K Poisson Distribution Factors

Decimal Confidence Level (c)	Poisson Distribution Confidence Factor B — Number of Failures (r)											
	0	1	2	3	4	5	6	7	8	9	10	
.999	6.908	9.233	11.229	13.062	14.794	16.455	18.062	19.626	21.156	22.657	24.134	.001
.99	4.605	6.638	8.406	10.045	11.604	13.108	14.571	16.000	17.403	18.783	20.145	.01
.95	2.996	4.744	6.296	7.754	9.154	10.513	11.842	13.148	14.435	15.705	16.962	.05
.90	2.303	3.890	5.322	6.681	7.994	9.275	10.532	11.771	12.995	14.206	15.407	.10
.85	1.897	3.372	4.723	6.014	7.267	8.495	9.703	10.896	12.078	13.249	14.411	.15
.80	1.609	2.994	4.279	5.515	6.721	7.906	9.075	10.232	11.380	12.519	13.651	.20
.75	1.386	2.693	3.920	5.109	6.274	7.423	8.558	9.684	10.802	11.914	13.020	.25
.70	1.204	2.439	3.616	4.762	5.890	7.006	8.111	9.209	10.301	11.387	12.470	.30
.65	1.050	2.219	3.347	4.455	5.549	6.633	7.710	8.782	9.850	10.913	11.974	.35
.60	0.916	2.022	3.105	4.175	5.237	6.292	7.343	8.390	9.434	10.476	11.515	.40
.55	0.798	1.844	2.883	3.916	4.946	5.973	7.000	8.021	9.043	10.064	11.083	.45
.50	0.693	1.678	2.674	3.672	4.671	5.670	6.670	7.669	8.669	9.669	10.668	.50
.45	0.598	1.523	2.476	3.438	4.406	5.378	6.352	7.328	8.305	9.284	10.264	.55
.40	0.511	1.376	2.285	3.211	4.148	5.091	6.039	6.991	7.947	8.904	9.864	.60
.35	0.431	1.235	2.099	2.988	3.892	4.806	5.727	6.655	7.587	8.523	9.462	.65
.30	0.357	1.097	1.914	2.764	3.634	4.517	5.411	6.312	7.220	8.133	9.050	.70

	1	2	3	4	5	6	7	8	9	10	11	
.25	0.288	0.961	1.727	2.535	3.369	4.219	5.083	5.956	6.838	7.726	8.620	.75
.20	0.223	0.824	1.535	2.297	3.090	3.904	4.734	5.576	6.428	7.289	8.157	.80
.15	0.162	0.683	1.331	2.039	2.785	3.557	4.348	5.154	5.973	6.802	7.639	.85
.10	0.105	0.532	1.102	1.745	2.432	3.152	3.895	4.656	5.432	6.221	7.021	.90
.05	0.051	0.355	0.818	1.366	1.970	2.613	3.285	3.981	4.695	5.425	6.169	.95
.01	0.010	0.149	0.436	0.823	1.279	1.786	2.330	2.906	3.508	4.130	4.771	.99
.001	0.001	0.045	0.191	0.429	0.740	1.107	1.521	1.971	2.453	2.961	3.492	.999
	1	2	3	4	5	6	7	8	9	10	11	Decimal Conf. Level (c)
					Number of Failures (r)							

Poisson Distribution Confidence Factor A

Applications of Table K

Total test time: $T = B_{r,c}/\rho_a$ for $\rho \leq \rho_a$ where ρ_a is a failure rate criterion, r is allowed number of test failures, and c is a confidence factor.

Confidence interval statements (time-terminated test); $\rho \leq B_{r,c}/T$ $\rho \geq A_{r,c}/T$

Examples: 1 failure test for a 0.0001 failures/hour criterion (i.e., 10,000-hr MTBF)

     95% confidence test: Total test time = 47,440 hr (i.e., 4.744/0.001)

5 failures in a total of 10,000 hr

     95% confident: $\rho \leq 0.0010513$ failures/hour (i.e., 10,513/10,000)

     95% confident: $\rho \geq 0.0001970$ failures/hour (i.e., 1,970/10,000)

     90% confidence: $0.0001970 \leq \rho \leq 0.0010513$

TABLE L   Weibull Mean: Percentage Fail Value for Given Weibull Slope

Weibull Slope	Percent Failed at the Mean	Weibull Slope	Percent Failed at the Mean
0.1	98.9	2.1	53.9
0.2	92.6	2.2	53.5
0.3	85.8	2.3	53.1
0.4	80.1	2.4	52.7
0.5	75.7	2.5	52.4
0.6	72.1	2.6	52.0
0.7	69.2	2.7	51.7
0.8	66.9	2.8	51.4
0.9	64.9	2.9	51.2
1.0	63.2	3.0	50.9
1.1	61.8	3.1	50.7
1.2	60.5	3.2	50.5
1.3	59.4	3.3	50.3
1.4	58.4	3.4	50.1
1.5	57.6	3.5	49.9
1.6	56.8	3.6	49.7
1.7	56.1	3.7	49.5
1.8	55.5	3.8	49.4
1.9	54.9	3.9	49.2
2.0	54.4	4.0	49.1

TABLE M1   Two-Level Full and Fractional Factorial Designs, 4 Trials

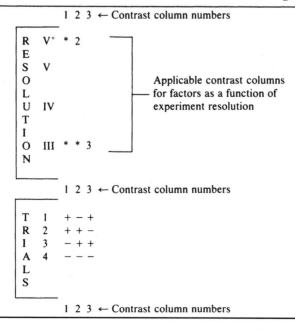

1 2 3 ← Contrast column numbers

```
R    V⁺  * 2
E
S    V
O                        Applicable contrast columns
L                      — for factors as a function of
U    IV                  experiment resolution
T
I
O    III  * * 3
N
```

1 2 3 ← Contrast column numbers

```
T  1   + − +
R  2   + + −
I  3   − + +
A  4   − − −
L
S
```

1 2 3 ← Contrast column numbers

TABLE M1 (*Continued*)

Instructions for Tables M1–M5: Creating a Two-Level Factorial Test Design Matrix[a]

---

1. Choose for the given number of two-level factors a table (i.e., M1–M5) such that the number of test trials yields the desired resolution, which is defined to be the following:

V^+: Full two-level factorial.

V: All main effects and two-factor interactions are not confounded with other main effects or two-factor interactions.

IV: All main effects are not confounded by two-factor interactions. Two-factor interactions are confounded with each other.

III: Main effects confounded with two-factor interactions.

The maximum number of factors for each trial matrix resolution is noted in the following:

	Experiment Resolution			
Number of Trials	V^+	V	IV	III
4	2			3
8	3		4	5–7
16	4	5	6–8	9–15
32	5	6	7–16	17–31
64	6	7–8	9–32	33–63

2. Look at the row of asterisks and numerics within the selected table corresponding to the desired resolution.

3. Begin from the left identifying columns designated by either an asterisk or numeric until the number of selected contrast columns equals the number of factors.

4. Record for each contrast column identified within step number three, the level states for each trial. Columns are included only if they have the asterisk or numeric resolution designator. A straightedge can be helpful to align the contrast numbers tabulated within the columns.

---

[a] See Example 30.1.

TABLE M2   Two-Level Full and Fractional Factorial Designs, 8 Trials[a]

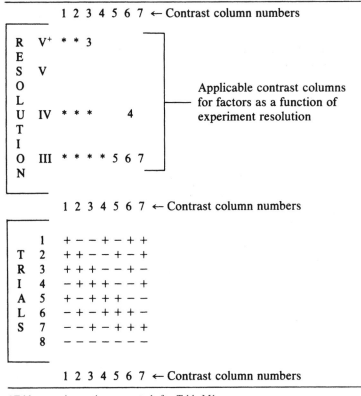

```
               1 2 3 4 5 6 7  ← Contrast column numbers

     R    V⁺   * * 3
     E
     S    V                                   Applicable contrast columns
     O                                    ─── for factors as a function of
     L                                        experiment resolution
     U    IV   * * *     4
     T
     I
     O    III  * * * * 5 6 7
     N
```

```
              1 2 3 4 5 6 7  ← Contrast column numbers

         1    + − − + − + +
    T    2    + + − − + − +
    R    3    + + + − − + −
    I    4    − + + + − − +
    A    5    + − + + + − −
    L    6    − + − + + + −
    S    7    − − + − + + +
         8    − − − − − − −

              1 2 3 4 5 6 7  ← Contrast column numbers
```

[a] Table usage instructions are noted after Table M1.
The 8, 16, 32, and 64 trial matrices in Tables M2–M5 were created from a computer program described by Diamond (1989).

TABLE M3 Two-Level Full and Fractional Factorial Design, 16 Trials[a]

Contrast column numbers →

		1	2	3	4	5	6	7	8	9	10	11	12	13	14	15
R	V+	*	*	*	4											
E																
S	V	*	*	*	*						5					
O																
L																
U	IV	*	*	*	*					*		6	7	8		
T																
I											1	1	1	1	1	1
O	III	*	*	*	*	*	*	*	*	9	0	1	2	3	4	5
N																

Applicable contrast columns for factors as a function of experiment resolution

Contrast column numbers →

TRIALS	1	2	3	4	5	6	7	8	9	10	11	12	13	14	15
1	+	−	−	+	−	−	+	+	−	+	−	+	+	+	
2	+	+	−	−	−	+	−	−	+	+	−	+	−	+	+
3	+	+	+	−	−	−	+	−	−	+	+	−	+	−	+
4	+	+	+	+	−	−	−	+	−	−	+	+	−	+	−
5	−	+	+	+	+	−	−	−	+	−	−	+	+	−	+
6	+	−	+	+	+	+	−	−	−	+	−	−	+	+	−
7	−	+	−	+	+	+	+	−	−	−	+	−	−	+	+
8	+	−	+	−	+	+	+	+	−	−	−	+	−	−	+
9	+	+	−	+	−	+	+	+	+	−	−	−	+	−	−
10	−	+	+	−	+	−	+	+	+	+	−	−	−	+	−
11	−	−	+	+	−	+	−	+	+	+	+	−	−	−	+
12	+	−	−	+	+	−	+	−	+	+	+	+	−	−	−
13	−	+	−	−	+	+	−	+	−	+	+	+	+	−	−
14	−	−	+	−	−	+	+	−	+	−	+	+	+	+	−
15	−	−	−	+	−	−	+	+	−	+	−	+	+	+	+
16	−	−	−	−	−	−	−	−	−	−	−	−	−	−	−

Contrast column numbers →

[a] Table usage instructions are noted in Table M1.

TABLE M4 Two-Level Full and Fractional Factorial Design, 32 Trials[a]

← Contrast column numbers

	1	2	3	4	5	6	7	8	9	10	11	12	13	14	15	16	17	18	19	20	21	22	23	24	25	26	27	28	29	30	31
R V+	*	*	*	*	*	5																									
E V	*	*	*	*	*	*	*																								
S																															
O						6																									
L V	*	*	*	*	*	*	*	7	8	9	10	11	12	13	14	15	16														
U IV	*	*	*	*	*	*	*	*7	8	9	10	11	12	13	14	15	16														
T																															
I III	*	*	*	*	*	*	*	*	*	*	*	*	*	*	*	*	17	18	19	20	21	22	23	24	25	26	27	28	29	30	31
O																															
N																															

Applicable contrast columns for factors as a function of experiment resolution

← Contrast column numbers

	1	2	3	4	5	6	7	8	9	10	11	12	13	14	15	16	17	18	19	20	21	22	23	24	25	26	27	28	29	30	31
1	+	−	−	−	+	−	−	+	−	−	+	−	+	+	−	+	+	+	−	+	+	−	−	−	+	−	−	+	+	−	+
2	+	+	−	−	−	+	−	−	+	−	−	+	−	+	+	−	+	+	+	−	+	+	−	−	−	+	−	−	+	+	−
3	+	+	+	−	−	−	+	−	−	+	−	−	+	−	+	+	−	+	+	+	−	+	+	−	−	−	+	−	−	+	+
4	+	+	+	+	−	−	−	+	−	−	+	−	−	+	−	+	+	−	+	+	+	−	+	+	−	−	−	+	−	−	+
5	+	+	+	+	+	−	−	−	+	−	−	+	−	−	+	−	+	+	−	+	+	+	−	+	+	−	−	−	+	−	−
6	−	+	+	+	+	+	−	−	−	+	−	−	+	−	−	+	−	+	+	−	+	+	+	−	+	+	−	−	−	+	−
7	−	−	+	+	+	+	+	−	−	−	+	−	−	+	−	−	+	−	+	+	−	+	+	+	−	+	+	−	−	−	+
8	+	−	−	+	+	+	+	+	−	−	−	+	−	−	+	−	−	+	−	+	+	−	+	+	+	−	+	+	−	−	−

	Trial	1	2	3	4	5	6	7	8	9	10	11	12	13	14	15	16	17	18	19	20	21	22	23	24	25	26	27	28	29	30	31
	9	+	+	−	−	+	+	+	+	+	−	−	−	+	+	−	+	+	+	−	+	−	+	−	−	−	−	+	−	−	+	−
	10	−	+	+	−	−	+	+	+	+	+	−	−	−	+	+	−	+	+	+	−	+	−	+	−	−	−	−	+	−	−	+
	11	+	−	+	+	−	−	+	+	+	+	+	−	−	−	+	+	−	+	+	+	−	+	−	+	−	−	−	−	+	−	−
T	12	−	+	−	+	+	−	−	+	+	+	+	+	−	−	−	+	+	−	+	+	+	−	+	−	+	−	−	−	−	+	−
R	13	−	−	+	−	+	+	−	−	+	+	+	+	+	−	−	−	+	+	−	+	+	+	−	+	−	+	−	−	−	−	+
I	14	+	−	−	+	−	+	+	−	−	+	+	+	+	+	−	−	−	+	+	−	+	+	+	−	+	−	+	−	−	−	−
A	15	−	+	−	−	+	−	+	+	−	−	+	+	+	+	+	−	−	−	+	+	−	+	+	+	−	+	−	+	−	−	−
L	16	−	−	+	−	−	+	−	+	+	−	−	+	+	+	+	+	−	−	−	+	+	−	+	+	+	−	+	−	+	−	−
S	17	−	−	−	+	−	−	+	−	+	+	−	−	+	+	+	+	+	−	−	−	+	+	−	+	+	+	−	+	−	+	−
	18	−	−	−	−	+	−	−	+	−	+	+	−	−	+	+	+	+	+	−	−	−	+	+	−	+	+	+	−	+	−	+
	19	+	−	−	−	−	+	−	−	+	−	+	+	−	−	+	+	+	+	+	−	−	−	+	+	−	+	+	+	−	+	−
	20	−	+	−	−	−	−	+	−	−	+	−	+	+	−	−	+	+	+	+	+	−	−	−	+	+	−	+	+	+	−	+
	21	+	−	+	−	−	−	−	+	−	−	+	−	+	+	−	−	+	+	+	+	+	−	−	−	+	+	−	+	+	+	−
	22	−	+	−	+	−	−	−	−	+	−	−	+	−	+	+	−	−	+	+	+	+	+	−	−	−	+	+	−	+	+	+
	23	+	−	+	−	+	−	−	−	−	+	−	−	+	−	+	+	−	−	+	+	+	+	+	−	−	−	+	+	−	+	+
	24	+	+	−	+	−	+	−	−	−	−	+	−	−	+	−	+	+	−	−	+	+	+	+	+	−	−	−	+	+	−	+
	25	+	+	+	−	+	−	+	−	−	−	−	+	−	−	+	−	+	+	−	−	+	+	+	+	+	−	−	−	+	+	−
	26	−	+	+	+	−	+	−	+	−	−	−	−	+	−	−	+	−	+	+	−	−	+	+	+	+	+	−	−	−	+	+
	27	+	−	+	+	+	−	+	−	+	−	−	−	−	+	−	−	+	−	+	+	−	−	+	+	+	+	+	−	−	−	+
	28	+	+	−	+	+	+	−	+	−	+	−	−	−	−	+	−	−	+	−	+	+	−	−	+	+	+	+	+	−	−	−
	29	−	+	+	−	+	+	+	−	+	−	+	−	−	−	−	+	−	−	+	−	+	+	−	−	+	+	+	+	+	−	−
	30	−	−	+	+	−	+	+	+	−	+	−	+	−	−	−	−	+	−	−	+	−	+	+	−	−	+	+	+	+	+	−
	31	−	−	−	+	+	−	+	+	+	−	+	−	+	−	−	−	−	+	−	−	+	−	+	+	−	−	+	+	+	+	+
	32	−	−	−	−	−	−	−	−	−	−	−	−	−	−	−	−	−	−	−	−	−	−	−	−	−	−	−	−	−	−	−
	← Contrast column numbers	1	2	3	4	5	6	7	8	9	10	11	12	13	14	15	16	17	18	19	20	21	22	23	24	25	26	27	28	29	30	31

[a] Table usage instructions are noted within Table M1.

TABLE M5 Two-Level Full and Fractional Factorial Design, 64 Trials^a

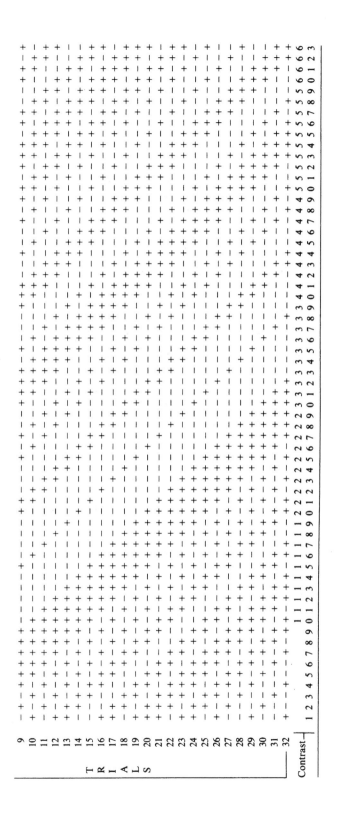

TABLE M5 (*Continued*)[a]

Contrast: 1 2 3 4 5 6 7 8 9 10 11 12 13 14 15 16 17 18 19 20 21 22 23 24 25 26 27 28 29 30 31 32 33 34 35 36 37 38 39 40 41 42 43 44 45 46 47 48 49 50 51 52 53 54 55 56 57 58 59 60 61 62 63 64 65 66

TRIALS 43–64

[a] Table usage instructions are noted within Table M1.

TABLE N1 Two-Factor Interaction Confounding in the Contrast Columns of the Tables M1–M5 Resolutions V Fractional Factorial Designs[a]

4 Trials

1	2	3
*A	*B	AB

8 Trials
Not Applicable

16 Trials

1	2	3	4	5	6	7	8	9	10	11	12	13	14	15
*A	*B	*C	*D	AB	BC	CD	ABD CE	AC	BD	ABC DE	BCD AE	ABCD *E	ACD BE	AD

32 Trials

1	2	3	4	5	6	7	8	9	10	11	12	13	14	15	16	17	18	19	20	21
*A	*B	*C	*D	*E	AC	BD	CE	ACD	BDE	AE	ABC	BCD	CDE	ACDE BF	ABCDE *F	ABDE CF	ABE	AB	BC	CD

22	23	24	25	26	27	28	29	30	31
DE	ACE	ABCD EF	BCDE AF	ADE	ABCE DF	ABD	BCE	AD	BE

64 Trials

1	2	3	4	5	6	7	8	9	10	11	12	13	14	15	16	17	18	19	20	21
*A	*B	*C	*D	*E	*F	AB	BC	CD	DE	EF	ABF	AC	BD	CE	DF	ABE	BCF	ABCD *G	BCDE	CDEF

22	23	24	25	26	27	28	29	30	31	32	33	34	35	36	37	38	39	40	41	42
ABDEF GH	ACEF *H	ADF	AE	BF	ABC DG	BCD AG	CDE	DEF	ABEF	ACF EH	AD	BE	CF	ABD CG	BCE	CDF	ABDE	BCEF	ABCDF FG	ACDE

43	44	45	46	47	48	49	50	51	52	53	54	55	56	57	58	59	60	61	62	63
BDEF GH	ABCEF BH	ACDF	ADE	BEF	ABCF	ACD BG	BDE	CEF AH	ABDF	ACE FH	BDF	ABCE	BCDF	ABCDE EG	BCDEF	ABCDEF	ACDEF DH	ADEF	AEF CH	AF

[a] The higher-order terms were used when generating the design. Main effects are denoted by an asterisk.

TABLE N2 Two-Factor Interaction Confounding in the Contrast Columns of the Tables M1–M5 Resolutions IV Fractional Factorial Designs[a]

8 Trials

1	2	3	4	5	6	7
*A	*B	*C	AB	BC	ABC	AC
			CD	AD	*D	BD

16 Trials

1	2	3	4	5	6	7	8	9	10	11	12	13	14	15
*A	*B	*C	*D	AB	BC	CD	ABD	AC	BD	ABC	BCD	ABCD	ACD	AD
				DE	AF	EF	*E	BF	AE	*F	*G	CE	*H	BE
				CF	DG	BG		EG	CG			DF		FG
				GH	EH	AH		DH	FH			AG		CH
												BH		

32 Trials

1	2	3	4	5	6	7	8	9	10	11	12	13	14	15	16	17	18	19	20	21
*A	*B	*C	*D	*E	AC	BD	CE	ACD	BDE	AE	ABC	BCD	CDE	ACDE	ABCDE	ABDE	ABE	AB	BC	CD
					DF	EG	GI	*F	*G	FJ	*H	*I	*J	EF	*K	AG	*L	CH	AH	AF
					BH	FH	DJ			IK				GH		HJ		FI	DI	BL
					GK	CI	HL			BL				AJ		CK		JK	GJ	EJ
					EM	KM	AM			CM				BK		DL		EL	LM	KL
					JN	LN	FN			DN				IL		IM		GN	KN	MN
					IO	AO	KO			GO				DM		BN		DO	FO	HO
					LP	JP	BP			HP				CN		EO		MP	EP	GP
														OP		FP				

22	23	24	25	26	27	28	29	30	31
DE	ACE	ABCD	BCDE	ADE	ABCE	ABD	BCE	AD	BE
BG	*M	BF	CG	*N	FG	*O	*P	CF	DG
CJ		DH	EI		EH			HI	IJ
HK		AI	BJ		DK			GL	FK
FM		EK	AK		CL			JM	AL
AN		JL	FL		BM			EN	HM
LO		GM	HN		IN			BO	NO
IP		CO	MO		JO			KP	CP
		NP	DP		AP				

TABLE N2 (Continued)[a]

64 Trials

1	2	3	4	5	6	7	8	9	10	11	12	13	14	15	16	17	18	19	20	21
*A	*B	*C	*D	*E	*F	AB	BC	CD	DE	EF	ABF	AC	BD	CE	DF	ABE	BCF	ABCD	BCDE	CDEF
						FG	FI	BM	GJ	GH	*G	GI	GK	HL	HJ	*H	*I	IK	EM	JL
						EH	AL	EN	CN	DO		BL	CM	DN	AK			DL	BN	FN
						CL	DM	KP	FO	JQ		FP	AQ	BR	IM			AM	IO	CO
						JO	GP	LQ	HQ	IR		MQ	NR	OS	EO			HN	JP	ES
						IP	ER	FS	MR	NS		HR	IS	JT	GQ			CQ	DR	HT
						DQ	KT	GT	TU	LU		KS	PT	GU	CS			GS	KU	QU
						ST	QX	JU	AV	KV		NV	HV	IW	LT			FT	LV	PV
						MX	NY	AX	BY	BW		UW	OW	VX	PX			OU	SW	MW
						VY	WZ	RY	SZ	CZ		DX	LX	MY	WY			RV	HX	IY
						UZ	Ha	OZ	Xa	Pa		Ea	EY	FZ	NZ			BX	CY	DZ
						Ra	Sb	Va	Wb	Yb		Tb	Fb	Aa	Bb			JZ	Qa	Ka
						Kb	Vc	Ib	Lc	Tc		Yc	ac	Qc	Uc			Ya	Zb	Rb
						Nc	Od	Hc	Id	Md		Jd	Zd	bd	Rd			Pb	Ac	Gc
						de	Je	Wd	Pe	Xe		Oe	Ue	Ke	ae			Ec	Fd	Bd
						Wf	Uf	ef	Kf	Af		ZJ	Jf	Pf	Vf			We	Ge	Ae
																		df	Tf	Xf

22	23	24	25	26	27	28	29	30	31	32	33	34	35	36	37	38	39	40	41	42
ABDEF	ACEF	ADF	AE	BF	ABC	BCD	CDE	DEF	ABEF	ACF	AD	BE	CF	ABD	BCE	CDF	ABDE	BCEF	ABCDF	ACDE
*J	HI	*K	BH	AG	*L	*M	*N	*O	EG	*P	FK	AH	BI	*Q	*R	*S	DH	EI	*T	IJ
	JM		KO	CI					FH		LM	JK	GL				FJ	MO		HM
	KN		LR	LP					DI		BQ	MN	NO				LN	HP		AN
	EP		IU	KQ					OQ		PS	CR	AP				GO	FR		OP
	GR		DV	MS					PR		IT	PU	DS				EQ	AU		QR
	BU		GW	JV					NT		EV	QV	QT				SU	TV		CV

Design column assignments (columns 43–63). Generators (bold, higher‑order terms) are shown with the effects in each alias set; main effects are marked with an asterisk.

Col	Generator	Entries
43	BDEF	AJ, HK, IN, BO, RS, GV, DW, UX, FY, MZ, Ta, Eb, Pc, Cd, Le, Qf
44	ABCEF	*U
45	ACDF	CK, GM, DP, IQ, JR, AS, BT, FX, UY, VZ, Oa, Lb, Wc, Hd, Ee, Nf
46	ADE	*V
47	BEF	*W
48	ABCF	CG, AI, FL, KM, JN, BP, QS, DT, EU, HZ, Wa, Xb, Oc, Vd, Ye, Rf
49	ACD	*X
50	BDE	*Y
51	CEF	*Z
52	ABDF	DG, EJ, BK, HO, MP, FQ, LS, CT, NU, VW, IX, Ab, Zc, ad, Re, Yf
53	ACE	*a
54	BDF	*b
55	ABCE	CH, EL, NQ, AR, JS, OT, FU, MV, PW, XY, GZ, Ba, Dc, Kd, be, If
56	BCDF	DI, KL, FM, PQ, OR, BS, AT, UV, NW, GX, YZ, Ja, Cb, Ed, He, cf
57	ABCDE	*c
58	BCDEF	*d
59	ABCDEF	CJ, GN, LO, KR, HS, ET, DU, IV, WX, PY, QZ, ab, Fc, Ad, Be, Mf
60	ACDEF	*e
61	ADEF	BJ, EK, AO, NP, RT, MU, FV, QW, GY, XZ, Sa, Hb, Ic, Ld, Ce, Df
62	AEF	*f
63	AF	AF, BG, DK, IL, CP, MT, RU, OV, HW, SX, JY, Za, Qb, cd, Ne, Ef

Upper‑portion (continuation) blocks:

1	CU, AW, KY, LZ, Ia, Vb, Sc, Xd, Me, Bf
2	BV, KW, RX, AY, TZ, Ma, Cc, Pd, Ie, bf
3	JW, CX, HY, Na, Gb, Rc, Ud, Ze, Of
4	SV, LW, OX, TY, AZ, Fa, bc, Qd, De, Cf
5	NX, QY, PZ, Ca, Jb, Mc, Td, Se, Ff
6	EW, TX, OY, RZ, Ua, Db, Nd, ce, Hf
7	TW, EX, LY, KZ, Da, Ub, Bc, Gd, Fe, Sf
8	FW, DY, IZ, La, Ob, Xc, Sd, Te, Ve, af
9	HU, RW, KX, EZ, Mb, Jc, Yd, Ve, af
10	CW, JX, SY, BZ, Ga, Nb, Kc, Dd, Qe, If

[a] The higher-order terms were used when generating the design. Main effects are denoted by an asterisk.

TABLE N3 Two-Factor Interaction Confounding in the Contrast Columns of the Tables M1–M5 Resolutions III Fractional Factorial Designs[a]

8 Trials

1	2	3	4	5	6	7
*A	*B	*C	AB	BC	ABC	AC
BD	AD	BE	*D	*E	CD	DE
EF	CE	DF	CF	AF	AE	BF
CG	FG	AG	EG	DG	*F	*G
					BG	

16 Trials

1	2	3	4	5	6	7	8	9	10	11	12	13	14	15
							ABD			ABC	BCD	ABCD	ACD	
*A	*B	*C	*D	AB	BC	CD	DE	AC	BD	CE	DF	EG	AG	AD
BE	AE	BF	CG	*E	*F	*G	*H	EF	FG	AF	BG	CH	FH	BH
CI	CF	DG	EH	DH	EI	FJ	AJ	*I	AH	GH	HI	IJ	DI	GI
HJ	DJ	AI	BJ	FI	GJ	HK	GK	BK	*J	BI	CJ	DK	JK	EJ
FK	IK	EK	FL	CK	AK	BL	IL	HL	CL	*K	*L	AL	EL	KL
LM	GL	JL	KM	GM	DL	EM	CM	JM	IM	DM	AM	*M	BM	FM
GN	MN	HM	IN	LN	HN	AN	FN	DN	KN	JN	EN	BN	*N	CN
DO	HO	NO	AO	JO	MO	IO	BO	GO	EO	LO	KO	FO	CO	*O

32 Trials

1	2	3	4	5	6	7	8	9	10	11	12	13	14	15	16	17	18	19	20	21
*A	*B	*C	*D	*E	AC	BD	CE	ACD	BDE	AE	ABC	BCD	CDE	ACDE	ABCDE	ABDE	ABE	AB	BC	CD
CF	DG	AF	BG	CH	*F	*G	*H	DF	EG	FH	BF	CG	DH	EI	FJ	AJ	BK	CL	AL	AI
EK	FL	EH	FI	GJ	DI	EJ	FK	*I	*J	*K	GI	HJ	IK	JL	KM	GK	HL	IM	DM	BM
NO	OP	GM	HN	AK	HK	IL	JM	GL	HM	IN	*L	*M	*N	AN	BO	LN	MO	NP	JN	EN
JQ	KR	PQ	QR	IO	BL	CM	DN	KN	LO	MP	JO	KP	AO	*O	*P	CP	DQ	ER	OQ	KO

```
PR  GT  *U  HV  SX  WZ  Qa  Lb  Jc  Fd  Ye
FS  *T  GU  RW  VY  PZ  Ka  Ib  Ec  Xd  He
*S  FT  QV  UX  OY  JZ  Ha  Db  Wc  Gd  Ke
*R  ES  PU  TW  NX  IY  GZ  Ca  Vb  Fc  Jd  Ae
*Q  DR  OT  SV  MW  HX  FY  BZ  Ua  Eb  Ic  de
CQ  NS  RU  LV  GW  EX  AY  TZ  Da  Hb  cd  Ie
BP  MR  QT  KU  FV  DW  SY  CZ  Ga  bc  Hd  Xe
LQ  PS  JT  EU  CV  RX  BY  FZ  ab  Gc  Wd  Me
OR  IS  DT  BU  QW  AX  EY  Za  Fb  Vc  Ld  Ne
NQ  HR  CS  AT  PV  DX  YZ  Ea  Ub  Kc  Md  We
GQ  BR  OU  CW  XY  DZ  Ta  Jb  Lc  Vd  Se
FP  AQ  NT  BV  WX  CY  SZ  Ia  Kb  Uc  Rd  De
EO  MS  AU  VW  BX  RY  HZ  Ja  Tb  Oc  Cd  Pe
LR  UV  AW  QX  GY  IZ  Sa  Pb  Bc  Od  Te
KQ  TU  PW  FX  HY  RZ  Oa  Ab  Nc  Sd  Ve
JP  ST  OV  EW  GX  QY  NZ  Mb  Rc  Ud  ae
RS  NU  DV  FW  PX  MY  La  Qb  Tc  Zd  Be
MT  CU  EV  OW  LX  KZ  Pa  Sb  Yc  Ad  Je
LS  BT  DU  NV  KW  JY  Ra  Xb  Id  ce
AS  CT  MU  JV  IX  QZ  Wa  Hc  bd  Ee
BS  LT  IU  HW  MX  PY  VZ  Gb  ac  Dd  Re

31  BE   DJ  MN  IP  AR  KS  HT  GV  LW  OX  UY  Fa  Zb  Cc  Qd  *e
30  AD   CI  LM  HO  JR  GS  FU  KV  NW  TX  EZ  Ya  Bb  Pc  *d  Qe
29  BCE  BH  KL  GN  IQ  FR  ET  JU  MV  SW  DY  XZ  Aa  Ob  *c  Pd  Ce
28  ABD  AG  JK  FM  HP  EQ  DS  IT  LU  RV  CX  WY  Na  *b  Oc  Bd  Ze
27  ABCE IJ  EL  GO  DP  CR  HS  KT  QU  BW  VX  MZ  *a  Nb  Ac  Yd  Fe
26  ADE  HI  DK  FN  CO  BQ  GR  JS  PT  AV  UW  LY  *Z  Ma  Xc  Ed  be
25  BCDE GH  CJ  EM  BN  AP  FQ  IR  OS  TV  KX  *Y  LZ  Wb  Dc  ad  Ue
24  ABCD FG  BI  DL  AM  EP  HQ  NR  SU  JW  *X  KY  UZ  Va  Cb  Zc  Td  Oe
23  ACE  EF  AH  CK  DO  GP  MQ  RT  IV  *W  TY  JX  UZ  Ba  Yb  Sc  Nd  Le
22  DE   BJ  CN  FO  LP  QS  HU  *V  IW  TY  AZ  Xa  Rb  Mc  Kd  Ge
```

TABLE N3 *(Continued)*[a]

64 Trials

1	2	3	4	5	6	7	8	9	10	11	12	13	14	15	16	17	18	19	20	21
*A	*B	*C	*D	*E	*F	AB	BC	CD	DE	EF	ABF	AC	BD	CE	DF	ABE	BCF	ABCD	BCDE	CDEF
						*G	*H	*I	*J	*K	FG	GH	HI	IJ	JK	EG	FH	GI	HJ	IK

22	23	24	25	26	27	28	29	30	31	32	33	34	35	36	37	38	39	40	41	42
ABDEF	ACEF	ADF	AE	BF	ABC	BCD	CDE	DEF	ABEF	ACF	AD	BE	CF	ABD	BCE	CDF	ABDE	BCEF	ABCDF	ACDE
JL	KM	LN	MO	BF	CG	DH	EI	FJ	GK	HL	IM	JN	KO	DG	EH	FI	GJ	HK	IL	JM
PQ	QR	AP	BQ	AL	AH	BI	CJ	DK	EL	FM	GN	HO	IP	AN	BO	CP	DQ	ER	FS	GT
*V	*W	RS	ST	NP	BM	CN	DO	EP	FQ	GR	HS	AQ	BR	LP	MQ	NR	OS	PT	QU	RV
Ua	Vb	*X	*Y	CR	OQ	PR	QS	RT	SU	TV	UW	IT	JU	JQ	KR	LS	MT	NU	OV	PW
Wb	Xc	Wc	Xd	TU	DS	AS	BT	CU	DV	EW	FX	VX	WY	CS	DT	EU	FV	GW	HX	IY
Gd	He	Yd	Ze	*Z	UV	ET	FU	GV	HW	IX	JY	GY	HZ	KV	LW	MX	NY	OZ	Pa	Qb
De	Ef	If	Jg	Ye	*a	VW	WX	XY	YZ	Za	ab	KZ	La	XZ	Ya	Zb	ac	bd	ce	Ac
TJ	Ug	Fg	Gh	af	ZJ	*b	*c	*d	*e	*f	*g	bc	cd	la	Jb	Kc	Ld	Me	Nf	df
Xh	Yi	Vh	Wi	Kh	bg	ag	bh	ci	dj	Ai	Bj	*h	Af	Mb	Nc	Od	Pe	Qf	Rg	Og
Kj	Lk	Zj	ak	Hi	Li	ch	di	ej	fk	ek	fl	Ck	*i	de	ef	fg	gh	hi	ü	sh
Fm	Gn	Ml	Nm	Xj	ij	Mj	Nk	Ol	Pm	Qn	Ro	gm	Dl	Bg	Ch	Di	Ej	Fk	Gl	jk
Oo	Pp	Ho	Ip	bl	Yk	Jk	Kl	Lm	Mn	No	Op	in	hn	*j	*k	*l	*m	*n	*o	Hm
Rp	Sq	Qq	Rr	On	cm	Zl	am	bn	co	dp	eq	Sp	jo	Em	Fn	Go	Hp	lq	Jr	*p
Aq	Br	Tr	Us	Jq	Po	dn	eo	fp	gq	hr	is	Pq	Tq	io	jp	kq	lr	Ar	Bs	Ks
Ir	Js	Cs	Dt	Ss	Kr	Qp	Ap	Bq	Cr	Ds	Et	fr	Qr	kp	lq	mr	ns	ms	nt	Ct
ks	It	Kt	Lu	Vt	Tt	Ls	Rq	Sr	Ts	Ut	Vu	ji	gs	Ur	Vs	As	Bt	ot	pu	ou
Zt	au	mu	nv	Eu	Wu	Uu	Mt	Nu	Au	Bv	Cw	Fu	ku	Rs	Si	Wt	Xu	Cu	Dv	qv
gu	hv	bv	cw	Mv	Fv	Xv	Vu	Ww	Xx	Yy	Qx	Wv	Gv	ht	iu	Tu	Uv	Yv	Zw	Ew
cv	dw	iw	jx	ow	Nw	Gw	Yw	Zx	ay	bz	Zz	Dx	Xw	lv	mw	jv	kw	Vw	Wx	ax
mw	ox	ex	fy	dx	px	Ox	Hx	by	Jz	Ka	cα	Ry	Ey	Hw	Lx	nx	Ax	lx	my	Xy
Sy	Ay	py	qz	ky	ey	qy	Py	Qz	Ra	Sβ	Lβ	aa	Sz	Yx	Zy	Jy	oy	By	Cz	nz
Ez	Tz	Bz	Ca	gz	lz	fz	rz	sa	tβ	uγ	Tγ	dβ	bβ	Fz	Ga	az	Kz	pz	qα	Da
YB	Fα	Uα	Vβ	rα	ha	ma	ga	Hβ	iγ	jδ	vδ	Mγ	eγ	Ta	Uβ	Hβ	ba	La	Mβ	rβ
Iγ	Zγ	Gβ	Hγ	Dβ	sβ	iβ	nβ	oγ	pδ	qe	ke	Uδ	Nδ	cγ	Aγ	Vγ	Iγ	cβ	dγ	Nγ
aδ	mδ	aδ	be	Wγ	Eγ	sγ	jγ	kδ	le	mζ	rζ	we	xζ	fβ	dδ	Bδ	Wδ	Jδ	Aδ	eδ
ie	Bε	ne	cζ	Iδ	Xδ	Fδ	uδ	ve	wζ	χη	mη	lζ	mη	Oe	ge	ee	Ce	Xe	Ke	Be
Mζ	jζ	γζ	δη	cζ	Je	Ye	Ge	Hζ	Lη	Jθ	yθ	sη	tθ	Wζ	Pζ	hζ	fζ	Dζ	Yζ	Lζ
Cη	Nη	kη	lθ	pη	dη	Kζ	Zζ	aη	bθ	cι	dκ	oθ	pι	yη	Xη	Qη	iη	gη	Eη	Zη
Hθ	Dθ	Oθ	Pι	eθ	qθ	eθ	Lη	Mθ	Nι	Oκ	PA	zι	αχ	nθ	zθ	Yθ	Rθ	Sι	hθ	Fθ
Bι	lι	Eι	Fκ	mι	ζι	rι	fι	gκ	Bκ	CA		Lχ	MA	uι	oι	aι	Zι	αχ	kι	iι
Nκ	Cκ	Jκ	KΛ	Qκ	nκ	ηκ	sκ	tΛ	hΛ			eλ		qκ	vκ	pκ	βκ	γΛ	Tκ	lκ
xλ	OΛ	DΛ		GΛ	RΛ	oΛ	θΛ							βΛ	rΛ	wΛ	qΛ		bλ	UΛ

TABLE N3 (Continued)[a]

43	44	45	46	47	48	49	50	51	52	53	54	55	56	57	58	59	60	61	62	63
BDEF	ABCEF	ACDF	ADE	BEF	ABCF	ACD	BDE	CEF	ABDF	ACE	BDF	ABCE	BCDF	ABCDE	BCDEF	ABCDEF	ACDEF	ADEF	AEF	AF
KN	LO	MP	AJ	BK	CL	AI	BJ	CK	DL	EM	FN	GO	HP	IQ	JR	KS	LT	MU	AK	AF
HU	IV	JW	NQ	OR	AR	DM	EN	FO	GP	AO	BP	CQ	DR	ES	FT	GU	AU	BV	NV	BL
AV	BW	CX	KX	LY	PS	BS	CT	DU	EV	HQ	IR	JS	KT	LU	MV	NW	DW	EX	CW	OW
SW	TX	UY	DY	EZ	MZ	QT	RU	SV	TW	FW	GX	HY	IZ	Ja	Kb	Lc	OX	PY	JX	DX
QX	RY	SZ	Ob	Wa	Fa	Na	Ob	Pc	Qd	UX	VY	WZ	Xa	Yb	Zc	Lc	Ad	Ne	FY	KY
JZ	Ka	Lb	Hc	Fa	Xb	Gb	Hc	Id	Je	CY	DZ	Ea	Fb	Gc	Hd	Lc	Md	Ne	QZ	GZ
Rc	Sd	Te	Zd	Ub	Vc	Yc	Zd	Re	Kf	Re	Sf	Tg	Uh	Vi	Wj	Xk	Ne	be	Be	Ra
Bd	Ce	Df	Xe	Nd	Oe	Wd	Xe	Kf	Zg	KJ	Lg	Mh	Ni	Oj	Pk	Ql	Jf	cf	Of	Cf
eg	fh	gi	Pf	Ae	Bf	Pf	Qg	ae	bf	ah	dh	ei	fj	gk	hl	im	Ne	be	dg	Pg
Ph	Qi	Rj	Cg	Vg	Wh	Cg	Dh	Yf	Si	cg	bi	cj	dk	Oj	hl	im	Yl	Kg	Lh	eh
Ti	Uj	Vk	Xi	Fh	Gi	Xi	Yj	Rh	Fj	Tj	Uk	Vl	Wm	Xn	Yo	Zm	Sn	Zm	an	Mi
kl	lm	Al	Hj	ik	jl	Hj	Ik	Ei	al	Gk	Hl	Im	Jn	Ko	Lp	Eo	ho	ko	To	bo
In	An	mn	km	Tl	Um	km	Am	Zk	Km	bm	cn	do	ep	fq	gr	hs	it	ip	lp	Up
*q	Jo	Bo	Vn	Xm	Yn	Vn	In	Jl	Co	Ln	Mo	Np	Oq	Pr	Qs	Rt	Su	Gq	jq	mq
Lt	*r	Kp	Zo	Cn	Do	Zo	Wo	Bn	np	Dp	Eq	Fr	Gs	Ht	Iu	Jv	br	Gq	Hr	kr
Du	Mu	*s	Ep	op	pq	Ep	ap	mo	Yq	Zr	as	bt	cu	dv	ew	fx	Os	Fr	cs	ls
pv	Ev	Nv	qr	Dq	Er	qr	rs	Xp	cr	ds	et	fu	gv	hw	ix	jy	it	Pt	dt	dt
rw	qw	Fw	Fs	Mr	Ns	Fs	Gt	bq	Hs	It	Ju	Kv	Lw	su	tv	uw	Su	ju	Gu	Qu
Fx	sx	rx	Ot	*u	*v	Ot	Gi	Gr	tu	uv	vw	wx	r	Pr	Qs	Jv	Kw	Tv	kv	Hv
by	Gy	ty	*w	Px	Qz	*w	*x	st	Iv	bt	as	Kv	cu	Ht	Iu	fx	vx	Lx	Uw	lw
Yz	cz	Hz	Rz	Hy	Iz	Rz	Sa	Hu	Rw	Jw	Kx	wx	Lw	su	tv	fy	gy	wy	My	Vx
oα	Zα	da	Iα	tα	uα	Ja	Pu	Iv	*z	Sx	Ty	Ly	cu	dv	ew	fy	gy	hz	xz	Nz
Eβ	pβ	aβ	vβ	vβ	wβ	va	*x	*z	Aβ	*α	Az	Uz	xy	hw	ix	Oz	kz	hz	ia	ya
sγ	Fγ	qγ	wγ	Jγ	Kγ	vβ	Kβ	Tβ	Uγ	Bγ	*β	wx	Mz	yz	za	aβ	Pa	la	iα	jβ
Oδ	tδ	Gδ	xδ	fδ	gδ	xγ	wy	Ly	Mδ	Vδ	Az	Ly	Va	Na	Oβ	Bγ	Qβ	Qβ	mβ	nγ
fε	Pε	uε	yδ	cε	dε	yδ	yδ	xδ	yε	Nε	*β	Uz	Vα	Wβ	Xγ	Yδ	By	By	Rγ	Sδ
Cζ	gζ	Qζ	Mζ	sζ	iζ	he	Me	ze	aζ	zζ	We	De	Cβ	Dγ	Eδ	Fe	Ze	Re	δε	eζ
Mη	Dη	hη	iη	Iη	Jη	eζ	iζ	Nζ	Oη	βη	Oζ	Xζ	Yη	Dγ	*ζ	Aζ	Gζ	δε	Sζ	Tη
aθ	Nθ	Eθ	uθ	wη	xθ	uη	fη	Jη	kθ	Pθ	αη	ββ	Yη	*ε	Aη	Bθ	Hη	aζ	bη	cθ
Gι	bι	Oι	Kι	xθ	Tι	Kθ	vθ	gθ	gι	lι	Qθ	ββ	Qθ	Zθ	Gθ	Cθ	Hη	Hη	lθ	Jι
jκ	Hκ	Pκ	yι	ji	kκ	yι	Li	wι	xκ	ix	Qι	δ	γι	Rι	aι	Hι	Cι	*ι	Dι	Jι
mλ	kλ	dλ	Vλ	Gκ	HΛ	IΛ	zκ	Mκ	Nλ	yλ	mκ	Rκ	εκ	δκ	Sκ	bκ	Iκ	Dκ	*κ	Eκ
				QΛ	HΛ	IΛ	VΛ	aλ	NΛ	yΛ	jΛ	nΛ	SΛ	ζΛ	eΛ	TΛ	cΛ	JΛ	EΛ	*Λ

[a] The higher-order terms were used when generating the design. Main effects are denoted by an asterisk.

TABLE O Pass/Fail Functional Test Matrix Coverage

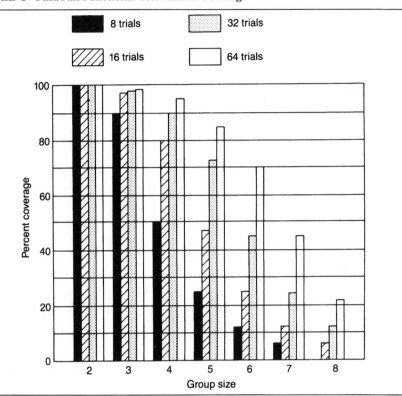

TABLE P Generic Percent Plot Positions (F_i) for Probability Papers [$F_i = 100(i - 0.05)/n$]

Ranking Number i	Sample Size (n)												
	1	2	3	4	5	6	7	8	9	10	11	12	13
1	50.0	25.0	16.7	12.5	10.0	8.3	7.1	6.3	5.6	5.0	4.5	4.2	3.8
2		75.0	50.0	37.5	30.0	25.0	21.4	18.8	16.7	15.0	13.6	12.5	11.5
3			83.3	62.5	50.0	41.7	35.7	31.3	27.8	25.0	22.7	20.8	19.2
4				87.5	70.0	58.3	50.0	43.8	38.9	35.0	31.8	29.2	26.9
5					90.0	75.0	64.3	56.3	50.0	45.0	40.9	37.5	34.6
6						91.7	78.6	68.8	61.1	55.0	50.0	45.8	42.3
7							92.9	81.3	72.2	65.0	59.1	54.2	50.0
8								93.8	83.3	75.0	68.2	62.5	57.7
9									94.4	85.0	77.3	70.8	65.4
10										95.0	86.4	79.2	73.1
11											95.5	87.5	80.8
12												95.8	88.5
13													96.2

Sample Size (n)

Ranking Number i	14	15	16	17	18	19	20	21	22	23	24	25	26
1	3.6	3.3	3.1	2.9	2.8	2.6	2.5	2.4	2.3	2.2	2.1	2.0	1.9
2	10.7	10.0	9.4	8.8	8.3	7.9	7.5	7.1	6.8	6.5	6.3	6.0	5.8
3	17.9	16.7	15.6	14.7	13.9	13.2	12.5	11.9	11.4	10.9	10.4	10.0	9.6
4	25.0	23.3	21.9	20.6	19.4	18.4	17.5	16.7	15.9	15.2	14.6	14.0	13.5
5	32.1	30.0	28.1	26.5	25.0	23.7	22.5	21.4	20.5	19.6	18.8	18.0	17.3
6	39.3	36.7	34.4	32.4	30.6	28.9	27.5	26.2	25.0	23.9	22.9	22.0	21.2
7	46.4	43.3	40.6	38.2	36.1	34.2	32.5	31.0	29.5	28.3	27.1	26.0	25.0
8	53.6	50.0	46.9	44.1	41.7	39.5	37.5	35.7	34.1	32.6	31.3	30.0	28.8
9	60.7	56.7	53.1	50.0	47.2	44.7	42.5	40.5	38.6	37.0	35.4	34.0	32.7
10	67.9	63.3	59.4	55.9	52.8	50.0	47.5	45.2	43.2	41.3	39.6	38.0	36.5
11	75.0	70.0	65.6	61.8	58.3	55.3	52.5	50.0	47.7	45.7	43.8	42.0	40.4
12	82.1	76.7	71.9	67.6	63.9	60.5	57.5	54.8	52.3	50.0	47.9	46.0	44.2
13	89.3	83.3	78.1	73.5	69.4	65.8	62.5	59.5	56.8	54.3	52.1	50.0	48.1
14	96.4	90.0	84.4	79.4	75.0	71.1	67.5	64.3	61.4	58.7	56.3	54.0	51.9
15		96.7	90.6	85.3	80.6	76.3	72.5	69.0	65.9	63.0	60.4	58.0	55.8
16			96.9	91.2	86.1	81.6	77.5	73.8	70.5	67.4	64.6	62.0	59.6
17				97.1	91.7	86.8	82.5	78.6	75.0	71.7	68.8	66.0	63.5
18					97.2	92.1	87.5	83.3	79.5	76.1	72.9	70.0	67.3
19						97.4	92.5	88.1	84.1	80.4	77.1	74.0	71.2
20							97.5	92.9	88.6	84.8	81.3	78.0	75.0
21								97.6	93.2	89.1	85.4	82.0	78.8
22									97.7	93.5	89.6	86.0	82.7
23										97.8	93.8	90.0	86.5
24											97.9	94.0	90.4
25												98.0	94.2
26													98.1

TABLE Q1 Normal Probability Paper

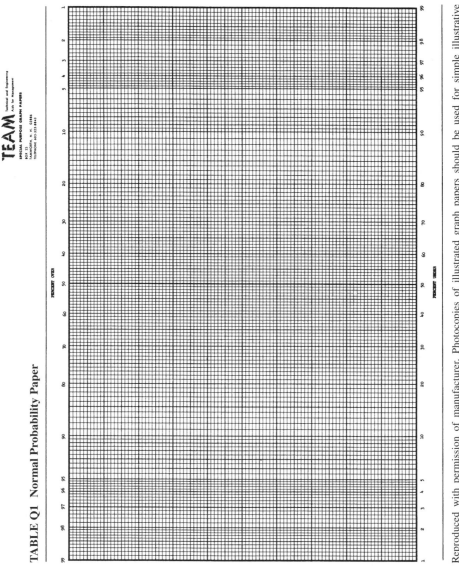

Reproduced with permission of manufacturer. Photocopies of illustrated graph papers should be used for simple illustrative purposes only. Photocopy distortions change the mathematical relationships between horizontal and vertical scale grids which then causes errors in parameter estimates taken from the graph.

TABLE Q2 Log-Normal Probability Paper

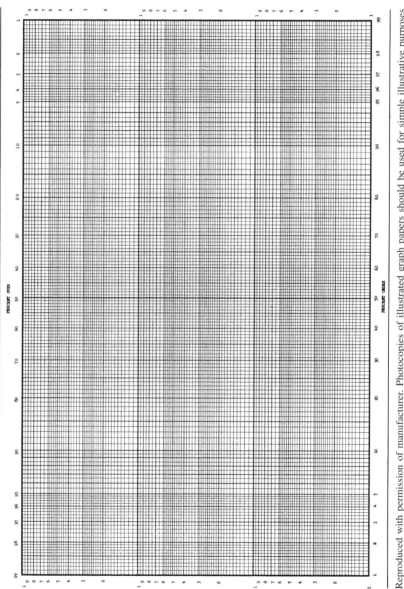

Reproduced with permission of manufacturer. Photocopies of illustrated graph papers should be used for simple illustrative purposes only. Photocopy distortions change the mathematical relationships between horizontal and vertical scale grids which then causes errors in parameter estimates taken from the graph.

TABLE Q3 Weibull Probability Paper

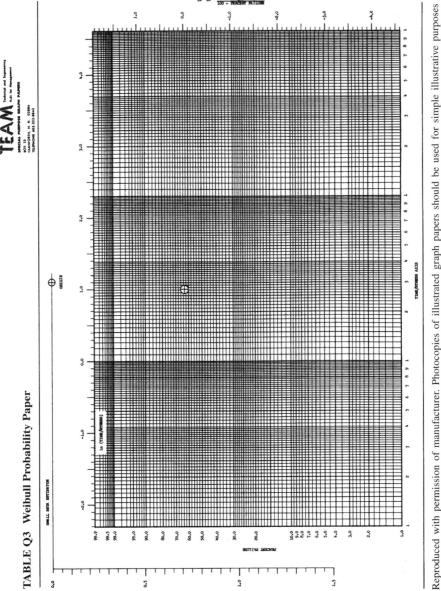

Reproduced with permission of manufacturer. Photocopies of illustrated graph papers should be used for simple illustrative purposes only. Photocopy distortions change the mathematical relationships between horizontal and vertical scale grids which then causes errors in parameter estimates taken from the graph.

TABLE R1 Normal Hazard Paper

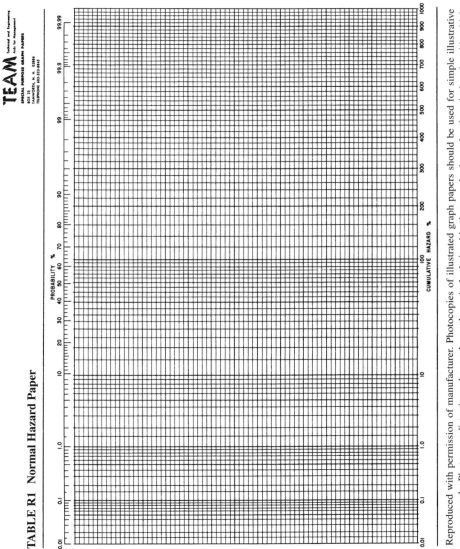

Reproduced with permission of manufacturer. Photocopies of illustrated graph papers should be used for simple illustrative purposes only. Photocopy distortions change the mathematical relationships between horizontal and vertical scale grids which then causes errors in parameter estimates taken from the graph.

TABLE R2 Log-Normal Hazard Paper

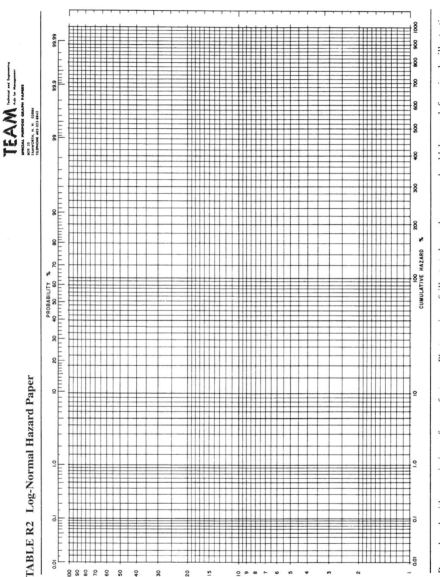

Reproduced with permission of manufacturer. Photocopies of illustrated graph papers should be used for simple illustrative purposes only. Photocopy distortions change the mathematical relationships between horizontal and vertical scale grids which then causes errors in parameter estimates taken from the graph.

TABLE R3 Weibull Hazard Paper

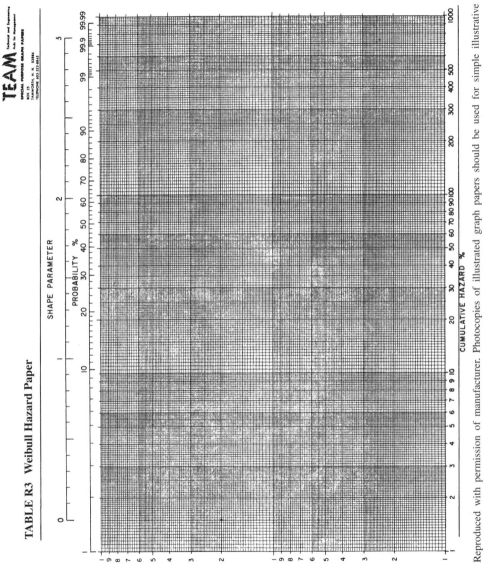

Reproduced with permission of manufacturer. Photocopies of illustrated graph papers should be used for simple illustrative purposes only. Photocopy distortions change the mathematical relationships between horizontal and vertical scale grids which then causes errors in parameter estimates taken from the graph.

TABLE S Conversion Between ppm and Sigma

+/− Sigma Level at Spec. Limit*	Percent within spec.: Centered Distribution	Defective ppm: Centered Distribution	Percent within spec.: 1.5 Sigma Shifted Distribution	Defective ppm: 1.5 Sigma Shifted Distribution
1	68.2689480	317310.520	30.232785	697672.15
1.1	72.8667797	271332.203	33.991708	660082.92
1.2	76.9860537	230139.463	37.862162	621378.38
1.3	80.6398901	193601.099	41.818512	581814.88
1.4	83.8486577	161513.423	45.830622	541693.78
1.5	86.6385542	133614.458	49.865003	501349.97
1.6	89.0401421	109598.579	53.886022	461139.78
1.7	91.0869136	89130.864	57.857249	421427.51
1.8	92.8139469	71860.531	61.742787	382572.13
1.9	94.2567014	57432.986	65.508472	344915.28
2	95.4499876	45500.124	69.122979	308770.21
2.1	96.4271285	35728.715	72.558779	274412.21
2.2	97.2193202	27806.798	75.792859	242071.41
2.3	97.8551838	21448.162	78.807229	211927.71
2.4	98.3604942	16395.058	81.589179	184108.21
2.5	98.7580640	12419.360	84.131305	158686.95
2.6	99.0677556	9322.444	86.431323	135686.77
2.7	99.3065954	6934.046	88.491691	115083.09
2.8	99.4889619	5110.381	90.319090	96809.10
2.9	99.6268240	3731.760	91.923787	80762.13
3	99.7300066	2699.934	93.318937	66810.63
3.1	99.8064658	1935.342	94.519860	54801.40
3.2	99.8625596	1374.404	95.543327	44566.73
3.3	99.9033035	966.965	96.406894	35931.06
3.4	99.9326038	673.962	97.128303	28716.97
3.5	99.9534653	465.347	97.724965	22750.35
3.6	99.9681709	318.291	98.213547	17864.53
3.7	99.9784340	215.660	98.609650	13903.50
3.8	99.9855255	144.745	98.927586	10724.14
3.9	99.9903769	96.231	99.180244	8197.56
4	99.9936628	63.372	99.379030	6209.70
4.1	99.9958663	41.337	99.533877	4661.23
4.2	99.9973292	26.708	99.653297	3467.03
4.3	99.9982908	17.092	99.744481	2555.19
4.4	99.9989166	10.834	99.813412	1865.88
4.5	99.9993198	6.802	99.865003	1349.97
4.6	99.9995771	4.229	99.903233	967.67
4.7	99.9997395	2.605	99.931280	687.20
4.8	99.9998411	1.589	99.951652	483.48
4.9	99.9999040	0.960	99.966302	336.98
5	99.9999426	0.574	99.976733	232.67

TABLE S (*Continued*)

+/− Sigma Level at Spec. Limit*	Percent within spec.: Centered Distribution	Defective ppm: Centered Distribution	Percent within spec.: 1.5 Sigma Shifted Distribution	Defective ppm: 1.5 Sigma Shifted Distribution
5.1	99.9999660	0.340	99.984085	159.15
5.2	99.9999800	0.200	99.989217	107.83
5.3	99.9999884	0.116	99.992763	72.37
5.4	99.9999933	0.067	99.995188	48.12
5.5	99.9999962	0.038	99.996831	31.69
5.6	99.9999979	0.21	99.997933	20.67
5.7	99.9999988	0.012	99.998665	13.35
5.8	99.9999993	0.007	99.999145	8.55
5.9	99.9999996	0.004	99.999458	5.42
6	99.9999998	0.002	99.999660	3.40

*Sometimes referred to as sigma level or sigma quality level when considering process shift.

LIST OF SYMBOLS

Symbols used locally in the text are not shown.

$A_{r;c}$	Factor from the Poisson distribution that is tabulated in Table K
ABC	Activity based costing
AFR	Average failure rate
ANOM	Analysis of means
ANOVA	Analysis of variance
AQL	Accept quality level
ARL	Average run length
ASQ	American Society for Quality (Previously ASQC, American Society for Quality Control)
ASTM	American Society for Testing and Materials
A_t	Acceleration test factor
$B_{r;c}$	Factor from the Poisson distribution tabulated in Table K
b	Weibull distribution shape parameter (slope of a Weibull probability plot); a parameter used in the NHPP with Weibull intensity model
c	Confidence factor used in Table K
c chart	Control chart for nonconformities
°C	Celsius temperature
CL	Center line in an SPC chart
CDF	Cumulative distribution function
C_p	Capability index (AIAG 1995b) (In practice, some calculate using "short-term" standard deviation, others calculate using "long-term" standard deviation)

746

C_{pk}	Capability index (AIAG 1995b) (In practice some calculate using "short-term" standard deviation, others calculate using "long-term" standard deviation)
cP	Centipoise (measure of fluid viscosity)
CUSUM	Cumulative sum (control chart approach)
C_4	Controlled collapse chip connection points within electronic chip components
C&E	Cause and effect (diagram)
COPQ	Cost of poor quality
CTC	Critical to cost
CTD	Critical to delivery
CTP	Critical to process
CTQ	Critical to quality
d	Discrimination ratio (Poisson distribution sequential testing)
df	Degrees of freedom
DFM	Design for manufacturability
DOA	Dead on arrival
DOE	Design of experiments
DPMO	Defects per million opportunities
dt	Calculus expression used to describe an infinitesimally small increment of time t
EVOP	Evolutionary operation
$\exp(x)$	$= e^x = (2.71828...)^x$
°F	Fahrenheit temperature
F_0	Test criterion value from the F distribution (Table F)
$F_{\alpha;\nu1;\nu2}$	Value from the F distribution for α risk and ν_1 and ν_2 degrees of freedom (Table F)
F_i	Probability plot positions determined from Table P
FIT	Failures in time
FMEA	Failure mode and effects analysis
$F(x)$	Describes the CDF where the independent variable is x
$f(x)$	Describes the PDF where the independent variable is x
Gauge R&R	Gauge repeatability and reproducibility
GLM	General linear modeling
H_0	Null hypothesis
H_a	Alternative hypothesis
HPP	Homogeneous Poisson process
in.	Inches
K	Temperature in degrees Kelvin (273.16 + °C); Boltzmann's constant
k	Characteristic life or scale parameter in the Weibull distribution
KCA	Knowledge centered activity
KPIV	Key process input variables

KPOV	Key process output variables
L_a	Length run for AQL (in CUSUM charting)
LCL	Lower control limit (in SPC)
LDL	Lower decision level (in ANOM)
ln	$\log_e = \log_{2.718}$
log	$\log_{10}$
L_r	Length run for RQL (in CUSUM charting)
mph	Miles per hour
MR	Moving range (in SPC)
MS	Mean square
MSA	Measurement Systems Analysis
msec	Milliseconds
MTBF	Mean time between failures
n	Sample size
np (chart)	SPC chart of number of nonconforming items
NGT	Nominal group technique
NHPP	Nonhomogeneous Poisson process
$NID(0, \sigma^2)$	Modeling errors are often assumed to be normally and independently distributed with mean zero and a constant but unknown variance
NTF	No trouble found
OC	Operating characteristic curve.
ORT	Ongoing reliability test
p (chart)	SPC chart of fraction nonconforming
P	probability
P	Test performance ratio (ρ_t/ρ_a)
PDF	Probability density function
PDCA	Plan do check act
PDSA	Plan do study act
ppm	Parts per million (defect rate)
P_p	Performance index (AIAG 1995b) (calculated using "long-term" standard deviation)
P_{pk}	Performance index (AIAG 1995b) (calculated using "long-term" standard deviation)
P/T	Precision to tolerance ratio
QFD	Quality function deployment
ROI	Return on investment
RQL	Reject quality level
R	Range (in SPC)
RMR	Rejected material review
RPN	Risk priority number (in FMEA)
RSM	Response surface methodology
r	Number of failures, correlation coefficient
R^2	Coefficient of determination
$r(t)$	System failure rate at time (t) for the NHPP model
s	Standard deviation of a sample

SOD	Severity, occurrence, and detection (used in FMEA)
SPC	Statistical process control
SS	Sum of squares
S^4	Smarter Six Sigma Solutions
T	Total test time used in Table K
t	Time
t_0	Test criterion value from the t distribution (Tables D or E)
T_q	$q\%$ of the population is expected to be below this value for a population
$t_{\alpha;\nu}$	Value from the t distribution for α risk and ν degrees of freedom (Tables D and E)
UCL	Upper control limit (SPC)
UDL	Upper decision level (ANOM)
U_0	Test criterion value from the normal distribution (Table B or C)
U_α	Value from the normal distribution for α risk (Table B or C)
U_β	Value from the normal distribution for β risk (Table B or C)
u (chart)	SPC chart of number of nonconformity's per unit
VIF	Variance inflation factor
Xmr (chart)	SPC chart of individual and moving range measurements
$\underline{x}_0$	Three-parameter Weibull distribution location parameter
x	Mean of a variable x
$\bar{x}$ chart	SPC chart of means (i.e., x-bar chart)
$\tilde{x}$	Median of variable x
Z_α	Normal distribution value for α risk (Table A)
α	Alpha, risk of rejecting the null hypothesis erroneously
β	Beta, risk of not rejecting the null hypothesis erroneously
Δ	Delta, effect of contrast column
δ	Delta, an acceptable amount of uncertainty
θ	Theta, the parameter in the exponential distribution equation (mean of the distribution)
λ	Lambda, hazard rate; intensity term in the NHPP equation
μ	Mu, population true mean
$\hat{\mu}$	Estimate of population mean
ν	Nu, degrees of freedom
ρ	Rho, actual failure rate of population, correlation coefficient between two variables
ρ_a	A single failure rate test criterion
ρ_t	The highest failure rate that is to be exhibited by the samples in a time-terminated test before a "pass test" statement can be given
ρ_1	Higher failure rate (failures/unit time) involving β risk in Poisson sequential testing (typically assigned equality to failure rate criterion ρ_a)

ρ_0	Lower failure rate (failures/unit time) involving α risk in Poisson sequential testing
ρ_α	Used when calculating sample size for a fixed length test; the failure rate at which α is to apply
ρ_β	Used when calculating sample size for a fixed length test; the failure rate at which β is to apply
Σ	Mathematical summation
σ	Sigma, population standard deviation
$\hat{\sigma}$	Estimate for population standard deviation
$\chi^2_{\alpha;v}$	Chi-square value from the chi-square distribution for α risk and v degrees of freedom (Table G)
χ^2_0	Test criterion value from the chi-square distribution (Table G)
$\parallel$	Mathematical symbol used to denote the absolute value of a quantity

GLOSSARY

Abscissa: The coordinate representing the distance from the y axis in a two-dimensional plot.

Accelerated testing: The testing of equipment in an environment so that the time will be shortened for failures to occur. For example, high temperature is often used to create failures sooner during a reliability test of electronic components. The acceleration test factor (A_t) is the test time used to perform the accelerated testing divided into the expected "normal usage time" that the test is pulling on the device under test.

Accept quality level (AQL): In a sampling plan the maximum proportion of defective units that can be considered satisfactory as the process average.

Accuracy: The closeness of agreement between an observation value and the accepted reference value.

Activation energy (E_0): A constant in the Arrhenius equation that is a function of the type of failure mechanism during a high-temperature accelerated test of electrical components.

Active experimentation: Experiments are conducted where variable levels are changed to assess their impact on a response(s).

Affinity diagram: A methodology where a team can organize and summarize the natural grouping from a large number of ideas and issues.

Algorithm design: A methodology to choose experiment design trials when fitting a model (e.g., quadratic). With these designs a computer creates a list of candidate trials and then calculates the standard deviation of the value predicted by the polynomial for each trial. The trial with the largest standard deviation is picked as the next trial to include in the design. The coefficients of the polynomial are next recalculated using this new trial, and the process is repeated.

Alias: *See* Confounded.

Alpha (α) risk: Risk of rejecting the null hypothesis erroneously. It is also called type I error or producer's risk.

Alternative hypothesis (H_a): *See* Hypothesis testing.

Analysis of goodness: The ranking of fractional factorial experiment trials according to the level of a response. An attempt is then made to identify factors or combination of factors that potentially affect the response.

Analysis of means (ANOM): A graphical analysis approach to compare the means of several groups of size n.

Analysis of variance (ANOVA): A statistical procedure that can be used to determine the significant effects in a factorial experiment.

Arrhenius equation: A common model that is used to describe the test acceleration on electronic components in a high-temperature environment.

Attribute data: The presence or absence of some characteristic in each device under test (e.g., proportion nonconforming in a pass/fail test).

Average: *See* Mean.

Average run length (ARL): The average number of points required before an out-of-control process condition is indicated.

Balanced (design): A fractional factorial experiment design where for each factor an equal number of trials is performed at each level state.

Bar charts: Horizontal or vertical bars that graphically illustrate the magnitude of multiple situations.

Bathtub curve: A curve used to describe the life cycle of a system/device as a function of usage. When the curve has its initial downward slope, the failure rate is decreasing with usage. This is the early-life region where manufacturing problems are typically encountered. The failure rate is constant during the flat part of the curve. When the curve begins sloping upward, the failure rate is increasing with usage. This region describes wear-out of a product.

Best estimate: A value where there is a 50% chance that the true reading is higher/lower than the estimate.

Beta (β) risk: Risk of not rejecting the null hypothesis erroneously. Also called type II error or consumer's risk.

Bias: The difference between the observed average of measurements and the reference value. Bias is often referred to as accuracy.

Bimodal distribution: A distribution that is a combination of two different distributions resulting in two distinct peaks.

Binomial distribution: A distribution that is useful to describe discrete variables or attributes that have two possible outcomes (e.g., a pass/fail proportion test, heads/tails outcome from flipping a coin, defect/no defect present).

Blocking: A technique that is used to account for "nuisance" variables when structuring fractional factorial experiment test trials.

Boldness: The term used to describe the choosing of the magnitude of the variable levels to use within a response surface design. The concept suggests that the magnitudes of variables should be large enough to capture the minimum and maximum responses of the process under test.

Boltzmann's constant: A constant of 8.617×10^{-5} eV/K used in the Arrhenius equation for high-temperature accelerated testing.

Bootstrapping: A resampling technique that provides a simple but effective methodology to describe the uncertainty associated with a summary statement without concern about details of complexity of the chosen summary or exact distribution from which data are calculated.

Brainstorming: Consensus building among experts about a problem or issue using group discussion.

Bugs: A slang term used to describe problems that may occur in a process or in the use of a product. These problems can result from errors in the design or the manufacturing process.

Burn-in: Stress screen at perhaps high temperature or elevated voltages conducted on a product for the purpose of capturing failures inside the manufacturing facility and minimizing early-life field failures. *See* Screen.

Canonical form: A transformed form of a response surface equation to a new coordinate system such that the origin is at the maximum, minimum, or saddle point and the axis of the system is parallel to the principal axis of the fitted quadratic response surface.

Catapult: A teaching aid originally developed by Texas Instruments (TI). With this device, teams of students project plastic golf balls, where the distance from the catapult at impact is the response. There are many adjustments on the catapult that affect the throw distance. Contact the author for information about availability.

Cause-and-effect diagram (C&E diagram): This is a technique that is useful in problem solving using brainstorming sessions. With this technique, possible causes from such sources as materials, equipment, methods, and personnel are typically identified as a starting point to begin discussion. The technique is sometimes called an Ishikawa diagram or fishbone diagram.

Cell: A grouping of data that, for example, comprises a bar in a histogram.

Censored datum: The sample has not failed at a usage or stress level.

Central composite rotatable design: A type of response surface experiment design.

Central Limit Theorem: The means of samples from a population will tend to be normally distributed around the population mean.

Certification: A test to determine whether, for example, a product is expected to meet or be better than its failure rate criterion.

Characteristic life (k): A parameter that is contained in the Weibull distribution. In a reliability test, the value of this parameter equates to the usage when 63.2% of the devices will fail.

Checks sheets: The systematic recording and compiling of data from historical or current observations.

Chronic problem: A description of the situation where a process SPC chart may be in control; however, the overall response is not satisfactory (i.e., common causes yield an unsatisfactory response). For example, a manufacturing process has a consistent "yield" over time; however, the average yield number is not satisfactory.

Class variables: Factors that have discrete levels.

Coded levels: Regression analysis of factorial or response surface data can be performed where the levels are described in the natural levels of the factors (e.g., 5.5 and 4.5 V) or the coded levels of the factors (e.g., -1 and $+1$).

Coefficient: *See* Regression analysis.

Coefficient of determination (R^2): The square of the correlation coefficient. Values for R^2 describe the percentage of variability accounted for by the model. For example, $R^2 = 0.8$ indicates that 80% of the variability in the data is accounted for by the model.

Combinational problem: A term used in this text to describe a type of problem where the occurrences of a combination of factor levels cause a *logic* failure. Pass/fail functional testing is a suggested procedure to identify whether such a problem exists in a unit under test. This term is very different from the term "interaction."

Common Causes: *See* Chronic problem.

Component: A device that is one of many parts of a system. Within this text components are considered to be nonrepairable devices.

Confidence interval: The region containing the limits or band of a parameter with an associated confidence level that the bounds are large enough to contain the true parameter value. The bands can be single-sided to describe an upper/lower limit or double sided to describe both upper and lower limits.

Confounded: Two factor effects that are represented by the same comparison are aliases of one another (i.e., different names for the same computed effect). Two effects that are aliases of one another are confounded (or confused) with one another. Although the word "confounded" is commonly used to describe aliases between factorial effects and block effects, it can more generally be used to describe any effects that are aliases of one another.

Consumer's risk: *See* Beta (β) risk.

Continuous distribution: A distribution used in describing the probability of a response when the output is continuous (*See* Response).

Continuous response: *See* Response.

Contrast column effects: The effect in a contrast column, which might have considerations that are confounded.

Control chart: A procedure used to track a process with time for the purpose of determining if sporadic or chronic problems (common or special causes) exist.

Control: The term "in control" is used in process control charting to describe when the process indicates that there are no special causes. "Out of control" indicates that there is a special cause.

Correlation coefficient (*r*): A statistic that describes the strength of a relationship between two variables is the sample correlation coefficient. A correlation coefficient can take values between -1 and $+1$. A -1 indicates perfect negative correlation, while a $+1$ indicates perfect positive correlation. A zero indicates no correlation.

Cost of poor quality: Cost of quality issues are often given the broad categories of internal failure costs, external failure costs, appraisal costs, and prevention costs.

Coverage: *See* Test coverage.

Cumulative distribution function (CDF) [*F*(*x*)]: The calculated integral of the PDF from minus infinity to x. This integration takes on a characteristic "percentage less than or percentile" when plotted against x.

Cumulative sum (CUSUM) (control chart): An alternative control charting technique to Shewhart control charting. CUSUM control charts can detect small process shifts faster than Shewhart control charts can.

Customer: Someone for whom work or a service is performed. The end user of a product is a customer of the employees within a company that manufactures the product. There are also internal customers in a company. When an employee does work or performs a service for someone else in the company, the person who receives this work is a customer of this employee.

Dead on arrival (DOA): A product that does not work the first time it is used or tested. The binomial distribution can often be used to statistically evaluate DOA (i.e., it works or does not work) scenarios.

Decision tree: A graphical decision-making tool that integrates for a defined problem both uncertainties and cost with the alternatives to decide on the "best" alternative.

Defect: A nonconformity or departure of a quality characteristic from its intended level or state.

Defective: A nonconforming item that contains at least one defect, or having a combination of several imperfections causing the unit not to satisfy intended requirements.

Degrees of freedom (*df* or *v*): Number of measurements that are independently available for estimating a population parameter. For a random sample from a population, the number of degrees of freedom is equal to the sample size minus one.

Delphi technique: A method of "predicting" the future by surveying experts in the area of concern.

Design of experiments (DOE): Experiment methodology where factor levels are assessed in a fractional factorial experiment or full factorial experiment structure.

Discrete distribution: A distribution function that describes the probability for a random discrete variable.

Discrete random variable: A random variable that can only assume discrete values.

Discrimination (of a measurement system): The concern when selecting or analyzing a measurement system. Discrimination or resolution of a measurement system is its capability to detect and faithfully indicate even small changes in the measured characteristic.

Discrimination ratio (d): Poisson sequential testing relationship of failure rate considerations (ρ_1 / ρ_0).

Distribution: A pattern that randomly collected numbers from a population follow. The normal, Weibull, Poisson, binomial, and log-normal distributions discussed in this text are applicable to the modeling of various industrial situations.

Double-sided test: A statistical consideration where, for example, the mean of a population is to be equal to a criterion, as stated in a null hypothesis.

Early-life failures: *See* Bathtub curve.

Effect: The main effect of a factor in a two-level factorial experiment is the mean difference in responses between the two levels of the factor, which is averaged over all levels of the other factors.

Efficiency: A concept due to R. A. Fisher, who said that one estimator is more efficient than another if it has a smaller variance. Percentage efficiency is 100 times the ratio of the variance of the estimator with minimum variance to the variance of the estimator in question.

Error (experimental): Ambiguities during data analysis caused from such sources as measurement bias, random measurement error, and mistake.

Evolutionary operation (EVOP): An analytical approach where process conditions are changed structurally in a manufacturing process (e.g., using a fractional factorial experiment design matrix) for the purpose of analytically determining changes to make for product improvement.

Experiment: A process undertaken to determine something that is not already known.

Experimental error: Variations in the experimental response under identical test conditions. Also called "residual error."

F test: A statistical test that utilizes tabular values from the F distribution to assess significance.

Factorial experiment: *See* Full factorial experiment and Fractional factorial experiment.

Factors: Variables that are varied to different levels within a factorial designed experiment or response surface experiment.

Failure: A device is said to fail when it no longer performs its intended function satisfactorily.

Failure mode and effects analysis (FMEA): Analytical approach directed toward problem prevention through the prioritization of potential problems and their resolution. Opposite of fault tree analysis.

Failure rate: Failures/unit time or failures/units of usage (i.e., 1/MTBF). Sample failure rates are: 0.002 failures/hour, 0.0003 failures/auto miles traveled, 0.01 failures/1000 parts manufactured. Failure rate criterion (ρ_a) is a failure rate value that is not to be exceeded in a product. Tests to determine if a failure rate criterion is met can be fixed or sequential in duration. With fixed-length test plans the test design failure rate (ρ_t) is the sample failure rate that cannot be exceeded in order to certify the criterion (ρ_a) at the boundary of the desired confidence level. With sequential test plans failure rates ρ_1 and ρ_0 are used to determine the test plans.

Fault tree analysis: A schematic picture of possible failure modes and associated probabilities. Opposite of failure mode effects analysis.

Fire fighting: An expression used to describe the process of performing emergency fixes to problems.

Fixed-effects model: A factorial experiment where the levels of the factors are specifically chosen by the experimenter (as opposed to a random effects or components of variance model).

Fold-over: Resolution IV designs can be created from resolution III designs by the process of fold-over. To fold-over a resolution III design, simply add to the original fractional factorial design matrix a second fractional factorial design matrix with all the signs reversed.

Force field analysis: Representation of the forces in an organization are supporting and driving toward a solution and which are restraining progress.

Fractional factorial experiment: A designed experiment strategy that assesses several factors/variables simultaneously in one test, where only a partial set of all possible combinations of factor levels are tested to more efficiently identify important factors. This type of test is much more efficient than a traditional one-at-a-time test strategy.

Freak distribution: A set of substandard products that are produced by random occurrences in a manufacturing process.

Full factorial experiment: Factorial experiment where all combinations of factor levels are tested.

Gauge: Any device used to obtain measurements. The term is frequently used to refer specifically to shop floor devices, including go/no-go devices.

Gauge repeatability and reproducibility (R&R) study: The evaluation of measuring instruments to determine capability to yield a precise response. Gauge repeatability is the variation in measurements considering one part and one operator. Gauge reproducibility is the variation between operators measuring one part.

General linear modeling (GLM): A statistical procedure for univariate analysis of variance with balanced/unbalanced designs, analysis of covariance, and regression.

Goodness of fit: *See* Lack of fit.

Go/no-go: A technique often used in manufacturing where a device is tested with a gauge that is to evaluate the device against its upper/lower specification limit. A decision is made that the device either meets or does not meet the criterion.

Group size: A term used in this text to describe how many factors are considered when making a combinational "test coverage" statement within a pass/fail functional test.

Half-normal probability plot: A normal probability plot where the absolute data measurements are plotted.

Hazard paper: Specialized graph paper (*See* Tables R1 to R3 in Appendix D) that yields information about populations similar to that of probability paper. In this text this paper is used to plot data that contain censored information.

Hazard rate (λ): The probability that a device will fail between times x and $x + dx$, after it has survived time (usage) x (i.e., a conditional probability of failure given survival to that time). At a given point in time, the hazard rate and instantaneous failure rate are equivalent.

Hidden factory: Reworks within an organization that have no value and are often not considered within the metrics of a factory.

Histogram: A graphical representation of the sample frequency distribution that describes the occurrence of grouped items.

Homogeneous Poisson process (HPP): A model that considers that failure rate does not change with time.

Hypergeometric distribution: A distribution that has a similar use to that of the binomial distribution; however, the sample size is "large" relative to the population size (e.g., sample size is greater than 10% of the size of the population).

Hypothesis testing: Consists of a null hypothesis (H_0) and alternative hypothesis (H_a) where, for example, a null hypothesis indicates equality between two process outputs and an alternative hypothesis indicates nonequality. Through a hypothesis test a decision is made whether to reject a null hypothesis or not reject a null hypothesis. When a null hypothesis is rejected, there is α risk of error. Most typically there is no risk assignment when we fail to reject the null hypothesis. However, an appropriate sample size could be determined such that failure to reject the null hypothesis is made with β risk of error.

Indifference quality level (IQL): Quality level is somewhere between AQL and RQL in acceptance sampling.

Inner array: The structuring in a Taguchi-style fractional factorial experiment of the factors that can be controlled in a process (as opposed to an outer array).

In control: The description of a process where variation is consistent over time (i.e., only common causes exist).

Intensity function: A function that was used to describe failure rate as a function of time (usage) in the NHPP.

Interaction: A description for the measure of the differential comparison of response for each level of a factor at each of the several levels of one or more other factors.

Interrelationship digraph (ID): A methodology that permits systematic identification, analysis and classification of cause-and-effect relationships. From these relationships, teams can focus on key drivers or outcomes to determine effective solutions.

Knowledge-centered activity (KCA): A term used within this text that means striving to *wisely* obtain knowledge and *wisely* utilize knowledge.

Lack of fit: A value determined by using one of many statistical techniques stating probabilistically whether data can be shown not to fit a model. Lack of fit is used to assess the goodness of fit of a model to data.

Lambda plot: A technique to determine a data transformation when analyzing data.

Least squares: A method used in regression to estimate the equation coefficients and constant so that the sum of squares of the differences between the individual responses and the fitted model is a minimum.

Levels: The settings of factors in a factorial experiment (e.g., high and low levels of temperature).

Linearity: The difference in the bias values through the expected operating range of the gauge.

Location parameter (x_0): A parameter in the three-parameter Weibull distribution that equates to the minimum value for the distribution.

Logic pass/fail response: *See* Response.

Logit (transformation): A type of data transformation sometimes advantageous in factorial analysis when data have an upper and lower bound restriction (e.g., 0–1 proportion defective).

Loss function: A continuous "Taguchi" function that measures the cost implications of product variability.

Main distribution: The main distribution is centered around an expected value of strengths, while a smaller freak distribution describes a smaller set of substandard products that are produced by random occurrences in a manufacturing process.

Main effect: An estimate of the effect of a factor measured independently of other factors.

Mallows C_p statistic: A regression parameter that is used to determine the smallest number of parameters that should be used when building a model. The number of parameters corresponding to the minimum of this statistic is the minimum number of parameters to include during the model-building process.

Mean: The mean of a sample $(\bar{x})$ is the sum of all the responses divided by the sample size. The mean of a population (μ) is the sum of all responses of the population divided by the population size. In a random sample of a population, $\bar{x}$ is an estimate of the μ of the population.

Mean square: Sum of squares divided by degrees of freedom.

Mean time between failure (MTBF): A term that can be used to describe the frequency of failures in a repairable system with a constant failure rate. MTBF is the average time that is expected between failures MTBF = 1/ failure rate.

Measurement system: The complete process of obtaining measurements. This includes the collection of equipment, operations, procedures, software, and personnel that affects the assignment of a number to a measurement characteristic.

Measurement systems analysis: *See* Gauge repeatability and reproducibility (R&R) study.

Median: For a sample the number that is in the middle when all observations are ranked in magnitude. For a population the value at which the cumulative distribution function is 0.5.

Mixture experiments: Variables are expressed as proportions of the whole and sum to unity. Measured responses are assumed to depend only on the proportions of the ingredients and not on the amount of the mixture.

Multicollinearity: When there exists near linear dependencies between regressors, the problem of multicollinearity is said to exist. *See* Variance inflation factor (VIF).

Multimodal distribution: A combination of more than one distribution that has more than one distinct peak.

Multi-vari chart: A chart that is constructed to display the variance within units, between units, between samples, and between lots.

Natural tolerances of a process: Three standard deviations on either side of the mean.

Nested data: An experiment design where the trials are not fully randomized sets. In lieu of full randomization, trials are structured such that some factor considerations are randomized within other factor considerations.

Nominal group technique (NGT): A voting procedure to expedite team consensus on relative importance of problems, issues, or solutions.

Nonhomogenous Poisson process (NHPP) with Weibull intensity: A mathematical model that can often be used to describe the failure rate of a repairable system that has a decreasing, constant. or increasing rate.

Nonrepairable device: A term used to describe something that is discarded after it fails to function properly. Examples of a nonrepairable device are a tire, spark plug, and the water pump in an automobile (if it is not rebuilt after a failure).

Nonstationary process: A process with a level and variance that can grow without limit.

Normal distribution: A bell-shaped distribution that is often useful to describe various physical, mechanical, electrical, and chemical properties.

Null hypothesis (H_0): *See* Hypothesis testing.

One-at-a-time experiment: An individual tries to fix a problem by making a change and then executing a test. Depending on the findings, something else may need to be tried. This cycle is repeated indefinitely.

One-sided test: *See* Single-sided test.

One-way analysis of variance: *See* Single-factor analysis of variance.

Ordinate: The coordinate representing the distance from the x axis in a two-dimensional plot.

Orthogonal: The property of a fractional factorial experiment that ensures that effects can be determined separately without entanglement.

Outlier: A data point that does not fit a model because of an erroneous reading or some other abnormal situation.

Outer array: The structuring in a Taguchi-style fractional factorial experiment of the factors that cannot be controlled in a process (as opposed to an inner array).

Pareto chart: A graphical technique used to quantify problems so that effort can be expended in fixing the "vital few" causes, as opposed to the "trivial many." Named after Wufredo Pareto, an European economist.

Pareto principle: 80% of the trouble comes from 20% of the problems (i.e., the vital few problems).

Pass/fail functional test: A test strategy described in this text to determine whether a failure will occur given that the response is a logic pass/fail situation. *See* Response.

Passive data analysis: Data is collected and analyzed as the process is currently performing. Process alterations are not assessed.

Path of steepest ascent: A methodology used to determine different factor levels to use in a follow-up experiment such that the expected response will be larger than previous responses.

Percent (%) R&R: The percentage of process variation related to the measurement system for repeatability and reproducibility.

Point estimate: An estimate calculated from sample data without a confidence interval.

Poisson distribution: A distribution that is useful, for example, to design reliability tests where the failure rate is considered to be constant as a function of usage.

Population: The totality of items under consideration.

Precision: The closeness of agreement between randomly selected individual measurements or test results.

Precision-to-tolerance ratio: Indicates the amount of tolerance spread that could be used up by measurement error.

Probability (P): A numerical expression for the likelihood of an occurrence.

Probability density function (PDF) [$f(x)$]: A mathematical function that can model the probability density reflected in a histogram.

Probability paper: Various types of graph papers (see Tables Q1 to Q3 in Appendix D) where a particular CDF will plot as a straight line.

Probability plot: Data are plotted on a selected probability paper coordinate system (e.g., Tables Q1 to Q3) to determine if a particular distribution is appropriate (i.e., the data plots as a straight line) and to make statements about percentiles of the population.

Problem solving: The process of determining the cause from a symptom and then choosing an action to improve a process or product.

Process: A method to make or do something that involves a number of steps. A mathematical model such as the HPP (homogeneous Poisson process).

Process capability indices (C_p and C_{pk}): C_p is a measurement of the allowable tolerance spread divided by the actual 6σ data spread. C_{pk} has a similar ratio to that of C_p except that this ratio considers the shift of the mean relative to the central specification target.

Process flow diagram (chart): Path of steps of work used to produce or do something.

Producer's risk: *See* Alpha (α) risk.

Qualitative factor: A factor that has discrete levels. For example, product origination where the factor levels are supplier A, supplier B, and supplier C.

Quantitative factor: A factor that is continuous. For example, a product can be manufactured with a process temperature factor between 50°C and 80°C.

Quality function deployment (QFD): A technique that is used, for example, to get the "voice of the customer" in the design of a product.

Randomizing: The procedure used in statistics to avoid possible bias due to the influence of systematic disturbances that are either known or unknown.

Random: Having no specific pattern.

Random effects (or components of variance) model: A factorial experiment where the variance of factors is investigated (as opposed to a fixed effects model).

Range: For a set of numbers, the absolute difference between the largest and smallest value.

Ranked sample values: Sample data that are listed in order relative to magnitudes.

Regression analysis: Data collected from an experiment are used to empirically quantify through a mathematical model the relationship that exists between the response variable and influencing factors. In a simple linear regression model, $y = b_0 + b_1 x + \varepsilon$, x is the regressor, y is the expected response, b_0 and b_1 are coefficients, and ε is random error.

Regressor: *See* Regression analysis.

Reject quality level (RQL): The level of quality that is considered unsatisfactory when developing a test plan.

Reliability: The proportion surviving at some point in time during the life of a device. A generic description of tests evaluating failure rates.

Repairable system: A system that can be repaired after experiencing a failure.

Repeatability: The variation in measurements obtained with one measurement instrument when used several times by one appraiser while measuring the identical characteristic on the same part.

Replication: Test trials that are made under identical conditions.

Reproducibility: The variation in the average of the measurements made by different appraisers using the same measuring instrument when measuring the identical characteristics on the same part.

Residuals: In an experiment the differences between experimental responses and predicted values that are determined from a model.

Residual error: Experimental error.

Resolution III: A fractional factorial designed experiment where main effects and two-factor interaction effects are confounded.

Resolution IV: A fractional factorial designed experiment where the main effects and two-factor interaction effects are not confounded; however, two-factor interaction effects are confounded with each other.

Resolution V: A fractional factorial designed experiment where all main effects and two-factor interaction effects are not confounded with other main effects or two-factor interaction effects.

Resolution V+: Full factorial designed experiment.

Response: In this text, three basic types of responses (i.e., outputs) are addressed: continuous, attribute, and logic pass/fail. A response is said to be continuous if any value can be taken between limits (e.g., 2, 2.0001, and 3.00005). A response is said to be attribute if the evaluation takes on a pass/fail proportion output (e.g., 999 out of 1000 sheets of paper on the average can be fed through a copier without a jam). In this text a response is said to be logic pass/fail if combinational considerations are involved that are said to either always cause an event to pass or fail (e.g., a computer display design will not work in combination with a particular keyboard design and software package).

Response surface methodology (RSM): The empirical study of relationships between one or more responses and input variable factors. The technique is used to determine the "best" set of input variables to optimize a response and/or gain a better understanding of the overall system response.

Risk priority number (RPN): Product of severity, occurrence, and detection rankings within an FMEA. The ranking of RPN prioritizes design concerns; however, issues with a low RPN still deserve special attention if the severity ranking is high.

Robust: A description of a procedure that is not sensitive to deviations from some of its underlying assumptions.

Robust design: A term sometimes used to describe the application of Taguchi philosophy (i.e., reducing variability).

Rotatable: A term used in response surface designs. A design is said to be rotatable if the variance of the predicted response at some point is a function of only the distance of the point from the center.

Run: A consecutive number of points, for example, that are consistently decreasing, increasing, or on one side of the central line in an SPC chart.

Run chart: A time series plot permits the study of observed data for trends or patterns over time, where the x axis is time and the y axis is the measured variable.

Run-in: A procedure to put usage on a machine within the manufacturing facility for the purpose of capturing early-life failures before shipment. *See* Screen (in manufacturing).

Sample: A selection of items from a population.

Sampling distribution: A distribution derived from a parent distribution by random sampling.

Sample size: The number of observations made or the number of items taken from a population.

Scale parameter: *See* Characteristic life (k).

Scatter diagram: A plot to assess the relationship between two variables.

Screening experiment: The first step of a multiple factorial experiment strategy, where the experiment primarily assesses the significance of main effects. Two-factor interactions are normally considered in the experiments that follow a screening experiment. Screening experiments should typically consume only 25% of the monies that are allotted for the total experiment effort to solve a problem.

Screen (in manufacturing): A process step in the manufacturing process that is used to capture marginal product performance problems before the product is "shipped" to a customer. A burn-in or run-in test is a test that could be considered a screen for an electro-mechanical device.

Sequential testing: A procedure where items are tested in sequence. Decisions are "continually" made to determine whether the test should be continued or stopped (with either a pass or fail decision). Decision points of the tests are dependent on the test criteria and the α and β risks selected.

Shape parameter (b): A parameter used in the Weibull distribution that describes the shape of the distribution and is equal to the slope of a Weibull probability plot.

Shewhart control chart: Dr. Shewhart is credited with developing the standard control chart test based on 3σ limits to separate the steady component of variation from assignable causes.

Sigma: The Greek letter (σ) that is often used to describe the standard deviation of data.

Sigma level or sigma quality level: A quality that is calculated by some to describe the capability of a process to meet specification. A Six Sigma quality level is said to have a 3.4 ppm rate. Pat Spagon from Motorola University prefers to distinguish between sigma as a measure of spread and sigma used in sigma quality level (Spagon 1998).

Significance: A statistical statement indicating that the level of a factor causes a difference in a response with a certain degree of risk of being in error.

Single-factor analysis of variance: One-way analysis of variance with two levels (or treatments) that is to determine if there is a significant difference between level effects.

Single-sided test: A statistical consideration where, for example, an alternative hypothesis is that the mean of a population is less than a criterion value.

Simplex lattice design: A triangular spatial design space used for variables that are mixture ingredients.

Six Sigma: A term coined by Motorola that emphasizes the improvement of processes for the purpose of reducing variability and making general improvements.

Smarter Six Sigma Solutions (S^4): Term used within this book to describe the *wise* and often unique application of statistical techniques to creating meaningful measurements and effective improvements.

Smarter Six Sigma Solutions assessment (S^4 assessment): Using statistically based concepts while determining the "best" question to answer from the point of view of the customer. Assessment is made to determine if the right measurements and the right actions are being conducted. This includes noting that there are usually better questions to ask (to protect the "customer") than "What sample do I need?" or "What one thing should I do next to fix this problem?" (i.e., a one-at-a-time approach). S^4 resolution may involve putting together what often traditionally are considered "separated statistical techniques" in a "smart" fashion to address various problems.

Space (functional): A description of the range of factor levels that describe how a product will be used in customer applications.

Special causes: *See* Sporadic problem.

Specification: A criterion that is to be met by a part or product.

Sporadic problem: A problem that occurs in a process because of an unusual condition (i.e., from special causes). An out-of-control condition in a process control chart.

Stability (or drift): The total variation in the measurements obtained with a measurement system on the same master or parts when measuring a single characteristic over an extended time period.

Standard deviation (σ, s): A mathematical quantity that describes the variability of a response. It equals the square root of variance. The standard deviation of a sample (s) is used to estimate the standard deviation of a population (σ).

Standard error: The square root of the variance of the sampling distribution of a statistic.

Stationary process: A process with an ultimate constant variance.

Statistical process control (SPC): The application of statistical techniques in the control of processes. SPC is often considered a subset of SQC, where the emphasis in SPC is on the tools associated with the process but not product acceptance techniques.

Statistical quality control (SQC): The application of statistical techniques in the control of quality. SQC includes the use of regression analysis, tests of significance, acceptance sampling, control charts, distributions, and so on.

Stress test: A test of devices outside usual operating conditions in an attempt to find marginal design parameters.

Subcause: In a cause-and-effect diagram, the specific items or difficulties that are identified as factual or potential causes of the problem.

Sum of squares (SS): The summation of the squared deviations relative to zero, to level means, or the grand mean of an experiment.

System: Devices that collectively perform a function. Within this text, systems are considered repairable, where a failure is caused by failure of a devices(s). System failure rates can either be constant or change as a function of usage (time).

Taguchi philosophy: This text supports G. Taguchi's basic philosophy of reducing product/process variability for the purpose of improving quality and decreasing the loss to society; however, the procedures used to achieve this objective often are different.

Test coverage: The percent of possible combinations of group sizes (e.g., 3) evaluated in an pass/fail functional test (e.g., for a given test, there might be 90% test coverage of the levels of three factor combinational considerations).

Test performance ratio (ρ): For a reliability test using the Poisson distribution, the ratio of the sample failure rate to the criterion (ρ_t/ρ_a).

Testing: A means to determine whether an item is capable of meeting specified requirements by subjecting the item to a set of physical, environmental, chemical, or operating actions/conditions.

Time-line chart: Identification of the specific start, finish, and amount of time required to complete an activity.

Treatment: *See* Levels.

Trend chart: A chart to view the resultant effect of a known variable on the response of a process. *See* Scatter diagram.

Trial: One of the factor combinations in an experiment.

t **test:** A statistical test that utilizes tabular values from the *t* distribution to assess, for example, whether two population means are different.

Type I error: *See* Alpha (α) risk.

Type II error: *See* Beta (β) risk.

Type III error: Answering the wrong question.

Two-sided test: *See* Double-sided test.

Uncensored data: All sample data have failed or have a reading.

Uncertainty (δ): An acceptable amount of change from a criterion. The parameter is used when considering β risk in sample size calculation.

Uniform precision design: A type of central composite response surface design where the number of center points is chosen such that there is more protection against bias in the regression coefficients.

Unimodal: A distribution that has one peak.

Usage: During a life test, the measure of time on test. This measurement could, for example, be in units of power-on hours, test days, or system operations.

Variable data: Data that can assume a range of numerical responses on a continuous scale, as opposed to data that can assume only discrete levels.

Variables: Factors within a fractional factorial designed experiment or response surface experiment.

Variance (σ^2, s^2): A measure of dispersion of observations based upon the mean of the squared deviations from the arithmetic mean.

Variance inflation factor (VIF): A calculated quantity for each term in a regression model that measures the combined effect of the dependencies among the regressors on the variance of that term. One or more large VIFs can indicate multicollinearity.

Verification: The act of establishing and documenting whether processes, items, services, or documents conform to a specified requirement.

Wear-out failures: *See* Bathtub curve.

Weibull distribution: This distribution has a density function that has many possible shapes. The two-parameter distribution is described by the shape parameter (b) and the location parameter (k). This distribution has an x-intercept value at the low end of the distribution that approaches zero (i.e., zero probability of a lower value). The three-parameter has, in addition to the other parameters, the location parameter (x_0) which is the lowest x-intercept value.

Weibull slope (b): *See* Shape parameter (b).

Worst-case tolerance: The overall tolerance that can be expected if all mating components were at worst-case conditions.

REFERENCES

Affourtit, B. B. (1986), Statistical Process Control (SPC) Implementation Common Misconceptions, *Proc. 39th Ann Quality Cong.,* American Society for Quality Control, pp. 440–445.

AIAG (1995a), Automotive Industry Action Group, *Measurement Systems Analysis (MSA) Reference Manual,* Chrysler Corporation, Ford Motor Company, General Motors Corporation.

AIAG (1995b), *Statistical Process Control (SPC) Reference Manual,* Chrysler Corporation, Ford Motor Company, General Motors Corporation.

AIAG (1995c), *Potential Failure Mode and Effects Analysis (FMEA) Reference Manual,* Chrysler Corporation, Ford Motor Company, General Motors Corporation.

Agresti, A. (1990), *Categorical Data Analysis,* Wiley, New York.

Anderson. V. L., and McLean, R. A. (1974), *Design of Experiments,* Marcel Dekker, New York.

American Society for Quality (1983), *Glossary and Tables for Statistical Quality Control,* ASQ, Milwaukee, WI.

American Society of Testing Metals (1976), *ASTM Manual on Presentation of Data and Control Charts Analysis STPJSD,* ASTM, Philadelphia, PA.

Ash, C. (1992), *The Probability Tutoring Book,* IEEE Press, Piscataway, NJ.

Ball, R. A., and Barney, S. P. (1982), *Quality Circle Project Manual,* UAW–Ford Employee Involvement, Rawsonville, MI.

Barlow, R. E., Fussell, J. B., and Singpurwalla, N. D. (1975), *Reliability and Fault Tree Analysis: Theoretical and Applied Aspects of System Reliability and Safety Assessment,* Society for Industrial and Applied Mathematics, Philadelphia, PA.

Bisgaard, S. (1988), *A Practical Aid for Experimenters,* Starlight Press, Madison, WI.

Bisgaard, S., and Fuller, H. T. (1995), Reducing Variation with Two-Level Factorial Experiments, *Quality Engineering,* **8**(2): 373–377.

Bothe, D. R. (1997), *Measuring Process Capability,* McGraw-Hill, New York.

Box, G. E. P. (1966), Use and Abuse of Regression, *Technometrics,* **8**(4): 625–629.

Box, G. E. P. (1988), Signal to Noise Ratios, Performance Criteria and Transformations, *Technometrics,* **30**(1): 1–40 (with discussion).

Box, G. E. P. (1991), Feedback Control by Manual Adjustment, *Quality Engineering,* **4a:** 331–338.

Box, G. E. P. (1996) and Behnken, D. W. (1960), Some New Three Level Designs for the Study of Quantitative Variables, *Technometrics,* **2**(4): 455–475.

Box, G., and Luceno, A. (1997), *Statistical Control by Monitoring and Feedback Adjustment,* Wiley, New York.

Box, G. E. P. and Meyer, R. D. (1986), An Analysis of Unreplicated Fractional Factorials, *Technometrics,* **28**: 11–18.

Box, G. E. P. and Tiao, G. C. (1973), *Bayesian Inference in Statistical Analysis,* Addison-Wesley, Reading, MA.

Box, G. E. P., Hunter, W. G., and Hunter, S. J. (1978), *Statistics for Experimenters,* Wiley, New York.

Box, G., Bisgaard, S., and Fung, C. (1988), An Explanation and Critique of Taguchi Contributions to Quality Engineering, *Quality and Reliability Engineering International,* **4**(2): 123–131.

Box, G. E. P., Jenkings, G. M., and Reinsel, G. C. (1994), *Time Series Analysis: Forecast and Control,* 3rd ed., Prentice-Hall, Englewood Cliffs, NJ.

Boyles, R. (1991), The Taguchi Capability Index, *Journal of Quality Technology,* **23**(1): 17–26.

Brassard, M., and Ritter, D. (1994), *The Memory Jogger II,* GOAL/QPC, MA.

Breyfogle, F. W. (1988), An Efficient Pass/Fail Functional Test Strategy, IBM Technical Report Number TR 51.0485.

Breyfogle, F. W. (1989a), Software Test Process, *IBM Technical Disclosure Bulletin,* **31**(8): 155–157.

Breyfogle, F. W. (1989b), Random Failure Graphical Analysis, *IBM Technical Disclosure Bulletin,* **31**(8): 321–322.

Breyfogle, F. W. (1989c), Stress Test Scenario Assessment Process, *IBM Technical Disclosure Bulletin,* **31**(8): 355–356.

Breyfogle, F. W. (1989d), Method to Provide a Software Overview Assessment, *IBM Technical Disclosure Bulletin,* **31**(10): 278–282.

Breyfogle, F. W. (1989e), Comparing Hadamard and Taguchi Matrices, IBM Technical Report Number TR51.0527.

Breyfogle, F. W. (1991), An Efficient Generalized Pass/Fail Functional Test Procedure, IBM Reliability and Applied Statistics Conference, East Fishkill, New York, pp. 67–74.

Breyfogle, F. W. (1992), *Statistical Methods for Testing, Development, and Manufacturing,* Wiley, New York.

Breyfogle, F. W. (1992), Process Improvement with Six Sigma, *Wescon/92 Conference Record,* Western Periodicals Company, Ventura, CA, pp. 754–756.

Breyfogle, F. W. (1993a), Taguchi's Contributions and the Reduction of Variability, *Tool and Manufacturing Engineers Handbook, Volume 7 Continuous Improvement,* Society of Manufacturing Engineers, Dearborn, MI, pp. 10-14–10-19.

Breyfogle, F. W. (1993b), Measurements and Their Applications, *ASQ Quality Management Division Newsletter,* Fall, ASQ, Milwaukee, WI, **19**(3): 6–8.

Breyfogle, F. W. (1993c), Self Evaluation: Ask the Right Question, *ASQ Quality Management Division Newsletter,* ASQ, Milwaukee, WI, **19**(2): 1–3.

Breyfogle, F. W. (1994a), Do It Smarter: Ask the Right Question, *International Test and Evaluation Association Journal of Test and Evaluation,* ITEA, Fairfax, VA, **15**(3): 46–51.

Breyfogle, F. W. (1994b), Reducing Variability Using Contributions from Taguchi, *ASQ Quality Management Division Newsletter,* ASQ, Milwaukee, WI, **20**(2): 3–5.

Breyfogle, F. W. (1994c), Quantifying Variability Using Contributions from Taguchi, *ASQ Quality Management Division Newsletter,* ASQ, Milwaukee, WI, **20**(1): 1–3.

Breyfogle, F. W. (1996), Implementing "The New Mantra" Described by Forbes, *ASQ Quality Management Division Newsletter,* ASQ, Milwaukee, WI, **22**(2): 3–5.

Breyfogle, F. W., Gomez, D., McEachron, N., Millham, E., and Oppenheim, A. (1991), A Design and Test Roundtable—Six Sigma: Moving Towards Perfect Products, *IEEE Design and Test of Computers,* Los Alamitos, CA, June, pp. 88–99.

Breyfogle, F. W., and Abia, A. (1991), Pass/Fail Functional Testing and Associated Coverage, *Quality Engineering,* **4**(2): 227–234.

Breyfogle, F. W., and Davis, J. H. (1988), Worst Case Product Performance Verification with Electromagnetic Interference Test Applications, *Quality and Reliability Engineering International,* **4**(2): 183–187.

Breyfogle, F. W., and Steely, F. L. (1988), Statistical Analysis with Interaction Assessment, *IBM Technical Disclosure Bulletin,* **30**(10): 234–236.

Breyfogle, F. W., and Wheeler, S. (1987), Realistic Random Failure Criterion Certification, *IBM Technical Disclosure Bulletin,* **30**(6): 103–105.

Breyfogle, F. W., Le, T. N., and Record, L. J. (1989), Processor Verification Test Process, *IBM Technical Disclosure Bulletin,* **31**(10): 324–325.

Brown, D. K. (1991), personal communication.

Brush, G. G. (1988), *How to Choose the Proper Sample Size,* American Society for Quality Control, Milwaukee, WI.

Burkland, G., Heidelberger, P., Schatzoff, M., Welch, P., and Wu, L. (1984), An APL System for Interactive Scientific-Engineering Graphics and Data Analysis, APL84 Proceedings, Helsinki, pp. 95–102.

Chan, L. K., Cheng, S. W., and Spiring, F. A., (1988), A New Measure of Process Capability: C_{pm}, *Journal of Quality Technology* **20**(3): 162–175.

Cheser, R. (1994), "Kaizen is More than Continuous Improvement, *Quality Progress,* pp. 23–25.

Clopper, C. J., and Pearson, F. S. (1934), The Use of Confidence or Fiducial Limits Illustrated in the Use of the Binomial, *Biometrika,* **26:** 404.

Cochran, W. G. (1977), *Sampling Techniques,* Wiley, New York.

Coffin, L. F., Jr. (1954), A Study of the Effects of Cyclic Thermal Stresses on a Ductile Metal, *Transactions of ASME,* **76:** 923–950.

Coffin, L. F., Jr. (1974), Fatigue at High Temperature—Prediction and Interpretation, James Clayton Memorial Lecture, *Proc. Inst. Mech. Eng. (London)*, **188**: 109–127.

Cornell, J. (1981), *Experiments with Mixtures: Designs, Models, and the Analysis of Mixture Data*, Wiley, New York.

Cornell, J. A. (1983), *How to Run Mixture Experiments for Product Quality*, American Society for Quality Control, Milwaukee, WI.

Cornell, J. (1984), *How to Apply Response Surface Methodology*, American Society for Quality Control, Milwaukee, WI.

Cornell, J. (1990), Embedding Mixture Experiments inside Factorial Experiment, *Journal of Quality Technology*, **22**(4): 265–276.

Cornell, J. A., and Gorman, J. W. (1984), Fractional Design Plans for Process Variables in Mixture Experiments, *Journal of Quality Technology*, **16**(1): 20–38.

Cox, D. R. (1958), *Planning of Experiments*, Wiley, New York.

Crocker, O. L., J. S. L. Chiu, and C. Charney (1984), *Quality Circle a guide to participation and productivity*, Facts on File, New York.

Crow, Larry H. (1974), "Reliability Analysis for Complex, Repairable Systems, Reliability and Biometry, Statistical Analysis of Lifelength," *SIAM* 379–410.

Crow, Larry H. (1975), "On Tracking Reliability Growth," *Proceedings 1975 Annual Reliability and Maintainability Symposium*, IEEE, New York, NY 1292 75RM079.

Croxton, Frederick E. (1953), *Elementary Statistics with Applications in Medicines*, Prentice-Hall, Englewood Cliffs, NJ.

Cunnane, C. (1978), Unbiased Plotting Positions—A Review, *Journal of Hydrology*, **37**: 205–222.

D'Agostino, R. B., and Stephens, M. A., eds. (1986), *Goodness-of-Fit Techniques*, Marcel Dekker, New York.

Daniel, C. (1959), Use of Half-Normal Plots in Interpreting Factorial Two-Level Experiment, *Technometrics*, **1**(4): 311–341.

Daniel. C. (1976), *Applications of Statistics to Industrial Experimentation*, Wiley, New York.

Daniel, C. and Wood, F. S. (1980), *Fitting Equations to Data*, 2nd ed. Wiley, New York.

Davies, O. L. (1967), *Design & Analysis of Industrial Experiments*, 2nd ed., Hafner Publishing, New York.

Deming, W. F. (1982), *Quality, Productivity and Competitive Position*, MIT Center for Advanced Engineering Study, Cambridge, MA.

Deming, W. F. (1986), *Out of the Crisis*, Massachusetts Institute of Technology, Cambridge, MA.

Dettmer, H. W. (1995), Quality and the Theory of Constraints, *Quality Progress*, **April:** 77–81.

Deutsch, C. H. (1998), Six Sigma Englightment—Managers Seek Corporate Nirvana Through Quality Control, *New York Times–Business Day*, The New York Times, New York, NY, Dec. 7.

Dewar, D. L. (1980), *Leader Manual and Instructional Guide*, Quality Circle Institute, Reb Bluff, CA.

Diamond, William J. (1989), *Practical Experiment Designs for Engineers and Scientists*, Van Nostrand Reinhold, New York.

Dixon, W. J. (1957) and F. J. Massey, *Introduction to Statistical Analysis,* 2nd ed., McGraw-Hill, New York.

Dixon, W. J., and F. J. Massey, Jr. (1969), *Introduction to Statistical Analysis,* 3rd ed., McGraw-Hill, New York, pp. 246, 324.

Dixon, P. M. (1993), The Bootstrap and the Jackknife: Describing the Precision of Ecological Indices, in Scheiner, S. M., and Gurevitch, J., eds., *Design and Analysis of Ecological Experiments,* New York: Chapman & Hall, pp. 290–318.

Dobyns, L., and Crawford-Mason, C. (1991), *Quality or Else,* Houghton Mifflin Company, Boston.

Draper, N. R., and Smith, H. (1966), *Applied Regression Analysis,* Wiley, New York.

Duane, J. T. (1964), Learning Curve Approach to Reliability Monitoring, *IEEE Transactions on Aerospace,* **2**(2): 000–000.

Duncan, A. J. (1986), *Quality Control and Industrial Statistics,* 5th ed., Irwin, Homewood, IL.

Efron, B. E. and Tibshirani, R. J. (1993), *An Introduction to the Bootstrap,* Chapman and Hall.

Engelmaier, W. (1985), Functional Cycles and Surface Mounting Attachment Reliability, *Circuit World,* **11**(3): 61–72.

Environmental Sciences (1984), *Environmental Stress Screening Guidelines for Assemblies,* Institute of Environmental Sciences, Mount Prospect, IL.

Fedorov, V. V. (1972), *Theory of Optimal Experiments,* Academic Press, New York.

Ferrell, F. B. (1958), Probability Paper for Plotting Experimental Data, *Industrial Quality Control,* **XV**(I):000–000.

Fisher, R. A., and Yates, F. (1953), *Statistical Tables for Biological, Agriculture, Medical Research,* 4th ed., Oliver and Boyd, Edinburg.

Flynn, M. F. (1983), What Do Control Charts Really Mean? *Proceedings of the 37th Annual Quality Congress,* American Society for Quality Control, Milwaukee, WI, pp. 448–453.

Flynn, M. F., and Bolcar, J. A., (1984), The Road to Hell, *Proceedings of the 38th Annual Quality Congress,* American Society for Quality Control, Milwaukee, WI, pp. 192–197.

Freund, J. F. (1960), *Modern Elementary Statistics,* 2nd ed., Prentice-Hall, New York.

GE (1997), *General Electric Company 1997 Annual Report.*

Goldmann, L. S. (1969), Geometric Optimization of Controlled Collapse Interconnections, *IBM Journal of Research and Development,* **13**: 251.

Goldratt, E. M. (1992), *The Goal,* 2nd ed., North River Press, New York.

Gorman, J. W., and Cornell, J. A. (1982), A Note on Model Reduction for Experiments with both Mixture Components and Process Variables, *Technometrics,* **24**(3): 243–247.

Grant, F. L., and Leavenworth, R. S. (1980), *Statistical Quality Control,* 5th ed., McGraw-Hill, New York.

Griffith, G. K. (1996), *Statistical Process Control Methods for Long and Short Runs,* ASQ Quality Press, Milwaukee, WI. 1996.

Gunther, B. H. (1989), The Use and Abuse of C_{pk} (parts 1–4), *Quality Progress,* Jan. 1989 (pp. 72–76), Mar. 1989 (pp. 108–112), May 1989 (pp. 79–83), July 1989 (pp. 86–90).

Gunther, B. H. (1991, 1992), Bootstrapping: How to Make Something from Almost Nothing and Get Statistically Valid Answers, *Quality Progress,* Dec. 1991 (pp. 97–103), Feb. 1992 (pp. 83–86), April 1992 (pp. 119–122), June 1992 (pp. 79–83).

Halpern, S. (1978), *The Assurance Sciences—An Introduction to Quality Control & Reliability,* Prentice-Hall, Englewood Cliffs, NJ.

Hall, P. (1992), *The Bootstrap and Edgeworth Expansion,* Springer-Verlag, New York.

Harry, M. J. (1987), The Nature of Six Sigma Quality, Technical Report, Government Electronics Group, Motorola. Inc., Scottsdale, AZ.

Harry, M. J. (1994a), *The Vision of Six Sigma: A Roadmap for Breakthrough,* Sigma Publishing Company, Phoenix, AZ.

Harry, M. J. (1994b), *The Vision of Six Sigma: Tools and Methods for Breakthrough,* Sigma Publishing Company, Phoenix, AZ.

Harry, M. J. (1998), Six Sigma: A Breakthrough Strategy for Profitability, *Quality Progress,* **May:** 60–64.

Hauser, J. R., and Clausing, D. (1988), The House of Quality, *Harvard Business Review,* **May–June:** 63–73.

Hoerl, R. (1995), Enhancing the Bottom-Line Impact of Statistical Methods, *ASQ Statistics Division Newsletter,* **15**(2).

Hunter, J. S. (1986), The Exponentially Weighted Moving Average, *Journal of Quality Technology,* **18:** 203–210.

Hunter, J. S. (1995), Just What Does an EWMA Do? (Part 2), *ASQ Statistics Division Newsletter,* Fall, **16**(1): 4–12.

Hunter, J. S. (1996), Beyond the Shewhart Paradigm, Council for Continuous Improvement General Session Presentation Notes.

Hunter, J. S. (1989), A One Point Equivalent to the Shewhart Chart with Western Electric Rules, *Quality Engineering,* **2**(1): 13–19.

IBM (1984), *Process Control, Capability and Improvement,* International Business Machines Corporation, Thornwood, NY.

Ireson, W. G. (1966), *Reliability Handbook,* McGraw-Hill, New York.

Jensen, F., and Petersen, N. F. (1982), *Burn-in: An Engineering Approach to the Design and Analysis of Burn-in Procedures,* Wiley, New York.

John, Peter W. M. (1990), *Statistical Methods in Engineering and Quality Assurance,* Wiley, New York.

Johnson, L. G. (1964), *The Statistical Treatment of Fatigue Experiments,* Elsevier, New York.

Jones, D. (1998), Firms air for Six Sigma Efficiency, *USA Today,* 7/21/98 Money Section.

Juran, J. M. (1988), *Juran's Quality Control Handbook,* 4th ed., McGraw-Hill, New York.

Juran, J. M., and Gryna, F. R. (1980), *Quality Planning & Analysis,* 3rd ed., McGraw-Hill, New York.

Juran, J. M., Gryna, F. M., and Bingham, R. S. (1976), *Quality Control Handbook,* 3rd ed., McGraw-Hill, New York.

Kano, N., Seraku, N., Takashashi, F., and Tsuji, S. (1984), Attractive Quality and Must Be Quality, *Nippon QC Gakka,* 12th annual meeting, **14**(2): 39–48.

Kemp, K. W. (1962), The use of cumulative sums for sampling inspection schemes, *Applied Statistics,* **11:** 16–30.

Kempthorne, O., and Folks, J. L. (1971), *Probability, Statistics and Data Analysis,* Iowa State University Press, Ames, IA.

Kepner, C. H., and Tregoe, B. B. (1981), *The New Rational Manager,* Kepner–Tregoe, Princeton, NJ.

Khuri, A. I., and Cornell, J. A. (1987), *Response Surfaces Design and Analyses,* Marcel Dekker, New York.

Kiemele, M. J., Schmidt, S. R., Berdine, R. J. (1997), *Basic Statistics Took for Continuous Improvement,* Air Academy Press, Colorado Springs, CO.

Kiemele, M. J. (1998), Information presented in this paragraph was contributed by J. Kiemele, Ph.D., of Air Academy Associates.

King, B. (1987), *Better Designs in Half the Time, Implementing QFD in America,* Goal/QPC, Methuen, MA.

King, J. R. (1980), *Frugal Sampling Schemes,* Technical Aids for Management (TEAM), Tamworth, NH.

King, J. R. (1981), *Probability Charts for Decision Making,* Technical Aids for Management (TEAM), Tamworth, NH.

Koselka, R. (1996), The New Mantra: MVT, *Forbes,* March 11, 1996, pp. 114–118.

Kroehling, H. (1990), Tests for Normality, ASQC—Electronics Division, *Technical Supplement* Issue 14, Winter.

Lane, T., and Welch, P. (1987), The Integration of a Menu-Oriented Graphical Statistical System with Its Underlying General Purpose Language, *Computer Science and Statistics: Proceedings of the 19th Symposium on the Interface,* Philadelphia, PA, pp. 267–373.

Laney, D. B. (1997), *Control Charts for Attributes Without Distributional Assumptions,* BellSouth, Birmingham, AL.

Lentner, C. (1982), *Geigy Scientific Tables,* Vol. 2, Ciba-Geigy, Basel, Switzerland.

Lipson, C., and Sheth, N. J. (1973), *Statistical Design & Analysis of Engineering Experiments,* McGraw-Hill, New York.

Lloyd, D. K., and Lipow, M. (1976), *Reliability: Management, Methods, and Mathematics,* 2nd ed., Prentice-Hall, Englewood Cliffs, NJ.

Lorenzen, J. (1989), personal communications.

Lorenzen, J. (1990), personal communications.

Lowe, J. (1998), *Jack Welch Speaks,* Wiley, New York.

Mallows, C. L. (1973), Some Comments on $C(p)$, *Technometrics,* **15**(4): 661–675.

Mann, N. R., Schafer, R. F., Singpurwalia, N. D. (1974), *Methods for Statistical Analysis of Reliability and Lift Data,* Wiley, New York.

Manson, S. S. (1953), Behavior of Materials Under Conditions of Thermal Stress, NACA-TN-2933 from NASA, Lewis Research Center, Cleveland, OH.

Manson, S. S. (1966), *Thermal Stress and Low-Cycle Fatigue,* McGraw-Hill, New York.

Marwah, B. S. A General Model for Reliability Testing, IBM Toronto Technical Report 74.027.

Massey, F. J., Jr. (1951), The Kolmogorov–Smirnov Test for Goodness of Fit, *Journal of the American Statistical Association,* **4:** 68–78.

Mauritzson, B. H. (1971), Cost Cutting with Statistical Tolerances, *Machine Design,* Nov. **25:** 78–81.

McFadden, F. R. (1993), Six-Sigma Quality Programs, *Quality Progress,* **June:** 37.

McWilliams, T. P. (1990), Acceptance Sampling Plans Based on the Hypergeometric Distribution, *Journal of Quality Technology,* **22**(4): 319–327.

Messina, W. S. (1987), *Statistical Quality Control for Manufacturing Managers,* Wiley, New York.

Miller, I., and Freund, J. (1965), *Probability & Statistics for Engineers,* Prentice-Hall, Englewood Cliffs, NJ.

Minitab (1998), *Minitab Statistical Software,* Release 12, State College, PA.

Moen, R. D., Nolan, T. W., and Provost, L. P. (1991), *Improving Quality Through Planned Experimentation,* McGraw-Hill, New York.

Montgomery, D. C. (1985), *Introduction to Statistical Quality Control,* Wiley, New York.

Montgomery, D. C. (1997), *Design and Analysis of Experiments,* Wiley, New York.

Montgomery, D. C., and Peck, F. A. (1982), *Introduction to Linear Regression Analysis,* Wiley, New York.

Moody, P. F. (1983), *Decision Making: Proven Methods for Better Decisions,* McGraw-Hill. New York.

Nachlas, J. A. (1986), A General Model for Age Acceleration During Thermal Cycling, *Quality and Reliability Engineering International,* **2:** 3–6.

Natrella, M. G. (1966), *Experimental Statistics,* National Bureau of Standards Handbook 9, Washington, D.C.

Navy (1979), Navy Manufacturing Screening Program, NAVMAT P-9492, May.

Nelson, Lloyd S. (1983), Exact Critical Values for Use with the Analysis of Means, *Journal of Quality Technology,* **15**(1): 40–42.

Nelson, L. S. (1993), Personal communication during critique of *Statistical Methods for Testing, Development, and Manufacturing,* Wiley, New York.

Nelson, Wayne (1982), *Applied Life Data Analysis,* Wiley, New York.

Nelson, Wayne (1990), *Accelerated Testing: Statistical Models, Test Plans, and Data Analyses,* Wiley, New York.

Nishimura, A., Tatemichi, A., Miura, H., and Sakamoto, T. (1987), Life Estimation of IC Plastic Packages Under Temperature Cycling Based on Fracture Mechanics, *IEEE Trans. Comp., Hybrids, and Mfg. Tech,* **CHMT-12:** 637–642.

Norris, K. C., and Landzberg, A. H. (1969), Reliability of Controlled Collapse Interconnections, *IBM Journal of Research,* **May.**

Pearson, E. S., and Hartley, H. O. (eds.) (1958), *Biometrika Tables for Statisticians,* Vol. 1, Cambridge University Press.

Peck, D. S., and Trapp, O. D. (1978), *Accelerated Testing Handbook,* Technology Associates, Portola Valley, CA.

Plackett, R. L. and Burman, J. P. (1946), "Design of Optimal Multifactorial Experiments," *Biometrika,* **23:** 305–325.

Pyzdek, Thomas (1993), "Process control for short and small runs," *Quality Progress,* April 1993.

Pyzdek, Thomas (1998), "How do I computer σ? Let Me Count the Ways," *Quality Digest,* May 1998.

Ramig, Pauline F. (1983), "Applications of the Analysis of Means," *Journal of Quality Technology,* **15**(1): 19–25.

Ramsey, Patricia P. and Philip H. Ramsey (1990), "Simple Tests of Normality in Small Samples," *JQT,* **22**(2): 299–309.

Roberts, S. W. (1959), Control chart tests based on Geometric Moving Averages, *Technometrics,* **1:** 239–250.

Ross, P. J. (1988), *Taguchi Techniques for Quality Engineering,* McGraw-Hill, New York.

Saari, A. F., Schafer, R. F., and VanDenBerg, S. J. (1982), Stress Screening of Electronic Hardware, RADC-TR-82-87, Hughes Aircraft Company, Rome Air Development Center, Griffiths Air Force Base, NY.

Scheffe, H. (1958), Experiments with Mixtures, *Journal of the Royal Statistical Society, B,* 344–360.

Schmidt, S. R., and Launsby, R. G. (1997), *Understanding Industrial Designed Experiments,* Air Academy Press, Colorado Springs, CO.

Schmidt, S. R., Kiemele, M. J., Berdine, R. J. (1997), *Knowledge Based Management* Air Academy Press & Associates, Colorado Springs, CO.

Scholtes, P. R. (1988), *The Team Handbook: How to Use Teams to Improve Quality,* Joiner Associates, Madison, WI.

Searle, S. R. (1971a), *Linear Models,* Wiley, New York.

Searle, S. R. (1971b), Topics in Variance Component Estimation, *Biometrics,* **27:** 1–76.

Senge, P. M. (1990), *The Fifth Discipline: The Art and Practice of the Learning Organization,* Doubleday/Current, New York.

Shainin, D., and Shainin, P. (1989), PRE-Control versus $\bar{x}$ and R Charting: Continuous or Immediate Quality Improvement?, *Quality Engineering,* **1**(4): 419–429.

Stamatis, D. H. (1995), *Failure Mode and Effect Analysis, ASQ Quality Press,* Milwaukee, WI.

Shao, J. and Tu, D. (1995), *The Jackknife and Bootstrap,* Springer-Verlag, New York.

Shapiro, S. S. and Wilk, M. B. (1965), Analysis of Variance Test of Normality (Complete Samples), *Biometrika,* **52:** 591–611.

Shewhart, W. A. (1931), *Economic Control of Quality of Manufactured Product,* Van Nostrand, New York.

Snedecor, G. W., and Cochran, W. G. (1980), *Statistical Methods,* 7th ed., Iowa State University Press, Ames, IA.

Spagon, P. (1998), personal communications.

Sporting News (1989), **July 3:** 7.

Steiner, S. H. (1997), PRE-Control and Some Simple Alternatives, *Quality Engineering,* **10**(1): 65–74.

Sutterland, R. R., and Videlo, I. D. F. (1985), Accelerated Life Testing of Small-Geometry Printed Circuit Boards, *Circuit World,* **11**(3): 35–40.

Taguchi, G. (1978), Off-line and On-line Quality Control Systems, Proc. International Conference Quality Control, Tokyo Japan, pp. B4-1–B4-5.

Taguchi, G. and Konishi, S. (1987), *Taguchi Methods® Orthogonal Arrays and Linear Graphics,* American Supplier Institute Inc., Center for Taguchi Methods®, Dearborn, MI.

Taylor, W. A. (1991), *Optimization and Variation Reduction in Quality,* McGraw-Hill, New York.

TEAM, Technical and Engineering Aids for Management, Box 25 Tamworth, NH 03886.

Tobias, P. A., and Trindade, D. (1995), *Applied Reliability,* second edition, Van Nostrand Reinhold, New York.

Traver, R. W. (1985), Pre-control: A Good Alternative to $\bar{x}$ and R Charts, *Quality Progress,* **Sept:** 11–14.

Traver, R. W. (1989), *Industrial Problem Solving,* Hitchcock Publishing Company, Carol Stream, IL.

Tummala, R. R., and Rymaszewski, E. J. (1989), *Microelectronics Packaging Handbook,* Van Nostrand Reinhold, New York.

US Department of Defense (1957), Sampling Procedures and Tables for Inspection by Variables for Percent Defective, MIL-STD 414, U.S. Government Printing Office, Washington, DC.

US Department of Defense (1963), Sampling Procedures and Tables for Inspection by Attributes, MIL-STD 105, U.S. Government Printing Office, Washington, DC.

US Department of Defense (1978), Military Standard-Reliability Growth Testing, MIL-STD-1635(EC), U.S. Government Printing Office, Washington, DC, 3 February.

US Department of Defense (1980), Procedures for Performing Failure Mode Effects and Criticality, US MIL STD 1629, Naval Publications and Forms Center, Philadelphia, PA.

US Department of Defense (1981a), Military Handbook-Reliability Growth Management, MIL-HDBK-189, US Government Printing Office, Washington D.C., 13 February.

US Department of Defense (1981b), Single- and Multi-Level Continuous Sampling Procedures and Tables for Inspection by Attributes, MIL-STD 1235, US Government Printing Office. Washington, DC.

US Department of Defense (1986), Military Standard-Reliability Testing for Engineering Development, Qualification, and Productions. MIL-STD-781, US Government Printing Office, Washington, DC, 17 October.

US Department of Defense (1987), Military Handbook-Reliability Test Methods, Plans, and Environments for Engineering Development, Qualification, and Productions, MIL-HDBK-781, US Government Printing Office, Washington DC, 14 July.

Urban, G. L., Hasser, J. R. (1980), *Design and Marketing of New Products,* Prentice-Hall, Englewood Cliffs, NJ.

Wald, A. (1947), *Sequential Analysis,* Wiley, New York.

Western Electric (1956), *Statistical Quality Control Handbook,* Western Electric Co., Newark, NJ.

Wheeler, B. (1989), *E-CHIP™ Course Text,* ECHIP Inc., Hockessin, DE.

Wheeler, D. J. (1990), Evaluating the Measurement Process When Testing Is Destructive, *Statistical Process Controls Inc.*

Wheeler, D. J., and Lyday, R. W. (1989), *Evaluating the Measurement Process,* 2nd ed., SPC Press, Knoxville, TN.

Wheeler, D. J. (1991), *Short Run SPC,* SPC Press, Knoxville, TN.

Wheeler, D. J., (1995a), *Aavanced Topics in Statistical Process Control,* SPC Press, Knoxville, TN.

Wheeler, D. J. (1995b), "Just What Does an EWMA Do?", *ASQ Statistics Division Newsletter,* Summer.

Wheeler, D. J. (1996), Charts for Rare Events, *Quality Digest,* December, p. 43.

Wheeler, S. G. (1990), personal communications.

Wortman, B. (1990), *The Quality Engineer Primer,* Quality Council of Indiana, Terre Haute, IN.

Wynn, H. P. (1970), The Sequential Generation of D-Optimum Experimental Designs, *Annals of Mathematical Statistics,* **41:** 1655–1664.

Yashchin, F. (1989), personal communications.

Zinkgraf, S. (1998), conversation, exercise is given in a Six Sigma workshop he conducts.

Index